THE CHARIOT OF ISRAEL

Also by Harold Wilson

NEW DEAL FOR COAL (1945)

IN PLACE OF DOLLARS (1952)

THE WAR ON WORLD POVERTY (1953)

THE RELEVANCE OF BRITISH SOCIALISM (1964)

PURPOSE IN POLITICS (1964)

THE LABOUR GOVERNMENT 1964–1970 (1971)

THE GOVERNANCE OF BRITAIN (1976)

A PRIME MINISTER ON PRIME MINISTERS (1977)

FINAL TERM: THE LABOUR GOVERNMENT 1974–76 (1979)

THE CHARIOT
OF ISRAEL

Britain, America and the State of Israel

HAROLD WILSON

W·W· NORTON & COMPANY
New York • London

Printed in the United States of America.

The maps in the text are taken from Martin Gilbert's *The Arab-Israeli Conflict: Its History in Maps,* copyright © Martin Gilbert 1974, 1976, 1979, and are reproduced with his kind permission.

W. W. Norton & Company, Inc. 500 Fifth Avenue, New York, N.Y. 10110
W. W. Norton & Company Ltd. 37 Great Russell Street, London WC1B 3NU

1 2 3 4 5 6 7 8 9 0

ISBN 0-393-01591-2

Contents

Illustrations

The Balfour Declaration, 2 November 1917 (*by permission of the British Library*).

The Zionist Commission arriving in Palestine, 1918 (*Central Zionist Archives*).

Winston Churchill in Jerusalem, 1921 (*Israel State Archives*).

A reception for Sir Alfred Mond, 1921 (*Felix Gluck Archives*).

Chaim Arlosoroff and Dr Weizmann meet Trans-Jordan leaders, 1933 (*photo: Zvi Oron, reproduced by permission of Mrs R. Legum*).

Prime Minister Neville Chamberlain presides over the Jewish representatives at the unsuccessful London conference, February 1939 (*Central Zionist Archives*).

Charles Orde Wingate, the British soldier and Zionist (*Central Zionist Archives*).

The Allenby Bridge after it had been blown up, 1946.

An illegal boat carrying immigrants captured by the British, 1946 (*Central Zionist Archives*).

Ernest Bevin, British Foreign Secretary, 1947 (*BBC Hulton Picture Library*).

Clement Atlee, whose government went back on the Balfour-Churchill assurances about *the* Jewish National Home (*Weidenfeld Archives*).

President Harry Truman, 1948 (*Popperfoto*).

Ben Gurion reads out the Declaration of Independence, 14 May 1948 (© *Jewish Agency, Jerusalem*).

The Israeli delegation to the United Nations after the new state had just been admitted as a member of the UN, 11 May 1949 (*United Nations Photo*).

French Foreign Minister Christian Pineau, Sir Anthony Eden, French Premier Guy Mollet and Selwyn Lloyd discussing the Suez crisis, September 1956 (*Popperfoto*).

Colonel Nasser meets Sir Robert Menzies, leader of the Council of Five trying to find a solution to the Suez crisis, September 1956 (*Popperfoto*).

Moshe Dayan with his troops during the Sinai campaign, 1956 (*Weidenfeld Archives*).

Harold Wilson with Golda Meir (*Photo-Emka Ltd.*).

Harold Wilson giving a lecture at the memorial evening for Yigal Allon, Tel Aviv, 13 April 1980 (*Photo: Michal Roche, Tel Aviv University*).

Maps

Preface

THIS BOOK SETS OUT to examine the role of British and, where relevant, United States policies which led to the creation in 1948 of the State of Israel. It inevitably has to start much earlier with a brief account of the dispersal (Diaspora) of the Jews as a result of successive conquests and pogroms by her Middle Eastern neighbours, until in the last quarter of the nineteenth century, as the Czars of St Petersburg embarked on anti-semitic policies, a distinctively Zionist movement began to develop in Europe, later supported by powerful groups in America.

With the very existence of Israel, even as this book goes to press, again threatened by neighbouring powers, it inevitably deals with the varying motives, from fear or a racialist drive for conquest, which have forced her almost continuously to regard herself as a small embattled community, not however lacking powerful friends from Jewish groups and statesmen of almost every religious persuasion in the Western world.

In Britain, as in the United States, there has been and is very strong support for Israel and her people, from politicians and communities extending far beyond the relatively small numbers of Jews who are our citizens. How far this is due to admiration for the courage and tenacity of the Israelis, how far – as is certainly true in my own case – it is in part a response to the teaching of religious history in our day schools and Sunday schools, chapels, churches, kirk and conventicles, I would find it hard to say. I shall not be surprised to hear that many of those who come to read the following pages will do so for one or other of these reasons, in many cases, a majority perhaps, for both of them.

'The chariot of Israel, and the horsemen thereof.'

2 KINGS ii.12

INTRODUCTION

The Diaspora

THE JEWISH PEOPLE have been wanderers on the face of the earth for more than twenty-five centuries: the history of the Diaspora which has been set out in countless books over the years.

These works show that the principal authority for the earlier years is the Old Testament, supported and amplified as year succeeded year by archaeological studies in the Holy Land and neighbouring countries, illumined particularly in recent years by the excavations of Professor Yigael Yadin.

However, perhaps the clearest and most readable account for the years before and after Christ is not in a conventional history but in the report of a Royal Commission, not normally a product of great historical writing. While drawing on the works of some writers in Israel itself and in the Western world, this introduction mainly follows the exposition in the Report of the Royal Commission on Palestine, chaired by Lord Peel (grandson of Sir Robert Peel, the nineteenth-century Prime Minister) appointed in August 1936. It reported in June 1937 and its first chapter begins:

> In the course of the second millennium BC, the lands that lie along the eastern coast of the Mediterranean were subject to periodical incursions of Semitic tribesmen pressing seawards across the Arabian desert from the barren steppes of the North. In Palestine these immigrants became known as Hebrews, and one tribe or group of tribes, who claimed descent from Abraham of Ur, acquired the name of Israelites from Abraham's grandson, Jacob or Israel . . .

The Hebrew tribes appear to have come to Canaan from Mesopotamia, 'not primitive desert nomads, but the product of a region in which Sumer, Akkad and Babylon had built a long tradition of civility and enterprise'[1] and had already become subject both to Babylonian and Egyptian traditions.

The migration of Israelites to Egypt, their persecution by the Pharaohs and the Old Testament's record of their return under the leadership of Moses, led to the historical fact that the Israelites had, by around 1000 BC, occupied most of the hill country in Palestine. They were differentiated, by their religion, from the coast peoples – the Phoenicians or Philistines – and from the Semites of the desert across the river Jordan.

Their religion was distinctive in that it involved the worship of one God, whose commandments were passed on to the Jewish people through their leader Moses, as against the polytheistic worship which characterized their neighbours and others of the ancient world.

Peel draws on the Old Testament to trace their history from the book of *Judges*, the period of Joseph, Jacob, Joshua and Moses: a people characterized by tribal disunion and recurring conflict with their neighbours. These pressures caused them to create a monarchy. Under King David (*c.* 1010–970 BC) of the tribe of Judah, and his son King Solomon (*c.* 970–930 BC) the Israelites overcame their enemies, and their rule embraced the whole of Palestine, north and south, encompassed by the Egyptian and Syrian empires. Their dynasty lasted over a century.

After Solomon's death the people of the coast won back their independence; the northern people seceded and formed a separate kingdom centring on Samaria; and it was in the kingdom of Judah that the tradition of Hebrew thought and culture was henceforth mainly concentrated, largely because of the Temple which Solomon had built at Jerusalem. For two hundred years the rival kingdoms and the men of the coastal region survived as separate nations, until Samaria succumbed in the early years of the eighth century BC to the Assyrians. Some Samaritans were deported far afield, and soon not only they but also the southern kingdom bent the knee to Assyrian rule.

By this submission the southerners escaped annihilation or dispersion until about 585 BC, when the new Babylonian conquerors of Nebuchad-nezzar's army subjugated Judah. Jerusalem was sacked and its historic buildings were destroyed.

By the rivers of Babylon, there we sat down, yea and wept, when we remembered Zion.[2]

Less than half a century later, however, Babylon itself was occupied by Cyrus of Persia, and he allowed the Judaean exiles to return. Historians have estimated that forty thousand returned to the land of their fathers and immediately undertook the rebuilding of the Temple. Nehemiah gave them political leadership and the prophet Ezra their spiritual inspiration.

During the next three or four hundred years the Judaeans were in their 'Dark Ages', little being recorded of this time: Peel simply states that the Jews lived as part of the fifth Satrapy of the Persian Empire, and later came under the Ptolemaic successors of Alexander the Great. However, modern research, the Commission records, ascribes to this dark period a flowering of

Hebrew culture:

> It was the period, it was held, when the Mosaic Law or Torah took on its final form and became the binding code of social life as well as of religious observance, and when such varied achievements of Jewish thought and art as Job, Ruth, the Song of Songs, Ecclesiastes, Proverbs and some of the finer Psalms were composed.

Palestine next fell to the Syrian Seleucid rulers, and with them came the first persecution of the Jewish faith *per se*. The religious emphasis was now Hellenic, and the Jews came under brutal pressure to abandon the Torah and worship the Greek gods and adopt Greek ways. A Jewish revolt was led by the Hasmonean family, notably Judas Maccabaeus and John Hyrcanus, and from about 150 BC on they won back the independence of Judaea and extended their sway north, south and east until it virtually covered the area of the kingdoms of David and Solomon. But this freedom did not survive. Maccabaeus was killed in a feudal war, and the country returned to a state of division between ruling princes and despots. Pharisees and Sadducees were engaged in deadly theological conflict; the fratricidal Hasmonean dynasty was totally incapable of secular leadership. When an all-conquering Rome appeared on the scene there was no one to offer any coherent resistance. A group of Jewish zealots retired to the citadel-rock of Masada, where later almost all the nine hundred and sixty of them took their own lives rather than yield to the Romans. Pompey captured Jerusalem in 63 BC and, in the words of the Peel Commission, 'Never since then has Palestine been an independent State.'

For nearly two centuries Palestine was virtually a Roman province; unruly, but not free. Judah was a Roman province in AD 26–39, a period which included the crucifixion of Christ by Pontius Pilate. The subjugation of the Jews was carried out by Vespasian, who hastened to Rome on the death of Nero and successfully claimed the Imperial Throne. An uprising by the Jews in AD 64 led to bitter fighting: the Jews were in no shape to resist the counter-attack which ensued. Many of the Sadducees collaborated with the conquerors or were busy upholding their privileged class position. The Pharisees were preoccupied with their religious problems. Jerusalem was captured and sacked in AD 70 by Titus, son of Vespasian, who burned to the ground the Temple where the final resistance was mounted. In AD 115 and 132 the Jews fought back again; the latter rising proved so damaging to the Romans that they destroyed Jerusalem and ploughed up its very site.

Hadrian, who for a time held out hopes of rebuilding the Temple, changed his mind and decided to rebuild Jerusalem as a 'Great City', Aelia Capitolina. It was this which brought about the major revolt led by Bar-Kochba, still a folk-hero of the Jewish people. He succeeded in capturing Jerusalem and services were held on the site of the destroyed Temple. But

Sextus Severus was called from Britain to head the tenth legion, who rapidly recaptured Jerusalem and destroyed Bar-Kochba and his army at Bethar, a few miles south. Many Jews were executed, many more taken as slaves. From then on, Peel records, Palestine steadily sank into obscurity. Its population fell still further: at the time of the destruction of the Temple, it is estimated that some 300,000 Jews were living in Palestine and a further million or more in Egypt, Syria, Asia Minor and Babylon. This figure is to be set against an estimated population of the entire Greco-Roman world in the last century BC of sixty to seventy million.

It is interesting to see how Abba Eban, as a Jew, highlights the hopes which surrounded the mission of Jesus Christ.

Jesus was a Pharisaic Jew. He lived among the common people of Galilee and was the spokesman of their ideas. Galilee was the stronghold of a robust Jewish patriotism, which found resonance in the teachings of Jesus in so far as they conformed with those of the ancient prophets. He never considered himself a universal prophet outside the Jewish context. It cannot even be said that he was indifferent to the external forms of religion. He meticulously kept Jewish laws, made a pilgrimage to Jerusalem on Passover, ate unleavened bread and uttered a blessing when he drank wine. He was a Jew in word and deed.

Jesus articulated the ideas and manners of the masses. Even his attacks on the hypocritical leaders were not unprecedented. He himself declared in the Sermon on the Mount that he 'had not come to destroy the law but to fulfil it'. Nourished by the ideas of Pharisaic Judaism, he stressed the Messianic hope, predicting its fulfilment in his own time. The terms 'Messiah' and 'King of the Jews' were used by him in their spiritual significance. But in the atmosphere of the time they resounded like a call to revolution. The Roman authorities saw Jesus's activities as a token of subversion. His arrest, trial and execution reflected the intolerance of an insecure regime which had experienced many a Jewish revolt arising out of religious fervour.

After his death, a small circle of Jesus's followers began to spread his teachings among the Jews of Palestine. It was not until the moral crusade of Paul that this teaching spread among the gentile population in the form of a new religion.

The Jew had come, through the Torah, to a comprehension of God. To Paul, Christ was the incarnation of the Law, and even its substitute. Jesus had sacrificed himself in order to emancipate man from the burden of the Law. He was an intermediary between God and man. The principle of Christ as mediator became the cornerstone of the new faith, as Paul denounced the original Jewish Law as burdensome to Jew and Gentile alike.

Gradually the Jewish Christians were won over in increasing numbers to his views. As the new faith broke more and more sharply with the old institutions and the old prohibitions against deification, a final split became inevitable. In time Christianity, in contact with the Roman world, grew more and more distinct from the parent Jewish faith.

If the Bible had not been translated into Greek, there would have been few converts among the Greek-speaking gentiles, and Christianity would hardly have become a world religion in the course of three centuries. The Septuagint had kindled a flame of religious yearning among the Hellenic population of the Empire . . . the Jewish diaspora was deeply rooted from the first century onward throughout the Hellenistic Middle East. The dispersion gave strong impetus to Christian teaching. The oldest Christian communities, established by immediate followers of Jesus, consisted of Aramaic-speaking Jews of Palestine, and Greek-speaking Jews of Cyrene, Alexandria, Syria and Cilicia. When the apostle Stephen was stoned in Jerusalem, his colleagues went to Phoenicia and Antioch, preaching the word to Jews of a more tolerant and less orthodox disposition . . .[3]

For five hundred years Palestine remained under Roman and Byzantine rule, and then in the seventh century it was reconquered, this time by Islam. Between 632 and 713, the followers of Mahomet invaded and conquered Syria, Iraq, Persia, Egypt and then the whole length of the North African coast, and finally Spain. In south-eastern and south-central Europe, they were defeated by Constantine in 717–18 and by the Franks at Poitiers in 732. Nevertheless, they controlled the Mediterranean seaboard from southern Spain to the Middle East. Their sea power was dominant in the Indian Ocean, and battling for supremacy in the Mediterranean. Their trade extended from Cadiz to Cairo, Baghdad and Zanzibar and beyond to India and China. They were also intellectual leaders: scholars from Central and Northern Europe came to Arab universities when academic studies on the continental mainland were still in the Dark Ages.

The Palestinians had rebuilt Jerusalem, and established a university there as well as one of the greatest historic places of worship, the Dome of the Rock, where Mahomet is believed by the faithful to have leapt through the skies to Paradise on his Arab horse.

But the Arab Empire, too, went the way of the others. All the Arab states in the Near East were defeated by the Seljuk Turks. From the end of the eleventh century, the West intervened through the Crusades, aiming at recovering the Holy Sepulchre, and actually maintained a 'Kingdom of Jerusalem' until the late twelfth century, when the Mameluke dynasty in Egypt took it over, together with Syria, a rule punctuated by repeated Mongol raids. The Ottoman Turks conquered the territory in 1517; from then on, except for the time of Napoleon's brief invasion and Mohammed Ali's brief occupation, they held the Holy Land in fief up to the 1914–18 war.

The Peel Commission's history of the Diaspora is just as valuable in setting the stage as it is for its recommendations on the problem it had been appointed to resolve. The Diaspora is nearly as old as Jewry itself. When in 538 BC the Jews had been allowed to return to their homes, a significant number stayed in Iraq, with their own educational institutions, but working closely with the Baghdad Caliphate: the same occurred in Egypt, where some were 'assimilated' (went native). The destruction of Jerusalem in AD 135 led to immigration into Iraq, Egypt, Syria, the Yemen and indeed to Greece and Italy. Centuries later Jews were to follow the conquering Arabs to the north-east of Africa and Spain: in Spain, Peel records, they rose to high positions in diplomacy, finance, science, medicine, and what we would now call higher-level civil servants. Again, most of the Jews in Spain were assimilated.

The era of persecution which was wholly to transform the conditions of life in the Diaspora, the Peel Commission says pointedly, 'began not in the Moslem world but in the Christian'. In feudal Europe the immigrant Jew could find no place in what would now be called the 'Establishment', i.e. on the land or in the exclusive industrial guilds. He became a middleman, merchant or itinerant pedlar, and with usury forbidden to Christians by the canon law of the Church, a moneylender. In career terms the Jews were driven in on one another, a closer and tighter community which meant one hated and ultimately persecuted.

> In the eyes of the Church, moreover, they were the worst of Heretics. They did not seek, it was true, to convert others, but none refused so obstinately to be converted. And behind that was the general idea that on all Jews, in all times and places, lay the guilt of the Crucifixion.
>   This complex of ill-feeling came to a head in the period of the Crusades. The wrath of the Crusaders fell as much on Jew as on Moslem; and it soon seemed as much an act of piety to kill Jews in Europe as to kill Saracens in the Holy Land. A wave of persecution, increasingly cruel in its methods, spread all over Europe.[4]

First England and then France took up the cause of expropriation, torture and massacre. Hundreds of Jewish communities were pillaged. They were accused of poisoning wells, even blamed for the Black Death which decimated Europe in the fourteenth century. The Mongol invasion of Germany was blamed on them. Some countries expelled them; others persecuted them. Between 1182 and 1321 the Jews of France were expelled and readmitted four times, each time to face further persecution.

Jews had come to England with William the Conqueror. He had, in fact, a Jewish doctor, and was friendly with the community – even challenging them, as a joke, to convert him: the nobles were not amused. In the fourteenth century they were well established. Legally they were regarded as the property of the Crown: only they, the doctrine ran, were allowed to lend money and receive interest. The prevailing rate was about 50 per cent, sometimes rising to $66\frac{2}{3}$. They could and were taxed at the King's own discretion, and on their death their entire property was taken over by the

Crown, usually being sold to their heirs for a swingeing percentage. In return, the Jews were given every facility by the Crown to pursue their debtors, the Crown then levying a proportion of the amount paid.

Paul Johnson, in *The Offshore Islanders,** comments on their central role in financing not only agriculture but the arts. One of them, Aaron of Lincoln, he records, operated in twenty-five counties, and numbered among his clients the King of Scotland, the Archbishop of Canterbury and 'a score of bishops, abbots and earls', financing the building of Lincoln Cathedral and the abbeys of Peterborough and St Albans. So rich did he become that, on his death, the Crown set up a separate financial establishment, the *Scaccarium Aaronis*, to realize as much as possible of his wealth.

Inevitably their power led to a sharp reaction, not least from the Church, whose representatives in Stephen's reign were assiduous in spreading tales of ritual murders, particularly of children. In London, Norwich, Stamford and Lincoln pogroms took place – in York, 150 Jews who had taken refuge in the royal castle were murdered. When King John was forced by the barons at Runnymede to sign Magna Carta, three specifically anti-semitic clauses were included:

> If anyone shall have borrowed money from the Jews, more or less, and die before the debt be satisfied, no interest shall be taken upon such debt so long as the heir be under age, of whomsoever he may hold; and if the debt should fall into Our hands we will only take the chattel mentioned in the Charter. And if anyone die indebted to the Jews his wife shall have her dower and pay nothing of that debt; and if the children of the said deceased be left under age they shall have necessaries provided for them according to the condition of the deceased, and the debt shall be paid out of the residue, saving the Lord's service; and so it shall be done with regard to debts owed to other persons than Jews. (Sanders translation)

Later in the century, Simon de Montfort's rebellion led to further pogroms. A dedicated anti-semite, he burnt as a heretic an archdeacon who married a Jewess, and introduced rules requiring Jews to wear distinctive symbols of disgrace on their garments. In 1290, Edward I expelled the Jewish community from his realms, and for generations agriculture suffered through lack of the financial investment which the Jews had organized.

In Spain, too, the atmosphere changed. Where the Jews had been welcomed, they were now hunted down by the Inquisition and burnt as heretics. In 1492 all Jews who refused to be converted were expelled. Some fled to Portugal, but were thrown out when King Manuel II, about to marry the daughter of Ferdinand and Isabella, obtained their consent only on giving an undertaking to expel the Jews. In 1536 Portugal, too, introduced

* London, 1972, pp. 106–7

the Inquisition, which immediately directed itself against those Jews who had adopted the Christian religion.

Venice introduced the ghetto; other communities such as Prague and Frankfurt followed. European Rabbis had created a policy: build a frame around the Torah.

The migration changed direction: not from east to west but from west to east, to the Turkish Empire, the Balkans, even Egypt and Asia Minor.

The mass movement of Spanish Jews, Sephardim, is still important in the life of Israel, where they on the one hand, and the Russians and Germans, or Ashkenazim, on the other, are still regarded as quasi-separate communities.

Some Jews from Germany, France and England sought refuge in Eastern Europe, in Lithuania, Poland, and Hungary, and soon more than half the world's Jews lived in that area. The Polish kings changed their policy from one of protection to one of persecution. The Cossacks came and conquered, and then came Russian rule with the 'Pale of Settlement' – what Peel calls a sort of 'territorial ghetto' – which was established from the Baltic north of Warsaw to the Black Sea near Odessa to prevent the Jews from permeating Russia. Chaim Weizmann was to be one of many born and living within the 'Pale' who, at the end of the nineteenth century, escaped and started a new life in the West.

The hope of the Diaspora, as Peel records, now swung back from east to west. It was in France and England, once leaders in persecution, that a new spirit of tolerance first developed. Oliver Cromwell, not always credited with such a spirit, threw Britain's doors open to the Jews. This was partly due to the infiltration of the Marranos, enlightened, assimilated Spanish Jews who were soon in financial business with their opposite numbers in Hamburg and Amsterdam. Many of the petty German princelings had their 'Court Jew', charged with raising loans in the money markets, providing supplies for the armed forces and investment advice to his sovereign. The Jews were less popular with the leading citizens, but the Great Elector Frederick William of Brandenburg declared, 'The Jews and their commerce, far from being a detriment to the land, are a decided benefit', and appointed three Jewish financiers as his advisers and managers. Elsewhere there were restrictions. A Jew could remain, but if he had sons, only one could remain with him. Jews were not allowed to engage in agriculture or to acquire property. In Prussia and Austria, where outwardly there was toleration, the Jews were kept in check by discriminating taxation, the *Leibzoll*, a poll tax on Jews entering a city or crossing a frontier.

In France, where the regime though moving towards emancipation was still markedly anti-Jewish, reformers pressed for easement. Mirabeau worked for emancipation but he was fighting a strong tide. Anti-semitism was particularly vigorous in Alsace and Lorraine, where the number of Jews was limited by law: in all France by 1789 there were only 50,000. After the revolution the National Assembly were finally prevailed on to grant French Jews the right to take the oath of citizenship.

The Jews were thus emancipated in France in 1790, whence the invading French armies carried the attack on the ghetto to Holland, Germany and Italy. Napoleon however only addressed himself to the question after Austerlitz in 1805. His first reaction was to restrict them, despite the emancipation already proclaimed, then to soak them. 'It would be a weakness to chase away the Jews: it would be a sign of strength to correct them.' Usury was to be attacked, and Jews interviewed individually. If they gave satisfactory answers about their behaviour, their religion and practices, and affirmed their loyalty to France until death, they were told '*Sa Majesté veut que vous soyez Français*'. To this end he reconvened the Sanhedrin, the group of wise men who went back to Biblical times in Jewish history. Napoleon went a long way towards making the Jews French, loyal to him; but for all that he is one of the few dictators who could be accused of toleration.

In Britain anti-Jewish restrictions were relaxed, but not finally abolished until 1890. Meanwhile a man of Jewish birth, Benjamin Disraeli, had become Prime Minister, though he had joined the Church of England a third of a century before he became the Queen's First Minister. In 1858 a de Rothschild, a professing Jew, had become a Member of Parliament; in 1885 his son, Baron Lionel de Rothschild, was created a peer and took his seat in the House of Lords.

In the nineteenth century it was in Russia that oppression continued, relieved only by reformist Czars for short periods. Since the sixteenth century a succession of Czars had refused to allow Jews into the country, but with the several partitions of Poland in the late 1700s the number of Jews within the Czar's jurisdiction rose to 900,000. This was when the 'Pale' came into being. Briefly after 1802 there were easements, but with the succession of Nicholas I persecution became acute. Conscription into the army was imposed on a selective and humiliating basis. In 1835 the 'Pale of Settlement' was further constricted. Institutions of education barely existed. Jews, whose economic activities were severely restricted, had to club together to ensure a minimum education service. When Alexander II, who emancipated the serfs, was assassinated, the Jews were blamed. Nicholas II, his successor, was pressed to accept the authenticity of a Franco-Russian forgery, the 'Protocols of the Elders of Zion'. He refused – and a quarter of a century later this was quoted to explain the Russian revolution, for was not Trotsky a Jew?*

* As were Zinoviev, Kamenev, Sverdlov and Sokolnikov.[5]

The Peel Report comments:

The Jews' exclusion from all Russia except Poland was the least of their misfortunes. A series of massacres deliberately incited by anti-Jewish fanatics and acquiesced in, if not connived at, by the Government was imitated and repeated from time to time until as late as 1910. Tens of thousands of Jews were murdered. More were rendered homeless and destitute. Again, therefore, there was a mass migration westwards. Between 1880 and 1910 at least three million Jews fled from Eastern Europe. Many found refuge on British soil, in England, Canada, Australia and South Africa; but the great majority made for the United States. In 1870 the number of American Jews was roughly about a quarter of a million, it is now about four and a half million. Of the other twelve million Jews in the world, some ten million are in Europe and of these about nine million are in central and Eastern Europe.*[6]

Meanwhile anti-semitism became acute in Western countries, in Italy with Papal support. In Germany Jewish financiers were blamed for the economic depression which was affecting the industrial world. Bismarck, who began by persecuting the Catholics through the *Kultur Kampf*, presided beamingly over the 1879 campaign directed against the Liberals, with whom the Jews were identified. Nor was literature neutral. Treitschke and Friedrich Nietzsche lent their pliant pens to the campaign.

In Austria-Hungary the 1880s saw a similar course of action, with an anti-semite appointed to the Chair of Theology at Prague University. Accusations of ritual murder followed as a matter of course.

Before long in country after country a spurious intellectualism was devoted to stirring up racialism. In Hungary even the socialists employed an agitator in this cause. The Aryan myth was already a tool of German racialism, with its emphasis on the blond, blue-eyed Nordic, the epitome of physical perfection, the hereditary characteristic of the Teuton and the rest of Central European manhood. Against this paragon was set the undersized dark-haired, dark-eyed Jew. Even Richard Wagner campaigned against the 'decay of German folk by the fact that it is now exposed without defence to penetration by the Jew'. More than half a century before the Nazis came to power the intellectuals were sowing the seed: Hitler could put forward no higher claim to history's judgment than that of a charnel-house operator.

France, smarting from her defeat at Sedan and Metz, sought solace in anti-semitic, anti-Freemason and anti-liberal bear-baiting. French Jews were one in 400 of the population; their well-backed and highly publicized adversaries advocated the expropriation of all Jewish property. One book dedicated to this end ran into 140 editions, a free enterprise operation which made even the propagation of *Mein Kampf* look amateur.

It was in 1894 that the Western world was set alight by the Dreyfus affair.

* These figures relate to 1937.

His sensationally publicized trial, conviction and sentence to Devil's Island provided the proof the anti-semitic Establishment was seeking.

Many years ago I commented that in the world of politics every action designed to provide a specific political response is capable of generating an equal, opposite, and more than likely greater, political reaction. It was the Dreyfus Affair which more than any other single event, if it did not create Zionism, made it articulate and created a counter-force which would not rest until the Jews of Europe and the wider Diaspora were granted a national home in what is now Israel.

The Peel Commission ends its first chapter with an analysis of Zionism; at the time it was being written (1936-7), the numbers seeking to go to Palestine were greatly increased by the growth of persecution in Nazi Germany. Peel, published on 7 July 1937, draws a sharp distinction between the Zionism which on its negative side is a creed of escape, and Zionism for its own sake.

The troubles in France, Germany and Russia in the last decades of the nineteenth century and the early years of the twentieth, Peel shows, increased the number of Jews in Palestine from about 25,000 in 1881 to over 80,000 in 1914, most of them settling in Jerusalem and the growing towns of Haifa and Jaffa, but 12,000 of them going to one of the forty-three 'colonies', i.e. agricultural settlements, such as those sponsored by Baron Edmond de Rothschild between 1883 and 1900.

Peel then analyses the motives for Zionism, refers to Herzl and, even earlier, Shaftesbury's proposal in 1840 for a scheme of Jewish colonization under international guarantee, and the support for the Zionist ideal of George Eliot and Laurence Oliphant, Disraeli and Sir Moses Montefiore.

It is to the work of 'the Zionists' in that formative period, 1880 to 1914, that we now turn.

CHAPTER 1

The Zionists

THE MANY HISTORIES of the Zionist movement pay tribute to three men: Leon Pinsker, Theodor Herzl and Chaim Weizmann. Two were Russians, one, Herzl, Austro-Hungarian.

Pinsker, graduating in law in Odessa, found that he was unable to practise in his chosen profession, and turned to medicine. The Odessa pogrom in 1871, and still more those of 1881, led him to Zionism. He travelled extensively in West European countries. In London a Jewish Member of Parliament persuaded him to write a book, which was published under the title *Auto-Emancipation: An Admonition to his Brethren from a Russian Jew*.[1] 'To the living, the modern Jew is a dead man. To the native born he is a stranger, to the long settled a vagabond, to the wealthy a beggar, to the poor a millionaire and exploiter, to the citizen a man without country, to all classes a competitor.' Jews therefore had no alternative but to become a nation once more and possess their own territory. Pinsker did not much care where that territory was. Palestine was one possibility, but 'not the only one'. Further persecution followed, for example in Kunavina in 1884. In that same year a conference of Jews from Russia, Britain, Germany, France and Romania took place in Upper Silesia. Pinsker urged the need for Jews to work on the land in Palestine.

It has been said of him that having brooded darkly on the Jewish future during the Russo-Turkish war, he 'finally diagnosed anti-semitism as an endemic psychic deformity for which legal adjustment was a wholly inadequate remedy'. He called for a national home for the Jews, yet despite his support of the existing Palestine settlements did not commit himself to Palestine as the site for the Jewish National Home until late in life, when he finally agreed with this idea. Nahum Sokolov, another Russian, stressed the need for industrial development there. Funds were raised to help two projects already established at Petah Tikvah and Yesud ha-Ma'alah.

If it was Chaim Weizmann who saw Israel through to nationhood, it was Theodor Herzl, at the age of forty-three very near to death, who was the first notable Western Zionist. He presided over the sixth Zionist Congress in Basle, which Weizmann as a young chemistry student attended as one of the 592 delegates; indeed he made a speech highly critical of Herzl who, as we shall see, having failed to persuade the Sultan of Turkey to sanction the establishment of a Jewish National Home in his fief, Palestine, was commending Uganda as a staging-post on the way to the Holy Land.

Herzl's youth and upbringing and his early writings gave no indications of his future ideals, still less of his status as the acknowledged leader of world Jewry. He was born in Budapest in May 1860 of rich, assimilated Jewish parents, who soon afterwards moved to the other capital city of the Austro-Hungarian Empire, Vienna. In his youth neither he nor his parents paid much regard to Jewish affairs or aspirations. After a brief period at a Jewish school, he attended a series of secular schools and and ultimately the university. His thirteenth birthday was celebrated not as a *Bar Mitzvah* but a 'confirmation'. He was recorded at that time as attacking Judaism with 'mocking cynicism'.

His ambitions from boyhood were literary. He was for ever writing plays, with scant success until he became famous. But, after leaving university, he secured a post on the *Neue Freie Presse* of Vienna, mainly as literary reviewer, and was sent to Paris where his dramatic criticisms, and above all his vignettes and *feuilletons* soon won a large and appreciative Viennese readership. In 1891 his paper appointed him as Paris correspondent, which widened his interests to cover the political scene – eventually to provide the shock of the Dreyfus Affair. He served on the *Neue Freie Presse* until his death.[2]

Many times he feared that he would be dismissed by his employers because of his Zionist activities, particularly when he came to be involved in prolonged absences at Congresses or in the Chancelleries of Europe. The owners of the *Presse* had no sympathy with his Zionism, and even when the world's press was recording his movements and achievements, these were not referred to in his own paper. When he died they printed a lengthy obituary on the front page, but confined to two bare sentences the account of his Jewish activities. His anxieties about keeping his job were mainly financial. Though he was born of a rich family, his father had lost a great part of his fortune in a rash speculation, and while Herzl himself had adequate private resources, he used them without stint for the cause – out of his own pocket, for example, providing the substantial *baksheesh* required by both the servants and the ministers (including the Grand Vizier) of the Sultan.

Accounts of his early life reveal a strange psychologically mixed-up character: arrogant, petulant, an avid frequenter of the *demi-monde*, even it is thought contracting a venereal disease. His marriage with a neurotic was far from happy, though he was devoted to his children, and in later years also to his wife. In his youth he sought to live as a more or less 'assimilated' Jew, and as such was treated as an outsider by gentiles and as a renegade by devout Jews. His son, born in 1891, was not circumcised. It was not until 1895, with only nine years to live, that Herzl experienced a vision and transformation as dramatic as that of St Paul on the road to Damascus. He himself was not sure whether he was going insane, as he pounded the Paris avenues, composing what became *The Jewish State, An Attempt at a Modern Solution of the Jewish Question.* In his diary he wrote, 'I believe that my life had ended and world history begun'. He was warned by a fellow journalist who had had medical training to see a doctor. Amos Elon in his biography of Herzl records that in his wild scribblings he compared himself with Bismarck, Savonarola and Napoleon, and quotes from his voluminous scribbles,

> The promised land – nobody has thought of looking for it where it really is – within ourselves. . . . The promised land is where we shall take it. . . . The promised land, where we may at last have hooked noses, black and red beards, bow legs, without being despised for it . . . where we can at last live as free men on our soil . . . where the offensive cry of 'Jew' may become an honourable appellation like German, Englishman; in short, like all civilized people.[3]

As his paper's political correspondent in France he had already been involved in reporting *causes célèbres* reflecting the growing anti-semitism of his time – the lawsuit brought against a raving anti-semite, Edouard Drumont, who had accused the deputy speaker of the French Parliament of being in the pay of the Jews. As feeling grew there were frequent duels between Jewish army officers and anti-semitic fanatics who stirred up doubts about their loyalty. One was killed by an anti-semitic Marquis; Herzl, still at this time a detached observer rather than a participant, walked with 50,000 Jewish mourners in his funeral procession. The violence and the duels spread to other professions, finance, the press, politics. A million copies of Drumont's *La France Juive* were sold between 1885 and the early 1890s.

In 1892 France was rocked by the Panama Canal Company bankruptcy, destroying the savings of thousands of small investors. No Jews were on the board, but two had been implicated in some of the disreputable secondary financial dealings. At once this was widened to attacks on the whole Jewish community in France. Herzl heard, for the first time, raucous street demands, '*A mort, à mort les Juifs*'. He began to transform his far from successful theatrical ambitions into wild, deluded dramas he would enact in real life. He would challenge to a duel one of the three leading enemies of Austrian Jewry.* He would either contrive to get himself shot – his death, to

---

* Prince Alvis of Liechtenstein, George Schonerer and Karl Lueger.

use his own words, 'might at least improve the hearts and minds of man' – or, were he to kill one of his chosen anti-semites, he would use his subsequent trial as a world platform for converting the Austrian people against his persecutors, and at the same time ensure his acquittal and indeed his election to Parliament. He never carried out his mad plan, and later referred to it as 'a dream' he had had while still uncertain where to turn.

His next scheme was no less visionary, and still no more Zionist. He would go to the Pope and say:

> Help us against anti-semitism. In return *I* [author's italics] shall initiate a great mass movement for the free and honourable conversion of all Jews to Christianity – a diplomatic peace treaty concluded behind closed doors.[4]

But he would be celebrated in public, with pageants in the capitals of Europe, involving Emperors and Archbishops – he even drew up the specification of the frock-coat he would be wearing, and of the peal of bells which would reflect his glory. The Archbishop of Vienna and even the Pope would be *dramatis personae*. He tried to sell the idea to his newspaper's proprietors and editors: the message he received in reply was in the spirit, 'Don't ring us: we'll ring you'. To them he was a literate journalist, a good dramatic critic, and a worthwhile Paris correspondent: no more.

He continued to ponder the answer to the growing anti-semitism he met everywhere. He nearly went berserk at an anti-semitic insult flung at him. Still anti-Zionist, he decided to visit Palestine to see the Jewish agricultural settlements established by rich European Jews, notably the Rothschilds. Meanwhile he returned to writing plays. Suddenly the situation was transformed for him, as for others, by the Dreyfus Affair.

Alfred Dreyfus, an officer in the French Army and a Jew, was court-martialled in December 1894 on a charge of high treason. The evidence, contained in a letter, was thin and unconvincing, but he was nevertheless found guilty, condemned to public degradation and deportation to Devil's Island, Guiana, for life.

Herzl's first reaction to the Dreyfus Affair had been to assume the captain guilty, and he so reported to his newspaper – who, strangely, were sceptical. But before the trial ended he was convinced of Dreyfus's innocence and so reported home. What undoubtedly affected him most was the outburst of anti-semitism in Paris, and indeed throughout France:

> For by now the howl of the Paris mob on the place de la Concorde, screaming 'Down with the Jews' like dogs baying at the moon, was rising almost daily into Herzl's hotel window in the nearby rue Cambon. . . . As he watched the demonstrations, he sensed a kind of evil-smelling fog rise from the massed crowd, only to redescend on it like poisoned vapour. He thoroughly disliked Dreyfus as a man, but he decided that for psychological reasons Dreyfus simply could not be guilty.[5]

Five years later doubts about Dreyfus's guilt led to a formidable campaign for a fresh trial. The Vice-President of the Senate, Auguste Scheurer-Kestner, convinced Georges Clemenceau, a leading politician by this time a journalist, of Dreyfus's innocence. Clemenceau denounced the court-martial, and the writer Emile Zola wrote an open letter to the President of the Republic, published in Clemenceau's *L'Aurore*, in January 1898. The literary and moderate political establishment supported him, while the right wing, for different reasons, also demanded that Zola be brought to trial.

He was sentenced to a heavy fine and a year in prison, but the army officer who had denounced Dreyfus had himself by this time been found guilty, and committed suicide. A fresh trial was ordered which again found Dreyfus guilty; but although he was again sentenced to imprisonment, the authorities remitted the remainder of the sentence. Dreyfus accepted the clemency but continued his campaign to prove his innocence. In 1906 the verdicts condemning him were annulled, and Dreyfus went on to fight in the First World War and to become a lieutenant-colonel. He died in 1935. The Dreyfus trial was a turning-point in Herzl's career, and more than any other factor led to the revival of Zionism in France and the wider Western world.

Herzl was now determined to devote his life to the cause of Zionism. His zeal was heightened by the wave of anti-semitism which swept France and other countries in Europe. In his own country the Lower Austrian Diet was moving towards an anti-semitic majority. The same was threatened in France, where a proposal to ban all Jews from the public service was defeated by a majority of only 268 to 208. Herzl himself came under surveillance by the French police, who in a report referred to his 'hostility to France'. Meanwhile, anti-semitism grew more powerful in the German Reichstag and in Russia.

Herzl had been in court when Dreyfus was found guilty and sentenced to life imprisonment, and later witnessed the condemned man's 'degradation' as his sword was broken and he was stripped of his uniform and insignia and taken away in chains, while his fellow officers shouted 'Judas! Traitor'. Herzl saw this not as the hounding of one man, but as the persecution of an entire race. He walked home in what he called a 'state of strange agitation'. His mind was made up. For the rest of his life he would lead a campaign for the Jews. In his home country the anti-semites, in the Diet, the municipal government and the streets, were triumphant. Political bully-boys demanded the expulsion of 'four million Jews, who don't work. . . . Why shouldn't this people, this goddamned rabble, be exterminated from the face of the earth?' His own report to his Vienna paper on the growth of French anti-semitism, headed by him 'Death to the Jews', was changed by his editors to 'Death to the traitors'.

As in Vienna, so on a more organized scale in Russia hysteria and official persecution was directed against the Jews. K. P. Pobiedonostsev, 'Procurator of the Holy Synod', was exploiting anti-Jewish feeling by accusations of profiteering during the Russo-Turkish war of 1877–8. Alexander III, driven by Pobiedonostsev, was ready to accuse the Jews as murderers of Christ: 'In my heart I am very glad when they beat the Jews, even though this practice cannot be permitted.' His solution for the problem of Russian Jews was that one-third should be harried to destruction, one-third should emigrate, and the remainder be converted from their faith.

Most of the Jews were restricted to the West and South, the Ukraine, White Russia, the Polish provinces and Bessarabia, the notorious 'Pale of Settlement'. It was not long before they were being blamed for financial manoeuvrings, exploiting the poor, controlling stock markets and the banks, even the press. Was not that notorious Jew Benjamin Disraeli responsible for Holy Russia's humiliation at the Congress of Berlin?[6]

Herzl, in his mental confusion, toyed with writing a novel which would convert or confute the anti-semites, but rejected it in favour of political action – political action in favour of a new Exodus, financed by wealthy Jews in the Diaspora, supplemented by donations from European governments who would be glad to see the back of the Jews once and for all. Finally he acted. He wrote a letter to Baron Maurice de Hirsch, a multi-millionaire Jew, seeking an interview. Hirsch had established the Jewish Colonial Organization, with vast resources, originally considering Palestine for his projected settlements, later deciding on Argentina, but only 20,000 went there under his scheme. Herzl's tactless approach led to a refusal, with Herzl leaving him swearing that he would raise a fund of ten million marks.

He went away to begin his diaries – *Book One of the Jewish Cause* – 'begun around Whit Sunday [sic] 1895'. He locked himself up in his hotel room and, inspired by Wagner's music, wrote a fourteen-point plan for raising the money and organizing his Exodus (Mark II). The Germans would finance it. He began his appeals by a letter to the Viennese Chief Rabbi, read it over to a former doctor, by that time a journalist, who noted that 'he had gone mad'. He approached Rothschild* with a thundering and totally ill-calculated memorandum: Rothschild formed a similar opinion, but later began to listen – the English and French Rothschilds had already begun to subsidize agricultural settlements of Jewish émigrés in Palestine.** Herzl wrote to Bismarck, but received no reply. Anti-Jewish riots broke out in Vienna, but by this time the frightened Chief Rabbi began to feel that Herzl

*Baron Nathaniel Rothschild.
**See pp. 26–7 below.

was showing signs of inspiration: 'Remain as you are', he advised. 'Perhaps you are the one called of God.'

The French anti-semites made further gains in the municipality and took control of City Hall. Herzl returned to Vienna, and in a city seething with riots began his new Zionist mission to the Jews. He was met by ribald comments such as 'I'm all in favour of a Jewish state provided that they appoint me as ambassador to Vienna.' In his diary he said, 'I shall be the Parnell of the Jews.' To his surprise the Austro-Hungarian Prime Minister offered him the editorship of a new state-owned newspaper, which led him to negotiate with his own paper's proprietors, with a view to their placing a Sunday issue at his disposal, the front page to be devoted to his clarion call, 'The Solution to the Jewish Question'. But right to the end of his life his friendly and admiring publishers refused him a platform, even when he had become world famous and a regular visitor to the courts of the crowned heads of Europe.

He visited England, where there had been continuing work on 'Zionist' settlement programmes for thirty years, supported by Lord Shaftesbury, Palmerston, biblical scholars, and the authoress George Eliot, who wrote a novel, *Daniel Deronda*, about a Jew who settled in Palestine to create a national home for the Jews. He met Sir Samuel Montagu, who had earlier petitioned the Sultan of Turkey, to whose domains Palestine belonged, to grant 250,000 acres east of the Jordan for colonization by European Jews. In 1896 his eighty-six-page book, *The Jewish State: An Attempt at a Modern Solution of the Jewish Question* was published in Vienna, dedicated to winning support for a sovereign state, either in Palestine or in Argentina. It created a stir in his own country, but most of the comments were hostile. Not all: the poet Richard Beer–Hofmann wrote:

> At long last here is a man who carries his Judaism not like a burden, or as disaster, in resignation, but as the legitimate legacy of an ancient civilization.[7]

In England Holman Hunt, the Pre-Raphaelite painter, gave him public support, even prophesying that the Arabs who already lived in Palestine would happily work for their incoming Jewish masters. Sir Samuel Montagu published a statement that Palestine could be bought for £2 million. New supporters joined him, including Nathan Birnbaum, who had coined the word 'Zionism' a few years before.

Nicholas Sokolov, 'later his closest lieutenant, attacked Herzl's ideas, describing Herzl himself as a *feuilletoniste* who dabbled in diplomacy. It was in the East, in Russia, where, as Elon puts it, the message of Herzl's book 'fell like a torch on dry straw'. In the Jewish enclave of Plonsk the young Ben-Gurion, later Israel's first Prime Minister, heard the message – half a century later referring to a rumour that 'the Messiah had arrived, a tall handsome man, a learned man of Vienna, a doctor no less: Theodor Herzl'.

It was in the Pale of Russia that five million Jews lived in what was a large, tightly guarded concentration camp. Where the assimilated Jews of Western Europe were cool, or did not want to know, the Russian Jews leapt at the new vision which had reached them. Chaim Weizmann, born in Russia and by this time a student at the Berlin Institute of Technology, recorded that Herzl's tract hit him and his associates 'like a bolt from the blue'. Jews in Poland and other East European countries rallied to his support. In Bulgaria the Chief Rabbi proclaimed Herzl as the Messiah. What had up to this time been a one-man mission became organized and endowed with resources when David Wolffsohn, a Russian-born wealthy timber merchant living in Germany, joined him: Wolffsohn was later to succeed to the Zionist leadership on Herzl's death.

Then came what might have seemed a combination of the sublime with the ridiculous, 'in the person of a long-bearded, eccentric English parson', the Reverend William Hechler, Chaplain to the British Embassy in Vienna. The account needs to be read in Elon's original: ' "Here I am," cried the Chaplain. "That I can see," replied Herzl, "but who are you?" Hechler replied, "You are puzzled, but, you see, as long ago as 1882 I predicted your coming to the Grand Duke of Baden. Now I am going to help you." ' Elon's account quoted Hechler's visions of the future, based on a prophecy dating from the reign of the Caliph Omar in the seventh century that in 1,260 years, i.e. 1897 and 1898, Palestine would be restored to the Jews.

The account of this first meeting reads like a novel but Hechler, with his position at the German Court, had access to the Kaiser himself, and the Kaiser could open the doors that counted – those of the palace of the Sultan of Turkey and his Grand Vizier. An appointment was made with the Grand Duke Friedrich who, in turn, arranged for Herzl to see the Kaiser, though the Kaiser failed to keep the appointment. Hechler then produced a Count de Nevlinski, a Polish contact-man of dubious origins who nevertheless had access to the Sultan of Turkey, in whose domains lay historic Palestine. Nevlinski, duly hired by Herzl, put before the Sultan a plan under which Turkey would lease Palestine to the Jews either as an independent or as a self-governing Turkish vassal: in return Herzl was to ensure that Jewish millionaires of Europe would assume responsibility for the Sultan's huge national debt, and thenceforth manage his finances. Turkey would thus escape from her degrading subservience to British and French creditors.

The Sultan had no criticism to make of the plan, except that as Jerusalem was – as it is today – a holy place for the Moslems as well as for the Jews, it could not be negotiated away. Herzl agreed to accept that Jerusalem would become extra-territorial. 'It will belong to nobody, and to all – a holy place in the joint possession of all believers.'

After further exchanges and the outpourings of moneys into Turkish palms, Herzl went with Nevlinski to Constantinople. Leading Turks they met in the train told them that there was no possibility of purchase, but that vassalage was a possibility. The train stopped at Sofia, and a large concourse of Bulgarian Jews hailed Herzl as the saviour, the 'leader', 'the heart of Israel' and its hope. 'Next year in Jerusalem', they shouted as the train left the station, 'Long live Herzl: long live the Jews'.

On arrival he met the Grand Vizier, who was encouraging, but Herzl refused to discuss terms until he met the Sultan:

> I could state the exact scope of our proposals only directly to his Majesty the Sultan; if they are accepted in principle, Sir Samuel Montagu of London would present our financial programme.

Elon points out that sales or exchanges of territory were by no means unusual in the last quarter of the nineteenth century. Marx saw nothing odd in the subservience of India and China; Engels had welcomed the British occupation of Egypt, which was still a Turkish vassal; in 1878 Disraeli had bought Cyprus from Turkey for an 'annual tribute of £92,000 and 4,166,220 okes of salt'. Herzl negotiated with determination, regardless of the fact that he had no mandate from Western countries, or Jewish financiers, no organization, not a penny from any of his potential backers. Yet he was promising Turkey a cancellation of her international debts to the tune of £100 million.

Other officials, such as the Secretary-General of the Foreign Ministry, accepted the plan – 'C'est superbe' – though there might be doubt in his case whether His Excellency was referring to the plan, or to his bribe. The next step, Herzl was led to believe, was to see the Sultan. Herzl pressed Nevlinski to arrange an audience. He was invited to see him at his court ceremonies, and after further talks with the Grand Vizier and other officials, received a stalling message. He would receive Herzl 'as a friend', but first Herzl must do something for him, namely 'use his influence with the international press to treat Turkey more kindly, especially as regarded the Armenians', who should submit directly to him, instead of stirring up the press of Europe. Day after day the Sultan stalled. Yes, he would see him, but not yet – 'sooner or later'. Then he queried the basic plan – must the Jews have Palestine? What about another province? Herzl grew more and more impatient, worried perhaps too about the lack of an ounce of gold backing for the 100 million demanded of him. Nevlinski urged patience:

> I am convinced the Turks want to give us Palestine. The Sultan is just like a woman, willing to surrender, but coy about it. I say she is a whore. I don't know why. I just feel she's a whore.

Still deferring an audience, the Sultan conferred upon him through an intermediary a box containing the Commander's Cross of the Ottoman Medjidiye Order. Finally realizing that the Sultan was not going to see him, Herzl returned to the West, well satisfied and full of hope, but much poorer through the steady drain of *baksheesh*, and conscious that when the appeal was renewed he must come bearing proof that in return for a Jewish National Home, the Sultan's debts would be taken over.

His immediate target must be London and his first approach Montagu. But Montagu refused to accept responsibility. Though three months earlier he had said publicly that Palestine could be bought for £2 million, he now made conditions. He must have the prior consent of the great powers; the Hirsch foundation would have to put up £10 million; and he would need the support of Edmond de Rothschild. De Rothschild had helped Jewish colonists to settle on farmland of dubious viability, but he was in no way committed to a Zionist state. Herzl's visit to London, despite popular acclaim, was a failure. Jewish audiences cheered him but the money was not forthcoming to buy the Sultan's agreement. Herzl wrote off de Rothschild, and turned again to the Cologne timber merchant, David Wolffsohn.

He was planning an International Zionist Congress in Zurich with a preparatory conference in Vienna, the first of six he was to hold before his death, seven years later. News from Turkey became more depressing. The French Government and French Jews were moving towards a rescue operation for the Sultan, without any Zionist conditions. The Chief Rabbi of Vienna, who only eighteen months earlier had encouraged Herzl – 'You remind me of Moses. . . . Perhaps you are the one called of God' – deserted him and attacked the very concept of Zion. Despite the backing of Gladstone, now retired from public life, and Alphonse Daudet, Herzl lacked mass support: above all, he lacked money. The conference in Vienna was a failure; he set up a new conference in Basle in 1897.

This was a crowded and enthusiastic Congress. Sixteen countries were represented by 208 delegates. Herzl controlled the Congress, with the author Max Nordau as his deputy. The Basle Programme which was agreed stated: 'The task of Zionism is to secure for the Jewish people in Palestine a publicly recognized, legally secured homeland.' But the phrase 'homeland' was not an assertion of a monopolistic Jewish settlement in Palestine. The conference simply agreed on a Fabian programme in favour of settlement and international Jewish co-operation. But Herzl was moved to write in his diary:

> At Basle I founded the Jewish state. If I said this aloud today, I would be answered by universal laughter. Perhaps in five years, and certainly in fifty, everyone will know it.

His forecast of 'fifty' written in September 1897 was uncannily prophetic. In

1947 Britain, the post-war mandatory power, referred the question to the United Nations, and in 1948 handed the administration over to the Israelis.

Among the delegates to the Second Congress in Basle was the young Russian chemistry student, Chaim Weizmann, then aged twenty-four. The Congress was preceded by vicious pogroms in Galicia and Romania; France was still overrun by the anti-semitism aroused by the Dreyfus affair. National delegations in Basle were factious and Herzl had a difficult time arousing any spirit of unity, though in the end he emerged triumphant over those who saw the future only in terms of driblets of agricultural colonists.

Any gloom he may have felt was ended by the receipt of a friendly communication from the Ottoman Emperor, responding to the message the Congress had sent him as paramount sovereign of Palestine. Still better, the moment Congress was over he received an invitation from his German contacts inviting him to visit the Grand Duke of Baden on the eve of the Kaiser's pilgrimage to Palestine. On arrival he again became the world statesman. The German ambassador in Constantinople, on instruction, had asked the Turkish court about the Sultan's attitude to Herzl's scheme: the answer was that he regarded it 'with favourable eyes'. The Kaiser also was said to be warming to it once again, and the German ambassador in Vienna, Count von Eulenburg, had been asked to report to the Kaiser on the project. To Herzl the Grand Duke said: 'German influence in Constantinople is now unlimited. England has been crowded out completely, to say nothing of the other powers.... If our Kaiser drops one word to the Sultan, it will certainly be heeded.'

Herzl was losing faith in Britain. 'We need a protectorate.... A German protectorate would suit us best.' There was great optimism that the Kaiser would have little difficulty in winning support from the Sultan. After further consultations with Baden, he told Eulenburg, who had been extremely forthcoming:

> Our movement exists. I expect that one or another of the great powers will espouse it. I once thought it would be England. It lay in the nature of things. I would like it much more to be Germany.

Von Bülow, the German Foreign Minister, received Herzl the next day and was even more encouraging.

Herzl was himself due to go to Palestine, and he was encouraged to believe that he would meet the Kaiser there; indeed he was given to understand that he would be received there as the head of a Zionist delegation. He went via Constantinople where he saw the Kaiser, who was still encouraging, though tension arose when Herzl showed his resentment at what he felt was anti-semitism on His Imperial Majesty's part. The Kaiser had encouraged a mass movement of Jews from Germany, he told

Herzl, so that his country could be rid of the usurers who were waxing rich at the expense of the farming community. Herzl commented on this bitterly, but encouraged the Kaiser to think that if he was worried about Jewish membership of revolutionary parties, a mass move to Palestine would be good for Germany as well as for Zionism. As the conversation warmed again, the Emperor asked Herzl exactly 'in one word' what he should ask of the Sultan. The answer was 'a chartered company under German protection'. The chartered company was becoming a fashionable instrument in colonization, as witness Cecil Rhodes's chartered company in Southern Africa. 'Good,' answered the Kaiser, 'a chartered company.' Herzl left him and caught his own ship, the Russian *Imperator Nicholas II*, from Constantinople to Alexandria, en route for his first visit to the Holy Land. He left behind him, for the Kaiser to give to the Sultan, his memorandum on the future of Zionism and Palestine.

Disappointment awaited him. Before the Kaiser's conversations with the Sultan, the German delegation had watered down his document, excising all references to German participation. The Turks had clearly been hostile to even the hint of such a development, and when Herzl finally met the Kaiser in Jerusalem there was only discouragement. Instead of his earlier phrase, that he was 'fire and water' for the scheme, he was now totally non-committal. 'I thank you for your communication. It interests me very much. The matter, in any case, still requires careful study and further discussions.'

Herzl's cup of bitterness was full. He now feared for his life, in an unknown country with no protection, and the new suspicion that Turkish patrols in Palestine might be under orders to eliminate him. He fled during the night to Jaffa and joined a ship for Alexandria. When he saw the official communiqué there was nothing in it to lift his heart. The approach to Palestine through Potsdam had failed. From then on Herzl's life was marked by failure, ill-health and the emergence of a new generation in the Zionist leadership.

His first reaction to the Turkish disappointment was to seek the intercession of the Czar, followed by a fresh approach to the German court. Both failed. He sent his lieutenant, Nevlinski, to Turkey, but on arrival there Nevlinski had a stroke and died. His hopes for Palestine suffered a further reverse when Yussef Ziah el-Khaldi, a former mayor of Jerusalem, then living in Constantinople as a Jerusalem member in the Ottoman Imperial Parliament, laid claim to the sole rights of the Turks and Arabs as guardians of the Holy Places, asserting that these rights would never be shared with the Jews.

These events were bad auguries for the third Zionist Congress, again held at Basle, in August 1899. The delegates were highly critical, in particular attacking Herzl for over-optimism; though he retained control, Congress broke up yet again with cheers and shouts of 'Next year in Jersalem'.

But Jerusalem seemed as far away as ever. Herzl began to listen to those who were advocating halfway houses. Cyprus had attractions, it was – as it were – a staging-post on the way to Israel, and Lord Salisbury, the British Prime Minister who had been involved with Disraeli in the organization of the island following the Congress of Berlin, was himself a supporter of Zionism. At the 1899 Congress there was strong opposition when the Cyprus project was mentioned, and still more at the fourth Congress, held in London in 1900. Herzl was seriously ill before the meetings began and was only a shadow of his past self. Delegates were impatient and demanding, not least the four hundred Russians, inflamed by the ritual murders and pogroms in Russia itself and in Poland and Romania. He planned one more visit to Turkey, following a message that the Sultan – again in need of Western finance – would give him an audience. But all he received was an offer of a limited colonization, five families here, five there. Herzl recorded in his diary that he thought – though he did not say – 'so you may plunder and slay them all the more easily'.

The 1901 Congress in Basle, therefore, met with little more hope than its immediate predecessors, though progress had been made, especially with the establishment of the Jewish Colonial Bank, with its main office in London. It was at this Congress that Chaim Weizmann first became known. There was a new move for a specifically 'Jewish culture', which would become a positive force instead of basing the movement's philosophy purely on resistance to anti-semitism. Weizmann formally proposed action to create a Jewish university to be established, he hoped, in Jerusalem.

After yet another approach to Turkey, Herzl discussed with the British Government a proposal which had already proved divisive in past Congresses: a staging-post on the way to Palestine. Cured of his German flirtation he had spoken in the fourth Congress in warm terms about Britain:

> England, great England, England the free, England commanding all the seas
> – she will understand us and our purpose.

Two possible staging-posts were Cyprus and the Sinai Peninsula, and Britain controlled both.

Joseph Chamberlain, an expansionist and imaginative Colonial Secretary, agreed to see him. First he approached Lord Rothschild, who had written to him saying that he would

> view with horror the establishment of a Jewish Colony pure and simple. Such a colony would be *imperium in imperio*; it would be a ghetto with the prejudices of the ghetto: a small petty Jewish state, orthodox and illiberal, excluding the Gentiles and the Christians.

Herzl raised the Cyprus and the Sinai Peninsula proposals, but Chamberlain made it clear that his writ did not run to Sinai, which came under the Foreign Office. Cyprus he felt was out of the question, because of the violent opposition which would come from its Greek and Moslem inhabitants. But he arranged for him to meet Lord Lansdowne, the Foreign Secretary, on the Sinai question. Lansdowne was forthcoming, but said he would have to consult Lord Cromer, British Consul and, in fact, virtually Pro-Consul in Egypt. Cromer at first was encouraging, but suggested a *cordon sanitaire* between Turkish Palestine and British-controlled Sinai.

A mission was arranged, sponsored by Lord Cromer and organized by Thomas Cook. Delays occurred mainly because of Turkish opposition, so Herzl, though desperately ill, decided to join the mission. The problem of settling Palestine, it was said, was water, though Herzl was convinced that given time this could be solved. When Herzl saw Chamberlain on his return, the Colonial Secretary commented on the adverse report, and came up with an alternative – Uganda.* Herzl was opposed to this: it must be in or near Palestine, but he would not oppose a secondary settlement in Uganda. He went the rounds of London and Paris to raise funds for Sinai, but failed.

Suddenly and tragically the need for a national home for the Jews was underlined by developments in Russia. In Kishinev (Bessarabia) a pogrom occurred; there was good reason to feel that it had been promoted on the orders of the Czarist Government, in fact through Konstantin Pobiedonostsev, author of the 'three-thirds' policy for the Jews.** This added urgency to Herzl's Sinai project, but it also brought to the centre of the stage Chamberlain's project that European Jews should seek immediate refuge in Uganda. Herzl, while realizing how strong would be the Zionist reaction, felt he had to consider it, and entrusted a firm of London lawyers to conduct the negotiations – the head of which was David Lloyd George, shortly to become Chancellor of the Exchequer in Asquith's Government, and later to succeed Asquith as Prime Minister. There was, inevitably, a sharp reaction from one hundred per cent Zionists: Herzl was concerned with saving lives. But first, gravely ill though he now was, he decided to visit Russia, meeting the evil Plehve and Serge Witte, the Finance Minister who had vetoed the sale of shares in the Jewish Colonial Trust. He was met with smooth words; clearly the Russians would facilitate their first Exodus. London met the crisis by re-emphasizing their offer of a home in North Africa. It was what he had seen and heard in Russia that led him to commend Uganda to the forthcoming (sixth) Congress in Basle.

It was Herzl's last Congress, and for him the worst. He was traduced by

* The site was always referred to as Uganda but was, in fact, a little distance away.
** See p. 17 above.

many who a year or two earlier would have died for him, among them Chaim
Weizmann. He argued that, if pressed, the British Government would make
a better offer. What Herzl was prepared to accept, he said, was 'a symptom
of a sickness I have warned against for years'. The Congress in fact voted for
Uganda by 295 to 175, yet Weizmann pointed out, a majority of the Russian
delegation, at a time when anti-semitic persecution was again becoming
acute, voted against. Herzl almost admiringly said, 'These people have a
rope around their necks, and still they refuse!'[8]

On 3 July 1904 Herzl died, and Weizmann, about to leave Geneva to work
in Britain, wrote to his fiancée, 'I feel that a heavy burden has fallen on my
shoulders, and the shoulders are weak and tired.' In 1949, Herzl was buried
in Jerusalem on what is now Mount Herzl.

Herzl's Zionist crusade was not the only or even the first movement to create
a national Jewish home in Palestine. His appeal was to temporal powers to
permit the designation of part of Turkish Palestine for Jewish settlement, an
entirely political approach to the chancelleries of Europe. But even before
his conversion in Paris in 1895, the practical work of settlement had begun.
In the early 1880s the settlement of Rishon le Zion (First in Zion), south of
Jaffa, on the Jerusalem road, was created. Petah Tikvah, a project of three
hundred acres which was bought by three Jerusalem Jews – Stampfer,
Salamon and Guttman – had already been founded, though one might have
regarded this as a form of speculative development, in that there was an
intention to sell off the farms when they were operating successfully. By
1881 Petah Tikvah failed and was almost totally abandoned. Rishon was
little more successful, and it was Baron Edmond de Rothschild, head of the
French branch of the House of Rothschild, who came to the rescue. When
he intervened to save Rishon he said: 'I am not a philanthropist. . . . I have
set out on this enterprise to see whether it was possible to establish Jews on
Palestine soil.' Fifteen years later he declared to the Rishon settlers:

> I did not come to your aid because of your poverty and suffering for, to be
> sure, there were many other similar cases of distress in the world. I did it
> because I saw in you the realisers of the renaissance of Israel and of that ideal
> so dear to us all, the sacred goal of the return of Israel to its ancestral
> homeland.

He was not a committed Zionist: he was trying to establish whether Zionism
was an economically viable aspiration. But it had to be Zion, Palestine; here
he distanced himself from Pinsker who, in committing himself to what he
called 'Auto-Emancipation', never tied himself to Palestine as the place
where it should necessarily become a reality.

Simon Schama's *Two Rothschilds and the Land of Israel*,[9] which is the

authoritative account of the Palestinian settlement movement, sums up
Baron Edmond's approach:

> From modest beginnings, the Palestinian opportunity grew until it
> overflowed into every corner of his life. By nature he was the opposite of a
> dilettante and the trials and tribulations of the colonies drew from him that
> extraordinary relentlessness which all those who knew him at first hand
> commented on. No detail was too petty, no datum too trivial to escape his
> omniscient attention and his role as mentor and benefactor, far from being
> confined to the formal provision of means, was a work of exhaustive planning
> and management. Characteristically, he was criticized if anything for doing
> too much, not too little, and made the same stringent demands on all those
> who worked for him . . .
>
> Behind it all was an increasingly passionate identification with the fate of
> the Jewish people and a conviction that Palestine would have a central role to
> play in its future, but at the same time he was concerned to harness the
> technical expertise of the West so as to put into the hands of the Palestinian
> settlers the practical tools of their social as well as moral emancipation. Jewish
> Palestine had first to be a working economic organism or it could be nothing.
> As time went on success in that task seemed to recede rather than grow
> nearer. . . . But as the work grew more daunting in its ramifications so
> Edmond's own determination grew more resolute.[10]

Although the Baron in 1899 withdrew from personal direction of the
Palestine colonies, wine from the Rishon le Zion vineyards was awarded a
gold medal in the Paris Exhibition of 1900, taking its place alongside the
historically acclaimed 1899 vintages of Margaux and Château-Lafite.

Edmond's own assessment of his achievement in relation to the political
decision to create a national home for the Jews was made when Turkey
entered the 1914–18 war as an ally of Germany, which led to the hope that a
defeated Turkey and her possessions would be broken up:

> When I created my colonies in Palestine I had in view that a time might come
> when the fate of Palestine could be in the balance, and I desired that the world
> should have to reckon with the Jews there at such a time. We did a good deal in
> the last ten to fifteen years; we want to do still more in the years to come; the
> present crisis has caught us in the middle of our activities, still one has to
> reckon with the facts and now we have to use the opportunity which will
> probably never return again.[11]

But all the work of Herzl, the de Rothschilds and other pioneers would have
been in vain, but for the dedication of the greatest builder of them all, Chaim
Weizmann. On 29 November 1947 the United Nations General Assembly,
by a vote of 33 to 13 created independent Arab and Jewish states. The
following May, Chaim Weizmann in New York received a telegram from
the first leaders of the new state, David Ben-Gurion, Golda Myerson
(Meir), David Remez and Eliezer Kaplan:

> On the occasion of the establishment of the Jewish State, we send our

greetings to you, who have done more than any living man towards its creation. Your stand and help have strengthened all of us. We look forward to the day when we shall greet you at the Head of the State, established in peace.

There was not a breath of exaggeration in that simple statement. Without Weizmann there would have been no State of Israel, in 1948 or in all probability up to today, more than thirty years later.

Chaim Weizmann was born in Czarist Russia in the small township of Motol in the district of Kobrin in the Department or *Guberniya* of Grodno, close to the Polish border, in 1874. Motol was situated, to quote Weizmann himself,

> in one of the darkest and most forlorn corners of the Pale of Settlement, that prison house created by Czarist Russia for the largest part of its Jewish population. Throughout the centuries alternations of bitter oppression and comparative freedom – how comparative a free people would hardly understand – had deepened the consciousness of exile in these scattered communities, which were held together by a common destiny and common dreams.[12]

He went as did all the Jewish children to a *cheder*, a one-room all-form school, and at the age of eleven to a Russian school in the nearby town of Pinsk, during the years of repression which followed the murder of the liberal Alexander II in 1881. The pogroms which began that year were reinforced by the so-called May Laws, officially known as 'Temporary Legislation Affecting the Jews' which were by 1885 at their harshest period of enforcement. In his autobiography Weizmann comments that nothing in Czarist Russia was as enduring as 'Temporary Legislation'. The period of reaction and persecution they created lasted until the overthrow of the Romanov dynasty by the Bolsheviks thirty-six years later; while they lasted, the flow of ukases interpreting them and intensifying them

> broadened and prolonged and extended until it came to cover every aspect of Jewish life . . . one obtained the impression that the whole cumbersome machinery of the vast Russian Empire was created for the sole purpose of inventing and amplifying rules and regulations for the hedging in of the existence of its Jewish subjects until it became something which was neither life nor death.[13]

Throughout Weizmann's writings and those of his contemporaries we are to find a deep difference in the attitudes of Western Jews and of those who emigrated from Russia, and this goes a long way to explain some of the divisions in successive Zionist Congresses in the early years of this century and indeed later.

It was held by some to be the anti-Jewish outbreak at Demnate in

Morocco which prompted the eleven-year-old Chaim Weizmann to write his often quoted letter to his headmaster about the future of the Jews, though Isaiah Berlin considers it may have been inspired by the death at the age of 101 of Sir Moses Montefiore, one of the earliest British Zionists:[14]

> My teacher, my mentor, Schlomo Sokolvsky, I am sending you one of my ideas so that you can see about the Society of lovers of Zion and Jerusalem in our land. How great and lofty was the idea which inspired our brother Jews to found this society.... Through it we can save our down-trodden and despondent brethren who are scattered in all corners of the world and have no place in which to pitch their tents. We are being persecuted everywhere and the Jew is a burden on all people, and on all the kings of Europe generally and on the king of Russia in particular. Yet this may be the beginning of our redemption. We must therefore support this esteemed Society, and we must thank all the supporters of this Society, such as Dr Yassinovsky and Dr Pinsker and all who rallied underneath the flag of this Society. But we must also thank two Jewish patriots, and they are Moses Montefiore and Rothschild. Finally, we must thank this Society, because we are able to see what lies before us and the evil which threatens us. Therefore the obligation lies upon us to find some place of refuge. Because, even in America, where knowledge prevails, they will persecute us and in all the countries of Africa and especially in the State of Morocco they will persecute us and have no mercy upon us. So let us carry our banner to Zion. Let us return to our original mother, on whose knees we were reared. For why should we expect mercy from the kings of Europe, that they should, in their pity for us, give us a resting place? In vain. All have decided that the Jew is doomed to death, but England will have mercy on us. Nonetheless, let us turn to Zion. Jews, to Zion let us go.
>
> From me, your pupil, Chaim Weizmann

After his final exams at Pinsk at the age of eighteen, he had to decide where to continue his studies. Kiev and St Petersburg he considered, but decided to join the 'stampede' to the West. Through a friend of the family he obtained a teaching job in Hebrew and Russian in the village of Pfungstadt, an hour's train journey from Darmstadt in Germany, whence he could commute to Darmstadt Polytechnic. The problem of getting there was increased by the cost of a Russian domestic passport and the problem of escaping from the Pale. He solved it by briefly embracing his father's profession, a raft worker on the river timber transport system to Danzig. At Thorn, the first stop in German territory, he 'picked up his bundles and skipped'.

The Pfungstadt-Darmstadt experience was not a success, and trying to earn a living, with the constant travelling, affected his health. After two terms he returned to Pinsk, where his family were by this time living, and worked for a time in a small chemical factory. But his father had started a business with one of his sons-in-law and this was proving so successful that the two of them decided to finance Chaim's further education – this time at the Berlin Polytechnic, one of the best scientific colleges in Europe, and one which had a significant number of German and Russian Jewish students. It was there that he made friends with whom he was to be working through the greater part of his life, the most notable being Asher Ginsberg, later better known under his pen-name of Ahad Ha-Am ('One of the People'), who became famous in Zionism with his *Truth from Palestine*. Weizmann said of him:

> For him Zionism was the Jewish renaissance in a spiritual-national sense. Its colonizational work, its political programme had meaning only as an organic part of the re-education of the Jewish people. A façade of physical achievement meant little to him, he measured both the organization in exile and in the colonies in Palestine by their effect on Jewry. His first concern was with quality. When he organized his society, the *Bnai Moshe* – the training school of many of the Russian Zionist leaders – he put the emphasis on perfection. The membership was never more than one hundred, but every member was tested by high standards of intelligence and devotion . . .

Weizmann took to propaganda and discussion in the suburbs and villages, returning during the summer vacation to Russia, a militant Zionist in a land where Zionism was illegal.

It was in his second year in Berlin that Herzl published *Der Judenstaat* (*The Jewish State*) – creating not so much a concept, Weizmann commented, as a historic personality. Where the greatness lay, in his view, was in Herzl's role as a man of action, particularly in his founding of the Zionist Congress. Even so he regarded the entire approach simplistic and doomed to failure. He had no time for Herzl's wooing of rich Jews such as Edmond de Rothschild. Still more Weizmann regarded him as a Westerner, uninspired by the experiences and vision which animated the Jews of Russia.

But Weizmann had become sufficient a figure in Zionism to be nominated a delegate to the first Congress. He did not attend because of his work. He had made a discovery in dyestuffs chemistry, and was sent by his professor to Moscow in the hope of selling the process to a Russian industrialist. He had to stay longer in Moscow than he intended and missed the Congress. The following year he did attend the second Congress, playing, as he put it, an insignificant part. His studies took him to Freiburg, which enabled him to spend a great deal of time in nearby Berne. Here there was a large Russian-Jewish student colony. Moreover, as he put it, it was the 'cross-roads of Europe's revolutionary forces'. Lenin and Plekhanov made it their centre. Trotsky was frequently there. Weizmann took issue strongly with the revolutionaries – they did not want Russian Jews to be Jewish with their first aim a Jewish national home; they wanted them to be first and foremost

Russians, with their aim the destruction of Czarism.

What Weizmann and his associates did was to challenge the old guard by founding a distinctively Zionist society, *Ha-Schachar* (The Dawn). A *Bierhalle* meeting, lasting three nights and two days, at 4 a.m. carried a resolution overwhelmingly in favour of active Zionism and dissociation from Lenin, Plekhanov *et al.*, whom Weizmann called the 'assimilatory revolutionists': 180 students enrolled in the Zionist society. These and others to whom the gospel spread in other centres began to form the weight of opposition to Herzl and became increasingly effective in Zionist Congresses.

Herzl was clear-headed enough to realize the challenge he faced, but he continued his contacts with crowned heads and millionaires. It was his willingness to flirt with the Uganda scheme which caused the new movement to dissociate itself from him:

> We opposed him within the movement because we felt that the Jewish masses needed something more than high diplomatic representatives, that it was not good enough to have two or three men travelling about interviewing the great of the world on our behalf. We were the spokesmen of the Russian-Jewish masses who sought in Zionism self-expression and not merely rescue.[15]

Nevertheless when Weizmann came to know Vienna and Western Jewry he came to understand Herzl better and to pay tribute to his greatness and 'the profundity of his intuition'.

> He was the first – without a rival – among the Western leaders, but even he could not break the mould of his life. Within the limitations of that mould, and with his magnificent gifts and his complete devotion, he rendered incalculable service to the cause. He remains the classical figure in Zionism.[16]

His scientific work was beginning to make him more economically independent, particularly some of his discoveries which were taken up by industry, including I. G. Farben. In 1900 he attended the fourth Congress, held in London – his first visit. It was there that the Jewish National Fund was created, to purchase land in Palestine 'as the inalienable property of the Jewish people'.

In Geneva Weizmann and his colleagues founded the first Zionist publishing-house, *Der Jüdische Verlag*; it was there also that progress was made on the concept of the Hebrew University, first raised in the 1897 Congress. An office was opened for it, and strong support came from Jewish students, a thumbs-down from the revolutionaries.

Also in 1900 Weizmann met a young medical student, Vera Chatzman, from Rostov-on-Don, whom he was to marry six years later. In 1903, returning from a Russian tour, he met in Poland Nahum Sokolov, head of the Warsaw committee for the projected Hebrew University, and editor of

Ha-Zefirah, a leading Hebrew periodical. It was while they were meeting in Warsaw that news came of the murderous pogrom at Kishinev. He returned to Pinsk and helped to organize a Jewish corps for self-defence, which soon afterwards saved a nearby town, Homel, where a further pogrom had been mounted.

At the sixth Congress a heated debate took place on the offer from Joseph Chamberlain, Colonial Secretary in Balfour's Government, to provide a Jewish home in, or rather near, Uganda. Many delegates were angered to see behind Herzl's chair a map, not of Palestine, but of part of Africa. Weizmann advised rejection: 'If the British Government and people are what I think they are, they will make us a better offer.' But Nordau supported Uganda, and Sokolov abstained. The Uganda proposal was carried by 295 to 175, with about a hundred abstentions. What Weizmann noticed was that the visiting Russian delegation, actually from Kishinev, voted against Uganda despite their sufferings. Once again there was a split between East and West.

Herzl's final speech was heard in silence, despite the vote later recorded. He died the following year, and it was at the seventh Congress held in 1905 that the Uganda proposal was decisively rejected.

Between the two Congresses Weizmann decided to visit London to size up the Uganda proposal. There he met Lord Percy, Under-Secretary of State for the Colonies, who surprised Weizmann by expressing his astonishment that leading Jews had been willing to support Uganda or any other country than Palestine: 'If I were a Jew I would not give a halfpenny for the proposition.'[17]

Weizmann also inquired into British Government proposals to permit Jewish colonization of a strip of territory in the El Arish area. This idea fell through because of lack of water, though it would in any case have been too narrow a strip of territory to satisfy Zionist aspirations.

The following year Weizmann emigrated to Britain. He felt that neither his Zionist campaigning nor his scientific work was making enough progress in Geneva. He decided to go to Manchester. He had a letter of introduction to Professor Perkin of the University there, himself the son of a pioneer in dyestuffs chemistry, and the creator of 'Aniline blue' or mauve. Weizmann was provided with a laboratory which he had to prepare and scour out, as well as pay rent for its use. His successes there, both with the production of carcinogenic substances for cancer research, anthracene and dyestuffs soon improved his desperate financial position, particularly when Charles Dreyfus, director of Clayton Aniline and Chairman of the Manchester Zionists, gave him an industrial research contract.

Weizmann had known hardly a word of English when he arrived in Manchester, and this precluded his being appointed to a lectureship. But by the end of the year he was granted a university research scholarship and began lecturing. It was many months before he had time to throw himself into Zionist work, to which he was introduced by Dreyfus. His political loneliness became lessened, however, when Ahad Ha-Am came to live in London, enabling them to meet from time to time.

It was in early 1906, the year in which Chaim Weizmann and Vera were married, that destiny took a hand and led to the historic meeting between Weizmann and Arthur James Balfour.

CHAPTER 2

Balfour, Churchill and the Mandate: 1905–22

CONTINENTAL ZIONISTS had dreamed dreams. But British statesmen could see visions and possessed the political power to begin to make them a reality. It was the actions, first of Arthur James Balfour, and then of Winston Churchill, which brought the concept of a 'Jewish National Home' in Palestine on to the agenda of the British Parliament and the world stage – both of them urged on by the vision of Chaim Weizmann.

It began in Manchester. Balfour had succeeded his uncle, the Marquess of Salisbury, as leader of the Conservative Party and Prime Minister in July 1902. After nearly ten years of Tory rule, in 1905 he resigned and let the Liberals in. They immediately called a General Election. Balfour lost the election of January 1906 in a Liberal landslide, losing his own seat, East Manchester, at the same time. During the election, Balfour met Weizmann. His niece and biographer, Blanche Dugdale, put it in these words:

> Balfour's interest in the Jews and their history was lifelong. It originated in the Old Testament training of his mother, and in his Scottish upbringing. As he grew up, his intellectual admiration and sympathy for certain aspects of Jewish philosophy and culture grew also, and the problem of the Jews in the modern world seemed to him of immense importance. He always talked eagerly on this, and I remember in childhood imbibing from him the idea that Christian religion and civilization owes to Judaism an immeasurable debt, shamefully ill repaid.[1]

It was Charles Dreyfus, Balfour's constituency party chairman, who brought the two together. Dreyfus had been a supporter of the Uganda scheme; Balfour mentioned that he would like to meet one of the Jewish leaders who had rejected Uganda. Dreyfus suggested Weizmann, hoping that Balfour would convince him that he had been wrong. In fact the tutorial went the other way: it was Weizmann who was to educate Balfour.

The sources for what was said at the meeting are two: Blanche Dugdale, to whom Balfour gave a full account, and Weizmann himself.[2] There is no conflict between them, though that of Weizmann is fuller:

34

I was taken to Balfour in a room in the old-fashioned Queen's Hotel in Piccadilly, which served as his headquarters. The corridors were crowded with people waiting for a word with the candidate. I surmised that Mr Balfour had consented to see me for a few minutes – 'a quarter of an hour,' Dreyfus warned me – simply to break the monotony of his routine. He kept me for well over an hour.

I had been less than two years in the country, and my English was still not easy to listen to. I remember how Balfour sat in his usual pose, his legs stretched out in front of him, an imperturbable expression on his face. We plunged at once into the subject of our interview. He asked me why some Jews, Zionists, were so bitterly opposed to the Uganda offer. The British Government was really anxious to do something to relieve the misery of the Jews; and the problem was a practical one, calling for a practical approach. In reply I plunged into what I recall as a long harangue on the meaning of the Zionist movement. I dwelt on the spiritual side of Zionism, I pointed out that nothing but a deep religious conviction expressed in modern political terms could keep the movement alive, and that this conviction had to be based on Palestine and on Palestine alone. Any deflection from Palestine was – well, a form of idolatry. I added that if Moses had come into the sixth Zionist Congress when it was adopting the resolution in favour of the Commission for Uganda, he would surely have broken the tablets once again. We knew that the Uganda offer was well meant, and on the surface it might appear the more practical road. But I was sure that – quite apart from the availability and suitability of the territory – the Jewish people would never produce either the money or the energy required in order to build up a wasteland and make it habitable, unless that land were Palestine. Palestine had this magic and romantic appeal for the Jews; our history has been what it is because of our tenacious hold on Palestine. We have never accepted defeat and have never forsaken the memory of Palestine. Such a tradition could be converted into real motive power, and we were trying to do just that, struggling against great difficulties, but sure that the day would come when we would succeed.

I looked at my listener, and suddenly became afraid that this appearance of interest and courtesy might be nothing more than a mask. I felt that I was sweating blood and I tried to find some less ponderous way of expressing myself. I was ready to bow myself out of the room, but Balfour held me back, and put some questions to me regarding the growth of the movement. He had heard of 'Dr Herz' – a very distinguished leader, who had founded and organized it. I ventured to correct him, pointing out that Herzl had indeed placed the movement on a new footing, and had given the tradition a modern political setting; but Herzl had died young; and he had left us this legacy of Uganda, which we were trying to liquidate.

Then suddenly I said: 'Mr Balfour, supposing I were to offer you Paris instead of London, would you take it?'

He sat up, looked at me, and answered: 'But Dr Weizmann, we have London.'

'That is true,' I said. 'But we had Jerusalem when London was a marsh.'

He leaned back, continued to stare at me, and said two things which I remember vividly. The first was: 'Are there many Jews who think like you?'

I answered: 'I believe I speak the mind of millions of Jews whom you will never see and who cannot speak for themselves, but with whom I could pave the streets of the country I come from.'

To this he said: 'If that is so, you will one day be a force.'

Shortly before I withdrew, Balfour said: 'It is curious. The Jews I meet are quite different.'

I answered: 'Mr Balfour, you meet the wrong kind of Jews.'

Lady Blanche Dugdale records Balfour's impression:

It was from that talk with Weizmann that I saw that the Jewish form of patriotism was unique. Their love for their country refused to be satisfied by the Uganda scheme. It was Weizmann's absolute refusal even to look at it which impressed me.[3]

She concludes this part of her biography with these words:

I hold [Balfour said] that from a purely material point of view the policy that we initiated is likely to prove a successful policy. But we have never pretended – certainly I have never pretended – that it was purely from these materialistic considerations that the Declaration of November 1917 originally sprang. I regard this not as a solution, but as a partial solution, of the great and abiding Jewish problem . . .[4]

Weizmann's contacts with Manchester Zionists were spreading. Charles Dreyfus and Nathan Laski, father of Harold Laski, were the leaders of the community. He had already met Harry Sacher, a prominent journalist and a lawyer: through him he was to meet Simon Marks and Israel Sieff.

He found that the majority of German Jews in Manchester were assimilated, 'dissociated from their people', as were many of the Sephardic Jews who were involved in the import trade in raw cotton from Egypt and India. But by far the largest concentration of Manchester Jews were Weizmann's own people, Russians.

From 1906 to 1914 Weizmann was busy spreading his gospel in the northern towns both sides of the Pennines, and travelling when he could to keep up his contacts with Ahad Ha-Am, Norman Bentwich, Albert Einstein, Ernest (later Lord) Rutherford and Leon Simon. Meanwhile he was advancing his research programme, including a method for synthesizing the production of isoprene and for its polymerization to a form of rubber, which soon proved commercially unviable as the price of natural rubber collapsed on world markets.

But the Manchester school was rapidly becoming the headquarters of Zionist advance. Simon Marks and Israel Sieff were not originally Zionists, but joined the cause through hearing Weizmann's speeches. Sacher, who had gone to Fleet Street, returned to the north, to write leading articles for the *Manchester Guardian*.

In 1907 Weizmann made his first visit to Palestine.

A dolorous country it was on the whole, one of the most neglected corners of the miserably neglected Turkish Empire. Its total population was something above six hundred thousand, of which about eighty thousand were Jews. The latter lived mostly in the cities, Jerusalem (where they formed a majority of the population), Hebron, Tiberias, Safed, Jaffa and Haifa. There were twenty-five colonies on the land. But neither the colonies nor the city settlements in any way resembled, as far as vigour, tone and progressive spirit are concerned, the colonies and the settlements of our day . . .

The further he travelled, however, the more positive he felt.

I made up my mind that I would go back to Europe to press with redoubled energy for immediate practical work in Palestine; and it was then, I think, that I laid out the programme of my Zionist work for the next eight years . . . between 1906 and 1914 we accumulated a body of experience, anticipated our future problems and laid the foundations of our institutions. . . . By 1914 we had increased the Jewish population from eighty thousand to one hundred thousand, our agricultural workers from five hundred to two thousand. The turnover of the Palestine office had grown thirty-fold. We had founded the Jewish National Library, and the Technikum of Haifa . . .[5]

Moreover, in addition to founding new 'colonies', like Kinneret and Deganiah, he felt that existing establishments had been enlivened by the influx of young people. He later was impressed by a conversation with Baron Edmond de Rothschild, who on a visit to Palestine saw for the first time the shape of the new country and the change overtaking settlements and kibbutzim alike, commenting, 'Without me, the Zionists could have done nothing, but without the Zionists my work would have been dead.'

Weizmann's preoccupation with higher education had begun well before his visit. In 1902, with Martin Buber and Berthold Feiwel he had published the first pamphlet proposing a Hebrew University – *Die Jüdische Hochschule*. Because of the Uganda scheme and other diversions the project languished, but appeared on the agenda of the 1913 Congress in Vienna. Arthur Ruppin, who at the seventh Congress had been appointed director of the newly created Palestine Department, had acquired a plot of land on Mount Scopus designed to be the site of the University. Concurrently the Haifa *Technikum* (Technical College) was being planned. Haifa was chosen since it was scheduled to be the principal industrial centre in the new state. The first building was planned by the German Foreign Ministry, and a great battle was fought on the question, should the college be named *Technikum*, the German word, or *Technion*? Further, should the language used in teaching be German or Hebrew? Weizmann, favouring Hebrew, was defeated by the pro-German faction by one vote, but the outbreak of war put the Germans in baulk, and General Allenby's occupation of the country settled the issue for all time.

Weizmann himself was hoping to settle in Haifa to research and teach at the *Technion*: 'when I get the Chair of Biochemistry in the *Technikum*', he wrote in a letter to Ahad Ha-Am in 1912, and soon afterwards he wrote to a friend in Berlin,

> As you know, I want to go to Palestine in three or four years. But I want to go to Palestine not when I have nothing to lose here, but on the contrary, after having achieved everything here.[6]

His plans were wrecked by the outbreak of war in August 1914. With his family he was on holiday on the continent when the Kaiser's armies invaded France: he just managed to get home to England after a three-week journey. In Paris, on the way home, he met Baron Edmond de Rothschild. Weizmann and his wife had already begun to speculate about the effects of the war on the Palestine dream. The world would be re-ordered, perhaps the Jewish homeland would be part of the wider settlement. The Baron, too, was thinking ahead: things looked black, but the Allies would win the war, and that would be 'the time for us to act, so that we do not get forgotten'. He believed that the war would spread to the Middle East, 'and there things of great significance to us will happen'. He urged Weizmann, on returning to England, to get in touch with leading statesmen.

Two months after returning to Manchester, Weizmann came to know C. P. Scott, the legendary editor of the *Manchester Guardian*. They met by accident at a party given by a German half-Jewish family who took an interest in Vera Weizmann's work in the 'Schools for Mothers'. Weizmann told Scott of the Zionist struggle, of their hopes for the future. At the end of the conversation, Scott said: 'I would like to do something for you. I would like to put you in touch with the Chancellor of the Exchequer, Lloyd George.' He went on, 'You know you have a Jew in the Cabinet, Mr Herbert Samuel',[7] at which Weizmann exploded: Samuel was in his eyes an assimilated Jew.

On 3 December 1914 Scott told Weizmann as they left the Manchester train at Euston, 'We're going to have breakfast at nine o'clock with Mr Lloyd George.' In addition to Lloyd George, Herbert Samuel, President of the Local Government Board and a Cabinet Minister, and Josiah Wedgwood were there. Weizmann was surprised to find them not only polite, but 'favourably disposed', and on his side. Lloyd George said that he should talk with Balfour as well as with Asquith, the Prime Minister. Herbert Samuel then said that he was preparing a memorandum on the subject of a Jewish state, to present to the Prime Minister.

It was, in fact, of no use to look to Asquith. He turned Samuel's memorandum down flat. In his diary, subsequently published, he wrote on 28 January 1915:

I have just received from Herbert Samuel a memorandum headed 'The Future of Palestine'. He goes on to argue, at considerable length and with some vehemence, in favour of the British annexation of Palestine, a country the size of Wales, much of it barren mountain and part of it waterless. He thinks we might plant in this not very promising territory about three or four million European Jews, and that this would have a good effect upon those who are left behind. It reads almost like a new edition of 'Tancred' brought up to date. I confess I am not attracted by this proposed addition to our responsibilities, but it is a curious addition to Dizzy's favourite maxim that 'race is everything' to find this almost lyrical outburst proceeding from the well-ordered and methodical brain of H.S.[8]

And again,

I think I have already referred to Herbert Samuel's dithyrambic memorandum, urging that in the carving up of the Turks' Asiatic dominion we should take Palestine, into which the scattered Jews would in time swarm back from all the quarters of the globe, and in due course obtain Home Rule. Curiously enough, the only other partisan of this proposal is Lloyd George who, I need not say, does not care a damn for the Jews or their past or their future, but thinks it will be an outrage to let the Holy Places pass into the possession or under the protectorate of 'agnostic, atheistic France'.*[9]

In December 1916 Asquith, challenged by Lloyd George, and deserted by the Conservative leader, Bonar Law, found himself unable to carry on as Prime Minister. A new Government was formed under Lloyd George, who appointed Balfour Foreign Secretary.**

Asquith had never been cast for the role of a wartime Prime Minister, least of all in a war of the virulence of that of 1914–18. Modern readers of his various biographies are amazed to see how much he diverted his attention from the conduct of the war to pursue his obsession with Venetia Stanley. On the darkest days of the war on the Western Front he would sit at his place in Cabinet writing soppy letters to her, charged with violent comments on his colleagues; and he would frequently desert his duties to be with her, as

* On a visit to the Holy Land many years later, after losing his seat in the 1924 General Election, he reports:

There are less than a million people in the country, which is roughly the size of Wales – of whom about one-tenth are Jews and the remainder Christians and Arabs, the Arabs being three-fourths of the whole. I suppose you could not find anywhere a worse representation of any of the three religions, especially of the Christians.

The Jews are increasing (mainly from the less civilized parts of the East of Europe) as the result of the Zionist propaganda, and no doubt are much better looked after and happier here than they were in the wretched places from which they were exported. But the talk of making Palestine into a Jewish 'National Home' seems to me as fantastic as it always has done.[10]

** When offered the Foreign Office, according to Beaverbrook, *Politicians and the War*, vol. 2, London, 1932, p. 502, Balfour said, 'Well, you hold a pistol to my head – I must accept.' He was, in fact, delighted.

well as take her on holiday.* He was shattered by her sudden decision to marry Edwin Montagu, in the same week that Fisher resigned from the Admiralty. Her defection undoubtedly hit Asquith harder than did that of the Admiral. Montagu, who joined Lloyd George's Government six months after its formation, was to play a significant role in the events leading up to the Balfour Declaration. He was one of the assimilated Jews who opposed Zionism, and by his opposition he certainly succeeded in delaying the Declaration. Montagu's marriage to Venetia Stanley had the opposite effect. Asquith was no longer capable of acting as a wartime Prime Minister. Had he remained, it is arguable that no Cabinet power-grouping could have carried the Balfour Declaration. The combination of Lloyd George and Balfour saw it through.

For long periods in the early war years Weizmann was engaged on urgent war work. Britain was in danger of running out of naval munitions. The effectiveness of the Royal Navy guarding Britain's supply routes against the ever more deadly U-boat fleet was in peril and the Germans were poised to blockade the British Isles. By 1915, Weizmann was working for the British Admiralty. His invention of a process to produce acetone by fermenting maize proved to be a signal contribution to the British war effort, enabling England to maintain vital supplies of explosive. The process was a development of his work on isoprene. Regular commuting between Manchester and London proved too much for him and, in 1916, he and his wife moved into a small flat in Campden Hill Road.

A further meeting with Balfour was arranged by Professor S. Alexander, the Jewish philosopher. Alexander reintroduced Weizmann, and received a postcard from Balfour: 'Dear Sam, Weizmann needs no introduction. I still remember our conversation in 1906.'** After a quick word of greeting, Balfour said, 'You know, I was thinking of that conversation of ours, and I believe that when the guns stop firing you may get your Jerusalem.' In 1916, as First Lord of the Admiralty, he was closely involved with Weizmann. He set up a Department of Invention and Research, renamed in 1919 the Committee for Scientific and Industrial Research,*** and appointed Weizmann to it because of his research on acetone. Lloyd George was wrong in his *War Memoirs*[11] in suggesting that the Jewish National Home was a reward for Weizmann's war work.

---

* See Roy Jenkins, *Asquith*, London, 1964, over the period 1910 to 1916. During the first three months of 1915 Asquith wrote to her on 141 separate occasions. On one day, 30 March, he wrote her by hand four letters which ran to 4,000 words in all (Jenkins, op. cit., p. 346).

** Weizmann, *Trial and Error*, p. 195, is wrong in saying that Balfour was at that time First Lord of the Admiralty. Balfour was in fact not in the Cabinet, but in October 1914 had been invited by Asquith to become a full member of the Committee of Imperial Defence.

*** Later the Department for Scientific and Industrial Research (DSIR).

It was in the following year that Weizmann was apprised of a significant development in an allied political strategy with a clear bearing on his life's ambition. This was the 'Sykes-Picot' agreement. Sir Mark Sykes, sixth baronet of Sledmere, East Yorkshire, was born in 1879 and succeeded to the title on his father's death in 1913. He became private secretary to George Wyndham, Conservative Chief Secretary for Ireland. But it was for the Near East that he yearned, and Wyndham managed to get him appointed an honorary attaché in Constantinople in 1905. In 1907 he became prospective Conservative candidate for Buckrose in East Yorkshire, but was defeated in both the elections Asquith called in 1910. In 1911 he was elected for Central Hull in a by-election caused by the unseating of the Unionist MP on an election petition. By this time he had published a learned history of Islam and the Ottoman Empire.

When war came in 1914, as a Lieutenant-Colonel in the Territorial Army he was called to the colours, and briefly went to France, then returned to train his Territorials. But his mind continued to dwell on the Near East. In August 1914 he had written to Churchill, First Lord of the Admiralty, warning him that Germany was trying to get Turkey into the war. Churchill was somewhat disbelieving, but by November Britain had declared war on the Ottoman Empire. Sykes supported Churchill in the Gallipoli invasion and was then offered a post on General Maxwell's staff in Cairo. This, however, was quashed by his appointment to Kitchener's personal staff where one of his first memoranda to the War Secretary was called 'Considerations on the fall of Constantinople'. This led to his appointment as Kitchener's personal representative to an interdepartmental committee set up to consider the future of Asiatic Turkey. He visited Cairo, Aden and India. On the way back he wrote a long memorandum for his Whitehall masters, recommending that Great Britain should make an agreement with France, Russia and Italy about the future of Asiatic Turkey and the status of Jerusalem. On his return, despite the failure of Gallipoli, he found the climate changing. His ideas were getting to the top, and he himself was invited to the Palace for an audience with King George V. Balfour did not rule out a Near East political and military initiative: Lloyd George was strongly for it. He was called to Asquith's war committee, the main war policy committee. Crewe, acting Foreign Secretary, who was an Asquith man, would not go farther than suggesting that HM Ambassador in Paris be consulted about Sykes visiting Paris to discuss his ideas.

Meanwhile, Sykes was actively selling the idea of an Arab Bureau to be set up in Cairo to harmonize the work and ideas of the principal departments, the Foreign Office, the India Office, the Admiralty, the War Office and the Government of India, on the basis of weekly reports on German and Turkish policies. The proposal was approved and the Bureau established.

By this time Sykes was where he wanted to be, talking to the French in the person of François Georges Picot, a diplomat with long experience in the Near East. Following Gallipoli, the French also were thinking of a permanent Near East foothold. Picot had come to London while Sykes was overseas, and made clear that France was determined to have all Syria and all Palestine except for the Holy Places. But Picot was aware of British interest in the area, and was moving towards a division of the territory. Provided France had its sphere of influence in the proposed Arab territory, and controlled the coast of Syria, Britain might have one Palestine port in return for French control of Mosul. The FO Permanent Under-Secretary arranged that discussions should take place between Sykes and Picot. The two were to 'outline the requirements of the various parties', namely the Arabs, France, Britain and the religions concerned with the Holy Places. Sykes already had a map which he had prepared for the earlier departmental talks. The Arab 'confederation' would be divided into a northern area under French protection and a southern area under British protection.[12]

When the map, amended by agreement, finally emerged, Alexandretta was in the French (Blue) Zone, and the ports in Britain's (Red) Zone were to be Haifa and Acre. Palestine, described as a 'Brown' area surrounding Jerusalem, should be under international administration. The Mosque of Omar was to be under uniquely Moslem control, the Latin and Orthodox religions should receive equal treatment in Palestine, and 'the members of the Jewish community throughout the world have a conscientious and sentimental interest in the future of the country'. This was the first time that the Diaspora, the Jewish community throughout the world, was mentioned as having a vital guaranteed stake, as opposed to the still small number of Jews living in the kibbutzim and settlements. When the draft was put to the Permanent Under-Secretary's Committee of officials, Whitehall was nearly united in attacking it, even though different members chose different reasons based on individual departmental interests. The Sykes-Picot understanding was grounded, but only for the moment.

In the debate on the King's Speech in February Sykes, as an MP, despite his Whitehall position, made a blistering attack on Asquith's conduct of the war, which won him praise from the leading newspapers, regardless of political affiliation. Soon afterwards he travelled to Russia, and after visiting the Russian army on the Caucasus front, Sykes met the Czar. It was, perhaps, the Russian visit more than anything which turned Sykes's already receptive mind towards Zionism. Picot was also in Russia and the two talked of how the Allies might win Jewish support. One idea was a Zionist chartered company in Palestine: Sykes was perhaps basing his thinking on Cecil Rhodes's Chartered Company in what later became Rhodesia. Referring to the Zionists, he told the Foreign Under-Secretary, if they want us to win they will do their best, which means they will (A) Calm their activities in Russia (B) Pessimise in Germany (C) Stimulate in France, England and Italy (D) Enthuse in the USA.

On returning to London Sykes sought to learn more about Zionism and talked to Samuel who introduced him to the man who became his tutor in Zionism, Dr Moses Gaster;* later he met Aaron Aaronsohn, a Palestine pioneer who felt his local knowledge would be useful to the spreading of the Zionist cause in England. Lloyd George by this time had become Prime Minister, and Sir Maurice Hankey, Secretary of the Committee of Imperial Defence, recommended Sykes as one of the two new chief political assistants of Lloyd George's new War Cabinet Secretariat. The other was Leopold Amery, an adherent of Zionism until his death. He was involved with Vladimir Jabotinsky's proposal** to establish a Jewish military force from refugees from the Turks: while Amery favoured the idea, Sykes, by this time no less of a pro-Zionist, feared that it might upset the French and provoke Turkish massacres in Palestine. Through his contacts Sykes met Weizmann, whom he asked to prepare for him a memorandum on Zionist aims.

Sykes, while warning the Jews about propaganda which in today's language would be called 'counter-productive', did go so far as to offer to provide official telegraph facilities to enable Weizmann and his colleagues to communicate securely with leading Zionists in the French, Russian, Italian and American capitals. He further sought to bring in the US as the protector of the new Palestine he envisaged. This was partly to assuage the French who were beginning to feel that Sykes was over-trumping Picot with every card he played. Sykes, however, no doubt had in mind, as did Balfour, that a pro-Jewish line would be of great importance in the US. Indeed, it was not long before London was considering how they should react to information Whitehall was receiving that the Germans were planning to come out in favour of a Jewish Palestine in the hope of winning support for Germany in the US and neutralizing the pressures there for the newly elected President, Woodrow Wilson, to make common cause with the Allies.

Weizmann, too, was fearful of a German move on Zionism:

> . . . it is noteworthy that only about two or three months ago, the German press wrote comparatively little about the Zionist Movement, although there is a very powerful Zionist Organization in Germany and Austria, which has

* Sykes was later to say that it was Gaster who 'opened my eyes to what Zionism meant'.
** Vladimir Jabotinsky was a Jew from Odessa, whose literary abilities attracted the attention of Maxim Gorki and Leo Tolstoy. Weizmann was sufficiently impressed by his manner and his style at the early Congresses to describe him as a boy wonder.[13] One of the few active Zionists who throughout the First World War believed that the Allies would win, he founded the Jewish Legion and brought one of the Jewish regiments to Palestine in 1918 to serve alongside Allenby's forces.

increased in strength and vitality still more since the occupation of Poland and Lithuania. . . .[14]

He therefore prepared the memorandum Sykes had asked for, urging the British Government to make a declaration about Zionist proposals for the future of Palestine: 'Outline of Programme for the Jewish Resettlement of Palestine in Accordance with the Aspirations of the Jewish Movement'. The essential points are set out by Weizmann. The first – 'national recognition' – was as follows:

> The Jewish population of Palestine (which in the programme shall be taken to mean both present and future Jewish populations) shall be officially recognized by the Suzerain Government as the Jewish Nation, and shall enjoy in that country full civic, national and political rights. The Suzerain Government recognizes the desirability and necessity of a Jewish resettlement of Palestine.[15]

Weizmann also made his intention clear to Sykes in summary form:

> Palestine to be recognized as *the Jewish National Home* [author's italics][16] with liberty of immigration to Jews of all countries, who are to enjoy full national, political and civic rights; a charter to be granted to a Jewish Company, local Government to be accorded to the Jewish population, and the Hebrew language to be officially recognized.

Both of these quotations underline the fact that Weizmann was no longer talking of 'a Jewish National Home in Palestine', but was asserting that Palestine would be *the* National Home. There is little doubt that Weizmann was thinking of partition,* not necessarily with the boundaries set out by Sykes-Picot. But it was against the background of these two statements that the Balfour Declaration was to be made nine months later. During these months Sykes had made an extended tour of the Near East in preparation for a definitive political settlement, the more urgent in his eyes since he expected – wrongly as it turned out – that General Allenby would blast his way through Palestine before 1917 was too far advanced.

Allenby moved into GHQ Cairo in 28 June 1917, reconstituted the army's command structure, sent home a number of staff officers who had been having a good war propping up the bar at Shepheard's Hotel, and moved into operational headquarters in Gaza, where the army under Sir Archibald Murray had been twice halted by the German-Turkish forces under van Falkenhayn.[17] T. E. Lawrence was sent to take Aqaba and secure the South, also providing, should it be needed, a new port from which

---

* As will be seen, the ultimate solution for Palestine did involve partition. Had this been accepted from the start Britain need not have gone through the agonies of 1945–7. But not only was Bevin violently opposed to the concept until it was forced on him, but it became clear that the British Mandate itself was not compatible with a partition solution (see pp. 181–3 below).

equipment could be brought by the Navy round Africa.* His plan was to confuse the Turks into thinking that he would make a third effort to break through at Gaza, meanwhile driving south-east to Beersheba and then north-east straight into Jerusalem. His Chief Intelligence Officer, Colonel Meinertzhagen, who had already fixed radio apparatus on top of the Great Pyramid to monitor Turkish signals, carried through a daring deception of the Turks. Twice a staff officer, carrying a haversack containing money, maps and plans for a drive through Gaza, went near the enemy lines in the hope of being chased away and dropping his decoy plans. Twice the Turks failed to respond. On the third occasion, Meinertzhagen himself carried through the operation, and this time the Turks responded. The Turks, delighted with their find, issued an order warning their own officers under no account to go near the front line bearing operational plans, meanwhile basing their immediate strategy on what they thought they had learnt. So highly did Allenby regard this operation that on Meinertzhagen's Army Confidential Report to the War Office, he wrote: 'This officer has been largely responsible for my success in Palestine.'**

In the last week of October the assault began with an artillery barrage on Gaza, supported by a naval bombardment by British and French warships. While the German High Command awaited a landing behind Gaza, Allenby's troops under Chetwode marched off and captured Beersheba with a surprise attack. Two days later Gaza was captured, and a pincer movement from Gaza and Beersheba respectively captured Jaffa, Jerusalem's port. On 16 November the advance guard went on to take Jerusalem, evacuated by the enemy. Two days later Allenby, dismounting at the Jaffa Gate, entered Jerusalem on foot. 'Thus did the Christian nations return to Jerusalem after 730 years.'[18] The secular arm of Allied strategy had done its work just seven

---

* Lawrence was not employed on military tasks only. Highly secret papers, recently made public by the Government, show that Churchill employed him to organize subsidy payments to certain Arab rulers, principally Ibn Saud, Sultan of the Nejd, and Hussein, King of the Hedjaz. Churchill answered a question in the Commons on 2 March 1922, saying that £18,000 had been advanced to Hussein. The secret papers now published after more that fifty years were summarized in an article by Peter Hennessy in *The Times* of 11 February 1980, under the heading, 'Lawrence's secret Arabian "slush fund" '. Hennessy's account suggests that one of Churchill's aims was to get Hussein to sign away his family's Hashemite claim to Palestine. It also shows that Churchill was less than frank in his Commons statement about the sums involved, this leading to strictures by the Comptroller and Auditor General, a House of Commons officer independent of Government, in his report to Parliament. Hussein's luck did not hold. In 1924, Ibn Saud forced him to abdicate in favour of his son, who was then eliminated by Ibn Saud, that monarch then merging both kingdoms to form Saudi Arabia. Hussein, exiled to Cyprus, duly received compensation in the form of a GCB.

** Just before the decisive battle began, Allenby received news that his only son, Michael, had been killed on the Western front near Nieuport.

days after the promulgation of the Balfour Declaration.

Allenby's action in entering the Holy City on foot illustrated one of the main inspirations of British support for the Zionists. It was understood, and is well put, by Weizmann himself in his autobiography, *Trial and Error*:[19] '. . . men like Balfour, Churchill, Lloyd George, were deeply religious and believed in the Bible, that to them the return of the Jewish people to Palestine was a reality, so that we Zionists represented to them a great tradition for which they had enormous respect.'

Weizmann's last pressure for an early declaration on the National Home had been finally given a fair wind late in 1916 by the fears that Germany would herself propose such a course, in concert with her Turkish allies, while leaving Palestine still under Turkish suzerainty. Sykes by this time had moved into a more neutral attitude as he became more and more aware of the likely Arab reaction. The French, who since the Sykes-Picot agreement felt that their concerns had been met further north and east, were content. Thanks to the campaigning of Mr Justice Brandeis of the US Supreme Court, the Americans were happy, and indeed were pressing.

In March 1917 Balfour was, however, still worried about French attitudes, and said that should these difficulties persist, the Zionists might find the best course was a joint Anglo–American protectorate. The following June, Weizmann and Lord Rothschild visited Balfour at the Foreign Office and pressed that a declaration be made without delay. A committee under Sokolov prepared a draft, for which Balfour had asked. Balfour still had a fight on his hands with the assimilated Jews, and particularly with his Cabinet colleague, Edwin Montagu, Secretary of State for India. But by this time he had on his side a new argument, that such a declaration might have a favourable effect on the Russian revolutionary leaders. Lenin and Trotsky in fact came to power in the very week of the promulgation of the Declaration.

Weizmann was greatly helped by a leading article by Wickham Steed in *The Times* in June, written after an hour's talk with Weizmann, which vehemently rejected the views of the 'assimilationists' in Britain. Immediately afterwards he went to see Balfour, pressing

that the time had come for the British Government to give us a definite declaration of support and encouragement. Mr Balfour promised to do so, and asked me to submit to him a declaration which would be satisfactory to us, and which he would try and put before the Cabinet.

A draft was handed by Lord Rothschild to Balfour on 18 July 1917.

On 17 August, Weizmann wrote to Felix Frankfurter in the US:

The draft has been submitted to the Foreign Office and is approved by them, and, I heard yesterday, it also meets the approval of the Prime Minister . . .

About 18 September, according to Weizmann's record, he

> learned that a draft resolution had been discussed at a Cabinet meeting from
> which both Mr Lloyd George and Mr Balfour were absent, and that the sharp
> intervention of Edwin Montagu had caused the withdrawal of the item from
> the agenda.

Weizmann thereupon asked for an interview with Balfour, which took place on the following day. Rothschild saw the Foreign Secretary on the 21st. On that day also, General Smuts, a member of the War Cabinet, gave his support to the proposed declaration.

On 9 October, Weizmann cabled the definitive text to Brandeis, who suggested only one amendment: the replacement of the phrase 'Jewish race' by 'Jewish people'.

On 2 November, Weizmann records:

> After a final discussion in the War Cabinet, Balfour issued the Declaration in
> the form of a letter to Lord Rothschild.*

He had been chosen by Weizmann as the recipient, in his capacity as President of the British Zionist Federation.

> While the Cabinet was in session, approving the final text, I was waiting
> outside, this time within call. Sykes brought the document out to me, with the
> exclamation: 'Dr Weizmann, it's a boy!'

Weizmann failed to secure acceptance for his more grandiose demand, that Palestine should be recognized as *the* Jewish National Home. Indeed, Balfour had succeeded in getting the Declaration through Cabinet only by playing down any idea of exclusivity, even of automatic and early independence. The relevant Cabinet Minutes of 1917 show that Balfour interpreted 'national home' [no capitals] as

> some form of British, American or other protectorate, under which full
> facilities would be given to the Jews to work out their own salvation, and to
> build up, by means of agriculture, education and industry, a real centre of
> national culture and focus of national life . . . it did not necessarily involve the
> early establishment of an independent Jewish State, which was a matter of
> gradual development in accordance with the ordinary laws of political
> evolution.

Nevertheless, the Declaration was received by Weizmann and his colleagues in Britain, America and Palestine with great enthusiasm. Even in his most depressed moments he could not have imagined that another World War

---

* A reproduction of the letter to Lord Rothschild appears as plate 1 of the illustrations.

would have to take place, and the Zionists would have to wait over thirty more years, before Balfour's declaration of intent became a reality with the creation of *Eretz Israel*, with himself as first President.*

Christopher Sykes also censures a statement of Sokolov in 1918:

> It has been said and is still being repeated by anti-Zionists again and again, that Zionism aims at the creation of an independent 'Jewish State'. But this is wholly fallacious. The 'Jewish State' was never a part of the Zionist programme.[21]

He then goes on to examine the inconsistencies of Zionist statements:

> Excusable as they are in the low light of political morality, they left a lasting blemish on the political conduct of Zionism. In later years it became a Zionist habit to speak not only in two but in several voices to run several lines of persuasion at the same time . . .

Weizmann himself, as we have seen, spoke in two very different voices, aiming high or low, as Zionist prospects varied.

Britain was now in military occupation of Turkey's former territory in dispute between Jews and Arabs. In January 1918, with the outcome of the war still in perilous uncertainty, the Middle East Committee of the Cabinet resolved to send a Zionist Commission to Palestine, under Weizmann's leadership, to help to establish 'friendly relations between the Jews on the one hand and the Arabs and other non-Jewish communities on the other'. Its terms of reference clearly stated its task of 'restoring and developing the Jewish colonies', and of reporting on 'the possibilities of future Jewish developments in Palestine in the light of the declaration of His Majesty's Government'. Balfour wrote to Allenby asking him to facilitate the visit, emphasizing the need for the Commission to go into the wider question of Palestine's future economy. Mark Sykes meanwhile was working on the Emir Feisal to reassure the Arabs of their future, and a meeting was arranged between Feisal and Weizmann. Feisal for his part was more

---

* I an indebted to Christopher Sykes, son of Sir Mark, for pointing out, in contrast to many of the books written on this period, the key role of Lord Robert Balfour (A.J.'s cousin). Lord Robert was Parliamentary Under-Secretary of State at the Foreign Office from 1915–18, deputizing for Balfour on the latter's frequent absences. When Balfour was away, Lord Robert acted on these occasions as Foreign Secretary 'in the full meaning of the term', a fact 'in no way resented by Balfour which shows how close their sympathy must have been. When Lord Robert was made Assistant Foreign Secretary in 1918 (I believe a unique appointment) it seems to have been a regularization of accepted fact . . . helped by the fact that from 1916 onwards he was Minister of Blockade with a seat in the Cabinet. It followed that in the crucial period for Zionist fortunes, when Balfour was absent in the United States during the spring and early summer of 1917, Lord Robert was in charge of the Foreign Office.' Mr Sykes is correct in regarding this as a critical period in the developments leading to the Balfour Declaration. He is also correct in stating that Lord Robert as Blockade Minister sat in the Cabinet.[20]

relaxed about the Jews than the vast majority of his race:

> On general grounds I would welcome any good understanding with the Jews.
> I admit that some ignorant Arabs despise the Jews, but ignorants everywhere
> are the same, and on the whole such incidents compare favourably with what
> the Jews suffer in more advanced lands.

The Cabinet were in fact investing a great deal in Feisal, the son of Hussein, Sharif of Mecca, and he was soon designated as the intended monarch of Syria. (In the event he was later forced out and switched to Iraq.)

Accompanying Weizmann's Commission were Mark Sykes and advisers from Italy and France, together with James de Rothschild, son of Baron Edmond, who was to act as a liaison officer with the Palestine Jewish Colonization Association (PICA). Weizmann was soon disillusioned by the coldness – hostility even – of many of the military and the diplomats, but he was kindly received by Allenby. He also got on well with Feisal who was to enter Damascus with Allenby, the way having been prepared by Arab forces led by Lawrence. Weizmann told Allenby:

> You have conquered a great part of Palestine and you can measure your
> conquest by one of two yardsticks: either in square kilometres – and in that
> sense your victory, though great is not unique: the Germans have overrun
> vaster areas – or else by the yardstick of history. If this conquest of yours be
> measured by the centuries of tradition which attach to every square kilometre
> of its ground, then yours is one of the greatest victories in history. And the
> traditions which make it so are bound up with the history of my people. The
> day may come when we shall make good your victory, so that it may remain
> graven in something more enduring than rock – in the lives of men and
> nations. It would be a great pity if anything were done now – for instance by a
> few officials or administrators – to mar this victory.[22]

Allenby was a little shaken by this allocution, but expressed his best wishes to Weizmann in his task.

The mission's objective was in part to make contact with the settlements – many of whose members had taken up arms to help the Allies – and to bring the old-established *Yishuv* not only into that task, but to seek to harmonize them into what he saw as the future role of the country. Weizmann also arranged for further talks with Feisal, assisted by Lawrence. One object in which Feisal undertook to co-operate was to secure the support of Hussein, in which he was successful.

This visit also enabled Weizmann to perform a ceremony perhaps nearer to his heart than any of his diplomatic tasks, the laying of the foundation stones of the Hebrew University on Mount Scopus on 24 July, a task entrusted to him by Balfour. Allenby, who had begun by advising against such a ceremony, was present.

It was arranged that Feisal should meet Weizmann again, in London. On 3 January 1919 an agreement was signed. Paragraphs 3 and 4 read:

In the establishment of the Constitution and Administration of Palestine, all
such measures shall be adopted as will afford the fullest guarantees for
carrying into effect the British Government's Declaration of November 2nd,
1917.

All necessary measures shall be taken to encourage and stimulate
immigration of Jews into Palestine on a large scale, and as quickly as possible
to settle Jewish immigrants on the land through closer settlement and
intensive cultivation of the soil. In taking such measures the Arab peasant and
tenant farmers shall be protected in their rights and shall be assisted in
forwarding their economic development.[23]

In March the Supreme Council of the Allies involved in the peace
negotiations in Paris received a deputation headed by Weizmann and
Sokolov. The thrust of their demands was that Ukrainian, Polish and other
East European Jews should be given an undertaking about immigration into
Palestine. The American Secretary of State asked Weizmann for
clarification of the phrase 'Jewish National Home'. Did it mean an
autonomous Jewish Government? Weizmann, totally disregarding his
earlier interpretation, said that it did not:

The Zionist Organization did not want an autonomous Jewish Government,
but merely to establish in Palestine, under a Mandatory Power, an
administration, not necessarily Jewish, which would render it possible to send
into Palestine 70,000 to 80,000 Jews annually. The Organization would
require to have permission at the same time to build Jewish schools, where
Hebrew would be taught, and to develop institutions of every kind. Thus it
would build up gradually a nationality and so make Palestine as Jewish as
America is American or England English . . .

Later on, when the Jews formed the large majority, they would be ripe to
establish such a Government as would answer to the state of development of
their country and to their ideals.

But Whitehall, or at least the Foreign Office, had very different ideas.
Curzon, the Foreign Secretary, on being briefed by the Chief Administrator
of Palestine, wrote to Balfour:

He has much to say about that country. But his main point, and that of
Allenby, is that we should go slow about the Zionist aspirations and the
Zionist State, otherwise we might jeopardize all that we have won. A Jewish
Government in any form would mean an Arab rising, and the nine-tenths of
the population who are not Jews would make short shrift with the
Hebrews. . . . As you know, I share these views and have for long felt that the
pretensions of Weizmann and Company are extravagant and ought to be
checked.

Nor would Balfour's reply to Curzon have pleased Weizmann in his more
demanding moods:

As far as I know, Weizmann has never put forward a claim for the Jewish
Government of Palestine. Such a claim is, in my opinion, certainly

inadmissible and personally I do not think we should go further than the original declaration which I made to Lord Rothschild.

Curzon received further ammunition from the Zionist Conference held in March, complaining that the delegates had committed themselves to

1. Absolute control of immigration;
2. All Jewish holidays to be observed officially;
3. Immediate control of water-rights, carrying with it control of the land;
4. Jewish nationalization of all public land and of the surplus land of all private estates exceeding a certain size;
5. Complete control of all public works;
6. Jewish supervision of all Educational Institutions;
7. Use of Hebrew as main language in all schools.

On his visit to Palestine in 1883 Curzon had written:

> Palestine is a country to see once, not to revisit. The scenery is not often picturesque or even pretty. There is much greater need of cultivation than in Greece and much less chance of making it pay. For the surface in many places is all rocks and stones. No Jew with his eyes open (and you never saw one with them shut) would think of going back: and if the millennium is only to arrive when they have returned, our descendants will still be expecting it in 3000 AD.

Curzon was a senior member of the Lloyd George Government, which in 1917 approved the Balfour Declaration. But his personal hostility was implacable, particularly after he had replaced Arthur Balfour himself as acting Foreign Secretary at the beginning of 1919. Writing to Balfour in March about reports of the new Zionist programme, he said:

> I confess that I shudder at the prospect of our country having to adjust ambitions of this description with the interests of the native population or the legitimate duties of a Mandatory Power, and I look back with a sort of gloomy satisfaction upon the warning that I ventured to utter a year and a half ago in the Cabinet as to the consequences of inviting the Hebrews to return to Palestine.

In August Curzon wrote again to Balfour:

> This is merely a line to say how much startled I am at a letter from Dr Weizmann to you, dated July 23, in which that astute but aspiring person claims to advise us as to the principal politico-military appointments to be made in Palestine; to criticize sharply the conduct of any such officers who do not fall on the neck of the Zionists (a most unattractive resting place); and to acquaint us with the 'type of man' whom we ought or ought not to send.
>
> It seems to me that Dr Weizmann will be a scourge on the back of the unlucky Mandatory, and I often wish you would drop a few globules of cold water on his heated and extravagant pretensions.

Having determined in 1883 that Palestine was an unsuitable home for the

Jews of the Diaspora, he seems to have resented every stage in their subsequent reunion as a personal affront.[24]

Weizmann, however, was under the more urgent compulsion forced on him by a wave of pogroms in the Ukraine, involving the death of 60,000 Jews, in March 1919, followed by other outrages, and in April the Arabs broke loose in Jerusalem. Churchill, by this time Colonial Secretary, reported to Parliament on 29 April that in Jerusalem there had been 250 casualties, nine-tenths of them Jewish. Jabotinsky was immediately sentenced to fifteen years' imprisonment, later reduced to a year. Churchill came under great pressure in the House. On 29 April he had to answer questions by seven Members, including Lieutenant Commander Kenworthy and Ormsby-Gore, later Under-Secretary for the Colonies. Churchill said that he was looking into the question of the fifteen-year sentence. He had only received abridged reports from the War Office. He was in touch with Lord Allenby, but had not yet received his answer.[25] He went so far, however, as to endorse MPs' tributes to Jabotinsky's action in raising the first Jewish regiment to fight alongside the British Army in Palestine.

Another problem faced Britain. The Paris Peace Conference was set to institute the new system of mandates to be laid down by the proposed League of Nations whereby leading powers would be granted, subject to reporting to the Mandates Commission, executive governmental powers over colonial-type countries. There was a strong section in the Cabinet, including Curzon and Montagu, which would have liked to see the responsibility for Palestine transferred to the broad shoulders of the United States. But Lloyd George, with strong backing from Balfour, insisted on Britain taking the responsibility and she was accordingly assured of the Mandate by a decision of the San Remo Conference on 24 April 1920, though formal ratification of the Commission had to await a vote of the League of Nations on 22 July 1922.

Churchill had used his last few weeks in the War Office to work on a new interdepartmental structure for Middle East affairs, based on the Colonial Office. In August 1920 he had proposed the establishment of a special Department for Middle Eastern Affairs, to co-ordinate government policy in the area and, as he strongly urged, to save money. His proposals to concentrate the existing separate responsibilities of the War Office, the India Office, the Foreign Office and the Colonial Office in a single Department, the Colonial Office, were accepted by Cabinet on 31 December. On 1 January 1921, Lloyd George, who with Churchill was part of a house party as guests of Sir Philip Sassoon, asked him if he would take the Colonial Office. Churchill played for time, wanting to be quite sure that he would have full control of the new interdepartmental arrangements for the Middle East. On 4 January he wrote to the Prime Minister provisionally accepting the post, but formally asking for the powers of co-ordination necessary, on which he had sent Lloyd George a memorandum. With his letter he enclosed a further paper in elaboration of the first. By this time, still as War and Air Secretary, he was effectively exercising the powers of those departments. On 12 February he sent yet another letter:

> Now that I am leaving the War Office for the Colonial Office, it is essential that there should be a similarly clear understanding about the military aspect. It is absolutely necessary for me to have effective control of the general policy and to be able to communicate directly with the Commander-in-Chief in Mesopotamia, and to move the Secretary of State for War to change the Commander-in-Chief at the time I consider convenient. It will be convenient for me to send all my communications to the GOC, Mesopotamia, through the War Office in the same way as I have been communicating with Sir Percy Cox through the India Office. All actual orders should be sent as at present by the War Office, but in general accordance with the policy I am pursuing subject to Cabinet approval. Unless in this way I secure the effective initiation and control of the whole policy, I could not undertake the task with any prospects of success.[26]

Lloyd George accepted, and Churchill went to work on his master plan for Middle Eastern policy.

Churchill was a committed Zionist. Martin Gilbert[27] quotes a letter he had drafted (but did not send) to a Manchester constituent in 1908, dissociating himself from the Uganda scheme:

> Jerusalem must be the only ultimate goal. When it will be achieved it is vain to prophesy: but that it will some day be achieved is one of the few certainties of the future.

In an article he wrote as War Minister he referred to the 'inspiring movement' of Weizmann. The Jews, under the protection of the British Crown, could establish a Jewish state of three to four million inhabitants.

Now Colonial Secretary, Churchill moved quickly with his plans for a visit to Cairo and Mesopotamia; but just before being moved to the Colonial Office from the War and Air Office, he had decided to confine himself to a long-drawn-out conference in Egypt. This was mainly concerned with the question of Transjordan and its separation from Palestine. The two were still to come under the jurisdiction of a single High Commissioner, wearing two hats. But the Zionist issue was also covered under the headings, 'Policy in Palestine under the Mandate', and 'Special Subjects'. The conference over, Churchill went to Palestine* where he was much occupied with the

---

* Where, it appears, he and Samuel were greeted in Gaza by great crowds, yelling their heads off. They acknowledged their reception unaware that the crowd was demanding a massacre of the Jews.[28]

Transjordan problem. His message to the Arabs was that there was a great deal of groundless apprehension on their part, particularly the fear that 'hundreds of thousands of Jews' were going to pour into the country in a very short period and dominate the existing population: there were over half a million Arabs in Palestine and not more than 80,000 Jews. Immigration from Europe would be a slow process and 'the rights of the existing non-Jewish population would be strictly preserved'. His pledges to Abdullah in effect put paid to Weizmann's demand for Jewish settlement not only west but also east of the Jordan. But the Arabs memorialized Churchill with considered warnings against Jewish immigration, and specifically demanded:

First: The principle of a National Home for the Jews be abolished.

Second: A National Government be created, which shall be responsible to a Parliament elected by the Palestinian people who existed in Palestine before the war.

Third: A stop be put to Jewish immigration until such a time as a National Government is formed.

Fourth: Laws and regulations before the war be still carried out and all others framed after the British occupation be annulled, and no new laws be created until a National Government comes into being.

Fifth: Palestine should not be separated from her sister (*scilicet* Arab) States.

Churchill replied in categorical terms. He refused to repudiate the Balfour Declaration. The British Government were committed to a National Home for the Jews and this had been ratified by the victorious Allies at the end of the war. He argued that their reunion in a National Home would be good for the Jews, the British Empire and also 'for the Arabs who dwell in Palestine'.[29] During his visit he went to the site of the Hebrew University on Mount Scopus. After receiving a 'scroll of the Law' and planting a tree, he said:

Personally my heart is full of sympathy for Zionism. This sympathy has existed for a long time, since twelve years ago, when I was in contact with the Manchester Jews. I believe that the establishment of a Jewish National Home in Palestine will be a blessing to the whole world, a blessing to the Jewish race scattered all over the world, and a blessing to Great Britain. I firmly believe that it will be a blessing also to all the inhabitants of this country without distinction of race and religion. This last blessing depends greatly upon you. Our promise was a double one. On the one hand we promised to give our help to Zionism, and on the other, we assured the non-Jewish inhabitants that they should not suffer in consequence. Every step you take should therefore be also for the moral and material benefit of all Palestinians. If you do this Palestine will be happy and prosperous, and peace and concord will always reign; it will turn into a paradise, and will become as is written in the scriptures you have just presented to me, a land flowing with milk and honey, in which sufferers of all races and religions will find a rest from their sufferings. You Jews of Palestine have a very great responsibility; you are the representatives of the Jewish nation all over the world, and your conduct should provide an example for, and do honour to, Jews in all countries.

The hope of your race for so many centuries will be gradually realized here, not only for your own good, but for the good of the world.[30]

He was particularly impressed by the settlements or 'Jewish colonies' as he called them, and was anxious to communicate his enthusiasm to the Commons. On 14 June he reported fully on his negotiations about the leadership of Arab states neighbouring on Palestine, and went on:

The Arabs believe that in the next few years they are going to be swamped by scores of thousands of immigrants from Central Europe, who will push them off the land, eat up the scanty substance of the country and eventually gain absolute control of its institutions and destinies . . .

There is really nothing for the Arabs to be frightened about. All the Jewish immigration is being very carefully watched and controlled both from the point of view of numbers and character. No Jew will be brought in beyond the number who can be provided for by the expanding wealth and development of the resources of the country. There is no doubt whatever that at the present time the country is greatly under-populated. Anyone who has seen the work of the Jewish colonies which have been established during the last 20 or 30 years in Palestine will be struck by the enormous productive results which they have achieved. I had the opportunity of visiting the colony of Rishon le Zion about 12 miles from Jaffa, and there, from the most inhospitable soil, surrounded on every side by barrenness and the most miserable form of cultivation, I was driven into a fertile and thriving country estate, where the scanty soil gave place to good crops and good cultivation, and then to vineyards and finally to the most beautiful, luxurious orange groves, all created in 20 or 30 years by the exertions of the Jewish community who live there. Then as we went on we were surrounded by 50 or 60 young Jews, galloping on their horses, and with farmers from the estate who took part in the work. Finally, when we reached the centre, there were drawn up 300 or 400 of the most admirable children, of all sizes and sexes, and about an equal number of white-clothed damsels. We were invited to sample the excellent wines which the establishment produced, and to inspect the many beauties of the groves.

I defy anybody, after seeing work of this kind, achieved by so much labour, effort and skill, to say that the British Government, having taken up the position it has, could cast it all aside and leave it to be rudely and brutally overturned by the incursion of a fanatical attack by the Arab population from outside . . .[31]

This statement went some way to damp down criticism from Jewish circles about a statement made twelve days earlier by Samuel, and approved by Churchill. All Jewish immigration would be limited, he had said, by the 'economic capacity' of Palestine to absorb new immigrants. At the same time he amended Samuel's draft by objecting to 'any paraphrase of the words National Home' and rejected Samuel's proposal for a 'non-Jewish agency', an advisory Committee of Christians and Moslems. Even so, there were protests both in Palestine and Britain: Sokolov went to the Colonial Office and was reassured by Churchill, adding that he had given instructions for exemplary punishment of Arabs responsible for the Jerusalem outrages.

Meanwhile the Cabinet was reconsidering the question of the Mandate. Should Britain propose that it be assumed by the United States, as Lloyd George at one point suggested? Churchill was attracted by the suggestion, but the Prime Minister then had second thoughts.

Later in June the Imperial Cabinet of Dominion Prime Ministers had a report from Churchill on Middle Eastern affairs. The Canadian Prime Minister, Arthur Meighen, pressed Churchill for a definition of the phrase, Jewish 'National Home' – did it mean control of the Government? Churchill replied that if, in the course of many years, they became a majority in the country, they would naturally take it over. This was after flatly rejecting any idea that the Arabs, then in a majority, should have powers of government, or even a national assembly. But Churchill faced Conservative criticism, partly for his pro-Zionist stance, but in particular for his support of the 'Rutenberg scheme'.* This was a major public works project, sponsored by the Jewish Agency, to generate electricity by harnessing the waters of the Jordan and Auja rivers, involving the transfer not only of government-held land, but of Arab land too, to private enterprise. By its very nature it had to be a monopoly, and there was no question of throwing the concession open to competition: hydroelectric engineers were very thin on the ground. The Foreign Office defended the monopoly in a statement to Washington at the end of the year:

> So far as Palestine is concerned, Article II of the Mandate expressly provides that the administration may arrange with the Jewish Agency to develop any of the national resources of the country, in so far as these matters are not directly undertaken by the Administration.

The project was raised in debate in the House of Lords on 21 June 1922, when Lord Islington moved

> That the Mandate for Palestine in its present form is unacceptable to this House, because it directly violates the pledges made by His Majesty's Government to the people of Palestine in the Declaration of October, 1915, and again in the Declaration of November, 1918, and is, as at present framed, opposed to the sentiments and wishes of the great majority of the people of Palestine; that, therefore, its acceptance by the Council of the League of Nations should be postponed until such modifications have therein been effected as will comply with pledges given by His Majesty's Government.[32]

* Pinchas Rutenberg was an immigrant Jewish engineer, born in Russia.

The Noble Lord, making it clear 'that I speak in no sense in hostility to the Jewish race', embarked on a well-ordered criticism of the Mandate, with particular reference to the rights of the Arab majority, and, on the subject of the Rutenberg concession, arguing that a number of other possible firms could have been offered the contract. He was immediately followed by Balfour, Lord President of the Council, making his maiden speech in the Upper House.[33] His speech covered the whole ground, including the League of Nations' conferment of the Mandate, his concern for Arab rights and the procedures which led to Rutenberg obtaining the hydroelectric concession. But he was not able to convince their Lordships' House. When a division was called, the vote was 60 'Contents' in favour of Lord Islington's motion: 29 'Not-Contents' against.

The Government decided to take no notice of the vote. The debate opened by Churchill a week before had not been pressed to a division; an attempt to force a vote by Evelyn Harmsworth had failed, as the hour for moving on to 'next business' had arrived. There can be little doubt that the Commons as a whole would have endorsed the policy put forward by Churchill.

There were no further major debates until 1922 was halfway through. On 15 February, in written answers to Parliamentary questions, Churchill confirmed that the High Commissioner's Advisory Council would be nominated by Sir Herbert Samuel and would be purely consultative, and stated that the 'principle governing the policy of immigration into Palestine is that the number of immigrants at any time shall be adapted to the economic capacity of the country to absorb them'.[34] On 27 February Sir Gordon Hewart, the Attorney-General, confirmed that the legal status of Palestine in international law was that of occupied enemy territory, as Turkey had still not signed a peace with the Allies.[35]

On 9 March Churchill introduced the Supply Estimates providing the necessary finance for Britain's activities in Palestine. After referring to an abortive riot in Jerusalem in November, and in Jaffa the previous May, he said that

> broadly speaking, the country has been tranquil, though I do not for a moment pretend that the feeling of irritation, suspicion and inquietude has disappeared from the minds of the Arab population. The Jewish immigration has been closely watched and controlled from the point of view of policy. Every effort has been made to secure only good citizens who will build up the country. We cannot have a country inundated by Bolshevist riffraff [sic] who would wish to subvert institutions in Palestine as they have done with success in the land from which they came. Altogether, about 9000 have come in this year, and they bring with them the means of their own livelihood, the Zionist Association expending nearly a million a year in the country.[36]

In the same speech he also reported on the manoeuvrings about Abdullah. A vote was challenged on the Estimates, which were carried by 162 against 56.

Churchill, also answering questions on 14 March, gave Parliament an analysis of immigrants according to nationality. From September 1920 to December 1921, 33 per cent were Polish, 15 per cent Russian, 5 per cent Rumanian, 11 per cent 'Ukraine, etc.', British $3\frac{1}{2}$ per cent, Central Asia 10 per cent, the United States 2 per cent, and 'other nationalities' $20\frac{1}{2}$ per cent.[37]

On 21 March he confirmed that no subventions were given by His Majesty's Government for settlement, the cost of this being met by Jewish sources.[38]

On 16 May the Under-Secretary for Foreign Affairs, Cecil Harmsworth, drew the attention of Parliament to an Anglo-United States agreement issued by the State Department, for the text of which he referred Hon. Members to newspaper reports of the previous day.[39]

On 15 June Churchill answered an oral question on Palestine's overseas trade. In 1921, imports into Palestine were £5,665,000, and exports £824,000. Thirty-four per cent of the imports came from the United Kingdom, $18\frac{1}{2}$ per cent were from India, Australia and Egypt. Sixty-nine per cent of her exports went to Egypt, $15\frac{1}{2}$ per cent to Britain.[40]

Four days later he answered a question about military involvement and casualties. In a written answer about the troops he said that 1,192,511 had taken part in the fighting in Palestine and Egypt; 16,366 had been killed there, or had died of wounds or disease.[41]

The first major debate since June 1921 took place on 4 July. Technically it was a debate on Supply, i.e. a motion to approve a grant to cover part of the Colonial Office's expenditure for the year. But a decision of the House to refuse Supply is tantamount to a censure of the Government, threatening indeed the life of the Government unless it is speedily reversed by a motion expressing confidence in the Government, or some similar judgment by Parliament.

The debate was opened by the Under-Secretary of State for the Colonial Office, Edward Wood, later Lord Halifax. This was appropriate as the debate was bound to roam over Colonial Office administered territories the world over. Churchill, while ready to answer questions raised on any area covered by his departmental duties, wanted to have the last word on Palestine. Moreover, Sir William Joynson-Hicks, later as Home Secretary known to the country as 'Jix', had given notice of an amendment which he was to move. This stated that 'in the opinion of this House' the acceptance of the Palestine Mandate by the Government should receive the prior sanction of Parliament, and then went on, secondly, to propose that the Rutenberg contracts should be referred to a specially appointed Select Committee of the House for consideration and report. His speech pulled no punches on either part of his subject. He was particularly effective in quoting Weizmann, who had referred to Sir Herbert Samuel in terms suggesting that he was no more than the good doctor's poodle, as saying:

> I was mainly responsible for the appointment of Sir Herbert Samuel to Palestine. . . . There is no one who had more to do with, or was more pleased at the appointment of Sir Herbert Samuel than I . . .
>
> Sir Herbert Samuel is our friend and has worked loyally with us from the first moment. At our request, fortified by our moral support, he accepted the difficult position. We put him in that position. He is our Samuel; he is the production of our Jewry . . .[42]

Joynson-Hicks later went on to refer to a public statement the previous August by Samuel, technically an official, about the broader world question of the Jews. Samuel had said:

> They have a right to be considered. They ask for the opportunity to establish a home in the land which was the political, and has always been the religious centre, of their race. They ask that this home should possess national characteristics in language, in customs, in intellectual interests and in religious and political institutions.

Joynson-Hicks then charged that 'with the assent of Sir Herbert Samuel, Zionist political control has been gradually created in the administration of Palestine', and quoted Weizmann again, to show what Samuel was asserting:

> I declare that in the Jewish national home the conditions would be such that we should be allowed to develop our institutions, our schools and the Hebrew language, that there should ultimately be such conditions that Palestine would be Jewish as America is American and England is English.[43]

Those last words were frequently to be quoted against Weizmann and the British Government for more than a generation. As we have seen, Weizmann, as enthusiasm or depression took hold of him, though frequently not without careful calculation, would oscillate between the concept of Palestine as 'the National Home' and that of a minority stake in a mainly Arab land.

Joynson-Hicks went on to warn that if the Zionists aimed to import thousands and thousands until they secured a majority over the Arabs, then the latter were entitled to say at once:

> We represent 90 per cent of the population. We are entitled to self-determination and to decide what immigration laws are to be provided in our own country.[44]

He was issuing a clear warning, and was later that evening to force a division against the Government, purely, as he explained, against the Rutenberg concession. As Colonial Secretary he was to prove a steadfast friend of the Jewish cause in the years ahead.[45]

Winding up, Churchill indeed claimed him as a former pro-Zionist, quoting him:

> I will do all in my power to forward the views of the Zionists, in order to enable the Jews once more to take possession of their own land . . .

and devoted a considerable time to defending the Rutenberg concession (or monopoly as Joynson-Hicks claimed in an interruption). But the main theme of his speech was to emphasize his hopes for the Jewish national home. Referring to the Balfour Declaration, Churchill went on:

> At the same time that this pledge was made to the Zionists, an equally important promise was made to the Arab inhabitants in Palestine – that their civil and religious rights would be effectively safeguarded, and that they should not be turned out to make room for newcomers. If that pledge was to be acted upon, it was perfectly clear that the newcomers must bring their own means of livelihood and that they, by their industry, by their brains, and by their money, must create new sources of wealth on which they could live without detriment to or subtraction from the well being of the Arab population. It was inevitable that, by creating these new sources of wealth, and bringing this new money into the country, they would not only benefit themselves, but benefit and enrich the entire country among all classes and races of its population.
>
> What sources of new wealth were opened? In the first place, there was a greatly extended and revived agriculture. As I explained to the House when I addressed Hon. Members a year and a half ago, anyone who has visited Palestine recently must have seen how parts of the desert have been converted into gardens, and how material improvement has been effected in every respect by the Arab population dwelling around. On the sides of the hills there are enormous systems of terraces, and they are now the abode of an active cultivating population; whereas before, under centuries of Turkish and Arab rule, they had relapsed into a wilderness. There is no doubt whatever that in that country there is room for still further energy and development if capital and other forces be allowed to play their part. There is no doubt that there is room for a far larger number of people, and this far larger number of people will be able to lead far more decent and prosperous lives.
>
> Apart from this agricultural work – this reclamation work – there are services which science, assisted by outside capital, can render, and of all the enterprises of importance which would have the effect of greatly enriching the land none was greater than the scientific storage and regulation of the waters of the Jordan for the provision of cheap power, and light needed for the industry of Palestine, as well as water for the irrigation of new lands now desolate. This would have been carrying out your policy, not only the policy of the Government, and it was the only means by which it could be done without injuring vitally the existence of the Arab inhabitants of the country. It would create a new world entirely, a new means of existence. And it was only by the irrigation which created and fertilized the land, and by electric power which would supply the means of employing the Arab population, that you could take any steps towards the honest fulfilment of the pledges to which

this country and this House, to an unparalleled extent of individual commitment, is irrevocably committed.

What better steps could we take, in order to fulfil our pledge to help them to establish their national home, without breaking our pledge to the Arabs that they would not be disturbed, than to interest Zionists in the creation of this new Palestinian world which, without injustice to a single individual, without taking away one scrap of what was there before, would endow the whole country with the assurance of a greater prosperity and the means of a higher economic and social life? Was not this a good gift which the Zionists could bring with them, the consequences of which spreading as years went by in general easement and amelioration – was not this a good gift which would impress more than anything else on the Arab population that the Zionists were their friends and helpers, not their expellers and expropriators, and that the earth was a generous mother, that Palestine had before it a bright future, and that there was enough for all?[46]

The vote at the end of the day was technically a motion to reduce the Secretary of State's salary. This was defeated by 292 to 35, more Conservatives voting for the Government than against.

In the last few months of the Lloyd George administration Churchill was greatly involved in the Irish crisis, and then in the Chanak affair.[47] In October 1922 the Conservative revolt, headed by Bonar Law and supported at the last minute by Baldwin, drove Lloyd George and his Cabinet out of office and, losing Dundee in the subsequent General Election, Churchill out of Parliament. But he had left his imprint on the history of Palestine. When, nearly a third of a century later, Attlee and Bevin came into office, acting as though the Balfour Declaration had never been made, Churchill, leading the Opposition, was again to speak in almost the same language as he had used in the dying months of the Lloyd George administration.

Though Weizmann's Zionists and the British Cabinet had reached agreement on the greatest advance ever recorded up to that time in Zionist history, complications began to develop in the United States. From October 1914, Weizmann had been working with the American Provisional Executive Committee for Zionist Affairs, with Louis Brandeis (Mr Justice Brandeis from July 1916) at its head. In the months preceding the Balfour Declaration, leading British Zionists* met under the chairmanship of Dr Moses Gaster on 17 February 1917. They were agreed in seeking a Jewish homeland in the form of a British protectorate, and set their faces decisively against any idea of a condominium or protectorate involving any country but Britain: only Jerusalem's Holy Places should be internationalized. Weizmann records:[18]

* Lord Rothschild, Herbert Samuel, Sir Mark Sykes, James de Rothschild, Nahum Sokolov, Joseph Cowen, Herbert Bentwich, Harry Sacher and Chaim Weizmann.

Of one country we could speak with official authority. Mr Brandeis, the head of the Zionist movement in America, and adviser to President Wilson on the Jewish question, was in favour of a British protectorate, and utterly opposed to a condominium.

This was the position, too, of the Russian and German Zionists; but Sir Mark Sykes who, Weizmann records, 'placed all his diplomatic skill at our disposal', warned that while Russia, with whom he had been in touch, was unlikely to cause much difficulty, Italy would act on the principle of asking for whatever the French wanted, and 'France was the real difficulty', since she wanted both the whole of Syria 'and a great say in Palestine'.

When Weizmann met Asquith, he found him helpful, despite, he says, 'what we have seen, from private notes published years later, of Asquith's personal unfriendliness to the Zionist ideal'.[49] Asquith and Balfour, Weizmann notes, did not mention the Sykes-Picot treaty, of which he learnt on 16 April, though on 22 March Balfour had gone so far as to suggest that if France proved difficult, the Zionists should approach the US with a view to creating an Anglo-American protectorate over Palestine.

Weizmann reported these developments to Brandeis on 8 April, warning of the French problem. On 20 April Balfour, on his visit to the US, met Brandeis, whom he described to Lord Eustace Percy, a member of his mission, as 'the most remarkable man in America'. Brandeis confirmed that he and his supporters wanted to see a specifically British Administration in Palestine, though it was clear that President Wilson's concern for 'open covenants openly arrived at' could cause trouble in connection with the Sykes-Picot agreement, firm in its commitments, but not a treaty, and certainly not open. But when the Balfour Declaration was promulgated, not only Brandeis but President Wilson gave it their support in principle, though the President did not commit himself on the exact text. Weizmann had telegraphed Brandeis requesting such a statement as soon as he was shown the text of the Declaration. Brandeis cabled Weizmann suggesting the use of the phrase 'Jewish people' instead of 'Jewish race' in all public statements, and this phrase was in fact used in the final text.

Brandeis greeted the Balfour Declaration with a plan for the reconstruction of Palestine and, in June 1918, a convention of American Zionists adopted his proposals, under the title *The Pittsburg Programme*:

1. We declare for political and civil equality irrespective of race, sex or faith for all inhabitants of the land.

2. To insure in the Jewish National Home in Palestine equality of opportunity we favour a policy which, with due regard to existing rights, shall tend to establish the ownership and control by the whole people of the land, of all natural resources and of all public utilities.

3. All land, owned or controlled by the whole people, should be leased on such conditions as will insure the fullest opportunity for development and continuity of possession.

4. The co-operative principle should be applied so far as feasible in the organization of all agricultural, industrial, commercial and financial undertakings.

5. The system of free public instruction which is to be established should embrace all grades and departments of education.

With the end of the war, however, differences began to develop between Weizmann and Brandeis. They began when Brandeis, following a rushed visit to Palestine, deprecated any attempts to promote a large-scale programme of immigration, until major schemes of drainage and road-building had been undertaken. Brandeis was critical, too, of some of the historic settlements dating back to the 1890s and the early years of the twentieth century.

The disagreements became articulate at the twelfth Zionist Conference, held in London in 1920, seven years since the previous meeting. Immediately the argument about Palestine's economic development plans flared. Still more serious, Brandeis seemed to Weizmann to be opposing any political organization or development in the country: the Zionist movement was no longer relevant; in particular there was no need to recruit support among non-Zionists. This led to further disputes about the funding of the Zionist movement; against Weizmann's target of £2 million, Brandeis and his US colleagues asserted that no more than £100,000 could be raised. The real break occurred when Weizmann taunted the Americans by saying that he would have to go to the US to raise what was needed. Weizmann was to comment later that he doubted whether Brandeis ever forgave him for that remark. Before the conference ended, Weizmann was dealing only with a break-away group from Brandeis headed by Louis Lipsky. The London conference, however, maintained a fictional degree of co-operation by appointing Brandeis Honorary President, Weizmann, President of the Organization and Sokolov, Chairman of the Executive.

When Weizmann went to America in April 1921, he was presented with a policy on behalf of Brandeis and his colleagues. World Zionism, as Weizmann interpreted the document, was to consist of strong local organizations linked by a loose confederal structure. He saw this, and the Brandeis group's limited financial target, as a proof that the objective was simply to give help to private investment on an individual project basis, in contrast to the Jewish people, in its corporate, national capacity making the financial effort which would create the foundations of the Homeland.

What we had here was a revival, in a new form and a new country, of the old

cleavage between 'East' and 'West', in Zionism and Jewry; and the popular
slogan called it, in fact, 'Washington *v*. Pinsk', a convenient double allusion to
Brandeis and myself, and also to the larger ideological implication.[50]

Weizmann's task in fighting the Brandeis school was not an easy one. On
territory foreign to him he had to stand by the full Zionist philosophy, while
not alienating the hundreds of friendly souls, many of them not of the
Jewish faith, who contributed generously to the development of Palestine.
Before his American tour ended he formally broke off relations with the
Brandeis group and decided to extend to the United States the European
Keren Hayesod (the Palestine Foundation Fund),* which had been founded
in the previous year. Finally, at the twenty-fourth convention of the Zionist
Organization of America, at Cleveland in June, he appealed over the heads
of the Brandeis group and others, proclaiming the *Keren Hayesod* as
officially established in America. Its first year's income, Weizmann claims,
was four times the half-million dollars which Brandeis had regarded as the
maximum obtainable.

Meanwhile, the Brandeis group was losing ground in America to an
opposition organization set up by Louis Lipsky and Abraham Goldberg.
Weizmann maintained his grip on the Zionist scene, in America as in
Europe, and Brandeis and thirty-six of his friends resigned from the
American National Executive Committee of the World Zionist Organi-
zation, following a motion of no confidence at the Cleveland conference in
June 1921. In the same month, Brandeis resigned from his position as
Honorary President. American Zionism again became a mere provincial
centre within the World Zionist Organization and Zionism lost great men of
ideas and experience. 'Washington had lost out to Pinsk.'

Brandeis and his friends, having resigned from the World Organization,
began to concentrate on practical help for Israeli settlements. They set up
the Palestine Development League to encourage private enterprise and gave
help to Palestine's infant Co-operative Movement. Brandeis opposed those
who sought to keep Palestine a two-race state.

Despite his Supreme Court status, Brandeis's connections with the
Haganah led him to be an active supporter of illegal immigration. When the
Nazis took over Germany he worked to ease emigration restrictions in
America and Europe, and to ease the British immigration controls. Brandeis
University, founded in his memory, remains a worthy memorial to his work
and his ideals.[51]

* Later the Jewish National Fund, see p. 67.

CHAPTER 3

The Partition Question

BRITAIN'S MANDATE FOR PALESTINE was assured by the Peace Conference decision at San Remo in April 1920, though it was not formally ratified by the League of Nations until July 1922. Even the great imperialist pro-consul, Lord Milner, whose record went back to his days as High Commissioner in South Africa from 1897 to 1905, welcomed the Mandate in a debate in the Lords on 27 June 1923. He declared himself 'a strong supporter of Arab policy. . . . I believe in the independence of the Arab countries. . . . I look forward to our Arab Federation', but

> Palestine can never be regarded as a country on the same footing as the other Arab countries. You cannot ignore all history and tradition in the matter. You cannot ignore the fact that this is the cradle of three of the greatest religions of the world. It is a sacred land to the Arabs, but it is also a sacred land to the Jew and Christian: and the future of Palestine cannot be left to be determined by the temporary impressions and feelings of the Arab majority in the country of the present day.[1]

As the Peel Commission was to point out more than a decade and a half later, referring to the Mandate:

> The recognition of Jewish rights was thereby linked with the recognition of Arab rights. Jews were admitted to be in Palestine by right. The little Jewish minority was to be helped to grow by immigration. To facilitate the establishment of the Jewish National Home was a binding international obligation on the Mandatory. The Mandate also imposed specific obligations towards the Arabs. Their civil and religious rights and their position as affected by immigration and land-settlement were not to be prejudiced. But the acceptance of these specific and negative obligations towards the Arabs did not, of course, release the Mandatory from the general and positive obligations implicit in the first recital of the Preamble and in the first paragraph of Article 22 of the Covenant. If Arab claims in Palestine were subject to the rights of others, so were Jewish claims.
>
> It is clear, then, that the policy of the Balfour Declaration was subjected to the operation of the Mandate System in 1919 in the belief that the obligations thereby undertaken towards the Arabs and the Jews respectively would not

conflict. And this belief was still held when the draft Mandate was confirmed by the Council of the League in 1922. Already by then the Arab leaders had displayed their hostility to the Mandate and all it involved; but it was thought that this hostility to the Mandate would presently weaken and die away. Mr Churchill spoke of his 'Statement of Policy' as a basis on which he believed that a 'spirit of co-operation' might be built up, and the ground of this belief in the compatibility of the obligations was no less clear. It was assumed that the establishment of the National Home would mean a great increase of prosperity for all Palestine. It was an essential part of the Zionist mission to revivify the country, to repair by Jewish labour, skill and capital the damage it had suffered from centuries of neglect. Arabs would benefit therefrom as well as Jews. They would find the country they had known so long as poor and backward rapidly acquiring the material blessings of Western civilization. On that account it was assumed that Arab fears and prejudices would gradually be overcome.[2]

The Peel Report is the most useful public document on Palestine in the period from the acceptance of the Mandate to the outbreak of the Second World War.

In 1922, it records, the population was estimated as 589,000 Moslems, 83,000 Jews and 71,000 Christians. By 1936, when the report was drawn up, the Jewish population had risen to some 400,000, a third of the total population. Surveying the five years from 1920 to 1925, it records some half a million pounds sterling being made available, mostly in small amounts, to cultivators. Nearly 200 primary schools were provided by the Government in country districts. Through drainage and other measures malaria, which in 1920 had been rife not only in unhealthy low-lying areas but also in the towns, was eliminated from all the large towns bar Haifa and from considerable areas in the plains. A campaign was successfully launched against eye diseases; hospitals, child-welfare centres and clinics were built, and training provided for nurses and midwives. Jerusalem obtained an adequate water-supply; hundreds of miles of new roads were built and the railway system reorganized – 'a vigorous beginning had been made by 1925 in providing backward Palestine with the material equipment of a modern state'. The report pays tribute too to Christian missions, philanthropic bodies, medical work such as that of the Hadassah Medical Organization in the US, though the Jews insisted on themselves organizing education, just as the colonists took charge of draining the swamps. The Peel Commission, reviewing these schemes, both state-help and self-help, went on record to say that they were more to the benefit of the Arabs than the Jews.[3]

Immigration was gathering momentum, and Sir Herbert Samuel as High Commissioner had to undertake what he called 'the invidious task' of preventing it getting out of hand. They quoted from Samuel's review of his five years' administration a moving description of the origins of the newly arrived population, Palestine-orientated Jews from Bokhara, Persia and Iraq, university men and women from New York and Chicago:

> There are Jews from the Yemen . . . good craftsmen in silver and ivory and good labourers on the farms; and there are agricultural experts from the colleges of France, engineers from Germany, bankers from Holland, manufacturers and merchants from Poland and Russia . . . students and writers, doctors and lawyers, architects and musicians, organizers and social workers, from Eastern Europe and Western, from Asia and America.[4]

At least half the 1925 Jewish population, the Peel Report went on, was from Eastern Europe; of the total population those strictly orthodox in religion were a minority, those wholly irreligious also a minority with the mass in between. Those regarded as 'revolutionary' or 'Bolshevist' were numerically negligible. Three-quarters of the Jewish population lived in the towns and a quarter in the agricultural colonies.

The financing of entry, colonization and settlement was in the main undertaken by the International Zionist Executive, but a notable part was played by the Palestine Jewish Colonization Association (PICA), which had grown out of Edmond de Rothschild's society. Agricultural training had begun before the war under the aegis of the Anglo-Jewish Association and the *Alliance Israelite Universel*, as well as the Jewish National Fund (*Keren Hayesod*). From the war to 1925 about £6 million had been spent on these schemes, 236,000 square miles* of land had been bought, and some 100 villages created, with about 25,000 settlers.

Peel describes the varied 'social organization of the colonies' – orange plantations in private ownership, settlements of individual farmers or small-holders; co-operative settlements, some working the land on an individual basis, some working it in common – and the few communal settlements where no wages were paid, but food, clothing and essential needs were met out of the common purse.

Pre-war Jewish villages were growing into collective and country towns. The report instances Petah Tikvah, which had grown from 700 acres with a population of 125 to 5,000 acres with a population of 4,000; Rehovot, with less than 300 citizens in 1890 and over 1,400 in 1925.[5] There were the new suburbs of Jerusalem and Haifa, Tel Aviv, to the north of Jaffa, with 2,000 individuals in 1914, now with a population of 30,000 – 'the only town in the world which is wholly Jewish'. The development is also recorded of trade union and political organizations, Histadrut, the General Federation of Jewish Labour, and on the political side the General Assembly of 314 members, elected by the votes of all adult Jews of both sexes, with political

---

* 944,000 'dunums' or 'dunams', each equalling about a quarter of a square mile – a half-mile square.

parties emerging; the National Executive Council of political Jewry, the Va'ad Leumi, chosen by the Assembly, an embryo Cabinet; Tel Aviv's elected Municipal Council; with the religious affairs of the community regulated by a Rabbinical Council. Democratic organizations were following the spade and the trowel.

But the Commission, with its membership of experienced British politicians, administrators and pro-consuls, was clear in its analysis of the new, growing Palestine community, and fearless in its comments on the hubris of the immediate post-Balfour years:

> We believe that the British Government and Parliament have always maintained the moral assumption on which ... the Mandate was based, namely, that in course of time Arabs and Jews could and would sink their differences in a common Palestinian citizenship. It was for the achievement of that concord, not merely for the future growth in size and strength of the National Home, that they insisted on delay. In other words a national self-government could not be established in Palestine as long as it would be used to frustrate the purpose of the Balfour Declaration. Even so, the crux was plain enough to Arab eyes. It was the Balfour Declaration and the embodiment in the draft Mandate and nothing else which seemingly prevented their attaining a similar measure of independence to that which other Arab communities already enjoyed. And their reaction to this crux was logical. They repudiated the Balfour Declaration. They protested against its implementation in the draft Mandate. 'The people of Palestine', they said, 'cannot accept the creation of a National Home for the Jewish people in Palestine.' And they refused to co-operate in any form of government other than a national government responsible to the Palestinian people.[6]

Churchill's solution, the Commission noted, had been the establishment of a Legislative Council – Moslem Arabs, Christian Arabs and Jews, plus officials under the presidency of the High Commission. But the Arabs refused to co-operate.[7] It was this which created a new situation for which no provision, either in London or Jerusalem, had been made.

The Duke of Devonshire, who had succeeded Churchill in the Colonial Office, had proposed the establishment of an Arab Agency to occupy a position parallel to the Jewish Agency under Article 4 of the Mandate. This was flatly rejected by the Arabs. His threefold proposal of a Legislative Council, an enlarged Advisory Council, and the Arab Agency, set out in a telegram of 9 November 1923, proved unacceptable:

> Towards all these proposals Arabs have adopted the same attitude, viz. refusal to co-operate. His Majesty's Government have been reluctantly driven to the conclusion that further efforts on similar lines would be useless and they have accordingly decided not to repeat the attempt.[8]

The Commission clearly regarded this as a turning-point in Palestine history and policy. The earlier hopes of co-operation between the two communities were dead, and the Commission's detailed survey of relations over the next few years gave them still less hope of a tolerant, give-and-take, side-by-side creation of a viable two-party state. Even though Jewish immigration was declining, and for a brief period was exceeded by the numbers emigrating, population was still increasing. After the brief slump, immigration increased, and soon there were ugly incidents in Jerusalem, where the Wailing Wall – sacred equally to Jews and Arabs – and the respective temples were the scene of continuing inter-communal violence.*

The clashes were disastrous. Peel estimated that 133 Jews and 116 Arabs were killed, and 339 Jews and 232 Arabs wounded. This led to the inquiry conducted by Sir Walter Shaw, an experienced Colonial Office Governor, who in a full report made this pronouncement:

> There can, in our view, be no doubt that racial animosity on the part of the Arabs, consequent upon the disappointment of their political and national aspirations and fear for their economic future, was the fundamental cause of the outbreaks of August last.

Shaw and his fellow-Commissioners spelt out the Arab fears still further, and in economic as well as political terms:

> In pre-war days the Jews in Palestine, regarded collectively, had formed an unobtrusive minority; individually many of them were dependent on charity for their living, while many of the remainder – in particular the colonists – brought direct and obvious material benefits to the inhabitants of the area in which they settled. The Jewish immigrant of the post-war period, on the other hand, is a person of greater energy and initiative than were the majority of the Jewish community of pre-war days. He represents a movement created by an important international organization supported by funds which judged by Arab standards, seem inexhaustible. To the Arabs it must appear improbable that such competitors will in years to come be content to share the country with them. These fears have been intensified by the more extreme statements of Zionist policy and the Arabs have come to see in the Jewish immigrant not only a menace to their livelihood but a possible overlord of the future . . .
>
> Though Jewish immigration and enterprise have been of great advantage to Palestine, the direct benefit to individual Arabs, which alone is likely to be appreciated, has been small, almost negligible, by comparison with what it might have been had the pre-war methods of settlement been continued. When trade depression and unemployment followed the period of heavy immigration the indirect benefits which Jewish activities had brought to many parts of Palestine were forgotten and everywhere among the Arab people the Zionist movement was regarded as the cause of the economic

---

* The wall was sacred to the Jews as having been part of the Temple exterior, to the Arabs it was sacred as being the western face of the platform of the Haram-esh-Sharif. The Dome of the Rock was one of the Arabs' holiest places, from where Mahomet was said to have ascended to Paradise. But, as the Peel Report pointed out,[9] to the Jews it was once the site of the Temple.

problems of the country. The sale of the Sursock lands and other Jewish land purchases in districts where the soil is most productive were regarded as showing that the immigrants would not be content to occupy undeveloped areas and that economic pressures upon the Arab population was likely to increase.

In other words, those consequences of Jewish enterprise which have most closely affected the Arab people have been such that the Arab leaders could use them as the means of impressing upon their followers that a continuance of Jewish immigration and land purchases could have no other result than that the Arabs would in time be deprived of their livelihood and that they, and their country, might ultimately come under the political domination of Jews. Racial antipathy needed no other stimulus, but it was further encouraged by a spirit of mutual intolerance which has unfortunately been a marked feature of the past decade in Palestine. From the beginning the two races had no common interest. They differed in language, in religion and in outlook. Only by mutual toleration and by compromise could the views of the leaders of the two peoples have been reconciled and a joint endeavour for the common good have been brought about. Instead, neither side had made any sustained attempt to improve racial relationships. The Jews, prompted by eager desire to see their hopes fulfilled, have pressed on with a policy at least as comprehensive as the White Paper in 1922 can warrant. The Arabs with unrelenting opposition, have refused to accept that document and have prosecuted a political campaign designed to counter Jewish activities and to realize their own political ambitions.[10]

Shaw and his colleagues called for a follow-up report on the control of immigration and the issue of immigration certificates, and Sir John Hope Simpson was appointed as investigator. Commenting on his report,* the Peel Commission later noted:

It was the Arab rather than the Jewish point of view that had prevailed, that the Report was based on a calculation which, if it were accurate, cut at the very root of the National Home. It had hitherto been taken for granted that a substantial amount of cultivable land was still available for the further expansion of Jewish colonization without injury to Arab interests.

Simpson had deduced, the Peel Report commented:

1. If all the cultivable land in Palestine were divided up among the Arab agricultural population, there would not be enough to provide every family with a decent livelihood.
2. Until further development of Jewish lands and of irrigation had taken place and the Arabs had adopted better methods of cultivation, 'there is no room for a single additional settler, if the standard of life of the fellaheen is to

* Cmd 3686, Peel, p. 71, pointed out that the Zionists felt that 16,000,000 dunams (about 4 million square miles) were needed; the Commission of Lands had proposed 10,592,000, Sir John Hope Simpson 6,544,000 – all these excluding the Beersheba district.

remain at its present level'. On State lands, similarly, there is no room, pending development, for Jewish settlers.

But Sir John Hope Simpson went on to record his 'personal belief . . . that with thorough development of the country there will be room, not only for all the present agricultural population on a higher standard of life than it at present enjoys, but for not less than 20,000 families of settlers from outside'. In order, therefore, to carry out the obligations of the Mandate towards both Arabs and Jews he recommended 'an active policy of agricultural development, having as its object close settlement on the land and intensive cultivation by both Arabs and Jews'.

It would take time for the fruits of this development policy to mature, and meanwhile Sir John Hope Simpson was clearly opposed to the admission of any more Jewish immigrants as settlers on the land. Nor, at first sight, was he much more encouraging with regard to industrial immigration. At that time there was no statistical material available – it is still insufficient – to form a scientific opinion on the amount of Arab unemployment in the country. While refusing, therefore, to dogmatize on the subject, Sir John Hope Simpson was convinced that Arab unemployment was 'serious and widespread': and 'it is wrong', he argued, 'that a Jew from Poland, Lithuania, or the Yemen, should be admitted to fill an existing vacancy, while in Palestine there are already workmen capable of filling that vacancy who are unable to find employment'. 'This policy', he added, 'will be unacceptable to the Jewish authorities.' He was right: but in point of fact he had added a rider to his judgment which went far to meet the Jewish case.

It has been pointed out that Jewish capital will not be brought into Palestine in order to employ Arab labour. It will come in with the definite object of the employment of Jewish labour and not otherwise. The principle of 'derived demand' would justify the immigration of Jewish labour even when there are Arab unemployed in the country if the newly imported Jewish labour is assured of work of a permanent nature, through the introduction of Jewish capital to provide the work on which that labour is to be employed. It is clearly of no advantage to the unemployed Arab that Jewish capital should be prevented from entering the country, and he is in no worse position by the importation of Jewish labour to do work in Palestine for which the funds are available by the simultaneous importation of Jewish capital. In fact, he is better off, as the expenditure of that capital on wages to Jewish workmen will cause, ultimately, a demand for the services of a portion of the Arab unemployed.[11]

Weizmann not unnaturally protested that the White Paper was

inconsistent with the terms of the Mandate and in vital particulars marks the reversal of the policy hitherto followed by His Majesty's Government in regard to the Jewish National Home.[12]

He further told the Colonial Secretary, Lord Passfield, that he had resigned his dual office of President of the Zionist Organization and the Jewish Agency. There was wide British support among MPs and others against the Government's new stance. The Government responded by inviting the Jewish Agency to confer with Ministers on the offending document. The outcome was unsatisfactory and inconclusive. No amendment was made to the 'Statement of Policy', and the Government followed Hope Simpson with a White Paper (Cmd 3692).

The Arabs re-named the White Paper the 'Black Letter'.[13] A deputation to London complained not only of Shaw's handling of land purchase and immigration, but also of his comments on the question of self-government. The Government rejected their demands as rendering it impossible for them to carry out their Mandatory responsibilities. What was emerging, and highlighted by the Arabs' resort to violence in 1929–30, was the fact that Whitehall and Parliament had for so long underrated the Arabs' deep hostility to Jewish immigration, and had in fact over many years too easily accepted the comfortable doctrine that anything that was good for the Jews would be good for the Arabs. As Peel was to report six years after this uprising, British inability to appreciate the reasons for Arab resentment of Jewish immigration and land purchase was based on the 'old original assumption that the two races could and would learn to live together'.*

Peel's judgment was to be that all Ministers, Commissioners of inquiry and Jewish leaders had unanimously reaffirmed this assumption:

> Only one voice was missing from the chorus – the Arab voice. Not once since 1919 had any Arab leader said that co-operation with the Jews was even possible. The response of Arab nationalism to the assumption to which all the other parties in the case so stubbornly adhered was an equally stubborn denial. *Obstat natura*.[14]

Meanwhile, immigration had begun to pick up after the year of net emigration, 1928. In 1929 Jewish net immigrants totalled 3,503; in 1930,

---

* Peel, pp. 77–8, listed a succession of Ministerial statements – from Churchill in 1922, Devonshire in 1923, the White Paper of 1930, the Prime Minister's letter of 1931, and also of reports of inquiries, the Haycroft Commission, 1921, Shaw in 1930, Snell's Note of Reservations and Hope Simpson. All had stressed the need for the two communities to work together – using such words as 'co-operation' and 'understanding', 'not merely by the acceptance, but by the willing co-operation' of the communities; 'acceptance by the Arabs of the declared policy ... on the subject of the Jewish National Home' (Haycroft), 'corresponding growth of good will between the two peoples' (Snell), 'joint endeavour of the two great sections of the population' (Hope Simpson). Peel quotes also successive resolutions of the Zionist Congress in 1921, 1922 and 1930 expressing the determination of the Jewish people to live with the Arab people on terms of concord and mutual respect and together with them to make the common home into a flourishing community.

3,315; and 3,409 in 1931. In 1932 gross immigration leapt to 9,553,* with a more than threefold increase to 30,327 in 1933. But these figures were of legal immigration only. In 1931 the Government had accepted as permanent residents 6,000 Jews who had entered illegally, and went on in 1933 to make honest immigrants of thousands more who had entered the country as 'travellers' and had settled, as well as many 'self-smugglers'. During this period, Peel was to report later, the economic position of the Arabs was improving, in terms of earnings, market sales and the provision of economic and social capital such as roads, bridges, irrigation and schools. But Arab hostility remained as violent as ever, murders were rife, orange trees were destroyed, Jewish-owned cattle maimed; Arabs withdrew more and more from service on intercommunal government committees (including one on education), from municipal corporations and the River Board.

The new Jewish entrants continued to rise: 42,359 (legal) immigrants in 1934, 61,854 in 1935 (see Appendix 1).** The Arab reaction was predictable and aggravated the Administration's reply to protests that immigration had not exceeded the 'absorptive capacity of the country'. Violence intensified, and it became known that a 'terrorist' band had been established in the Hills of Galilee, under the leadership of Sheikh Izzed of Qassam. Their capture by the police and the Sheikh's death in a clash with security forces led to Arab demonstrations, and it was in fact the subsequent violence between the races which led to the appointment of the Royal Commission headed by Earl Peel. That part of its report which refers to the demonstrations, with its criticism of extremists on both sides, does not concern us. What does is the Commission's deep and great consideration of the underlying causes.

Because of the French shipping strike the Commission were delayed three weeks before they could reach Palestine. Once there, with great help from the High Commission, they speedily undertook their investigation, first into the actual disturbances, their immediate causes and the response of the authorities to them, second into the underlying causes of the fighting. Even in this task they were hampered by Arab refusal to give evidence until almost the last minute. The Commission summarized the views of the Arabs in these terms:[15]

> They frankly stated that, though they considered that they have complaints as to the way in which the Mandate had been carried out, they do not rest their case upon these grievances but that their quarrel is with the existence of the Mandate itself. They do not accept the interpretation of the McMahon letter as set out in the Government's statement of British policy in Palestine in June 1922. They deny the validity of the Balfour Declaration. They have never

* No figures were given of emigration in 1932–4: in 1935 it was just 396.
** See p. 382 below.

admitted the right of the Powers to entrust a Mandate to Great Britain. They hold that the authority exercised by the Mandatory is inconsistent with the Covenant of the League of Nations and with the principle of self-determination embodied in that Covenant. We have examined these controversial issues in an earlier chapter; and the point which concerns us here is not whether these Arab claims are justified or not, but simply that they are their claims, and that the overriding or setting-aside of them was the main cause of the disturbances.

In support of these claims, the Arab Higher Committee reaffirmed the conviction, maintained by Arab leaders ever since the War, that Palestine west of the Jordan was not meant to be excluded from the McMahon Pledge. They asserted that they were not an oppressed people under Turkish rule but that they had as full a share as any other Turkish citizens in the government of the country. It was not to escape oppression but to secure independence that they assisted the British forces and threw in their lot with the Allies. King Hussein called upon all the Arab territories to take their share, and volunteers from Palestine were among the first to join in a revolt which had a single end in view – the independence of the Arab lands, including Palestine. The Arabs of Palestine put their trust in the Proclamation from Lord Allenby issued in 1918 in the name of the Governments of Great Britain and France that it was the solemn purpose of the Allies to further the cause of Arab self-determination and to establish Arab national governments. They understood this Proclamation to be the renewed assertion of the promise made to King Hussein in the McMahon letter.

The Arab Higher Committee further claimed that the League of Nations recognized in principle the independence of all the Arab countries which were separated from the Turkish Empire. They were classed together in a group, to which what were called 'A' Mandates were to be applied: i.e., they were to be subject to the temporary advice and supervision of a Mandatory Government, and in the selection of the Mandatory the public opinion of the state concerned was to have a determining voice. The Arabs were therefore indignant when Palestine, without any consultation of its inhabitants by the Allied Powers, was severed from Syria and placed under a British Mandate in which the Balfour Declaration was enshrined. Again, though the Mandate was ostensibly based on Article 22 of the Covenant of the League of Nations, its positive injunctions were not directed to the 'well being and development' of the existing Arab population but to the promotion of Jewish interests. Complete power over legislation as well as administration was delegated to the Mandatory, who undertook to place the country under such political, administrative and economic conditions as would secure the establishment of the Jewish National Home. In actual fact, the Arab witnesses maintained, the rights and position of Arabs have been prejudiced by the fall in their numerical proportions in Palestine from about 90 per cent, in 1922, to 70 per cent today. As their aspirations to self-rule have been disappointed they have been unable to administer their own country and their national existence is threatened with annihilation through the entering into the country of another race.

One member of the Arab Higher Committee dealt more closely with the legal argument. He remarked that the terms of the Mandate are inconsistent with the provisions of Article 22 of the Covenant of the League of Nations. Paragraph 4 of that Article recognizes the existence of two juristic persons – one the community which should govern independently and the other the foreigner who is to assist and advise until the former is able to stand alone. But in Palestine there is one person who governs and who assists himself. Your Majesty is the Mandatory and Your Majesty's Government and their nominees are the Government of Palestine and, while the Preamble speaks of a Mandate, Article 1 denies the existence of a Mandate in the proper sense by conferring upon what is called the Mandatory full powers of legislation and administration. The community which is to be provisionally recognized as independent has no existence. This, it was argued, does not meet the provisions of Paragraph 4 and is contrary in principle to the treatment of other territories which were, like Palestine, released from the Government of Turkey. The Arabs maintain that all 'A' Mandates were or are being governed by this section with the exception of the Mandate for Palestine; and they claim that the Arabs of Palestine are as fit for self-government as the Arabs of 'Iraq or Syria'. They think that Article 22, and particularly Paragraph 4 of that Article, is really their charter and the Mandate represents – or should represent – its by-laws. They submit that the by-laws are inconsistent with the charter. They complain that the terms of the Mandate are drafted in such a manner that the student might understand that there existed in Palestine a Jewish majority and non-Jewish minority, the other sections of the population. On the contrary the Arab inhabitants of Palestine form the overwhelming majority and are the owners of the territory for the welfare of which the Mandate system was created; yet throughout the Mandate they are referred to as the 'non-Jewish' population – a misleading and humiliating term. The Jews, in fact, are to live in Palestine, to quote the words of the Churchill Statement of Policy, 'as of right and not on sufferance'; while the Arabs, on the other hand, are to live in Palestine as on sufferance and not of right. Again, in Article 2 the country is to be placed under such administrative, economic and political conditions as will secure the establishment of a Jewish National Home, while the Arab owners and inhabitants of the land are merely to have their religious and civil rights safeguarded. Under Article 4 a Jewish Agency is to be established to assist the Mandatory in all Jewish affairs. This provision has not only created a state within a state, but has formed a Mandate over a Mandatory in that country.

The Arab Higher Committee further maintained that the faith of the Arabs in the British Government was shaken by this outcome of their efforts in the War, and that subsequent actions of the Government had deepened their distrust. In particular the substitution of Mr MacDonald's letter for the White Paper of 1930 and the recent rejection by Parliament of the proposals in a Legislative Council had convinced them that Jewish influence was too powerful to permit justice to be done.

The desire for the removal of the Mandate and the establishment of national independence was thus put forward by the Arab Higher Committee as the primary cause of the disturbances. With it was associated both by Arab and non-Arab witnesses the fear of Jewish domination, political and economic. The Arabs are afraid of the Jews: they are impressed and alarmed by their pertinacity, their wealth, their ability and growing numbers. They cannot attempt to emulate the £70 million or more of capital which the Jews in the last 20 years have brought into the country. They view with mistrust the extent of land which has passed into Jewish hands: they fear that as the result of high prices and weakness of some of their fellow-countrymen more land will pass into the hands of the Jews. They note that land once acquired by the Jewish National Fund can never, by terms of the trust, be resold to the Arab. They point to the destruction of villages and the decay of the social structure of village life. If they have fears for themselves, these fears are multiplied a thousandfold for their children, whose whole future seems to be threatened by the advancing tide of Jewish immigrants. No doubt, too, among the less-educated Arabs at any rate, the fear is wide-spread that Jewish domination might affect the Holy Places and influence the freedom of religious observance.

On the other hand, the Commission assessed the Jewish evidence in these terms:[16]

The Jewish witnesses agreed with the Arab in regarding the 'underlying causes' of the disturbances as political. They questioned whether Arab nationalism was so strong or so coherent as it might seem to be on the surface in Palestine or outside it: but they admitted that the opposition of Arab nationalism to the Balfour Declaration and the Mandate was the mainspring of all the trouble. 'The underlying cause', said a Jewish witness, 'is that we exist.'

But this opposition, it was argued, would have been restrained and its expression in violence and rebellion discouraged if the Mandatory Government had shown a more positive sympathy with the policy of the Jewish National Home and a greater resolution in carrying it into effect. As it was, the official tendency in Palestine to take up a defeatist, almost an apologetic, attitude on this cardinal issue had helped to foster a belief in the Arab mind that the National Home was not an immutable point of policy and that, if the Arab resistance to it were sufficiently obstinate and forcible, the Mandatory Power might presently be worried or even frightened into giving it up. In this connexion Jewish witnesses laid stress on the Government's failure to maintain law and order, on its hesitation to make use of Jewish loyalty, particularly in police-service, on its toleration of inflammatory attacks on the National Home in the Arab Press, and on its permitting Palestine to become a centre of Pan-Arab and Pan-Islamic propaganda.

On the negative side the Jews asserted that the trouble had not been caused either by the economic effects on the Arabs of Jewish immigration or by its increase. The growth of the National Home had benefited the Arabs as a whole; and, though the high figure of immigration in 1935 might have helped to precipitate the outbreak the following year, the outbreaks of 1920 and 1921 had occurred when immigrants were relatively few, and that of 1929 had followed on two years of greatly reduced immigration.

After examining this and other evidence and studying the course of events in Palestine since the War, we have no doubt as to what were 'the underlying causes of the disturbances' of last year. They were:

(1) The desire of the Arabs for national independence.
(2) Their hatred and fear of the establishment of the Jewish National Home.

We make the following comments on these two causes:

(i) They were the same underlying causes as those which brought about the 'disturbances' of 1920, 1921, 1929 and 1933.
(ii) They were, and always have been, inextricably linked together. The Balfour Declaration and the Mandate under which it was to be implemented involved the denial of national independence at the outset. The subsequent growth of the National Home created a practical obstacle, and the only serious one, to the concession later of national independence. It was believed that its further growth might mean the political as well as economic subjection of the Arabs to the Jews, so that, if ultimately the Mandate should terminate and Palestine become independent, it would not be national independence in the Arab sense but self-government by a Jewish majority.
(iii) They were the only 'underlying' causes. All the other factors were complementary or subsidiary, aggravating the two causes or helping to determine the time at which the disturbances broke out.

The other factors may be summarized as follows:

(i) The effect on Arab opinion in Palestine of the attainment of national independence first by Iraq, to a less complete extent by Trans-Jordan, then by Egypt and lastly, subject to a short delay, by Syria and the Lebanon. The weight of this factor had been augmented by close contact between Arabs in Palestine and Arabs in Syria, Iraq and Saudi Arabia and by the willingness shown by the Arab rulers to do what they properly could to assist them.
(ii) The pressure on Palestine exerted by World Jewry in view of the sufferings and anxieties of the Jews in Central and Eastern Europe. The increase of this pressure from the beginning of 1933 onwards and the consequent high figures of Jewish immigration gravely accentuated Arab fears of Jewish domination over Palestine.
(iii) The inequality of opportunity enjoyed by Arabs and Jews respectively in putting their case before Your Majesty's Government, Parliament, and public opinion in this country; and the Arab belief that the Jews can always get their way by means denied to the Arabs. Based in general on the status of the Jewish Agency both in Jerusalem and in London, this belief was greatly strengthened by the publication of Mr [Ramsay] MacDonald's letter to Dr Weizmann in 1931 and by the debates in Parliament on the proposals for a Legislative Council early last year.
(iv) Associated with this last factor, the growth of Arab distrust, dating back

to the time of the McMahon Pledge and the Balfour Declaration, in the ability, if not the will, of Your Majesty's Government to carry out their promises.

(v)   Arab alarm at the continued purchase of Arab land by Jews.

(vi) The intensive character of Jewish nationalism in Palestine; the 'modernism' of many of the younger immigrants; the provocative language used by irresponsible Jews; and the intemperate tone of much of the Jewish as well as the Arab Press.

(vii) The general uncertainty, accentuated by the ambiguity of certain phrases in the Mandate, as to the ultimate intentions of the Mandatory Power. This uncertainty has aggravated all the difficulties of the situation, and in particular has (a) stimulated the Jewish desire to expand and consolidate their position in Palestine as quickly as may be, and (b) made it possible for the Arabs to interpret the conciliatory policy of the Palestine Government and the sympathetic attitude of some of its officials as showing that the British determination to implement the Balfour Declaration is not whole-hearted.

It was this searching and new analysis which led them to a conclusion – the 'unmentionable almost, the forbidden topic' – namely partition.

Chapter XXII of the report was headed 'A Plan for Partition', together with the surrender of the Mandate. Their terms of reference, they said, had implied the hope that they would be able to make recommendations which in their opinion would make it possible to bring about a lasting settlement without abandoning the Mandate. But, as the inquiry proceeded, they became more and more persuaded that, if the existing Mandate continued, there was little hope of lasting peace in Palestine, and 'at the end we were convinced that there was none'. Therefore they proposed

A Treaty System[17]

The Mandate for Palestine should terminate and be replaced by a Treaty System in accordance with the precedent set in Iraq and Syria.

A new Mandate for the Holy Places should be instituted to fulfil the purposes defined in Section 2 below.

Treaties of Alliance should be negotiated by the Mandatory with the Government of Trans-Jordan and representatives of the Arabs of Palestine on the one hand and with the Zionist Organization on the other. These Treaties would declare that, within as short a period as may be convenient, two sovereign independent States would be established – the one an Arab State, consisting of Trans-Jordan united with that part of Palestine which lies to the east and south of a frontier such as we suggest in Section 3 below; the other a Jewish State consisting of that part of Palestine which lies to the north and west of that frontier.

The Mandatory would undertake to support any requests for admission to the League of Nations which the Governments of the Arab and the Jewish States might make in accordance with Article 1 of the Covenant.

The Treaties would include strict guarantees for the provision of the minorities in each State, and the financial and other provisions to which reference will be made in subsequent actions.

Military Conventions would be attached to the Treaties, dealing with the maintenance of naval, military and air forces, the upkeep and use of ports, roads and railways, the security of the oil pipe line and so forth.

The report[18] then went on to set out its proposals for the Holy Places and for the frontier dividing the separated states (see Map 1).

The next two sections embodied the financial proposals. Since the Jews were in fact the richer community and were already, through the existing tax system, in effect, subsidizing the Arabs, it was suggested that the Jewish state should pay a subvention to the Arab state when partition came into effect. Further, the proposed Finance Commission should recommend how the £4.5 million Public Debt of Palestine be divided by the successor states. At the same time since Transjordan, a much poorer state than Palestine, was to be incorporated in the Arab state, the Commission suggested that in the event of an appropriate Treaty coming into force Parliament should be asked to make a grant of £2 million to the Arab state. Later sections dealt with 'Tariffs & Ports', 'Nationality', 'Civil Services', 'Industrial Concessions', 'Exchange of Land & Population'.

The Commission also made provision for action necessary during the period of transition, in respect of Land, Immigration, Trade, a joint Advisory Convention, Local Government and Education.

An imaginative report ended with a statesmanlike final chapter of just two-and-a-half pages, setting out the advantages to the Arabs, the advantages to the Jews, and finally, the advantages to Britain. The last two paragraphs were simple and moving:

There is no need to stress the advantage to the British people of a settlement in Palestine. We are bound to honour to the utmost of our power the obligations we undertook in the exigencies of war towards the Arabs and the Jews. When those obligations were incorporated in the Mandate, we did not fully realize the difficulties of the task it laid on us. We have tried to overcome them, not always with success. They have steadily become greater till now they seem almost insuperable. Partition offers a possibility of finding a way through them, a possibility of obtaining a final solution of the problem which does justice to the rights and aspirations of both the Arabs and the Jews and discharges the obligations we undertook towards them twenty years ago to the fullest extent that is practicable in the circumstances of the present time.

Nor is it only the British people, nor only the nations which conferred the Mandate or approved it, who are troubled by what has happened and is happening in Palestine. Numberless men and women all over the world would feel a sense of deep relief if somehow an end could be put to strife and bloodshed in a thrice hallowed land.

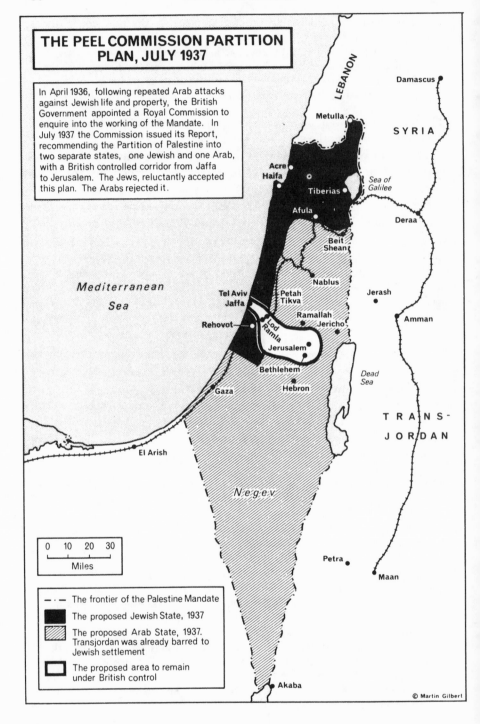

THE PEEL COMMISSION PARTITION PLAN, JULY 1937

In April 1936, following repeated Arab attacks against Jewish life and property, the British Government appointed a Royal Commission to enquire into the working of the Mandate. In July 1937 the Commission issued its Report, recommending the Partition of Palestine into two separate states, one Jewish and one Arab, with a British controlled corridor from Jaffa to Jerusalem. The Jews, reluctantly accepted this plan. The Arabs rejected it.

LEBANON

Damascus

Metulla

SYRIA

Acre
Haifa

Sea of
Galilee

Tiberias

Afula

Deraa

Beit
Shean

Mediterranean
Sea

Nablus

Jerash

Tel Aviv
Jaffa

Petah
Tikva

Ramallah

Amman

Rehovot

Lod
Ramla

Jericho

Jerusalem

Bethlehem

Dead
Sea

Gaza

Hebron

T R A N S -

J O R D A N

El Arish

Negev

0   10   20   30
Miles

Petra

Maan

— · — The frontier of the Palestine Mandate

■ The proposed Jewish State, 1937

▨ The proposed Arab State, 1937.
Transjordan was already barred to
Jewish settlement

□ The proposed area to remain
under British control

Akaba

© Martin Gilbert

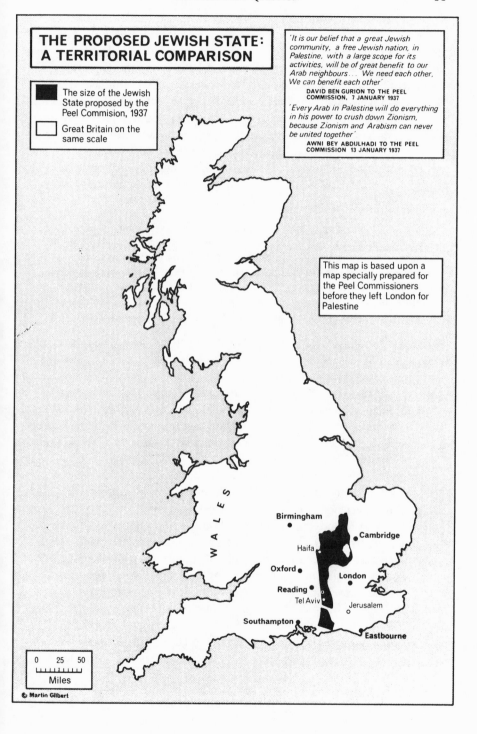

THE PROPOSED JEWISH STATE:
A TERRITORIAL COMPARISON

The size of the Jewish State proposed by the Peel Commision, 1937

Great Britain on the same scale

'It is our belief that a great Jewish community, a free Jewish nation, in Palestine, with a large scope for its activities, will be of great benefit to our Arab neighbours... We need each other, We can benefit each other'

DAVID BEN GURION TO THE PEEL COMMISSION, 7 JANUARY 1937

'Every Arab in Palestine will do everything in his power to crush down Zionism, because Zionism and Arabism can never be united together'

AWNI BEY ABDULHADI TO THE PEEL COMMISSION 13 JANUARY 1937

This map is based upon a map specially prepared for the Peel Commissioners before they left London for Palestine

WALES

Birmingham

Cambridge

Haifa

Oxford

London

Reading

Tel Aviv

Jerusalem

Southampton

Eastbourne

0 25 50
Miles

© Martin Gilbert

The Peel Report was published on 7 July 1937 and debated by the Commons on 21 July 1937, on a motion to approve 'the policy of His Majesty's Government relating to Palestine as set out in Command Paper No. 5513'. The White Paper they were debating was the Government's response to Peel. It stressed that the report was unanimous, and His Majesty's Government 'find themselves in agreement with the arguments and conclusions of the Commission'. They recorded that they and their predecessors had to take the view, as the tenor of the Mandate implied, that Britain's obligations to Arabs and Jews were not incompatible, and that in the process of time the two races would so adjust their national aspirations as to render possible the establishment of a single commonwealth under a unitary government. But

> in the light of experience and of the argument advanced by the Commission, they are driven to the conclusion that there is an irreconcilable conflict between the aspirations of the Arabs and the Jews in Palestine, that their aspirations cannot be satisfied under the terms of the present Mandate, and that a scheme of partition on the general lines recommended by the Commission represents the best and most hopeful solution of deadlock. His Majesty's Government propose to advise His Majesty accordingly.

They therefore, having regard to their existing treaty obligations, called on the League of Nations to give them freedom 'to give effect to a scheme of partition, to which they earnestly hope that it may be possible to secure an effective measure of consent on the part of the communities concerned'.

While such a scheme was being worked out, the Government would take steps, *ad interim*, to prohibit any land transaction which might prejudice such a scheme. On immigration they proposed a limit of 8,000 persons for the eight months August 1937 to March 1938, 'provided that the economic absorptive capacity of the country was not exceeded'.*

Ormsby-Gore moved the Government motion, after outlining the high quality and experience of every single member of the Royal Commission: 'no more impartial body, no more varied body could have been selected to go fundamentally into this question of Palestine . . .'[19] He made a great point that, despite the wide drafting of the terms of reference, the conclusions were unanimous. After a long account of the Palestine story since 1916 (he himself had been on the staff of the Arab Bureau under Sir Henry McMahon) he took the House through the Balfour story, asserting that the Balfour Declaration had, in fact, been drafted by Lord Milner. He outlined the nature of the pledge, a specific pledge both to Jews and non-Jews to promote their independence. He subjected the terms of the Mandate

---

* This phrase was coming into frequent use on all occasions. It was in the debate on Peel that Ormsby-Gore, the Colonial Secretary, correctly attributed it to Churchill.

to an unprecedented Parliamentary exegesis, in particular emphasizing that Article 2 had bound the Mandatory to promote self-governing institutions – in the plural. Since purely municipal institutions were dealt with in a separate article, this must have meant institutions in the country as a whole. To give effect to the Mandate required partition. Ormsby-Gore went on,

> The Commission are of opinion that the ideals of the two peoples and the intolerable burden upon His Majesty's Government can only be resolved by giving Jews and Arabs sovereign independence and self-government, not over the whole of Palestine but each over a part of it. With that conclusion His Majesty's Government agree. Only by partition can the ideals of both be realized, only by partition can peace be restored to these two nationalities, so that they will be able in the future one to help the other without fear of domination by either. It is the fear of domination of Jew by Arab and of Arab by Jew that is the root of the trouble, and the only way that can be removed is by partition and self-government. That is provided for in Article 28 of the Mandate which, being a Mandate, always envisaged the termination and the fruition of the mandatory period. We are only temporarily trustees in Palestine; trustees on behalf of the League. It is not our territory.[20]

Though there was widespread support for the Government's line, the Labour Opposition was doubtful. Their spokesman, Morgan Jones, MP for Caerphilly, moved a reasoned amendment calling on the House to refer the Royal Commission proposals to a Joint Select Committee, before there could be any question of Parliament's being committed – the last resort of an Opposition which is divided, or does not know where it is going, or both. He made the not unfair point that Ormsby-Gore, despite having spoken for fifty minutes, 'almost completely forgot to advance to the House any reason for the partition', and then made the strong point that while the Commission, after the long delay in getting to Palestine because of the strike, had taken much evidence, it had taken none on the partition issue. He drew attention to the small area the Jews would have. Even so, as well as the 258,000 Jews living there, there would be 225,000 Arabs. It was, he said, a question in political mathematics: 'If 1,000,000 Arabs cannot live and work with 400,000 Jews, how can 225,000 Arabs live and work with 258,000 Jews?'[21] The size of the suggested Jewish state would be 2,000 square miles, with a seaboard of eighty miles. The original proposal at the end of the war had been, he said, 45,000 square miles, including Transjordan.*

Churchill left his intervention until late. The debate was due to end at midnight, and he rose just after 10 p.m., when in those spacious days he could count on a fair post-prandial attendance. His speech was brief – only fourteen minutes. He took issue with Ormsby-Gore's attempts to re-write the history of the Balfour Declaration:

* A reference presumably to Sykes-Picot.

It is a delusion to suppose that this was a mere act of crusading enthusiasm or quixotic philanthropy. On the contrary, it was a measure taken, as the right Hon. Gentleman who led us in the crisis of the war knows,* in the dire need of the War with the object of promoting the general victory of the Allies, for which we expected and received valuable and important assistance . . . having studied this question as far as I can and having some personal connection and responsibility for it, I should have preferred the Government to have persevered in the old policy of persuading one side to concede and the other to forbear, and to carry forward that policy, hard and heavy though it may be, with all its inconveniences . . .[22]

He went on to praise 'the magnificently written state document, the result of months of inquiry by men of very high character and ability . . .', but,

All the same I must say that I could not vote for the Government Motion that we should approve now the principle of partition. I cannot do so because it seems to me it would be premature for the Government to ask the House to commit itself finally to this main principle. The principle cannot be judged fairly apart from the details by which it is expressed. Take the military aspect alone. The gravest anxieties arise about that. There are two sovereign States, one a rich and small State more crowded than Germany, with double the population to the kilometre of France, and then in the mountains in the surrounding regions, stretching up to . . . the Assyrians and the desert tribes to the south, the whole of this great Arab area confronting this new Jewish State, and in between the two the British holding a number of extremely important positions with responsibilities at present altogether undefined . . .

It seems to me that this is a matter on which we must know more before we can approve. How can we decide at this moment that we will stand between these two sovereign States and keep the peace between them without knowing at all to what we are committing ourselves? The Secretary of State says that these details have not been worked out; they are coming at the next stage. What is the next stage? It is one for further exploration and inquiry and discussion with the League of Nations; the next stage is discussing with the various parties through the committees which will be set up. We have not got before us at this moment any of the vital data upon which we should be able to commit ourselves finally to the principle of partition. It may happen that the League of Nations may not approve of the Government's proposals, and it may happen that they may break down in detail. It may happen that the two parties, under the pressure of these proposals, may come to a better solution than is open to them at the moment. Therefore, I feel great difficulty at this stage and at this moment in committing myself to the principle of partition, and if it were the only alternative I should have no choice but to vote against it.

On the other hand, we have to be fair to the Commission and to the Government who are carrying this matter forward. The Report and proposals

* Lloyd George was in the House and indeed later moved a revised version of Churchill's own amendment.

of the Commission should be tested to the full, and the government have in their connection with the League of Nations a claim for certain advice and authority. At the present time, obviously, it would be harsh for Parliament, even if it had the power, to prevent this matter going forward and being considered at the League of Nations. I have been looking about and walking about during the course of the afternoon to find some way by which, without hampering the forward movement and the treatment of this policy, those who do not feel inclined to commit themselves to the principle of partition may nevertheless agree with the next necessary step. It is of the greatest importance that we should be united on this problem. It is a problem where all the world is looking to see whether Great Britain behaves in an honourable manner, in a courageous manner and in a sagacious manner. I hope those who have been associated in this policy and have played some part in it will at any rate endeavour to walk together up to the point where it is perfectly clear that division arises.

There is also the question of the value of time. I do want to see some time before the House of Commons passes a definite vote of approval of the principle of partition. There are, I believe, signs on both sides that people are thinking that perhaps rather than this they might make some mutual concessions. They have heard of the judgment of Solomon, and how wise that was, in which a baby was held up in order to see which was the true mother. But if sufficient time had not been given for the true mother to proclaim herself by her feelings, I very much doubt whether that parable would have commended itself so much to subsequent generations . . .[23]

He therefore gave notice that at the end of the debate he would move an amendment, calling for the proposals contained in Command Paper 5513

to be brought before the League of Nations with a view to enabling His Majesty's Government, after adequate inquiry, to present to Parliament a definite scheme in accordance with the policy set out in that Paper.[24]

The main debate ended at midnight. Churchill then rose to move his amendment. Clement Attlee for the Labour Opposition sought to prevent a vote being taken. His objection to the Churchill amendment was that it would seem to bind the House to a decision 'here and now' to accept partition. It was not a party matter, simply one of finding the best way of dealing with the issue 'in the interests of the Arab people, the Jewish people and the whole world'.

George Buchanan, the left-wing Labour Clydesider, then moved that 'the Debate be now adjourned'. Churchill's amendment had been moved without enough notice for members to consider their position on 'the most important policy with which this country has had to deal possibly with during the present Parliament'.

Herbert Morrison[25] rose to support the motion for the adjournment. The Government, he argued, had said that they would take the issue to the

League. When that had been done and the matter discussed there, let the Government come back with their recommendation: the House of Commons will remain 'free and unfettered and will come to a proper and free conclusion' on the Government's proposals following the Geneva discussions.

A vote was forced as an amendment to the motion for the adjournment; in the event only three MPs, all Clydesiders, voted against the Government's main proposal, which was then finally carried. But in so far as this could be regarded as a vote for partition, which the Command Paper it endorsed had urged, it was anything but a lasting victory. Within weeks another commission was at work.

The military strategists advising the Cabinet were concerned about the likely reaction of the Arab states and threats to the Suez Canal, with Hitler menacing not only the West, but south-eastern Europe as well. Partition, as Peel had recommended, and continued immigration could turn the Middle East against the Western democracies. Since, therefore, it could be claimed that Peel's partition plan meant a permanent *de facto* or even *de jure* recognition of a Jewish state, Peel must be 'updated', that is to say, repudiated. So a retired Indian Judge, Sir John Woodhead, was wheeled in to head another Commission. (It was not called Royal, but the term Commission was intended to place it above the rank of a committee.) The new inquiry was not, in fact, to go over the whole ground covered by Peel: it was a 'technical' Commission on partition. This was how Sir John Woodhead and his colleagues interpreted their terms of reference. Reporting on 9 November 1938,[26] they defined their task in these words:

> that our functions will be 'to act as a testimonial Commission, that is to say [they] will be confined to ascertaining facts and to considering in detail, the practical possibilities of a scheme of partition'; and again 'to submit to His Majesty's Government . . . proposals for a detailed scheme of partition . . .'
> After setting out our terms of reference the despatch goes on to indicate that it will be for His Majesty's Government to decide whether, as a result of our investigations, a scheme of partition is equitable and practicable. We ourselves are nowhere directed to report upon the equity or practicability of partition in general. The majority of us have interpreted these directions to mean:
>
> (i)   that His Majesty's Government desire us in any case to produce the best scheme of partition that we can; but in so far as it may fail to satisfy any of the specified conditions, or may seem to be impracticable, to say so and give our reasons;
> (ii) that we are not directed, or entitled, to call in question the equity or morality of partition as a general principle. We were appointed as a technical body, and we conceive that we shall best assist His Majesty's Government if we are careful not to let our views on technical matters be

coloured by any views that we may have formed as individuals on the question of principle involved.

Further, we wish to emphasize that the question of practicability is one of degree, on which it is not possible to express a final opinion without taking into consideration other matters such as the consequences of rejecting partition and the equity and practicability of any alternative solution, which were left outside our terms of reference.

In their Conclusions they quote the Permanent Mandates Commission's Report to the Council of the League:

Any solution to prove acceptable should therefore deprive the Arabs of as small a number as possible of the places to which they attach particular value, either because they are their present homes or for reasons of religion. And, further, the areas allotted to the Jews should be sufficiently extensive, fertile and well situated from the point of view of communications by sea and land to be capable of intensive economic development, and consequently of dense and rapid settlement . . .

The facts adduced in our report show that these objectives are irreconcilable. If the Arabs are to be deprived of the smallest possible number of their homes, and if the fewest possible Arabs are to be included in the Jewish state, as our terms of reference direct, the Jewish state cannot be a large one, nor can it contain areas capable of development and settlement in the sense which the Permanent Mandates Commission evidently had in mind. Does this fact alone render the plan impracticable? We think not, so long as provision can be made for the continued immigration of Jews, subject to control, into the greater part of those areas which we propose should be retained under British Mandate, and for the development of those areas with a view to Jewish settlement therein, also under control. But this will necessitate heavy expenditure from public funds on development and other services in the Mandated Territories, and this expenditure (which we suggest should be limited to sums not exceeding £1 million on non-recurrent services, and not exceeding £75,000 per annum for 10 years on recurrent services) can only be provided by the United Kingdom Government, since the Government of the Mandated Territories will be unable anyhow to balance its budget . . .

They then proceeded to summarize their findings on 'The Attitude of the Arabs and the Jews':

in our opinion there is a deep-seated hostility to partition in any form among the Arab population of Palestine, and . . . we are convinced that the plan recommended by the Royal Commission would lead to an outbreak of general rebellion which could only be put down by stern and perhaps prolonged military measures.

But they reported that on one of the possible plans (the Commission's 'Plan C') no Arab came forward to give a view.

On the attitude of the Jews, they simply reported the categorical decisions of the twentieth Zionist Congress at Zurich in August 1937, rejecting Peel's finding that 'the Mandate has proved unworkable', and empowering the Executive to negotiate with the British Government for the proposed establishment of a Jewish state. The Woodhead Commission were, in fact, encouraged by the Jews to take them into their confidence about possible boundaries, while insisting that Haifa, Galilee and part of Jerusalem must be included; but the Jewish leaders would not give any definite decision until His Majesty's Government had made clear what the position would be if there were no partition.

Woodhead and his colleagues were rightly concerned about the size of the Arab minority in a Jewish state, and what its future might be. But while the Commission was sitting, the Colonial Secretary had made clear in a despatch on 23 December that the Government had not accepted a proposal for compulsory transfer. Pointing out that the Peel Commission's plan would have meant Jewish areas where the number of Arabs already living there would be almost equal to the number of Jews, the Commission said that the Colonial Secretary's intervention meant that it could not be right to produce a report where 60,000 rather than 300,000 Arabs would have to be forcibly transferred.

> Pushed to its logical extreme, this argument would obviously rule out all possibility of partition, since it is impossible to draw boundaries in such a way as to include no Arabs at all in the Jewish State. But it is inconceivable that either the Royal Commission in advocating partition, or His Majesty's Government in accepting it as the best and most hopeful solution of the problem, regarded this fact as in itself a fatal objection to any partition scheme; and indeed our terms of reference imply that His Majesty's Government were prepared for the inclusion of Arabs in the Jewish State and vice versa, albeit the fewest possible. It would seem to be recognized, therefore, that the question is one of degree, rather than of principle.[27]

After examining the implications of these issues for defence and administration, they turned to finance, where they produced the intimidating estimate that partition would cost the UK taxpayer £1,250,000 a year, without provision for defence. Moreover, these calculations were being made on a static basis, i.e. on community populations as they then were, not on the basis of continuing, indeed increasing, Jewish immigration in – without using the words – the age of Hitler:

> The economic future of the Jewish State, depending as it will upon a unique combination of economic, political, racial and emotional factors, is exceptionally difficult to foresee. Jewish witnesses have agreed with the suggestion that, if the Jewish State should adopt an active immigration policy, it must expect to encounter set-backs and to pass through periods of depression, but our impression is that they were inclined to under-estimate the violence of the economic fluctuations to which the Jewish State is likely to be exposed when as an independent state it takes over full responsibility for

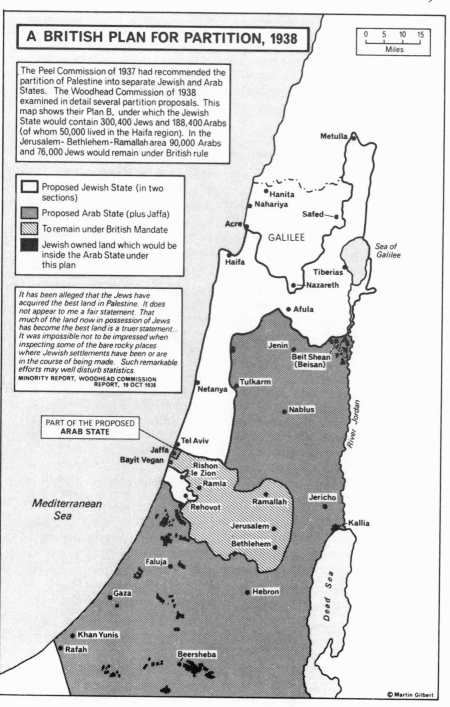

A BRITISH PLAN FOR PARTITION, 1938

0 5 10 15
Miles

The Peel Commission of 1937 had recommended the partition of Palestine into separate Jewish and Arab States. The Woodhead Commission of 1938 examined in detail several partition proposals. This map shows their Plan B, under which the Jewish State would contain 300,400 Jews and 188,400 Arabs (of whom 50,000 lived in the Haifa region). In the Jerusalem- Bethlehem-Ramallah area 90,000 Arabs and 76,000 Jews would remain under British rule

☐ Proposed Jewish State (in two sections)

▨ Proposed Arab State (plus Jaffa)

▨ To remain under British Mandate

■ Jewish owned land which would be inside the Arab State under this plan

It has been alleged that the Jews have acquired the best land in Palestine. It does not appear to me a fair statement. That much of the land now in possession of Jews has become the best land is a truer statement... It was impossible not to be impressed when inspecting some of the bare rocky places where Jewish settlements have been or are in the course of being made. Such remarkable efforts may well disturb statistics.
MINORITY REPORT, WOODHEAD COMMISSION REPORT, 19 OCT 1938

PART OF THE PROPOSED
ARAB STATE

Metulla

Hanita
Nahariya
Safed

Acre
GALILEE
Sea of
Galilee

Haifa
Tiberias
Nazareth

Afula

Jenin
Beit Shean
(Beisan)

Tulkarm
Netanya
Nablus

River Jordan

Jaffa
Tel Aviv
Bayit Vegan
Rishon
le Zion
Ramla
Ramallah
Jericho

Rehovot
Jerusalem
Kallia
Bethlehem

Mediterranean
Sea

Faluja

Gaza
Hebron

Dead Sea

Khan Yunis
Rafah
Beersheba

© Martin Gilbert

immigration. The same witnesses, anxious to explain to us the future policy of
the Jewish State on this subject, assured us that the volume of immigration 'to
be admitted at any given time will, so far as immigrant workers are concerned,
fall to be determined by reference to the openings for employment that are in
sight and to the resources available for financing such employment'. We do
not doubt that such will be the intention of the leaders; but we feel
considerable doubt whether they will be able to maintain so rigid a line in the
face of the urgent pressure that will be brought to bear upon the newly formed
state to receive the hundreds of thousands of distressed Jews who will be
demanding a refuge in the Jewish State as a national right.

The Commission was fearful of the effects of economic depression,
especially on the Arab population. The relative cheapness of Arab wages led
to a considerable employment of Arabs by Jewish farmers.* Partition would
mean that many Arab villages outside the newly defined Jewish state would
be 'deprived of an important subsidiary means of livelihood, the loss of
which will have a serious effect on their economic position'.[28]

The Commission proceeded to their 'Conclusion':

We can now sum up the position. The question whether partition is
practicable involves considerations of two kinds: practical and political. The
former concern chiefly finance and economics; the administrative difficulties
are great, but they cannot be called insuperable, if the will to find a solution is
present. But the financial and economic difficulties, as described in this
chapter, are of such a nature that we can find no possible way to overcome
them within our terms of reference. Rather than report that we have failed to
devise any practicable plan, we have proposed, in paragraph 506, a
modification of partition, which, while it withholds fiscal autonomy from the
Arab and Jewish States, seems to us, subject to certain reservations, to form a
satisfactory basis of settlement, if His Majesty's Government are prepared to
accept the very considerable financial liability involved.

There remain the political difficulties. We cannot ignore the possibility
that one or both of the parties may refuse to operate partition under any
conditions. It is not our duty, as a fact-finding Commission, to advise what
should be done in that event. But there is still the possibility that both sides
may be willing to accept a reasonable compromise. We cannot feel confident
that this will happen, but we put forward proposals in this chapter in the hope
that they form the basis of a settlement by negotiation.[29]

In fact partition, the essential consequence of Peel, was dead, as far as the
pre-war world was concerned, not so much because of the Woodhead
Report, but because Neville Chamberlain and Malcolm MacDonald
completely reversed the policies of a generation. Eight years later Attlee and
Bevin, after their own formidable and determined rearguard action, were
forced to accept it.

* The Commission estimated the wages of permanent Jewish workers in average areas at
200–300 mils per day, as against 150–200 mils per day for Arabs (1000 mils at that time
corresponded to £1 in sterling).

CHAPTER 4

Holocaust and War

ON 30 JANUARY 1939 HITLER told the Reichstag in Berlin on a day he said 'would be memorable for others as well as for us Germans', that he was going to fulfil his pledge, made before assuming power, that he would 'settle the Jewish problem'. The Jewish laughter, he said, had been uproarious, but 'I think that for some time now they have been laughing on the other side of their faces'. He went on to warn,

> If the international Jewish financiers in and outside Europe should succeed in plunging the nations once more into a world war, then the result will not be the bolshevization of the earth, and thus the victory of Jewry, but the annihilation of the Jewish race in Europe![1]

Three days earlier, Malcolm MacDonald, Ramsay's son and Chamberlain's Colonial Secretary, had told Cabinet:

> He was satisfied that we could not afford to forfeit the confidence and friendship of a large part of the Moslem world. If we lost that now, we would lose it for a long time, whereas if we reached a settlement in Palestine along the lines proposed, Jewish criticism in America would not have any permanent effect on Anglo-American relations.[2]

On 2 February, the British Consul in Dresden reported to the Berlin Embassy on conditions at the concentration camp at Buchenwald. 'There was not even enough water to drink and there were only 20 lavatories for 10,000 men.' A doctor who was released later had told of seeing men flogged with barbed wire 'birches'. Of 10,000 prisoners, including professors and other leading Jews, 350 had died since the previous November. On 25 February the Foreign Office received, via the Tel Aviv Association of Jewish Settlers, a detailed account of 133 atrocities committed against German and Austrian Jews.[3]

President Roosevelt was urging international action to find an alternative refuge for the Jews, and suggested Angola. This was turned down by the British Foreign Office – 'it would be difficult to justify pressing the Portuguese' – though Sir Alexander Cadogan, Permanent Under-Secretary, was moved to propose that a British colony such as Northern Rhodesia be opened for the purpose, and unsuccessfully minuted Lord Halifax, the Foreign Secretary, in that sense.

For Hitler, anti-semitism was not an instrument of policy, it was an ingrained prejudice which had begun to obsess him twenty-five years before he came to power. In 1908, as a youth of nineteen, he came to live in Vienna, and immediately became obsessed with the Jews he saw there – as is clear from reading *Mein Kampf*.

> The odour of these people in caftans often used to make me feel ill. . . . Was there any shady undertaking, any form of foulness, especially in cultural life, in which at least one Jew did not participate?

Vienna was something of a breeding-ground for anti-semitism, indeed had been so since the 1870s. Herzl, as we have seen, was shocked by the outburst of anti-semitism there in the 1890s.[4] Hitler was drawn to the teachings of Karl Lueger, leader of the Catholic party, and a dedicated anti-semite. As mayor of Vienna and a devastating speaker he had a big following. Hitler was drawn, too, to the anti-Jewish pamphlet, 'Protocols of the Elders of Zion', first published in Russia in 1905. He avidly swallowed their message, and indeed *Mein Kampf* shows their influence upon him. They were in fact proved to be a forgery around the time that Hitler adopted them.

In Munich, on 24 February 1920, a new party was formed and, taking its lead from Hitler, devoted eight of the twenty-five points in its manifesto to attacking German Jewry. He proposed that they be totally excluded from the rights and privileges of citizenship. Point 4 laid down:

> Only those who are members of the nation can be citizens . . . only those who are of German blood, without regard to religion, can be members of the German nation. No Jew can, therefore, be a member of the nation.

Therefore all Jews who had entered Germany since 1914 were to be expelled. All Jews regardless of their date of entry or even their birth in Germany must leave the country if there was a severe shortage of food. No Jew should be allowed to edit a newspaper, or even contribute to the press. In his Munich speech, Hitler pledged that his new party would 'free you from the power of the Jew'. He called for a new slogan: 'Anti-Semites of the World, Unite! People of Europe, Free Yourselves!'[5]

Thirteen years later, on 30 January 1933, he became German Chancellor. Persecution, as HM Ambassador in Berlin, Sir Horace Rumbold,* reported to the Foreign Secretary, had become serious. Bruno Walter had been banned from conducting a Leipzig concert; Jewish musicians were banned from orchestras, Jewish actors from the stage and Jewish judges from sitting

---

* Later Vice-Chairman of the Peel Commission.

in court. Reports to London suggested that 40,000 Jews and Socialists were in prison. Rumbold reported, less than two months after Hitler had become Chancellor, that the Nazi Party had instructed their local organizations the length and breadth of Germany to 'carry on anti-Jewish propaganda among the people'. In the same week Hitler called for a total boycott of all Jewish shops on 1 April. Jewish doctors and lawyers were to be boycotted and persecuted. When even Mussolini's ambassador advised moderation, Hitler rejected such pressure, and said that with 'absolute certainty' his name would be honoured in all lands in five or six hundred years' time, 'as the man who once and for all exterminated the Jewish pest from the world'.

By April, too, Rumbold was reporting the creation of 'large concentration camps, one near Munich was capable of holding 5,000 prisoners'. In the same week, the *Manchester Guardian*, which was conscientiously monitoring Nazi actions, published descriptions of many atrocities, including:

> A few days ago a man was sentenced to a year's imprisonment for spreading the 'false rumour' that a Jew had been hanged by Brown Shirts – the 'rumour' as a matter of fact, was true: the Jew . . . was beaten by Brown Shirts and hanged by his feet, so that his head was suspended off the ground. When the Brown Shirts had finished with him he was dead.

A Committee of Chamberlain's Cabinet on 7 April discussed reports from Germany. Its conclusion in the Palestine context was

> The number of Jewish refugees who could be allowed to enter the country is strictly conditioned by what the country can absorb. The matter is strictly one for the High Commissioner [*sic*], but there is no reason to suppose that room could be found in Palestine in the near future for any appreciable number of German Jewish refugees.[6]

Nevertheless, 30,000 Jews entered Palestine in 1933, a record; 13,000 of these were from Poland, 5,000 from Germany. The new entrants thus accounted for 15 per cent of the Jewish population at the level at which it had stood at the beginning of the year. The following year 42,000 entered, and in 1935, 61,000, the three years thus accounting for a figure equal to two-thirds of the January 1933 Jewish population.

In addition to Zionist-sponsored immigration, sixteen 'illegal' immigrant ships in 1934 sailed from the Black Sea to Palestine ports. Between 1934 and 1939 nearly fifty ships made the journey; many of them were intercepted and turned back. The Colonial Secretary, from March 1934 onwards, was complaining to his colleagues about this illegal immigration, particularly as the Jewish Agency were now employing Jewish labour only, instead of spreading available work over the Arab population as well. This new development was endorsed, he said, by Weizmann and other Jewish leaders:

> If the Arabs were clever propagandists, they could put their case against

exclusive Jewish employment in a very telling way. They could say that the charge against Hitler is that he had refused Jews employment in Germany: is it reasonable that Jewish immigrants to Palestine, entering in increasing numbers, should refuse employment to the Arab population?[7]

The Jews in Palestine were concerned about the case that could be made, and indeed in one area (the Huleh basin) allocated enough of their own land to increase the Arab reservations by half.

While Cabinet ministers were arguing about how many Jewish immigrants should be allowed to dance on the point of a needle, Hitler, on 15 September 1935, introduced new and unprecedented measures against the Jews, the Nuremberg Laws. These forbade marriage (and extra-marital relations) between Jews and non-Jews: no Jew could employ a non-Jewish German woman under forty-five. New regulations under the Nuremberg code barred Jews from all official and professional life. Hitler defined a Jew as any person whose grandparents were Jews: he also invented the concept of 'fractional Jews', of first or of second degree according to the number of Jewish grandparents.

Pictorial presentations on Nazi persecution, annotated with facts and statistics, are to be found in Martin Gilbert's *The Holocaust*.* That on the persecution of German Jews in the first five years of Nazi rule (1933–8) tabulates the main events: 30 January 1933, Hitler becomes Chancellor; 9 March 1933, the first anti-Jewish riots in Berlin; 13 March 1933, all Jewish lawyers and judges expelled from the law courts of Breslau; 13 March 1933, Jewish-owned shops in Braunschweig ransacked and destroyed; 1 April 1933, the boycott of all Jewish shops in Berlin; 10 May 1933, Nazis in Berlin held a public burning of books by Jewish and certain other authors; October 1933, all Berlin Hospitals declared 'free' of Jewish doctors, who were then denied any other hospital work; also in 1933 Thüringen (the first province to take this action) eliminated Jews from all official and professional positions; 15 September 1935, the Nuremberg Laws, creating second-class citizens and driving Jews from public and professional life; 1935, 100,000 German children in Franconia swore 'eternal enmity' to the Jews; 9 June 1938, synagogue destroyed in Munich; 10 August 1938, Nuremberg's synagogue destroyed; 15 November 1938, all German schools closed to German Jewish children; 1938, 191 synagogues set on fire in Germany; 1933–8, concentration camps established at Sachsenhausen, Esterwegen, Columbia Haus (Berlin), Buchenwald and Dachau.

In the early days of the Nuremberg Laws, the Nazi Government seemed anxious to see as many Jews as possible leave peaceably. One-third of the 120,000 who left under this policy went to Palestine, whither, under a

* For an account of Hitlerite persecution in other European countries, see Raphael Patai, *The Vanished Worlds of Jewry*, London, 1981.

system known as *Haavara*, they were able to export part of their property.

The free nations of the world retreated in the face of Hitler's persecution. An international conference on refugees was convened at Evian in July 1938, looked at the problem straight in the face, passed a few half-hearted resolutions and adjourned. At the end of the year there was a furious intensification of persecution following the murder of Ernst von Rath, a German diplomatic official, in Paris by a Polish Jewish youth on 12 December 1938. The only response to the spirit of Evian was from the little Dominican Republic (with an area of 19,000 square miles) who volunteered to provide homes for German Jews.

In another way, too, 1938 compounded the virulence and geographical spread of Nazi persecution. On 12 March German troops crossed the frontier into Austria, and Hitler formally incorporated the state into Nazi Germany. All German race edicts, including the Nuremberg Laws, became part of the law of Austria, just as the techniques of persecution became part of the practice. Dachau was designated as the concentration camp for Austrian Jews. Hitler's torturers now had 180,000 Austrian Jews to add to their clientele; another 40,000 of Jewish descent were racially designated as Jews, despite the fact that many had been baptized as Christians. A young Jewish witness was later to put the facts on record:[8]

> Jewish men, and especially women, were arrested in the streets and, under the scornful laughter of the Viennese, were forced to wash away the slogans painted during the desperate few weeks while Austria's fate lay in the balance. Jewish shops were broken into and plundered by the mob while Jews specially apprehended for the purpose stood in front (guarded by SA men, armed to the teeth) holding signs saying 'Aryans, don't buy at the Jews'.
>
> When dusk fell the shops were emptied by the looters. The SA then would collect the Jews who had been posted before the shops in one street, force them into a procession surrounded by Viennese of all ages, and, while their Austrian neighbours mocked and spat into the Jews' faces, led them down the road into some dark alleyway where the Austrians were allowed to beat them viciously.
>
> Jews were evicted from their flats by their own landlords or by jealous neighbours. Jewish students were turned out of their schools. The prisons became full of innocent people simply because they were Jews.

The British Consul-General in Vienna, on 31 May, informed HM Ambassador in Berlin that:

> The distress and despair amongst the Jews are appalling. This consulate-general is literally besieged every day by hundreds of Jews who have been told to leave the country and who come vainly searching for a visa to go anywhere.

The horrors of Hitler's persecution, torture and massacre of the Jews would require a book in itself, or indeed a series of books. In fact Dr Martin Gilbert has produced them. Reference has been made to *Exile and Return* and *Holocaust*. His most recent book up to the time of writing, *Final Journey*,[9] covers 216 pages of closely printed testimony, together with maps and 187 horror pictures of Jews being shot in the head, being forced to dig their own group graves before being shot, hundreds of naked corpses, German soldiers filming the shooting of Jews, and carrying away the bodies on handcarts, the corpses of hanged Jews dangling in the air, the shooting of naked pregnant women, and the death ovens and gas chambers. The story covers the first deportations of German Jews, the Lublin Poles, the Treblinka Death Camp, France, Holland, Belgium, Italy, and the record of Eichmann in Hungary, all in the fulfilment of Hitler's announced Final Solution to the Jewish 'problem'.* The coldest, most factual account is to be found in the record of the Eichmann trial in Jerusalem in 1961, after a Jewish task-force had hijacked him in his refuge in Argentina.[10]

It was a tragedy for Britain and the world that the only man in a position to lead Europe against Hitler was Neville Chamberlain. The United States, even under Roosevelt, had not shaken off the isolationist doctrines that had dominated her external relations for the previous two decades. Churchill, eight years before, had surrendered to Baldwin his automatic right to return to office whenever the Conservatives reassumed power, because of his obsession with the Indian problem.[11]

Neville Chamberlain had succeeded the by now ageing Stanley Baldwin in May 1937. Arguments still swirl around his memory and reputation,[12] particularly his record of 'appeasement' in his dealings with Mussolini and Hitler. His headstrong policy and apparent disregard of the Nazis' extermination of the Jews in concentration camps have brought bitter comment in wartime and post-war assessments, not least in the context of his policy, as Mandatory, in relation to Palestine. Those who would defend him can point to the fact that if war was coming, the dictators would be certain to seek control of the vital sectors of the Middle East. Pledges which had been made or – as it was more and more argued – had *not* been made in and after the First World War, mattered little compared with seeking allies in the Arab countries and not driving them into Hitler's arms. This argument seemed of increasing importance to Chamberlain and to most of his Cabinet as Hitler's aggression in Europe gathered momentum.

Chamberlain's appeasement began with Mussolini, and he evinced a contemptuous attitude to his Foreign Secretary, Anthony Eden, who came to remonstrate with him just as he had finished a letter to Mussolini, to be sent personally via Grandi, the Italian Ambassador in London. Eden was trying to persuade Chamberlain to respond to Roosevelt's first attempt to

---

* Sir Bernard Braine MP told me of a visit to British forces in North West Germany in 1947, which led to his meeting some of the survivors of the Holocaust from Belsen and other terror camps. His account of what they told him is reproduced in Appendix II, see pp. 383–4.

intervene in European affairs and halt the drift to war. Chamberlain dismissed the Roosevelt move, and Eden recorded in his diary for 18 January 1938:

> I fear that fundamentally the difficulty is that Neville believes that he is a man with a mission to come to terms with the dictators. Indeed one of his chief objections to Roosevelt's initiative was that with its strong reference to International Law it would greatly irritate the dictator powers . . .

Chamberlain's diary speaks for itself:

> In July I had a meeting with Grandi in the course of which I wrote a letter to Mussolini in friendly terms and this was followed by a very cordial reply from him in which he declared his readiness to open conversations with a view to the removal of all points of difference. I did not show my letter to the Foreign Secretary for I had the feeling that he would object to it.

To quote Eden's diary again:

> N.C. made it clear that he knew exactly what he wanted to do. He wanted to . . . open conversations at once. . . . I demurred, pointing out that we had still made very little progress in the Spanish affair. . . . N.C. became very vehement, more vehement than I had ever seen him, and strode up and down the room saying with great emphasis, 'Anthony, you have missed chance after chance. You simply cannot go on like this.'

Eden replied: 'Your methods are right if you have faith in the man you are negotiating with.' Chamberlain's answer was: 'I have.'[13] Eden resigned from the Cabinet on 21 February 1938.

Against this strategy and against, too, the background of the Holocaust, Chamberlain and his Cabinet were month by month taking decisions about Palestine. No less than twenty-one Cabinet meetings during this period involved decisions about Palestine and Jewish immigration.

On 2 March 1938 the Colonial Secretary, Ormsby-Gore, proposed to Cabinet the continuation of restrictions on immigration into Palestine, due to expire a month later, for a further twelve months. 'With a view to mitigating Jewish hostility towards this extension', he proposed to announce that as soon as the boundaries between Jewish and Arab territories had been drawn, Jewish immigration would be related to 'economic absorptive capacity'. This phrase going back to Churchill's period at the Colonial Office (and indeed earlier) was repeatedly to feature in Parliamentary debate right up to the outbreak of war, and again throughout the post-war exchanges between Bevin and Churchill.

The Woodhead Commission, as we have seen, had in fact been set up to invalidate the Peel Report and reject partition. At a Cabinet meeting on 19 October the Colonial Secretary, Malcolm MacDonald, who had succeeded Ormsby-Gore in April, recommended the appointment of a Cabinet

Committee, which reported to the Cabinet in November, when it was agreed that a White Paper rejecting partition should be issued, and an invitation issued to Jewish and Arab leaders to come to a conference in London. (The Arab leaders invited, however, were to exclude the trouble-making Mufti.)

In a memorandum to the Cabinet MacDonald pointed out that the Woodhead Commission, agreeing unanimously to reject partition, had disagreed on the number of Jewish immigrants to be allowed over the next five years. Three plans were considered: 'Plan A' envisaged a total population of 304,900; 'Plan B', 300,000 and 'Plan C', 383,400.* MacDonald himself considered that, in the short term, Jewish immigration should be within a fixed limit and should be related only to certain defined areas. There should be a real measure of local self-government. In the long term he would like to see the defined Jewish area extended, with Arab agreement, into something 'like a Jewish state', composed of a part of Palestine, while an area in Transjordan might be established as part of a federation of Arab states – to include Palestine, Syria, Lebanon, Transjordan, and perhaps Iraq and Saudi Arabia. (When these proposals were published the precise list of countries was omitted.)

Cabinet met again on 9 November to consider the outline of the statement. It was reported that the French would be against the inclusion of Syria and Lebanon as they were against the formation of a federation. It was proposed that the Yemen be included in the grouping, since the Italians had been attempting to exert influence over the Yemenis. It was reported that the High Commission felt that the statement of policy would have little effect. At the 16 November meeting of the Cabinet it was reported that the statement (Cmd 6019) had gone down well with the Arabs but that there was criticism of the exclusion of the Mufti from the proposed London conference of Jews and Arabs.

Cabinet considered the subject again on 23 November, and on 21 December when the defence departments gave their opinion:

The Secretary of State for Air: The view of the Air Staff was that if another crisis should find us with a hostile Arab world behind us in the Middle East, our military position there would be quite untenable in that with the loss of our military position would go the loss of our vital land, air and sea communications to the Far East.

The Minister for Co-ordination of Defence: In previous applications the Chiefs of Staff had only touched in a general way on the question of hostility of individual Arab states. They had assumed that in the event of war with Italy, both Iraq and Egypt would be on our side and that Ibn Saud would at any rate

* These included assumed populations for Jerusalem and the inclusion of Galilee in the Jewish area.

not be against us. If however the Arab world was to be united against us, the whole of the existing Staff Appreciations and also those now under preparation would have to be recast.

The Secretary of State for Foreign Affairs considered: that there was no disagreement (in the Cabinet) on the extreme desirability of our not arousing antagonism with the Arabs, and that the forthcoming negotiations at the London conference must be so conducted as to ensure that the Arab states would be friendly towards us. But until the conference met, we could not say how far we should have to go in order to meet their views.

In December MacDonald issued the invitation to the 'Tripartite Conference' of Britain, the Arabs and the Jews to meet in St James's Palace on 7 February. Chamberlain opened the conference; in reply, Weizmann, stretching the truth more than a little, spoke of the Jewish nation's 'unshaken confidence in British good faith'. Hussein, leading the Palestinian delegation, put forward the united view of the Arabs. MacDonald later recorded: 'We had terrible trouble, because for days neither side would sit round the same table in the same room. We had to talk to the Arabs in the morning, the Jews in the afternoon.' Indeed, as Weizmann explains, Chamberlain's address of welcome had to be read twice, once to the Jews and once to the Arabs. The Arabs, he adds, 'insisted on using different entrances to the palace to avoid embarrassing contacts'.[14]

Weizmann and Halifax, according to the former, had a somewhat bitter, partly theological dispute, centring on the refusal of the British authorities to permit refugees to land in Palestine from the *Patria*, when he said:

Look here, Lord Halifax, I thought the difference between the Jews and the Christians is that we Jews are supposed to adhere to the letter of the law, whereas you Christians are supposed to temper the letter of the law with a sense of mercy.[15]

Halifax did what Weizmann asked.

Weizmann's dialectical powers were not always well designed to win friends and influence people. A devout Christian, as Halifax was, was not going to warm to Weizmann's lecture on, as he himself puts it, law and ethics, and the immorality [*sic*] of the White Paper 'which was not really a law but a ukase such as might have been issued in the systematic persecution of the Jews'.

By the last days of February the Jewish delegation, feeling that they were friendless, decided to play the American card. Two American Zionists who were members of the Weizmann delegation spoke to Joseph Kennedy, the US Ambassador in London, and hinted at a direct approach to President Roosevelt. Part of the orchestration was a démarche signed by 9,000 American Jews living in Palestine: they had, they said, invested $80 million in Palestine, 'only because we had and still have unlimited confidence in our

United States Government'. They had come to Palestine, they said, to build the National Home, not to be a minority in an Arab state; they claimed that the 1924 Anglo-US Convention on the Mandate forbade Britain to abandon its policy as now proposed without American consent. The State Department rejected this argument, and the Jewish delegation withdrew from the formal conference. Strangely it was only after this, when Zionist participation was informal, that Jews and Arabs (though not the Palestinians) formally met with their British hosts round the conference table. Weizmann was prepared to accept the Arab view that in view of the progress the Zionists had made in settling Palestine they should 'consolidate' for a while, after which immigration could perhaps be resumed, but only with Arab consent. Weizmann, however, was overruled by Ben-Gurion and Shertok.*

On 2 March Cabinet met to hear a report on the progress of the conference. The Lord Chancellor concerned himself with the McMahon correspondence with Hussein. It was difficult, he said,

> to interpret the letter of 24th October 1915 as a specific exclusion of Palestine. However it would be very undesirable to abandon a view which we had maintained constantly for 20 years [sic]; more especially since the Arabs were suspicious people and appeared to regard all our actions as dishonest.

He continued by saying that 'it was important that we should make it clear that we favoured the establishment of an independent Palestine state when the conditions were ripe, and not within any specified period'.

In other words, in God's good time but not in his. The Colonial Secretary confirmed that this was the intention and went on to give an account of the progress of the negotiations:

> the Palestine Arabs had pressed for the immediate recognition of an independent Arab State. We had rejected the demand for recognition of an Arab State and for immediate recognition, but we said we were prepared to recognize an independent Palestine State in due course.
>
> The representatives of the neighbouring Arab States had become more and more insistent on some action being taken at once which, in form, would meet the demand for independence. They had taken the view that, if we met the claim for independence, it would be possible to reach agreement on immigration and land sales. They had pressed for the setting up of a provisional Government on the Iraq model, under which Palestine Ministers would nominally take over control of departments, with British advisers to run the show.
>
> We had rejected this claim for the establishment of a provisional Government. At the same time, the Foreign Office had been anxious that we should take action which would satisfy the neighbouring Arab States; he

---

* Shertok (Moshe Sharett) was described in one of the relevant Cabinet Minutes as one of the 'extreme Zionists'.

entirely agreed as to the importance of this, and, after consultation with the Secretary of State for Foreign Affairs, certain proposals had been submitted to the Cabinet Committee on Palestine. Very briefly these proposals were as follows:

1. The British Government should declare that it was their intention that *the Mandate should in due course come to an end and that an independent Palestine State should be created in treaty relations with Great Britain* [author's italics].
2. That a Round Table Conference should be summoned to work out the Constitution of the proposed Palestine State and the terms of the proposed treaty with Great Britain. This Round Table Conference would have to consider:
   (a) the transitional period;
   (b) provisions for the unique character of Palestine as a Holy Land sacred to three religions;
   (c) safeguards for various communities in Palestine, especially for the Jewish National Home. This was not an ordinary, but an extraordinary, minority, which required extraordinary safeguards;
   (d) safeguards for the protection of British interests, e.g. our important military interests;
   (e) United States interests, e.g. missions.
3. As an earnest of our good intentions, and the impending inauguration of the Round Table Conference, representatives of the Arab and Jewish communities in Palestine should be added to the Executive and Advisory Council.

The Secretary of State for the Colonies said he had put these proposals before the Delegations. The Jews had objected to many of the proposals, but nevertheless the discussions with them had at first gone quite well, and we had been able to make it clear that we could meet many of their objections. That had been the position late on Saturday night. Over the week-end, there had been a leakage of information in Egypt where a summary of our proposals with very misleading comments had been published. The result had been disastrous, and there had been great Arab demonstrations of joy in Palestine, followed by Jewish anger which had taken the form of bombing reprisals. Great pressure had been put on the Jewish representatives to leave the Conference, with the result that conversations with them had been broken off. He had, however, succeeded in getting them to continue discussions on an informal basis.

The Jews complained, in the first place, that there was no mention in our proposals of the Balfour Declaration or of the Mandate. The answer to this was that our proposals took these matters for granted, and dealt only with suggestions for the future.

The second objection raised by the Jews had been that it was quite impossible for them to accept the suggestion of an independent Palestine State until they knew what the safeguards would be. It was not enough to say that the safeguards would be worked out at the Round Table Conference. To meet this point of view, various alternative safeguards which might be adopted had been worked out and submitted to Dr Weizmann, who appeared to be fairly well satisfied with them. It appeared, however, that Dr Weizmann was having great difficulty with his own supporters, notably with Mr Ben-Gurion, the leader of the Palestine Jews. There was still a risk that the Jews might break off negotiations after tomorrow. He thought, however, that Dr Weizmann would be ready to continue discussions, subject to the reservations indicated above.

In the case of the Arabs, the neighbouring Arab States had accepted the proposals, and were doing their best to get the Palestine Arabs to accept them. Indeed, of the Palestine Arabs, the representatives of the Defence Party and two representatives of the Mufti's Party were in favour of acceptance. The rest of the delegates were still hankering after an independent Arab State on the Iraq model, with a transitional period of no more than three years. It had now been decided to set up a small Committee on Policy to consider in detail our proposals and those of the Palestine Arabs. On this Committee we should have the general support of the representatives of the neighbouring Arab States.

As to immigration and land sales these really depended on the settlement of the constitutional question. The proposal which we had made to the Arabs had been that there should be a five years' programme of, say, 100,000 immigrants. It was proposed to settle at the Round Table Conference what machinery should be used to determine immigration at the end of that period. The neighbouring Arab States were favourably disposed to us in this matter, and they were pressing the Palestine Arabs to accept a solution on these lines, though with perhaps a reduced total of 50,000 or 60,000 immigrants in the next five years.

On land sales the proposal was that the High Commissioner should have power to prohibit entirely or restrict land sales, according to the area concerned. The Arabs were asking for complete prohibition.

Although the Conferences had reached a very difficult stage, the Secretary of State thought that, as he thought there was still a faint hope of an agreement, it was worth while to continue negotiations for some days further. If, at the end of that time, the possibilities of agreement had been exhausted, the Conferences should be brought to an end. This, however, would only be done after there had been close consultation with the representatives of the neighbouring Arab States as to the proposals which we should put forward on our own responsibility. We hoped that we should obtain their sympathy for these proposals, though not, perhaps, their own support. The neighbouring Arab States might, however, come out with a declaration of their own that they hoped that strife would cease and that the Arabs would be content for the time being with the concessions which they had obtained.

In conclusion, the Secretary of State for the Colonies asked the Cabinet to give their general approval to the suggestions outlined above. He thought that these proposals represented an equitable solution and it was still just possible that, on the basis of their proposals, we might be able to reach an agreement with the representatives of both Jews and Arabs. If, however, agreement did not result, our position, though no doubt difficult, would be honourable. Indeed it would in some ways be a strong one which could be defended in Parliament.

In reply to the Secretary of State for India, *the Secretary of State for the Colonies* said that *he had informed the Jewish representatives of the proposal that we should make a public declaration that in our view the Balfour Declaration did not mean the establishment of a Jewish State in Palestine. He thought that for some time they had been reconciled to this* [author's italics].

The Secretary of State for Home Affairs thought that the position of the Jewish representatives was bound to be difficult, so long as no precise safeguards had been elaborated. He asked if it was possible, either to expedite the Round Table Conference, or to proceed at once to negotiate with regard to safeguards, thereby cutting out the proposed Round Table Conference.

The Secretary of State for the Colonies said that he appreciated the need for making progress on the question of safeguards, and for that reason he set out what seemed to us to be the various possible alternatives. He thought, however, that it would be very risky to have a Round Table Conference without adequate preparation. He wished himself to visit the neighbouring Arab States, and it was proposed that Dr Weizmann should visit Ibn Saud. The preparation might take as long as six months.

The Secretary of State for Dominion Affairs referred to the discussion which had taken place in the Palestine Committee on the word 'independent'. He hoped that any declaration which we made, would make quite clear the limitations which would be imposed on the so-called independent Palestine State. Otherwise we should be sowing trouble for the future.

The Secretary of State for India pointed out that the High Commissioner preferred the use of the word 'autonomous' rather than 'independent', to which *the Secretary of State for the Colonies* replied that the word 'independent' had a psychological value in the negotiations.

The Lord Chancellor expressed the fear that the Arabs would use any promise of an independent State as a basis for accusations of bad faith in the future. He thought it was important that we should make it clear that we favoured the establishment of an independent Palestine State when the conditions were ripe, and not within any specified period.

The Secretary of State for the Colonies confirmed that this was the intention.

As regards our Defence requirements, he did not think we were likely to encounter much difficulty.

On the proposal of the Prime Minister, the Cabinet agreed,

> to give general approval to the proposals outlined by the Secretary of State for the Colonies in the Minutes of the Meeting of the Palestine Committee held on 23rd February, 1939 (CP 56 (39)) and in the course of discussion.

The one dissident in the Cabinet was Walter Elliot, the Minister of Health. The MacDonald figures, he said, were a far cry from what had been originally proposed, and the projected Arab veto over Jewish immigration might lead to serious trouble in the United States and Palestine. MacDonald put him down: he had, he said, with some reluctance come to the view that the MacDonald plan was inevitable.

Bethell records in his book[16] a conversation with MacDonald, who felt that, given the strength of feeling in Cabinet and in Whitehall, he did as well as he could by his former Zionist friends in getting the final batch of 75,000 for the next five years.

> Our impression [said MacDonald] was that this would offend the Arabs grossly, but we could get by with it. So we fixed the quota of Jewish immigration and the spread of years at the maximum we thought the Arabs would swallow.

Bethell adds that Walter Elliot went from the 8 March Cabinet meeting to lunch at the Carlton Grill with Baffy Dugdale and the Weizmanns, where he broke all Cabinet rules by telling them of the decisions which had been taken.[17] Baffy wrote in her diary that

> it was a filthy trick to place future immigration to Palestine, which was a matter of survival for the Jews of Europe, as a bargaining counter against an independent Palestine State, which was only a matter of politics. And the supposed agreement with the Arab countries was 'Dead Sea fruit'.

Within a week of the Cabinet meeting Hitler invaded Czechoslovakia and 118,000 Czech Jews were listed under the infamous Nuremberg laws. The same day both Arabs and Jews rejected the MacDonald plan. Weizmann told the US Consul in Jerusalem that with its publication he must 'declare himself irrevocably in opposition and commit the Zionist movement to a policy of non-co-operation with Great Britain'.

The discussions on 15 and 22 March and 10 and 19 April on the Palestine issue, and in the Palestine Committee of the Cabinet, were mainly concerned with questions of procedure, timing and presentation. MacDonald was clearly coming under some pressure from leading British Zionists.[18] But Chamberlain was quite clear where he himself stood. At the meeting of the Cabinet Palestine Committee on 20 April, MacDonald is recorded as saying:

> One must admit to be quite honest that the Government scheme in its latest form includes certain features which would not have been there if we had been allowed to give our undivided attention to devising the best plan for the future good government of Palestine. This situation was of course due to our having incorporated in the scheme to placate the Arabs features as to which we ourselves were not convinced on merits.
>
> *Prime Minister : If we must offend one side let us offend the Jews rather than the Arabs* [author's italics].

By this time the Cabinet was preoccupied with preparing its White Paper on Palestine. Successive drafts came before Cabinet on 26 April, 1 and 3 May when MacDonald reported the criticisms made by the representatives of the neighbouring Arab states after they had seen the draft. (They had invited the Palestinians to meet them and in the light of Palestinian comments had toughened their attitude.) Their conditions for co-operation were:

1. Immediately after the restoration of peace and security a Ministry should be formed of Palestinians with British advisers to co-operate in the administration of the country.
2. The number of Jewish immigrants within the next five years should not exceed 75,000 and the proportion of the Jewish population in Palestine should in no way exceed one third of the whole population. [This point, noted the Secretary of State in his paper to Cabinet, 'did not present any serious difficulties, though the Egyptian Prime Minister had explained that the Palestinian Arabs were anxious that a census should be held at once'.]
3. The question of sale of lands should be settled by mutual understanding between the High Commissioner and the Palestinian Ministers.
[The MacDonald exegesis on this said 'it must be made clear that by "full consultation" we did not necessarily mean "agreement" '.]
4. The Arab States hope that within the next three years, after peace and order have been established, a constituent assembly will be formed for the purpose of drawing up a Constitution.

MacDonald's view was that after five years there should be an inquiry by experts, whose findings would be put to a Constituent Assembly.

On 17 May the Cabinet considered how matters should be handled when they formally reported to the Mandates Commission of the League of Nations on their new policies, as they were required to under the Mandate. There was a danger that the League authorities might refer the matter to the International Court at the Hague. The Foreign Secretary viewed this possibility with some anxiety:

he would much prefer it if the League of Nations could be induced, either to approve our policy as being consistent with the Mandate, or to say that the Mandate should be modified so as to make it consistent with our policy . . .
The Colonial Secretary agreed with this view, but thought that the Council of the League, on the advice of the Mandates Commission, which was much under the influence of Zionist opinion, might not be prepared to act without obtaining the opinion of the Hague Court.

The Chancellor then asked whether the White Paper wording might be misinterpreted as meaning that the Jewish National Home had not yet been established. The existing draft, he said, referred to facilitating 'the establishment of the Jewish National Home by further immigration'. 'After discussion', the Minutes record, 'it was agreed to alter the relevant words of the paragraph to read: "to facilitate the further development of the Jewish National Home by immigration".'

The Colonial Secretary then 'gave some account of his contacts with the

Press'. He said that it was very clear that the White Paper would have a very mixed reception, and agreed with a suggestion that he should get in touch with provincial newspapers. He was also concerned that it would have a bad reception from the Arabs: Britain's ambassadors to Baghdad and Cairo had warned that if the Government pressed on with their plan to refuse the Mufti permission to enter Palestine, neighbouring Arab states would not support the White Paper proposals publicly. The Cabinet adhered to their previous decision to keep the Mufti out. At the end the Colonial Secretary sought to cheer his colleagues:

> it was clear that the policy in the White Paper would be opposed by both sides. That, however, was some indication that it was a just settlement, and he was satisfied that the policy was one which could be defended and to which the approval of Parliament could be obtained.

The argument that we shall be criticized by both sides is a traditional tactic of statesmen: right or wrong, always appear to go straight down the middle, and make sure you are attacked by both sides. It is then easy to claim the highest common factor of agreement.

On 9 May in Downing Street a Cabinet Committee on Refugees confirmed the rejection of a proposal to settle 500 Jewish families in British Guiana: the Chancellor, Sir John Simon, had originally turned down the proposition on grounds of cost. When British Jews offered to finance the scheme, the proposal was finally rejected, the reason given this time being that the Jews would become citizens of British Guiana after five years and would have the right to re-emigrate – to Britain.

Meanwhile the Colonial Office was hard at work on the White Paper. Finalized in late April, it was laid before Parliament on 21 May, less than four months after Hitler's Reichstag speech, two months after the rape of Czechoslovakia. *Palestine, Statement of Policy*[19] was the ultimate in the retreat from Balfour. Recalling that in the *Statement on Palestine* of the previous November the Government had announced their intention of inviting Arabs of Palestine and certain neighbouring countries and the Jewish Agency to confer in London, the White Paper had to record that proposals put by the Government to the Arab and Jewish delegations had been rejected by both sides:

> Accordingly His Majesty's Government are free to formulate their own policy, and after careful consideration they have decided to adhere generally to the proposals which were finally submitted to and discussed with the Arab and Jewish delegations.[20]

Setting out the principal requirements of Articles 2, 6 and 13 of the Mandate, MacDonald proceeded, quoting the Royal Commission Report in aid, to draw attention to ambiguities in the Balfour Declaration, causing uncertainty and in consequence unrest and hostility between Arabs and Jews. Therefore 'a clear definition of policy and objectives is essential':

> It has been urged that the expression 'a national home for the Jewish people' offered a prospect that Palestine might in due course become a Jewish State or Commonwealth. His Majesty's Government do not wish to contest the view, which was expressed by the Royal Commission, that the Zionist leaders at the time of the issue of the Balfour Declaration recognized that an ultimate Jewish State was not precluded by the terms of the Declaration, but, with the Royal Commission, His Majesty's Government believe that the framers of the Mandate in which the Balfour Declaration was embodied could not have intended that Palestine should be converted into a Jewish State against the will of the Arab population of the country . . .

In support of this he quoted from the 1922 White Paper's[21] condemnation of the phrase (Weizmann's) 'Palestine is to become as Jewish as England is English'. The terms of the Declaration, the Command Paper continues, 'do not contemplate that Palestine as a whole should be converted into a Jewish National Home, but that such a home should be founded *in Palestine*'.[22] The 1922 Command Paper is further quoted in support of this assertion.

The Government had therefore decided on a ten-year transitional period, during which the Government hoped to bring the population into an increasing share in government and to promote good relations between the Arabs and the Jews. Within the ten years an independent Palestine would come into being, with treaty relations with Britain 'providing satisfactorily for the commercial and strategic requirements of both countries in the future'.[23] At this point the Mandate would be terminated. HMG would be required to be satisfied, first, on 'the security of, and freedom of access to, the Holy Places', and the protection of the interests and property of the various religious bodies: second, on the Government's obligations to both Arabs and Jews and 'for the special position in Palestine of the Jewish National Home', as well as on the arrangements required for security.

The Paper then came to its next main heading, 'Immigration', quoting the 1922 Command Paper:

> It is necessary that the Jewish community in Palestine should be able to increase its numbers by immigration. This immigration cannot be so great in volume as to exceed whatever may be the economic capacity of the country at the time to absorb new arrivals. It is essential to ensure that the immigrants should not be a burden upon the people of Palestine as a whole, and that they should not deprive any section of the present population of their employment.[24]

It went on to quote also a letter sent by Ramsay MacDonald to Weizmann in February 1931,[25] laying down that economic absorptive capacity was the sole criterion. Yet the text of Cmd 6019 went on somewhat confusingly to say 'nor do they find anything in the Mandate or in subsequent Statements of Policy to support the view that the establishment of a Jewish National Home in Palestine cannot be effected unless immigration is allowed to continue indefinitely'.[26]

The Government then went on to prepare the way for a basic change from the days of 1917 and 1922:

It has been the hope of British Governments ever since the Balfour Declaration was issued that in time the Arab population, recognizing the advantages to be derived from Jewish settlement and development in Palestine, would become reconciled to the further growth of the Jewish National Home. This hope has not been fulfilled. The alternatives before His Majesty's Government are either (i) to seek to expand the Jewish National Home indefinitely by immigration, against the strongly expressed will of the Arab people of the country; or (ii) *to permit further expansion of the Jewish National Home by immigration only if the Arabs are prepared to acquiesce in it* [author's italics]. The former policy means rule by force. Apart from other considerations, such a policy seems to His Majesty's Government to be contrary to the whole spirit of Article 22 of the Covenant of the League of Nations, as well as to their specific obligations to the Arabs in the Palestine Mandate. Moreover, the relations between the Arabs and the Jews in Palestine must be based sooner or later on mutual tolerance and goodwill; the peace, security and progress of the Jewish National Home itself require this. *Therefore His Majesty's Government after earnest consideration, and taking into account the extent to which the growth of the Jewish National Home has been facilitated over the last twenty years, have decided that the time has come to adopt in principle the second of the alternatives referred to above* [author's italics].

It has been urged that all further Jewish immigration into Palestine should be stopped forthwith. His Majesty's Government cannot accept such a proposal. It would damage the whole of the financial and economic system of Palestine and thus affect adversely the interests of Arabs and Jews alike. Moreover, in the view of His Majesty's Government, abruptly to stop further immigration would be unjust to the Jewish National Home. But, above all, His Majesty's Government are conscious of the present unhappy plight of large numbers of Jews who seek a refuge from certain European countries, and they believe that Palestine can and should make a further contribution to the solution of this pressing world problem. In all these circumstances, they believe that they will be acting consistently with their Mandatory obligations to both Arabs and Jews, and in the manner best calculated to serve the interests of the whole people of Palestine, by adopting the following proposals regarding immigration:

1. Jewish immigration during the next five years will be at a rate which, if economic absorptive capacity permits, will bring the Jewish population up to approximately one-third of the total population of the country. Taking into account the expected natural increase of the Arab and Jewish populations, and the number of illegal Jewish immigrants now in the country, this would allow of the admission, as from the beginning of April

this year, of some 75,000 immigrants over the next five years. These immigrants would, subject to the criterion of economic absorptive capacity, be admitted as follows:

(a) For each of the next five years a quota of 10,000 Jewish immigrants will be allowed, on the understanding that a shortage in any one year may be added to the quotas for subsequent years, within the five-year period, if economic absorptive capacity permits.

(b) In addition, as a contribution towards the solution of the Jewish refugee problem, 25,000 refugees will be admitted as soon as the High Commissioner is satisfied that adequate provision for their maintenance is ensured, special consideration being given to refugee children and dependants.

2. The existing machinery for ascertaining economic absorptive capacity will be retained, and the High Commissioner will have the ultimate responsibility for deciding the limits of economic capacity. Before each periodic decision is taken, Jewish and Arab representatives will be consulted.

3. *After the period of five years no further Jewish immigration will be permitted unless the Arabs of Palestine are prepared to acquiesce in it* [author's italics].

4. His Majesty's Government are determined to check illegal immigration, and further preventive measures are being adopted. The numbers of any Jewish illegal immigrants who, despite these measures, may succeed in coming into the country and cannot be deported will be deducted from the yearly quotas.

His Majesty's Government are satisfied that, when the immigration over five years which is now contemplated has taken place, they will not be justified in facilitating, nor will they be under any obligation to facilitate, the further development of the Jewish National Home by immigration regardless of the wishes of the Arab population.[27]

The White Paper further went on to announce that the Government through the High Commissioner would take powers to regulate the sale of land by Arabs to Jewish settlers.[28]

This provocative announcement, issued when most people were expecting Hitler to start the Second World War, as he did only a little over three months later, caused a violent reaction. Its philosophy and its specific proposals could only be interpreted as a repudiation of the Balfour Declaration. The limits on immigration – 25,000 on the High Commissioner's being satisfied that adequate provision could be made for them – followed by 10,000 a year for five years, were bad enough. What was worse was to make any further immigration dependent on Arab consent.

Command Paper 6019 undoubtedly represents an all-time nadir in the long history of Britain's relations with the Jewish people. That it could command acceptance even in Chamberlain's Cabinet almost passes comprehension. Where it was not going to have so easy a passage was in the

House of Commons, where a two-day debate took place on 22 and 23 May. The vote at the end of the debate, 268 to 179, inevitably confirmed the Government's Statement by a majority of 89, but this was a humiliation for a Government normally assured of a majority of over 240 as a result of the 1935 election, confirming, with some loss of Government seats, the landslide results of 1931.*

The Colonial Secretary opened the debate[29] by moving a motion to approve Government policy as set out in Cmd 6019. His speech made clear that he came to bury Balfour, though not without praising him. The authors of the Declaration – and MacDonald mentioned President Wilson's support – did not proclaim 'a Jewish State'. They had high hopes, but

> deliberately, they chose a phrase 'a National Home for the Jewish people' which could mean a Jewish State in Palestine, but which also might mean something very much less . . .

He quoted assurances given to the Arabs at that time, that Jewish immigration should be allowed in so far as it was compatible with the economic and political freedom of the existing population: moreover, no group of people in Palestine should be subject to another. He went on to question the meaning both of the Balfour Declaration and the Mandate, by quoting the overriding condition that immigration should not exceed the absorptive capacity of the country, a phrase Winston Churchill immediately greeted by claiming as his own. MacDonald expressed his surprise that Churchill 'should own parentage of so awkward though understandable a phrase'. What Churchill in his Colonial Office heyday could never have envisaged was that his phrase would be so interpreted by Malcolm MacDonald.**

The Secretary of State referred to the pledge given to the Arabs:

> What British Government was it that gave this solemn promise to the Arabs? It was the same Government of which Mr Balfour was still Foreign Secretary, the author of the Balfour Declaration. There cannot have been any misunderstanding. There cannot have been any conflict between those two promises given by the same Cabinet.[30]

He went on:

> I do not think that conditions are suitable for immigration. Under the Mandate we have to encourage immigration 'under suitable conditions'. That

---

* In 1931 the Conservative-dominated coalition had a majority of 493; in 1935 of 243.

** My criticisms of MacDonald in the context of Palestine, and under the constraints of a Chamberlain Government, should not be taken as derogating in any way from the great admiration I expressed for him as a Commonwealth statesman in *The Labour Government, 1964–70* and *Final Term, The Labour Government, 1974–76*.

is the instruction. I do not think that conditions are suitable for immigration, if that immigration, however advantageous it may be in certain other directions, is the direct cause of distrust and hatred which threaten fatally for a long time to come to destroy the welfare of Jews and Arabs alike in Palestine. Critics say that we can crush the Arab rebellion and that we had already overcome it before we made our announcement of policy. I believe that is true. But if the soldiers remove every rifle, every bomb and every land mine that is stored by Arab villagers, they cannot remove the distrust and fear and hostility which are lodged in these people's hearts. This is not a military problem. It is a political problem, and if we do not do something to remove the unrest which the Arab feels, if we merely go back to a policy of unlimited immigration which would confirm and augment his fears of being dominated, then we are only sowing dragon's teeth which one day will spring up again as armed men. There is no knowing how far that conflict will spread. There are Jews and Arabs in Iraq. There are Jews and Arabs in Egypt. There are Jews and Arabs in Yemen. This House should have a sober sense of responsibility towards a situation which is pregnant with tragic possibilities in more countries than one.

Moreover, let me remind the House that the Mandate lays down another condition which is to govern the extent to which we permit Jewish immigrants into Palestine. We are to facilitate immigration as long as it does 'not prejudice the rights of the non-Jewish inhabitants in the country'. What are the rights of the Arab population? They have lived in Palestine for centuries. Do their rights give them any title to say that beyond a certain point they should not have imposed upon them a population which may dominate them, even though we do recognize that the people coming in have a historic connection with and rights in the land? Is there no point at which we, in consideration of our obligations to the Arabs under the Mandate, should pay heed to their opinions on a matter so vital to them? Let me take a simple test. Suppose that instead of 1,000,000 Arabs in Palestine, there were 1,000,000 Americans, or Englishmen, or Frenchmen whose ancestors had lived in the country for generations past.[31]

He denied that immigration was to stop: it would continue for five years.

Labour spokesmen charged MacDonald with destroying in one year and two days what it took a great war and many years' efforts of Allied statesmen to build up: Tom Williams, speaking for the Opposition, said, 'The Right Hon. Gentleman has destroyed the very basis of the Balfour Declaration.'[32] He effectively quoted the then Chancellor of the Exchequer, Philip Snowden, and Lord Hailsham who had attacked the Labour Government when it was suggested that it was about to cut down immigration.

It was Colonel Wedgwood, Labour MP for Newcastle-under-Lyme, who perhaps got nearest to the truth when he described the debate as the culmination of a struggle which had been going on for twenty years between this House and officialdom, as represented principally by the administration in Palestine and by the permanent officials in the Colonial Office.[33] Leopold

Amery, a hard-line right-wing Conservative who was at the same time a strong supporter of the Jewish cause, posed two direct questions:

> If all the arguments which the Right Hon. Gentleman used today for putting an end to the development of the policy of the Balfour Declaration and of the Mandate are sound and good, why were they not sound and good three years ago, or indeed many years ago . . .?
>
> Why did not the Secretary of State tell us something, at any rate, of the reasons that have been responsible for all the changes in the policy of the British Government during the last three years?[34]

Why were the recommendations of the Royal Commission and the Woodhead Commission rejected? Going back to the days when he and Mark Sykes worked together on these matters, Amery challenged the Government to defend their reversal of the 1922 policy, a policy of equal rights neither assuming nor precluding an eventual Jewish majority.

Stafford Cripps, in a brief but lethal backbench intervention, condemned the Government's plan to stop Jewish immigration after five years 'which is an odd way of facilitating it under the Mandate'. He demanded that the Jewish people in Palestine must be protected for the next ten years, and proposed a scheme of temporary partition together with the development of Arab self-government in the rest of Palestine.

Philip Noel-Baker, winding up the first day's debate for the Opposition, quoted the Government's White Paper as saying that the Government did not contest the view of the Royal Commission 'that the Zionist leaders at the time of the Balfour Declaration, recognized that an ultimate Jewish State was not precluded by the terms of the Declaration'.[35] This was, he went on, a very disingenuous version of what the Royal Commission actually said, which was that 'The Jews understood that if the experiment succeeded the National Home would develop in course of time into a Jewish State.' And why did the Jews understand that to be the case? Because from 1918 to 1920 they had been told so by the rulers of the world, President Wilson, Lord Balfour and Lloyd George. They had been told so again by Ramsay MacDonald in 1931 in a letter confirming – as did the Peel Commission – that the primary purpose of the Mandate was to promote the establishment of a Jewish National Home. R. A. Butler, winding up, stated the Government's case with much loyalty, little passion, and, it would appear, less enthusiasm.

The second day was dominated by Churchill:[36]

> It is often supposed that the Balfour Declaration was an ill-considered sentimental act largely concerned with the Right Hon. Member for Caernarvon Boroughs (Mr Lloyd George), for which the Conservative Party had no real responsibility, and that, as the Secretary of State said yesterday, it

was a thing done in the tumult of the War. But hardly any step was taken without great deliberation and responsibility. I was glad to hear the account which my Right Hon. Friend the Member for Sparkbrook [Amery] gave, derived from the days when he was working in the Secretariat of the War Cabinet, of the care and pains with which the whole field was explored at that time. Not only did the War Cabinet of those days take the decision, but all Cabinets of every party after the War, often examining it in the varying circumstances which have arisen, have endorsed the decision and taken the fullest responsibility for it. It was also endorsed in the most cordial and enthusiastic terms by many of the ablest Conservative Private Members who came into the House when a great Conservative majority arrived after the General Election at the end of 1918. It was endorsed from the very beginning by my Right Hon. Friend the Prime Minister.

I make him my apologies for going back as far as twenty years, but when you are dealing with matters which affect the history of two or three thousand years there is no reason why the continuity of opinion should not be displayed. My Right Hon. Friend [Chamberlain], on 13th October 1918, said:

> The sympathy of the British Government with Zionist aspirations does not date from yesterday.... My father* was anxious to find such a territory within the limits of the British Constitution.... Today the opportunity has come. I have no hesitation in saying that were my father alive today he would be among the first to welcome it and to give it his hearty support.[37]

Churchill then pointed out that a number of MPs, now leading Ministers in the Chamberlain administration, had been strong adherents of the Balfour Declaration – he mentioned in particular Chamberlain and Inskip.

> We, the undersigned, having cordially welcomed the historic Declaration made on 22 November 1917, by His Majesty's Government

– that is the Balfour Declaration –

> that it would use its best endeavours to facilitate the establishment of a Jewish National Home in Palestine . . . now respectfully and solemnly urge upon His Majesty's Government the necessity of redeeming this pledge by the acceptance of a Mandate under the League of Nations.[38]

He continued:

> I think when all is said and done that Zionists have a right to look to the Prime Minister to stand by them in the days of his power. They had a special right to look to him because he was not only giving effect to his own deep convictions, but was carrying forward the large conceptions of his father whose memory he reveres and whose renown he has revived . . .[39]

He went on to quote his own pledge of those days:

> This is what I said in paragraph (I):

* Joseph Chamberlain had been Colonial Secretary.

His Majesty's Government have no intention of repudiating the obligation into which they have entered towards the Jewish people.

I then proceeded to say that the Government would refuse to discuss the future of Palestine on any basis other than the basis of the Balfour Declaration. Moreover, the whole tenor of the dispatch was to make it clear that the establishment of self-governing institutions in Palestine was to be subordinated to the paramount pledge and obligation of establishing a Jewish National Home in Palestine. In taking up this position on behalf of the Government of the day I really was not going any further than the views which were ardently expressed by some of the ablest and most promising of our back-benchers at that time. The fact that they are leading Ministers today should, I think, have gained for the problem of Palestine a more considered and more sympathetic treatment than it has received.

Last night the Under-Secretary of State for Foreign Affairs used a surprising argument. He suggested that the obligation to introduce self-governing institutions into Palestine ranked equally with the obligation to establish a Jewish National Home. In this very dispatch of mine, which represented the views of the entire Government of the day, the greatest pains were taken to make it clear that the paramount duty was the establishment of a National Home. It was said on page 6:

> The position is that His Majesty's Government are bound by a pledge which is antecedent to the Covenant of the League of Nations, and they cannot allow a constitutional position to develop in a country for which they have accepted responsibility of the principal Allied Powers which may make it impracticable to carry into effect a solemn undertaking given by themselves and their Allies . . .

Now I come to the gravamen of the case. I regret very much that the pledge of the Balfour Declaration, endorsed as it has been by successive Governments, and the conditions under which we obtained the Mandate have both been violated by the Government's proposals. I select the one point upon which there is plainly a breach and repudiation of the Balfour Declaration – the provision that Jewish immigration can be stopped in five years' time by the decision of an Arab majority. That is a plain breach of a solemn obligation. I am astonished that my Right Hon. Friend the Prime Minister, of all others, and at this moment above all others, should have lent himself to this new and sudden default.

To whom was the pledge of the Balfour Declaration made? It was not made to the Jews of Palestine, it was not made to those who were actually living in Palestine. It was made to world Jewry and in particular to the Zionist Associations. It was in consequence of and on the basis of this pledge that we received important help in the War, and that after the War we received from the Allied and Associated Powers the Mandate for Palestine. This pledge of a home of refuge, of an asylum, was not made to the Jews in Palestine but to the Jews outside Palestine, to that vast, unhappy mass of scattered, persecuted, wandering Jews whose intense, unchanging, unconquerable desire has been for a National Home – to quote the words to which my Right Hon. Friend the Prime Minister subscribed in the Memorial which he and others sent to us:

the Jewish people who have through centuries of dispersion and persecution patiently awaited the hour of its restoration to its ancestral home.

Those are the words. They were the people outside, not the people in. It is not with the Jews in Palestine that we have now or at any future time to deal but with world Jewry, with Jews all over the world. That is the pledge which was given, and that is the pledge which we are now asked to break, for how can this pledge be kept, I want to know, if in five years' time the National Home is to be barred and no more Jews are to be allowed in without the permission of the Arabs?

I entirely accept the distinction between making a Jewish National Home in Palestine and making Palestine a Jewish National Home. I think I was one of the first to draw that distinction. The Government quote me, and they seem to associate me with them on this subject in their White Paper, but what sort of National Home is offered to the Jews of the world when we are asked to declare that in five years' time the door of that home is to be shut and barred in their faces? The idea of home to wanderers is, surely, a place to which they can resort. When grievous and painful words like 'breach of peace', 'repudiation' and 'default' are used in respect of the public action of men and Ministers who in private life observe a stainless honour – the country must discuss these matters as they present themselves in their public aspect – it is necessary to be precise, and to do them justice. His Majesty's Government have been brutally precise. On page 11 of the White Paper, in Sub-section (3) of paragraph 14 there is this provision:

After the period of five years no further Jewish immigration will be permitted unless the Arabs of Palestine are prepared to acquiesce in it.

Now, there is the breach; there is the violation of the pledge; there is the abandonment of the Balfour Declaration; there is the end of the vision, of the hope, of the dream. If you leave out those words this White Paper is no more than one of the several experiments and essays in Palestinian constitution-making which we have had of recent years, but put in those three lines and there is the crux, the peccant point, the breach, and we must have an answer to it.

There need be no dispute about this phrase 'economic absorptive capacity'. It represented the intentions of the Government and their desire to carry out the Palestinian Mandate in an efficient and in a prudent manner. As I am the author of the phrase, perhaps I may be allowed to state that economic absorptive capacity was never intended to rule without regard to any other consideration. It has always rested with the Mandatory Power to vary the influx of the Jews in accordance with what was best for Palestine and for the sincere fulfilment – one must presuppose the sincere fulfilment – of our purpose in establishing a Jewish National Home there. It was never suggested at any time that the decision about the quota to be admitted should rest with the Jews or should rest with the Arabs. It rested, and could only rest at any time, with the Mandatory Power which was responsible for carrying out the high purpose of the then victorious Allies. Yesterday the Minister responsible descanted eloquently in glowing passages upon the magnificent work which the Jewish colonists have done. They have made the desert bloom. They have started a score of thriving industries, he said. They have founded a great city on the barren shore. They have harnessed the Jordan and spread its electricity throughout the land. So far from being persecuted, the Arabs have crowded into the country and multiplied till their population has increased more than even all world Jewry could lift up the Jewish population. Now we are asked to decree that all this is to stop and all this is to come to an end. We are now asked to submit – and this is what rankles most with me – to an agitation which is fed with foreign money and ceaselessly inflamed by Nazi and by Fascist propaganda.

It is twenty years since my friend used these stirring words:

A great responsibility will rest upon the Zionists, who, before long, will be proceeding, with joy in their hearts, to the ancient seat of their people. Theirs will be the task to build up a new prosperity and a new civilization in old Palestine, so long neglected and misruled.

Well, they have answered his call. They have fulfilled his hopes. How can he find it in his heart to strike them this mortal blow?

The debate was wound up by Sir Thomas Inskip, Dominions Secretary and a former Attorney-General, of whom Churchill once said, on his appointment as Minister for the Co-ordination of Defence, 'the most incredible appointment since the Emperor Caligula made his horse a Pro-Consul'.*

The vote, as has been said, was an easy but humiliating victory for the Government. In addition to the Labour Party, a number of Conservatives voted in the 'No' Lobby and many abstained. Partition was dead. This increased Jewish suspicions that the Conservatives of the 1930s were going back on Balfour. There was to be no specific National Home in Palestine. The constant harping on Churchill's phrase 'economic absorptive capacity' had led many to fear that this was to become a device to limit and ultimately to block immigration, a fear which became a reality in 1939. As Europe approached war, defence briefings and ministerial prejudices were moving to acceptance of a new political strategy. If war were to come in Europe, we should at all costs avoid driving the world's Moslems into the Nazi camp. Recalling Churchill's judgment on the First World War, 'the allies floated to victory on a sea of oil', the Chamberlain Government, backed by a spineless Establishment press and the feeblest political entourage Britain has ever seen since the great days of Ethelred, was not only ready to appease Hitler and Mussolini, but was seen to be increasingly taking the Arab side in Middle East affairs.

The Second World War broke out with Hitler's invasion of Poland on 1

* Nevertheless when Churchill formed his war administration in 1940 he appointed Inskip, by this time Viscount Caldecote, Lord Chancellor.

September 1939, followed by the Anglo-French declaration of war. Most realistic statesmen had regarded it as inevitable from Munich onwards. One of the most tragic photographs in the histories of these days shows Weizmann and his colleagues at the twenty-first Zionist Congress in Geneva hearing the news of the signature of the Molotov-Ribbentrop pact.

Weizmann immediately wrote to Chamberlain pledging the willingness of the Jewish Agency 'to enter into immediate arrangements for utilizing Jewish manpower, technical ability, resources, etc.' in the service of the war. Chamberlain's reply noted that Britain could rely 'upon the whole-hearted co-operation of the Jewish Agency'. Christopher Sykes[40] is right to comment that from that very moment there was a degree of wilful misunderstanding. Weizmann and the Agency had in mind the formation of a Jewish Army. Chamberlain interpreted the offer of 'whole-hearted co-operation' as meaning that the lion and lamb would lie down together in Palestine, and that the Zionists would accept the MacDonald policy of limited immigration for five years, after which no further immigration would take place without the specific consent of the Palestinian Arabs

Weizmann's proposal was in no sense to be interpreted as cashing in on the war. It was a plan to help win the war against the common enemy, the Nazis and all they stood for. Indeed it was so interpreted by the newly appointed Chief of the Imperial General Staff, Sir Edmund Ironside, who proposed the idea of creating a Jewish legion. The Secretary of State for War was Leslie Hore-Belisha, a Jew, but very much an assimilated one, with, moreover, high political ambitions. He turned it down 'for the present'. MacDonald and his chief could not see beyond the aridities of the White Paper, not even, apparently, to foresee what further atrocities Hitler would be likely to commit against the German Jews and those of the territories the Nazis had overrun. The British pro-consuls in Jerusalem took a similar line, actually arresting and passing long terms of imprisonment on forty-three young Jews, including the young Moshe Dayan, for the crime of drilling in secret.

Ben-Gurion, chairman of the Executive of the Jewish Agency, a moderate Zionist leader always suspected by Whitehall as being an extremist and indeed treated as one, had announced that 'We shall fight with Great Britain in this war as if there was no White Paper, and we shall fight the White Paper as if there was no war.' Sykes fairly commented that:

> This openly paradoxical call to arms ... unlike most slogans ... exactly defined policy. To fight Hitler and the White Paper became Zionist purposes which were carried through during the war years. Neither purpose was ever laid aside, and it followed inevitably that the Jews of Palestine became people of divided mind.[41]

Churchill's arrival in Downing Street in May 1940 raised Jewish hopes.

Lord Lloyd succeeded MacDonald who was sent to Canada in the ambassadorial post of High Commissioner, just as Halifax went to Washington as Ambassador. Churchill's dealings with Weizmann were mainly concerned with the recruitment of the Jewish Army. On 6 September 1940, at the height of the Battle of Britain, he told Weizmann that he had the Government's full and official support for the army project, and a War Office conference, presided over by Anthony Eden, with Lord Lloyd in attendance, met Weizmann and a Zionist delegation. Eden then formally told Weizmann that:

> the Government have decided to proceed with the organization of a Jewish army, on the same basis as the Czech and Polish armies.* Its size, to begin with, would be 10,000 including 4,000 from Palestine. They would be trained and organized in England and then dispatched to the Middle East.**⁴²

More good news for Weizmann was that Churchill on 2 October had told the Cabinet of his intention to repudiate the MacDonald White Paper, and again, later in the month, that Cabinet had ratified the project for a Jewish Army. But Army and official circles in Whitehall and Palestine were determined to have none of it, Churchill or no Churchill. Downing Street disposes, but before long the rats get at it, in this case the Colonial Office, the military and the Palestine administration.

There was a further and deeper grievance. Jewish refugees escaping from Europe in the so-called 'little death ships' were intercepted by the Governor in Cyprus, on the high seas by the Royal Navy or on arrival in Haifa. The treatment of the *Milos*, the *Pacific* and the *Atlantic* have passed into Israeli legend. When the *Atlantic* reached Haifa, her 1,800 refugee passengers, and 1,800 other immigrants immured in the Athlit camp, were transferred to the *Patria*, a capture from the French. The Jewish Agency's defence force, the Haganah, had formed a plot to prevent her sailing by blowing a hole in her side as indeed they planned to do with any other ship refused permission to land immigrants. But the Haganah technicians blundered in their task: 200 people drowned. An even worse case was the *Struma*, overcrowded with 769 passengers from the Balkans. The Administration in Jerusalem refused entry, and all but one of the 769 were drowned. English and Hebrew placards arraigned the Governor of Palestine for 'murder'. Even Lord Moyne's report to Parliament was guarded, so far as the actions of the Administration were concerned.

The new Colonial Secretary, Lord Lloyd, sought to force the return of

---

* Both formed from Czech and Polish refugees in Britain.

** The effect was diminished, however, by a decision that the pro-Zionist Orde Wingate, whose leadership would have been invaluable in Palestine, had been accepted for service by Lord Wavell, but was in no circumstances to be deployed in Palestine. He was sent to Ethiopia.

some 13,000 immigrants who had entered Palestine in twenty-three different ships, but was overruled by Cabinet, Lloyd pointing out that 35,000 Jews had entered the country in eighteen months, nearly half the White Paper quota of 75,000 for five years. The Cabinet's decision was resented by the C.-in-C. Lord Wavell, who was about to enter Egypt to deal with the Italians under Graziani, and feared the effect of the *Patria* decision on the Arabs. Churchill, however, wrote him a private letter smoothing him down.[43]

In February 1941 plans for the Jewish Army were still going forward and Weizmann met the General, ex-Indian Army, who had been selected. Later that month, however, Lord Lloyd suddenly died, and Lord Moyne, an intimate friend of Churchill, was appointed to succeed him. Problems with Wavell, who was short of supplies for the impending North Africa campaign, led to the proposal for a Jewish Army being put into cold storage, originally for six months. Christopher Sykes has expressed the view that at its conception, the hope had been that an army consisting of both Jews and Arabs might lead to a growth of understanding – perhaps camaraderie – which could endure into the post-war period. Temporarily a minimal force had been created in September 1940 by adding a Palestinian battalion to the East Kent Regiment. The fourteen companies, it had been decided, were to be 50-50 as between Jews and Arabs, but this failed, and in the event the Jewish participants tended to predominate, company by company.* The grouping was later expanded and called the Palestine Regiment, though Sharett (Shertok) said that this was only a shadow of what the Jews had wanted.

On the other hand many Jews from Palestine as well as, of course, from Britain, joined the United Kingdom forces. In October 1941, at the expiry of Churchill's six months' deferment, Lord Moyne had to tell Weizmann and Ben-Gurion that the plan still could not go ahead, because of the need for aid to Russia. Again and again, through 1942 and 1943, no action was taken, and in April 1944 fifty-three Members of Parliament tabled a motion calling for action. The Government spokesman in the Lords answered a call in the Upper House for action by saying that the possibility was being carefully studied. On 20 September 1944, five years after Weizmann's offer and eight months from the end of the war, the Government agreed to the establishment of a Jewish Brigade Group, embodying the existing Jewish companies, which took the field with its own standards bearing the Star of David.

But one factor dominated all others in Anglo-Zionist relations – the policy for Jewish immigration into Palestine from Nazi Europe. Reference has been

* Partly, says Sykes, because the Jews volunteered in larger numbers and the Arabs were more prone to desert.

made to Hitler's *Endlösung* (Final Solution) for the German Jews. By December 1942 the West knew what this meant, and the Allied Governments issued a formal joint communiqué condemning 'this bestial policy of cold-blooded extermination'. Nevertheless, the embattled nations and many others in Central and South America refused to open their doors to such victims as could escape the concentration camps and death-camps. But increasingly the phrase 'Final Solution' became understood in all its horror as reports began to come through of the gas chambers and deaths by drowning. Western Governments – and their fighting men – realized they were dealing with a monster, but the United States Government was still uncommitted, even though its citizens were becoming less and less neutral towards Germany's challenge to humanity.

Among the first to express their horror were the delegates to a Zionist conference held in New York, at the Biltmore Hotel in May 1942. Six hundred American Jews – not all of them Zionists – attended, and sixty-seven visiting Zionists, including Weizmann and Ben-Gurion. The Holocaust turned their minds still more to the future of their people, when Nazism was destroyed. Ben-Gurion stole the show on an unprecedentedly radical policy, both on immigration and on a demand for partition. Weizmann's line was moderate, because his first priority was his negotiations with the British on the proposed army. But Ben-Gurion used as his main card an unusually radical article written by Weizmann for the New York journal *Foreign Affairs*, in which the veteran leader had demanded that the Arabs be

> clearly told that the Jews will be encouraged to settle in Palestine and will control their own immigration; that here Jews who so desire will be able to achieve their freedom and self-government by establishing a state of their own.

Ben-Gurion's draft resolution took over this demand, while making it more declamatory. The resolution was adopted with no votes against, though the American-Jewish Committee had refused to play any part in the proceedings, and the Mapai* delegation from Palestine abstained. Weizmann's counterattack was feeble and unconvincing, saying that his

---

* Mapai, the Palestine Workers' Party (Mifleget Poali Eretz Israel) was active in canvassing the idea of Israel's statehood from 1900. In 1944, Achdut Ha'avodah, a left-wing organization drawing much of its strength from the Kibbutz movement, broke away from Mapai and, after 1948, joined with a party from the still further left – again kibbutzim orientated – to form Mapam (Mifleget Poalim Meuchedit – the United Workers' Party). For a time the new organization showed considerable support for Moscow, but Achdut Ha'avodah dissolved its ties from Mapam. For a time, therefore, Israel had three Socialist parties, but they came together to fight the 1969 election, recording the highest vote of any grouping, though neither then nor later sufficient to give them an overall majority.[44]

article had not been intended as a specific policy initiative, but a formal statement of Zionism's ultimate goal. In fact Ben-Gurion's exuberance won the battle but lost him the campaign, as American Jewry turned against him. Nevertheless, with Weizmann unaccountably refusing to visit Palestine to press his arguments home, Ben-Gurion was successful in carrying the Zionist organization in Palestine itself. Yet once again he had overreached himself. German and Austrian Jews placed their entire reliance on a British victory and the overthrow of the Nazis. The American Ihud, or Union group in Palestine, founded by Henrietta Szold, creator of the powerful American women's Zionist organization, Hadassah, rejected the Ben-Gurion approach.

Meanwhile Weizmann and his supporters placed their faith in Churchill. By this time he was closely involved in action to relieve the problem of displaced Jews, following Hitler's new policy. Britain and the United States called a conference in Bermuda in 1943. Although it set up what became the United Nations Relief and Rehabilitation Administration (UNRRA), which later created a fine post-war record for its work, it was ineffective in helping the displaced Jews and those in occupied Europe threatened with displacement, or increasingly, by this time, with death.

A combination within Palestine of frustration and original sin led to an outbreak of terrorism. The Irgun Tzvai Leumi was in process of being taken over by Stern, and the Stern Gang, and the growing power of the murderous Menachem Begin who became the commander of Irgun. Begin totally dissociated himself from Ben-Gurion: as Sykes says, 'his denunciations of Ben-Gurion and his colleagues of the Agency could hardly be exceeded by a rabid anti-semite'.[45] The worst tragedy was still to come. Lord Moyne, Colonial Secretary and Churchill's close friend, was moved by Churchill to the position of Deputy Resident Minister of State, Middle East, and succeeded the Australian, R. G. Casey,* as Minister in January 1944. In November he was murdered in a Cairo street by two young members of the Stern Gang. The Jewish Agency totally dissociated the Zionist leadership – though not the Stern Gang – from the murder. (In fact, one of the leaders in the outrage was Itzhak Shamir, who in 1980 became a leading member of Menachem Begin's Cabinet.) One result was that with Agency support Haganah co-operated fully with the Administration's police, who succeeded in arresting 279 Sternists and Irgun supporters.

There is no doubt from what I heard at the time in Whitehall that Churchill was shattered by the murder of his friend. Rumours abounded that his pro-Zionist sympathies weakened in consequence. I would doubt this, though no doubt in Whitehall some officials hoped that out of this

---

* Lord Casey, 1960, Governor-General of Australia, 1965–9.

evil deed good might come in the shape of a reappraisal of the Zionist case
by the Prime Minister.

It was in this same month that Dr Weizmann paid his first visit to
Palestine since the dark days of 1939. Abba Eban records his unprecedentedly enthusiastic reception – 'the community surrounded him with
the emblems and ceremony befitting a beloved Head of State'. He warned
against violence, deplored the relapse of Haganah – or at least a part of it –
into terrorism, and emphasized the need for gradualism in the movement to
the National Home. He had told Churchill, and he told his hearers now, that
a transitional period of five years at least, possibly ten, was necessary before
a fully fledged Jewish Commonwealth came into being, and he emphasized
that during that period he wanted to see an immigration rate of 100,000 a
year. Weizmann knew better than anyone how the Moyne murder had
shocked Churchill and shaken his resolution. Two days after Weizmann
reached Palestine, Winston uttered the first words of doubt in more than a
quarter of a century:

> If our dreams for Zionism should be dissolved in the smoke of the revolvers of
> assassins and if our efforts for its future should provoke a new wave of
> banditry worthy of the Nazi Germans, many persons like myself will have to
> reconsider the position that we have maintained so firmly for such a long
> time.[46]

But the rapturous welcome Weizmann received was in a sense more of a
tribute to a prophet, to a statesman, a distinguished potential head of state
perhaps – not necessarily an endorsement of his cautious, statesmanlike
policies. A new generation had grown up which knew not the measured
periods of the 1920s and 1930s: a further generation had entered Palestine
from the haunted areas of Europe. All his experience and wisdom caused
him to urge partition, but the politicians on the ground had the people's
support in rejecting it. Weizmann was in the end proved right, but there
were to be four more years of brutal fighting and careful statesmanship
before the flag of the State of Israel would fly in Tel Aviv. And the
Government in Whitehall with which the Zionists would have to negotiate
statehood would no longer be Churchill, Eden and Oliver Stanley, but
Attlee and Bevin.

CHAPTER 5

Britain Puts Back the Clock

THERE ARE – OR OUGHT TO BE – three Western heroes in the Israeli pantheon: Balfour, Truman and Churchill. Perhaps, as will become clear, Lyndon Johnson and Arthur Creech-Jones should be given an honourable mention. Churchill, it is true, was from the Zionist point of view something of a disappointment during his Colonial Secretaryship in the early 1920s, but in the grim period of Chamberlain and Malcolm MacDonald in the immediate pre-war years, he was as active and eloquent in the Zionist cause as in his warnings about Hitler. Indeed, it is doubtful whether he could entirely separate the two issues in his own mind in those years of the Holocaust. Churchill lost the premiership in the landslide Labour victory of July 1945. Glorious in that dawn was it for Socialists to be alive and, so it seemed, for Zionists.

It would not have been possible for a political party to be more committed to a national home for the Jews in Palestine than was Labour. In the election the party had uncompromisingly demanded that the 1939 White Paper be rescinded. It pledged itself categorically not to prevent the Jews from achieving a majority in Palestine by immigration. This was not an election-eve manoeuvre. The party had supported the Jewish national home ever since the Balfour Declaration: indeed since 1917, when this theme had been incorporated in Labour's statement of war aims. It had been reiterated eleven times from then to May 1945. A generation of Labour spokesmen on foreign and colonial affairs was committed – Herbert Morrison, Hugh Dalton, Philip Noel-Baker, Tom Williams and Arthur Creech-Jones. Time after time Labour's official team on the Opposition front bench, denouncing Conservative support for 'corrupt pashas and effendis', had committed the party, on taking power, to sweeping away all restrictions on immigration into Palestine. Crossman has recorded[1] that Weizmann had discussed the future of the national home with Clement Attlee in 1943, the year when Labour's annual party conference went on record with a resolution in these terms:

The Conference reaffirms the traditional policy of the British Labour Party in favour of building Palestine as the Jewish national home. It asks that the Jewish Agency be given authority to make the fullest use of the economic capacity of the country to absorb immigrants to develop the country, including the development of unoccupied and undeveloped lands.[2]

Be it noted that the resolution ran 'building Palestine as the Jewish national home', not just 'a national home in Palestine'.

In 1944 the party adopted an NEC statement drafted by Hugh Dalton:

Here [Palestine] we have halted half-way, irresolute between conflicting policies. But there is surely neither hope nor meaning in a 'Jewish National Home' unless we are prepared *to let Jews, if they wish, enter this tiny land in such numbers as to become a majority* [author's italics]. There was a strong case for this before the war. There is an irresistible case now after the unspeakable atrocities of the cold and calculated German Nazi plan to kill all Jews in Europe. Here, too, in Palestine surely is a case on human grounds and to promote a stable settlement, for transfer of population. *Let the Arabs be encouraged to move out as the Jews move in* [author's italics]. Let them be compensated handsomely for their land and let their settlement elsewhere be carefully organized and generously financed. The Arabs have many wide territories of their own; they must not claim to exclude the Jews from this small area of Palestine, less than the size of Wales. Indeed, we should re-examine also the possibility of extending the present Palestinian boundaries, by agreement with Egypt, Syria or Transjordan. We should seek to win the full sympathy and support both of the American and Russian Governments for the execution of this Palestinian policy.[3]

Arthur Greenwood, who had just beaten Herbert Morrison for the key party office of Treasurer, and was still Lord Privy Seal in the Churchill war-time coalition, was put up to commend the statement:

In each year since the war started, the Labour Party has made a declaration of policy on Palestine. . . . They have not wavered in any way from the attitude they have taken previously on the Jewish problem. Therefore, the statement which was again in the report issued a week ago must be taken in conjunction with the statements they have already made. The declaration makes it clear that there is a desire for the establishment of the Jewish national home, and that cannot be satisfied until we are prepared to allow Jews, if they wish, to enter Palestine in such numbers as to become a majority.[4]

Finally, at the 1945 conference, on the eve of Labour's assumption of power, Hugh Dalton reinforced the party line:

It is morally wrong and politically indefensible to impose obstacles to the entry into Palestine now of any Jews who desire to go there. We consider Jewish immigration into Palestine should be permitted without the present limitations, and we have also stated very clearly that this is not a matter which should be regarded as one for which the British Government alone should

take responsibility . . . it is indispensable that there should be close agreement
and co-operation among the British, American and Soviet Governments . . .
and in my view, steps should be taken in consultation with those two
Governments to see whether we cannot get that common support for a policy
which will give us a happy, free and prosperous Jewish state in Palestine.[5]

Attlee was, in fact, fully committed to an independent state for the Jews in
Palestine – even to the extent of expelling some of the Arabs. As Party
Leader he was one of the principal signatories of the National Executive
Committee's Annual Report, quoted on the previous page.[6]

As Deputy Prime Minister in Churchill's Cabinet he had been involved
in all Churchill's Middle East policies, including the appointment of Lord
Moyne. He was as committed as the Prime Minister himself to action to resettle Europe's persecuted Jews in Palestine, and was backed by a far more
united party in favour of the National Home than Churchill could ever hope
to claim.

Moreover, the 1945 electoral landslide brought to the House a new and
younger generation of Labour MPs, very many of whom had been nurtured
in the pro-Zionist doctrines urged on MacDonald, Baldwin and
Chamberlain in the 1930s by leading members of the Parliamentary Labour
Party. Many of them had joined the party or become activists in protest
against Hitlerism and the persecution of the Jews.

Many, too, had seen active service in the Middle East and had returned
home with scant regard for the Egyptians. Others of the new intake had
attended Labour Party Conferences and supported the pro-Jewish line of
Harold Laski and other leading party figures. For many of us the 1944
Conference was the first we had attended, and it was there that Attlee moved
the acceptance of the relevant part of that report. At the end of a general
debate on overseas affairs, the record of the conference debates shows, 'The
Statement in the National Executive's Report on the subject [i.e.
International Affairs] was approved.'[7] There cannot have been in
twentieth-century British history a greater contrast between promise and
performance than was shown by the incoming Government over Middle
Eastern issues.

The explanation was the hold that Ernest Bevin possessed over Clement
Attlee. He was the only man to whom Attlee ever deferred. This apart,
contemporary comment on Attlee could not have been more perverted.
There was the silly newspaper story about an empty taxi-cab stopping
outside No. 10 and the Prime Minister getting out. Nothing is further from
the truth. He was more than a headmaster; he was a martinet who could
reduce the toughest of his colleagues to silence – I have seen Manny
Shinwell, Nye Bevan and Hugh Dalton treated like erring schoolboys.[8]

But never Ernest Bevin. Bevin filled a gap that was missing in Attlee's life.

Clem had never really met trade unionists, ordinary workers, apart from his time at Toynbee Hall and other East End settlements, and also in the First World War, where his relationship was that of a major with his rank and file. In the party he was revered, much respected, but he always seemed to be at a distance. Bevin was a tough leader of working-class origin who had fought Churchill during the General Strike of 1926, and who – all tribute to Churchill – was made Minister of Labour in 1940. He knew trade unionists; he had led, or rather commanded, them for more than a generation. He knew employers too, he liked and respected many but feared none. There was a story strongly believed in those days, the truth of which is still argued. It suggests that Clem Attlee submitted his Cabinet list to King George VI – it included Dalton as Foreign Minister and Bevin as Chancellor, a job for which he was well fitted. The King, it is said, used his constitutional rights and experience to query the post suggested for Dalton. Attlee, about to leave for the Potsdam summit, promptly switched the two.

That a switch occurred is confirmed by Attlee in his memoirs:

> It is already known that I hesitated for some hours as to whether Bevin or Dalton should take the Exchequer or the Foreign Office. Various reasons impelled me to take my final decision, which was, I think, justified in the event.[9]

Knowing Attlee I would certainly have expected him to use such a form of words if there had been Royal intervention.* One wonders how different Middle Eastern history might have been over the past thirty years had the original postings held firm. Economic policy would probably have been more robust; foreign affairs would have come more fully under Attlee's direction.

As Foreign Secretary Bevin commanded his own ship. In nearly four years in Attlee's Cabinet I never once heard Attlee query any policy put forward by Bevin, nor indeed query Bevin's view on a domestic matter if it related to industry or trade unionism. On foreign affairs there was some criticism by senior ministers hardly ever made articulate in Cabinet – that too many issues were settled à deux, and not referred, sometimes not even

---

* In fact Sir John Wheeler-Bennett, in his *Life of King George VI*, p. 638, confirms the truth of the story by quoting the King's diary:

> I then saw Mr Attlee and asked him to form a government. He accepted and became my new Prime Minister. I told him he would have to appoint a Foreign Secy. and take him to Berlin. I found he was very surprised his Party had won, and had had no time to meet or discuss with his colleagues any of the Offices of State. I asked him whom he would make Foreign Secy. and he suggested Dr Hugh Dalton. I disagreed with him and said that Foreign Affairs was the most important subject at the moment and I hoped he would make Mr Bevin take it. He said he would but he could not return to Berlin till Saturday at the earliest. I told him I could hold a Council on Saturday to swear in the new Secy. of State. I hoped our relations would be cordial and said that I would always be ready to do my best to help him.

reported, to Cabinet. In many respects Bevin's foreign policy was sound, often inspired. He was one of the first to see the dangers in Europe, with the Soviet Union asserting an increasing control over her neighbours to the West, whom she had 'liberated' from Nazi Germany.* He was one of the first statesmen of any country to be able to read political problems in economic terms, and to foresee the imminent collapse of Western Europe if the United States failed to abandon their ancient policy of isolation, and also one of the first to identify the dangers of Russian penetration of the old Turkish Empire. The awesome fact is that by his Palestinian policies he so far angered the White House – even to the point of making at least one cheap anti-Truman gibe – that he could have imperilled his grand designs for Europe in both economic and diplomatic terms.

On Palestine policy and the Middle East generally he never accepted the conference commitments and election pledges of the Labour Party. Nor did he for a single moment suggest during this critical period that he paid any account whatsoever to the Balfour Declaration. Commitments entered into by Lloyd George,** Baldwin, Churchill and a generation of Labour leaders up to 1945 played no part in his policy, except as tiresome undertakings to be got round, or, if he was provoked, challenged head on. To this end he was prepared to risk Anglo-American initiatives of great moment for Europe, and to endanger any prospect of American economic aid for Europe, a prospect which became a reality with the announcement of Marshall Aid for Europe in June 1947. The nadir of Anglo-American relations came in his contemptuous outburst at the Labour Party Conference in 1946, when, heckled over Palestine, he retorted that President Truman had been so insistent on the immediate issue of the 100,000 UK immigration certificates

* I was privileged to see him at work in Moscow, warning the American Chief of Staff of the dangers of appeasing the Soviets. The occasion was the last of the tripartite meetings of the wartime alliance, before the cold war blanket came down. Bevin had had a serious heart attack: his doctor told me 'he had nearly lost him the previous week'. Attlee had sent for me, created me Secretary for Overseas Trade, and told me to 'go and hold Ernie's hand, and relieve him of as much as possible'. In particular, he told me, Ernie, seeing the break-up of the Council of Foreign Ministers, was anxious to keep a link with Moscow through trade. I was to stay on and seek to negotiate a trade agreement. My first morning there, Bevin said before a breakfast to which he had invited the American Chiefs of Staff, 'Watch this. I'm going to warn these American service chiefs. The State Department is too soft.' They got no breakfast until he had given them a tutorial, with maps slung over an easel, showing the dangers of Soviet penetration through the Black Sea to the warm water of the Eastern Mediterranean.

** Lloyd George had accepted the British Mandate in principle at the Peace Conference in 1919. The Cabinet – and indeed the French Government – ratified this decision at the same time. H. A. L. Fisher, the historian, who had joined the Cabinet as Minister of Education, recorded in his diary that he had proposed that the Mandate should go to America, but was overruled. Britain's mandatory position was not in fact ratified by the League of Nations until 1922.

into Palestine because 'they didn't want too many Jews in New York'.[10]

Bevin's first initiative – the Anglo-US mission – together with the tragic history of the illegal immigrant ships and the Arab–Israeli clashes directly led to the surrender of the Mandate. A contributory factor certainly was Ernest Bevin's growing ennui with the whole subject, and, no less, the fact that he was answerable in Parliament not only for the main strategy and the political decisions, but also for the practicalities of control, responsibility for the police, the welfare and above all the safety of the troops stationed there. The *Hansard* index from the formation of the Attlee Government in July 1945 to the reference back to the United Nations in February 1947 records no fewer than 500 Parliamentary questions and ten major debates on Palestine. Bevin proved to be a highly effective Parliamentarian, even if brusque, both in answering questions and in debate, but he made no secret, at least in Cabinet and private conversation, of the fact that he hated the House. Once in Attlee's Cabinet when I was warning that a particular proposal which a colleague had put forward would lead to trouble in the House of Commons, I made a slip of the tongue and referred to it as the 'House of Trouble'. Ernie seized on the phrase and ever afterwards called the lower house of the legislature the House of Trouble.

His exercise of the Mandate covered two phases: first, by the establishment of the Anglo-US mission he hoped to secure a sharing of the responsibilities Britain had assumed; second, when Truman became insistent on a change of policy, Bevin got his head down and stuck to his policy and prejudices with scant regard to either the US or the UN.

In world terms he was acting from weakness for the economic prospect facing Britain and Europe was in its way as formidable as the political threat presented by Russia. Britain was bankrupt, empty of foreign currency. It was not until General Marshall's Harvard speech in June, rapidly snapped up by Ernest Bevin as a commitment,[11] that massive economic aid began to flow to Europe under the Marshall Plan, one of the most imaginative acts of this century. No European politician of those days looking back now over a gap of more than thirty years could assert that he had any real confidence that Western Germany, Italy, or even France could have survived the westward march of Communism. That this is so is to the undying credit of Marshall and Bevin. The fact that Bevin was equally alert to the fact that Russian expansionism involved a simultaneous *Drang nach Südosten* through Turkey and towards the Middle East goes a long way to explaining his preoccupation with the Arabs. Moreover, Britain's world debtor position was reflected in her bilateral accounts with Egypt and other Middle Eastern Arab states. Wartime military operations, however helpful to Egypt and others, involved money. By June 1945 Iraq held a sterling balance in London of some £70 millions, Egypt one of £396 millions. Their new independence of their previous tutelage to Britain and other Western powers which dominated their planning was to take the form of capital-intensive investment. Britain's industry could not supply the capital goods required. But with all that money in the Bank of England, Egypt demanded full convertibility into more desirable currencies at the very time that Britain was ending its brief, disastrous experiment with convertible sterling.

By Congressional law, Lend–Lease had to end simultaneously with the end of the war with Japan. Unexpectedly, the atomic bomb on Hiroshima brought Japanese capitulation just three months after the end of the fighting in Europe. President Truman's only option was the American loan to Britain, negotiated with Congress with the greatest difficulty, and then made dependent on full convertibility into other European currencies. Every exporter to Britain demanded payment in dollars. Within a few weeks the loan had run out and Britain could not meet her overseas bills.* Despite this crisis, Britain made £15 million of convertible currency available to Iraq.** Egypt, who had left the sterling area in anger at Britain's inevitable refusal to grant her convertibility, was given a succession of small but costly 'sweeteners' over the next four years. Even, therefore, if one discounts Bevin's prejudices against Zionism, compounded by his feelings about President Truman's political motives, he was clearly subject to serious economic pressures pushing him into a pro-Arab line on Middle Eastern affairs.

The unfortunate fact was that Britain's handling of the Middle East question came perilously close to endangering relations with the United States when it was of paramount importance that we should be working in complete harmony, on both economic and Euro-policy grounds. But there was another factor working on the Foreign Secretary – the Foreign Office. The Foreign Office is often accused of a built-in prejudice against Israel and the Jews. To say this is unfair: the truth is not as simple as that. What is true is that at any given time there will be significantly more officials working in the Foreign Office in Whitehall who have had experience of service in Arab countries, than those with experience of Israel (or Palestine in Bevin's day). Today around two-score ambassadors are accredited to Arab states in the Middle East, a figure which excludes predominantly Moslem Iran and

* In Cabinet, Dalton whimpered like a child and blamed the Bank of England. Morrison, who for some reason of his own was quarrelling with Dalton, smoothly demanded that the Cabinet set up an independent inquiry into the Bank, and the Cabinet gave the task to me, then Secretary for Overseas Trade. By the time the report was completed I had joined the Cabinet as President of the Board of Trade; my findings entirely exonerated the Bank. Dalton had in fact been the victim of *force majeure* due to the influence of the Cobdenite Will Clayton at the State Department, supported by the academic theorists who infested Washington's decision-making agencies.

** 'Almost quixotic generosity', commented *The Times* on 21 August 1947.

Pakistan. During the last days of the Mandate there were six ambassadors so accredited. Others would have served in the Middle East Supply Centre, others again attached to the armies of Generals Alexander and Montgomery. Thus, if the average period of accreditation is three to four years, at any one time there would be several still serving who had in-post Arab experience.* Against that there have over the years been very few exambassadors to Israel in the Office. For some reason it has for long periods been the practice for HM Ambassador to Israel to be in his last overseas post, more than once moving there from Finland. So on leaving Israel the ambassador has usually gone into retirement. The Foreign Office Establishment was backed by its State Department counterpart. As we shall see, at all critical times the President had to veto initiatives – and sell-outs – not least the attempt by the US Ambassador to the UN to go back on a firm decision to create the State of Israel.

On 22 August 1945, less than a month after taking office, Attlee appointed a Cabinet Committee on Palestine under the chairmanship of Herbert Morrison. They were instructed to prepare a full report for Cabinet. Morrison headed a circular[12] announcing the Committee's appointment with a covering note, enjoining complete secrecy not only about its proceedings, but even about the fact that the Committee had been appointed and about the identity of its chairman. At its first meeting it had to consider the question of the number of immigrants to be allowed into Israel in the immediate future:

> The Committee recommends that His Majesty's Government should, in respect of the immigration to be permitted during the interval between the exhaustion of the White Paper quota and the promulgation of a new long-term policy, continue to conform to the existing arrangements as prescribed in the White Paper. Under those arrangements, no further Jewish

---

* I had an amusing experience created by the widespread Foreign Office diaspora in Middle East Arab posts in November 1974. Golda Meir, then Israeli Prime Minister, was invited to the Labour Party Conference, postponed because of the October Election and held in London. As in a normal seaside conference, regional parties, trade unions and fringe bodies put on evening receptions. Making my usual evening tour of some seven or eight of these, I called in at the dinner held by Labour Friends of Israel. Soon after I had sat down, Golda arrived and was loudly cheered. I naturally rose, embraced her and kissed her. A photographer was present, and it appeared that copies were sent to a high proportion of the countries represented in the United Nations. A few days later my Foreign Office Secretary at No. 10 informed me that the FO were perturbed at the number of telegrams received from HM representatives in the Middle East, protesting at the press reports and photographs. What answer should each give to the solemn protests registered at the Embassy? I felt these representations were sent with some satisfaction by the ambassadors concerned, mixed with a sense of humour. All were minuted to me personally, with a formal request for instruction. I simply replied, 'Tell the FO to say to the Embassies concerned that I shall kiss whom I like, and in the case of Golda it was a pure case of sex.' No further diplomatic action was reported to me from the Middle East.

immigration will be admissible during this interval unless Arab acquiescence on it can be obtained. Every effort must, of course, be made to secure such acquiescence . . .

This was a reference to the noted 1939 White Paper of Malcolm MacDonald.[13]

The report went on to say that it seemed clear that there should be no question of permitting, during that interval, the mass immigration for which the Zionist organizations were now pressing: whether or not such mass immigration should be allowed in the future was a matter for examination in connection with the formulation of a long-term plan. The most that could reasonably be contemplated without prejudicing long-term policy in advance would be the temporary continuance of immigration at approximately 'the rate now permissible, namely about 1,500 immigrants a month; that would be an extension of the 75,000 maximum contemplated in the White Paper'. The number, it went on, would in any case be comparatively small.

Indeed, the continuance of immigration during this period is of more importance when viewed as a measure designed to appease Jewish sentiment in the matter than when viewed as a genuine contribution to the solution of the real problems of World Jewry.

There were two courses possible, it was suggested:

(a) to continue to conform temporarily to the White Paper policy and, after the exhaustion of the White Paper quota, to permit no further immigration unless Arab acquiescence can be obtained;

(b) to continue to permit Jewish immigration after the exhaustion of the White Paper quota, the Arabs being consulted in the matter, although His Majesty's Government have already reached their decision on the question.

Then came a very key qualification:

It may be mentioned that the White Paper refers specifically to the acquiescence of the Arabs of Palestine. In actual fact, however, *it will be the Arab States which will have the prevailing voice. The question is bound to be referred to the Arab League, on which the Palestine Arabs are represented, and the latter would be most unlikely to stand out against any decision arrived at by the States* [author's italics].

We rule out the possible alternative of continuing immigration without consultation with the Arabs. Mr Churchill, President Roosevelt and President Truman have all given assurances to various Arab rulers that they will be consulted before any change is made in the basic situation in Palestine. Moreover, the Viceroy and the majority of His Majesty's Representatives in the Middle East take the view that more serious reaction would be evoked by failure to consult than by consultation, even if unsuccessful.

It was pointed out that in the previous June the Viceroy of India, HM representatives in Washington and the Middle East, and the High Commissioner for Palestine had been consulted about the likely reaction in their territories to the two alternatives listed above. The Chiefs of Staff in Britain were simultaneously asked for an assessment of the commitments HM Forces might have to take on as a result of the soundings. The response was predictable. The ambassadors in the Arab states might agree to continued immigration at the current low level: the Viceroy held that maintenance at the proposed rate was the only policy which would prevent criticism and agitation in India.* HM Ambassador in Washington, Lord Halifax, advised that adherence to the White Paper, if, but only if, accompanied by further Jewish immigration with Arab consent would be accepted without much difficulty by American opinion.

The Cabinet document went on to warn of possible terrorism by the Jews: were the proposals unacceptable, the Jews would resort to violence. The Chiefs of Staff advised the Committee that the troops in Palestine would need to be reinforced by two divisions, about 9,000 men, of whom a large number would be required for administration, possibly by the end of 1945. The Morrison Committee then went on to study the two alternative courses in depth. The 'acquiescence' by the Arabs, posited in the first, was unlikely. There would be 'extreme agitation' in Egypt if they were consulted and their advice subsequently disregarded. In the Levant states consultation would be 'hailed as a mockery'. While King Ibn Saud was more reasonable than most Arab leaders, 'if he were asked to acquiesce in further Jewish immigration in accordance with the White Paper process, he would interpret any departure from that process as a breach of faith and as a personal betrayal'. Similar warnings were put on the record in respect of the Palestine Arabs. It was noted that the Viceroy had warned of the possibility of a revolt in the Moslem provinces.

The Committee proceeded to its recommendations:

(a) That His Majesty's Government should continue to conform to the existing arrangements as prescribed in the White Paper in respect of immigration during the interval between the exhaustion of the quota therein prescribed and the promulgation of a new long-term policy, every effort being made to persuade the Arabs to agree to a continuation of immigration during this interval at the rate at present permissible.

(b) That, before the approach is made to the Arabs, the Government of the United States should be informed of the position, of the fact that the formulation of a new long-term policy for Palestine is under the urgent consideration of His Majesty's Government; but His Majesty's

* At that time, of course, the Indian Empire included the Moslem provinces which, following Lord Mountbatten's negotiations in 1947, were to become Pakistan.

Government intend to refer the long-term policy to the World Organization* in due course, and that they propose, in the meantime, to act as stated.

(c) That the Chiefs of Staff should be asked to take immediate steps to reinforce the Middle East garrison to the extent necessary to meet the military commitments involved in (a).

On 11 September the Cabinet, with Attlee in the chair, considered the report of Morrison's Committee. A complication had arisen meanwhile. A pilgrimage to Mecca was about to take place. The Foreign Secretary recommended that there should be no question of suspending immigration until after the pilgrimage. Cabinet Minutes in those days usually summarized the principal arguments put forward, without attribution to individual ministers. This was wise, because otherwise individuals would want to be on the record, if not for posterity (which for ministers includes memoirs) at any rate for their report back to their officials, in respect of whom ministers like to maintain the fact or fiction of great virility. Later, in Clem Attlee's administration, the Minutes became more personalized. Still more recently, attribution has been reduced, with the main arguments merely summarized. At the 11 September meeting these were:

(a) whatever action we took we were likely to find ourselves exposed to sharp criticism from one side or the other. It was important to take the United States with us. Opinion there was at the moment very free in its criticism of our policy in that the US Government had not so far been prepared to accept any responsibility for helping in the handling of the situation. [This contribution to the Cabinet discussion was almost certainly Bevin's.]

(b) some ministers urged that since ultimately we would have to go to the 'World Organization' [UN], would not the wise course be for us to make it clear that this was so? It would help us *vis-à-vis* the Jews, since Jewish opinion would recognize that matters were taking a new form [*sic*] and it might be hoped that there would be a tendency to concentrate on the preparation of the case for the World Organization [*sic*] with a corresponding easing of the situation in Parliament.

(c) if this were so, should we not make an early statement to this effect?

(d) should we not also approach the Jewish Agency and acquire their understanding and support for such temporary suspension of immigration as might be necessary pending the working out of such a policy?

Attributed statements include that of the Colonial Secretary who said he had been in touch with the Jewish Agency, 'but that body, which was now under considerable pressure by extreme elements, had adopted a quite uncompromising line of war'. He felt that the Agency was primarily

* The United Nations Organization was at that time in course of establishment.

concerned to make it clear that the White Paper was dead.

The Foreign Secretary was content with scoring a point, saying that the Agency had declined to accept the offer of 3,000 immigration certificates offered to them and had demanded a quota of 100,000, a fact which he had now communicated to the Americans and which had clearly made a marked impression on them. The Chancellor, Hugh Dalton, who must have found all these querulous points difficult to reconcile with the party policy as he and others had propounded it at party conferences over the previous ten years, stressed the importance of 'the economic development of this backward area'. A great part of the discussion was concerned with the grave military situation in Palestine.

The Prime Minister, summing up, said that it was clear that there were strong arguments for a public statement on the policy of His Majesty's Government and of their intention in due course to put this matter to the World Organization. On the question of timing, which was of critical importance, he suggested that he should have a meeting with the Secretary of State for the Colonies, together with Bevin and Morrison, to consider arrangements. In fact the tragedy was that Bevin clearly persuaded his colleagues not to go to the UN; an even greater tragedy was that he was confident that he could get Parliamentary and international acceptability for a personal policy totally at variance with everything the Labour Party had stood for over a generation, and at a time when Winston Churchill and the Conservative Opposition were more than ready to back the Government in any forward policy, but not to support the recidivist lurch back to the exclusively pro-Arab position Bevin was seeking.

Where Bevin and Halifax totally miscalculated was the attitude of President Truman. The State Department was not far in its attitudes from those of the Foreign Office, and each worked on the other. But the Washington power system is entirely different from ours. The President's executive writ runs absolutely, subject to a veto by Congress, enforceable by the withholding of finance or any necessary legislation. There is, of course, a 'Cabinet', appointed by the President, but its power is in the last resort no more than advisory: containing the appointed heads of the main Departments – State, Treasury, Commerce, etc. – it corresponds more to a committee of what we call permanent secretaries, except that they are not permanent. The classical text-book reference goes back to Lincoln's time during the Civil War, when the President summed up the proceedings:

Noes, seven, ayes one, the ayes have it.[14]

Truman's view was unequivocal from the outset. He referred to the

solemn promise that had been made [to the Jews] by the British in the Balfour

Declaration of 1917. . . . This promise, I felt, should be kept, just as all promises made by responsible civilized governments should be kept.[15]

He had already taken up this question with Winston Churchill in a letter dated 24 July 1945, with a view to discussing it with him at the Conference of the Allies at Potsdam. It was sent just before the counting of the votes in Britain's General Election held on 5 July. (The votes were not counted until the 26th as three weeks were required to collect the service men's votes from overseas.) The election led to an overall Labour majority in the House of Commons of 146 in a House of 640. On 27 July Attlee kissed hands as Prime Minister. Thus it was Attlee who replied to Truman. Truman's letter, referring to Churchill's 'deep and sympathetic interest in Jewish settlement in Palestine', had gone on to 'venture to express to you the hope that the British Government may find it possible without delay to lift the restrictions of the [1939] White Paper on Jewish immigration into Palestine'.* On 31 July Attlee sent a brief note of acknowledgment, promising that it would receive attention. Returning home after private talks that took place at the Potsdam Summit, Truman, in answer to press questions, said:

> The American view on Palestine is that we want to let as many of the Jews into Palestine as it is possible to let into that country. Then the matter will have to be worked out diplomatically with the British and the Arabs, so that if a state can be set up there they may be able to set it up on a peaceful basis. I have no desire to send 500,000 American soldiers there to make peace in Palestine.[16]

Truman records that the State Department continued to feel that the US should stay out of any activity that might offend the Arabs, and the Near Eastern Affairs Division prepared a memorandum for him in September 1945, which proposed: 'Unless the Arabs agreed, there would be no further Jewish immigration.'[17]

The President was having none of this. It was not for him just a question of honouring the Balfour Declaration. There was an immediate crisis in Europe. There were hundreds of thousands of homeless, rootless Jews in Germany, the minority who had survived the concentration camps and many more who had fled from Eastern European countries as Stalin's troops moved further and further west. Before Truman wrote to Churchill he had already sent the Dean of the Pennsylvania Law School, Earl G. Harrison, on a mission (in June 1945) to investigate the conditions of those displaced persons known as 'non-repatriables', temporarily housed – 'and a great many of them were Jews' – in camps. Harrison reported:

> some reasonable extension or modification of the British White Paper of 1939 ought to be possible without too serious repercussions. For some of the

---

* The texts of this exchange of letters between the two Heads of Government and of others during the 1945–8 period are reproduced in Appendix III, see pp. 384–7.

European Jews there is no acceptable or even decent solution for their future
other than Palestine.[18]

His report went on to support the petition of the Jewish Agency of Palestine
that 100,000 additional immigration certificates should be made available.
On 31 August 1945 Truman wrote to Attlee pressing for action on Harrison's
recommendation. The letter was taken personally by Secretary of State
Byrnes to Attlee.

When the Cabinet met on 4 October to discuss Truman's approach,
Attlee began by saying that, since these documents had been circulated,
there had been a marked increase in the agitation on this question in the
United States, 'where our difficulties with regard to the immediate problem
of immigration into Palestine were not clearly understood'. He had just
received a telegram from Lord Halifax – which he asked the Foreign
Secretary to read out – giving the Ambassador's impression of US opinion
on Palestine. He and Bevin opposed the 100,000 programme. He stressed
that with Parliament reassembling the Government would be pressed to
make a statement and to give facilities for a debate. A statement could not be
deferred beyond the week beginning 15 October (eleven days later).

The discussion in Cabinet showed that Attlee and Bevin did not receive
unanimous backing:

> In discussion, stress was laid on the importance of making a full statement of
> the facts of the situation. The admission of 100,000 Jews to Palestine, while it
> would lead to an explosion in the Middle East, would not solve the problem of
> the Jews in Europe. The same opportunity should be taken of correcting the
> impression that all the Jews in Europe were still living in intolerable
> conditions.

This was, of course, a strange approach to the facts. Six million had died in
the Holocaust. Others were just crawling out of their hide-holes, and further
to the East, as the Soviet grip tightened, many of those who had survived
Hitler's Eastern drive now began to live again in fear. Other Cabinet voices
were now beginning to be heard, as the Minutes record:

> it was urged that no announcement by His Majesty's Government could
> afford to ignore the present situation in Europe, where Jews were living in
> conditions of great hardship and were still subject, in some areas, to
> persecution. In the British zone of Germany everything possible was being
> done to ameliorate the conditions under which the Jews were still suffering
> persecution and were, in some areas, being driven from their homes. Could
> not a Commission be sent to Europe forthwith, to establish the facts with
> regard to the present plight of the Jews?

I did not become a member of the Cabinet until two years later, but I
would guess that the Minister responsible for the words just quoted was

either Hugh Dalton or Aneurin Bevan, either of whom would almost certainly be pressing sub-paragraph (d) below. 'Other points raised in discussion' were:

(a) How far would German Jews be unwilling to remain in Germany now that the Nazi régime, with its freeze on emigration, had been abolished?

(b) Would it be desirable that the Prime Minister or Foreign Secretary should see Dr Weizmann? [The Foreign Secretary explained that he had arranged to do so.]

(c) The Home Secretary said that he had received representations from the Chief Rabbi in favour of the admission to this country of Jews who did not wish to settle in Germany.

(d) The importance of dissociating any future statement of policy from the White Paper of 1939 was strongly urged.

The Foreign Secretary then imposed his *massif central* on the meeting. In the light of the views expressed by his colleagues and of the telegram he had received from Lord Halifax, he said, he would like to have the opportunity to consider a fresh approach to the problems; he would consult the Colonial Secretary and submit further proposals. Long-term problems, of course, should be referred to the United Nations Organization, but HMG must do more than suggest a reference to the UN if they were to avoid the criticism that they were evading the urgent issues. What he had in mind – Ernie was a genius at inserting into a Cabinet meeting under the phrase 'in the light of the discussion' something he had been working out for weeks – was a solution based on the immediate establishment of an Anglo-American Parliamentary Commission which would be given the following tasks:

(i) To examine what could be done immediately to ameliorate the position of the Jews in Europe;

(ii) To consider how much immigration into Palestine could reasonably be allowed in the immediate future; and

(iii) To examine the possibility of relieving the position in Europe by immigration into other countries, including the United States and the Dominions . . . in this connection the possibility of using as temporary quarters the camps in North Africa under the control of UNRRA should be considered.

The Commission would be instructed to consult the Arabs and the Jews jointly, both with regard to the proposals for immigration into Palestine in the immediate future, with a view to the submission of recommendations to the Governments concerned, and with regard to the problem of a long-term policy, with a view to making recommendations to the United Nations Organization.

He went on to suggest that Field Marshal Smuts might be invited to preside, and said that further thought should be given to the idea that the Australian

Government might be asked to nominate a representative. The Cabinet asked the Foreign and Colonial Secretaries to submit proposals along the lines suggested by the Foreign Secretary to the Palestine Committee in time for its next meeting.

This 'last-minute proposal' was a superb example of Bevin Cunctator at his best. The idea that these carefully worked out proposals were a brainwave 'in the light of the discussion' is inadmissible. They had clearly been prepared in advance. Moreover Ernie, despite his qualities of initiative and brusque dismissal of his colleagues' thoughts, was not a draftsman. His spoken word could be persuasive, on occasions devastating, but even his Foreign Office staff must have taken several days (including discussions with the Secretary of State himself) to get this draft right. From his point of view it had everything. Nothing was to change for the duration of his experiment. There would be no increase in the minimal rate of immigration. The Americans would be smoked out. President Truman occupied the White House by succession, not by popular vote. Before long he would have to face election, with the odds strongly against him. Truman could not turn his back on Israel. Moreover, Bevin calculated, this might be the ploy which would loosen Washington's purse-strings. If Truman would provide cash and even troops, this would be welcome; still more so would be his identification with British, *scilicet* Bevinist, policy in the Middle East. On the other hand, if Truman refused to co-operate Bevin could fairly claim, to twist an aphorism of Truman himself, that those who won't enter the kitchen can't get a cut off the joint.

It was a brilliant Foreign Office manoeuvre, and one can see FO officials and Foreign Secretary in an orgy of mutual congratulations on their achievement. Unfortunately it underrated Harry Truman. He had not reached the White House as a political innocent. What is more he would certainly be facing the electorate, against all the odds, in three years' time. New York State was vital; so was Chicago, Illinois; so was California. Truman would know the exact number of Jewish voters in those three key states, measured in millions.* They were not the lobby-fodder of a

* The Jewish vote in the United States is very much more important than that of Britain. In recent times the Jewish population in Britain has been a little above 400,000. Allowing for children and for those Jews who have not acquired the residence qualifications necessary for enfranchisement, the Jewish electorate would be around 150,000, a very small proportion of the total vote. Nevertheless, its concentration in certain areas could, and in fact does, affect local voting. About two-thirds of Britain's Jews live in the Greater London area; and in some constituencies, e.g. Hampstead, Hendon and Ilford, it can in some elections prove an important factor. The Prime Minister, Mrs Thatcher, has a substantial Jewish following in Finchley, not entirely unconnected with her responsive attitude to Middle East questions. In other areas such as Leeds and part of the Manchester conurbation, the Jewish vote is quite important. But except in conditions where Israel is threatened and the British Government is taking an identifiable pro- or anti-Jewish line, there is little evidence of a national pattern of

Transport and General Workers' Conference in Ernie Bevin's heyday. At their very lowest – and American electoral considerations are capable of plumbing the depths – politics demanded a successful démarche over Israel. But that was not all. In my view Truman would have taken a strong pro-Israeli line if there had not been a vote in it either way. I knew him well. Our first meeting was during his presidency. Years later, whenever I went to New York as Prime Minister and found him there, which I frequently did, we would go and have a drink together at the Carlyle, and most often go for a walk in Central Park. (That was in the days when it was safe to walk in Central Park.) Inevitably, we touched on politics: I am certain that Truman would have been prepared to break with Bevin over Israel. Indeed, as we shall see, on the eve of the mid-term elections in 1946, he threw Bevin over rather than allow Dewey to get his hands on the New York Jewish vote in readiness for the Presidential election due to follow two years later.

On 5 October Truman received a message from Attlee saying that the Cabinet were making serious efforts to come up with an answer to the Palestine problem.[19] Two weeks later the Washington Embassy presented to the Secretary of State Britain's formal proposal for the joint Anglo-American inquiry into the problems of Palestine. Truman clearly regarded the proposal as a delaying tactic to avert the immigration of 100,000 refugees from Europe. Moreover, he was worried that the question of Jewish immigrants 'would be only one of a number of things to be considered by the Committee'.

> The British expected to deal with the Palestine issue in three stages. First, they would consult the Arabs with a view to an arrangement which might insure that for the time being there would be no interruption of Jewish immigration at the then current monthly rate. Then they would explore, with the parties primarily concerned, the possibility of devising other temporary arrangements for dealing with the Palestine problem until a permanent solution of it could be reached. And, third, they would prepare a permanent solution for submission to the United Nations. For the immediate future, however, the British Government had decided that the only practicable course was to maintain the present arrangements for immigration.

Jewish voting. Many Jewish voters are prosperous and, indeed, important in financial and industrial undertakings: their voting record is not, in normal times, different from that of others in similar positions in industry and finance; their financial contributions to political parties would almost certainly show a bias in favour of the Conservatives. Working-class Jews again tend to vote on similar lines to their non-Jewish neighbours. I would think that most Jewish MPs of both major parties would feel that the fact that they are Jews neither helps nor hinders their electoral prospects, though in the Conservative Party (less so with Labour and Liberals) it may be more difficult, perhaps only marginally, for them, other things being equal, to get themselves selected as Parliamentary candidates.

Truman goes on:

> I instructed Secretary Byrnes to prepare a reply which would indicate that we
> were willing to take part in the proposed committee inquiry, but that we
> wanted to concentrate on speedy results. Furthermore, I suggested that
> Palestine should be the focus of the inquiry and not just one of many points. I
> wanted it made plain that I was not going to retreat from the position which I
> had taken in my letter to Attlee on August 31st. I did not want the United
> States to become a party to any dilatory tactics.
>
> The British were none too happy with our reaction. Bevin wrote to Byrnes
> [Truman's Secretary of State], insisting that the inquiry should extend to
> places other than Palestine as potential settlement areas for European Jews.
> We held to our point of view, however, lest the inquiry result in drawing
> things out interminably, and when the proposed meeting was held, this point
> of view prevailed.

Truman was to be no better pleased when he found that the British draft of
the terms of reference for the Committee covered no fewer than forty-three
points.[20] The Foreign Office must have had a field-day.

On 13 November Bevin informed the Cabinet that the United States
Government had now accepted the invitation to set up the Committee of
Inquiry, but Washington had made it clear

> that they were not in full accord with the views expressed to them by HMG
> on the subject of short-term immigration into Palestine, and President
> Truman had intimated that he still adhered to the views expressed on this
> aspect of the matter in the letter he had addressed to the Prime Minister on 31
> August.

Bevin read over to Cabinet the text of the statement he intended to make in
the House that afternoon, while making clear that he would not expect the
American Government to endorse the whole of it. Cabinet also agreed that
the Foreign Secretary's statement would be followed by one from the Home
Secretary which would set out the scheme approved by the Cabinet a week
earlier for admitting into Britain a limited number of refugees from Nazi
oppression. Thus on 13 November 1945[21] Bevin announced the
establishment of the Committee with the following terms of reference:

1. To examine the political, economic and social conditions of Palestine as
   they bear upon the problem of Jewish immigration and settlement therein
   and the well-being of the peoples now living therein.

2. To examine the position of the Jews in those countries in Europe where
   they have been the victims of Nazi and Fascist persecution, and the
   practical measures taken or contemplated to be taken in those countries to
   enable them to live free from discrimination and oppression and to make
   estimates of those who wish or will be impelled by their conditions to
   migrate to Palestine or other countries outside Europe.

3. To hear the views of competent witnesses and to consult representative Arabs and Jews on the problems of Palestine as such problems are affected by conditions subject to examination under paragraph 1 and paragraph 2 above, and by other relevant facts and circumstances, and to make recommendations to His Majesty's Government and the Government of the United States for *ad interim* handling of these problems as well as for their permanent solution.

4. To make such other recommendations to His Majesty's Government and the Government of the United States as may be necessary to meet the immediate needs arising from conditions subject to examination under paragraph 2 above, by remedial action in the European countries in question or by the provision of facilities for emigration to and settlement in countries outside Europe.

After a moving and sensitive reference to Nazi persecution he fairly reported on the conditions in which so many Jews were still living in Europe, stressing the Government's actions in trying to improve their position.

The Jewish problem is a great human one. We cannot accept the view that the Jews should be driven out of Europe, and should not be permitted to live again in these countries without discrimination, and contribute their ability and their talent towards rebuilding the prosperity of Europe. Even after we have done all we can in this respect, it does not provide a solution of the whole problem.

But then he went into a full treatment of the situation created for the Arabs, in terms which recalled the minds of pro-Zionist MPs to what they would regard as the years of shame in 1936–9.

There have recently been demands made upon us for large-scale immigration into Palestine. Palestine, while it may be able to make a contribution, does not, by itself, provide sufficient opportunity for grappling with the whole problem. His Majesty's Government are anxious to explore every possibility which will result in giving the Jews a proper opportunity for revival.

The problem of Palestine is itself a very difficult one. The Mandate for Palestine requires the Mandatory to facilitate Jewish immigration and to encourage close settlement by Jews on the land, while ensuring that the rights and position of other sections of the population are not prejudiced thereby. His Majesty's Government have thus a dual obligation to the Jews on the one side and to the Arabs on the other. The lack of any clear definition of this dual obligation has been the main cause of the trouble which has been experienced in Palestine during the past 26 years. His Majesty's Government have made every effort to devise some arrangements which would enable Arabs and Jews to live together in peace and to co-operate for the welfare of the country, but all such efforts have been unavailing. Any arrangement acceptable to one party has been rejected as unacceptable to the other. The whole history of Palestine since the Mandate was granted has been one of continued friction between the two races, culminating at intervals in serious disturbances.

The fact has to be faced that since the introduction of the Mandate it has been impossible to find common ground between the Arabs and the Jews. The differences in religion and in language, in cultural and social life, in ways of thought and conduct, are difficult to reconcile. On the other hand, both communities lay claim to Palestine, one on the ground of a millennium of occupation, and the other on the ground of historic association coupled with the undertaking given in the First World War to establish a Jewish home. The task that has to be accomplished now is to find means to reconcile these divergences.[22]

His reference to a Jewish home got him into trouble. Sydney Silverman, MP, wrote to him and on 13 December Bevin sent him a handsome letter of correction which Silverman was to welcome not only for itself, but for the fact that it was written after the appointment of the Anglo-American Commission. Silverman, who, with others, had rightly feared that the Commission was a device to enable Bevin to abandon previous government commitments from Balfour onwards to a Zionist solution for Palestine, took this as an assurance from Bevin that the Commission did not represent a reversal of policy. In this he flattered Bevin, but Bevin's letter to him had been surprisingly categorical.

Dear Silverman,
    In answer to your letter of 6 December, I write to assure you that the phrase 'Jewish Home' which I used in the House of Commons on 13 November, was intended to be understood as an abbreviation of the phrase 'National Home for the Jewish people' which appears in the Balfour Declaration and in the preamble of the Mandate for Palestine.
    His Majesty's Government have no intention of evading their obligations under these instruments, which of course include the facilitating of the establishment in Palestine of a National Home for the Jewish people.

Silverman went on to point out that this 'reaffirmation of the general policy of Great Britain in this matter' had been made *after* the appointment of the Anglo-American Commission, and drew the conclusion that he was therefore entitled to rely on it as authority for stating that

the policy of creating a national home stands and that the Commission is investigating things, and will report on things that may be cognate, incidentally on a short view or on a long view, to the implementation of that policy, but is not entitled to make recommendations that go behind it.[23]

The Israelis were not satisfied as easily as Silverman had appeared to be. Abba Eban, widely regarded as a highly sober-sided diplomat, referring in his autobiography to Bevin's appointment as Foreign Secretary, said,

He immediately subjected the Jewish people to a shock of sadistic intensity. Instead of abrogating the 1939 White Paper, opening the gates of the Jewish National Home and offering salvation for the concentration-camp refugees in

Europe, he simply told the Jews 'not to push to the head of the queue', but rather to devote their efforts to the 'reconstruction of Europe'. On an unforgettable November 13, 1945, he made a statement shattering all the hopes that Jews had invested in the prospect of better times after the war. Bevin virtually confirmed the White Paper, repudiated the Labour Party's conference platform and observed piously, 'We cannot accept the view that the Jews should be driven out of Europe.'[24]

For the best account of the work of the Committee we have Richard Crossman to thank.* He kept full notes, not only of travels, interviews and committee meetings, but of his own mental development on the problems set out in the terms of reference. Despite his pre-war political and journalistic experience he had not addressed himself much to Middle Eastern questions, and he brought not only his inquiring mind but *tabula rasa* so far as his thinking and prejudices were concerned. He was certainly not a committed Zionist; some of the thoughts he committed to paper after the first discussions of the Committee are significant:

I am quite clear after reading the documents that historically – but not legally – the Arabs' case is indisputable. We did include Palestine in the area of their independence: we failed to tell the French we had done so. We negotiated an entirely incompatible division of the spoils with France and Russia. And then, on top of all, we promised the Jews a national home . . .

Discussing the MacDonald White Paper of 1939, he comments:

Normal people like myself, who in 1939 would have reacted violently against the White Paper as unjust, now tend to be sympathetic to its objectives and only regard its tactics as wrong.

Was it that we were all on the look-out in 1939 for *appeasement* and saw the Arabs as a Fascist force to which Jewish liberty was being sacrificed? Partly, perhaps. But I suspect that six years of this war have fundamentally changed our emotions. We were pro-Jew emotionally in 1939, as part of 'anti-Fascism'. We were not looking at the actual problems of Palestine, but instinctively standing up for the Jews, whenever there was a chance to do so. Now, most of us are not *emotionally* pro-Jew, but only rationally 'anti-antisemitic' – which is a very different thing.

I argued yesterday that in this world of 1945, Zionist assertions that the Jews *are a nation* are a reflex of anti-semitism. Whereas the few survivors of European Jewry should be liberated from that awful separateness which Hitler imposed and be reconstituted Europeans into full rights and duties, Zionism actually strengthens the walls of the spiritual concentration camp. It is only the other side of the Nazi shield, the Jewish reaction of the German disease. It is the anti-semites and racists who want to clear the Jews out of Europe and place them together in Palestine.[25]

* He was appointed as one of the Commons members, his first introduction to Middle Eastern problems.

These words of Dick Crossman have been set out not only to show what a brilliant intellect, previously unversed in Middle Eastern problems, could make of the case for Zionism: equally he was recording what other Committee members had said at the outset of their mission.

At the end of their travels and deliberations he was committed to the Zionist solution but believed that, having regard to pledges given to the Arabs and the majority stake they enjoyed in Palestine, the only way was partition. In this he was to be proved right. This was the decision of the United Nations after the surrender of the Mandate, but he did not press his view to the extent of a minority report, which would have derogated from the Committee's unanimous findings on the rescinding of the 1939 White Paper and the entry into Palestine of 100,000 Jews as a matter of urgency, together with policies to raise Arab living standards and a long-term immigration policy. The Committee was unanimous in rejecting proposals which had been urged on them for the creation of a single Arab-Jewish federal state.

On 27 November Cabinet considered a memorandum by the Colonial Secretary making recommendations about the treatment of certain Palestinian Arabs who had co-operated with the enemy during the war. The meeting recorded agreement

> that the Mufti, and the other Palestinian renegades whose return to Palestine was not desired by the Palestine Government,* should be sent to the Seychelles and detained there as political prisoners.

Cabinet further invited the Secretary of State to arrange for these men to be sent to the Seychelles without coming to the United Kingdom *en route*.

The year 1946 was ushered in by trouble on the ground in Palestine. The Colonial Secretary reported to Cabinet at its meeting on 1 January that on 27 December terrorist attacks had been made on police and military buildings in Jerusalem and Tel Aviv. Ten policemen and soldiers were killed and eleven wounded. The High Commissioner had seen David Ben-Gurion and Moshe Shertok (Sharett), the leading members of the Jewish Agency in Palestine. They had dissociated themselves entirely from the outrages, but said that the Agency was unable to assist in preventing such incidents while His Majesty's Government pursued their present policy. He had pointed out that the basis of the special status given to the Jewish Agency was that it should co-operate with the Government, and if it was now unable to co-operate in ensuring observance of the law, this basic condition was not being fulfilled. The High Commissioner considered that the defiant attitude of the Agency could not be ignored and that retaliatory action should be taken

---

* It should be noted that all references to the 'Palestine Government' meant the British occupying forces with their handful of civilian advisers.

against them. He had it in mind that the Agency's buildings should be occupied and that the members of the Executive should be placed under police supervision.

The advice of the Parliamentary Under-Secretary to the Colonies as given to the Cabinet (George Hall, the Secretary of State, was absent) was that he thought the disadvantages of such a course outweighed the advantages; it would throw power into the hands of the extremists and above all make it impossible for the Anglo-American Commission to carry out its work in Palestine. He proved to be right. This was one of many meetings where there was a very natural conflict between the consideration undoubtedly due to the Army and the development of a political strategy. The Army was in a near-impossible situation, carrying out a near-impossible job. They were constantly subject to sniping and surprise attacks in a quarrel which was not theirs. No one understood this better than the moderate leaders of the Zionist movement who were all the time subject to political take-over bids from the extremists, or even assassination at their hands.

The Cabinet (1) agreed that there should be no wholesale search for arms in Palestine; (2) decided that the moment was not opportune for active pressures against the Jewish Agency on the lines suggested by the High Commissioner; (3) invited the Foreign Secretary to expedite his proposed approach to the Arabs with a view to obtaining their consent on the continuance of immigration at the then rate of 1,500 a month, on condition that all the immigrants were near relatives of persons already in the country; and (4) resolved that in the meanwhile immigration at the then existing rates should continue.

The Army and the Palestine Government, under the High Commission, were left with the unenviable task of maintaining law and order in powder-keg conditions, while the slow processes of Whitehall policy worked themselves out through the Anglo-American mission, instead of in accordance with the fulfilment of solemn commitments of nearly thirty years' standing.

Cabinet was for the moment applying itself less frequently to Palestinian affairs, while the Anglo-American mission got on with its job. Its next formal consideration was not until 21 February. Again the issue was one of security. And again, simply because the departments refused to base themselves on a consistent strategy, they were still addressing the wrong questions to the answer. The Secretary of State 'brought to notice', the Minutes record, another speech by Shertok on 13 February which could have been the basis of a seditious charge, and would in any case have warranted Shertok's detention under the Defence (Emergency) Regulations, 1945. The Secretary of State, instead of bringing this to notice, would have done better by bringing him to London and getting to the bottom of the problem. Less than two years later Lord Mountbatten was bringing self-government to India (where there was a Moslem problem too), seeking success through direct personal negotiations with an entire generation who under imperial law were guilty of subversion and treason. But then he had plenary powers, with a time-limit for independence, and for him partition was not a dirty word.[26] (Nor was it eighteen months later for Bevin in the Palestine context.)

In the case of Shertok the Secretary of State advised against detention, since the Committee of Enquiry was due shortly to visit Palestine, and as Shertok had promised the co-operation of the Agency in giving evidence, the High Commissioner had decided to take no action against him. But the High Commissioner had satisfied himself by getting it on the record that relations with the Agency had become increasingly difficult: 'Their attitude has encouraged terrorist organizations.'

The Secretary of State's advice was accepted. The Prime Minister, summing up, described the situation as grave and said that the Secretary in his speech in the Commons that day should repeat the warning that His Majesty's Government would not be coerced by terrorist threats. The lull in Cabinet preoccupation with the Palestine situation continued until 24 April, when the Foreign Secretary said that the report of the Anglo-American Committee had been received. Preliminary consideration had been given to it at the Defence and Overseas Policy Committee that morning. It had been decided to appoint a committee of senior officials of the departments concerned and then to make recommendations to Cabinet, which met on Monday 29 April to study the report.

Considering the matter following that meeting, the Foreign Secretary told Cabinet that

> he believed that if the situation was skilfully handled in consultation with the United States Government, it might be possible to bring about a reasonable settlement on the basis of the Committee's recommendation. He was not in favour of an immediate reference to the Security Council. He thought that this would be regarded as a confession of failure and would have unfortunate effects on other aspects of foreign policy. The essence of our policy should be to retain the interest and participation of the United States Government in this problem . . .

It followed, he went on to argue, that His Majesty's Government should not define their attitude towards the report as soon as it was published. For the moment it would suffice to say that the report was being considered by the two Governments in consultation. We could then watch the reaction. He himself believed that there would not be so much violence as had been predicted by HM representatives abroad. In any event we should not be unduly alarmed by some initial clamour from the Arab states. The Chancellor of the Exchequer – an intransigent Zionist of 1944 – said that the settlement of 100,000 Jewish immigrants would cost £100 million. 'In view of the magnitude of our overseas expenditure we could not lightly accept further obligations.'

The Colonial Secretary agreed with the Foreign Secretary, but, conscious of the problems the Government and, above all, HM Forces were facing on the ground, said that if the Americans proved to be unwilling to help, there might be a case for referring the issue to the United Nations. The Cabinet should be prepared for some outbreak of disorder when the report was published. In discussion, the Minutes record, there was general agreement that the report (commissioned though it was to delay or defuse the Palestine situation) 'was likely to create a most difficult situation for us'. It would accentuate all the existing difficulties and create much trouble with both Jews and Arabs. Secondly, the Committee appeared to have made no serious attempt to grapple with the problem of the Jews in Europe. Their only practical recommendation, under this part of their terms of reference, was that a large number of those Jews should go to Palestine, and the whole responsibility for the serious consequences of such an influx 'was to be left on our shoulders'. It would be very difficult for HMG alone to carry out the Committee's recommendations. Every effort therefore should be made to persuade the US Government to shoulder some part of the responsibility, and this should extend to military and financial as well as political support.

The first step, it was urged, was the disarmament of the illegal organization in Palestine. We should not allow the United States Government to lose sight of the Committee's first recommendation which, after emphasizing that the whole world shared the responsibility for the Jewish victims of Nazi persecution and for the resettlement of all displaced persons, recommended that the British and American Governments should together and in collaboration with other countries, endeavour immediately to find new homes for them all. American action would, it was pointed out, require a change in US immigration laws. The United States should therefore be pressed to take their share in the resettlement of displaced persons. European Jews should be dealt with as part of the general problem of refugees. It is interesting that by this time, as the Minutes record, 'some Ministers felt that we should be considering how the situation could best be handled vis-à-vis the United Nations. If an attempt were made to keep it on an Anglo-American bilateral basis, the suspicions of the Soviet Government might be aroused.'

The Foreign Secretary moved briskly to oppose any reference to the UN. Such a notification could be made only to the Security Council and he would prefer that, if this matter came before the UN at all, it should not go to the

Security Council. He went on to say that, if his proposals were approved, no official statement would be made, on the publication of the report, about the attitude of His Majesty's Government towards its recommendations. It was, however, important that some 'unofficial guidance' should be given to the press. In particular, it should be made clear that the US could not expect to offer advice on this problem without assuming some share of the responsibility. ('Responsibility without power' to influence his policy was clearly what he had in mind.) It ought to be suggested that the proposals for Jewish immigration into Palestine should be viewed as part of the wider problem of the resettlement of European Jews and other displaced persons, and attention should be drawn to those passages in the report which described the illegal Jewish organization in Palestine. To condition the press on these lines he suggested that the Colonial Secretary should have 'a confidential talk with Lobby Correspondents* during the course of the following day'.

It was agreed to send copies of the report to Dominion Governments and also to the Conservative Opposition, explaining to them in confidence the line HMG was proposing to take. The Cabinet's decision endorsed the Foreign Secretary's proposals. Two days later, at a specially convened Cabinet on 1 May – not a regular time for a Labour Cabinet meeting – the only item on the agenda was Palestine. The Prime Minister recalled that at the meeting on 29 April the Cabinet had agreed that the announcement of their deliberations should be confined to a statement that HMG was in consultation with the United States Government.

> President Truman had, however, issued a statement welcoming the report and expressing, in particular, the hope that the transfer of the 100,000 Jews to Palestine would be accomplished with the greatest despatch.

It was therefore necessary for His Majesty's Government to make a further statement. There was some suggestion that it should simply be said that HMG was in discussion with Washington, but the Cabinet decided that the Government should at once give some indication of their attitude towards the report and should, in particular, draw public attention to the difficulties of implementing some of its recommendations. The Prime Minister was to make the statement that very afternoon. It was in the following terms:

> I desire to make a statement in regard to the publication of the Palestine Report.

* 'Lobby Correspondents' are journalists representing the principal newspapers, agencies and broadcasting authorities, with special access to Parliament, including, of course, attendance in the Gallery when the House is sitting, and the right to patrol certain corridors and the Commons Lobby. Their rules involve the protection of their sources and it has been very rare indeed that a single one of them has betrayed a confidence.

His Majesty's Government desire to express their appreciation for the care and trouble which the Committee have devoted to the preparation of the Report. They hope that it will prove to be a notable contribution to the solution of the problems of Palestine and of the Jews in Europe, both of which they have so much at heart. His Majesty's Government received the Report only last week. His Majesty's Government and the United States Government jointly appointed the Committee, and the Report is addressed to both Governments.

His Majesty's Government are now studying it and will consult with the Government of the United States as soon as possible.

The Report must be considered as a whole in its implications. Its execution would entail very heavy immediate and long term commitments. His Majesty's Government wish to be satisfied that they will not be called upon to implement a policy which would involve them single-handed in such commitments, and in the course of joint examination they will wish to ascertain to what extent the Government of the United States would be prepared to share the resulting additional military and financial responsibilities.

The Report recommends that 100,000 certificates for the admission of Jews to Palestine should be authorized immediately, and awarded so far as possible in 1946, and that actual immigration should be pushed forward as rapidly as conditions permit. The practical difficulties involved in the immediate reception and absorption of so large a number would obviously be very great. It is clear, from the facts presented in the Report regarding the illegal armies maintained in Palestine and their recent activities, that it would not be possible for the Government of Palestine to admit so large a body of immigrants unless and until these formations have been disbanded and their arms surrendered. As the Report points out, private armies constitute a danger to the peace of the world and ought not to exist. Jews and Arabs in Palestine alike must disarm immediately. The Committee have drawn attention to the failure of the Jewish Agency to co-operate in dealing with this evil, and have expressed the view that the Agency should at once resume active and responsible co-operation with the mandatory power. His Majesty's Government regard it as essential that the Agency should take a positive part in the suppression of these activities. They hope that both Jewish and Arab leaders will give counsels of patience and restraint. His Majesty's Government recognize that decisions must be taken as soon as possible but meanwhile the House will understand that I am unable to make any further statement.

When on 8 May Truman informed him that the report of the Anglo-American Committee in his view provided a basis for talks between the two Atlantic powers on the one hand, with, separately, the Jews and the Arabs, Attlee's reply was: 'Thank you very much indeed for your message of yesterday about Palestine and for your kindness in consulting me.' Two days later Attlee wrote a further letter which Truman clearly regarded as a further delaying tactic.[27] While consultations with Jews and Arabs should proceed quickly, Britain was engaged in important and delicate negotiations with Egypt; he suggested a postponement until 20 May or even later. He added that a period of two weeks for consultation with the Jews and the Arabs to prepare for the conference would be inadequate, and 'that a month would be better'. So far as the Egyptians were concerned, Attlee almost certainly was not delaying matters, despite Truman's suspicions; the Egyptian talks involved the settlement of the debts we had incurred in the war, and were both difficult and financially crucial.

On 16 May Truman, seeking to make progress, held a long conference with Dean Acheson, and wrote a letter to Attlee[28] about written messages to be handed by the two Governments to the Jews and Arabs respectively, meanwhile hedging on Attlee's proposals 'for an eventual conference which would include Jewish and Arab representatives'. Again he suspected that London was working to a Greek Kalends timetable. He was not pleased either when Attlee, announcing to the House of Commons the publication of the Anglo-American report, added that His Majesty's Government would ask the United States to share the additional military and financial responsibilities he foresaw. Truman was clearly nettled about British press comments. Writing years afterwards he recorded that at this time London papers were saying or implying 'what Ernest Bevin, the Foreign Secretary, later said in a speech on 12 June that our interest in helping the Jews enter Palestine was due to our desire not to have them in the United States'.[29]

On 9 May, when the Cabinet met for its regular meeting, Palestine was again on the Agenda. The Foreign Secretary was in Paris. The Minutes record that

> The Prime Minister informed Cabinet that he had received a telegram from President Truman setting out the steps he proposed to take to enable his Government to decide their policy on the report of the Anglo-American Committee on Palestine. He [President Truman] proposed that his Government should now initiate the consultation with Jews and Arabs to which both Governments were committed. He intended to ask the Jewish Agency, the various Arab States and a number of Jewish and Arab organizations, to submit their comments on the report within two weeks. The United States Government would then consult His Majesty's Government and would proceed to determine their attitude towards the report as a whole and to issue a public statement as to the extent to which they were prepared to accept it as the basis for their Palestine policy. The President wished to know whether His Majesty's Government would take a concurrent action.

The Cabinet, of course, living in a dream world of their own, 'welcomed this' as a further admission by the US of some share of responsibility. True, it did not this time mention financial or military assistance. Again it was suggested that this point might be raised with the President, and again

Cabinet decided against such a course – which if it had had any success whatsoever would certainly have drawn from the President a counter demand for acceptance of the programme for 100,000 immigrants.

The Prime Minister deferred any decision. He would, he said, like to have the views of the Foreign Secretary before he sent a definite reply to the President. He had sent the Foreign Secretary the text of the American message, and hoped to discuss the matter with him at the end of the week. Thus, when the Cabinet met again on Monday 13 May, the Prime Minister was able to say that he had discussed the issue with the Foreign Secretary, who while in Paris had had preliminary discussions with the US Secretary of State. He now proposed to reply to Truman on the following lines:

> To start consultations with Arabs and Jews at this moment would prejudice the Egyptian negotiations and cause an uproar in the Middle East. It would be well that these consultations should be deferred for a few days: in any event it would be difficult to complete them within a fortnight. At some stage, preferably before the consultations with Jews and Arabs, *experts of the United Kingdom and the United States Governments should examine the financial and military implications* of carrying out the Committee's recommendations [author's italics].* After the consultations with Jews and Arabs there should be a conference of all interested parties, including Jewish and Arab representatives. The Prime Minister said he was arranging to see British members of the Anglo-American Committee.

The Cabinet took note with approval of the lines on which the Prime Minister proposed to reply to President Truman's message.

What is surprising in this catalogue of events, as is clear from our earlier chapters, is the fact that every Cabinet decision, every approach to Washington, Cairo or Tel Aviv recorded in this chapter, every Foreign Office manoeuvre, seems to have been taken without reference to the Balfour Declaration – almost as though it had never been made – and successive commitments made on Britain's behalf, to say nothing of the firm pledges made time and time again by the Labour Party in the years leading up to 1945, indeed by leaders who were to occupy high positions in the Cabinet. It was as though Balfour, Lloyd George – and Churchill – had never lived. What seems equally incredible is that ministers could hope, by one manoeuvre, consultation or meeting of experts after another, to delude Washington, at the very time when, with Soviet imperialism seeking new areas to infiltrate, and economic paralysis spreading over Western Europe, Anglo-American co-operation should have been a primary objective of British policy. Was it perhaps that Bevin regarded Truman as one of the secondary dockyard managers he had out-manoeuvred in his Transport

---

* There is no doubt that these words were similarly italicized in the minds of senior ministers and officials who had been considering for nearly a year how to raise the issue.

Workers' days?* Or had he judged, either through his own ratiocination, or on the reports he was receiving from his pro-consuls in the Lutyens monastery on Massachusetts Avenue, that Truman could be written off in the Presidential election of November 1948, two-and-a-half years away?

On 20 May Cabinet met again, to be informed of further messages between the Prime Minister and the President.

> It had now been agreed that the two Governments would independently but simultaneously invite the Jews and Arabs to submit within one month their views on all the recommendations in the (joint) report. These invitations were to be issued that day. Thereafter, a joint study of the implications of the report would be carried out by experts nominated by the two Governments. President Truman was selecting a group of experts for this purpose, and we had undertaken to indicate the subjects which we wished to be covered in their joint study. President Truman had also undertaken to consider our suggestion that at a later stage there should be a conference convened by the two Governments but attended by representatives of the Jews and Arabs.

The Foreign Secretary, the Minutes show, welcomed the evidence in this exchange of messages that the United States was ready to contemplate some practical steps in the responsibility for Palestine. 'They now seemed to be willing to remove this question from the realms of propaganda and to study its implications on a business-like footing.' Cabinet decided that there should be no announcement in Parliament about the invitation to Jews and Arabs – it was too late to concert an agreed form of words with the United States Government. Any questions which might be put in Parliament the next day should be answered by reference to the announcement made on behalf of the Cabinet.

A week later, on 27 May, Cabinet met yet again. The Prime Minister briefly reported his exchanges with President Truman on behalf of the two Governments. On the same day, Truman records, Attlee 'cabled' him with the 'catalog' of forty-three subjects London wanted the experts to discuss.

> My reaction was that this procedure would only serve to postpone any relief for the 100,000 homeless Jews that we still wanted to see admitted into Palestine. I replied therefore that their problem should be taken up without delay, even before the experts might be ready to go into the other subjects listed by the British.

The President said that he was willing to help with transportation and temporary housing, but

> The Prime Minister's reply to my proposal was negative. . . . In my answer I

---

* More than once Bevin would recall for the benefit of his colleagues, at some critical point in the Palestine issue, how he had out-manoeuvred some employer and secured an agreement on his terms, at the eleventh hour plus fifty-nine minutes.

told Attlee that I could appreciate his point of view, but that I saw no reason why it should not be possible to make all arrangements for the admission of the 100,000 at once so that there would be no further delay once the experts had reached agreement on the more general questions.[30]

London and Washington could hardly have been further apart, on objectives, methods or timing. Attlee certainly had one grievance, that their earlier exchanges on the admission of 100,000 Jews into Palestine had been leaked to the *New York Herald Tribune* (of 30 September 1945), who reported that Truman had made this request but that Attlee, after a month, had not replied. This Attlee repudiated, and it quickly came out, in a Senate debate, that the reply had been a flat rejection. Meanwhile London contrived to produce a fresh provocation for the President.

During the Whitsun recess the Labour Party Conference took place in Bournemouth. The Foreign Secretary was replying to the debate on Foreign Affairs. A considerable part of his speech referred to the Western alliance and the threatening behaviour of the Soviet Union, but he included a strong passage on Palestine. Referring to the 1939 White Paper he said:

> I came to the conclusion that the mere wiping out of the White Paper would not lead us very far. There has been the agitation in the United States, and particularly in New York, for 100,000 Jews to be put into Palestine. I hope I will not be misunderstood in America if I say that this was proposed with the purest of motives. They did not want too many Jews in New York . . .*
>
> If we put 100,000 Jews into Palestine tomorrow, I would have to put another division of British troops out there. I am not prepared to do it . . .
>
> President Roosevelt and the British Government both gave a pledge that we would consult the Arabs and the Jews. The famous Palestine Mandate leaves me with a feeling that it is so drawn that it can be argued both ways. 'How happy would I be with either were t'other fair charmer away'.

There was no further meeting of the Cabinet on Palestine for a month, nor were there any serious exchanges with the United States.

When Cabinet met on 20 June the emphasis was on further military activity in the Jewish area of Palestine. There had been a further outbreak of violence, including attacks on the bridges over the Jordan. The railway workshops at Haifa had been severely damaged and five British officers had been kidnapped from the officers' club. The High Commissioner had urged on the Government that no further discussions on the subject of the admission of the 100,000 Jews into Palestine should take place until the kidnapped officers were safely returned. The Prime Minister read to the

---

* He was *not* 'misunderstood in America'. Truman understood perfectly and never forgave Bevin, or for that matter Attlee. It was just over six weeks later that Truman responded by cutting the ground from under the Government's feet halfway through a major two-day Parliamentary debate (see p. 174 below).

Cabinet a telegram from the Foreign Secretary, who was still in Paris, urging that strong action should be taken, the United States Government being enlisted for support. There should also be a publicity campaign in Britain and the United States on the reasons for Britain's actions.

'In discussion' the point was made that it was certainly the case that the actions had been taken by the Jews, but historically the illegal organizations had in some part originated as a protection against Arab violence. It was also urged that it was important to break the illegal organization rather than undertake the wholesale disarming of both Jews and Arabs – which might follow later – but this would be difficult and likely to involve a heavy military commitment. There was 'clear evidence' that the Jewish Agency was connected with Haganah and it would probably be necessary, in suppressing illegal organizations, to raid its premises and to arrest some of its members. 'The complete suppression of the Agency as such would however be undesirable.'

The Minister of State at the Foreign Office (Philip Noel-Baker) reported on the mysterious movements of the Mufti, who the Cabinet had had reason to think was in baulk. The Cabinet had earlier decided to prevent him from returning to the Middle East, but he had by this time left France and arrived in Egypt.

Cabinet further considered the Palestine situation at its meeting on 24 June. On the 'outrages' it was reported that two of the kidnapped officers had been released, but the other three had not. Ministers were informed of the progress of the consultations between British and United States officials about the proposed admission of the 100,000. The talks might be completed during that week, but there was no information about the date of arrival of the main party of US officials to discuss the Anglo–American report, now getting somewhat frayed round the edges. Meanwhile, the proceduralists had settled their lines of battle on the question of the next steps for discussing Truman's 100,000. The report on this issue should not be made in the form of a report to the two Governments: it should be a memorandum for the use of the main conference of officials who were to discuss the Anglo-American report as a whole. There was no report of Balfour turning in his grave. Dr Weizmann was reserving for himself a dignified silence, and earning criticism from his impatient Zionist colleagues. The time was coming for 'a healthy growl' from Winston Churchill.[31]

It will have become clear that in the policy clashes between Britain and the US, and the murderous clashes between Jew and Arab, there was a further dimension – the virtually intolerable role of the British armed forces in Palestine, a role which was to become totally anomalous in the twilight period between the decision to transfer the issue to the United Nations and the final assertion of Israeli sovereignty in 1948. Throughout 1946 and 1947, indeed right up to independence, they had a job to do, sometimes executed with a wooden, even prejudiced, inspiration. Though they were sometimes prone to panic-inspired actions, this was not so much a reproach to them and the High Command, as to Whitehall. A clear policy directive from London could have ensured that Cabinet, the Foreign Office, the Horse Guards HQ, the Palestinian command and the High Commissioner were working as one. After all this was not the War of American Independence, when it took seven weeks for a ship to convey a message from George III to the New England colonies: there was a telegraph system, radio, and the communications advances of the Second World War. The problem was the greater – though in some ways a rerun of the months before the events leading up to 1776 – in that the troops were there to maintain a *status quo* unacceptable to the lusty inhabitants of the smaller part of the region they were policing. In this case there was the further complication of the Arab majority. It was as if George III in his dealings with the colonists had to be concerned about the need to consult the Indian tribes at every turn. The Army understandably was not influenced by strictly policy issues such as the Balfour Declaration, the Peel Commission or the role of the United Nations.

In the absence of any instructions to the contrary, their task was to maintain law and order. They were the secular arm of the administration, which was ruling in a colonial context. The Secretary of State for the Colonies was responsible to Cabinet and Parliament, though in departmental terms and, personally, in policy terms he was very much under the thumb of the Foreign Secretary. In many respects the position was analogous to that of India: indeed telegrams from the Viceroy and ministerial representations from the Secretary of State for India repeatedly warned of the catastrophic consequences that would follow there if softness were shown to the religious fanatics of Palestine. After all, India had its Gandhi. Moreover, any policy in Palestine which appeared to grind the faces of the Arabs could provoke sharp reactions from India's Moslems in the area which substantially, as a result of Lord Mountbatten's statesmanship, was to become Pakistan. Until 1947 India had its Viceroy; Palestine had its High Commissioner, but his role was in no way parallel to the High Commissioners accredited to Australia, New Zealand and Canada. He was very much a colonial governor, supported by the forces of law and order in the shape of the Palestine Police Force (more or less parallel to a colonial police force) backed up by the Army. It was indeed a classical colonial situation. The Zionist political leaders had the support of the Haganah and the 'National Council', Irgun Tzvai Leumi, who were admittedly responsible for many of the murders, bombings, kidnappings and physical destruction the Army was fighting to prevent. Weizmann, when appealed to by the Armed Forces, usually intervened to discourage and indeed publicly denounce terrorism, but the High Commissioner and successive Commanders-in-Chief claimed to be certain of their evidence of responsibility on the part of such leaders as Moshe Shertok and Ben-Gurion. Far more committed, and admitting it, to the policy of terrorism and murder was Menachem Begin, thirty years later to become Israel's first Likud Prime Minister. He had escaped from Poland via Iran to Palestine in 1942, and, joining the underground, issued his statement of commitment to British rule[32] in 1944. While Britain was in the course of destroying Hitler, arch-exterminator of Jewish lives in Germany, in Begin's homeland – Poland – and in other occupied countries, he would not attack the Army: his struggle would be against the police and relevant parts of the colonial civil administration.

What must be said is that of the 100,000 British soldiers subject to surprise sorties and callous murder, in a quarrel which was not Britain's and served no British interest whatsoever, a high proportion were National Service men, enlisted for the war with Hitler, conscious that US soldiers were being demobilized and for this purpose using British liners handed over for US use in wartime.

It is not the role of this book to trace the history of Britain's armed forces in Palestine, except to refer to incidents which led to policy decisions by Cabinet or the departments, to debates in Parliament or to international initiatives or clashes. It will be necessary likewise to quote some of the public statements of Army leaders, such as General Barker, which, however understandable in view of the provocation he faced, created propaganda leverage in the West and fomented trouble in Parliament for Bevin (who in the main agreed with them, possibly regarding them as under-statements).

At the weekend following the 24 June meeting there was a showdown, carefully planned six days earlier, with the Jewish Agency and the principal Jewish military organizations. This was provoked by the kidnapping of the five British officers and pressed on the Cabinet by General Montgomery, Chief of the Imperial General Staff, who had visited Palestine earlier in the month. On Saturday 29 June, the Jewish Sabbath, the forces of order struck, Attlee informing Truman by telegram at 1.45 a.m. on the morning the action was due to take place. The Jewish Agency was occupied by the troops. Five members of the Executive, 2,659 men and 29 women were arrested and put into security camps. The offices of the principal organizations – the Histadrut (the Jewish Labour movement corresponding to the TUC), the Agricultural Workers' Organization and the Women's International movement – were searched.* The traditionally militant Kibbutz Yagur on the slopes of Mount Carmel was searched by the security

---

* In the case of Histadrut and the agricultural workers, the offices had been locked for the Sabbath, and the doors were blown open with explosives.

forces.* A hundred thousand troops and ten thousand police, it was reported, took part in the raids. The surprising thing is that there was no attack on the headquarters of the terrorists, Begin, Irgun or the Stern Gang, who were repeatedly condemned by moderate leaders, particularly Chaim Weizmann. Yet Shertok and other Agency leaders were interned.

The Jewish Agency executives in London condemned the Government's action as 'a clear act of aggression against the Jewish people', and a violation of Britain's obligation under the 1922 Mandate.[33] The British authorities claimed that the documents captured revealed evidence that the so-called moderates, Shertok and his colleagues, were clearly involved in relations with the terrorist organizations.

At the Cabinet on the following Monday, 1 July, a report was made on the weekend's activities. Sydney Silverman had given notice of a Private Notice Question, which the Speaker was likely to accept, and it was decided that the Prime Minister should reply. If, as was likely, an emergency debate was demanded under Standing Order 8, Attlee was to reply to the debate. In his reply to Silverman,[34] the Prime Minister made a full and frank statement. Quoting the Anglo-American Committee's reference to illegal armed forces as 'a sinister feature of recent years in Palestine', he referred to the Haganah, estimated at 70,000 strong, with a striking force, the Palmach, about 5,000 strong. He referred also to Irgun Tzvai Leumi, specializing in assassination, and to warnings repeatedly given to the Jewish Agency which he had drawn to the attention of the House when the report was published. Despite these warnings the situation had not improved: on the contrary.

> Within the past three weeks, sabotage of road and rail communications, including the blowing up of the principal bridges over the Jordan, has caused damage estimated at well over a quarter of a million pounds. On the night of 17th June the railway workshops at Haifa were seriously damaged by explosions and fire. The climax came on 18th June, when six British officers were kidnapped, and two others were seriously wounded. Three of those kidnapped are still held captive. These are the culminating events in a campaign of violence which since December has caused the death of 16 British soldiers and five police (including the seven soldiers murdered in cold blood at Tel Aviv on 25th April). The material damage has exceeded £4,000,000.

Assessing the situation after a year of Bevinite policies produces a grim reckoning. Britain was now in a classical colonialist posture. A hundred thousand troops were holding down a country where a national home and democratic self-government had been pledged nearly thirty years before.

* This Kibbutz, dating back to the third *Aliyah* in the early 1920s, had always had a record for radicalism from its earliest days. I should mention that my younger son spent a year there in 1972–3, working on the land.

Repressive action was being taken not only, indeed not so much, against the terrorists and other disturbers of the peace as against certain of the moderates who were the acknowledged custodians of that pledge. At a time when the Soviet threat from the East and the prospect of European bankruptcy meant that Britain and Europe had most to fear from an American relapse into isolation, Anglo-American relations were strained by a policy which, while self-consciously seeking American financial and even military participation in the solution to the Palestine problem, was obdurately opposed to immigration and the policies on which the American President and Congress were insisting. Strained too by offensive words uttered in public, scorning the President's motives, by the spokesmen for a party totally committed for a generation to a national home for the Jews. When Labour was in a position to celebrate a majority in Parliament greater than had ever been won by a single party, that party was divided and that majority was being humiliatingly cut back when Parliament had to vote on the Palestine issue. Cabinet, too, was divided on the issue – though not in public – at a time when unity was essential if Britain were to summon up the reserves of strength and trust needed to meet the economic and international challenge.

Oliver Stanley for the Conservatives and Clement Davies for the Liberals expressed their full support for the Government's action, and Stanley welcomed the Prime Minister's statement that a White Paper would be published setting out the evidence. Kenneth Pickthorn, the highly academic member for Cambridge University, asked the Prime Minister if it would not be better to use the word 'Zionist' in future rather than 'Jewish'. This proposal was in fact at once adopted by the Cabinet.

There was, of course, pressure for an early debate and the Prime Minister supported consultations 'through the usual channels' to this end. In fact, the debate came earlier than expected. Silverman succeeded at the end of the exchanges in getting the Speaker's approval, and the required support of forty members to obtain an emergency debate under Standing Order 8 at 7 p.m. that evening. Opening the debate,[35] he succeeded in clarifying and defining the basic issues before the House, as did Clement Attlee in his reply. For Silverman the events of the weekend were

> plain naked war upon the Jewish national home, war of the White Paper of 1939 condemned by the Right Hon. Gentleman, by this party, by members sitting on the Front Bench now and by the Leader of the Opposition [Attlee] at the time.

Referring to the Prime Minister's reference to Haganah's deploying a strength of some 70,000 to 80,000, he pointed out that the total Jewish population, male and female, old and young, was 600,000.

Can it be denied that the attempt by the Administration by naked force to disarm 80,000 people out of a population of that kind means nothing else than war, war on every city in Palestine, war in every settlement?

Britain held the Mandate; yet there was no consultation of any of the other Powers involved. 'The mandatory Power and the Agency are co-trustees' – there was no consultation with the US, whom Britain were pressing to join in sharing the responsibility.

Not one thing could His Majesty's Government find to do alone, except this one thing – attacking the Jewish Agency and putting it out of action.

His strongest point was:

I listened in vain in that statement for any accusation that the Jewish Agency, or any member of its Executive was responsible, directly or indirectly, for any act of terror.

Again,

It is said that the Jewish Agency failed to co-operate. Co-operate in what? What was its duty? It was to co-operate with the mandatory Power in facilitating immigration and building up the Jewish national home. The mandatory Power, the British Government, stopped doing that in 1938. What was there to co-operate with? To co-operate with the Administration in implementing the White Paper, to co-operate in keeping refugee Jews out of Palestine, to co-operate with destroyers in firing upon wretched little ships, overcrowded almost to sinking point with people who had escaped with their lives . . .

Dick Crossman, seconding the motion,[36] picked up the point about the Haganah, 'a private army' – saying that although that phrase had occurred in the Anglo-American report which he had signed, Haganah was in fact 'a very large scale conscript organization, both male and female'. To say that it was a private army 'is as far fetched as the Haganah view that they could challenge us to war without the risk of war'.

When, therefore, the Prime Minister speaks of the necessity of restoring law and order, it is important to remember that what he really means is the restoration of the authority of the police, the restoration of the authority of a state hated both by Jew and Arab . . .

I must say frankly to the House that what we are trying to impose on the Jewish community is a reimposition of the White Paper, something which no Jew in Palestine accepts as either law or order. No Jew anywhere, least of all Dr Weizmann or the Haganah, can be won over to support the Government by the arrest of thousands of their brothers.

Constructively he advised the Government to

call on the Jewish Agency in return for our acceptance of what we all believe anyway, to join once again in the suppression of the Irgun Tzvai Leumi and the Stern Gang. Let them go further. Let them call on the Jewish Agency to do what it can do, namely to tell the Haganah to come out and become what it once was, the territorial force of the Jews in Palestine, co-operating actively with the British Government. That would not be refused. None of those things would be refused, but I must remind the House that no request for Jewish co-operation has been made since the publication of the Anglo-American report.

The debate went on for the full three hours allowed. Winding up, the Prime Minister[37] began by repudiating Silverman's idea that 'we were in Palestine as partners with the Jewish Agency for the creation of a Jewish state'.

That is not so. The Jewish Agency has a position to co-operate on the economic and social side with the Government, but the Government of Palestine is the Government of the mandatory Power.

Attlee understandably based himself on the intolerable and murderous attacks by the terrorists on the security forces, including the murders of soldiers and police, the destruction of bridges and the disruption of the railways. He referred to what he regarded as 'a very close tie-up between the Jewish Agency and the Haganah and the Irgun', and indicated that he would table a report to support the Government's allegations:

We want to keep the Jewish Agency doing magnificent work, but the Jewish Agency cannot be a cover for running an illegal army in illegal actions.

He did not distinguish between the Haganah and the Irgun, as he had evidence of co-operation between them, and 'the Haganah acts under the general direction of members of the Jewish Agency, I am not saying all the members but certainly some members of the Executive of the Jewish Agency'. He denied a suggestion in an intervention by Silverman that his view was that no solution arising out of the Anglo-American report or otherwise, even if agreed with the United States, would be applied, unless the Arab community concurred:

I said nothing of the sort. What I said was that you have to examine this very fully because it is not our policy to enforce a policy on Palestine at the point of a bayonet, whether that policy is dictated by one side or the other in favour of one side or the other. . . . In this matter we are trying to deal fairly with the Jews and with the Arabs in Palestine. It is really no good suggesting that we have not an obligation to Arabs as well as Jews. That is our Mandate.

What must have worried Attlee was the cool reaction of Truman to the developments in Palestine and to the British Government's political strategy. This is clear from Truman's memoirs,[38] as the account of one month succeeds another. He records the atrocities committed by Jewish terrorists: on 16 June they destroyed bridges near the Transjordan frontier; there were the Haifa explosions, 'the pitched battle between British troops and Jews in Haifa, the kidnapping of British officers, and the discovery of an extremist plot to kidnap the British Commander-in-Chief'.[39] He rightly felt that

> my efforts to persuade the British to relax immigration restrictions in Palestine might have fallen on more receptive ears if it had not been for the increasing acts of terrorism that were being committed in Palestine.

Attlee had informed Truman on 28 June of the plans to occupy the Jewish Agency headquarters, to search the Histadrut and other offices, and to arrest known militants. He replied on 2 July:

> Replying to your message of 28 June, I join with you in regretting that drastic action is considered necessary by the Mandatory Government while discussions of the reports of the Anglo-American Committee are in progress. I also join with you in a hope that law and order will be maintained by the inhabitants of Palestine while efforts are being made toward a solution of the long-term policy.

This was much more an expression of sympathy than an endorsement of British policies.

But further, and worse, atrocities lay ahead.

CHAPTER 6

Bevin Moves the Reference Back

AT THE CABINET MEETING on Thursday 4 July, the Prime Minister reported that British and United States officials had completed their consultations on the second recommendation of the Anglo-American report (the American proposal to allow 100,000 immigrants to be allowed to enter Israel without delay), but despite pressing Truman to expedite matters, the main party of US officials due to discuss the implications of the report was not due to arrive until 15 July. He asked the Cabinet to decide what could be said on behalf of the Government in the debate which it had been agreed should take place before the Summer Recess early in August.

> If no agreement had been reached with the US by that time it might become necessary [he said] for His Majesty's Government to indicate that they were prepared to adopt a specific given line in Palestine if they were assured of the support and co-operation of the United States Government. The Cabinet should consider this during the following week on the basis of memoranda to be submitted to Cabinet by the Secretary of State for the Colonies. These should summarize the recommendations of the Anglo-American Committee on Palestine and the difficulties which the responsible departments of His Majesty's Government saw in giving effect to those recommendations, and should outline alternative policies which might be adopted.

The Cabinet should also receive a further report on the military situation. A suggestion was made that a delegation of Members of Parliament should go to Palestine; this was turned down, as was a proposal for a similar mission to South Africa on the question of South African Jews.

The following Monday 8 July, Cabinet met again. The Prime Minister informed the Cabinet that it had been suggested by the United States Secretary of State that, with a view to easing the forthcoming discussions in Congress on the United Kingdom loan, it would be well if some reassuring statement could be issued on Palestine. The Cabinet, the conclusions record, felt that it would be a mistake to issue any statement which might appear to have been made for this purpose. They also thought it unlikely that any general statement which could be made at this stage on the issues dealt with in the report of the Anglo-American Committee would have the desired effect on opinion in the United States. These objections would not, however, apply to the release of news about the progress of the current operations in Palestine. And it would be convenient if the High Commissioner for Palestine was now able to announce that these operations were virtually concluded, that the Jewish Agency's buildings were being handed back and that a substantial number of those detained had been released. It was 'unlikely', however, that this announcement could include further evidence of the connection between the Jewish Agency and Haganah; the examination might not be completed for some little time; also it might compromise sources.

It was at this meeting that the Cabinet accepted Mr Pickthorn's suggestion in the previous debate that it would be advisable in future statements on Palestine to use the word 'Zionist' rather than 'Jew' or 'Jewish' wherever possible, as there were many Jews both in the United Kingdom and the United States who were not in sympathy with Zionist policy.

Three days later (11 July) the Cabinet assembled for a set-piece discussion on Palestine problems. After the first two routine subjects, items 3 and 4 on the Agenda were 'The Present Situation and Illegal Immigration' and 'Report of Anglo-American Discussions'. The Secretary of State for the Colonies reported on the current security situation, the return of the Jewish Agency buildings, and the numbers detained who were still in custody. Meanwhile, it was reported, for the moment the influence of Dr Weizmann and the moderates was increasing. Dr Weizmann had told the Chief Secretary on 7 July that he had held a meeting with leading members of the Jewish community and had impressed on them the need for preventing any more terrorist activities. The Chief Secretary had made it clear that the basis of any negotiations with the Government must be a guarantee by the Jewish Agency that the illegal activities of the Haganah and the Palmach would cease, and that the Palmach would be disbanded. The decision to bring the Haganah under government supervision and control would be made effective. Dr Weizmann, it was reported, was leaving for England on 16 July; Rabbi Wise and Mr Lipsky also had visas. Ben-Gurion, who represented the more extreme element, was still in Paris: there was clear evidence, the Secretary of State said, that he had been associated with illegal activists.

The Minister of State said that it had been reported in the American press that there was to be a meeting of Jewish Agency representatives in Paris. The record continues:

> Discussion showed that it was the general view of the Cabinet that everything possible should be done at this stage to strengthen the hands of Dr Weizmann and his associates. For this purpose it might be advisable to hold discussions

with him and other Jewish leaders when he arrived in this country, though it should be made clear that these discussions would be confined to the immediate situation resulting from recent operations in Palestine and would not extend to the issues raised by the report of the Anglo-American Committee, on which there should be simultaneous discussions with Jews and Arabs after the discussions with the United States representatives had been completed.

The Chancellor reported that according to the latest reports from Washington, the prospects of Congress approving the United Kingdom Loan were now more favourable. It was agreed that it would be a mistake for His Majesty's Government to issue any further public statement on Palestine until the debate on the loan was completed. The Secretary of State for the Colonies reported on the arrival of further illegal immigrants.

The Cabinet turned to Item (4), a paper by the Colonial Secretary summarizing the difficulties which would arise in giving effect to the recommendations of the Anglo-American Committee, and one by the Chiefs of Staff on the military implications. A further paper by the Colonial Secretary summarized various statements by President Truman on the proposal to admit 100,000 Jewish immigrants. His third paper proposed that the future constitution of Palestine should be such that one race would be unable to dominate the other, but no proposals were put forward to this end, except continuing the Mandate.

The Foreign Secretary was not at the meeting, being in attendance at the Paris Peace Conference; Sir Norman Brook, the Secretary of the Cabinet, had been sent over to get his views on the papers before the meeting. He reported that the Foreign Secretary was anxious to avoid being put in a position in which he would have to oppose the recommendations for the admission of 100,000 Jewish immigrants into Palestine. He proposed to inform the American Secretary of State, Mr Byrnes, that he would not oppose this recommendation, so long as there was proper consultation with representatives of the Jews and the Arabs. What he had in mind was that there should be a conference in London, preferably in the early part of September, before the meeting of the General Assembly of the UN, at which British and American representatives could discuss with representatives of both Jews and Arabs all the issues raised by the report of the Anglo-American Committee. He proposed, however, to tell Byrnes that Arab opposition to this particular recommendation about Jewish immigration would be substantially reduced if an early announcement could be made that a substantial number of Jewish immigrants from Europe would be admitted to the US, even though this would mean increasing the current quota. He intended to press strongly for an early concession on these lines from the US Government.

He favoured the Colonial Office Paper, CP (46) 259, and said it should be explored in the forthcoming discussion with American officials. He doubted, though, whether a scheme of provincial autonomy which this would mean would provide a lasting solution of the Palestine problem, and suggested therefore that the Foreign and Colonial Offices should consider, with the Chiefs of Staff, whether it would be practicable to adopt, as our long-term aim, a scheme under which the major part of the Arab province would be assimilated in the adjacent Arab states of Transjordan and the Lebanon, and the Jewish province established as an independent Jewish state, with perhaps a somewhat larger territory than that suggested by the Colonial Office. He hoped that any intermediate solution on the lines proposed in the Colonial Office would contain nothing which was inconsistent with this long-term aim.

For Jerusalem, Bevin suggested a special Council, representing all interested religions, to control the Holy Places there, and this should be incorporated on the understanding that the administration of the City would remain a responsibility of the mandatory Power. If his long-term proposals were realized, he would hope that Jerusalem would become an international area under the United Nations, the control of the Holy Places remaining in the hands of the special Religious Council.

On Anglo-American collaboration on Palestine, the Foreign Secretary felt that the US Government should certainly be pressed to promise Britain full political support in announcing a new policy for Palestine, in negotiating this with representatives of the Arabs and the Jews, and in defending it, if necessary, to the United Nations. He did not, however, contemplate continuing American participation in the administration of Palestine. The American Government should also be asked for financial assistance, not only in the settlement of Jewish immigrants, but also in whatever measures were agreed to be necessary for raising the standard of living of the Arabs in Palestine. As regards military assistance, we should make it clear that if it became necessary to impose a solution by force, we were neither willing nor able to do this alone and should have to ask for active American assistance. This should be used as an argument to persuade the United States Government to join with us in seeking a solution which would not have to be imposed by force and in making every effort to get such a policy agreed with the Arabs and the Jews before it was put into effect.

In the Cabinet's discussion, the Minutes record, 'there was general agreement that the recommendation in the report of the Anglo-American Committee offered no practical prospect of progress towards a solution of the constitutional problem in Palestine, and discussion turned on the alternative policy put in CP (46) 259'. The view was expressed, the record goes on, that if the Cabinet were disposed to agree that the ultimate solution was to be found in *partition* [author's italics], it would be advantageous if the suggestions thrown out by the Foreign Secretary for a long-term plan were put forward at once in the forthcoming discussions as a solution of the immediate problem. If a separate Jewish state were created now, the Jews could be left to fix the limit for immigration and to bear the whole cost of settling the immigrants. Our own strategic needs in this area might be secured through Treaty arrangements with the Arab states, which, under the Foreign Secretary's proposals, would be taking over the Arab parts of Palestine. We could then look forward to early release from the political and financial commitments involved in our obligations under the Mandate. Against this, it was pointed out that proposals for the immediate partition of Palestine would encounter strong opposition. The Anglo-American Committee had themselves felt unable to recommend partition as the solution.* If independent sovereign states were to be created, long and difficult negotiations would have to be undertaken over frontiers, customs barriers and the rest, all of which were avoided by the intermediate scheme proposed in CP (46) 259. The 'intermediate scheme', it was argued, had the great advantage that it separated sovereignty from cultural autonomy. It would also afford a valuable period of actual experience of separate administration during which means of surmounting some of the practical problems of partition could be devised. The Cabinet decided not to put forward proposals for partition because of possible military implications.

On the tactics of the talks with the American officials it was agreed that it was 'inexpedient for the delegates to confine themselves to destructive criticism', as had been recommended in the Cabinet Paper analysing the Anglo-American Committee proposals. For tactical reasons the Anglo-American report should not be overthrown at once, but *used* [author's italics] while seeking the right moment to bring forward the scheme as set out in CP (46) 259 – 'the weaknesses of the Anglo-American report having been exposed'. The process of argument should begin with the problem of the Jews at present in Europe. 'Arab opposition to the admission of 100,000 Jewish immigrants into Palestine would be substantially strengthened if this movement began before there was any indication that other countries outside Europe would make their contribution towards the solution of their problem.' Fiorello La Guardia had just announced on behalf of UNRRA his intention that 120,000 Jews should be admitted to the United States, all unused immigration quotas being made available for that purpose. This would reinforce the suggestion which the Foreign Secretary was proposing to make to Secretary Byrnes: the

---

* But see Crossman's account (p. 144 above) of his decision not to press the idea of partition to which he had been converted because of his keenness not to destroy the unanimity of the Commission or its other recommendations.

British delegation might ask whether the US Government would be willing to make an early announcement of their attitude to these proposals. It was important, however, to maintain the principle that the settlement of Jewish and other displaced persons from Europe was an international, not an Anglo-American, responsibility; likewise that remedial action should be taken through the machinery of the United Nations. It might be some time before the UN established an effective organization for handling the refugee problem as a whole. Any appeal to governments to make an interim contribution by receiving a proportion of these displaced persons in territories under their control should be made by the UN, not by the Governments of Britain and America.

The Cabinet approved the Colonial Office proposal CP (46) 259 subject to any modifications necessary to meet the Foreign Secretary's views on the Council for the Holy Places in Jerusalem. Subject to any comments received from the Chiefs of Staff, Cabinet authorized the British delegation to the forthcoming Anglo-US talks to put the proposals forward at an appropriate stage during the discussions with the American officials.

The day after the Cabinet meeting, 12 July, President Truman's emissary, Ambassador Henry F. Grady, came to London with the American team to join in discussions with the British officials. Truman was anything but keen on these talks. He regarded them as part of London's desire to play out time, and was well aware that both sides of Downing Street, No. 10 and the Foreign Office, were hoping to secure American financial participation, and if possible military assistance. Truman had no intention of agreeing to either. He wanted speed and 100,000 Jews moving into Israel. What he was seeing was the Royal Navy under strict orders to intercept, deflect and, if necessary, board any immigrant ship bound for Israel. Morrison took over the talks from the British side, and by late July was able to report a provisional agreement, *ad referendum* to Washington and London. Truman had appointed a top level group: in London the report was to go to Cabinet.

Presenting the report to Cabinet on 22 July, Morrison was able to record good progress. He needed, however, Cabinet guidance on a question which had come up at the meeting on 11 July. On that occasion the proposal for provincial autonomy in a unitary Palestine had been minuted 'subject to the comments of the Chiefs of Staff'. When so consulted, the three Chiefs, Lord Montgomery, Chief of the General Staff, Marshal of the Royal Air Force Lord Tedder, and Admiral Sir John Cunningham, First Sea Lord and Chief of Naval Staff, had expressed their anxieties:

No solution of the Palestine problem should be proposed which would alienate the Arab states, and . . . it was doubtful whether the scheme in CP (46) 259 satisfied that condition.

It was reported that the British delegation at the joint talks had therefore put forward 'tentative suggestions' for modifying the originally proposed provincial boundaries with a view to making the scheme more acceptable to the Arabs. The US delegation had made counter-suggestions for expanding the Jewish province; and, after discussion, the issue had been narrowed down to the delineation of the southern boundary below Jaffa. The Chiefs of Staff commented fully, in particular pressing that of the three schemes to which, during the discussions, the original proposals had been narrowed down, they would prefer the one in which a viable airport would be 'transferred to' Arab, not Jewish, territory. The Cabinet agreed that the objective was to find proposals for putting to the US, the Arabs and the Jews, with the proviso that changes might have to be made as a result of the consultation with the two sides to the dispute.

The Foreign Secretary raised the question of the proposed conferences with the Arabs and the Jews, which he suggested should take place towards the end of August. Should the United States be invited to take part? There were indications, he said, that they would not wish to be one of the main parties to the consultations, but would prefer that the United Kingdom Government as Mandatory should alone negotiate a scheme previously agreed with them. They might be willing to send observers to the conferences. Cabinet authorized Bevin to proceed on those lines. Approval was given also to a White Paper to be presented on the complicity of the Jewish Agency in terrorist outrages. That very day, the catalogue of outrages was aggravated by the events at the King David Hotel.

The King David Hotel was the headquarters of the occupying British forces and secretariat. The Irgun, with Haganah, decided to strike in retaliation for the occupation of Zionist premises and the arrests of Black Saturday. The operation was under the general direction of Menachem Begin, with Amihai Paglin as his Chief of Operations. At 11 a.m. on 22 July, milk churns containing explosives were taken into the hotel through the service entrance and timing devices attached. A security officer was shot dead. A warning by one of the conspirators was telephoned through to the hotel to warn all personnel to evacuate. Soon after noon the hotel went up as the mines went off; ninety-one people were killed, including twenty-eight British servicemen and civilians. Begin claimed to have inflicted even more casualties than the figures quoted. General Barker's anger and grief caused him to make one comment, later much publicized, about a boycott of, indeed closure of, Jewish shops and businesses, in order 'to hit the Jews in their pockets'; clearly the most vulnerable target so far as they were concerned. He also forbade any social contacts between soldiers and Jews. When, following a court-martial, three Jewish terrorists were hanged, there was a savage retaliation. Two British sergeants were hanged and booby-trap bombs attached to their bodies. When they were cut down the bombs went off, killing a Captain of the Royal Engineers.

The 22 July Cabinet had approved the line to be taken in the two-day Commons debate on 31 July and 1 August, as agreed between the Anglo-American experts. Attlee and Bevin had to be in Paris, so Morrison and Cripps were to be the main speakers for the Government. Morrison rose to present the new plan for provincial autonomy in a unitary State of Palestine, despite the fact that it had not been approved by the White House. News of its terms had been spread around quite widely, almost certainly by the Americans, and had been rejected by Weizmann as being worse than the old 1937 scheme. What the Lord President had to put forward was a contraption rather than a constitution, a municipal scheme for Palestine he would have scorned when he was Leader of the London County Council in his great days.

He naturally began his speech[1] with a strong reference to the outrages in the King David Hotel, and an account of the actions taken to pursue the perpetrators in Tel Aviv, where, he said, 'some, if not all, of the persons responsible for the Jerusalem crime came from'. At the same time he dissociated himself and the Government from the provocative statement made earlier by General Barker, the GOC. He then went on to refer to the unanimous recommendations of the joint meeting of American-British experts. The Committee recognized that Palestine alone could not meet the immigration needs of the Jewish victims of Nazi and Fascist persecution. So the first aim would be to resettle as many as possible in Europe, though this could deal only with part of the problem. The second recommendation was for the establishment of an International Refugee Organization. At the forthcoming General Assembly of the United Nations an appeal would be made to all member governments to receive displaced persons. Britain had accepted a commitment to resettle 235,000 Polish troops, civilians and their dependents, in addition to the refugees accepted during the period of Nazi persecution, of whom 70,000 Jews were still in Britain. He then turned to the recommendations for the future of Palestine. They accepted the recommendation of the Anglo-American Parliamentary Committee that Palestine should be neither a Jewish nor an Arab state. This was not to be challenged, but as the conflict between the irreconcilable aspirations of the two communities in Palestine was too bitter to secure that massive co-operation between Arab and Jew which would make possible a unitary system of government,

> the only chance of peace, and of immediate advance towards self-governing institutions, appears to lie in so framing the constitution of the country as to give to each the greatest practicable measure of power to manage its own affairs. The experts believe that, in present circumstances, this can best be

secured by the establishment of Arab and Jewish Provinces, which will enjoy a large measure of autonomy under a central Government.

He outlined the scheme:

for this purpose Palestine shall be divided into four areas, an Arab Province, a Jewish Province, a District of Jerusalem, and a District of Negev. The Jewish Province would include the great bulk of the land on which Jews have already settled and a considerable area between and around the settlements. The Jerusalem District would include Jerusalem, Bethlehem and their immediate environs. The Negev District would consist of the uninhabited triangle of waste land in the South of Palestine beyond the present limits of cultivation. The Arab Province would include the remainder of Palestine; it would be almost wholly Arab in respect both of land and of population. The provincial boundaries would be purely administrative boundaries, defining the area within which a local legislature would be empowered to legislate on certain subjects and a local executive to administer laws. They would have no significance as regards defence, Customs and communications, but, in order to give finality, boundaries, once fixed, would not be susceptible of change except by agreement between the two Provinces. A provision to this effect would be embodied in any trusteeship agreement, and in the instrument bringing the plan into operation.

The provincial governments would have power of legislation and administration within their areas with regard to a wide range of subjects of primarily provincial concern. They would also have power to limit the number and determine the qualifications of persons who may take up permanent residence in their territories after the introduction of the plan. The provincial governments would be required by the instrument of government which establishes the fundamental law to provide for the guarantee of civil rights and equality before the law of all residents, and for the freedom of inter-territorial transit, trade and commerce. The provincial governments would have the necessary power to raise money for the purpose of carrying out their functions.

There would be reserved to the Central Government exclusive authority as to defence, foreign relations, Customs and Excise. In addition, there would be reserved initially to the Central Government exclusive authority as to the administration of law and order, including the police and courts, and a limited number of subjects of all-Palestine importance. The Central Government would have all powers not expressly granted to the provinces by the instrument of Government. An elected Legislative Chamber would be established in each Province. An executive, consisting of a chief Minister and a Council of Ministers, would be appointed in each Province by the High Commissioner from among the members of the Legislative Chamber after consultation with its leaders. Bills passed by the Legislative Chambers would require the assent of the High Commissioner. This, however, would not be withheld unless the Bill is inconsistent with the instrument of Government, whose provisions would afford safeguards for the peace of Palestine and for the rights of minorities.

It would also be necessary to reserve to the High Commissioner an emergency power to intervene if a provincial government fails to perform, or exceeds, its proper functions. The executive and the legislative functions of the Central Government would initially be exercised by the High Commissioner, assisted by a nominated Executive Council. Certain of the departments of the Central Government would be headed, as soon as the High Commissioner deems practical, by Palestinians. The High Commissioner would establish a Development Planning Board and a Tariff Board composed of representatives of the Central Government and of each province. In the Jerusalem District, a council would be established with powers similar to those of a municipal council. The majority of its members would be elected, but certain members would be nominated by the High Commissioner. The Negev District would be administered, for the time being, by the Central Government.[2]

The Lord President went on to say what such a plan for provincial autonomy could mean for immigration. Clearly the American delegation had been willing to go along with HMG's views about the constitution in return for a move on immigration, and the Government were willing to make a concession on the hundred thousand *in return for the Americans not pressing the Balfour concept of a Jewish national home in Palestine* [author's italics]. While final control over the pace of immigration would continue to rest with the Central Government, that is for the time being with the High Commissioner, his decision would be based on recommendations by the provincial governments, so long as 'the economic absorptive capacity of the province was not exceeded'.

So Morrison was able to announce that 'the experts' had agreed to suggest acceptance of the Anglo-American Committee's recommendation for the immediate admission of 100,000 Jewish immigrants into Palestine. They had prepared a plan for the movement of the hundred thousand from Europe 'into the Jewish area of Palestine', and this plan could be set in motion as soon as the decision had been taken to put the scheme into effect. Priority would be given to building craftsmen and agricultural workers, young children, the infirm and the aged, from Germany, Austria and Italy; and only orphan children from Eastern and South-Eastern Europe. The United States were to bear the full cost of shipment and food supplies to last two months after arrival. The situation in Palestine, Morrison said, 'will brook no delay', thus qualifying for, though not receiving, Ernest Bevin's favourite comment 'clitch after clitch after clitch'. After the delaying mechanisms such as the Anglo-American Committee and the forty-three proposals, this was indeed progress. Morrison summarized the consequences of the Agreement.[3]

The Jews will be free to exercise a large measure of control over immigration into their own Province, and to forward there the development of the Jewish

National Home. The Land Transfer Regulations will be repealed. It will be open to the Government of the Arab Province to permit or to refuse permission to Jews to purchase land there, but the area of the Jewish Province will be larger than that in which Jews are free to buy land at present. The Arabs will gain, in that the great majority of them will be freed once and for all from any fear of Jewish domination. The citizens of the Arab Province will achieve at once a large measure of autonomy, and powerful safeguards will be provided to protect the rights of the Arab minority left in the Jewish Province. To both communities the plan offers a prospect of development, of which there would be little hope in a unitary Palestine.

In the long term, the plan leaves the way open for peaceful progress and constitutional development either towards partition, or towards federal unity. The association of representatives of the two Provinces in the administration of central subjects, may lead ultimately to a fully developed federal constitution. On the other hand, if the centrifugal forces prove too strong, the way is open towards partition. Our proposals do not prejudge this issue either way. We believe that this plan provides as fair and reasonable a compromise between the claims of Arab and Jew as it is possible to devise, and that it offers the best prospect of reconciling the conflicting interests of the two communities. This, however, must be made clear. The full implementation of the experts' plan as a whole depends on United States co-operation. I hope that that will be forthcoming. If not, we shall have to reconsider the position, particularly as regards the economic and financial implications, and this is bound to affect the tempo and extent of immigration and development.

That Truman, whose patience was exhausted after a year of delays, did not ratify the Agreement, provides good reason for not summarizing the rest of the two-day debate. The Conservative spokesman, Oliver Stanley, rebuked the Government for the long delay in holding the debate, not least since leakages meant that the press were free to comment where MPs were not, and proceeded to devote the greater part of his speech, understandably, to the security situation and the problems the troops were facing. But Stanley went some way to confirm others' suspicions of deliberate dilatory tactics by saying that the solution announced by Morrison had been in the Colonial Office the previous September, ten months ago:

We could have got as far as we are today last November; and the policy, which we can only hope now will be implemented in the next two or three months, might have been in force at the end of the year. Instead of that, everything has been at a standstill for a Report of a Committee, which, as soon as it is received, is abandoned.[4]

The debate was primarily important for the speech of Winston Churchill, who followed Cripps's opening speech the following day. He had been challenged the previous day by the Liberal leader, Clement Davies, for having voted with his party for the restriction on immigration in 1939. Bringing a bulky volume of *Hansard* into the House, Churchill was able to show that he had indeed voted against the Conservative Government of the day on that issue. He spoke with clarity, consistency and a deep sense of history:[5]

> The position which I, personally, have adopted and maintained dates from 1919 and 1921, when as Dominions and Colonial Secretary, it fell to me to define, with the approval of the then Cabinet and Parliament, the interpretation that was placed upon our obligations to the Zionists under the Mandate for Palestine entrusted to us by the League of Nations. This was the declaration of 1922, which I personally drafted for the approval of the authorities of the day. Palestine was not to be a Jewish National Home, but there was to be set up a Jewish National Home in Palestine. Jewish immigration would be allowed up to the limit of the economic absorptive capacity – that was the phrase which I coined in those days and which seems to remain convenient – the Mandatory Power being, it was presumed, the final judge of what that capacity was. During the greater part of a quarter of a century which has passed, this policy was carefully carried out by us. The Jewish population multiplied, from about 80,000 to nearly 600,000. Tel Aviv expanded into the great city it is, a city which, I may say, during this war and before it, welcomed and nourished waifs and orphans flying from Nazi persecution. Many refugees found a shelter and a sanctuary there, so that this land, not largely productive of the means of life, became a fountain of charity and hospitality to people in great distress. Land reclamation and cultivation and great electrical enterprises progressed. Trade made notable progress, and not only did the Jewish population increase but the Arab population, dwelling in the areas colonized and enriched by the Jews, also increased in almost equal numbers. The Jews multiplied six-fold and the Arabs developed 500,000, thus showing that both races gained a marked advantage from the Zionist policy which we pursued and which we were developing over this period.

He took up Stafford Cripps's description of the previous twenty-five years as being the most unhappy Palestine had known:

> I imagine that it would hardly be possible to state the opposite of the truth more compendiously. The years during which we have accepted the Mandate have been the brightest that Palestine has known and were full of hope. Of course, there was always friction, because the Jew was in many cases allowed to go far beyond the strict limits of the interpretation which was placed upon the Mandate. Disturbances occurred in 1937 and in 1938; in 1939 Mr Chamberlain's Government produced the White Paper, which limited immigration other than on the ground of the economic absorptive capacity of the country. That, after a five-year interval, would have brought immigration to an end, except by agreement with the Arab majority, which would certainly not have been obtained. This was, in my view, a failure to fulfil the obligations we had accepted[6] ... but there is no dispute on the matter – this Labour Party, some of whom we see here today, gained a large majority in the House of Commons. During the Election they made most strenuous pro-Zionist

speeches and declarations. Many of their most important leaders were known to be ardent supporters of the Zionist cause, and their success was, naturally, regarded by the Jewish community in Palestine as a prelude to the fulfilment of the pledges which had been made to them, and indeed opening the way to further ambitions. This was certainly the least which everybody expected.

In fact, all sorts of hopes were raised among the Jews of Palestine, just as other hopes were raised elsewhere. However, when the months slipped by and no decided policy or declaration was made by the present Government, a deep and bitter resentment spread throughout the Palestine Jewish community, and violent protests were made by the Zionist supporters in the United States.

Had I had the opportunity of guiding the course of events after the war was won a year ago, I should have faithfully pursued the Zionist cause as I have defined it; and I have not abandoned it today. . . . I am against preventing Jews from doing anything which other people are allowed to do. I am against that and I have the strongest abhorrence of the idea of anti-semitic lines of prejudice. Secondly, I have for some years past – this is really the crux of the argument I am venturing to submit to the House – felt that an unfair burden was being thrown upon Great Britain by our having to bear the whole weight of the Zionist policy, while Arabs and Moslems – or Muslims, as they are called by a certain school of political thought – then so important to our Empire, were alarmed and estranged, and while the United States, for the Government and people of which I have the greatest regard and friendship, and other countries, sat on the sidelines and criticized our shortcomings with all the freedom of perfect detachment and irresponsibility. Therefore, I had always intended to put it to our friends in America, from the very beginning of the post-war discussions, that either they should come in and help us in this Zionist problem, about which they feel so strongly, and as I think rightly, on even terms, share and share alike, or that we should resign our Mandate, as we have, of course, a perfect right to do.

Indeed, I am convinced that from the moment when we feel ourselves unable to carry out properly and honestly the Zionist policy as we have all these years defined it and accepted it, and which is the condition on which we received the Mandate for Palestine, it is our duty at any rate to offer to lay down the Mandate. We should therefore, as soon as the war stopped, have made it clear to the United States that, unless they came in and bore their share, we would lay the whole care and burden at the feet of the United Nations organization; and we should have fixed a date by which all our troops and forces would be withdrawn from the country.[7]

But even before Churchill spoke the situation had been changed by a statement issued by the White House on 31 July:

The President has been considering certain recommendations of the alternates of the Cabinet committee with regard to Palestine, and has decided in view of the complexity of the matter to discuss the whole matter with them in detail. The President hopes that further discussion will result in decisions which will alleviate the situation of the persecuted Jews and at the same time contribute to the ultimate solution of the longer-term problem of Palestine.

The press had interpreted Truman's statement as indicating that he was likely to turn down the joint Committee's report. Churchill referred to the press stories:

> It was with very great regret that I read this morning of the non-agreement of the United States, and the Right Hon. and learned Gentleman who has just sat down, quite bluntly and bleakly told us that there was no agreement at the present time. I hope it is not the final word. This agreement was the one great goal to which we were invited to aspire; here was the one excuse the Government could put forward for the long delays and indecisions which have involved us in so much cost and serious bloodshed. If this Anglo-American co-operation fails, as it seems so far to have failed, then I must say that the record of the Administration during this year – and a Government must be judged by results – in the handling of Palestinian affairs will stand forth as a monument of incapacity.[8]

He came to his final words:

> Here is the action – action this day. I think the Government should say that if the United States will not come and share the burden of the Zionist cause, as defined or as agreed, we should now give notice that we will return our Mandate to UNO and that we will evacuate Palestine within a specified period. At the same time, we should inform Egypt that we stand by our treaty rights and will, by all means, maintain our position in the Canal Zone. Those are the two positive proposals which I submit, most respectfully to the House. In so far as the Government may have hampered themselves in any way from adopting these simple policies, they are culpable to the last degree, and the whole Empire and the Commonwealth will be the sufferers from their mismanagement.[9]

Once Truman had vetoed the experts' report – itself scant reward for a year's travail – it can only have been stubbornness on Bevin's part, with Attlee's backing, which caused him to get involved in a go-it-alone policy. Churchill had given the right advice – perhaps that rankled, too. But since in that very week Bevin's main assumption – Anglo-American co-operation – had been kicked from under him, there would have been little loss of face had Attlee and Bevin either surrendered the Mandate, or at least done what they had to do six months later, and seek the advice of the United Nations on how the Mandate should be operated. Even in an inflationary world, there is nothing so costly as a statesman's face, nor is there any known investment which carries a higher rate of interest to maintain it.

After the debate, a further meeting of the Cabinet was held on 7 August. The Colonial Secretary reported on a long talk he had had with Weizmann, who was seriously ill and due to go into hospital. Weizmann, he said, had not been unfavourable to the Government's proposals for future policy on Palestine. But he had made three points: (i) on the 'enclave proposal', the

Jewish province should not be smaller than the territory which had been proposed for the Jewish state as a consequence of the Peel Commission; (ii) the period of central (British) rule should not continue for more than three or at most five years; and (iii) the Negev should be handed over at once to the Jews who would, he was confident, be able to develop it. Most of the rest of the Cabinet's discussion related to illegal immigration, security and the Government's plan to evacuate 'non-essential personnel, especially women and children'. Plans for a clamp-down on immigration were discussed:

> an important factor in considering the timing of the action would be the probable effect on opinion in the United States. There was still a chance that President Truman might accept the plan for the future of Palestine prepared by the British and American experts. But news of the [security] action now proposed would inevitably strengthen the forces working against acceptance.

On 14 August, a brief discussion took place in Cabinet on the control of the would-be immigrants who had been taken to Cyprus.

Cabinet next had Palestine before it, again briefly, on 10 October. In a short discussion on the proposed Palestine conference, a report was made on talks with the delegations of the Arab states (not Palestinian Arabs) and a summary of informal conversations with representatives of the Jewish Agency designed to bring Jewish delegates to the conference.

Parliament had resumed on 8 October. On the first day of a two-day debate on Foreign Affairs on 21 October, Ernest Bevin spoke on foreign affairs, but made no reference to Palestine. For the hope that President Truman would accept the plan worked out by the officials had been formally laid to rest by a telegram he sent to Attlee on 12 September. The President saw no hope in the plan; what particularly irked him was that the admission of the 100,000 was

> conditional on its being accepted by the Arabs, so no relief was offered in that direction either . . . it seemed a retreat from the fine recommendation that had been made by the Anglo-American Committee of Enquiry earlier in the year. I therefore felt compelled to inform Attlee that the Government of the United States could not go along.[10]

The telegram was blunt:

> After further study of recommendation of American and British groups . . . and after detailed discussion in which members of my Cabinet and other advisers participated, I have reluctantly come to the conclusion that I cannot give formal support to the plan in its present form as a joint Anglo-American plan.
>
> The opposition in this country to the plan has become so intense that it is now clear it would be impossible to rally in favor of it sufficient public opinion to enable this Government to give it effective support.

In view of the critical situation in Palestine and of the desperate plight of homeless Jews in Europe I believe the search for a solution to this difficult problem should continue. I have therefore instructed our Embassy in London to discuss with you or with appropriate members of the British Government certain suggestions which have been made to us and which, I understand, are also being made to you.

Should it be possible to broaden the coming conference sufficiently to consider these suggestions, it is my earnest hope that the conference may make possible a decision by your government upon a course for which we can obtain necessary support in this country and in the Congress so we can give effective financial help and moral support.

Meanwhile he told the American Ambassador in London to press Whitehall to accept an alternative plan prepared by the Jewish Agency. This ended the hopes Attlee had nurtured that there would be a change of heart in Washington. On 18 September he telegraphed the President:

It is, of course, a great disappointment to us that you should feel yourself unable to give support to the plan recommended by the Anglo-American Expert Delegations. The discussion of the summary of this plan which we recently presented to Parliament will form the first item on the agenda at the coming conference. We earnestly hope that, as a result of the conference, some solution will emerge which, even if not fully accepted by either Arabs or Jews, may be possible of implementation without too gravely endangering the peace of Palestine or of the Middle East as a whole. But you will appreciate that any such solution must, as matters stand, be one which we can put into effect with our resources alone.

As regards the plan of partition submitted by the Jewish Agency, it is, as I have said, our intention to place the outlines of the provincial autonomy plan before the conference. On various matters, and in particular as regards the boundaries of the provinces and the degree of self-government to be conceded to them, we designedly refrained from committing ourselves in any way when presenting the plan to Parliament. While we are adopting the plan as the initial basis for discussion, we do not propose to take up an immovable position in regard either to the plan itself or to its constituent features in advance of the conference.

It is accordingly open to the Jews or to the Arabs, if they accept our invitation to attend the conference, to propose alterations in the outline plan as announced, to make recommendations as to its details or to submit counter-proposals. All such proposals and recommendations will be given due consideration.

On 23 October, Winston Churchill, opening the general debate on foreign affairs, said:

Before we separated for the Autumn Recess, I spoke about Palestine. I must refer to that subject, linked as it is with all other questions of the Middle East. If we are not able to fulfil our pledge to the Jews to create a national home for the Jewish people in Palestine – which is our undoubted pledge – we are entitled and, indeed, bound, in my view – I speak my personal view; there are differences on this subject in all quarters of the House – because it is our duty, and certainly we have a full right, to lay our Mandate at the feet of the United Nations Organization. The burden may yet be too heavy for one single country to bear. It is not right that the United States, who are so very keen on Jewish immigration into Palestine, should take no share in the task, and should reproach us for our obvious incapacity to cope with the difficulties of the problem . . .

From the moment when we declare that we will give up the Mandate – giving proper notice, of course – all difficulties will be considerably lessened, and, if other interested Powers wish us to continue, it is for them to make proposals and help us in our work. We have at this moment a large proportion of our overseas Army in Palestine engaged in a horrible, squalid conflict with the Zionist community there. This is a disproportionate exertion for us; a wrong distribution of our limited forces, and the most thankless task ever undertaken by any country. If we stand on the treaty with Egypt about the Canal zone, we have no need to seek a new strategic base of very doubtful usefulness in Palestine, and we can present ourselves to the world organization as a totally disinterested party. Superior solutions may then, for the first time, become open. I strongly commend this course of action to His Majesty's Government and to the House.[11]

His proposals were taken up by Oliver Stanley: he was not advocating the surrender of the Mandate, he said – 'what we have to face at the moment is at any rate a last attempt to make the existing situation work', and he expressed his sympathy with the Government in that task. He spoke of the need for American co-operation, but was gloomy at the prospect – 'that hope, upon which the Government have acted for the past year, is now doomed to disappointment'.[12]

On 4 November Cabinet held a brief discussion on security in which a report was given on resolutions adopted by the Council of the Jewish Agency dissociating themselves from terrorist activities. These resolutions, the Colonial Secretary said,

> were not as satisfactory as could have been wished, but in this particular situation the Council had taken a courageous stand against terrorism, which had been reinforced in public speeches subsequently made by senior members of the Jewish Agency.

He now proposed the release and re-entry into Palestine of certain Jewish leaders who had been detained without trial, and at the same time the release and readmission of a number of Palestinian Arabs who had been held in the Seychelles.

Another brief discussion took place at the Cabinet held on 21 November, mainly on the prospect of the forthcoming Zionist Congress at Basle, which was not likely to end before 23 December; until the new Executive was thus elected there would be no one who could speak with full authority on future policy on Palestine.

On 28 November Cabinet had before it telegrams from Washington and New York reporting conversations between the Foreign Secretary and the American Secretary of State, and also talks with representatives of the Jewish Agency.

> These showed that the Jewish Agency was pressing for some assurance that His Majesty's Government were favourably disposed towards Partition* as a solution of the Palestine problem. They had suggested that if they could be given in confidence some indication that His Majesty's Government were sympathetic towards this solution, this would have a beneficial effect on the forthcoming discussions at the Zionist Conference in Basle at which it would be decided whether Jewish representatives should attend the Palestine Conference.

Bevin was clearly beginning to move under American pressure, though he was to be an unregenerate opponent of any solution based on partition up to the day, and indeed *on* the day when he proposed reference of the Palestine issue to the United Nations, more than two months later. Nevertheless, Attlee virtually dissociated himself from Bevin's references to partition, and pronounced a very strong warning against reliance on such a proposal:

> While there were indications that opinion in various quarters was moving towards Partition as the only practical solution of the Palestine problem, it was important that His Majesty's Government should not commit themselves to support of this solution before all the alternatives had been fully discussed in the resumed proceedings of the Palestine Conference. It might well turn out that no agreed settlement could be reached, and that His Majesty's Government would be compelled to impose a solution; but it was essential that this result should emerge from the proceedings of the Conference itself and that His Majesty's Government should not at this stage prejudge issues which had still to be fully discussed with representatives of the two communities in Palestine. In these circumstances he thought that the Foreign Secretary's conversation in New York should continue to be purely exploratory. Even his discussions with members of the United States Administration should be on the basis of ascertaining the probable attitude of the United States Government towards the various probable solutions.

This intervention, clearly worked out in advance, should support other evidence in rejecting any idea that Attlee was throughout the Palestine story a creature of Bevin's, or going along with him for the sake of peace. Attlee was just as hawkish as the Foreign Secretary, and on this occasion apparently more so. He clearly thought that Ernie had temporarily caught

---

* The capital letter was in the Cabinet record.

some infection from the Americans. After this warning he read out the terms of a previously prepared draft telegram to the Foreign Secretary exactly following the lines of his intervention. This was approved by Cabinet.

On 10 December the Cabinet's discussion on Palestine was directed exclusively to the growing problem of illegal immigration. The First Lord of the Admiralty, George Hall (now Lord Hall),* submitted a memorandum proposing that officers commanding HM ships should be authorized to arrest on the high seas certain specified categories of vessels suspected of carrying Jewish immigrants to Palestine, and given a discretion to divert to Cyprus any such ship which was found to be carrying illegal immigrants – for, the First Lord urged, faster and heavier immigrant vessels had come into use. The Lord Chancellor, Lord Jowitt, said that he was not satisfied that the proposal could be reconciled with the requirements of international law. We had always looked jealously on any action by another government – for example the United States in connection with the enforcement of prohibition – that might be held to constitute an extension of the three-mile limit governing territorial waters. He felt that the legal implications of this policy should be more closely examined before it was approved. Cabinet invited the Lord Chancellor, after consultation with the legal advisers of the Foreign Office and the Admiralty, to submit his considered view on the legal implications of such action. On 19 December the Lord Chancellor duly reported to Cabinet that after these consultations 'he was satisfied that this proposal could not be justified in international law'.

On the first day of January 1947 the Defence Committee and, later that day, the Cabinet, met with the Prime Minister in the chair. What became clear were the divergent views of the War Office and the Colonial Office on the use of the armed forces in dealing with terrorism, a divergence which had developed ever since Creech-Jones had succeeded George Hall at the Colonial Office in October. But the meeting was notable for Bevin's contribution. Possibly as a result of his visit to the United States, he was himself beginning to question the policies – largely his own – which Britain had been following for nearly eighteen months. The issue of what action should be taken to deal with the immigration situation in Palestine, he said, was bound up with that of our ultimate intention in that country. He agreed that the recent recrudescence of terrorism must be dealt with, but before it was decided to endorse the War Office proposals it was important that the Cabinet should know what solution they were going to adopt and be sure in their own minds that they were not launching a short-term policy which they were not prepared to see through.

* He had been moved from the Colonial Office to the Admiralty the previous October.

On the long-term question, he felt that during the previous month our whole position in the Middle East had weakened, and the impression seemed to be growing that we had lost the ability and, indeed, the will to live up to our responsibilities. Without the Middle East and its oil and other protected resources, he saw no hope of our being able to achieve the standard of life at which we were aiming in Great Britain. If, as he believed, the retention of Palestine was *strategically essential** to the maintenance of our position in the Middle East, we should have to make up our minds on what solution we were going to impose, and recognize that any solution which we might think it right to impose would be met with opposition from both Jews and Arabs – a situation which the Chiefs of Staff had hitherto regarded as unacceptable. If we were to maintain our position in Palestine, three things would have to be done:

(i) we must establish law and order;

(ii) we must decide on our long-term policy and enforce it;

(iii) we must make it clear to the United States Government that we could no longer tolerate the anti-British activities which were being carried on by Zionists in the United States.

On the last point, he said he was ready to communicate with the United States Secretary of State and point out that US nationals were collecting money with which to undermine our efforts to maintain law and order in Palestine.

On 15 January 1947, Cabinet met again for a full-dress strategic discussion on what Britain's approach to the problem of Palestine should be. The Colonial Secretary and the Foreign Secretary had each prepared positive papers, which were laid before the Cabinet – still filed today with each page headed in large red capitals TOP SECRET. Especially sensitive parts of the Minutes of the meeting were not circulated in the usual way, but followed a rarely used formula of being printed as a Confidential Annex and kept in the Cabinet Secretary's Standard File of Cabinet Conclusions.** The Foreign Secretary's Minute, as circulated, noted that the London conference of Arabs and Jews on Palestine was due to reopen on 21 January. It was necessary to decide the line of policy for Britain to take. There were three choices:

* Author's italics: Churchill, of course, had repudiated the strategic argument.

** This was an integral part of the Cabinet's decisions, but its special security classification prevented its having the usual Cabinet paper circulation, being distributed strictly on a 'need to know' basis.

I would estimate that this was done during my near eight years as Prime Minister on not more than half a dozen occasions – Budget Cabinets excluded – even though my period covered the Six Day War and some very sensitive meetings with President de Gaulle and others.

(a) the plan for provincial autonomy drafted the previous July by the conference of British and American 'alternates' (announced by Morrison to Parliament on 31 July and repudiated by Truman);

(b) a unitary independent State, as proposed by the Arabs at Lancaster House; and

(c) partition, 'which the Zionists want'.*

It is quite clear that proposal (a) in its present form is unacceptable to either Arabs or Jews. Proposal (b) is unacceptable to the Jews. Proposal (c) is unacceptable to the Arabs.

To deal with (c) first, partition would also be unacceptable to the United Nations, and I am advised that we could not give effect to this policy without previously obtaining the consent of the United Nations. Personally I would have no very violent objection to partition if I thought it would prove to be a solution. But I cannot conceive of the British Government, even aided by the United States, being able to carry partition with the requisite majority.**

He went on:

We must therefore consider another line of action. We must take the proposals made by the British and American officials as our basis, while amending them in such a way that they point towards an independent unitary State and incorporating with them as much as possible of the Arab plan. We must of course make it clear that we cannot accept the Arab proposals on immigrants, though steps must be taken to prevent a real flooding of the country by Jewish immigrants.

With this as our aim, we can ask the British Delegates to re-open the Conference by telling the Arabs that we have not been convinced that their proposals deal adequately with the problem; that we have therefore not withdrawn our own plan, but that we are ready to examine with them the possibility of arriving at a compromise which would enable us to discharge our obligations in Palestine and to satisfy world opinion. The Delegation would report constantly to the Cabinet, and its course of action would be subject to review as the Conference proceeded.

If we allowed the Jews to insist on partition and the creation of a Jewish State (which was promised in the Balfour Declaration) then we would face defeat in the United Nations. Even if we follow the plan of merging the Arab and the British proposals, I think the issue will have to go before the United Nations. But in that event I am satisfied that we should get sufficient support.

The Confidential Annex reports the discussion. The Prime Minister said that it might become necessary to impose in Palestine a solution which would be actively resisted by one or both of the two communities there. He asked for the views of the Chiefs of Staff on the question whether law and order could be preserved in Palestine in such circumstances. The CIGS

* The Foreign Office memo, unlike the Cabinet Minutes, insisted on a small 'p' for partition.
** On this he was proved wrong, see p. 216 below.

replied that if there were active opposition from either Jews or Arabs the situation could be handled. If the proposals were resisted from both sides, reinforcements would be necessary, which would have to come from the Army of Occupation in Germany.

The Prime Minister, who was clearly concerned with first principles, asked the Chiefs for their assessment of the strategic importance of Palestine as a factor in the defence of the British Commonwealth. The Chief of the Air Staff said that it was essential that we should be able to fight from the Middle East in case of war there. Palestine was of special importance in the general scheme of defence. A Treaty of Alliance would not be enough if Palestine were to be divided into an Arab state, a Jewish state and a Jerusalem enclave alone. So far as Palestine was concerned it was, from the defence point of view, immaterial whether it was divided into two independent states or became a single independent state.

The Confidential Annex to the part of the discussion on the UN centred on the question whether, under the Mandate, it was legally possible for His Majesty's Government to impose a solution of the Palestine problem, either by way of partition or by the introduction of a system of Provincial Autonomy, without first obtaining the sanction of the United Nations. On this a paper had been submitted by the legal advisers of the Foreign and Colonial Offices, with a note showing that the Lord Chancellor and the Attorney-General concurred with the conclusion:

> That, before putting into effect a Partition solution, we should be legally obliged to obtain the approval of the United Nations; that we should not, from the strictly legal point of view, be obliged to obtain such previous approval for the introduction of the Provincial Autonomy plan, but that it would be politically inexpedient to attempt to introduce either solution without first bringing the matter before the United Nations.

The Colonial Secretary's approach differed considerably from that of the Foreign Secretary. Although the Zionists had just rejected participation in the London conference of HMG, Jews and Arabs, he reported that Ben-Gurion felt that, if immigration were stepped up, this would create 'the change in the situation' which had been asked for to ensure attendance at the conference. He said that representatives of the Palestine Arab High Commissioner would be attending. More important, he said, the High Commissioner for Palestine was anxious that the Government should realize the urgency of finding a solution. The Administration and the Military Forces in Palestine were working under great strain. Early action to relieve them was, in his view, essential. The High Commissioner's own opinion was that, despite the difficulties involved by the need for obtaining the approval of the United Nations, some form of partition provided the only practicable solution.

The Colonial Secretary said that he himself was more and more inclined to share this view, which he felt sure would also command more general acceptance in this country than any other solution. He appreciated that there would be differences in the United Nations, but these would also arise over any other possible solution. If the scheme were not accepted by the Assembly, the responsibility would then be on the Assembly to find a better solution. He himself could see no solution on the lines of the Arab plan for a unitary state, for the illegal immigration of Jews would continue and the present state of tension would be perpetuated – while Britain would still remain responsible for law and order. Nor did he favour the plan for Provincial Autonomy. The question was raised whether a plan based on partition required a two-thirds majority of the United Nations.

The Prime Minister said that, as he read it, the Charter did not so provide, but any member state might propose that a two-thirds majority was necessary and carry the proposal. This proposal was certain to be made in respect of the Palestine issue. The Foreign Secretary said that the Arab states would certainly oppose partition, and he believed that the Soviet Government and the Slav Group would also oppose it, partly because of a desire to support the Arabs against Britain and partly because they would expect us, in the event of partition, to secure military facilities by negotiating a Treaty with the independent states. It was unlikely that the United States would be able to secure the support of China for a partition solution; and India was also likely to vote against it. In these circumstances he saw no prospect of obtaining a two-thirds majority in favour of partition.* In discussion, the Minutes record, the view was expressed that if the Soviet Government must be expected to vote against partition for the reason given by the Foreign Secretary, there could be no assurance that they would support the alternative of Provincial Autonomy. The Foreign Secretary thought, however, that in certain circumstances the Arab states might support such a solution and that some of the Slav states might also be persuaded to support it.

> The view was also expressed in discussion, that if all the arguments in favour of Partition were set forth in the discussions at the Assembly, and the disadvantages of the alternative courses were fully explained, the possibility could not be wholly excluded that, by a combination of skilful debating and tactical manoeuvering . . . the necessary majority of this solution could be obtained.

Hugh Dalton and Aneurin Bevan stressed the urgency of the situation. Dalton said that his own view was that, on the whole, the best solution was

---

* In the event he was proved wrong on voting in the General Assembly. The United States, the Soviet Union, most of the Slav bloc, Australia, Canada and New Zealand voted for the partition proposal.

partition. Events had shown that Jews and Arabs could not, and would not, work together in Palestine. It was also clear that the Zionists were determined to insist on the right of Jews to enter, as immigrants, subject only to the control of a purely Jewish authority, some purely Jewish area in Palestine, however small it might be. That determination in effect ruled out all solutions other than partition.

Aneurin Bevan endorsed the views expressed by Dalton. It was essential that an early solution should be found. If it were not, the consequences would be continuing disorder in Palestine, which we would be called upon to repress by force, and a general outbreak of anti-semitism. This was a situation which 'this Government' could not contemplate. He considered that partition was the right solution; and he could not believe that it would be rejected by the United Nations if it were supported by the United Kingdom and the British Dominions, by the United States, and, as seemed probable, by some at least of the Governments of Western Europe. At the moment responsible Jews were ready to accept partition as a solution. This, therefore, was the moment at which to put it forward. The Cabinet 'agreed to resume their discussions at a later meeting'. Both Bevan and, in particular, Dalton, whose pre-1945 commitments have been recorded above, were clearly worried about Bevin's hard-line approach from the outset. Their respective positions are worth setting out.

In the second volume of his *Memoirs* Dalton records, quoting an entry in his diary for 1 August 1946, that 'In the twelve months since our election victory events in Palestine have not gone well': he

> felt some sense of personal responsibility over Palestine.
> For, as I have related elsewhere, it was I who had drafted in 1944, as part of our official declaration on the Post-War Settlement, a section on Palestine which had attracted wide attention. This section had been accepted, first by the National Executive of the Labour Party and then by our own Annual Party Conference in December, 1944, practically without opposition. It was, therefore, by the rules of the game, firmly Labour Party policy.[13]

He went on to quote the 'key passage on Palestine', rejecting Malcolm MacDonald's 1939 White Paper, which had provided for a 'pitiful trickle of immigration . . . for the next five years, after which there should be no more Jewish immigration at all without the consent of the Palestine Arabs'; recording also that the Labour Party in Parliament had opposed MacDonald's Land Regulations, limiting, 'almost to vanishing point, the possibility of the purchase of land in Palestine for settlement by Jews'. Against that, the Declaration of 1944 had ended the concept of 'illegal immigration': all the Jews would be free to come in. Dalton points out that not only the Zionists, but the Permanent Mandates Commission had held that the White Paper itself was illegal; moreover, that the party itself had rejected MacDonald's doctrine of 'economic absorptive capacity'.

Dalton examined Bevin's motives for throwing over party policy. His explanation laid emphasis on the 'striped pants boys' of the Foreign Office,* together with the Colonial Office and the Service Departments, who were advising that 'our Declaration, if it were acted on would be a major catastrophe'. Nevertheless Bevin's approach was somewhat different. His first approach was as a negotiator, based on his experience and training over a lifetime:

> He had great self confidence, and believed that, if he got the Jews and Arabs round a table with himself in the chair, he would persuade them to a settlement, practical and based on 'give and take'. Indeed he rashly promised, that 'if I don't get a settlement, I'll eat my hat'. He suffered, however, from an inhibition due to his belief, which I heard him more than once express, that 'the Jews are a religion, not a race, or a nation'. And I heard Attlee several times express the same opinion.[14]

Dalton makes clear that from pre-war days he had always supported 'some form of partition', as recommended by Peel: 'I did not find Bevin very responsive to it.' Dalton strongly criticizes Bevin's negative response to Truman's 1946 proposal that the 100,000 should be admitted without delay, considering that if this had been accepted Britain would have been in a stronger position to seek financial and perhaps also military help from the US 'to underpin a joint Anglo-American policy in Palestine'. Looking back on the rejection of Truman's proposals, he expresses the view also that a favourable attitude would have rallied the not inconsiderable influence of world Jewry behind Britain, and thirdly, that

> in Palestine itself, we should have increased the hope of finding a friend, an ally, a base if we needed one somewhere in the Eastern Mediterranean or the Middle East, *even perhaps a new and loyal member* [author's italics] of the British Commonwealth.[15]

But he honestly admits that he did not press this point in Cabinet, nor did any of his colleagues. 'We were all greatly preoccupied with a multitude of other problems.' He records that he supported the Morrison plan of August 1946, involving administrative devolution based on the four provinces, Arab, Jewish, Jerusalem and the Negev.[16]

He returns to the subject of Palestine in a chapter on 1947, 'Annus Horrendus'. Quoting his diary, he had welcomed the appointment of Creech-Jones as Colonial Secretary in place of George Hall. But, he says, Bevin and Attlee continued 'to try to tangle up the merits of various solutions with hypothetical discussions of who would vote for this or that at the UN'. He was still urging partition:

* Dalton takes the phrase from Truman's own reference to the 'striped pants boys' of the State Department.

> There must be a Jewish state – it is no good boggling at this – and, even if it is small, at least they will control their own immigration, so that they can let in lots of Jews, which is what they madly and murderously want.[17]

A series of quotations from his diary sets out his growing criticism of Bevin, despite his own disenchantment with Jews as a result of the decoying and murder of the British Army sergeants: it was only years later that he again became pro-Zionist.

> Bevin's great gift, as it once was, of seeing apparently separate problems as part of a wider whole, has now degenerated with weariness and ill-health and ill-success, into the opposite vice of not being able to keep separate things separate, or to settle, or make up his mind, on one problem at a time . . . some of us have been trying hard, for some time past, first of all to get a firm decision in favour of Partition, and then to discuss how to bring it about. But Bevin goes round and round with the Arabs and the Jews, and nothing ever happens except a growing series of outrages in Palestine, which are rapidly breeding anti-semites all through the British Army and administration.[18]

Dalton's comments on Bevin's Palestine policy, and the dissociative line he took at critical times in Cabinet, inevitably raises the question: would Britain's policy have been fundamentally different had the King not moved Attlee to switch the two round? The answer depends on one's assessment of Attlee's own attitude. Undoubtedly Bevin's policy and prejudices were or became acceptable to Attlee, and on at least one occasion, as we have seen, Attlee intervened to force a hard-line policy on Bevin when he appeared to be softening under the influence of the US Secretary of State. Nevertheless, recalling Attlee's own personal commitments in 1944, with Dalton well to the fore in deciding the party's line at that time, one is forced to assume that a more pro-Zionist policy would have been followed, not least because of American pressures. To go beyond that, and seek to speculate on the reaction such a policy would have created in the Middle East, would carry us beyond any reasonable barriers of human certainty.

The other significant Cabinet malcontent on successive developments of Palestine policy was Aneurin Bevan. With him, Cabinet Minutes apart, it is more difficult to trace the record. He left no diary or autobiography behind. His one significant written work was *In Place of Strife*, and this contains no reference to the Palestine question. In the Cabinet's discussion, Bevan said that it was not necessarily true that we must avoid estranging Arab states. A friendly Jewish state would be a safer military base than any we should find in any Arab state. If, however, India 'and other Muslim countries' [*sic*] passed under Russian influence, how long could we expect to retain a secure military base in an Arab Palestine? A. V. Alexander, the Minister of Defence, said that he would favour partition if it were possible to get both Arabs and Jews to accept it, but differed from Bevan on his assessment of the strategic issue. Shinwell supported partition and said that His Majesty's Government should strive to get the solution endorsed by the United Nations.

At Cabinet on 22 January the Foreign Secretary was in a more chastened mood and ready to accept the reference to the UN. He said that he had considered how to handle the discussions with the Arabs and Jews in London. *He was not opposed in principle to a solution by way of partition*, but he was impressed by the difficulties of imposing any solution against the active opposition of either community in Palestine. He hoped, however, that the Cabinet would not attempt to decide, before the negotiations began (with both sides) *what recommendations the Government should make to the United Nations* [author's italics] if they failed in this last attempt to secure an agreed settlement. The Colonial Secretary agreed that no decision should be taken on what should be done if the negotiations with the Arabs and the Jews were to break down. But for his part he felt that we should seek to reach agreement with the Arab and Jewish representation then in London in the hope of finding a solution acceptable to both, based on partition.

In subsequent discussions Ministers agreed that, failing an agreed settlement, any solution of this problem would have to come before the United Nations. The General Assembly was not due to meet until September; and, although a special meeting could no doubt be called earlier, the atmosphere would probably be more favourable at the September meeting. On the other hand, if the forthcoming discussions produced no agreement, it was doubtful whether the internal situation in Palestine could be held until September.

The Cabinet concluded that it would be a mistake to decide at this stage what policy should be followed if the forthcoming conversations broke down. During the conversations, Ministers should try their utmost to move the two parties from their present irreconcilable positions. The Cabinet should be kept informed of the progress of the discussions; and they should, in particular, be consulted further before any indication was given to either Arabs or Jews that His Majesty's Government would be prepared to support any particular solution of the problem.

On 7 February the Cabinet met again, to receive a joint report from the Foreign and Colonial Secretaries. This made clear that the conversations with representatives of the Arabs and the Jews had led nowhere.

> These conversations have confirmed our fear that there is no prospect of finding such a settlement.
>
> *The Arabs* have again put forward the plan which they presented at Lancaster House in the autumn – that Palestine should be given early independence as a unitary State with a permanent Arab majority. They have, however, indicated that they would be ready to discuss modifications of their

political proposals *if* they were first given a firm assurance that

(a) *we were prepared to exclude the possibility of partition as a solution, and*

(b) *we agreed that there should be no further Jewish immigration into Palestine* [author's italics].

The two Secretaries of State said that they were satisfied that 'there is no possibility of moving the Arab delegation from the first of these conditions', but went on to suggest that there were certain negotiating tactics possible on point (b). Continuing their summary of the positions of the two sides they went on:

The Jews still interpret the Balfour Declaration and the Mandate as implying a proviso that a Jewish State will be established in the whole of Palestine. Their first suggestion was that we should rescind the White Paper of 1939 and continue to hold the Mandate on a basis which would enable them to build the foundations of the State by unrestricted immigration and economic expansion. We made it clear that His Majesty's Government were not prepared to maintain in Palestine a purely military administration under the protection of which such a Jewish policy could be carried out. The issue we presented to the Jewish representatives was the need to find some practical means of initiating in Palestine self-government evolving towards inter-dependence.

The Jewish representatives then indicated that, while still maintaining the justice of their full claim, they would be prepared to consider as a compromise proposals for the creation of a 'viable Jewish State in an adequate part of Palestine'. They would not themselves propose a plan of Partition, but expressed willingness to consider such a proposal coming from His Majesty's Government.

The essential point of principle for the Jews is the creation of a sovereign Jewish State. And the essential point of principle of the Arabs is to resist to the last the establishment of Jewish sovereignty in any part of Palestine. These, for both sides, are matters of principle on which there is no room for compromise. There is, therefore, no hope of negotiating an agreed settlement.

The two Secretaries of State therefore said that in these circumstances they had tried to find a solution which, even though it might not be acceptable to the two communities in Palestine, would be one which could be conscientiously recommended and defended to public opinion in Britain and to the United Nations.

Setting out the proposed solution, they said that it could not be found along the lines of partition, Creech-Jones here clearly deferring to Bevin. For, in the first place, wherever frontiers might be drawn, large Arab minorities would be left within the Jewish state. The area which would be left to the Arabs would not be economically self-supporting, even if joined to the territory of Transjordan. Second, 'if we did advocate Partition, we should have to face the resolute hostility of the Arab world'. Further, it was argued, the existing Mandate gave the Government no authority to move in the direction of creating an independent Jewish state, whether under partition or otherwise – we would have to go to the UN. They therefore proposed an alternative, which would still be based on local autonomy, with Arabs and Jews 'collaborating at the centre'. Provision would be made also for the immigration of 100,000 Jews in the next two years, and thereafter by agreement between the two communities or, failing that, 'by arbitration under the United Nations'.

Cabinet met again on 14 February. There was every reason for finding a means for reducing the commitment in the Middle East. Britain was facing the worst of the 1947 economic crisis, with the balance of payments deficit soaring far beyond the power of the American loan to assuage. It was the coldest winter in living memory, with gale damage around the coasts, gas and electricity cuts, coal shortage, transport paralysed and industry on short time through lack of power and raw materials. Hours of broadcasting were restricted, and no BBC programmes were going out between 9 a.m. and 12 noon, or from 1.30 to 3.30 p.m. It was no time for indulging imperialist or proconsular fantasies in the Middle East or elsewhere – only six months before Lord Mountbatten was to be sent to India to negotiate the end of Britain's proudest Empire. The first item on the agenda was in fact a question arising out of the crisis. The Prime Minister reported that the Chairman and the Director General of the British Broadcasting Corporation had asked whether it would be helpful if the BBC were to arrange for 'a series of broadcasts by leading representatives of the Opposition, the Churches and both sides of industry appealing for national unity in the present crisis'. Attlee's view was that this should not be encouraged and Cabinet concurred.

Cabinet had before it a further joint paper by the two Secretaries of State. It began with a report back:

> At meetings held on 10 and 12 February respectively, Zionist representatives and the Arab delegates declined to accept these proposals as a basis for further negotiations. The explanations given in the paper were entirely predictable: the Arabs said that the proposals would lead to Partition, while the Jews said they would lead to a unitary State securing independence with the Jews as a permanent minority. We have reached the conclusion that it is impossible to arrive at a peaceful settlement in Palestine on any basis whatsoever, except with the backing of the United Nations.

Opening the discussion on the joint paper, the Foreign Secretary understandably went back over the whole history of the previous eighteen months, explaining how the problem had become more 'intractable'. American Jewry now had great influence on the comments of the Jewish Agency. He had made every effort to secure the assistance of the

United States Government, but in the event their intervention had only increased our difficulties.

> In the final stage of the negotiations the Jewish representatives had been prepared to consider a scheme of Partition, but when asked to define what they meant by that claim to 'a viable State in an adequate area of Palestine' they had made it clear that they claimed a far larger area than any which His Majesty's Government would be justified in proposing for the Jews under a Partition Scheme.

(A map indicating the extent of the Jewish claims was shown to the Cabinet, the Minutes record.) Bevin was here showing the old TGWU Secretary touch: he had known how much to outbid the employers and when to settle.

> The Foreign Secretary said that he had the impression that the representatives of the Jews had not believed that we should in fact refer the matter to the United Nations. He thought that both Jews and Arabs were anxious to avoid discussion in that forum, and it might be that if we announced our firm intention to take the matter to the United Nations Assembly, this might bring them to a more reasonable frame of mind. Even after such an announcement had been made, he would certainly continue his efforts to find a solution; and he had it in mind, in particular, to make a direct approach to the rulers of the Arab States. Even though we gave notice of our intention to submit the matter to the United Nations, we could subsequently withdraw it from the agenda of the Assembly if between now and September a solution could be found which was acceptable to both parties.

The Chief of the Air Staff on behalf of the Defence Chiefs stressed Britain's need to maintain our bases in Palestine.

The Chancellor said that he still believed partition would afford the best means of securing both peace in Palestine and our own strategic interests in the Middle East. He presumed that the proposition before the Cabinet did not exclude the possibility of a decision by the UN in favour of partition. The Foreign Secretary confirmed that 'Partition was not excluded'. Further discussion, the Minutes record, showed that it was the general view of the Cabinet that the right course was now to submit the whole problem to the United Nations. Such a submission would not involve an immediate surrender of the Mandate; but His Majesty's Government would not be under an obligation themselves to enforce whatever solution the United Nations might approve. If the settlement suggested by the UN was not acceptable to us, we should be at liberty to surrender the Mandate and leave the United Nations to make other arrangements for the future administration of Palestine.

The question was raised whether the UN decision would have to wait until the General Assembly next convened in September.

> After considerable discussion the Foreign Secretary undertook to enquire whether there were any means by which the United Nations could get in train preliminary enquiries and other preparatory measures with a view to ensuring that the General Assembly could proceed at once to a definitive discussion of the problem at its next regular Session in September.

The suggestion was made – though the Minutes do not record by whom – that the position might be eased if some concession could be made in respect of Jewish immigration in this interim period. The Prime Minister said that in his view the right course for His Majesty's Government would be to make every effort to maintain the *status quo* during this period, including the restriction of Jewish immigration to the present rate of 1,500 a month. Any concession on that point would excite the opposition of the Arabs and also would lead to pressure from the Jews for further concessions.

The Lord Chancellor said he had seen Simon Marks and Ben-Gurion, leaders respectively of British and Palestine Jewry, who had made it clear that the Jewish Agency would prefer not to try to force a final solution of the Palestine and this was bound to excite active hostility by the Arabs. They would be happy to see Britain still the Mandatory Power on the pre-1939 basis, but with an increased immigration programme. Bevin commented that the Jewish Agency representatives were saying this in the hope that they would attain by immigration a numerical majority in Palestine and this was bound to excite active hostility by the Arabs. Suggestions made at this Cabinet to increase the rate of immigration were resisted by the Prime Minister without further discussion.

The Cabinet:

1. Agreed that His Majesty's Government should now give notice of their intention to refer the problem of Palestine to the General Assembly of the United Nations on the basis proposed in CP (47) 59, paragraph 13.

2. Authorized the Secretary of State for Dominion Affairs and the Foreign Secretary, respectively, to communicate this decision to Dominion Governments and to the United States Government.

3. Agreed that a statement of the Government's intention should be made in both Houses of Parliament early in the following week.

4. Invited the Foreign Secretary to consider whether, in order to avoid further delay, preparatory measures could be initiated by the United Nations to ensure that the General Assembly could proceed to a definitive discussion of this problem when it met in September.

What Britain had not done was to surrender the Mandate. She was still the Mandatory Power, and as Bevin made clear in New York, he was inviting the views of the world community on how the Mandate could best be exercised. He had little confidence that they could suggest any better policy, or even that there would be any agreement on any policy at all.

At the Cabinet meeting held on 18 February, the Foreign Secretary said that he had now received from General Marshall, the United States Secretary of State, a message about the Government's decision to refer the Palestine problem to the United Nations. General Marshall was concerned about the further delay involved in waiting to submit the issue to the General Assembly in September, and had asked whether it might not be considered earlier by the Trusteeship Council. The Foreign Secretary had been advised that the Trusteeship Council would not be compelled to discuss the matter, as Palestine was not the subject of a Trusteeship Agreement. He had, however, decided in view of General Marshall's representation that in the announcement to be made in Parliament that afternoon he would avoid specific reference to the General Assembly and say merely that the matter was to be submitted to the UN. He could then continue to consider possible means of getting the matter discussed by the United Nations before September. General Marshall, he said, had also asked whether the rate of Jewish immigration into Palestine could not be increased in the interim period before the judgment of the United Nations was given. On this point the Foreign Secretary thought it inexpedient to hold out any hopes at the present time. If the United States Government was anxious that some such concession should be made to the Jews, they should consider what pressure they could bring to bear to secure the acquiescence of the Arab states.

Aneurin Bevan pressed for reconsideration. As there was now to be a further delay before a final settlement was reached, he thought it right that the rate of Jewish immigration should be increased in the interim period. If some concessions were made, the Jewish Agency would find it easier to give effective co-operation in checking both terrorists and illegal immigration. The Colonial Secretary said that this was only one of several questions which he would have to ask the Cabinet to consider regarding the administration of Palestine in the interim period before the judgment of the United Nations was given. He asked that no Cabinet decision should be made on this point until he had been able to consider the situation in the light of representations which would be made after the announcement of the Government's decision to submit the issue to the UN. The Cabinet 'took note' that the Colonial Secretary would submit a memorandum on the rate of Jewish immigration and other issues affecting the administration of Palestine in the interim period before the United Nations decision on long-term policy.

The Foreign Secretary, as he had proposed, reported the decision to Parliament that afternoon. It was a straightforward account of the efforts made and the meetings and conferences held since 1945, and of the irreconcilable positions of the Arabs and Jews respectively, almost in the words used in the joint paper to Cabinet, CP (47) 59:

> His Majesty's Government have of themselves no power under the terms of the Mandate to award the country either to the Arabs or to the Jews, or even to partition it between them. It is in these circumstances that we have decided that we are unable to accept either the scheme put forward by the Arabs or by the Jews, or to impose ourselves a solution of our own. We have therefore reached the conclusion that the only course now open to us is to submit the problem to the judgment of the United Nations.

He indicated that the Government would present to the UN an historical account of the way in which His Majesty's Government had discharged their trust in Palestine over the last twenty-five years, and would explain why the Mandate had become unworkable, owing to the obligations undertaken to the two communities there having themselves become irreconcilable. Churchill, who had been pressing for just this decision for over six months, was surprisingly critical:

> Are we to understand that we are to go on bearing the whole of this burden, with no solution to offer, no guidance to give – the whole of this burden of maintaining law and order in Palestine, and carrying on the administration, not only until September, which is a long way from February, not only until then, when the United Nations are to have it laid before them, but until those United Nations have solved the problem, to which the Right Hon. Gentleman has declared himself, after 18 months of protracted delay, incapable of offering any solution? How does he justify keeping 100,000 British soldiers in Palestine, who are needed here, and spending £30 million to £40 million a year from our diminishing resources upon this vast apparatus of protraction and delay?[19]

The Government had agreed to give time for a full day's debate, which took place a week later. It was very much an inquest and raised little new comment, except that Bevin strongly criticized the 1939 White Paper which he had inherited – and in fact operated. While deploring the failure of the Arab-Jewish conference he also drew a, for him, subtle distinction between British and American Jews:

> Those who have been trained in England and grown up under English customs and practice, wanted to come in, but the Jewish Agency, very largely dominated by New York, would not really come in, and it was with gentlemen from there that I had to deal so much.[20]

He was repeatedly interrupted with requests for elucidation, or questions of straight argument, and got himself more than a little rattled, as when he said in reference to the local government proposal:

> I am convinced that if the Jews and Arabs in Palestine – I emphasize in

Palestine – are given a chance to work together, they will work together and solve this problem, but if it is to be settled in accordance with the Jewish Agency's dictates, it will never be settled. I am speaking, I hope, impartially.[21]

He got involved with the Balfour Declaration: 'I know the reason for this Declaration. I know why it was made, but I do not believe it would help the discussion now.'* He went on, 'It was thought by most people prior to 1939 that the steps that had been taken up to that date, did really fulfil the Balfour Declaration.' Since he had earlier said that there were 600,000 Arabs and 400,000 Jews in Palestine, this was a difficult thesis to maintain, but he ran into fresh difficulties when he sought to commend the municipal solution as the fulfilment of Balfour:

we thought if we developed these municipal areas, if we transferred the land regulations, the laws and the police, and all this kind of thing, to majorities in that area, we should have established the National Home. We should have established the National Home within a unitary State, with a free chance to the Jews for their own development, which would have allowed them in the joint Parliament of Arabs and Jews, to have had their say in the affairs of the world.[22]

The point, of course, was that the municipal solution was rejected both by the Arabs and the Jews.

Despite the strong support in the Cabinet for partition, he went out of his way to damn the proposition:

May I now turn to the question of partition? A good many people have said that the way out of the difficulty is to have partition. I am sure that, if we had agreed to partition, we would have had a tremendous row as to where the frontier should be. We have drawn frontiers in the Provincial Autonomy Plan; I have seen the Jewish idea of partition in an American paper, but we really cannot make two viable States of Palestine, however we may try. We can make one viable State, and, so far as I can see, or as far as any student of the map could see, the only thing we could do would be transfer the rest to one of the Arab States, but I ask what trouble is that going to cause in the whole of the Arab world? That will set going a conflict which will be worse than the conflict we have tried to settle. It has been suggested that we could do it by knitting in Transjordan, and it is argued that we carried out partition when we created Transjordan. That may be, but, if we try now, with Palestine as we know it today, to make it into two viable States, I say that we cannot do it. If we try to take away the taxable capacity of the best areas of Palestine for productive purposes, and that taxation goes entirely to the Jewish portion, you cannot expect the others to accept it. You cannot expect to make the one State dependent upon somebody else. The best partition scheme, and the

* Probably he meant that the Balfour Declaration was made to get the Americans on the side of the Allies at a critical point in the war, with Germany possibly ready to make a similar offer.

most favourable one that I have seen up to now, has the effect that it would leave, at the present moment, 450,000 Jews and 360,000 Arabs in that Jewish State. I put that to the Arabs quite frankly, and what was their answer? The Arabs say: 'If it is wrong for the Jews to be in a minority of $33\frac{1}{3}$ or 40 per cent, in the whole country, what justification is there for putting 360,000 Arabs under the Jews? What is your answer to that?' I have no answer to that.

Therefore, you transfer one large issue in solving your problem by partition, and there are only two possible consequences. Either the Arabs in the partitioned State must always be an Arab minority, or else they must be driven out – the one thing or the other – and, on that basis, I am afraid that I should be led, and the Government would be led, to a worse position.[23]

Churchill was unable to attend the debate owing to a family bereavement, but Oliver Stanley, leading for the Opposition, developed the criticisms Churchill had made following Bevin's announcement a week earlier. He was gloomy – as Churchill had been – about the prospects for the UN reference.

I would like to know whether our reference to UNO in any way commits us to carry out a decision of the United Nations, however it is arrived at, with which we ourselves are not in agreement. Surely, it would be better to say now what we shall have to say in the end, namely that failing agreement between the United Nations upon some policy which we ourselves can support, we will surrender the Mandate of Palestine and leave it to the United Nations themselves to appoint a successor and frame a policy. The principle of fixing a date and saying that if by that date something does not happen, we should clear out, is not a principle to which His Majesty's Government have any objection. They are doing it in India in much more difficult circumstances, in much more complicated conditions of greater danger and in circumstances where there is no United Nations organization as a residuary legatee to whom we can hand back the responsibility which we feel no longer able to carry.[24]

I believe it might have a considerable effect upon the deliberations of the United Nations if we were to make this announcement now. If they were to know that their deliberations might be followed by certain consequences and that every nation who spoke and voted might have to take some part of the consequences of their speeches and their votes, it might have a very considerable effect upon their willingness to reach some sensible, practical and tolerable conclusion.

The debate ended without a vote. Creech-Jones wound up on a more constructive and indeed hopeful note than Bevin had shown. Whether by accident or design he went on right up to the moment of 10 o'clock when the debate lapsed. No one had exercised the right to jump up a moment or two before and 'move that the question be now put'. Perhaps no one knew what the question was. Still less the answer.

CHAPTER 7

Eretz Israel

The Lord shall set His hand again the second time to recover the remnant of His people. . . . He shall set up an ensign for the nations, and shall assemble the outcasts of Israel, and gather together the dispersed of Judah from the four corners of the earth.[1]

BEVIN HAD NOT SURRENDERED THE MANDATE. Technically what he had done was to seek the advice of the United Nations on what Britain as the Mandatory Power should do.

On 29 April Cabinet met. The UN General Assembly was due to meet later that day. The Cabinet had before them a memorandum by the Foreign Secretary on the question whether His Majesty's Government should commit themselves in advance to accept any recommendations the Assembly might endorse concerning the government of Palestine. Bevin was not himself present to speak to his own paper, as he had gone to Berlin, and it was accordingly introduced by Hector McNeil, Minister of State. He said that there had been adverse comment in the United States about the apparent reluctance of Britain to commit herself in advance to accept any decision the UN might take, and the point was likely to be urged on the British delegate as soon as the Assembly convened. The Foreign Secretary had taken the view that our representative in New York should be authorized to say, if strongly pressed, that recommendations made by the General Assembly, if carried by a two-thirds majority, would be accepted by HMG, 'but that they must reserve their position with regard to ourselves enforcing any such policy'. But, the Minister reported, the Foreign Secretary had now expressed a further view from Berlin: HMG should not commit themselves even to this extent in advance of the General Assembly's meeting to be held as usual in September. The Cabinet Minutes record that, 'in a preliminary discussion differing views were expressed on this question'.

On the one hand, it was urged, submission of the Palestine question to the UN necessarily implied willingness to accept the Assembly's recommendations. On the other hand it was unreasonable for His Majesty's Government alone to give such an assurance in advance. The Assembly's recommendations might prove to be wholly impracticable for political and other reasons, and HMG would be placed in a most difficult position if they had committed themselves in advance to accepting them:

> No analogy could properly be drawn with procedure in a court of law: we were seeking a settlement between the conflicting claims of Jews and Arabs which would be backed by greater moral authority than one Government could command; it was, however, a settlement which we were seeking and not a judgment.

'After further discussion it was agreed that the Prime Minister should discuss the matter with the Foreign Secretary', who had in fact just arrived back in London.

The UN General Assembly, later that day, duly met in New York to consider the 'Palestine Question'. There was no reason at all to assume that there would be anything like a majority in favour of an independent Israel. Abba Eban, still in London, was summoned to join the small Jewish staff at the UN. He describes his first reaction: to go to Foyle's bookshop in the Charing Cross Road and buy half a dozen books about the UN and its procedures.

> The dangers were evident. Surely the Soviet Union would express its anti-Zionist tradition. Surely the states of Latin America and some in Western Europe would be influenced by the Vatican, which had found it theologically difficult to accommodate itself to the idea of a Jewish state. Surely the wishes of their mother country would have a strong influence on the younger countries of the British Commonwealth. Surely we must understand that the Arabs had five votes in the Assembly of fifty-seven members, whereas we had none. In addition, there were countries whose attitude would be determined by their Moslem solidarities. All these 'certainties' were grave, but we had to make the most of our opportunities – and the least of our dangers.[2]

There was an immediate procedural problem. Zionists, from Weizmann downwards, had committed themselves in 1942 to the 'Biltmore Programme', which had rejected any idea of partition and had called for an undivided Palestine to be reconstituted as a single 'Jewish Commonwealth'. In 1946 Weizmann and Ben-Gurion had agreed on the concept of partition, provided that the boundaries were appropriate and the ultimate size of the new Jewish state adequate. In that same year Nahum Goldmann had been authorized by the Executive of the Jewish Agency to discuss this at the State Department with Dean Acheson, then Assistant Secretary of State, who had

The Balfour Declaration,
2 November 1917.

Foreign Office,
November 2nd, 1917

Dear Lord Rothschild,

I have much pleasure in conveying to you, on behalf of His Majesty's Government, the following declaration of sympathy with Jewish Zionist aspirations which has been submitted to, and approved by, the Cabinet

'His Majesty's Government view with favour the establishment in Palestine of a national home for the Jewish people, and will use their best endeavours to facilitate the achievement of this object, it being clearly understood that nothing shall be done which may prejudice the civil and religious rights of existing non-Jewish communities in Palestine, or the rights and political status enjoyed by Jews in any other country"

I should be grateful if you would bring this declaration to the knowledge of the Zionist Federation.

Yours,
Arthur James Balfour

The Zionist Commission
arriving in Palestine, 1918.

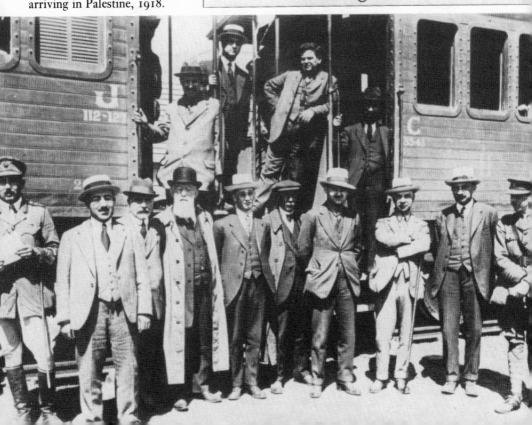

Winston Churchill in Jerusalem, 1921.

A reception for Sir Alfred Mond, 1921. *Left to right*: Dr Chaim Weizmann, Sir Alfred, his daughter Eva, Mr Meyer Dizengoff and Abraham Shapiro.

Chaim Arlosoroff and Dr Weizmann meet Trans-Jordan leaders, 1933.

Prime Minister Neville Chamberlain presides over the Jewish representatives at the unsuccessful London conference, February 1939.

Charles Orde Wingate, the British soldier and Zionist.

The Allenby Bridge after it had been blown up, 1946.

An illegal boat carrying immigrants captured by the British, 1946.

Above left: Ernest Bevin, British Foreign Secretary, 1947.

Above right: Clement Atlee, whose government went back on the Balfour-Churchill assurances about *the* Jewish National Home.

Right: President Harry Truman, 1948, who supported the proposed UN partition plan for Palestine and was one of the first to formally recognize the new State of Israel.

Ben Gurion reads out the Declaration of Independence, 14 May 1948. The portrait behind him is of Theodor Herzl, the founder of modern Zionism.

The Israeli delegation to the United Nations after the new state had just been admitted as a member of the UN, 11 May 1949. *Left to right*: Arthur Lourie, Abba Eban and Moshe Sharett.

Left to right: French Foreign Minister Christian Pineau, Sir Anthony Eden, French Premier Guy Mollet and Selwyn Lloyd discussing the Suez crisis, September 1956.

Below left: Colonel Nasser meets Sir Robert Menzies, leader of the Council of Five trying to find a solution to the Suez crisis, September 1956.

Below right: Moshe Dayan with his troops during the Sinai Campaign, 1956.

Harold Wilson with Golda Meir, Prime Minister of Israel during the Six Day War.

Harold Wilson giving a lecture at the memorial evening for Yigal Allon, Tel Aviv, 13 April 1980.

appeared to give the idea a fair wind provided that Britain was prepared to agree. Ben-Gurion took the same view. On 28 October 1946 he had written to Weizmann:

> We should in my opinion be ready for an enlightened compromise, even if it gives us less in practice than we have a right to in theory, but only so long as what is granted to us is really in our hands. That is why I was in favour of the principle of the Peel Report in 1937 and would even now accept a Jewish State in an adequate part of the country rather than a British Mandate with the White Paper in all the country.[3]

Weizmann replied, '. . . I can't help feeling that the inexorable logic of facts will drive [US opinion] towards partition.'

The odds at the UN seemed heavily weighted against the Jewish cause, but the small Jewish team in New York set out to organize a lobby, not of UN delegates but of their home governments, each member of the team being given a group of countries to approach. Eban describes how he was detailed to canvass France, Belgium, the Netherlands and Luxembourg – without, of course, possessing any diplomatic status, for Palestine was still an administered territory under the Mandate.[4] From Amsterdam he was summoned to New York (crossing the Atlantic for the first time) to help prepare a statement of the Zionist case to circulate to delegates.

In May the General Assembly appointed a Special Committee to visit the Middle East and then decide what recommendations should be made to Britain as Mandatory Power. It was decided that the major states should not be members: the eleven chosen were Sweden, the Netherlands, Canada, Australia, Peru, Uruguay, Guatemala, Czechoslovakia, Yugoslavia, India and Iran. They were an experienced team. For example, the Chairman was a Justice of the Supreme Court in Sweden, the Canadian a High Court Judge, the Australian a professional diplomat. The Dutchman was a former colonial governor in the Dutch East Indies – 'His experienced eye would detect whether the British colonial régime in Palestine had any chance of survival.'

Eban together with David Horowitz* were appointed by the Jewish Agency to act as liaison officers to the Special Committee. (The Palestine Arab Higher Committee refused to make a nomination, clearly an error with men like Eban and Horowitz active by night and by day on the other side.)

The 'United Nations Special Committee on Palestine', known at once and subsequently as UNSCOP, left New York in early June and flew first to Malta, where the British Government distinguished itself by providing a most churlish reception, housing the delegates in rough barracks and huts,

* Horowitz was a former director of the Economics Department of the Jewish Agency. After independence he became Governor of the Bank of Israel.

taking no trouble with food, and not even giving them a courtesy trip round the island. On 16 June they arrived in Jerusalem. Eban and Horowitz drafted a careful brief for Weizmann in preparation for his appearance before the Committee. Not for the first time, his eyes failed him; not for the first time, either, the speech he made extempore lifted the eyes of his hearers to his own breadth of political vision and approach. He believed strongly in the possibility of Arab-Jewish coexistence, but only on the basis of sovereign equality, which must mean partition. There can be little doubt, if Eban is right, of the impression he made on the Committee. But a still more powerful witness was to impress the Committee, just seventy-five miles away at Haifa.

UNSCOP's terms of reference required them to study the problem of the 'Jewish Displaced Persons'. Many of those from Germany and from Eastern Europe, being supernumerary to the immigrant quota, arrived in 'illegal' ships. There had been five of these in the six weeks before members of UNSCOP went to Haifa.* All the passengers had been sent back to Europe. It was while four UNSCOP members, including the Chairman, were in Haifa – taken there, not for the most innocent reasons – that the *President Warfield*, later known as *Exodus 1947*, reached Palestine waters. A British naval vessel had sought to intercept her and three Jews had been killed. She was brought into harbour under escort; her 4,500 refugee passengers were immediately transferred – British soldiers using hose pipes, rifle butts and tear gas – to another vessel, the *Empire Rival*, where they were locked in cages below decks and incontinently shipped, not even to Cyprus, but to France. Finally, after the passengers refused to land in France, *Empire Rival*, on Bevin's personal orders, went to Hamburg, back to German soil whence it had come, and from there the passengers were sent to a Displaced Persons Camp at Pöppendorf. The *Exodus* story, later filmed, was to pass into legend, and in both the US and Europe was to be a potent factor in stirring up anti-British feeling. Its effect on the UNSCOP Mission and the future of Israel was even more important. What perhaps was not so highlighted, either for the Mission or in Europe, was the murder of the British soldiers and the blasting of the King David Hotel. But the *Exodus* incident had done its work; Vladimir Simic, the Yugoslav member of the Special Committee, was later to say that the *Exodus 1947* incident 'is the best possible evidence we have'.

The events leading up to this incident are now described in more detail. On 1 May the Cabinet met – Whitehall was concerned about stopping the illegal flow of immigrants. The Prime Minister recalled that some months before, on 19 December, the Cabinet had considered a proposal that officers

---

* The *Guardian* with 2,552 illegal immigrants; the *Galata* with 769; the *Trade Winds* with 1,442; the *Orletta* with 1,457, and 399 on the *Anal*.

commanding His Majesty's ships should be authorized to arrest on the high seas certain specified categories of vessels suspected of carrying illegal immigrants to Palestine, but had rejected that proposal as the Lord Chancellor had advised that it could not be justified in international law. The Foreign Office and Colonial Office had subsequently put forward the alternative proposal that His Majesty's ships should be authorized to arrest on the high seas any illegal immigrant ship whose flag state had agreed to interception, and the Lord Chancellor had advised that this would not be open to the same objections. If the policy were approved it might be applied to the case of the *President Warfield*. The First Lord of the Admiralty opposed the proposal on two grounds: first, the conclusion of bilateral agreements with individual states for the right of interception might prove an embarrassing precedent. It might lead the state concerned to demand rights of interception and search of British vessels, which would be unacceptable to us. It was contrary to our long-term interests to encroach upon the doctrines of the inviolability of the high seas. Second, interception involved serious practical difficulties. Illegal immigrants usually sabotaged their ships' engines on interception and had to be towed into harbour. This created no particular difficulty when ships were intercepted off the Palestine coast and towed into a local port. If, however, they were intercepted on the high seas for towing into Cyprus, the immigrants were likely to resist being taken into tow and effective control of the intercepted ship could only be secured by placing a large guard on board. The Colonial Secretary urged that every possible step should be taken to prevent the arrival in Palestine of a ship carrying as many as 5,000 illegal immigrants. The Cabinet asked the Foreign Secretary to consider the problem with the Minister of Defence, the Secretary of State for the Colonies, the First Lord, and the Minister of Transport.

A Cabinet meeting as late as 31 July was still preoccupied with the *President Warfield*. It had sailed to Palestine, it was found, from a French port with some 4,500 illegal immigrants aboard, who had been furnished with forged Colombian travel documents; moreover, it had sailed without proper clearance from the French authorities. The Foreign Secretary had taken up the matter with M. Bidault, the French Foreign Minister, who had agreed that if a British ship were to intercept the *President Warfield*, the passengers might be returned to France. She had, in fact, the Foreign Secretary reported, been intercepted off the Palestine coast by a naval patrol and her passengers had been transferred to three other ships which were by this time in harbour. However, they had been refused permission to disembark. HM Ambassador in Paris had reported that the French Government was not prepared to act as requested and further attempts would be unlikely to produce any successful results. Ministers agreed that there was no question of sending the passengers to Palestine or Cyprus, and the Colonial Secretary said he was looking for a suitable British colonial territory for their reception. It was also reported that news had been received about the kidnapping of two British NCOs, but the authorities were unable to confirm or deny that they had been executed. What Ministers failed to realize was the impression made on members of the UNSCOP Mission, who had seen the *President Warfield* arrive and stayed to witness the actions taken by the British authorities.

Meanwhile, the Cabinet had met on 20 May. In the interval the creation of the State of Israel had been endorsed by the vote of the United Nations General Assembly. The Cabinet was by now concerned with the financial implications of the Palestine problem. The Colonial Secretary submitted a memorandum showing that the cost of security was already £8 million out of a total of £25 million, and was likely to increase. There was also the cost of the damage which had been done to the Shell Company's installations in Haifa Bay, over and above the contribution the Palestine Government had to make towards it. The Palestine Government also had to bear the cost of detaining illegal immigrants in Cyprus, which was described as 'substantial'. This demand for cash roused the anger of the Chancellor (usually expressed with a formidable quotient of decibels). He was, as we have seen, already out of sympathy with the handling of the Palestine problem: he was not going to jeopardize his already unhappy Budget prospects further for such purposes. The British taxpayer, he said,

> could not be expected to assume further burdens in respect of Palestine, and the local Government should lose no time in imposing additional taxation. There was no need or justification for taxation discriminating between Jews and Arabs.

He would deprecate the payment of compensation to the Shell Company which would place them in a favoured position *vis-à-vis* other private interests in Palestine: it was reasonable to expect the company to have insured against the risk of terrorist damage.

> The Cabinet
> (a) Asked the Secretary of State for the Colonies to inform the High Commissioner for Palestine that the Palestine Government should not look for further financial assistance from His Majesty's Government at the present time, and should take immediate steps to ensure a balanced budget by imposing additional measures designed to provide special compensation for the damage caused by terrorists to their Haifa Bay oil installations.

Cabinet met again on 8 July, confining its discussion, so far as Palestine was concerned, to the activities of the Mufti of Jerusalem. Currently in Beirut, he was said to be about to descend on Palestine. The Cabinet decided that the Secretary of State for the Colonies should instruct the High Commissioner that if the Mufti were to come within the jurisdiction of the Palestine Government, he should be arrested and deported immediately to the Seychelles for detention as a political prisoner. The Foreign Secretary, for his part, was invited to instruct HM Minister at Beirut to repeat the warnings already administered to the Lebanese Government against their allowing the Mufti to enter the Lebanon, and to say that His Majesty's Government counted on them to take all possible measures to prevent this from happening.

The accounts of the Cabinet meetings in the spring and early summer of 1947 suggest that Ministers, and above all Bevin, were getting bogged down with detail, mixed with a certain cattiness not normally associated with either Bevin or Attlee. It might have been their sense of relief that they were now, or soon would be, rid of the problem: it was in the hands of UNSCOP and then the UN Assembly. But there was more than that. Ernie had not won the battle. In his TGWU days be had not been used to defeat, and certainly he had never been worsted or out-fought by Jews. It was not only that he was unwell: he was sulking.

Meanwhile UNSCOP was hard at work taking evidence. Ben-Gurion impressed the Committee with a moving speech in which he praised Britain: 'It will be to the everlasting credit of the British people that it was the first in modern times to undertake the restoration of Palestine to the Jewish people.' In Britain itself, Jews 'were and are treated as equals. A British Jew can be and has been a member of the Cabinet, a Chief Justice, a Viceroy . . .'[5]

The UNSCOP members went to Geneva to prepare their report. Eban went to London, where a senior Foreign Office official flatly told him that there was no chance of a two-thirds majority in the UN Assembly, because the Great Powers were split. Bevin, as we shall see, was just as confident.

The Special Committee's labours at Geneva produced a report of sixty-seven printed foolscap pages. In addition to an account of their travels, the evidence they had received and the work done by sub-committees, they reported that they had held fifty-two meetings of the main committee. Their recommendations occupy three chapters (V, Va and VI) and distinguish between those where the Committee was unanimous and those where there had been a majority vote. The principal recommendations, together with their 'Comment' where appropriate, are set out below:

1 *It is recommended that*
The Mandate for Palestine shall be terminated at the earliest practicable date . . .

Comment: All directly interested parties – the mandatory Power, Arabs and Jews – are in full accord that there is urgent need for a change in the status of

Palestine. The mandatory Power has officially informed the Committee 'that the Mandate has proved to be unworkable in practice, and that the obligations undertaken to the two communities in Palestine have been shown to be irreconcilable'. Both Arabs and Jews urge the termination of the Mandate and the grant of independence to Palestine, although they are in vigorous disagreement as to the form that independence should take.

The outstanding feature of the Palestine situation today is found in the clash between Jews and the mandatory Power on the one hand, and on the other the tension prevailing between Arabs and Jews. This conflict situation, which finds expression partly in an open breach between the organized Jewish community and the Administration and partly in organized terrorism and acts of violence, has steadily grown more intense and takes as its toll an ever-increasing loss of life and destruction of property.

In the nature of the case, the Mandate implied only a temporary tutelage for Palestine. The terms of the Mandate include provisions which have proved contradictory in their practical application . . .

It may be seriously questioned whether, in any event, the Mandate would now be possible of execution. The essential feature of the mandates system was that it gave an international status to the mandated territories. This involved a positive element of international responsibility for the mandated territories and an international accountability to the Council of the League of Nations on the part of each mandatory for the well-being and development of the peoples of those territories. The Permanent Mandates Commission was created for the specific purpose of assisting the Council of the League in this function. But the League of Nations and the Mandates Commission have been dissolved, and there is now no means of discharging fully the international obligation with regard to a mandated territory other than by placing the territory under the International Trusteeship System of the United Nations . . .

The International Trusteeship System, however, has not automatically taken over the functions of the mandates system with regard to mandated territories. Territories can be placed under Trusteeship only by means of individual Trusteeship Agreements approved by a two-thirds majority of the General Assembly.

The most the mandatory could now do, therefore, in the event of the continuation of the Mandate, would be to carry out its administration, in the spirit of the Mandate, without being able to discharge its international obligations in accordance with the intent of the mandates system. At the time of the termination of the Permanent Mandates Commission in April 1946, the mandatory Power did, in fact, declare its intention to carry on the administration of Palestine, pending a new arrangement, in accordance with the general principles of the Mandate. The mandatory Power has itself now referred the matter to the United Nations.

II *It is recommended that*
Independence shall be granted in Palestine at the earliest practicable date.

Comment: Although sharply divided by political issues, the peoples of Palestine are sufficiently advanced to govern themselves independently . . .

The Arab and Jewish peoples, after more than a quarter of a century of tutelage under the Mandate, both seek a means of effective expression for their national aspirations . . .

It is highly unlikely that any arrangement which would fail to envisage independence at a reasonably early date would find the slightest welcome among either Arabs or Jews . . .

III *It is recommended that*

There shall be a transitional period preceding the grant of independence in Palestine which shall be as short as possible, consistent with the achievement of the preparations and conditions essential to independence.

Comment . . . A transitional period preceding independence is clearly imperative. It is scarcely conceivable, in view of the complicated nature of the Palestine problem, that independence could be responsibly granted without a prior period of preparation . . .

The importance of the transitional period is that it would be the period in which the governmental organization would have to be established, and in which the guarantees for such vital matters as the protection of minorities, and the safeguarding of the Holy Places and religious interests could be ensured . . .

A transitional period, however, would in all likelihood only serve to aggravate the present difficult situation in Palestine unless it were related to a specific and definitive solution which would go into effect immediately upon the termination of that period, and were to be of a positively stated duration, which, in any case, should not exceed a very few years.

IV *It is recommended that*

During the transitional period the authority entrusted with the task of administering Palestine and preparing it for independence shall be responsible to the United Nations.

Comment . . . The responsibility for administering Palestine during the transitional period and preparing it for independence will be a heavy one. Whatever the solution, enforcement measures on an extensive scale may be necessary for some time. The Committee is keenly aware of the central importance of this aspect of any solution, but has not felt competent to come to any conclusive opinion or to formulate any precise recommendations on this matter . . .

It is obvious that a solution which might be considered intrinsically as the best possible and most satisfactory from every technical point of view would be of no avail if it should appear that there would be no means of putting it into effect. Taking into account the fact that devising a solution which will be fully acceptable to both Jews and Arabs seems to be utterly impossible, the prospect of imposing a solution upon them would be a basic condition of any recommended proposal . . .

Certain obstacles which may well confront the authority entrusted with the administration during the transitional period make it desirable that a close link be established with the United Nations . . .

The relative success of the authority entrusted with the administration of

Palestine during the transitional period in creating the proper atmosphere and in carrying out the necessary preparations for the assumption of independence will influence greatly the effectiveness of the final solution to be applied. It will be of the utmost importance to the discharge of its heavy responsibilities that, while being accountable to the United Nations for its actions in this regard, the authority concerned should be able to count upon the support of the United Nations in carrying out the directives of that body.

Recommendation V dealt with Holy Places and Religious Interests, calling for the sacred character of the Holy Places to be preserved and access to them ensured.

Recommendation VI called on the General Assembly to undertake immediately 'the initiation and execution of an international arrangement whereby the problem of the distressed European Jews, of whom approximately 250,000 are in assembly centres will be dealt with as a matter of extreme urgency for the alleviation of their plight and of the Palestine problem'.

Recommendation VII – 'Democratic Principles and Protection of Minorities' – said that the constitution or other fundamental law of the new state 'shall be basically democratic, i.e. representative in character, and that this shall be a prior condition to the grant of independence'. It must provide specific guarantees on

> human rights and fundamental freedoms, including freedom of worship and conscience, speech, press and assemblage, the rights of organized labour, freedom of movement, freedom from arbitrary searches and seizures, and rights of personal property; and full protection for the rights and interests of minorities, including the protection of the linguistic, religious and ethnic rights of the peoples and respect for their cultures, and full equality of all citizens with regard to political, civil and religious matters.

Recommendation VIII required the constitutional provisions to incorporate the basic principle of the Charter of the United Nations, 'whereby all international disputes should be settled by peaceful means in such a manner that international peace and security, and justice are not endangered, and also the obligation to refrain from the threat or use of force against the territorial integrity or political independence of any State'.

Recommendation IX urged as a cardinal principle that the preservation of the economic unity of Palestine as a whole is indispensable to the life and development of the country and its people.

Recommendations X and XI called for the perpetuation of existing rights, privileges and immunities already enjoyed by states, including consular jurisdiction and other rights including those carried forward from the Ottoman Empire; and for an appeal against acts of violence.

All the above were unanimous recommendations of the Commission: the report went on to deal with one which was 'approved by a substantial majority', namely XII: 'any solution for Palestine cannot be considered as a solution of the Jewish problem in general'.

The recommendations in chapter VI set out their plan for 'Partition with Economic Union', 'Boundaries' and provisions for the City of Jerusalem. Reverting to Peel and setting aside Woodhead,* the Special Committee stated:

> The basic premise underlying the partition proposal is that the claims to Palestine of the Arabs and Jews, both possessing validity, are irreconcilable, and that among all of the solutions advanced, partition will provide the most realistic and practicable settlement, and is the most likely to afford a workable basis for meeting in part the claims and national aspirations of both parties.[6]

It went on to make proposals for the division of the existing social services and for customs revenue, setting out plans – as Peel had done – for a transfer of net revenue from the Jewish state to the Arabs. Then followed the formal recommendations for partition and independence, and the transitional period and constitution:

A. PARTITION AND INDEPENDENCE

1. Palestine within its present borders, following a transitional period from 1 September 1947, shall be constituted into an independent Arab State, an independent Jewish State, and the City of Jerusalem, the boundaries of which are respectively described in Parts II and III below.

2. Independence shall be granted to each State upon its request only after it has adopted a constitution complying with the provisions of section B, paragraph 4 below, has made to the United Nations a declaration containing certain guarantees, and has signed a treaty creating the Economic Union of Palestine and establishing a system of collaboration between the two States and the City of Jerusalem.

B. TRANSITIONAL PERIOD AND CONSTITUTION

1. During the transitional period, the present mandatory Power shall:
   (a) Carry on the administration of the territory of Palestine under the auspices of the United Nations and on such conditions and under such supervision as may be agreed upon between the United Kingdom and the United Nations, and if so desired, with the assistance of one or more Members of the United Nations;
   (b) Take such preparatory steps as may be necessary for the execution of the scheme recommended;
   (c) Carry out the following measures:
      (1) Admit into the borders of the proposed Jewish State 150,000 Jewish immigrants at a uniform monthly rate, 30,000 of whom are

* See chapter 3 above.

to be admitted on humanitarian grounds. Should the transitional period continue for more than two years, Jewish immigration shall be allowed at the rate of 60,000 per year. The responsibility for the selection and care of Jewish immigrants and for the organizing of Jewish immigration during the transitional period shall be placed in the Jewish Agency.

(2) The restrictions introduced by land regulations issued by the Palestinian Administration under the authority of Palestine (Amendment) Order-in-Council of 25 May 1939 shall not apply to the transfer of land within the borders of the proposed Jewish State.

2. Constituent assemblies shall be elected by the population of the areas which are to comprise the Arab and Jewish States, respectively. The electoral provisions shall be prescribed by the Power administering the territory. Qualified voters for each State for this election shall be persons over twenty years of age who are: (a) Palestinian citizens residing in that State and (b) Arabs and Jews residing in the State, although not Palestinian citizens, who, before voting, have signed a notice of intention to become citizens of such State. Arabs and Jews residing in the City of Jerusalem who have signed a notice of intention to become citizens, the Arabs of the Arab State and the Jews of the Jewish State, shall be entitled to vote in the Arab and Jewish States, respectively. Women may vote and be elected to the constituent assemblies.

3. During the transitional period, no Jew shall be permitted to establish residence in the area of the proposed Arab State, and no Arab shall be permitted to establish residence in the area of the proposed Jewish State, except by special leave of the Administration.

4. The constituent assemblies shall draw up the constitutions of the States, which shall embody chapters 1 and 2 of the Declaration provided for in C. below, and include *inter alia*, provision for:

(a) Establishing in each State a legislative body elected by universal suffrage and by secret ballot on the basis of proportional representation, and an executive body responsible to the legislature.

(b) Settling all international disputes in which the State may be involved by peaceful means in such a manner that international peace and security, and justice, are not endangered.

(c) Accepting the obligation of the State to refrain in its international relations from the threat or use of force against the territorial integrity or political independence of any State, or in any other manner inconsistent with the purposes of the United Nations.

(d) Guaranteeing to all persons equal and non-discriminatory rights in civil, political and religious matters and the enjoyment of human rights and fundamental freedoms, including freedom of religious worship, language, speech and publication, education, assembly and association.

(e) Preserving freedom of transit and visit for all residents and citizens of the other State in Palestine and the City of Jerusalem, subject to security considerations; provided that each State shall control residence within its borders.

(f) Recognize the rights of the Governor of the City of Jerusalem to determine whether the provisions of the constitution of the States in relation to Holy Places, religious buildings and sites within the borders of the States and the religious rights appertaining thereto, are being properly applied and respected, and to make decisions in cases of disputes which may arise with respect to such Holy Places, buildings and sites; also accord to him full cooperation and such privileges and immunities as are necessary for the exercise of his functions in those States.

5. The constituent assembly in each State shall appoint a provisional government empowered to make the Declaration and sign the Treaty of Economic Union, provided for in C. . . . below.

On making the Declaration and signing the Treaty of Economic Union by either State, and upon approval by the General Assembly of the United Nations of such instruments as being in compliance with these recommendations, its independence as a sovereign State shall be recognized.

If only one State fulfils the foregoing conditions, that fact shall forthwith be communicated to the United Nations for such action by its General Assembly as it may deem proper. Pending such action, the régime of Economic Union as recommended shall apply.

C. DECLARATION

A Declaration shall be made to the United Nations by the Provisional Government of each proposed State before the interim administration is brought to an end. It shall contain *inter alia* the following clauses:

General provision: The stipulations contained in the Declaration are recognized as fundamental laws of the State and no law, regulation or official action shall conflict or interfere with these stipulations, nor shall any law, regulation or official action prevail over them . . .

When Cabinet met on 20 September, they had before them the results of the UNSCOP Mission. Covering it was a memorandum by the Foreign Secretary summarizing the main recommendations, and proposing the line the Government should take when it came before the General Assembly. There was also a document from the Minister of Defence covering an appreciation by the Chiefs of Staff of the military and strategic implications of the plans proposed in the Majority Report and recommendations of the Special Committee. Introducing his paper, Bevin said the danger he saw was that representatives of other countries might be tempted to put forward unworkable proposals, relying on the fact that it would be for Britain to

implement them. To obviate this it was essential that the United Kingdom
delegation should make the attitude of Britain clear from the start. His own
view was that there would be grave disadvantage in any decision by HMG to
undertake the task of carrying out either the recommendations of the
Majority Report, or any alternative plan of partition which might be
proposed, or, for that matter, the proposals of the Minority Report:

> He had been reluctantly driven to the conclusion that the right course was for
> His Majesty's Government to announce their intention to surrender the
> Mandate, and, failing a satisfactory settlement, to plan for an early
> withdrawal of the British forces and of the British administration from
> Palestine. He did not wish to express any opposition to the recommendations
> in either Report, but he was satisfied that, unless His Majesty's Government
> announced their intention of abandoning the Mandate and of withdrawing
> from Palestine, there was no prospect of an agreed settlement, and he was not
> willing that British forces should be used to enforce a settlement which was
> unacceptable to either the Arabs or the Jews.

The Colonial Secretary was 'in general agreement with the views
expressed by the Foreign Secretary'. It was to be hoped that the proposed
arrangement would produce an agreed settlement, but it had to be realized
that no such support might be forthcoming, in which event HMG would
have to face the prospect of leaving Palestine in a state of chaos which would
make it difficult to safeguard British interests, such as airfields and oil
installations. The Minister of Defence said that if the proposed
announcements were to induce Arabs and Jews to co-operate and invite
HMG to assist them in drawing up a new constitution for the country, it
should be possible to satisfy the strategic requirements of the UN in
Palestine. If, however, there were no agreement HMG would be faced with
the choice between (i) ceasing to administer Palestine immediately and
merely maintaining such order as was necessary to ensure the withdrawal of
British forces and civilians, and (ii) assuming a date after which British
administration in Palestine would cease and the withdrawal would begin,
but attempting to maintain law and order throughout the whole country
until that date. The former course could be adopted without further military
reinforcements, but it would no doubt involve loss of life and property. On
the other hand, to maintain law and order over the whole country until a
specific date for withdrawal would require substantial reinforcements.

The Minister of Health said that HMG's first task should be to convince
all concerned 'that they did not wish to retain forces in Palestine for
imperialist reasons. If this were *made clear* it would have a very great effect
on opinion in the United States. Whatever statement was issued *should be
made clear*.' The Minister of Fuel and Power, Emanuel Shinwell, said that
if the proposal to relinquish the Mandate and withdraw the British

administration and British forces from Palestine was being put forward seriously and not merely as a threat to induce the contending parties to agree or other members of the UN to provide us with assistance to enforce the Majority Report, every effort should be made to enable the withdrawal to be carried out in an orderly way and to avoid its being interpreted as a confession of weakness on the part of HMG.

The Chancellor agreed that it should be made clear that HMG intended to relinquish the Mandate finally. Also a date for withdrawal of the administration and forces should be announced as soon as possible. If an agreed settlement could not be reached in Palestine, that country of no strategic value to HMG, and the maintenance of British forces in it merely led to a heavy drain on our financial resources and to the creation of a dangerous spirit of anti-semitism. Stafford Cripps supported the proposals. The Prime Minister said that in his view there was a close parallel between the position in Palestine and the recent situation in India. He did not think it reasonable to ask the British administration in Palestine to continue in present conditions, and he hoped that salutary results would be produced by a clear announcement that His Majesty's Government intended to relinquish the Mandate, and failing a peaceful settlement, to withdraw the British administration and British forces. The Cabinet approved the proposals outlined by the Foreign Secretary, and agreed that a statement following the lines of the Prime Minister's summing up be issued. It authorized the Commonwealth Office to send copies of the draft in its final form to Dominion Governments.

The crucial debate began in the General Assembly on 27 November 1947. Key to the decision was the position of the United States delegation, and the instructions which could be given to it at any time by President Truman two hundred miles away in Washington, DC. Weizmann had won the confidence of the President, who in any case, after the events of July and August 1946, was anything but an uncritical supporter of the British Government. Washington had been careful to avoid committing itself to partition in Palestine, and had equally avoided any contact with the UNSCOP Mission on its travels, and during the preparation of its report in Geneva. Now UNSCOP had come out plainly for partition and for the end of the Mandate. The US were concerned to emphasize the difference between what the world had accorded to the Arabs, with six independent countries each with delegates accredited to the United Nations, and Israel with neither independence nor international recognition. Following UNSCOP the US now came out in favour of partition in Palestine. They were followed by the Soviet delegation who equally supported partition. Samyon Tsarapkin, Soviet Ambassador to the UN, put it in declaratory form:

Every people, and that includes the Jewish people, has a full right to demand that their fate should not depend on the mercy or the good will of a particular state . . .

The members of the United Nations can help the Jewish people by acting in accordance with the principle of the Charter which calls for the guaranteeing to every people of their right to independence and self-determination . . .

The minority plan* had its merits and advantages since it is based on the idea of creating a single Arab-Jewish state in Palestine. However, relations between Arabs and Jews have reached such a state of tension that it has become impossible to reconcile their points of view on the solution of the problem. The minority plan therefore appears impracticable. In the circumstances therefore the partition plan proposed by the majority offers more hope of realization.

The Arab states played their cards unwisely. They were supposed to be co-ordinated by the Palestine Arab Higher Committee, but it was a simple matter to push them into a corner through their unremitting opposition to the partition plan. Their alternative lacked credibility, and despite UNSCOP and unlike the Jewish delegation, they had cut themselves off from any posture of negotiation or compromise. All they could do was to propose the establishment of an Arab state with no provision for the recognition of any Jewish persona. This had been rejected by UNSCOP. Moreover, their hard-line attitude to the Jews already living in Palestine extended even more to further Jewish immigration. For a generation there had been an international consensus in favour of continuing Jewish immigration, Hitler dissenting – and, for a short and unhappy period, Britain.

The issue was not going to be decided by a short debate followed by a vote. If, as many felt, it would be necessary to reduce the number of Arabs in the new Jewish state, and to open up again the disparity between the areas of the two new states, there was a 'committee-stage' job to be done. The sub-committee which was appointed, unlike UNSCOP, was no longer confined to middling and smaller countries. It was made up of the United States, the Soviet Union and Canada, as well as Czechoslovakia, Guatemala, Poland, South Africa, Uruguay and Venezuela. The Palestine Jewish representatives were worried about how federal countries might vote: for many of these countries federation was the alternative to disintegration. However, they were much reassured by the reply by·federal Canada to Pakistan's argument against enforced partition – a not unnatural viewpoint, Canada said, since Imperial India had been partitioned because of the seventy million Moslems living there. (Nor was it unnatural for Moslem Pakistan to support the Arab States.) No, said Canada,

* That is, the minority of the members of UNSCOP.

the representative of Pakistan has said here that partition should not take place without consent. But the question arises whether it is any better to try to maintain unity *without* [author's italics] consent.

Historical parallels, apposite as it happened, then took over. The Yugoslav delegate upheld the principle of federation but described 'the right of secession' as 'the democratic principle which may be considered the highest achievement of thought'. The Dutch delegate used a similar argument, referring to the separation of the Netherlands and Belgium after unification in Napoleonic times:

> Although our two peoples had very close ties, relations and interests of a cultural, historical, ethnological and economic nature, this unitary state ended rapidly and unsuccessfully. The differences between Arabs and Jews are much greater than those between Belgium and the Netherlands. Now, together with Luxembourg, our countries are reunited, not politically, but economically. And what counts more is not our political separation but our union for economic purposes. History has taught our countries this valuable lesson of independence combined with unity, for certain important but limited purposes.

Meanwhile, Britain was on the sidelines. There was a brief Cabinet meeting on 11 November. (The Prime Minister clearly did not expect it to last long, for although it was Armistice Day, it was called for 10.30.) Cabinet simply accepted a report from the Defence Committee recommending that 1 August 1948 be set as the final date for the withdrawal of the British administration and forces from Palestine.

On 25 November a further meeting was held on the eve of the United Nations' final determination of the proposals set out in the UNSCOP report. The Foreign Secretary said that the discussion there would shortly reach a stage at which a vote would be taken on the respective proposals for partition versus a unitary state. The United Kingdom representative had been instructed that, when this stage was reached, he should abstain from voting. In discussion a number of Ministers suggested that the time was approaching when HMG would be compelled to adopt a more positive attitude towards the problem. We should, in particular, have to decide whether we intended to facilitate the establishment of 'ultimate authorities to whom we could hand over our responsibilities when we withdraw from Palestine'. The Prime Minister said that the Cabinet must consider these matters as soon as it was known whether a two-thirds majority could be obtained in the UN for any particular solution of the Palestine problem.

Even the American position had been uncertain. While the issue had still remained in doubt, Weizmann, on 19 November, went to the White House to meet President Truman. He was rightly concerned about the attitude of the American delegation at the UN, and the instructions given to them by the State Department in Washington. In particular he sought the President's support for the incorporation of the Southern Negev in the proposed Israeli state. Without that, Israel would have no port giving them access to the Gulf of Aqaba, and thence to the high seas, so that Israeli cargoes would be cut off from Asia, Africa and the round-Africa route to the Western world. For Weizmann had no illusions that even if they could secure access to the waters bordering on Port Fuad they would have freedom of navigation through the Suez Canal.* His visit to the White House could not have been more timely. The US delegates in New York were holding out on State Department instructions against Jewish access to the southern waters. The American Ambassador to the UN, Hershel Johnson, had called a meeting with the Jewish Agency representatives, Moshe Sharett and David Horowitz, to inform them of the instructions he had received from the State Department in Washington. In the middle of the interview he was called to the telephone, but, saying he could not be disturbed, sent his deputy, General Hildring, to take the call. In very little time the General came to interrupt the Ambassador to tell him that the President himself was on the line. In due course he returned, and lamely said, 'What I really wanted to say to you was that we have no changes in the map you suggest.' As Horowitz put it later: 'We sighed with relief. Dr Weizmann's talk had been successful. The struggle for the frontier had ended in victory.' The President was to intervene yet again with equal decisiveness when the very issue of the creation of the State of Israel was in danger.

The geographical disputation, indeed the issue of partition itself, continued until late November. The Political Committee of the UN finally turned in a report, by 22 votes against 15 – with some 20 abstentions – in favour of partition. There was no guarantee whatsoever that the final vote would produce the required two-thirds majority. Taking into account the abstainers, the Committee's vote showed a pro-partition tally of less than one-third. Nor was the American delegation at the UN, despite Truman's intervention, helping to secure a majority for the partition solution. On 27 November, the General Assembly convened for the decision. Abba Eban, whose substantial figure was flitting from tree to tree like a large bird, set out the dubious prospects:

> Was there anybody in Manila who had access to the President? Might some friend in the United States have influence on the President of Liberia? What exactly were the motivations and impulses that would cause Haiti to vote with us? Was there some hope that Thailand would abstain? What was needed to bring France and Belgium into the Yes column? How could Moshe Tov** get

* Indeed Israel had to go through a bloody war in 1967 to ensure her right of navigation through the Straits of Tiran – see chapter 11 below.
** The Jewish Agency's contact man with the Latin American states.

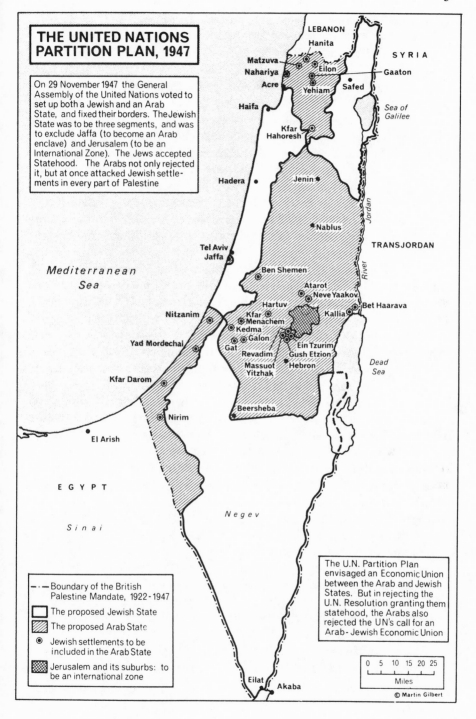

THE UNITED NATIONS PARTITION PLAN, 1947

On 29 November 1947 the General Assembly of the United Nations voted to set up both a Jewish and an Arab State, and fixed their borders. The Jewish State was to be three segments, and was to exclude Jaffa (to become an Arab enclave) and Jerusalem (to be an International Zone). The Jews accepted Statehood. The Arabs not only rejected it, but at once attacked Jewish settlements in every part of Palestine

LEBANON
Hanita
SYRIA
Matzuva
Nahariya
Eilon
Gaaton
Acre
Yehiam
Safed
Haifa
Sea of Galilee
Kfar Hahoresh
Hadera
Jenin
Jordan
Nablus
TRANSJORDAN
Tel Aviv
Jaffa
Mediterranean Sea
Ben Shemen
Atarot
Neve Yaakov
River
Hartuv
Nitzanim
Kfar Menachem
Kallia
Bet Haarava
Kedma
Galon
Yad Mordechai
Gat
Ein Tzurim
Revadim
Gush Etzion
Massuot Yitzhak
Hebron
Dead Sea
Kfar Darom
Beersheba
Nirim
El Arish
EGYPT
Negev
Sinai

The U.N. Partition Plan envisaged an Economic Union between the Arab and Jewish States. But in rejecting the U.N. Resolution granting them statehood, the Arabs also rejected the UN's call for an Arab-Jewish Economic Union

- – Boundary of the British Palestine Mandate, 1922-1947

The proposed Jewish State

The proposed Arab State

Jewish settlements to be included in the Arab State

Jerusalem and its suburbs: to be an international zone

Eilat
Akaba

0 5 10 15 20 25
Miles

© Martin Gilbert

us more Latin American votes? Here was the Jewish people at the threshold
of its greatest transition, and yet there was a danger that everything would be
lost through utterly marginal circumstances in countries ostensibly external
to the issue.[7]

But no vote was taken on the 27th. Alexandre Parodi, the French delegate,
perhaps because Paris was going through a reappraisal, moved the
postponement of the session, but without success. Zionist hopes were
slipping, but the Uruguayan delegate embarked on a lengthy speech which
Eban was to comment might not uncharitably have been regarded as a
filibuster. At least his eloquence moved the chairman, Oswaldo Aranha of
Brazil, to note that the hour was late; what was more, the following day was
Thanksgiving, the day on which loyal US citizens celebrate the reaping of
the first harvest by the Pilgrim Fathers, a national holiday. The debate and
the decision were deferred until the 29th. Thirty-six hours remained for
Eban and his colleagues to canvass the marginals.

A three-man committee, Iceland, Thailand and Australia, had been
appointed to see whether an agreed solution could be devised. The Thai,
Prince Wan, promptly left for Bangkok on the *Queen Mary*: he would have
been instructed by his Government against his own judgment to cast a
contrary vote, and an increasing expanse of sea-water was his best
protection. (General Carlos Romulo of the Philippines, who had spoken
against partition on the 27th, also suddenly remembered an urgent
engagement at home and disappeared from the scene.) The Icelander, Thor
Thors, was therefore called to the rostrum when the Assembly met in full
session. His main contribution was to reject any idea of a compromise
formula. His vote was accordingly cast for the new Jewish state. The chair
rejected a procedural motion by Camille Chamoun of the Lebanon* who
proposed an adjournment to discuss a proposal for federation. The Arabs –
and indeed the British delegation – were manoeuvring in favour of a further
delay. The Filipino alternate delegate announced his support of partition.
Liberia had swung to the Zionist cause, as did the Benelux countries.

After all the speeches had been heard, Chairman Aranha called for the
votes, in alphabetical order. Eban recounts the drama: Argentina? –
Abstain. Afghanistan? – No. Australia? – Yes. Belgium? – Yes. Bolivia? –
Yes. Byelorussia? – Yes (the first of the Soviet bloc). France emitted a loud
Oui. The votes mounted. The last country was called: Yugoslavia abstained
– it was the year when the Yugoslavs were beginning their own moves
towards independence of the Soviet Union.

Britain had abstained.

Aranha announced the result: 'Thirty-three in favour, thirteen against,

* A Lebanese Christian and a personal friend of the author while a refugee in Britain just
after the war.

ten abstentions, one absent. The resolution is adopted.' Adopted, in fact, by more than the required two-thirds majority.

In the Jewish towns of Palestine there was dancing in the streets. Moshe Dayan records in his memoirs:

> We were happy that night, and we danced, and our hearts went out to every nation whose UN representative had voted in favour of the resolution. We had heard them utter the magic word 'Yes' as we followed their voices over the air-waves from thousands of miles away. We danced – but we knew that ahead of us lay the battlefield.[8]

A two-day debate took place in the Commons on 11 and 12 December 1947, to discuss and ratify the decision of the General Assembly on 29 November. Creech-Jones rose to explain the change in Government policy which had led to this step, and to outline the Government's proposals for ending Britain's responsibilities under the Mandate. The reference to the UN had been necessary because Britain's record as mandatory had been based on the structure of a unitary state. (Morrison's limited 'partition' plan had of course simply envisaged a system of devolution within such a state.) But the Government, having moved towards partition, had been given the clearest legal advice that the Government had no mandatory authority to partition the state, nor to govern it after partition.

> A free judgment by the United Nations, without any suspicion or prejudice which might be engendered by Britain urging proposals of her own, seemed to His Majesty's Government, in all the circumstances, to be the wisest course to take . . .
>
> I made it clear at Lake Success that the British Government were not prepared to impose, by force of arms, a settlement which was not acceptable to both Arabs and Jews in Palestine and that, in the absence of such a settlement, the Government must plan for the early withdrawal of British Forces and administration from Palestine. . . . I made every effort to persuade delegations that enforcement must be regarded as an integral part of any new policy by the United Nations in Palestine.[9]

The announcement, he said, was universally welcomed, and he went on to report on the action taken by the UN, beginning with the appointment of UNSCOP and the acceptance of its report. While the new constitution, and in particular the partition lines for the new states were different from those which UNSCOP had recommended, Britain would not obstruct the decisions which had been taken.

> We have no desire to create new difficulties for the United Nations, or to encourage disorder and violence in Palestine, or to see undone, by resulting chaos, the great work which our Administration has performed since we took up the Mandate.[10]

Creech-Jones described the administrative arrangements for ending the Mandate and announced, subject to negotiations with the United Nations Commissioner appointed to supervise the UN decision, that Britain would withdraw troops on 1 August 1948. He spent some time emphasizing the problems the UN Commission would face, though perhaps with less satisfaction than Bevin would have shown, and pointed out that the Palestine Arab Higher Committee had already stated that 'it will not nurse the United Nations Commission in any way'. He described it as 'disturbing that the Commission will go to its task with inadequate support for its decisions', and stressed the danger of communal disturbances in mixed areas, such as Jerusalem and Haifa. British police would be moved to these areas from purely Jewish areas such as Tel Aviv, Petah Tikvah and Ramat Gan. He warned against any moves to speed up immigration during the period up to British withdrawal.

Oliver Stanley, for the Opposition, joined in the tributes the Secretary of State had paid to the British troops and administrators. While he had long been a supporter of the principle of partition, he expressed disagreement with many of the details laid down by the UN. He and his friends could see no alternative to the course being followed, but this did not mean that this was a moment at which they could feel either happiness or pride:

> Events in Palestine are in tragic contrast to the hopes of many in the past. I am afraid it will be a humiliating end to the honourable role which hitherto we have played in that country, very different indeed from the dream of those who first inspired the idea, very different from the object for which many thousands of our fellow citizens worked, indeed, died in Palestine.[11]

Among the backbenchers, Richard Crossman made one of the most knowledgeable speeches. Since his first indoctrination at the time of the Anglo-American Commission he had become an acknowledged authority on Palestine, though his strong Jewish sympathies had anything but endeared him to Attlee. There is no doubt that Attlee's feeling that Crossman had gone American in 1946–7 was the reason why Crossman was denied the ministerial rank many thought he should have had. Crossman was critical of the policy vacuum in the eighteen months prior to the reference to the UN,* though he said that once the matter was so referred, 'the attitude of the Government has been that of the skilful negotiator', and

---

* Crossman had felt so strongly about the Government's rejection of the Anglo-American Commission's recommendations that he had asked to see Attlee, who listened to his argument and then said, 'Saw your mother last week.' This story is vouched for by Sir David Hunt in his autobiography *An Ambassador Remembers*, London, 1975. Sir David Hunt had been Private Secretary to Attlee and later Churchill when they were Prime Ministers, before serving in Pakistan, Nigeria, Uganda, Cyprus and at the Foreign Office in London. From 1969–73 he was Ambassador to Brazil.

he went out of his way to pay a tribute to Creech-Jones. Forward-looking as ever, a great deal of his speech looked to the future, especially to relations with the Arabs. He wanted the UN Commission to get on the ground early, in contradiction to the views of the Colonial Secretary, and pressed the Government to ensure that both Americans and Russians were kept out of the area. The UNSCOP success had been due to the fact that it was widely representative of small and medium-sized nations, and that the Commonwealth (Dominions) was well represented.

The debate was wound up on the second day by Anthony Eden[12] and Ernest Bevin. Eden's speech was characteristically helpful and non-partisan: in particular he agreed that the Government were right to take the decision they had: 'I think that on one issue there will be general agreement; that the Mandate has proved unworkable.' He went on to pay tribute to the administrators and armed services, going right back to Herbert Samuel and Lord Plumer: 'To those who criticize from a distance the work of the Mandatory Power, I would say, "Could you have done any better?" ' His speech was practical, proposing for example a 'planned transfer of minorities' which, as he said, had been recommended by the Peel Commission, who had based themselves on the successful transfer of a million Greeks and a smaller number of Turks in 1922. He was also concerned about the arrangements for the Holy Places. He closed his speech with two eloquent messages to the Jews and to the Arabs:

To the Jews I would say,
'Now that you will shortly achieve the goal for which, through centuries, Jewish hearts have yearned, we ask you to exercise moderation in this moment when your hopes, in a great measure at least, are to be realized. Remember that this change of status is going to carry with it heavy responsibilities, responsibilities towards the United Nations for the maintenance of the settlement and for the respect of your new frontier; responsibilities towards your Arab neighbours, as well as towards a large Arab minority in your midst, to calm spirits and to avoid provocation of any kind, now or in the future.'
To the Arabs,
'Finally a word to the Arabs, which I feel perhaps justified in uttering because, in 1940, I had something to do with proposals which led to closer unity between the Arab States. I would say this to them. If, at the twelfth hour, the Arabs were prepared to submit to the Assembly a plan for a Federal State – as they were – composed of Jewish and Arab cantons, is it too much to ask of them, in the interests of peace and humanity, to go a step further and accommodate themselves to the new situation, and put an end, once and for all, to the strife and bloodshed which for ten years have torn asunder this land which, to Christian, Moslem and Jew alike, is sacred? I make a solemn appeal to all my Arab friends, sore at heart though they must be, to make this great effort in the interests of mankind.'

Bevin immediately, and movingly, associated himself with Eden's closing words. He defended the Government against those who had criticized the long delay in evacuating the administration and the troops. The date set for the former had been 15 May. Bevin pointed out that Israel would be a member of the sterling area, and there was a great deal to be done on currency, trade, 'and a variety of economic things'. He repeated that the troops were due to leave on 1 August. He referred to the vast and costly installations; time was needed to recover as much as possible on economic grounds. Thousands of service men and civil servants had to be brought home, and shipping was scarce. It would not be possible to complete the evacuation of the troops before 1 August – there was a massive demobilization plan associated with it. The immigration quota would remain while the troops were there. Arab Legion troops which had been serving under the orders of the British GOC would be returned to King Abdullah of Jordan as our own troops left.

The Foreign Secretary thanked those members who had pressed for compensation for government officials and others who would be retired, and pledged the administration to pay adequate monetary compensation. Without raising the temperature of the debate, he defended the Government against those who had criticized ministers for waiting for two years before placing the issue before the UN. To have laid down the Government's mandatory duties could have led to charges before the Security Council of endangering peace and security. He defended himself against the 'outrageous and inaccurate' charge that he had turned down the report of the Anglo-American Committee, characteristically blaming President Truman for US insistence on only one point – the 100,000 immigrants. He took credit on the Government's behalf for trying to secure acceptance of the Morrison partition plan. His Majesty's Government would not oppose the United Nations decision.

Ernest Bevin's speech reflected a very different tone from most of its predecessors, as Ian Mikardo said towards the close of the debate. There was no vote. At 3.55, the Government Chief Whip 'begged to ask leave to withdraw the motion', which was then, by leave, withdrawn, and the House passed on to a backbench member's speech, under the half-hour Adjournment debate procedure, on food supplies and the cuts in consumer rations.

When Dayan had said that ahead lay the battlefield, he failed to forecast also a political minefield. Despite the clear majority in the United Nations, the resistance movement of the international political establishment went to work. The State Department, the White House establishment, leading figures in the UN Secretariat, were beavering away to destroy what had been achieved. Even Truman weakened. He was irked by the persistence and orchestration shown by America's own counter-productive Zionists.

> I do not think I ever had as much pressure and propaganda aimed at the White House as I had in this instance. The persistence of a few of the extreme Zionist leaders – actuated by political motives and engaging in political threats – disturbed me and annoyed me . . .
>
> Individuals and groups asked me, usually in rather quarrelsome and emotional ways, to stop the Arabs, to furnish American soldiers to do this, that and the other . . .
>
> As the pressure mounted, I found it necessary to give instructions that I did not want to be approached by any more spokesmen for the extreme Zionist cause. I was even so disturbed that I put off seeing Dr Chaim Weizmann who had returned to the United States and had asked for an interview with me.[13]

Attlee and Bevin, to their credit, refused to see the American reaction against Zionism as an opportunity to snatch victory out of the jaws of defeat. The decision had been taken. As good democrats they accepted it – for a time. The Cabinet meetings of early 1948, in so far as they were concerned with Palestine at all, were nuts and bolts affairs, designed to ensure the speedy evacuation of administrative staff and the military from the country.

The meeting in Downing Street on 29 January was devoted to economic questions. Cabinet agreed to the steps necessary for excluding Palestine and Transjordan from the Sterling Area, and to other consequential action in bilateral terms, in consultation with the Dominions. The Chancellor was asked to arrange for the briefing of FO personnel at the UN on the consequential economic modalities.

On 5 February Cabinet met to consider a request from the UN about the timing of a visit to Palestine by the Commission appointed by them to 'oversee' the transfer of power. The Colonial Office had secured ministerial agreement to keeping them out until the last two weeks before the administration withdrew, though the Commission had asked for a longer period there. After a long but hardly world-shaking discussion, Cabinet agreed to allow the Commission to send a 'nucleus' of members of the Commission's staff ahead of the date they had fixed. There were also detailed proposals for the evacuation of the port of Tel Aviv in advance of the general evacuation. These were flatly rejected.

More important was the issue of partition, carried by the UN's endorsement of the majority UNSCOP report. Cabinet were told that the Jewish Agency had represented to the Security Council that the latter should send an international force to Palestine to enforce partition, and the UN itself, Cabinet was informed, was likely to make a similar request. Any international force would almost inevitably have to include a Soviet contingent, or one from a Soviet satellite. The establishment of such a force would greatly increase the likelihood of open intervention by the Arab states in Palestine. Moreover, the force could hardly be assembled and sent to Palestine in time to take effective action. HMG had already made it clear that they would not participate in enforcing partition. It was accordingly proposed that in any discussion about the establishment of an international force by the Security Council the United Kingdom delegate should express no opinion and should abstain from voting, while not, however, exercising any veto.

Cabinet critics of this proposal warned that participation by a British contingent in an international force might well lead to our having to carry the major part of the burden of enforcement, and would, in view of our previous declaration, expose us to the charge of bad faith. Moreover, there were good reasons for the view that, if any international force were established, it should not contain a UK contingent, on the ground that we had been too deeply involved in the past history of the Palestine problem. There were also serious objections to the expression of any opinion by the UK delegation on whether an international force should be established. If we supported the proposal, we should have difficulty in refusing to allow a UK contingent to participate and would probably find it impossible to resist a demand for the retention of the UK forces in Palestine until the international force was in a position to take over from them. On the other hand, any advice that we might give against the proposal would be construed as an attempt to obstruct the implementation of the United Nations plan.

The Cabinet agreed: that Tel Aviv should not be evacuated in advance of 15 May; that it would be impossible to contemplate the progressive transfer of power to the United Nations Commission in advance of 15 May, but that reasonable proposals for facilitating the transfer of responsibility on the termination of the Mandate might be discussed with the Commission when it visited London; that when the question of the establishment of an international force was discussed by the Security Council, the UK delegation should:

(i)   make it clear that it was for the Council to determine what support should be given to the United Nations Commission;

(ii) reaffirm statements made by the UK delegation to the General Assembly and by Government spokesmen in the debate on Palestine in the House of Commons on 11 and 12 December about the intention of HMG to withdraw their forces from Palestine by 1 August 1948,* and

---

* Much of the technical discussions in sub-committees and the Defence departments were directed to the maximum recovery and despatch of military and civil stores. Little was left for the Israelis. This was in marked contrast to the policies adopted by the Labour Governments of 1964–70 and 1974–6 in relation to Singapore. When the first run-down of the UK military and naval installations occurred in 1968, Lee Kuan Yew, the Singapore Prime

their unwillingness to undertake, either individually or collectively, in
association with others, to impose the UN decisions by force; and
(iii) abstain from voting but not exercise a veto.

The Cabinet went on to approve the proposal made with regard to the
attitude to be adopted by the UK delegates towards any resolution calling
for the use of sanctions against members of the Arab League. Ministers were
further told that the Bill to give effect to Britain's changed responsibilities in
relation to Palestine had been approved by the Legislation Committee of the
Cabinet on 4 February. The Cabinet decided that the Lord President of the
Council (who was Leader of the House of Commons), the Secretary of State
for the Colonies and the Chief Whip should discuss the possibility of
deferring the introduction of the Palestine Bill into Parliament until the
Security Council's discussions on Palestine were completed.

A meeting on 23 February confined itself to receiving a report of an
explosion the previous day in the Jewish quarter of Jerusalem which had
killed fifty Jews and injured seventy others. Ministers expressed concern at
the failure of the Palestine Government to issue a more categorical denial of
allegations that British troops were responsible for this outrage. Cabinet was
informed that a Private Notice Question had been tabled in the Commons
and this would enable the Minister to make a further condemnation of the
allegation.

Then a fresh crisis occurred. The State Department decided that the
UN decision was wrong and should be reversed. Even Truman was carried
along, irked again no doubt by the clamour of the extreme US Zionists.
Attlee called a special Cabinet on 22 March, a Monday – a day when
Cabinet meetings are most rare – to consider the problem raised by this
sudden action of the United States Government, in fact withdrawing their
support of the partition plan proposed for Palestine and suggesting that in
its place Palestine as a whole should be placed under UN Trusteeship, thus
reversing the UN's decision to create a Jewish state. The first question
raised was whether progress on the Palestine Bill already before the House
should be delayed, but it was agreed that this might create the wrong
impression abroad. The Bill would therefore go through its remaining

---

Minister, told me, although some military property was handed over to the Singapore
Government, much was rendered useless, e.g. telegraph poles were cut off a foot from the
ground. When the incoming Labour Government in 1974 announced its complete
evacuation from the territory, Lee Kuan Yew asked me to instruct the military to hand over
all property on a working basis. On a visit there in 1977 he showed me how imaginatively this
had been honoured: troops' quarters were handed over in perfect condition and the
dockyards retained all their equipment – two 250,000-ton tankers were being serviced there,
and Singapore has become a major ship-repairing and service centre for ships from all over
the world.

committee and other stages as arranged.

Cabinet was told that the Soviet representative on the Security Council would in all probability veto the US proposal to overturn the partition plan. There might then be a procedural vote on a proposal to withdraw the matter from the Council's agenda or to summon a special meeting of the Assembly. It was impossible to decide at that stage what attitude the United Kingdom representative should adopt towards such procedural proposals, but it should be borne in mind that his vote might be decisive. There was clearly, it was felt, no hope that the proposal for a trusteeship would be accepted either by the Jews or the Arabs, and there were various objections to a further suggestion which had been made in Washington that order should be maintained by a combination of forces from the US, the UK and France. Moreover, it might well be that in the new situation the Jews would go ahead and seek to establish a Jewish state covering such parts of the area allotted to them in the partition plan as they might reasonably expect to be able to defend, while the King of Transjordan might seek to assure control of other parts of Palestine, a move which would stir up trouble among the other Arab states, in addition to the disturbance which it would cause in Palestine itself. A further factor in the situation was that the United Nations Commission was now unlikely to be in Palestine on the date when the Mandate was surrendered and, indeed, there was some reason to believe that they might resign from their duties because of the danger of the reversal of policy in New York.

The Cabinet agreed that, although there should be no change in the date (15 May) fixed for the surrender of the Mandate, the British civil and military authorities in Palestine should make no effort to oppose the setting up of a Jewish state – or a move into Palestine from Transjordan – but should now concentrate on the task of withdrawing the civil administration and the British forces from Palestine. The Chiefs of Staff should examine the possibility of accelerating the rate of withdrawal of British forces in the light of the new situation. Particular care should be taken to avoid leaving isolated units either of the civil administration or of our forces in areas from which their retirement might be cut off. This should be avoided even at the cost of allowing the efficiency of our civil administration to run down over wide areas of Palestine before the surrender of the Mandate.

Other points in discussion were:

(a) The British authorities in Jerusalem had done everything possible to secure the co-operation of Jews and Arabs, in a scheme for safeguarding the Holy Places, and the United Kingdom representative on the Trusteeship Council had pressed strongly for the appointment of a Governor in order that he might recruit the necessary security forces. Unfortunately, however, the Trusteeship Council had postponed consideration of this matter until 28 April.

(b) No attempt should be made to transfer to the UK or to a British Colony Jews or Arabs now held in Palestine prisons for terrorist offences.

The Cabinet:

(1) Invited the Minister of Defence to arrange for the Chiefs of Staff to consider whether the withdrawal of British forces from Palestine could not be accelerated, in the light of the developments likely to result from the United States proposal that the partition plan should be abandoned.

(2) Invited the Secretary of State for the Colonies to consider whether the units of civil administration in Palestine could not be concentrated in such a way as to reduce the risk that individual units might become isolated.

But in the end it was not by British action or pressure that President Truman was caused to reverse the new trusteeship decision and revert to the original partition plan. Weizmann, who had been preparing to go to Palestine, was in London, and it was no accident that Abba Eban, watching all he had fought for turning to nought, had sent him a telegram on 23 January:

IN VIEW WORSENING SITUATION ADVISE YOU IF POSSIBLE RECONSIDER DECISION TO GO PALESTINE JANUARY. NO CONDITIONS EXIST THERE YOUR CONSTRUCTIVE POLITICAL ACTIVITY. EVERYTHING DEPENDING ON OUTCOME CRUCIAL NEGOTIATIONS LAKE SUCCESS AND WASHINGTON. MOST CRUCIAL PHASE OF ALL NOW APPROACHES HERE IN WHICH WE SORELY MISS YOUR PRESENCE ADVICE ACTIVITY INFLUENCE, AFFECTIONATELY EBAN.[14]

Weizmann, in London and in poor health, took much persuading to make the journey. In March he crossed the Atlantic. Truman was allergic to seeing him. It was his friend Eddie Jacobson, a Kansas Jew, but no Zionist, a former business partner with Truman in a clothing store which had failed, who bullied the President into receiving the Zionist leader. Jacobson went to see the President. Truman was not having it. Jacobson then played his ace. He gestured to a bust of Andrew Jackson:

He's been your hero all your life, hasn't he? You have probably read every book there is on Jackson. I remember when we had the store that you were always reading books and pamphlets and a lot of them were about Jackson. You put his statue in front of the Jackson County Court House in Kansas City when you built it. I have never met the man who has been my hero all my life, but I have studied his past like you have studied Jackson's. He is the greatest Jew alive, perhaps the greatest Jew who ever lived. You yourself have told me that he is a great statesman and a fine gentleman. I am talking about Dr Chaim Weizmann. He is an old man and a very sick man. He has travelled thousands of miles to see you, and now you put off seeing him. That isn't like you.

The President, Jacobson recounts, remained silent, looking out of the window. Then he said, 'All right you bald-headed son of a bitch, you win. Tell Matt [Truman's appointments secretary] to invite Dr Weizmann here.' Jacobson went himself to summon Weizmann to the White House. Truman described the meeting in his own record:

> We talked for almost three-quarters of an hour. He talked about the possibilities of development in Palestine, about the scientific work that he and his assistants had done that would sometime be translated into industrial activity in the Jewish State that he envisaged. . . . I explained to him what the basis of my interest in the Jewish problem was and that my primary concern was to see justice done without bloodshed. And when he left my office, I felt that he had reached a full understanding of my policy and that I knew what it was he wanted.[15]

There was still Foggy Bottom to contend with for the Washington traditional private enterprise system continued to function in the State Department there, busily organizing their own declaration of independence of the President. They stuck to their trusteeship fetish as though Truman did not exist.

The following day, 19 March, Warren Austin, US Ambassador to the United Nations, baldly announced the change they had effected in American policy, rejecting partition. The General Assembly should be specially summoned to ratify an American proposal that the UN should establish a 'trusteeship' over Palestine, 'without prejudice to the character of the eventual political settlement'. UNSCOP was dead, it seemed; UN resolutions discarded. Jews all over the United States rushed to denounce the administration. There was just one quiet voice, that of Weizmann, on the telephone to Jacobson, expressing his confidence that the President would make his promise good. (Eban records that the President was never to forget this act of faith.) The next day, Weizmann's colleagues were busy drafting a personal message for him to send to the President. It was not necessary. Truman had been reading the morning papers.

> Truman called Clark Clifford, his administrative assistant, at 7.30 Saturday morning, March 20. 'Can you come right down', he said, 'there is a story in the papers on Palestine and I don't understand what has happened.' In his office, Truman was as disturbed as Clifford had ever seen him. 'How could this have happened? I assured Chaim Weizmann that we were for partition, and would stick to it. He must think that I am a plain liar. Find out how this could have happened.'[16]

The word went forth but chaos and confusion continued at the UN. Grass-roots Zionist opinion soon began to make itself felt. Eban and the other Israelis intensified their canvassing. The State Department ground out their resolutions as though the White House was untenanted: the Mandate should be continued, on a multi-national, not specifically British, basis. Then Truman's order arrived. Sharett, in charge of the Jewish operation, gave Eban – who had drafted one successful speech for him that day – the task of preparing and delivering the Zionist definitive reply to the debate. Eban records:

> That evening I was among the guests, together with Sharett, at Trygve Lie's home in Forest Hills. Gromyko came up to me, pumped my hand warmly and said, 'You have helped to kill trusteeship'. Trygve Lie was similarly ebullient. In a corner cowered Ernest Bevin and his wife, both sending out waves of venom and hostility.[17]

From that time the trusteeship proposal was dead. So, at long last, was the State Department's revolt against the White House. Indeed their past indiscipline had turned sharply counter-productive. In April, Truman told Judge Samuel Rosenman, simply, 'I have Dr Weizmann on my conscience.' If the General Assembly continued to endorse partition, and the Jewish state was spontaneously created in Palestine, he would accord recognition immediately. As the time for the proclamation drew near and the Arab armies mobilized to destroy the Jewish state, as even American Jews lost their nerve and talked of postponing the creation of the new state, the American Secretary of State, Marshall, stood firm as a rock by Truman's policy.

Weizmann and his aides were pressing the Jewish leaders back home to declare the creation of the new state. To colleague after colleague he was demanding, 'Tell them to proclaim the state no matter what happens.' Sharett was leaving for Israel: 'Don't let them weaken, Moshe; it may be now or never', was Weizmann's message. Manoeuvrings in favour of this resolution, against that one, continued at Lake Success. Meanwhile, Weizmann was writing to Truman asking for American recognition of the Jewish state, once established. The letter was taken to Truman by Weizmann's assistant. Weizmann could not restrain his impatience with the Jewish leaders back home in failing to announce the creation of the state: '*Vos warten zey, die idioten.*' As the UN Political Committee on 14 May was debating details on trusteeship, the American Jewish leader, Abba Hillel Silver, at the Jewish Agency desk, announced to the Assembly:

> This morning at ten o'clock the Jewish state was proclaimed in Palestine. Thus what was envisaged in the resolution of the General Assembly last November has been, as far as the Jewish State is concerned, implemented. Thus too there has been consummated the age-old dream of Israel to be re-established as a free and independent people in its ancient homeland.

But would it be recognized? Would the nations continue to rage together in their fight for trusteeship and dependence? It was Weizmann who received the answer, from Truman himself in response to his own letter of 13 May. The President called a meeting – the Secretary of State, the Under-Secretary, Lovett, Clark Clifford and an official of the State Department. Weizmann's letter arrived, using the name 'Israel' as the title of the new State. At 6.15 p.m. Truman granted recognition. Even so, once again the channels of communication were fouled. The President's message had been sent to the UN by ticker-tape, but miscarried and was then accidentally filed – in Trygve Lie's waste paper basket! The screwed-up scrap of paper was finally handed to the American Ambassador: smoothing it out he went to the rostrum and announced:

> This Government has been informed that a Jewish State has been proclaimed in Palestine and recognition has been requested by the provisional government thereof. The United States recognizes the de facto authority of the new State of Israel.

The Soviet Union immediately recognized the new state, in fact, many months before Britain did.* Egypt responded to the announcement by an aerial bombardment of Tel Aviv. The new Government was embattled almost as soon as it was formed. But one thing the Israelis did not forget. As Weizmann rested in his hotel room a bell-boy entered, bearing a telegram from Tel Aviv:

> ON THE OCCASION OF THE ESTABLISHMENT OF THE JEWISH STATE WE SEND OUR GREETINGS TO YOU WHO HAVE DONE MORE THAN ANY LIVING MAN TOWARDS ITS CREATION. YOUR HELP AND STAND HAVE STRENGTHENED ALL OF US. WE LOOK FORWARD TO THE DAY WHEN WE SHALL SEE YOU AT THE HEAD OF THE STATE ESTABLISHED IN PEACE. BEN GURION   KAPLAN   MYERSON [Golda Meir] REMEZ   SHERTOK.

---

* The United Kingdom recognized Israel *de facto* on 30 January 1949 and *de jure* on 27 April 1950.

CHAPTER 8

Why Do the Nations . . .?[*]

BRITISH RULE IN PALESTINE was due to end on 15 May 1948. For months before the Israelis had been mobilizing against the expected Arab attack. All Haganah members were called up; 21,000 men and women, though arms were scarce. Ben-Gurion was concerned about where command would effectively lie, and decided to rely on senior regular commanders, many from abroad such as Colonel David Marcus (a former member of General Eisenhower's staff) and Ben Dunkelman (previously a Canadian infantry major). With the formation of the Israeli National Administration, Yigael Yadin,[**] at the age of thirty-one, took control of the Israel Defence Forces (IDF) field units. Yigal Allon, later Foreign Minister and Deputy Prime Minister, described by Professor Gunther Rothenburg[1] as 'perhaps the outstanding field commander of the War of Independence', was barely thirty.[†] Yitzhak Rabin, later Prime Minister, was twenty-six, and Shmuel Cohen, commander of the Yiftash Brigade, twenty-five. Moshe Carmel, another commander, was, according to Professor Rothenburg, considered old at thirty-seven. Six of the twelve brigade commanders had 'learned their trade' in the Palmach.

A history of the fighting properly plays no central part in this present

[*] The words in the title are taken from Handel's *Messiah*, an oratorio known to millions of Gentiles in the past two centuries and more.

> Why do the Nations so furiously rage together: why do the people imagine a vain thing?
> The kings of the earth rise up, and the rulers take counsel together: against the Lord, and against his Anointed.
> Let us break their bonds asunder and cast away their yokes from us.
> He that dwelleth in Heaven shall laugh them to scorn: the Lord shall have them in derision.
> Thou shalt break them with a rod of iron; thou shalt dash them in pieces like a potter's vessel. HALLELUJAH.

(Handel took the words from Psalms 1 and 2, and the Book of Revelation, chapters xix 6; xi.15 and xix.16.)

[**] Soldier and archaeologist; during the writing of this book he resigned his position as Deputy Prime Minister in Menachem Begin's coalition Government.

[†] Speaking at a memorial commemoration in Tel Aviv after Yigal Allon died in 1980, I referred to his age: 'rather old for an Israeli general in those days.'

book on Israel in British politics, so a brief summary, following Professor Rothenburg, serves to illustrate the precarious character of Israel's statehood and independence in the nine months which followed British withdrawal.[2] Even before Britain withdrew, the newly founded Jewish units were facing Arab Legion forces from Jordan and her allies, struggling to drive the Israelis out of Jerusalem and the Galilee region, where ancient Safed was under siege. Fighting was raging, too, in Haifa, Palestine's most important port, where the population of 130,000 was almost equally divided between Arabs and Jews. There were mopping-up operations in Tel Aviv, and in the north Allon and Israel Galili cleared lower Galilee and a critical part of the Jordan valley. With Britain's departure, the Palestine Arabs were reinforced by 10,000 Egyptians, 6,000 Jordanians, 4,000 Iraqis, 4,000 Syrians, 1,500 Lebanese, and smaller forces from Saudi Arabia, Yemen and as far away as Morocco. Key areas from Tel Aviv to the Degania settlements in Galilee were threatened. The Egyptians in fact penetrated to within twenty-three miles of Tel Aviv, as well as to Bethlehem, and joined the Arab Legion attacking the parts of Jerusalem held by the Israelis. The UN intervened to stop the fighting and a one-month truce was agreed on 11 June.

Fighting began again on 9 July. Allon forced the Arabs to withdraw from Lud and Ramleh, and relieved the pressure on Tel Aviv, while Latrun was also saved. A second truce, this time of unspecified duration, was called.

In New York Sir Alexander Cadogan proposed a cease-fire on the basis of terms for a truce, terms which included an instruction to the Mediator to make recommendations about an eventual settlement of Palestine – thus seeking to supplant the 33–13 vote of the Assembly on 29 November 1947. The Security Council ordered a cease-fire for four weeks, under the supervision of the Secretary-General of the UN, the Swedish Count Bernadotte, assisted by military observers. Bernadotte claimed that he had accepted the role of mediator 'unbound by any previous decision', and proceeded to issue a statement of nine new constitutional proposals, under which Palestine would become a Union comprising two members, one Arab and one Jew – a return in fact to the Morrison proposal. Further clauses would determine the boundaries. This was, of course, a total reversal of the UN decisions and of the creation of the State of Israel, though some of his other proposals, notably repatriation of Arabs from Israel to congenial neighbouring states, were more imaginative. Sharett (Shertok), the Israeli Prime Minister, issued a statement based on the UN decision:

But for the intervention of the Arab States, there would have been an overwhelming measure of Israel-Arab acquiescence in the establishment of the State of Israel. . . . When the Arab States are ready to conclude a peace treaty with Israel, this question [of repatriation] will come up for constructive solution as part of the general settlement and with due regard to our counter-claim in respect of the destruction of Jewish life and property.[3]

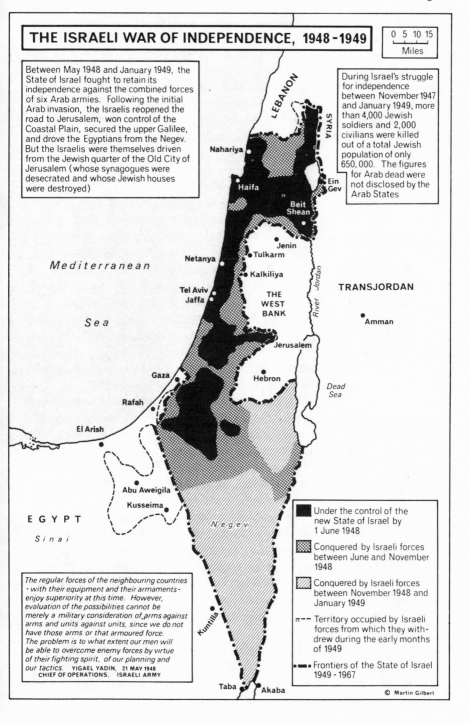

THE ISRAELI WAR OF INDEPENDENCE, 1948-1949

0 5 10 15
Miles

Between May 1948 and January 1949, the State of Israel fought to retain its independence against the combined forces of six Arab armies. Following the initial Arab invasion, the Israelis reopened the road to Jerusalem, won control of the Coastal Plain, secured the upper Galilee, and drove the Egyptians from the Negev. But the Israelis were themselves driven from the Jewish quarter of the Old City of Jerusalem (whose synagogues were desecrated and whose Jewish houses were destroyed)

During Israel's struggle for independence between November 1947 and January 1949, more than 4,000 Jewish soldiers and 2,000 civilians were killed out of a total Jewish population of only 650,000. The figures for Arab dead were not disclosed by the Arab States

LEBANON

SYRIA

Nahariya

Haifa

Ein Gev

Beit Shean

Jenin

Netanya   Tulkarm

Kalkiliya

Tel Aviv
Jaffa

THE
WEST
BANK

River Jordan

TRANSJORDAN

Amman

Jerusalem

Gaza

Hebron

Dead
Sea

Rafah

El Arish

Mediterranean

Sea

EGYPT

Sinai

Abu Aweigila

Kusseima

Negev

The regular forces of the neighbouring countries - with their equipment and their armaments - enjoy superiority at this time. However, evaluation of the possibilities cannot be merely a military consideration of arms against arms and units against units, since we do not have those arms or that armoured force. The problem is to what extent our men will be able to overcome enemy forces by virtue of their fighting spirit, of our planning and our tactics.   YIGAEL YADIN, 21 MAY 1948
CHIEF OF OPERATIONS, ISRAELI ARMY

Kuntilla

Taba   Akaba

■ Under the control of the new State of Israel by 1 June 1948

▨ Conquered by Israeli forces between June and November 1948

▧ Conquered by Israeli forces between November 1948 and January 1949

=-- Territory occupied by Israeli forces from which they withdrew during the early months of 1949

•—■ Frontiers of the State of Israel 1949 - 1967

© Martin Gilbert

Count Bernadotte's proposal of a truce, backed by a Security Council resolution under the 'threat to peace' Article 39 of the Charter – with the implied threat of sanctions – was not uncongenial to the Arabs, who had suffered heavily in the fighting. A body of international advisers was appointed to supervise the truce. Bernadotte's 'back to first base' proposals met with a flat rejection by both Arabs and Israelis. On 17 September 1948 he was murdered by a breakaway section of the Stern Group.* Just as the Stern Gang's murder of Lord Moyne had weakened Winston Churchill's wartime support of the Jews, so now the murder of Bernadotte caused a revulsion against the Israelis.

The truce ended in October, and the Israeli Defence Forces then mounted three major operations. The Egyptians were driven from the Negev, the Syrians from Galilee, and Israeli forces fought their way into the Lebanon. Another truce had been agreed on 22 October, but Fawzi el Kaukji, commanding a Lebanese unit, decided that he was not bound by the UN action in proclaiming a truce, and attacked a Jewish settlement near the Lebanese border. The Israeli counter-strike, 'operation Hirais', cleared out all the remaining Arab invaders and chased Fawzi into Lebanon. Two months later Allon consolidated the attack on the Negev, broke into Sinai and took El Arish, a town not far from the Canal and an Israeli target in subsequent wars.

To curb Israel's successes, Bevin tried to invoke the Anglo-Egyptian Treaty. On 31 December 1948 HM Ambassador in Washington warned the American Government that serious consequences could follow the crossing of the frontier by the Israelis. On 3 January 1949 the Israeli Foreign Office put out a statement accusing Britain of trying to use the Anglo-Egyptian Treaty to save Egypt from defeat. The next day the British Consul-General at Haifa softened the acerbity of the exchange by saying that Britain had no intention of declaring war on Israel, but had just asked the US to use her influence with Israel to prevent a direct dispute. RAF fighters in the Suez Canal made an armed reconnaissance over the Israeli lines and were shot down by Allon's troops. Professor Rothenburg concludes that 'the threat of British intervention, coupled with American pressure, saved the Egyptian army from total destruction'.[4] An armistice was agreed with Egypt on 24 February, but the other Arab states were still at war. The Israelis took advantage of this by an advance on the Negev, taking the fortress of Masada, dating back to the 'zealots' of Biblical times, and for good measure the port of Eilat.

On 26 January 1949 these developments were further debated in the

* Professor Rothenburg attributes this action to 'persons believed to be close to Lehi, "The Fighters for the Freedom of Israel" ', founded by Stern, and active against the British from 1941 onwards.

House of Commons, on a motion for the adjournment of the House. This
time the debate rapidly became a confrontation between Bevin and
Churchill: Churchill interrupted Bevin four times during his opening
speech, and was himself interrupted three times by Bevin, once by Creech-
Jones and once by Attlee.

Bevin indeed began by saying that he was 'unable' to confine the matter
within the narrow limits of the conflict which was going on in Palestine, 'but
rather must take the subject on the wider basis'. In fact, his speech was in the
main a historical survey of justification of his policy from 1945, and claimed
that at all times the Government had steadily supported all the resolutions of
the Security Council as regards both sides in the Palestine dispute: from
that policy His Majesty's Government 'are not going to be deterred an inch'.

> From 1919 to 1945 there has been within successive United Kingdom
> Governments a conflict of policy, and, as far as I can trace it, there was never
> unanimity about how to deal with the problems of the Middle East, and
> especially with Palestine. As a result of the break-up of the Turkish Empire,
> several independent Arab States were formed; but in Palestine the policy was
> to create, in fact, a bi-national State. It seems to me that during all that period
> this country has been trying to ride two very difficult horses at once, and we
> have always been balancing ourselves only with very great difficulty.
>
> Speeches have been made in all parties pledging support to one or other
> solution of the Palestine problem, now to the Jews and now to the Arabs.
>
> Most of the proposals made were incompatible with our obligations under
> the Mandate and were not realizable in practice. I have always been willing
> and eager to take note of and to consider any constructive proposals put
> forward, in this House or elsewhere, for trying to grapple with this problem. I
> have also been confronted with attacks, untruths, half-truths and abuse,
> reflecting not only on me personally, but on the British people who have done
> so much for the Middle East and for Palestine. Some of these things I must
> deal with today, although I have tried to keep mainly to a factual account, in
> the hope that this Debate may still contribute to a final settlement and to
> understanding between these two Semitic peoples . . .[5]
>
> The Government did not create the Palestine problem. I do not want to
> arouse controversy, but ever since I have had anything to do with it I have
> been conscious of one fundamental fact, that the Balfour Declaration
> promised the same thing to two peoples. If partition is difficult now it is
> because the statesmen in those days did not face the problem fearlessly,
> resolutely and finally. If they desired a National State for the Jews and not, as
> they said, a National Home, I cannot understand why they did not carve out a
> piece of territory and then say, 'This is Jewish and that is Arab'. They were
> dealing at that time with a fluid situation and it was no service to posterity to
> take refuge in contradictory statements to Arabs and Jews, leaving this
> problem to go on for 32 years under successive Governments and never
> bringing it to a final issue.
>
> The Right Hon. Gentleman the Member for Woodford [Mr Churchill]

was Colonial Secretary in 1922, and I admire his extraordinary ingenuity, but can he deny that he, too, was faced with a problem to which there was no real solution? In his Memorandum in 1922 entitled, 'British policy in Palestine', which was officially communicated in the name of His Majesty's Government in June of that year to both the Zionist organizations and to a Palestine Arab Delegation then in London, it was stated:

> It is essential to ensure that the immigrants should not be a burden upon the people of Palestine as a whole and they should not deprive any section of the present population of their employment.

I think he, too, is responsible for the rather undefined formula of 'economic absorptive capacity'. It is a commentary on this statement that today –

Mr Churchill: Those half a million Arabs came in during the period of the capacity'.

Mr Bevin: I accept the Right Hon. Gentleman's correction.

Mr Churchill: 'Up to the limits' is an important part of the phrase.

Mr Bevin: It is an important commentary on this statement that over half a million Arabs have been turned by the Jewish immigrants into homeless refugees without employment or resources.

Mr Churchill: Those half a million Arabs came in during the period of the 25 years of British administration, and were an addition to the Arab population, getting employment under the conditions we created.

Mr Bevin: I am adhering to my statement. Throughout the 'thirties successive Governments tried and failed to solve the Palestine problem. I am only dealing with the point that the criticism of this Government is that we have been unable to settle in three and a half years what everybody has been trying to solve by a succession of Commissions and White Papers. . . .[6] At the end of the war the pressure on Jewish immigration was greater than it had ever been, and the Government of Palestine were forced to take costly and unwelcome measures to control it. Jewish immigration was allowed to continue after the limit laid down by the 1939 White Paper, which was 70,000, was passed. I repeat that the professed aim of the Balfour Declaration was the establishment of a National Home, and when my Right Hon. Friend the Secretary of State for the Colonies and I came to deal with this problem we were faced not with a demand for a National Home but for a Jewish State . . .

This development made a more intense conflict with the Arabs inevitable. It also meant we would have to do a thing not contemplated by the Balfour Declaration nor by the League of Nations. It has been suggested that His Majesty's Government have been opposed to the establishment by the Jews of their own State of Israel in fulfilment of centuries of national and religious aspirations. Our original objective, which has been the objective of other Governments since 1917, was to persuade Jews and Arabs to live together in one State as the Mandate charged us to do. We failed in this. The State of Israel is now a fact, and we have not tried to undo it.

At the same time, the tide of Arab nationalism has been running high, and this has not been merely representative of Effendis or wealthy people. I can assure the House that this intensity of feeling on the part of the Arabs at the moment has bitten deep into the ordinary young Arab people, and it will produce a very serious situation unless handled with great care. At the same time it has been extremely difficult to get the Arab States to agree among themselves. There have been quarrels in which the Syrians, the Lebanese and the Iraqis have been involved. That is the situation we found ourselves in up to the point when we tried to grapple with this problem . . .

The Arabs feel as profoundly as the Jews that in the problem of Palestine right is on their side. They consider that for the Arab population, which has been occupying Palestine for more than 20 centuries, to be turned out of their lands and homes to make way for another race is a profound injustice. We understand how this strikes the Arabs – all the Arab people, not only their Governments – and we should consider how the British people would have reacted if a similar demand had been made on us. Suppose we had been asked to give up a slice of Scotland, Wales or Cornwall to another race, and that the present inhabitants had been compelled to make way. I think there might have been trouble in this House, and possibly outside . . .

The Arabs believe that for what they regard as a new and an alien State to be carved out of Arab land by a foreign force, against the wishes and over the protests of the inhabitants, is a profound injustice. The Arabs believe that it is contrary to the right of self-determination and to the principles of the United Nations. I am giving the House and the country their arguments, because there is so much propaganda on the other side and I think it is sometimes forgotten that the Arabs are in the world. They point to the fact that since Britain gave up the Mandate – and I repeat the figure I gave them just now – 500,000 Arabs have been driven from their homes. In Jaffa, which was an Arab town of 70,000, allotted to the Arabs by the Assembly Resolution of 1947, there are now, so I am informed, only 5,000 Arabs . . . [*Interruption*]

The fact is that 500,000 Arabs are gone; they are refugees; and I do not think they walked out voluntarily. I really do not think that it is any good either side being touchy. I am trying to make a balanced speech, and when I get through it will be found that I have done so. However I cannot accept the position that when anybody mentions Arabs he is [*Interruption*] – well, I will leave it at that; I will not use the phrase I was about to use.

Do let us be fair and just. If we proceed on those lines, then I think that in the end we shall get a solution. But I must state the facts, and the fact is that there are over 500,000 Arab refugees, and the marvel to me is that the conscience of the world has been so little stirred over that tragedy. I hate the refugee problem. I think that the driving of poor innocent people from their homes, whether it is in Germany by Hitler, or by anybody else, and making the ordinary working people of the place suffer, is a crime, and we really ought to join together to stop it if we can. Let those who want to quarrel, quarrel; but why visit spite and hate on ordinary people who are doing nothing but earn their living . . . ?

At this point Bevin returned to his old party conference stance and again paraded his sub-conscious feelings about President Truman:

His Majesty's Government were at this stage faced with a problem which had never faced Governments before the war. The United States had long been interested in Palestine, but it was not until 1945 that American interests in Palestine and pledges made in America became one of the determining factors. I have to be very careful what I say here, or I shall be accused of disturbing relations with America; but in defence of His Majesty's Government I ask the House to realize that at this point the whole question of who should be elected to certain offices in the United States turned on this problem, and the United Kingdom had very little latitude after that time. We had to consider the matter on an entirely different footing . . .[7]

He recounted the history of the Anglo-American Parliamentary Commission but was clearly misleading the House when he accused Truman of being willing only to 'accept one point, the immediate immigration of 100,000 Jews', while Britain was willing to accept all the recommendations including the 100,000. This was Ernie's New York obsession coming to the surface. The facts set out in chapter 5 make it clear that Truman welcomed the report as a whole, and that HM Government persistently refused to accept the proposal for the 100,000 until, late in the day, they began to toy with it provided that Truman would undertake to provide financial *and* military support. His account of Britain's responsibility for Bernadotte is equally interesting, as is his summary of the history of the period:

> In the first three months our effort was mainly to induce the Arabs to stop fighting. In the second period, from July 1948, until now, the effort has been to stop the Jews from fighting . . .[8]

But it was the Jewish actions, not those of the Arabs, he recounted. At no point did he accept that the fighting which began on Israel's achievement of statehood was initiated by the Arabs, though his criticism was valid that 'the Jewish side' had refused the United Nations observers access. He further pointed out that when HMG, in pursuance of the Security Council Resolution of 29 May, placed an embargo on the introduction of military personnel, Britain honoured the decision, but Czechoslovakia supplied arms to the Jews. He welcomed the statement of the US representative at the UN General Assembly in Paris, later endorsed by President Truman, that if the Jews were to retain areas occupied by them in Galilee, Jaffa and other portions of Palestine, they should give the Arabs compensation elsewhere.

One of the principal issues in the debate was British recognition of Israel.

> This matter has been under our attention for a long time. The way this question was treated initially was a little unfortunate. I will not take the trouble to go into it in detail now. The United Nations made a decision. The next morning a State was declared. We had been working together on this

problem of Israel with others but recognition was given without any notice. Indeed, recognition was given before the man on the United Nations Delegation* knew about it, and a peculiar situation was developing. There was a good deal of competition between two great Powers in this business which I do not think was the right way to deal with it. Recognition by this country of another country is worth something, and we have not been in the habit of dealing with this matter in a lighthearted way. We want to know first what the country is, what its frontiers are, and what its status is presumed to be. Those States which accorded their recognition have not recognized the State of Israel, but the Government of Israel, without prejudice to frontiers, as did the French Government . . .[9]

Now that armistice talks are at last proceeding, His Majesty's Government have considered whether the time has come when *de facto* recognition might contribute to peace and a settlement. I am glad to say that the United States Government have indicated that they intend to recognize the government of Transjordan, and this also is a material factor. His Majesty's Government have been in consultation with those Commonwealth governments which have not yet recognized Israel about *de facto* recognition of the Israel Government, and we are in close contact with them at the moment. We have also been in consultation with our Brussels Treaty Allies, and this matter will be discussed with the Foreign Ministers at the meeting in London tomorrow.

I should explain what I said a moment ago that recognition would not prejudice the question of the boundaries between Israel and her neighbours, and any recognition that might be given would be on that basis. I am sure that the House will join with me in expressing the hope that, if recognition is now accorded by His Majesty's Government and other Governments which have not yet done so, the Government of Israel will respond on their side by showing that they wish to make their contribution to a wise settlement and peaceful relations with their neighbours . . .[10]

But he made clear he would not act on recognition before he had consulted Commonwealth Governments, and 'there must be peace and no more fighting'. Thirdly, the settlement with Palestine should be on lines most likely to afford a hope of stability throughout the Middle East as a whole. Ernie had kept his options open.

Churchill began by expressing his full support for Bevin in resisting the Communist menace and encroachment, and in cultivating ever closer and more friendly relations with the United States.

But it is on this basis and with this background that we are forced this afternoon to consider the Right Hon. Gentleman's astounding mishandling of the Palestine problem. We feel that this has been so gross and glaring that we should fail in our duty if we did not expose it in the plainest terms. We shall not only do that in Debate; we shall support our criticism in the Lobby.** Only in this way can we make an effective protest and lead public opinion to the true conclusions.

* Presumably a reference to the United States Ambassador to the UN.
** i.e. the Division Lobby, by voting.

The Right Hon. Gentleman's Palestine plight is indeed melancholy and cannot be covered up with wide generalities. No one ever made such sweeping declarations of confidence in himself on this point as the Right Hon. Gentleman, and no one has been proved by events to be more consistently wrong on every turning-point and at every moment than he. Every opportunity for obtaining a satisfactory settlement was thrown away. Immediately after the end of the Japanese war, we had the troops in the Middle East and we had the world prestige to impose a settlement on both sides. That chance was missed. Instead, an Anglo-American Committee of Inquiry was set up to examine the problem. It was on that occasion that the Right Hon. Gentleman staked his political future on solving the Palestine problem. No more rash bet has ever been recorded in the annals of the British turf. Luckily, it is not intended that the wager shall be paid.[11]

He chided Bevin for failing to reach agreement with Truman. Yet, Churchill went on, though this decision was endorsed by the United Nations Assembly on 29 November 1947, His Majesty's Government, despite having referred the matter to the UN for a solution, were not prepared to accept their decision, and even refused to allow the UN Palestine Commission to enter the territory of Palestine until a fortnight before the end of the Mandate.

His Majesty's Government, in the whole of this matter, have always been one, or even two, and sometimes three, steps behind the march of events. When the State of Israel was proclaimed, it was recognized at once by the Americans. His Majesty's Government could at least have accepted the principle of partition laid down in the United Nations Resolution. When they finally accepted that principle in the Bernadotte Report of September last, why could they not have faced reality and accorded *de facto* recognition to Israel?

I have told the tale of different aspects of this story so often that I can but mention today the salient features. These have led us, through vast waste of money, to the repeated loss of British lives, to humiliation of every kind, to the fomenting of injurious hatreds, to a position where Britain has given up every interest she possessed and abandoned the task for which all parties in this island had laboured for a quarter of a century, and has quitted – or half quitted, because in some ways we have not; we still manage to get the disadvantages – the scene of so much valuable work and achievement, amid the scorn and hatred of Arab and Jew and the contemptuous disdain of the civilized world. That is what we are asked to believe deserves our general confidence and approbation as the victory of patience and phlegm in the long run . . .[12]

Churchill went on to press the Government to accord *de facto* recognition to the Israeli Government:

I am quite sure that the Right Hon. Gentleman will have to recognize the Israeli Government and that it cannot be long delayed – I regret that he has

not had the manliness to tell us in plain terms tonight, and that he preferred to
retire under a cloud of inky water and vapour, like a cuttlefish, to some
obscure retreat . . .[13]

He rejected any suggestion that recognition could not be accorded until
boundaries were finally settled.

Whether the Right Hon. Gentleman likes it or not, and whether we like it or
not, the coming into being of a Jewish State in Palestine is an event in world
history to be viewed in the perspective, not of a generation or a century, but in
the perspective of a thousand, two thousand or even three thousand years.
That is a standard of temporal values or time values which seems very much
out of accord with the perpetual click-clack of our rapidly-changing moods
and of the age in which we live. This is an event in world history. How vain it
is to compare it with the recognition, or the claims to recognition, by certain
countries, of the Communist banditti which we are resisting in Malaya or of
the anarchic forces which the Dutch are trying to restrain in Indonesia.

No one has done more to build up a Jewish National Home in Palestine
than the Conservative Party, and many of us have always had in mind that this
might some day develop into a Jewish State [interruption]. I am speaking for
myself anyhow . . . now that it has come into being, it is England that refuses
to recognize it, and, by our actions, we find ourselves regarded as its most
bitter enemies. All this is due, not only to mental inertia or lack of grip on the
part of the Ministers concerned, but also, I am afraid, to the very strong and
direct streak of bias and prejudice on the part of the Foreign Secretary.[14]

He not only made clear his impartiality as between Jews and Arabs, but
outlined what he had done for the Arab cause.

I speak of 25 years of British policy and the settlement made after the First
World War, supported by a Parliament with a great Conservative majority, in
which I was prominently concerned, and which placed Feisal on the throne of
Iraq – and his dynasty is there today. I myself, with the advice and guidance
of Lawrence, took steps to put Emir Abdullah at Amman, where he is still
after 25 years of shock and strain, always a good friend. We took all pains
when we liberated Syria during a difficult moment in the last war to make sure
that the Syrian Arabs had their full rights and independence, and although it
meant bitter controversy with General de Gaulle we insisted upon that at a
moment when, as everyone knows, our margin of control and subsistence was
not large.

I will not have it said that we have not behaved with loyalty to the Arabs or
that what has been asked for the Jews, which was supported and sustained by
the Conservative Party for so many years, to say nothing of the party opposite,
has gone beyond what was just and fair, having regard to the fact that both
these races have lived in Palestine for thousands of years side by side . . .[15]

He ended his fifty-five-minute speech, apologizing for its length, with one
final

protest against the course of action prolonged over nearly four years which has deprived Britain of the credit she has earned, and of the rights and interests she has acquired, and made her at once the mockery and scapegoat of so many States who have never made any positive contribution of their own.[16]

Oliver Stanley wound up for the Opposition, claiming that

everyone of every party who has either spoken or, after the Debate, is going to divide, has been oppressed with feelings of anxiety, feelings of regret, and I am sorry to say, feelings of humiliation.[17]

He explained that he had come to the problem with a different approach from that of Churchill. He had never been a Zionist, in the sense of having felt particularly the emotional appeal of the Zionist cause. He had, in fact, voted for the 1938 White Paper. It was his experience at the Colonial Office which led him to the conclusion that the only practical solution would be partition, despite its 'obvious difficulties and real dangers'. Who, he asked, has gained from all this? Not the Arabs, with 700,000 refugees placed upon the shoulders of the Arab states. Nor the Jews.

We have forfeited the friendship of Israel without gaining the gratitude of the Arabs. . . . Only one set of people has gained from this vacillation of the Government since the UNO Resolution, and they are the set of people who profit from chaos and confusion wherever it happens in the world. If Communism ever does come in Palestine, the Right Hon. Gentleman and his policy will have done most to encourage it.[18]

He ended his speech by making it clear that the official Opposition would go into the Division Lobby and record their vote against the Government, not only because the past conduct of the Government deserved censure, but because it was the only way to shock the Government out of its tragic complacency.

The Prime Minister wound up the debate. His speech as usual was taut, avoiding any kind of emotion, addressed to the facts as he saw them. He reported the Government's standard defence of the break with Truman, and 'nailed another mistake which has had great circulation', viz. the charge that HMG had urged the Arabs to take military action. His speech sought to hold the balance between Arabs and Jews, particularly condemning Arab extremists, including those who sought to cause trouble in Transjordan, and frankly stated that everybody knew there was a truce which was broken by the Arabs. On recognition, he thought it would have been ill-advised to rush into it, but the Government had now been engaged in talks to see whether the time had come to agree to *de facto* recognition. To that end the Government were in consultation with Commonwealth Governments and our Brussels Treaty allies.

Attlee then addressed himself to Churchill, who, he felt, had thought 'that it might be useful to make an attack on my Right Hon. Friend the Foreign Secretary'. The policy being followed was not that of the Foreign Secretary only, it was the policy of the Government. He repudiated the suggestion – 'I am not sure that the Right Hon. Member for Woodford [Churchill] did not make it' – that Bevin was activated by a dislike of the Jews. This he denied, but rather spoilt the effect by saying, 'My Right Hon. Friend has many good friends among the Jews . . .' Bevin had been

> thanked for his work by Jewish Labour for helping them in forming their federation, and getting them into the International Labour Office. Indeed I have seen a paper circulated in which my Rt Hon. Friend is put down – with many other eminent people – as one of the architects of Zionism. Yet there is this vendetta against him.

A not very effective speech ended with an attempt to fathom Churchill's motives. The explanation seemed to be that Churchill saw a General Election not so very far away, in eighteen months, and thought, 'What a good thing it would be if we could remove from the Government such a prominent person as the Foreign Secretary.' Equally, he felt, Churchill was hoping to persuade Labour backbenchers to abstain in the vote at the end of the debate. But 'in vain the net is spread in the sight of any bird'.

The House divided: Ayes, 193; Noes, 283. The Government's majority was more than 250 over all parties. Even allowing for the Liberals, some of whom voted with the Conservatives, the Government suffered a net loss of support of more than 150 votes.

One fact which rankled with the Israelis, and with Churchill, was the determination of the Government to bring home, or transfer to other British territories, the maximum possible equipment previously used by the armed forces rather than leave them as a birthday endowment to the new state.

With Britain's decision finally to recognize the State of Israel, the Arab-Jewish question became a minor and no longer divisive issue in British politics. Rather more than two years after the state was created, Winston Churchill again became Prime Minister, and Anthony Eden, later to succeed him, Foreign Secretary. In 1955 Clement Attlee retired and went to the Lords. He was succeeded by Hugh Gaitskell, who, though not a dedicated Zionist, was undoubtedly a supporter of Israel and had many friends in her Government and political parties. The Israelis got their heads down. The assimilation of immigrants from the Diaspora, whom she was now free to welcome as the result of her victories on the battlefield, absorbed the greater part of her energies. Between 1949 and 1956 the population rose from 1,174,000 to 1,873,000.* In 1949, Jews had accounted for 1,014,000, non-Jews 160,000. In 1956, there were 1,668,000 Jews and 205,000 others.

Dividing the Jewish population between those born in Israel and immigrants – and here we have to take different years – the records show that in 1948, 254,000 of the 717,000 Jews registered were Israeli-born: in 1961, 730,000 of a total Jewish population of 1,932,000 were Israeli-born, while 'non-Jews' had risen from 156,000 in 1948 to 247,000 in 1961, of whom 171,000 were classified as Moslems. In 1948, 5.7 per cent of the world's Jews lived in Israel; in 1951, 12.2 per cent; in 1954, 12.9 per cent, and in 1968, 17.7 per cent.

Taking countries of origin, before 1954 429,000 immigrants had been born in Europe or America; 102,000 in Africa, and 230,000 in Asia (excluding Israel itself).

Trade figures during this period showed gross exports rising from $28.5 million to $89.1 million in 1955, and $245.3 million in 1961. Gross imports in these three years were $253.7 million, $336.8 million and $592 million respectively, exports as a percentage of imports rising from 11.3 in 1949 to 26.6 in 1955 and 40.9 per cent in 1961.

Agricultural output (1967–8 = 100) rose from 24 in 1951–2, to 42 in 1956–7, and to 71 in 1961–2. The areas cultivated measured in thousands of dunams (roughly four dunams to the acre) rose from 1,650, of which 300 were irrigated, to 3,475 in 1951–2, of which 540 were irrigated; 3,820 in 1956–7, of which 1,110 were irrigated; and 4,150 in 1961–2 of which 1,360 were irrigated. Afforestation showed an increase from 53,000 dunams in 1948–9, to 133,000 in 1951–2, 231,000 in 1956–7, and 326,000 in 1961–2. The development of cultivated products, by groups, is set out over the period in the following table:[19]

	Field crops	Vegetables, potatoes, melons and pumpkins	Citrus fruits	Other fruit	Fish ponds	Miscellaneous, including flower farms and nurseries
1948–9	1,094	106	125	230	15	80
1951–2	2,676	248	135	275	30	111
1956–7	2,753	279	246	352	41	149
1961–2	2,915	267	340	413	53	162

* For comparison, it reached 3,653,000 by 1977. Different years are used in the population statistics set out in these pages because the current issue of the *Statistics Abstract of Israel 1975* tends to select different years for the early periods in different tables.

CHAPTER 9

*Tangled Web**

THE SUEZ CRISIS OF 1956 produced the greatest trauma in British politics since the Second World War. The major political parties were divided. The Prime Minister and white hope of the Conservative Party was destroyed after only twenty-one months in office. The leadership of the Labour Party, then in opposition, moved from support of Eden's first response to outright rejection of his policies, while being able to maintain total consistency through Hugh Gaitskell's early demand that no action be taken without United Nations approval and support. Families were divided, political parties were divided. Historians, a decade later, were practically all agreed that Suez marked the end of Britain's mission as a world power. In place of imperialism, she turned inward to a preoccupation with her possible place in a West European grouping.

It had been proved that Britain could no longer go it alone. Power had passed to the super-nations: America and Russia. Harold Macmillan, foremost among the hawks who joined in forcing Eden into the undeclared war over the Canal, the man who speedily became its principal political beneficiary, had, more than most Prime Ministers, a profound sense of history. For him the failure of the war was one of the climacterics of history, as is shown by his diary entry on becoming Prime Minister after Suez:

> The events of the last few months had been a grievous shock both to those who approved and to those who were opposed to the last Government's actions. The fact that France and Britain, even acting together, could no longer impose their will was alarming. Never before in history had Western Europe proved so weak.... Was I destined to be the remodeller or the liquidator of Empire?[1]

The Suez crisis has proved to be the theme for more histories and commentaries than any other event in Britain's story since the Second World War. A complete bibliography of those so far published, and more have

* 'O, what a tangled web we weave, when first we practise to deceive.' Walter Scott, *Marmion*, canto VI, section XVII.

243

appeared while this present book was being written, would occupy many, many pages. Apart from the memoirs of Eden, Macmillan, Selwyn Lloyd, Anthony Nutting, the relevant chapters of the biographies or autobiographies of their contemporaries, such as Hugh Gaitskell, George Brown and others, many more have been written by both political and military historians and by statesmen in Britain, America, Israel and elsewhere. What unfortunately has not yet been made available is the voluminous set of Cabinet papers and Minutes 'Conclusions' for the period. The 'Thirty Year Rule' prevents their publication in whole or in part until 1986.*

There is another problem. Few of the later memoirs – not those of Eden, Macmillan and, only to a limited extent, Selwyn Lloyd – have revealed the so-called 'conspiracy' between Britain, France and Israel to precipitate a war in order to destroy Egypt's President Nasser. No one today accepts the explanation given by the Government at the time, and for some years afterwards, that Britain and France intervened simply to separate the combatants, Egypt and Israel. Israel's attack on Egypt, and the Anglo-French intervention, were in fact planned by leading politicians at meetings in Paris, London and Chequers. Their plotting was well known in Washington, though severely disapproved of, to Eisenhower and Dulles.

On 26 July President Gamal Abdul Nasser of Egypt announced the unilateral nationalization of the Suez Canal.** The Prime Minister, Sir

* Until 1974 the close period for the publication of Cabinet papers was fifty years. My proposed twenty-five year rule would, in fact, have led to the documents relating to Suez seeing the light of day about the same time as the publication of this book. The change required the agreement of the Opposition, who were not willing to go below thirty years. I was not a member of the Cabinet in those years, so I did not have any access to the papers, as I had to the Labour Cabinet records relating to the Six Day War in 1967. The same prohibition applies to the Yom Kippur War of 1973 (see chapter 12 below). A Shadow Cabinet's knowledge of events is inevitably limited, except when, as is usually the case, the Prime Minister takes the Leader of the Opposition into his confidence in the national interest. It is then for the Opposition Leader to decide how much to communicate to his colleagues, a quantum directly related to the trust he has in them. In 1956 nothing was communicated by the Government to the Labour Front Bench beyond what was known to Parliament as a whole, and to the general public.

** Eden heard the news towards the end of a dinner in honour of King Feisal of Iraq and his Prime Minister, Nuri es-Said, attended by Hugh Gaitskell on behalf of the Opposition, a number of members of the Cabinet, the French Ambassador, the Chiefs of Staff, and the US Chargé d'Affaires, Andrew Foster. The members of the Cabinet present remained for a brief meeting.

It was not a night for humour. As the guests left, Nuri-es-Said, trying for a moment to relieve the tension, pointed to the bust of Disraeli in the corridor leading to the front door, and said, 'That's the old Jew who got you into all this trouble.' Eden was not amused. (Leonard Mosley, *Dulles*, New York, 1978, p. 405.)

Macmillan and Lord Salisbury were dining with Robert Murphy, the American Defence Secretary, and Macmillan took an extremely robust anti-Nasser line, which he later explained as being designed to stiffen the American administration.

Anthony Eden, made a brief holding statement in Parliament. He announced that monetary measures, including an order under the Exchange Control Act, had put Egypt outside the transferable account area and made all transactions in Egyptian-controlled sterling accounts subject to Treasury permission. A second measure was a statutory direction safeguarding the securities and gold of the Suez Canal Company. But, added Eden:

> This much, however, I can say. No arrangements for the future of this great international waterway could be acceptable to Her Majesty's Government which would leave it in the unfettered control of a single power which could, as recent events have shown, exploit it purely for purposes of national policy.[2]

Close touch was being maintained with the Commonwealth, and on the previous day the French Foreign Minister and Mr Robert Murphy of the State Department had arrived for consultations with Eden and the Foreign Secretary. These had continued until a late hour the previous night and were to resume that afternoon.

Selwyn Lloyd's memoirs of Suez[3] provide the most authoritative book written by any of those bearing ministerial responsibility at the time, though even his work is extremely perfunctory in its record of the conspiracy with the French, at least partly suggesting that he was not fully in the picture – or perhaps, to the extent that he was, viewing the whole thing with distaste. My opinion on this is based not only on the carefully considered, if somewhat bowdlerized, memoirs now published but on many long private discussions with him. As Speaker of the House of Commons from 1971–6 he was a very lonely figure, and I would often go up to his study of nights, right up to the time of his translation to the Lords.

Eden was tormented throughout and in the later stages was seriously ill. The Minister who never doubted that the policy was right, and who saw it through almost to the end, was Harold Macmillan, Chancellor of the Exchequer and guardian of Britain's gold reserves, who himself cracked when the Americans applied financial sanctions.

As the Prime Minister, Sir Anthony Eden, made clear in Parliament on 2 August 1956, following Nasser's action, the Canal, built by de Lesseps and opened in 1869, was the subject of two binding international agreements. The first was the 'Concession' under which the then Egyptian Government authorized the construction and management of the waterway by the Suez Canal Company, and which defined the rights and status of the Company, and the obligations of the Egyptian Government towards it. Indeed, less than seven weeks before Nasser's action, on 10 June, these understandings had been endorsed by the conclusion of a formal Financial Agreement between the Egyptian Government and the Company, which was to continue in force until the expiry of the original Concession in 1968.

The second instrument was the international Suez Canal Convention of 1888, which clearly laid down that the Canal should always be open, in time of war as in time of peace, to every vessel of commerce or of war without distinction of flag. The Convention had been signed by nine Powers, including the Sultan of Turkey on behalf of the Khedive of Egypt.[4]

Furthermore, Eden pointed out, so far as Britain was concerned, the Anglo-Egyptian Treaty of 1954 recognized that the Canal is a waterway which is economically, commercially and strategically of international importance, and expressed the determination of both parties to uphold the still valid 1888 Convention. He went on to stress not only the importance of non-discrimination in respect of passage through the Canal, but also the continuing growth in its traffic of about 7 per cent a year; oil traffic was developing particularly rapidly: ten million tons more oil had gone through the Canal in 1955 than in the previous year. Already, plans were in hand to increase its capacity at a cost of £20 million, and the Company had been accumulating capital for this purpose from the reserves of the Company and the shipping revenues. 'But', said Eden, 'Colonel Nasser has now announced his intention to divert these revenues from this vital international waterway to build a dam in Egypt.'

Eden was referring to the Aswan Dam project for developing the Nile valley. Britain and the US had offered to pay the foreign exchange costs of this project mainly because they feared that otherwise Moscow would step in as part of its drive for greater influence in the Middle East. In 1955 Egypt had approached the US for arms, and Washington had driven a hard bargain, asking for cash on delivery. Nasser then began to turn to the Soviet Union and Czechoslovakia. The Anglo-US offer on Aswan had been designed to turn Egypt away from the Russians, and to this end Selwyn Lloyd and Christian Pineau, heads respectively of the British and French Foreign Offices, visited Egypt. It was while they were there that a major political revolution occurred nearby. While the British Foreign Secretary was actually dining with Nasser, King Hussein of Jordan abruptly sacked General Glubb ('Glubb Pasha'), his pro-British military adviser and commander of the Arab Legion. Meanwhile Nasser heard that the French Socialist Government, headed by Guy Mollet, had supplied Mystère aircraft to the Israelis. As Nasser's publicity machine became more and more strident against France and Britain, and as East European influences seemed to be taking hold, the West turned cold on financing Aswan. The US Secretary for Finance had done his calculations and suspected that Egypt was so over-extended financially that she would even have had to default on the interest due on previous World Bank loans. On 19 July the US and, two days later, the British withdrew their offer of finance. (Nasser was to be further angered when the Russians, who had stepped into the financial breach, also cooled on Aswan; in fact, it took two more years before they put money on the table.) Within a week Nasser announced his take-over of the Canal.

Eden had no confidence in Nasser's assurances, still less in his intentions of compensating the Canal Company's shareholders. The net annual revenue of the Canal (after providing for taxation and reserves) was about £10 million. Compensation, the cost of Aswan and the development capital required for the Canal itself, Eden put at £70 million. Nor could the Western World even trust Nasser to maintain free passage through the Canal. In defiance of the Convention he had already denied passage to Israeli vessels for years. Eden was particularly critical, too, of the Egyptian action in compelling the Company employees, drawn from many countries, to remain at their posts under threat of imprisonment: 'certainly, to say the least, a violation of human rights'.[5] 'In these circumstances', he went on to tell the House 'of certain precautionary measures of a military nature'. These included the movement of Navy, Army and Air Force units, and the recall of reservists from Section A and B and Army Emergency Reserve Category I and II together with a number of officers from the Regular Army Reserve of Officers. This would require a Royal Proclamation.

Hugh Gaitskell's response, rightly applauded by Eden himself and most of the national press, began by making clear that while the Opposition had been critical of the Government's Middle East policy, and as recently as March had divided the House for a vote on the issue, nothing the Government had done in any way excused Nasser's action. The Labour Opposition was not opposed to the principle of nationalization, provided that fair compensation was paid – which Nasser was in no position to afford.

At this stage one must look at the issue from the point of view of each of the two front benches in the House of Commons, Cabinet and Shadow Cabinet. The line-up of Eden's ministers, now known in detail, was only partially clear at the time. Eden himself was in poor health. At one of the earlier crisis points, visiting his wife in hospital, he himself was taken ill. His chatterbox doctor, writing his own memoirs, has revealed the facts about the Prime Minister's liver-duct, from which he had become a semi-invalid following surgery; further American surgery only partially relieved his condition. But about Harold Macmillan's part in these events, there was never any doubt. In the course of the debates which marked the inquest on Suez I characterized his record as, 'First in, first out' – the last two words a reference to his demand on the day the war began for a withdrawal of British troops as a result of the American Government's carefully orchestrated Wall Street run on sterling.

Rab Butler was never an adherent of the Suez cause. Wishing to wound but fearing to strike, he went along with the mob, while all the time contenting himself with mental dissociation. When Eden resigned through illness early in 1957, it was Macmillan, not Butler, the obvious candidate, who succeeded (as indeed was to happen again six years later, when Macmillan and his friends were successful in blocking the choice of Butler as successor to Macmillan himself, instead securing the appointment of Lord Home). Kingsley Martin, editor of the *New Stateman and Nation*, fairly summed up the 1957 battle of succession when he said that the Conservative Party after Suez were like a group of men who had been out on a drinking party, and when they sat around the next morning with severe headaches and mouths feeling like the bottom of a parrot's cage, they turned, in their wrath, not against the man who had taken them on the night's dissipation, but against the one who went along and spent the whole night drinking tomato juice.

The problem facing the Shadow Cabinet from 26 July onwards in one way was not easy, not least because Hugh Gaitskell and George Brown had been for years in basic disagreement about the Middle East. Hugh Gaitskell was close to the Israelis, George was regarded by many pro-Jewish Labour MPs as a 'raging Arab'. It was true that he was closer to a number of Arab leaders, and was indeed later shattered almost to the point of tears when King Feisal and Nuri-es-Said of Iraq were murdered, Gaitskell expressing his sympathy at a Shadow Cabinet meeting.* When the Suez war began, George, in all fairness and within his rights, was able to insist that, as they had agreed that the party could not support aggression, the fact that the Israelis struck first meant that the PLP could not support them. Both of them, however, and indeed all of us, were agreed that we could not support any resort to war which did not receive UN approval. For George this insistence was a necessary condition and if only for this reason it was for Hugh Gaitskell an imperative in every statement he made. In fact, as this chapter and the next make clear, Israel had every reason to thank George Brown for his attitude throughout the months which followed Nasser's action.

While Gaitskell emotionally supported the Israelis, as many of us did, he nevertheless felt able to reconcile this with an insistence on opposing any military action which was not sanctioned by the Security Council of the United Nations. At one crucial stage it was the combined pressure of the Shadow Cabinet at home and Eisenhower across the Atlantic which was

---

* The Parliamentary Labour Party's collective leadership when in opposition is the elective Parliamentary Committee, more often known as the Shadow Cabinet. Its decisions and advice on Parliamentary strategy are reported to the PLP, the assembly of Labour MPs. I was a member of this Committee from 1954 to Labour's entry into Government in 1964, and all references are based upon personal recollection, fortified by checking the records publicly available.

decisive in forcing Eden's Government to go to the UN. And it was the Security Council's order of a cease-fire under American leadership which brought the Suez operation to an end.

Gaitskell made a fuller and more considered statement when Eden reported further to the House on 2 August. His reply was clear and consistent:

> The real objections, it seems to me, are three. In the first place, as the Prime Minister has rightly emphasized, this is not an ordinary Company, conducting ordinary activities. It is a Company controlling an international waterway of immense importance to the whole of the rest of the world. It is, therefore, bound to be a matter of international concern when it changes hands. Hitherto, it has been under the control and ownership very largely of the States using it, of the maritime Powers, and it is quite true, as the Prime Minister has said, also, that while I think that the interests of Egypt have been considered and taken into account, and, as Colonel Nasser has recently said, relations between the Company and the Egyptian Government have been amicable, nevertheless the Company has certainly taken care of the interests of the user countries.
>
> Now the ownership and control of the Company is to be transferred to a single Power, to the hands of one State controlling it and, therefore, in a position even more than before to decide how the Canal shall be run. It may be said there is no need for anxiety because we have had these assurances about the 1888 Convention. I am bound to say that it seems to me the strongest reason for having doubts in our minds as to whether we can accept those assurances has been the behaviour of the Egyptian Government in stopping Israeli ships from going through, and equally important – indeed, even more important – the clear defiance of the Resolutions of the United Nations condemning this action, passed in September 1951.
>
> The second reason why I think we must take strong exception to this is that any confidence we might have had in an action of this kind was profoundly shaken by the manner in which it was carried out. It was done suddenly, without negotiation, without discussion, by force, and it was done on the excuse that this was the way to finance the Aswan Dam project. Colonel Nasser himself, at the conclusion of his speech a week ago, said:
>
>> Thus, you will see that our wealth has been restored to us and that we shall not look forward to the Anglo-American financial aid amounting to 75 million dollars because we shall henceforth get from the profits of the Suez Canal the sum of 100 million dollars every year and in five years we shall secure 500 million dollars.
>
> That, in effect, means that he is proposing to take the whole of the gross revenues of the Canal – almost all of them transit dues – and divert them for the purpose of the Aswan Dam. Yet he has promised compensation. How can he at one and the same time both keep the Canal going, spend the necessary money on the repairs, extensions and reconstruction, pay the compensation or service the compensation loan to the shareholders, and also find money for the Aswan Dam . . .?

My third reason for thinking that we must object to this is that we cannot ignore – and this is a matter that the Prime Minister did not touch upon, no doubt for good reasons – the political background and the repercussions of the whole of this episode in the Middle East. We cannot forget that Colonel Nasser has repeatedly boasted of his intention to create an Arab empire from the Atlantic to the Persian Gulf. The French Prime Minister, M. Mollet, the other day quoted a speech of Colonel Nasser's and rightly said that it could remind us only of one thing – of the speeches of Hitler before the war.

Colonel Nasser has certainly made a number of inflammatory speeches against us and his Government have continued attempted subversion in Jordan and other Arab States; he has persistently threatened the State of Israel and made it plain from time to time that it is his purpose and intention to destroy Israel if he possibly can. That, if ever there was one, is a clear enough notice of aggression to come.

The fact is that this episode must be recognized as part of the struggle for the mastery of the Middle East. That is something which I do not feel that we can ignore.[6]

He went on to suggest that any control commission which was set up should be a United Nations agency. This was a theme to which he was to continue to return in the debates which lay ahead that heated summer and autumn.

In the debate which followed, a very different view was put by right-wing Conservative members. Lord Hinchingbrooke had a word for the Americans:

The USA exemplifies and puts into effect the international theme on every possible occasion. The headquarters of the United Nations and the United Nations Agencies resides in the United States. When it came to post-war action in Korea, the United States acted first and secured diplomatic assistance afterwards, and we ourselves were instant in our readiness to go to her aid and follow her in.

Shame on that country now, shame, I regret to say, on the country which gave my mother birth, that she should be behind us by days or even months in our endeavours jointly with the French to do for the Old World what she so successfully has done in the New.[7]

He called on the US to look on the isthmus of Suez as her history demanded that she must look upon the isthmus of Panama.[8]

Midway through the debate Selwyn Lloyd intervened, explaining that he had to go for discussions with the two Foreign Ministers then in London: Dulles, the US Secretary of State, and Pineau, the French Foreign Minister. He added little to the debate and wisely subtracted nothing, simply stressing the impossibility of leaving Nasser in unchallenged control of the Canal and of its employees, whom he was at that moment threatening. British subjects were involved – so were British ships:

Therefore, I think that the Government would be failing in their duty if they did not take precautionary measures. Nevertheless, whilst taking these precautionary measures, we still seek and will do our best to achieve an international solution of the matter.[9]

He went on to claim, fairly, that the Government could feel as a result of the debate that they had the support of almost the whole House in what they were doing.

The fact was that the House had no knowledge of what the Government was doing, or rather at that stage was planning, if only on a contingency basis. Nor indeed, of the torment through which Eden was going. It was not only that his long diplomatic experience led him to attach great importance to keeping the Middle East cauldron from boiling over which dominated his thinking. Nasser was not the first dictator Eden had had to deal with. Eden's resignation from the Foreign Office in February 1938 when he refused to tolerate any longer Chamberlain's vain and amateurish manoeuvring with Mussolini's Ambassador, and the six years of war which followed, had ingrained in him a detestation of dictators and a determination to act against any upsurge of dictatorial power by instant and resolute resistance:

> It is important to reduce the stature of the megalomaniac dictator at an early stage. A check to Hitler when he moved to re-occupy the Rhineland would not have destroyed him, but it would have made him pause. The world would then have had time to assess the truth, and the Germans occasion to question themselves. This process would have been altogether salutary. 'Though your enemy be an ant,' runs the Turkish proverb, 'imagine that he is an elephant.' Nowadays it is considered immoral to recognize an enemy. Some say that Nasser is no Hitler (or Mussolini). Allowing for a difference in scale, I am not so sure. He has followed Hitler's pattern even to concentration camps and the propagation of *Mein Kampf* among his officers.[10]

(Eden goes on to comment on the fact that a number of Arabic translations of *Mein Kampf* were found by the Israeli army in the possession of Egyptian officers after the Sinai campaign.)

The real truth about the planning of the Suez War, though soon known to Eisenhower and many members of his Administration, was not known to British or world public opinion for several years. Everyone was familiar with the main events, ending with the cease-fire on 6 November, but very few – Cabinet ministers, the French leaders and the Israeli high command apart – knew of the plotting with the Israelis. Harold Macmillan and Anthony Eden made no reference in their respective memoirs to the Sèvres meeting or to any such plotting.* Selwyn Lloyd's factual account of the diplomatic moves and the events which led to the cease-fire in his Suez book published in 1978 is

* See pp. 265–80 below. The names Sèvres, Villacoublay, Patrick Dean and Donald Nolan (Lloyd's private secretary), who were involved in these meetings, do not appear in Lloyd's index or in that of Macmillan.

extremely guarded about the Israeli role. It is doubtful how much he knew until late October but certain that he did not want to know. Nor did those of his colleagues closely involved in the plotting want him to know.

My own view, both from talks with Selwyn Lloyd and from his book, written after all the other disclosures from Professor Hugh Thomas onwards,* is that he knew of Israel's intended participation in any military moves which might take place to oust Nasser, but that he knew little until very late in the day of the scenario under which Israel would attack first, and Britain and France would then intervene to separate the combatants, getting rid of Nasser and reopening the Canal to traffic on the 1888 terms. His public utterances, that military force could not be ruled out in all circumstances, were a statement of the obvious, not related to any specific military plans to which he was at that time a party. Still less did MPs know of the pressures which would very quickly be put on Eden and Lloyd from the French, nor the perfidious lengths to which the French, without telling their British partners, would soon be going in their manoeuvrings with Israel.

France had a Socialist administration which had, for a French Government, an unusual degree of support in the Assembly. France also had a debilitating war in her North African Empire. Nasser was supplying arms and money to the Algerian rebels. French casualties were high and progress towards victory slow. Action to cut off the flow of Egyptian weapons to Algeria was urgent; hence any proposal to rock, better still destroy, the Nasser régime was timely and relevant.

Meanwhile the United States Government was considering its position. Eisenhower was touring the country on his campaign for re-election as President. It was Murphy, reporting on his London visit, and in particular his dinner with Macmillan and Salisbury, who alerted him to the position of the Westminster hawks. Having received Murphy's report, clearly coloured by what Macmillan in particular had told him, Eisenhower on 31 July wrote an anxious letter to Eden:

Dear Anthony:

From the moment that Nasser announced nationalization of the Suez Canal Company, my thoughts have been constantly with you. . . . Until this morning, I was happy to feel that we were approaching decisions as to applicable procedures somewhat along parallel lines. . . . But early this morning I received the messages, communicated to me through Murphy from you and Harold Macmillan, telling me on a most secret basis of your decision to employ force without delay or attempting any intermediate and less drastic steps.

* Hugh Thomas's *The Suez Affair* was published in 1966. Unaccountably I was told in 1979 when attempting to buy a copy of Hugh Thomas's work from one of London's leading bookshops, that it was out of print.

We recognize the transcendent worth of the Canal to the free world and the possibility that eventually the use of force might become necessary in order to protect international rights. But we have been hopeful that through a Conference, in which would be represented the signatories to the Convention of 1888, as well as other maritime nations, there would be brought about such pressures on the Egyptian government that the efficient operation of the Canal could be assured for the future . . .

I cannot over-emphasize the strength of my conviction that some such method must be attempted before action such as you contemplate should be undertaken. . . . Public opinion . . . would be outraged should there be a failure to make such efforts. Moreover, initial military successes might be easy, but the eventual price might become far too heavy.

I have given you my own personal conviction . . . as to the unwisdom even of contemplating the use of military force at this moment. Assuming, however, that the whole situation continued to deteriorate to the point where such action would seem the only recourse, there are certain political facts to remember. . . . Employment of the United States forces is possible only through positive action on the part of the Congress. . . . There would have to be a showing that every peaceful means of resolving the difficulty had previously been exhausted. Without such a showing, there would be a reaction that could very seriously affect our people's feeling toward our Western Allies. . . . This could grow to such an intensity as to have the most far-reaching consequences.

I realize that the messages from both you and Harold [Macmillan] stressed that the decision taken was already approved by the government and was firm and irrevocable. But I personally feel sure that the American reaction would be severe. . . . On the other hand, I believe we can marshal that opinion in support of a reasonable and conciliatory, but absolutely firm, position. So I hope that you will consent to reviewing this matter once more in its broadest aspects. It is for this reason that I have asked Foster [Dulles, Secretary of State] to leave this afternoon to meet with your people tomorrow in London . . .

The step you contemplate should not be undertaken until every peaceful means . . . has been thoroughly explored and exhausted. Should these means fail . . . then world opinion would understand how earnestly all of us had attempted to be just, fair and considerate, but that we simply could not accept a situation that would in the long run prove disastrous to the prosperity and living standards of every nation whose economy depends directly or indirectly upon East–West shipping.

With warm personal regard and earnest assurances of my continuing respect and friendship.

> As ever
> DE[11]

What is particularly worrying about the letter is that Eisenhower twice referred to messages from Eden *and Macmillan*. Macmillan had no status in the matter over and above that shared by every member of the Cabinet. His contribution had been made at the private dinner with Robert Murphy, and his (and Salisbury's) belligerent outbursts carried no Cabinet authority. The only legitimate channels to the White House and American administration were Eden himself and the Foreign Secretary.

On 31 July Dulles descended on London. Washington was remarkably relaxed, unlike Downing Street. Nasser, Dulles felt, would not be likely to cut off his toll revenue to spite his face. In any case, Suez was not Panama – the Panama Canal was American-constructed and American-owned. Chester Cooper, the US Central Intelligence Agency (CIA) representative in London, in fact argues that one reason why Dulles wanted to play Suez down was his fear that too provocative a line might lead the Panamanians to take over the Panama zone. Dulles met Eden and Pineau. The French Foreign Minister was extremely rude to his American opposite number. He blamed the Americans for causing the crisis by reneging on the Aswan Dam. In private, according to Pineau, Eden was as rude to him about Dulles as Pineau had been to Dulles's face. The American had in fact some soothing words for Eden. Of course it was 'intolerable' for Egypt to control the Canal without international supervision. Force – not to be ruled out – should be used only as a last resort. Nasser must be made to 'disgorge'. 'Those were forthright words', said Eden. 'They rang in my ears for months.'[12]

The tripartite meeting decided to summon an international conference to discuss the crisis and settled on 16 August. British shipowners, Eden told Dulles, had been told to pay their Council tolls to the Canal Company in London for the time being; Dulles could not forecast how US shipowners would react. In any case a considerable proportion of American ships sailed under flags of convenience: Liberian, Panamanian and others. The three powers issued an agreed statement:

> The present action involves far more than a simple act of nationalization. It involves the arbitrary and unilateral seizure by one nation of an international agency which has the responsibility to maintain and to operate the Suez Canal so that all the signatories to, and beneficiaries of, the treaty of 1888 can effectively enjoy the use of an international waterway upon which the economy, commerce and security of much of the world depends.[13]

At Dulles's suggestion Eden agreed to call a meeting of the eighteen nations who had signed the 1888 treaty or had later become dependent on the Canal.

By 8 August the British and French military had agreed on contingency plans for a joint attack on Egypt, and General Hugh Stockwell and Major General André Beaufre were appointed commander and deputy. The plan was for an attack on Alexandria from the sea followed by a French move towards the Canal and then on to Cairo. On that day Eden made a nationwide broadcast:

> The alternatives are clear for all to see. If we all join together to create an

international system for the Canal and spend its revenues as they should be spent . . . there will be wealth for all to share, including Egypt. There is no question of denying her a fair deal or a just return. . . . Meanwhile we have too much at stake not to take precautions. We have done so. That is the meaning of the movements by land, sea and air of which you heard in the last few days. We do not seek a solution by force, but by the broadest possible agreement. That is why we have called the conference . . .[14]

The 1888 Convention signatories' meeting convened in London as planned. Meanwhile Eisenhower and Dulles, worried about London's militancy, met leaders of Congress and warned them of possible fighting in the Middle East. The President described the situation as 'serious', and Dulles used the word 'grim'. But as early as 8 August Eisenhower at a press conference had said:

> I can't conceive of military force being a good solution, certainly under the conditions as we know them now . . . every important question in the world in which more than one nation is interested should be settled by negotiation.[15]

'Disgorging' was no longer in vogue. Eisenhower's Ambassador to Moscow in an interview with Premier Bulganin compared Nasser with Hitler. The Russians, however, were moving fast towards condemning the use of force, and at the meeting of 1888 Convention powers, Shepilov, the Foreign Minister said:

> We believe that the Egyptian government . . . was acting within the norms of international law . . . and therefore Suez cannot be the subject of discussion either at this or any other international conference.

The Conference of 'Eighteen' – by this time sixteen – decided to send Robert Menzies, Prime Minister of Australia, leading an international delegation, to Cairo to seek to persuade Nasser to withdraw his restriction. Eisenhower elaborated further on the American position in a letter to Eden on 8 September:

> Whenever, on any international question, I find myself differing even slightly from you, I feel a deep compulsion to re-examine my position instantly and carefully. But permit me to suggest that when you use phrases in connection with the Suez affair, like 'ignoble end to our long history' in describing the possible future of your great country, you are making Nasser a much more important figure than he is . . .
>
> The use of military force against Egypt under present circumstances might . . . cause a serious misunderstanding between our two countries because I must say frankly that there is as yet no public opinion in this country which is prepared to support such a move, and the most significant public opinion . . . seems to think that the United Nations was formed to prevent this very thing.
>
> It is for reasons such as these that we have viewed with some misgivings your preparations for mounting a military expedition against Egypt.
>
> At the same time, we do not want any capitulation to Nasser. We want to stand firmly with you to deflate the ambitious pretensions of Nasser and to

assure permanent free and effective use of the Suez waterway . . .

It seems to Foster and to me that the result that you and I both want can best be assured by slower and less dramatic processes than military force. There are many areas of endeavor which are not yet fully explored because exploration takes time.

We can, for example, promote a semi-permanent organization of the user governments to take over the greatest practical amount of the technical problems of the Canal, such as pilotage, the organization of the traffic patterns, and the collection of dues to cover the actual expenses. This organization would be on the spot and in constant contact with Egypt and might work out a *de facto* co-existence which would give the users the rights which we want . . .

Nasser thrives on drama. If we let some of the drama go out of the situation and concentrate upon the task of deflating him through slower but surer processes . . . the desired results can more probably be obtained . . . we could isolate Nasser and gain victory which would not only be bloodless, but would be more far reaching in its ultimate consequences than could be anything brought about by force of arms. In addition, it would be less costly both now and in the future.

Of course, if during this process Nasser himself resorts to violence . . . then that would create a new situation and one in which he and not we would be violating the United Nations charter.

I assure you we are not blind to the fact that eventually there may be no escape from the use of force. . . . But to resort to military action when the world believes there are other means available for resolving the dispute would set in motion forces that could lead, in the years to come, to the most distressing results . . .

> As ever your
> friend,
> DE

In his own public utterances, Eisenhower was in fact becoming almost garrulous – politicians in the middle of an election campaign frequently get that way. On 11 September, the eve of Eden's recall of Parliament, he addressed yet another press conference in words which must have been manna from heaven for Nasser. He was asked whether the US would back Britain and France if in the event they were to resort to force:

> Well . . . I don't know exactly what you mean by 'backing them'. As you know, this country will not go to war ever while I am occupying my present post unless Congress declares such a war; and the only exception to that would be in the case of unexpected and unwarranted attack on this nation . . . so, as far as going into any kind of military action under present conditions, of course, of course we are not.[16]

Referring to economic sanctions, he said 'that a programme of economic sanctions has never been placed before me as of this moment, never'. Asked about the UN, he replied:

I am certain that it will be referred to the United Nations before anything you would call a more positive, material – physical positive steps [*sic*] are taken. I don't know whether this is the exact time.[17]

At the beginning of September there had occurred a diversion which was to cause great annoyance to Eden, and indeed to Lloyd. Its author was John Foster Dulles, who was having a quiet weekend with his wife at their log cabin on Duck Island, Lake Ontario:

> It was on Duck Island during this particular weekend as he did the chores and watched the birds, that he conceived his brain-child the 'Users' Club (later to be called the Suez Canal Users' Association – SCUA). The users of the Canal should band themselves together, hire the pilots, manage the technical features of the Canal, organize the pattern of navigation, and collect the dues from the ships of member countries. Nasser had no right to make a profit out of the Canal. He would see money slipping out of his hands, and that would be better than the threat or the use of force.[18]

Lloyd received Dulles's message about this proposal on his way to Paris, where he immediately met Pineau. Lloyd was more concerned with his plan to take the Canal issue to the Security Council – for which the Labour Opposition as well as the TUC and the Scandinavians were pressing. Pineau was worried that this would cause a delay until it was too late to take military action. 'I agreed', says Lloyd, 'that this was a relevant matter, as the threat of force was an important element in the situation' – 'threat of force', not 'use of force', be it noted. He then told Pineau about 'Dulles's brain-child'. It was, in fact, a development of what Dulles had put to London when he had suggested that the 1888 Convention had given the users all the rights they needed. Now, he was pressing for the users to form their own club, operate the pilotage and other services, and collect the dues. Lloyd felt that this might attract European support, and indeed Luns of the Netherlands and Spaak of Belgium were robust in its support. It received little support in the House of Commons, and I myself in a speech in my constituency described it as a 'co-operative society which would pay no dividend'. But although the British and French were keeping their invasion plans from the Americans, Lloyd, even more than Eden, wanted to avoid a breach with the Americans, and was therefore in favour of pursuing the idea. In his book Lloyd says that 'we for our part believed that Dulles was acting in good faith', but goes on to quote Robert Murphy, Secretary of State (in a television programme some years later):

> If John Foster Dulles ever was actually convinced of the possibility of organizing a Canal Users Association to operate the Suez Canal, I was not aware of it. Perhaps he considered the idea useful as a negotiating device. Probably he thought that a legal case could be made, sound enough to be upheld in any tribunal, which could demonstrate the good faith of the

Association in keeping the Canal operating and in paying tolls to maintain it. A practical effect would be to divert tolls from Egyptian hands until a settlement and compensation for nationalization could be arranged. But Dulles did not spell this out and it seemed to me that he was skilfully working for time in the hope that public opinion in western Europe would harden against a military adventure.[19]

American timing was unfortunate. Robert Menzies had been sent to Egypt to negotiate with Nasser. He was at pains to leave Nasser in no doubt that France and Britain meant business. Nasser told his military commanders that the Franco-British mobilization measures were all bluff. Menzies in a private meeting with Nasser on 4 September had said that it would be a great mistake were he to exclude the possible use of force from his calculations. The following morning Menzies' move was kicked into touch by Eisenhower. Asked at an election press conference about the possible use of force, he replied, 'We are committed to a peaceful settlement of this dispute, nothing else.' It was just as Menzies was due to see Nasser that Eisenhower, who already knew about the plotting of the Cabinet hawks,* followed up his statement with a warning letter to Eden:

> I am afraid, Anthony, that from this point onward our views on this situation diverge. As to the use of force or the threat of force at this juncture, I continue to feel as I expressed myself . . . some weeks ago . . . new military preparation and civilian evacuation exposed to public view seem to be solidifying support for Nasser. . . . I must tell you frankly that American public opinion flatly rejects the thought of using force. . . . I really do not see how a successful result could be achieved by forcible means. . . . Before such action were undertaken all our peoples should unitedly understand that there were no other means available. . . . Seldom, I think, have [we been] faced by so grave a problem. . . . We must put our faith in the processes already at work to bring Nasser peacefully to accept the solution along the lines of the 18-nation proposal . . .[20]

The American pressures forced Lloyd, however unwillingly, to take the idea of a Users' Association more seriously, even to the point of endangering the timetable for the use of force which had been worked out by the French. Eden invited Mollet and Pineau to come to London, where it was decided – 'not very willingly', says Lloyd – that they should agree in principle to the Users' Club, given that the United States would join, and that dues, including those in respect of American ships, should be paid to the new organization. Provided that this plan was accepted by the Americans, they would agree not to take the issue, as had been planned, to the Security Council, but they would write to Hammarskjöld putting him in the picture.

---

* Considering that the military preparations were highly secret, there was a good deal of gossip by British military officers and their US opposite numbers.

When this was reported to the Cabinet, Macmillan, says Lloyd, was in favour of SCUA, but for a characteristically Macmillanist reason. In his view there would be no effective international control of the Canal without the use of force, and a SCUA which failed would be a step towards that. It would not, in Macmillan's view, itself produce a solution.

Meanwhile, the assiduous Dulles had defined the purposes of the Users' Club:

(a) to organize the use of the Canal by member-controlled vessels so as to promote safe, orderly, efficient and economical transit;
(b) to assure that such use will, as among member-controlled vessels, be impartial and uninfluenced for or against any ship or cargo by reason of the policies of any Government;
(c) to co-operate with Egypt in the discharge by Egypt of its obligation to take new measures for ensuring the execution of the 1888 Convention;
(d) to co-ordinate generally on behalf of the members the rights of users granted by the 1888 Convention with scrupulous regard for the sovereign right of Egypt in consonance with the 1888 Convention.[21]

On 15 September Nasser made a violent speech in which he described the Canal Users' Association as being an organization 'in truth for declaring war'. Dulles went on patiently with his plan.

In the same week that Dulles launched his SCUA proposals, Parliament was recalled for a two-day debate on 12 and 13 September. It was opened by Anthony Eden. Referring to the previous debate at the beginning of August, he claimed that there had been wide acceptance of the need for the Canal to be placed under an international system designed to secure the rights of all users – also acceptance of the view that the precautionary military measures had been justified. When there was a shout of 'No', he sought to quote Gaitskell in aid; in fact Gaitskell's only reference on 2 August had been to the call up of reservists and others. Eden went on:

Nothing which the Government have done since that debate took place has in any way changed the policy of my Right Hon. Friend the Foreign Secretary as I described in our speeches on that occasion. On the contrary, the Government have done and are doing everything in their power to obtain a peaceful settlement which takes account of Egypt's legitimate interests and which adequately safeguards, as it must, the interests of the many nations vitally concerned in the Canal.[22]

Considering how far the military planning had gone by that time it was a very cool claim to say that nothing had changed. He made a good point when he criticized the use of the word 'nationalization' by Nasser – what Egypt had done was to 'de-internationalize' the Canal. He went over the history of the six weeks since the previous debate, including the conference of the maritime powers, the Menzies mission, and the Dulles proposals for the Users' Association:

> But I must make it clear that if the Egyptian Government should seek to interfere . . . with the operations of the association, or refuse to extend to it the essential minimum of co-operation, then that Government will once more be in breach of the Convention of 1888. I must remind the House that what I am saying is the result of exchange of views between three governments. In that event Her Majesty's Government and others concerned will be free to take such further steps either through the United Nations, or by other means, for the assertion of their rights . . .

France and Britain, he went on, had addressed a letter to the President of the Security Council: 'it puts us in a position to ask for urgent action if that becomes necessary'.

Despite Dulles's efforts the Cabinet was going ahead with the military contingency plan (less of a contingency for some ministers than for others). The *Musketeer Plan* in its first form had been accepted by the Egypt Committee of the Cabinet on 10 August – at that time the Chiefs of Staff draft envisaged a full-scale assault on Alexandria, capturing the port and the airfield, followed by an attack on Cairo (to topple Nasser), then on to the Canal. The provisional date fixed was 15 September, deferred to 19 September a fortnight later. Just before Dulles outlined his SCUA alternative the Chiefs of Staff told ministers that the date had receded a further eleven days, i.e. to 30 September. Were there to be a further postponement, the last date must be 9 October: if that did not provide enough time a new plan would have to be prepared. But with the likely timetable for SCUA – the original meeting to approve it, followed by a conference of the eighteen states who might join – it became clear that the 9 October date was too early, and so the Cs OS were told to prepare a new plan *Musketeer Revise*. This substituted Port Said for Alexandria, and its three 'Stages' provided for the 'neutralization' of the Egyptian Air Force; a few days of aerial bombardment of selected targets, coupled with psychological warfare; and occupation of the Canal Zone by a seaborne attack on Port Said, supported with airborne landings as required.[23]

Eden was becoming impatient, but Lloyd had to ask for a little more time to meet Dulles's demands. The French had been for some time demanding stronger action, and on 10 September had visited London for talks with Eden. He succeeded in persuading the French to humour Dulles for a little longer, though Mollet and Pineau were by this time resolute on action. An Anglo-French communiqué stated that the two Governments had discussed the further measures to be taken and reached full agreement upon them – one of these agreed measures was to join in Dulles's SCUA-founding conference on 19 September.

The Users' Conference opened as planned. Dulles unveiled his scheme, also commenting on the pressures for a Security Council reference. This in his view should happen, though he wanted the users to have an agreed view first. In his speech, Lloyd said:

> We all want a world in which force is not used. True, but that is only one side of the coin. If you have a world in which force is not used, you have also got to have a world in which a just solution of problems of this sort can be achieved. I do not care how many words are written into the Charter of the United Nations about not using force; if in fact there is not a substitute for force, and some way of getting just solutions of some of these problems, inevitably the world will fall back again into anarchy and into chaos.

But any suggestion that SCUA would be even an effective buyers' cartel, let alone a political force, was killed by a passage in Dulles's opening speech:

> Membership in the Association would not, as we see it, involve the assumption by any member of any obligation. It would, however, be hoped that members ... would voluntarily take such action with respect to their ships and the payment of Canal dues as would facilitate the work of the Association. ... This action, I emphasize, would be entirely a voluntary action by each of the member governments if it saw fit to take it.

Lloyd comments that he did not think that anyone who heard the speech could have felt that if Nasser turned down the SCUA plan, and if no solution emerged from the Security Council, Dulles would then oppose the use of force, even though the US would not herself take part in military operations. The conference then reached its decision. SCUA came into being, the name, Lloyd records, being substituted for CASU (Co-operative Association of Suez-Canal Users) on the ground that CASU was a dirty word in Portuguese. (Cooper records that the name SCUA was parodied in Washington as 'Screwyer'.)[24]

After the conference had concluded by calling for a meeting of SCUA on 18 October, Dulles and Lloyd had a private discussion. Dulles, Lloyd records, repeated that it was imperative that Nasser should lose 'as a result of Suez'. How to achieve that was the problem – 'war would make him a hero'. It was better, Dulles said, for him to 'wither away'. He outlined a short list of what would now be called sanctions. Some, such as a ban on buying Egyptian cotton, would in fact have harmed the West more than it would harm Nasser. But consideration, Dulles suggested, should be given to action over the Nile waters, discouragement of Western tourists, and switching oil purchases to Western Hemisphere sources. Israel might help through the Jewish financial fraternity. Lloyd agreed to set up a Political Warfare Group to this end. But Dulles and Lloyd disagreed on an immediate reference to the UN. The American wanted to allow ten days to get a full membership for SCUA and then go – say – ten days later: time would be needed to set up the meeting and to lobby members. The Latin Americans, he said, under Panamanian pressure were unhelpful. Moreover SCUA should be functioning before the approach to the UN. Lloyd, conscious of other timetables, was in a hurry, but agreement was reached on a UN hearing in the week beginning 1 October, later than Lloyd would have wished.

Macmillan[25] by this time had been in the US for the annual conference of the International Monetary Fund. He was briefed on SCUA before he saw Eisenhower and Dulles on 25 September. Dulles was angry about Lloyd's decision to go to the UN, and complained that he had been badly treated; Britain would get nothing but trouble from New York. The UN meeting was in the event fixed for 5 October – around the date originally suggested by Dulles. Eden and Lloyd flew to Paris on 26 September to concert tactics for the Security Council meeting with the French.

Lloyd, in New York on 2 October, was shocked by a statement by Dulles to a press conference relating to SCUA: 'There is talk about teeth being pulled out of the plan, but I know of no teeth – there were no teeth in it so far as I am aware.'[26] He and Pineau were busy promoting an Anglo-French resolution in the Security Council. Lloyd did in fact, for a time, have considerable success with Fawzi, the Egyptian Foreign Minister. On 10 October, Fawzi expressed agreement with his proposition that the Canal should be insulated from the politics of any one country, and went over points arising from Article 8 of the 1888 Convention on the powers of representatives of the signatories to supervise the operation of the agreement; the Canal Code; the powers of the proposed SCUA, and the percentage of dues which should be set aside for development. He felt that some progress had been made with Fawzi, but 'there was still a wide gap'. The next day, when the parties met to discuss a draft prepared by Hammarskjöld, Fawzi seemed to be retreating on the question of 'politics of one country'.[27]

The Foreign Secretary then drafted a series of 'Six Principles', which later obtained the unanimous approval of the Security Council:

1. That there should be free and open transit through the Canal without discrimination, overt or covert;

2. That there should be respect for Egyptian sovereignty;

3. That the operation of the Canal should be insulated from the politics of any country;

4. That the level of dues should be fixed by agreement between users and owners;

5. That a fair proportion of the dues should be allotted to development;

6. That affairs between the Suez Canal Company and the Egyptian Government should be settled by arbitration, with suitable terms of reference and suitable provision for the payment of the sums found to be due.

Pineau, who, says Lloyd, had a bad cold, was difficult – moving from saying that he felt agreement was impossible and then fearing an expression of opinion by the Council 'which would tie our hands'. At a private session Hammarskjöld announced that there was agreement on the six principles: Lloyd warned against over-optimism and said that 'there were wide gaps between Egypt and ourselves'.

Dulles meanwhile was announcing his ideas on SCUA to a press conference, recognizing that it did not represent a permanent solution. 'Should that fail. . . .?' he was asked, and lamely he replied that 'the alternative for us at least would be to send our vessels round the Cape . . . we do not intend to shoot our way through.' This was no doubt possible, but the idea was far less attractive on geographical grounds to the countries of Southern and Western Europe.

Eden and Mollet were coming closer together: their first act was to call home British and French pilots from the Canal. Dulles was all this time bent on a still further devaluation of SCUA, his very own brain-child. Membership of it would not carry any obligation, he laid down, nor would Dulles order American ship-owners to pay their tolls to it – they were free to continue paying to the collectors of Port Said or Ismailia.* Eden, one part of whose mind was clinging to the hope that SCUA was the alternative to the military action which was being prepared on a contingency basis, was infuriated: 'And now,' he hissed at Nutting, 'what do you have to say for your American friends?'[28]

Lloyd, who was far less committed in his own mind to a military solution than Eden, was still somewhat lifted in spirits by Fawzi, the Egyptian Foreign Minister, who had made a constructive speech holding out hopes of a negotiated solution. The Council agreed that a meeting of Britain, France and Egypt should take place at Geneva on 29 October. But, whatever Lloyd's hopes may have been, there was no 29 October in Eden's Peace Calendar, still less in the minds of the French. Just at that moment Eisenhower, busy on his re-election campaign, again fouled the waters from Lloyd's and Hammarskjöld's points of view. He told his press conference on 12 October:

I have an announcement. I have got the best announcement that I could possibly make to America tonight. The progress made in the settlement of the

* Among the powers SCUA would have as set out in the declaration of the conference was 'to receive, hold and disburse the revenues from dues and other sums which any user of the Canal may pay to SCUA'. The operative word was 'may'.

Suez dispute this afternoon at the United Nations is most gratifying. Egypt, Britain and France have met through their Foreign Ministers and agreed on a set of principles on which to negotiate, and it looks like here is a very great crisis that is behind us. I do not mean to say that we are completely out of the woods, but I talked to the Secretary of State just before I came over here tonight and I will tell you that in both his heart and mine at least there is a very great prayer of thanksgiving.[29]

Lloyd 'protested strongly' to Dulles, who was clearly embarrassed by his President's words.

In the public session of the Council that evening, the Foreign Secretary suggested that a basis for negotiation existed with his six principles. Egypt had made some advance, but, quoting Dulles, the essence of the matter was the insulation of the Canal from the politics of any one country. SCUA, Lloyd said, had apparently been accepted, so he submitted on behalf of Britain and France new proposals, and said he would not press for a vote on Britain's 5 October resolution. Pineau supported the six principles, but said the three countries, France, Britain and Egypt, had been unable to agree on a coherent system to make them effective. Fawzi, for his part, was relaxed. He had reason to be. He had Eisenhower's statement of the previous day.

He clearly felt that the pressure was off, and even in that speech began to hedge about the phrase 'insulation of the operation of the Canal from the politics of any country'. He said that it was a rather unfortunate as well as misleading phrase. It allowed scope for various and contradictory interpretations.[30]

Dulles supported the British approach, now formulated as a resolution, embodying the six principles, with a second part calling on Egypt to propose a system which would conform with them. Shepilov, on behalf of Russia, said he would vote for the first part of the British resolution, setting out the six principles, but would oppose the second part. In a further session that evening, Dulles supported the resolution as did the Chinese. The Yugoslavs, following the Russians, would vote for Part I only.

The Council finally came to a vote. Eleven members voted for Part I. Nine voted for Part II, Yugoslavia and the Soviet Union against; under Security Council rules the Soviet vote constituted a veto. After the vote Lloyd took Dulles aside, following up a point made by Eisenhower in his letter of 8 September. What, he asked, were the 'pressures' Britain could bring to bear on Egypt to put forward reasonable counter-proposals. Lloyd was shocked (referring to 'my horror') when he learnt from Dulles that the idea was that the dues should be paid to SCUA and that 90 per cent of them should then go to Nasser – a larger proportion than he was receiving up to that time. Lloyd sent a full report by telegram to Eden, commenting that: 'There had been no resolution against the use of force, and if we had to come to it I thought there would be a more understanding reaction at the United Nations.'[31] On the credit side there had been a favourable 9–2 vote: on the debit side, 'the Egyptians would feel that the critical phase was past'.

Eden was at this time heavily involved in the Conservative Party Conference at Llandudno, where he received a rapturous reception for his references to the crisis. Salisbury was to have replied to the foreign affairs debate, but went down with heart trouble. Nutting at extremely short notice was told to stick to the speech prepared for Salisbury, and, despite his vehement reservations – he was within days of resigning – he stuck faithfully to the Cabinet line.

On Lloyd's return, Eden said that the two of them should go quickly to Paris to see Mollet and Pineau. Before they left, Lloyd produced an interesting balance-sheet of the successes and failures at the UN meetings. Meanwhile D-Day for the contingent naval/military operation had been pushed back from 15 September to a late October date: it could not be postponed beyond about the end of the month:

> Equipment loaded in the ships was deteriorating. Batteries were running down. Vehicles were becoming unserviceable. Equally important, the reservists were understandably becoming restive. They had responded willingly and in many cases enthusiastically to the recall to the colours but, as the weeks went by and nothing happened, they were getting fed up.[32]

Lloyd was worried too about Middle East reactions. Egypt and Syria were collaborating. Jordan linked up with the joint Arab military high command. What Lloyd, the Foreign Office and presumably the Intelligence Services did not fully realize was the developing collusion over the previous few weeks between Israel and the French.

In the very early weeks after Nasser's speech, the French had been in touch with the Israelis on an exclusively bilateral basis. At first the Israelis were cautious, but discussions progressed between the respective General Staffs. Ben-Gurion, the Israeli Prime Minister, was anxious not to get into a French-Israeli sideshow. France's principal aim was to see Nasser's intervention in Algeria brought to an end. Ben-Gurion's fear was that if Israel were to attack Egypt from the East, his country might be left high and dry as soon as France had cordoned off Egyptian aid from Algeria. But the Israelis themselves needed help against Nasser, who was responsible for combining damaging raids by fedayeen terrorists in the Gaza Strip and elsewhere with a blockade of the Straits of Tiran in the South, thus preventing Israel's world-wide commerce getting through to and from Eilat. Ben-Gurion would have been satisfied with clearing up the Gaza area and a quick attack on the Straits. What he feared was retaliatory air-raids from Egypt, with Nasser's new Russian aircraft, on Israel's main centres of population. In these circumstances, Israel could be defended only by bomber raids on the Egyptian bases. France was necessary but she did not have the heavy bombing capability. It was Britain, and Britain alone, who had bases near enough to provide the offensive power Israel needed. Military get-togethers were followed by diplomatic co-operation. Shimon Peres, Director-General of the Ministry of Defence (now leader of the Israel Labour Party) went to Paris – nominally to discuss the phasing of the payments for the Mystères and the tanks France was supplying. But soon the discussions were directed to an orchestration of the Middle East war both countries were avidly seeking. What had happened in fact was that Pineau's disappointment with the SCUA meeting, and the lack of British resolve, as he saw it, led him to another scenario. Peres was told that Pineau had told Eden that France might act alone and even be aided by Israel, Eden replying that he was not against the idea provided Israel refrained from attacking Jordan. 'The French Cabinet', Selwyn Lloyd recorded in his book twenty-two years later, 'then decided to invite Israeli representatives to come to Paris to discuss joint military action against Egypt'. It would appear that it was only then that Lloyd began to hear something of earlier Israeli-French discussions.

Dayan's memoirs recall that at their meeting on 29 September Pineau was off to New York, expecting nothing to be achieved. It was at that stage, before the Security Council's meetings, that 'there followed, so we are now told, detailed discussions of the military aspects of Franco-Israeli co-operation. A list of equipment required by the Israelis was handed over.'*[33] Hence, presumably, the Mystères, and a wide range of other equipment for which the Israelis indented on the French. Lloyd says that when he and Eden went to Paris on 16 October they had no idea of what the French had been up to.

The two Prime Ministers and their Foreign Ministers tried to agree on the facts of the situation. SCUA had failed. They then discussed Israel's intentions. The French said that the Israelis were in no mood to sit back and see their enemies, north and south, accepting more and more modern Russian weapons. Israel was getting desperate and would not for long hold her hand. Not an inkling was given of the modern arms France had provided nor of the close military co-operation which had developed.

How would an Israeli attack make out? What would Britain do if Israel attacked on her own? Eden repeated Britain's commitment to Jordan should Israel select her for attack. By this time France had decided to bring Britain into the picture. Mollet asked Eden to receive Albert Gazier, acting Foreign Minister in Pineau's absence. On Sunday 14 October the meeting took place

* The phrase 'so we are now told' written twenty years after Suez is a remarkable one to use.

at Chequers to maintain its secrecy, Gazier being accompanied by General Maurice Challe, Deputy Chief of Staff for the Air Force.* The French began by asking Eden to use his influence with Iraq to cease her pressures on Jordan. Nutting protested but Eden overruled him. It was one of the most bizarre incidents of the Suez period that Israel nearly became involved in hostilities with Jordan, with whom Britain had a treaty requiring her to intervene if Jordan was threatened. There was, for a moment, a real possibility that Britain would have been at war with Israel, a highly inconvenient development which the French were anxious to avoid. Nutting resigned on 31 October when the British armada was on its way from Malta to Port Said, and the RAF was revving up its engines in Cyprus for the bombing of Egypt's coastline and military installations. He was a passionate pro-Arab whose views were congenial to many of the top Foreign Office officials. At one point in those troubled days he records that Eden, ill and tortured with the crisis, turned on him, during the Jordanian crisis, and shouted down the telephone, 'I will not allow you to plunge this country into war merely to satisfy the anti-Jewish spleen of your people in the Foreign Office.'[34] Nutting further earned his chief's displeasure when at the Chequers meeting he passed a note to Eden suggesting that he ask the French to suspend delivery of their Mystère fighters to Israel, seventy-five having just been sent to follow the twelve whose supply had been cleared with Britain and the US earlier in the year.

The key issue at Chequers was Gazier's question: what would Britain's reaction be if Israel were to attack Egypt? Eden replied that this was a very difficult question: clearly the Tripartite Declaration would be invoked and we should be involved as signatories. 'But would you resist Israel by force of arms?' Gazier asked. According to Nutting, Eden replied with a half-laugh that he could hardly see himself fighting for Colonel Nasser, and then sought refuge in the idea that the 1954 agreement meant that we were not obliged to send troops if Egypt were attacked by Israel. Nutting replied that Britain's right to reactivate the base would apply only if Egypt were attacked by an outside power, and Israel had been specifically excluded by name from such a definition. But this did not nullify our obligations under the Tripartite Declaration to resist any attack across the armistice borders between Israel and her Arab neighbours. There was no getting away from

* Years afterwards I had occasion to look at the Visitors' Book at Chequers. For the Sunday in question the guests were listed, but strangely a civil servant's name was included, contrary to the usual practice. It seemed to me that a name had been scratched out by a sharp instrument, such as a razor-blade, and the official's name written in over it. At Chequers there is a powerful hand magnifying glass, used to illumine the locket of Queen Elizabeth I, and showing her own picture and that of her mother, Anne Boleyn. This confirmed that the rough surface had in fact been caused by a razor-like instrument. I concluded that the name excised had been that of an Israeli general. I was wrong. It was that of General Challe.

them. Gazier, however, revived Eden's spirits by saying that the Egyptians had recently argued that the Tripartite Declaration did not apply to Egypt. So, said Eden, 'that lets us off the hook. We have no obligation, it seems, to stop the Israelis attacking the Egyptians.'

Challe then outlined the French plan for Britain to get control of the Canal. Israel should be asked to attack Egypt across Sinai; France and Britain, having given the Israeli forces enough time to seize all or most of Sinai, should then order 'both sides'* to withdraw their forces from the Suez Canal, to permit an Anglo-French force to intervene and occupy the Canal on the pretext of saving it from being damaged by the fighting. We should then be in charge of the Canal, its operations and the terminal ports. Challe indicated that the Israelis had been sounded out on these ideas.

Selwyn Lloyd's account of the Paris meeting on 16 October is extraordinarily thin, a compound still perhaps of not knowing the whole story – he had not been at Chequers – and not wanting to know, above all a desire not to cross Eden. The discussions first covered the possibility of a satisfactory settlement by negotiation. Lloyd records that he thinks Mollet and Eden would have liked such a solution if the terms were adequate, but this was not possible without stronger American pressure. 'If only one or two Americans had spoken to Nasser as Menzies had done in Cairo, it could have been enough for success.'[35] The meeting then turned to a survey of Israeli intentions. Pineau emphasized arms supplies. The Israelis would not sit back and watch the Egyptians secure possession of more and more sophisticated Soviet weapons. Mollet and Pineau said 'several times' that the Israelis were getting desperate and they thought that, if an agreement about the Canal was not forced upon Nasser in a few days, the Israelis would act. This was in fact deceptive to a degree. Lloyd goes on:

> They told us very little about the military co-operation which was already taking place between Israel and France. I still thought that it was limited to the supply of some aircraft.[36]

The French went on to ask what Britain's attitude would be if Israel attacked Egypt. After a few ritual words about resisting Israel if Jordan was attacked, Eden agreed with Pineau that it would be impossible for Britain and France to commit troops to defend Nasser after his attitudes to France and Britain. The discussion continued about what would happen if Israel attacked first. Eden was clear that the Israeli forces would quickly destroy the Egyptian bases in Sinai – then there would be the fight for the Canal. Should this happen, both Prime Ministers agreed, subject to approval by their respective Cabinets, that Britain and France would intervene, on the basis of plans already prepared, in order to safeguard the Canal and stop the

* Nutting's quotation marks.

spread of hostilities. Lloyd's account shows him leaving Paris with no knowledge or assumption of any put-up job with the Israelis.

The result of the Paris meeting was the by now famous second meeting at Sèvres, of which nothing was known at the time or indeed for several years. Ben-Gurion represented Israel, and Selwyn Lloyd Britain – Dayan was later to record that when Mollet arranged the meeting, he included a note from Eden written before he left Paris on the 16th, proposing, according to Dayan, that if Israel were to invade Egypt, Britain and France would then ask both countries to withdraw their forces. Eden is also said to have guaranteed that if war were to break out between Israel and Egypt, Britain would not come to Egypt's help. Selwyn Lloyd and Ben-Gurion clearly did not get on. The account of the meeting in Lloyd's book is uninformative, in part concerned with regretting Ben-Gurion's unfavourable description of his personality. This he ascribes as possibly being due to his apparent ignorance of the French plan, on which Ben-Gurion perhaps thought Lloyd was fully informed. 'I was not aware', Lloyd says referring to later histories, 'that by that time France and Israel were virtually allies in an imminent offensive against Egypt.'[37]

Selwyn Lloyd returned to London to report to Eden. Peres and Dayan were working on Ben-Gurion and the original Israeli move was planned in considerable detail. Pineau flew to London. At 7 p.m. the secret protocol was ready for signature. Lloyd had been unable to return to Paris, though Pineau had taken it upon himself to report to Ben-Gurion and Dayan that Eden's approach had been far 'warmer' than Lloyd's.

The decisive meeting took place in Paris on 24 October. Lloyd was not there. His reason was that he had to reply to Foreign Office Questions in the Commons. It is, of course, not infrequent for ministers to miss Questions, given a good reason for absence, and the Foreign Office had ministers enough to stand in for him. Clearly the reason why he could not absent himself was that Opposition members on such occasions tend to shout, 'Where is he?' Lloyd's stand-in could hardly have said 'Paris': in any case the distaste in which Lloyd held the Sèvres plot was enough to keep him anchored firmly to the Commons front bench. The Foreign Office was represented in Paris, therefore, by Patrick Dean* and Donald Logan, one of Lloyd's Private Secretaries, an extraordinary proceeding, since it was at this meeting that the Suez collusion took shape. Lloyd, describing their report back, says[38] that the Israelis refused to give details of their operational plans, except their intention to capture the Tiran Straits. But he makes no bones about the plan to call on Israel and Egypt to stop hostilities. To this extent,

---

* He became Sir Patrick on Macmillan's recommendation to the Queen in his first honours list, Queen's Birthday, 13 June 1957.

Lloyd must have understood the basis of what had been agreed, the more so as Dean and Logan produced a plan which, he says:

> had been typed on plain paper in a neighbouring room and recorded the elements of the contingency plan which had been discussed, and the actions which could be expected to follow them in given circumstances. Dean and Logan had a word together about this development. There had been no earlier mention of committing anything to paper and no reason to regard the document as anything other than a record of the discussion on which the three delegations would report. As that, Dean signed it.[39]

What has later been called 'the secret protocol of Sèvres' has not been officially published, though Dayan and Pineau have themselves quoted slightly different versions:

1. On the afternoon of 29 October, Israel would launch a strong attack with the aim of reaching the Canal Zone the following day.

2. On 30 October Britain and France would appeal to both Egypt and Israel to withdraw all forces ten miles from the Canal and for a ceasefire.

3. At the same time Egypt would be asked to accept a temporary occupation of key positions on the Canal by Anglo-French forces.

4. If the Government of Egypt failed to agree within twelve hours to the terms of the Anglo-French appeal, early on 31 October an attack would be launched on the Egyptian forces.

5. The Israelis were given the freedom to attack and occupy the western shore of the Gulf of Aqaba and the islands in the Tiran Straits.

6. Israel would not attack Jordan during the period of hostilities, and the British agreed not to go to Jordan's aid if, during this time, she attacked Israel.

7. All parties were enjoined to the strictest secrecy.[40]

Dayan's account of the ending of the Paris meeting is worth recording. He left the conference room to send a 'most immediate' signal to his chief of operations, beginning 'Good Prospects for Operation Kadesh soonest', and ordering immediate and secret mobilization, as well as activating 'deception to produce impression that mobilization aimed against Jordan because of entry of Iraqi forces'.

> When I returned to the conference room, I found everyone standing around full of nervous tension and not quite knowing what to do with themselves. Planning to launch a campaign was not the kind of event over which one clinked glasses or indulged in comradely backslapping. However there was a general sense of deep satisfaction that the effort had been fruitful. The first to leave were the British, mumbling as they went words of politeness tinged with humour and not quite comprehensible.[41]

One wonders what Selwyn Lloyd, had he been there, would have been drinking, and how far he would have tinged his politeness with humour.

Lloyd's own reconstruction of the events of the weeks before the Suez campaign suggests that as late as 16 October he knew nothing of the meeting between Dayan and the French on 29–30 September, covering not only arms supplies but 'decisions about the operational plans of both countries when it was decided to go ahead'.[42] But he goes on: '*We now have* [author's italics] an account of what had been happening in Moshe Dayan's *Story of My Life*, Chapter 13.' By the time Lloyd wrote his book in 1978 he clearly knew that the French had been well advanced in their plotting with the Israelis by the time the meeting of 22 October took place, but did not know or suspect it at the time. On 16 October Pineau, according to Lloyd, went only so far as to say that the Israelis would not sit quietly and watch the Egyptians and Syrians assimilate more and more Russian weapons. He, Pineau, believed that the Israelis would attack soon. According to Lloyd, Mollet and Pineau said several times that the Israelis were getting desperate and if an agreement about the Canal was not forced on Nasser in a few days, the Israelis would act.

The French had, of course, completely and culpably misled Selwyn Lloyd. Dayan's memoirs show just how far the French and the British had gone in their joint planning.[43] In fact he himself goes much further than any other of the *dramatis personae* when he claims:

> After the first meeting of the French delegation with Eden in London, the governments of Britain and France resolved to launch a joint military operation to seize and hold the Suez Canal Zone, cancel the nationalization order, and restore their rights in the Canal Authority. It was also their aim to topple Nasser.

Nothing which is known, even today, justifies that claim. All the published writings of those concerned – politicians, soldiers and others – confirm that so far as Britain was concerned the Government never ruled out the use of force, but as with the Fawzi talks and the approach to the Security Council, they were prepared for alternative action provided that it would succeed in returning the Canal to international control and remove Nasser. Some ministers, as has been said, made little secret of their demand for military action, particularly Macmillan. At its lowest, his judgment was that it would have to come to that. Eden wavered, letting 'I dare not' wait upon 'I would', then showing resolution, and ultimately becoming obsessive about the destruction of Nasser. Not so the French. Dayan's two chapters were both significantly called 'The French Connection', not 'The Anglo-French

Connection'. It is worthwhile to judge the Anglo–French accounts by studying Dayan's much more frank story. Unlike French (and British) participants, Dayan has nothing to hide on grounds of domestic politics, and his account goes right back to 1 September.

> The first intimation that France was interested in co-ordinated action with Israel against Egypt reached us on September 1, 1956. It came in a 'Most Immediate' signal I received that morning from our military attaché in Paris informing me of Anglo–French plans and adding that Admiral Barjot held the view that Israel should be invited to take part in the operation. The message was brought to me while I was meeting with the General Staff. Ben-Gurion was present, and he instructed me to reply that in principle we were ready to co-operate. If what was required from us was only intelligence on Egypt's armed forces, this information would be furnished by the office of our military attaché. If the French had in mind the participation of the Israeli army in military action, the minister of defence was prepared to send me to Paris to discuss it.[44]

It was this message which led to the Israeli–French staff talks referred to above. Admiral Barjot, Dayan records, was anxious to know whether French aircraft would be able to land in Israel in case of necessity; also how far Israel could tie down Egyptian forces if Israel were to go for Sinai. The questions were, of course, Barjot told Dayan, 'only for enlightenment', though 'appropriate political conditions might arise in the immediate future for Israel to take part in the operation'.

Dayan was in fact much preoccupied with terrorist attacks from Jordan and, as we have seen, London was throughout concerned about the danger of any action which would activate the Anglo-Jordanian treaty commitment. But, even at this stage, he ordered the relevant sections of the General Staff to have a fresh look at existing contingency plans relating to Egypt, such as capturing the whole of Sinai, or just the Straits of Tiran, or alternatively the Gaza Strip. In his planning he emphasized the difference between the 'international' problems raised by the Paris talks and Israel's own objectives. Even at that stage he was not interested in going as far as the Canal and getting 'involved in that dispute'. His other preoccupation was the supply of arms and especially of modern fighters. Peres went to France with an up-to-date shopping list, at the same time briefed to discuss Israeli–French political co-operation in the Middle East. Peres, Dayan suggested, should ensure that the initiative should come from France, and care should be taken to avoid the further dimension of Jordan. After three days of talks, Peres was able to report by cable that Bourgès-Manoury, the French Defence Minister, had explored the possibility of joint French-Israeli action against Egypt without the British. Mollet and Pineau were irked by London's time-wasting preoccupation, as they saw it, with SCUA, evidence, it seemed to them, that Britain's brief period of militancy was fading away.

An exchange of letters between Bourgès-Manoury and Ben-Gurion showed the Israeli Prime Minister in agreement with the French on an early timing for operations, and made it clear that he was ready to act jointly with France, whether Britain was in the action or not.

At a Cabinet meeting on 25 September Peres reported on his Paris talks. Pineau's second London conference on 21 September, he had learned, had been a grave disappointment. He was convinced that the American SCUA operation was a negative proposal to 'nullify' any attempt to oppose Nasser's take-over of the Canal, and in particular to prevent the British from taking military action. There was strong opposition in Britain, even from some Conservative MPs. The French had told Peres that France might take independent action, possibly with Israeli help. Eden had said, it was reported, that he was not against this plan provided that Jordan was not attacked. It was decided to send Dayan again to Paris, taking with him a list of specific directives from Ben-Gurion.

> Israel would not launch war on its own. If our friends started, we would join. If we were asked to make a parallel start, we would consider it sympathetically.
>
> The United States should be apprised of the impending war and offer no objection (or at least express no specific opposition). We should be ensured that the United States would not impose sanctions or an embargo against Israel.
>
> Britain should be informed, should agree, and should undertake not to go to the assistance of the Arab States if they should join Egypt.
>
> It was our aim to gain control of the western shore of the Gulf of Aqaba so as to guarantee freedom of Israeli shipping through that waterway. Consideration might perhaps be given to the demilitarization of the Sinai peninsula, even under the supervision of an international force.

To these, Dayan says, 'I added three operational directives':

> The forces of each country would operate in separate sectors – ours in our sector, the French in theirs – even if there were a single overall headquarters. This affected primarily the land forces, less so the air forces.
>
> If we received aid in equipment, and if the French forces entered Egypt, Israel could take it upon herself to capture the eastern sector of the Suez Canal Zone [meaning the Sinai Peninsula].
>
> We should ask the French for equipment but not make their affirmative reply a condition of our participation in the operation.[45]

Ben-Gurion was concerned to ensure that this was a specifically Israeli-French operation. Dayan was afraid that Britain would join with Jordan against Israel.

The Paris talks, he records, began on Sunday morning, 29 September, with Pineau summarizing the position reached. After Nasser's action on 26 July, it had become clear to France that force must be used against Egypt. The US was opposed, not wanting any disturbance of their relationship with the Soviet Union, despite Russian help to Nasser, in particular Moscow's action in supplying 'pilots' for Canal shipping. The most suitable date for the French for military action was before 15 October, because of the expected deterioration in the weather from then on. Pineau himself had to go to New York for the Security Council meetings. Hammarsjköld was trying to propose a four-nation mediation committee, with representatives of Britain, France, the USSR and an Asian country, to mediate between Egypt and the West. Pineau regarded this, Dayan records, as a device to force the West to surrender, and France would not hesitate to use her veto to defeat the idea. France would, he said, try to convince the British that Anglo-French military measures were the only course, 'but he was doubtful that she would succeed'. Eden favoured action: Pineau blamed the Foreign Office officials. He went on to ask whether Israel was interested in taking military action against Egypt, together with France, if Britain withdrew from a joint operation. France would give Israel full military aid and such political backing as vetoing any anti-Israel resolution in the Security Council.

There were two possibilities: the first, Israel on her own, with French military aid, France sending in her forces after the action had begun; or, the second, action opened jointly by the forces of both countries. Dayan makes it clear that he agreed with the French view that the Nasser problem could not be dealt with by diplomatic means. There was now no alternative to military action. Israel regarded France as 'our friend and ally and agreed wholeheartedly to act jointly with her', but they had to be sure that there was no trouble with Britain especially over Jordan. The French gave their estimate of the answers to these questions on Jordan, Pineau recalling that during recent border clashes between Israel and Jordan, Eden had said, 'Pity they did not happen on the Egyptian border.'

But one problem, both sides came to agree, dominated the military discussions. France and Israel alone did not possess the bomber striking power necessary to the operation, particularly as regards the destruction at the outset of the Egyptian Air Force. Dayan records:

> For this and other reasons, the French returned to their suggestion that Israel open the campaign, and then they felt sure that Britain would join in – albeit at a later stage. On the other hand, they insisted that even if Britain agreed to a Franco-British action, it would be desirable for Israel to join the campaign later and capture the Sinai Peninsula east of Suez . . .[46]

– thus tying down a significant part of the Egyptian forces. Pineau went on to say that he hoped for a final decision by Britain about mid-October, after the Security Council discussions. France could not finalize her plans on Suez until she had Britain's decision, but wanted Israel's agreement to join the campaign, fighting in an independent sector, under a separate command, and *starting the war on her own before the British and French* [author's italics].

Dayan, looking back over the years, was in no doubt that Britain was the problem. If Britain pulled out, would France be far behind? That was Ben-Gurion's fear. France might not be able to stand up to the combined opposition of the US and the USSR.

Britain hated the very idea that her name might possibly be smeared as partners with Israel in military action against Arabs, but at the same time, she would welcome the chance of exploiting Israel's conflict with the Arabs to justify her action against Egypt. The most desirable development for Britain would be an Israeli attack on Egypt. She could then rush to Egypt's defense and drive out Israel's forces, and since British troops would then find themselves in the Suez area, they would automatically stay to control the Canal. The Foreign Office was convinced that under such circumstances, no one could accuse Britain of being either anti-Arab or the aggressor.

Moreover, Britain wished us to fulfil this exalted function of villain, or scapegoat, without her having to meet us and discuss it face to face. She knew that the very act of our sitting together would carry the implication of 'treaty making' – albeit limited to one-time action against Egypt – which would be highly unpopular in the Arab world. The British therefore wanted France to be their insulated link with Israel. Through France they would get us to do what was desirable for Britain while guaranteeing them freedom from contact with Israel.[47]

The following day the talks were transferred to direct military planning – an Israeli-French venture on the assumption that Britain would stay out or perhaps join in at a later stage. The Israeli idea was that their land sector should be east of the Canal, similarly with the Air Force, except for certain additional targets – such as the destruction of the Egyptian Air Force on the ground. The French were interested in the occupation of Cairo and the removal of Nasser. On timing, Dayan said five to seven days would be needed for Israel's mobilization. With the Security Council meeting ending on 12 October and a final political decision on the 15th, the Israeli forces would be ready for action on 20 October. Despite Ben-Gurion's concern about the Anglo-French proposals that Israeli action should trigger off the war, Dayan was not unduly worried. Here was an opportunity unlikely to recur – action against Egypt in co-operation with France, and possibly Britain as well – 'an historic chance'.

On his return to Israel Dayan issued the Early Warning Order to the General Staff. But Ben-Gurion still had his reservations, indeed they had grown, mainly about the lack of bombing power without the British. The French, too, and Dayan himself, were worried should the deployment of their mutual forces be inadequate to remove Nasser. Despite these anxieties, Ben-Gurion was becoming more reconciled to the operation. On 4 October he approved Dayan's request that the armed forces should go ahead with their preparation – without at that stage seeking Cabinet approval that the operations should take place: contingency plans only.

On 18 October came the cable from Guy Mollet inviting Ben-Gurion to Paris, which crossed a cable from Ben-Gurion making the same suggestion. As the Israelis were leaving, a Paris message told them of the two-paragraph declaration Eden had handed the French, intending it to be passed on to the Israelis. (By this time Eden's involvement had become clearer thanks to the meeting at Chequers.) Paragraph 1 said that Britain and France would demand that both Egypt and Israel should retire from the Canal Area, and if 'one side' refused, Anglo-French forces would intervene 'to ensure the smooth operation of the Canal'. This, records Dayan, would provide the legal, political and moral justification for the invasion of Egypt by Britain and France. Paragraph 2 said that Britain would not go to Egypt's aid if war broke out between her and Israel – accompanied, of course, by a reservation on Jordan. Britain would not, however, support Jordan if Jordan attacked Israel.

Ben-Gurion was still worried about a war-guilt clause, the arrangement that Israel was to be the aggressor. Ben-Gurion said he was not having a situation whereby 'Israel volunteered to mount the rostrum of shame so that Britain and France could lave their hands in the waters of purity'. Dayan tried to reassure his Prime Minister – this was an historic opportunity which would never recur. Miss it and any future confrontation would be a go-it-alone operation. All this and Sinai too – and the re-establishment of the freedom of shipping to Eilat.

The French sent an aircraft to pick up the Israeli team, and Dayan was annoyed by the attempt of two of the French who began to negotiate in his office without waiting to return to France. He was further infuriated, it is clear, by the use of the words 'pretext' and 'scenario', finally losing his temper when the word was used once too often, and asserting that Shakespeare was better at producing a scenario than the French. In any case spoiling the scenario from the French point of view, he makes clear, was the French refusal to come to Israel's aid if her cities were bombed in the first twenty-four hours.

> I, for one, would not support a partnership proposal based on the condition that one would do the job and the other two would come along and kick him out. If we had to fight the Egyptians alone, we ourselves would decide when and how to do so, being governed by what suited us best. In a partnership,

however, if Egyptian planes bombed Tel Aviv because our own planes were away preparing the path for the Anglo-French conquest of the Canal Zone, it was inconceivable that our partners would not come to our aid so as not to spoil the 'scenario'.[48]

He was clearly resistant to the idea of French aircraft being based in Israel.

As the Israeli party left by car for the airfield that night, Dayan told Ben-Gurion of the French visitors. Ben-Gurion, according to Dayan, wanted to cancel the flight on hearing that he would be pressed to accept the original plan, Israel's starting the war and then leaving the consequences of its management to others. He was persuaded to continue with the journey. The aircraft landed at Villacoublay, and the party went on to Sèvres.

Needless to say, Dayan's account of the meeting is considerably fuller than that of Selwyn Lloyd. The main theme was opened up by Ben-Gurion who presented a plan which Dayan himself regarded as fantastic, or at least naïve – a new and fundamental rearrangement of boundaries in the Middle East, with Iraq effectively taking over East Jordan, and Israel the Jordanian West Bank, not to mention boundary changes affecting Lebanon. Britain would 'exercise her influence over Iraq', and over the southern ports of the Arabian Peninsula. France would master-mind Lebanon and possibly Syria. There should be an approach to the US to secure her support: there should be no hurry with the military campaign but they should take the time necessary to review such possibilities. The French had not come all the way from the Hotel Matignon to Sèvres to listen to such dreams. The Americans in any case, Mollet said, would not be quickly persuaded to throw out Nasser. Pineau warned Ben-Gurion that in trying to solve all the problems, none would be solved. Not only the US, but Britain would be unready for such discussion. Eden was already having a rough time, not only with the Labour Opposition but with members of his own party, even with his own Cabinet. He went on to outline three reasons for urgency – the weather, with the Mediterranean subject to storms after October; the US, with their minds concentrated on the Presidential and Congressional elections, and the Soviet Union's preoccupations with problems in Poland and other satellite states.

The dialogue of the deaf continued. Ben-Gurion went on with his dream. Pineau and Bourgès-Manoury pointed out that if the attack was not launched within a few days, France would have to withdraw – not only were the ships and stores required, but the troops together with their heavy equipment were needed for Algeria.

This meeting was, of course, the one attended by Selwyn Lloyd. He and his secretary arrived at 7 p.m. and stayed outside the meeting room to be briefed by the French. As we have seen, Lloyd has stated in his own book that he was not put at all fully in the picture by the French, thus explaining

his limited contribution, and also explaining Dayan's unfriendly description
of him, about which Lloyd was clearly sensitive. Dayan's account of the
meeting is at variance with Lloyd's. Dayan recalls that, while Lloyd was still
out of the room, Pineau read out the 'principal moves and timetables' of
what he calls the 'British suggestion':

> Israel to start military action against Egypt.
> Franco-British ultimatum to be issued to Egypt and Israel demanding their
>   withdrawal from the Canal area.
> Egyptian airfields to be bombed after the expiry of the ultimatum.

The French then proposed that the delegations met *à trois*. Dayan
comments that Ben-Gurion and Selwyn Lloyd showed a surprising measure
of readiness to compromise, though – the words to which Lloyd later took
offence –

> His manner could not have been more antagonistic. His whole demeanour
> expressed distaste – for the place, the company and the topic. His opening
> remarks suggested the tactics of a customer bargaining with extortionate
> merchants.

Lloyd's theme – confirmed by him in his own book – was that Fawzi in
New York had been co-operative, and the Egyptians had agreed to recognize
SCUA, to set the Canal fees in advance, to guarantee international
supervision of the operation of the Canal, and to accept the imposition of
sanctions, in accordance with the UN Charter, if the Egyptians broke their
commitments. From this point the Dayan and Lloyd accounts diverge. Why
was Lloyd here if all was well?

> Because, he explained, such an agreement would not only fail to weaken
> Nasser, but would actually strengthen him, and since Her Majesty's
> Government considered that Nasser had to go, it was prepared to undertake
> military action in accordance with the latest version of the Anglo-French
> plan. This called for an invasion of Sinai by the Israeli army, whose units were
> to reach Suez within forty-eight hours. . . . Some time during those forty-
> eight hours the Anglo-French ultimatum would be issued to both sides
> ordering them to withdraw from the Canal. If Egypt rejected it, the Anglo-
> French attack would be launched to capture the Canal Zone and overthrow
> Nasser.[49]

It was now Ben-Gurion the dove who took on the hawks. He said he had
already rejected the plan as Lloyd had authorized it, reflecting his anxiety
about Egypt's bombing of Israeli cities. Dayan sought to reassure his
Prime Minister, pointing out the safeguards the scheme would provide
against such action on the part of the Egyptians. If Egypt turned down the
call to evacuate the Canal Zone, 'British and French air units would start
bombing Egyptian airfields the next morning'. At this Dayan states,

Selwyn Lloyd was not shocked. He did not even seem surprised at my plan. He simply urged that a military action be not a small-scale encounter but a 'real act of war'. Otherwise there would be no justification for the British ultimatum and Britain would appear in the eyes of the world as an aggressor.[50]

Ben-Gurion asked Lloyd 'directly' whether HMG had given thought to the damage that might be suffered by Israel's cities during the two days when Israel would be standing alone on the battlefield. Lloyd, Dayan says, replied that he had come to Paris only because he thought he would be discussing the plan as agreed upon between the British and the French, and here he was, being confronted by a new suggestion.[51] Pineau, Dayan goes on, was not happy about the report Lloyd would give to Eden on his return, so he 'got himself invited' to London to meet the Prime Minister the following evening. There would be a final 'summing up' in Paris on the 24th Meanwhile the French were angered by the reports that an Egyptian vessel, the *Athos*, had been caught out in the act of smuggling weapons sent by Egypt to the Algerian rebels.

The Israelis and French met again to discuss what Pineau should say in London. Though Ben-Gurion had still not approved the plan which had been discussed and was disappointed at the Anglo-French refusal to consider his broad vision of new international boundaries and groupings in the Middle East, he seemed at last ready to examine the Anglo-French plan on its merits with Dayan. Dayan's scheme was, of course, much less than what the French were asking for. The Israeli Air Force would be held back the first day, apart from dropping a paratroop battalion near the Canal – at Mitla about thirty miles from Suez – while a mechanized brigade would capture Egyptian border positions, and then push south through Sinai to Sharm-el-Sheikh. Israel would tell the British the size of her force but not the location of the paratroop landings or the other movements: 'that was not their affair'. (By selecting Mitla instead of El Arish, Dayan was keeping as far away from the Canal as he could, so that whatever plot was devised by the Europeans there would be no question of a loss of face by the enforced withdrawal which the original Anglo-French plan had envisaged.)

Ben-Gurion went so far as to authorize Dayan to put his ideas to Pineau, though on the understanding that it was Dayan's own proposition, not yet endorsed by higher political authority.

The following morning, 24 October, Ben-Gurion summoned Dayan and Peres for a further discussion. Clearly his views had changed. Dayan records that all his searching questions were of the 'how', 'what', and 'when' type, no longer 'if'. Dayan's list of the answers he gave indicates the nature of the questions put to him.[52]

Pineau returned from London in the afternoon, saying that representatives from the British Government would be arriving shortly. Eden's approach, he reported, he had found to be far warmer than that of Lloyd. As for the 'pretext', the British again emphasized that it must be a 'full-scale act of war'. They also agreed to advance the time of their 'response' and attack at dawn on the Wednesday. In the ultimatum to Egypt and Israel, now re-designated the 'appeal', Israel would be asked to cease fire and retire from the Canal.

A 'small group of us', Dayan says, 'adjourned to a nearby room to sum up our consultation.'[53]

The principles of the plan that emerged were as follows:

On the afternoon of October 29, 1956, Israeli forces would launch a large-scale attack on the Egyptian forces with the aim of reaching the Canal Zone by the following day.

After being apprised of these events, the governments of Britain and France, on October 30, 1956, would submit to the governments of Egypt and Israel, separately and simultaneously, appeals formulated in the spirit of the following basic lines:

To the government of Egypt:
Absolute cease-fire.
Withdrawal of all forces to ten miles from the Canal.
Acceptance of the temporary occupation of the key positions on the Canal by Anglo-French forces in order to guarantee freedom of passage through the Canal to the vessels of all nations until a final arrangement was secured.

To the government of Israel:
Absolute cease-fire.
Withdrawal of her forces to ten miles east of the Canal.

It would be reported to the government of Israel that the governments of France and Britain had demanded of the government of Egypt that she agree to the temporary occupation of the key positions on the Canal by Anglo-French forces. If either of the two governments rejected the appeal . . . the Anglo-French forces were liable to take the necessary measures to ensure that their demands were met.

The government of Israel would not be required to fulfil the conditions of the appeal sent to her in the event that the government of Egypt failed to accept the conditions of the appeal which she would receive.

If the government of Egypt failed to agree to the conditions presented to her in the allotted time, the Anglo-French forces would launch an attack on the Egyptian forces in the early-morning hours of October 31, 1956.

The government of Israel would dispatch forces to seize the western shore of the Gulf of Aqaba and the islands of Tiran and Sanapir in order to ensure freedom of navigation in that gulf.

Israel would not attack Jordan during the period of the operation against Egypt. But if by chance Jordan attacked Israel during that time, the British government would not go to Jordan's aid.[54]

CHAPTER 10

A Canal Too Far

AN ACCOUNT OF THE DETAILS of the campaign, the planning and the execution of the Suez operation is not directly relevant to the theme of this book. There is, in any case, a voluminous literature covering every detail, by military and other historians, including some of the commanders involved. What is relevant is the impact of politics, national and international (particularly American) on the military planning, and indeed on major strategic and tactical decisions during the brief period of fighting, and also the impact of the fighting on Whitehall and Westminster, and on the other Western capitals.

The Israeli operation, named *Kadesh* after the desert post where the Israelites had rested on their way to the Promised Land, began on 29 October. Israeli aircraft dropped 385 parachutists at the Israeli end of the Mitla Pass, thirty miles east of Suez, any warning to the Egyptians being averted by a daring and unprecedented raid in which Israeli fighters had cut the telephone wires with their propellers and wings. Dayan's strategy, clear in his own mind from the beginning, was to use the occasion for taking over Sinai as well as Sharm-el-Sheikh which held the key to the Straits of Tiran, and would thus restore Eilat as Israel's southern port.

In the afternoon of 30 October, Britain and France issued their ultimatum, requiring Egypt and Israel to cease fighting and calling on each of them to withdraw ten miles from the Canal. (Israel was nowhere near the ten-mile limit.) The Anglo-French message was certainly a speedy reaction: what was even more speedy was that the Anglo-French armada had set out from Malta the day before operation Kadesh began.

Much of the Fullick-Powell book *Suez: The Double War* draws attention to the chaos of the invasion, wrong plans, rapidly changed plans, loss of contact between commanders, inadequate contact between the sea, air and land forces, wrong equipment, and equipment too clapped out to be used (some of their accounts revealing a rare sense of humour) but their final conclusion nevertheless rejects popular post-Suez comment of a total SNAFU (politely translated 'Situation Normal, All Fouled Up') and concludes:

Undoubtedly the lessons drawn from the war against the Axis powers weighed heavily on British thinking, particularly in the use of airborne forces, in the meticulous planning of the assault, and in the build-up and logistic planning of the operation. In the event, the plan worked with few hitches of major consequence; Fergusson,* in fact, with some accuracy described the operation as being 'technically brilliant'. The planners had done their work well, but this was far from the same thing as saying that the plan was the right one in the circumstances. The problem with large-scale and elaborate projects is that once they build up a certain momentum their progress becomes self-generating and their achievement a sufficient purpose in itself – the true aim becomes overlaid or forgotten. The need for careful plans to bring superior forces to bear across a sea barrier against a determined and well-equipped army was self-evident when fighting the Germans and Japanese, but the Egyptians, as the Israelis were to demonstrate, were not such an enemy.[1]

The first change in the plan was a deferment for twelve hours of the bombing of the Egyptian Air Force bases by the British and French. Canberras, it had been discovered almost overnight, were not to be hazarded in daylight. Dayan grew suspicious.

At this stage Eisenhower intervened. He sent a tough demand to Israel that she should withdraw, and the US took the issue to the Security Council. The sequence of events on 30 October was that the Council was called for 11 a.m. but Britain and France secured a postponement until 5 p.m. in order to secure time to deliver their ultimatum to both sides. They then vetoed the American resolution which was strongly supported by the Soviet delegation. Neither country had previously used its UN veto since the establishment of the organization. A second motion from the Russians confining its censure to Israel was similarly vetoed. A year earlier, no one could have conceived of the US and the Soviet Union being at one in their condemnation of France and Britain. The US Ambassador in London, Winthrop Aldrich, was stymied when asking the Foreign Office for information about what was going on. Britain (and France) had in fact virtually frozen any flow of information to the Americans. Eisenhower later referred to what he described as 'our lack of clear understanding as to exactly what was happening in the Suez area, due to the break in our communications with the French and British. We were in the dark about what they planned to do.'**[2]

When the Security Council finally met, the US tried to invoke the Tripartite Declaration of 1950, embodying an undertaking by the US, UK

* Brigadier Bernard Fergusson, appointed Director of Psychological Warfare for the campaign.

** In fact, for weeks past, British defence officers had been talking freely to their American counterparts, one reason why the President's messages to Eden, recorded in the previous chapter, were so well-grounded in fact.

and France to oppose aggression by either Israel or one of the Arab States. Washington instructed its ambassadors in London and Paris to ask Lloyd and Pineau to explain their plans to implement the 1950 Declaration. The US Embassy in London had been kept so much at arm's length that Ambassador Aldrich regarded an inquiry as virtually useless. Only two days before he had been told that the British were pressing for a negotiated settlement. But, since his chief had demanded an approach to the Foreign Secretary, he went along. All he got was a vague suggestion that Britain was planning to arraign Israel at the UN as an aggressor, an all-time low in British deception of Washington. But, he was told, Britain would have to consult and would he call again. When he arrived, Lloyd was at the House of Commons. The Under-Secretary received Aldrich and handed him a copy of the Anglo-French ultimatum. This was hardly a 'special relationship' gesture to America, not even the timing: the text of the ultimatum was already monopolizing the ticker-tapes of five continents:

> The Governments of the United Kingdom and France have taken note of the outbreak of hostilities between Israel and Egypt. This event threatens to disrupt the freedom of navigation through the Suez Canal on which the economic life of many nations depends.
>
> The Governments of the United Kingdom and France are resolved to do all in their power to bring about the early cessation of hostilities and to safeguard the free passage of the Canal.
>
> They accordingly request the Government of Israel:
>
> (a) to stop all warlike action on land, sea and air forthwith;
>
> (b) to withdraw all Israeli military forces to a distance of ten miles east of the Canal.
>
> A communication has been addressed to the Government of Egypt, requesting them to cease hostilities and to withdraw their forces from the neighbourhood of the Canal, and to accept the temporary occupation by Anglo-French forces of key positions at Port Said, Ismailia and Suez.
>
> The United Kingdom and French Governments request an answer to this communication within twelve hours. If at the expiration of that time one or both Governments have not undertaken to comply with the above requirements, United Kingdom and French forces will intervene in whatever strength may be necessary to secure compliance.[3]

The British Ambassador, Sir Roger Makins, who was due to retire from his post to Whitehall duties, was conveniently not in Washington, and his replacement, Sir Harold Caccia, was not due to arrive for more than a week. This was probably a deliberate arrangement; certainly the Americans thought so. The Chargé d'Affaires and the French Ambassador, Hervey Alphand, called on Dulles with personal messages from their respective Prime Ministers. Nothing could have been more clumsy and insensitive than their official wording. Eden's letter was anything but convincing, and composed of weasel-words:

> My first instinct would have been to ask you to associate yourself and your country with the declaration. But I know the constitutional and other difficulties in which you are placed. I think there is a chance that both sides will accept. In any case it would help this result very much if you found it possible to support what we have done at least in general terms. We are well aware that no real settlement of Middle Eastern problems is possible except through the closest cooperation between our two countries. Our two Governments have tried with the best will in the world all sorts of public and private negotiations through the last two or three years and they have all failed. This seems an opportunity for a fresh start . . .
>
> Nothing could have prevented this volcano from erupting somewhere, but when the dust settles there may well be a chance for our doing a really constructive piece of work together and thereby strengthening the weakest point in the line against communism.[4]

Mollet, for his part, was more truculent, as he made clear later. Addressing the French Assembly later he said:

> When our American friends asked us 'why' [Mollet or Pineau did not warn them of the ultimatum], I told them: 'You would have stopped us.' I even added: 'We did not want you to be late: we did not want to go through the same periods of waiting that we went through from 1914 to 1917 and from 1939 to 1941.'[5]

Eisenhower issued a statement in strong terms:

> As soon as the President received his first knowledge, obtained through press reports, of the ultimatum, he sent an urgent personal message to the Prime Minister of Great Britain and the Prime Minister of the Republic of France. The President expressed his earnest hope that the United Nations Organization would be given full opportunity to settle the issue by peaceful means instead of by forceful ones . . .

He addressed his telegram to Eden not only as 'head of Her Majesty's Government', but as 'my long-time friend'. He then asked Eden to explain:

> exactly what is happening between us and our European allies – especially between us, the French and yourselves. We have learned that the French had provided Israel with a considerable amount of equipment . . . in excess of the amounts of which we were officially informed [and] in violation of agreements now existing between our three countries. . . . Last evening our Ambassador to the United Nations met with your Ambassador. . . . We were astonished to find that his government [i.e. Great Britain] would not agree to any action whatsoever to be taken against Israel. He further argued that the tripartite statement of May, 1950, was ancient history and without current validity.
>
> Egypt has not yet formally asked this government for aid. But . . . if the

United Nations finds Israel to be an aggressor, Egypt could very well ask the Soviets for help . . . and then the Mid East fat would really be in the fire . . . we may shortly find ourselves with a *de facto* situation that would make all our present troubles look puny indeed . . .[6]

Chester Cooper reports that there were Embassy rumours that in addition to Eisenhower's official *démarche*, the President had 'telephoned Eden and had given him unshirted hell'. This story, he comments, appears neither in Eisenhower's nor Eden's memoirs. Was Eden's memory being selective, he asks, and Eisenhower discreet? His explanation, from Embassy information, was that 'Ike . . . did call Downing Street, but mistook one of the Prime Minister's aides, who answered the call, for Eden himself. By the time that Eden got to the phone, Ike had finished his tirade and hung up.'[7]

Meanwhile the British Ambassador to Egypt, Sir Humphrey Trevelyan, heard the text of the ultimatum on the news ticker machine – the first he had heard of the proposed declaration of war. When he met Nasser and Fawzi later that evening he tried to defuse the message by describing it as 'a communication'. Nasser replied, 'We take it as an ultimatum.' Trevelyan tried to tell the Egyptian leaders that Britain and France were simply trying to 'stop the fighting and protect the Canal'; Nasser said flatly, 'We can defend the Canal and tomorrow we shall be defending it from more than the Israelis.' Nasser's message to the Security Council was a clear rejection of the ultimatum, and a request for an immediate meeting of the Council in view of the 'imminent danger, within a few hours from now, of British and French armed forces . . . occupying Egyptian territory'.

Meanwhile Abba Eban, Israel's Ambassador to the UN, hearing the terms of the ultimatum, was puzzled: 'Since we were nowhere near the Canal, we would have to "remove ourselves" forward in order to obey.'[8] Dayan had succeeded, as he had planned, in avoiding any serious demand for a withdrawal. His interests, in any case, lay in Sinai, now open to him as a result of the French and British move.

Whatever comfort the Anglo-French move might have given the Israelis, the Egyptians or themselves, there can be no doubt who were the real beneficiaries. Moscow revelled in her new cloak of comparative respectability: world attention had been diverted from Hungary to Egypt. Her UN Ambassador called for a meeting of the Security Council. Britain succeeded in getting its timing postponed so that they could take action on Israel's attack on Egypt and the Anglo-French ultimatum.

Eisenhower was in a fury. He was within a week of the vote which could endorse him or throw him out of the White House. He had concentrated his campaign, as a former victorious General, on the fight for peace, and the unity of Europe to which his proconsulship had so greatly contributed. There was a further thought. Eisenhower had welcomed Britain's emergence as he saw it, from the age of imperialism, and its unquestioned rule over Kipling's 'lesser breeds without the Law'. Now his friends – Eden; his old wartime crony in North Africa, Harold Macmillan; some of his former commanders – all of them seemed to have gone back a century in time.

Chester Cooper, who was in the closest touch with American official opinion on both sides of the Atlantic, has commented that the ultimatum was 'too clever by half for much of the world'. 'It fooled few and angered many not least the President of the United States and his Secretary of State.'[9] Nevertheless, Cooper recognized that Eden and Mollet were at long last able to take matters into their own hands – if they moved quickly enough neither friends nor enemies would notice, or even care, how transparent was their guise as selfless international guarantors of free passage through the Canal.

Two days after the Israeli move, at 4 a.m. London time, 6 a.m. Cairo time, the Anglo-French ultimatum expired. In Malta, more marine commanders in battle kit were boarding tank landing craft. British and French aircraft were landing in Cyprus in a round-the-clock operation. The largest naval concentrations since the Second World War, including battleships and five aircraft carriers, were said to be assembling in the eastern Mediterranean – the invasion fleet had in fact set out before the ultimatum. The operational plan laid down that the first Royal Air Force strikes were to begin on the morning of Wednesday 31 October, but this was postponed when the British and French heard that American aircraft were on the ground on Cairo's airfield, taking off American refugees. That evening the bombing began, to continue round the clock almost until the cease-fire seven days later.

The ostensible *casus belli* had already become inoperative. The Israelis had consolidated their groupings east of the Canal, and then proceeded to go about their own business in the Sinai, opening up the way to Sharm-el-Sheikh. The British and French, however, had secured the conditions printed on their own *carte d'entrée*: the Israelis had moved up towards the Canal and had moved away again, or so Dayan had allowed it to appear. But Egypt was still in command of the Canal through which, right up to the first bombing, merchant ships were moving freely, in large numbers and with no pilotage difficulties.

Almost at the last minute, Eden had changed the plan. The work of months had been based on the landing of troops at Alexandria, the troops then filtering off to the Canal and Cairo. Eden, however, decided that the paratroop drops should be limited to selected strategic points of the Canal. Cooper quotes a continuing comment in the officers' messes, 'Of the twelve different invasion places prepared, Eden chose the thirteenth.'[10]

Diplomatic relations between London and Washington were virtually non-existent by the Wednesday. The US Ambassador had been recalled to the States, and Embassy staff were instructed to 'keep their distance from Whitehall'. An exception, as we shall see, was Chester Cooper who was encouraged to keep his links with the Foreign Office and the 'friends' – security and intelligence units – in Whitehall.

Parliament met on 30 October. A technical motion for the adjournment of the House was moved at 4 p.m. to enable Sir Anthony Eden to make a statement.[11] After a brief reference to the tension which had been increasing on Israel's frontiers, and the establishment of a Joint Military Command between Egypt, Jordan and Syria, he said,

> Five days ago news was received that the Israel Government were taking certain measures of mobilization. Her Majesty's Government at once instructed Her Majesty's Ambassador at Tel Aviv to make inquiries of the Israel Foreign Affairs and to urge restraint.

There was, of course, not a word about the collusion, described in the previous chapter, providing for just such action on Israel's part. President Eisenhower, he went on, had called for immediate tripartite discussions between Britain, France and the US, which had been held on 28 and 29 October.

> While these discussions were proceeding, news was received last night that Israel forces had crossed the frontier and had penetrated deep into Egyptian territory. Later, further reports were received indicating that paratroops had been dropped. It appears that the Israel spearhead was not far from the banks of the Suez Canal. From recent reports it also appears that air forces are in action in the neighbourhood of the Canal.

He referred to Britain's obligations to Jordan and the assurance given by the Government during the previous few weeks that these obligations would be honoured. HM Ambassador in Tel Aviv, he went on, had the previous night received an assurance that Israel would not attack Jordan – an assurance, in fact, which had been obtained in the Paris talks two weeks earlier.

The Foreign Secretary, he said, had discussed the situation with the US Ambassador that morning, and the French Prime Minister and Foreign Minister had come to London 'at short notice' at the invitation of Her Majesty's Government. 'I must tell the House that very grave issues are at stake, and that unless hostilities can quickly be stopped, free passage through the Canal will be jeopardized.'* He went on to point out that any fighting on the banks of the Canal would endanger ships actually in passage, involving many hundreds of passengers and crew members: the value of ships in passage was about £50 million, excluding the value of the cargoes.

---

* Israel, as we have seen, had never been anything like so close.

Her Majesty's Government and the French Government have accordingly agreed that everything possible should be done to bring hostilities to an end as soon as possible. Their representatives in New York have, therefore, been instructed to join the United States representative in seeking an immediate meeting of the Security Council. This began at 4 p.m.

In the meantime, as a result of the consultations held in London today, the United Kingdom and French Governments have now addressed urgent communications to the Governments of Egypt and Israel. In these we have called upon both sides to stop all warlike action by land, sea and air forthwith and to withdraw their military forces to a distance of 10 miles from the Canal.[12] Further, in order to separate the belligerents and to guarantee freedom of transit through the Canal by the ships of all nations, we have asked the Egyptian Government to agree that Anglo-French forces should move temporarily – I repeat, temporarily – into key positions at Port Said, Ismailia and Suez.

The Governments of Egypt and Israel have been asked to answer this communication within 12 hours. It has been made clear to them that, if at the expiration of that time one or both have not undertaken to comply with these requirements, British and French forces will intervene in whatever strength may be necessary to secure compliance.

Hugh Gaitskell, for the Opposition, began by saying that the Prime Minister had made a statement of the utmost gravity, adding that it would be unwise to comment until the House had had an opportunity of thinking over what Eden had said. He went on to make three points. The first was that Britain was obliged under the Tripartite Declaration to do everything we could to stop aggression, either by Israel against the Arab states or by the Arab states against Israel – and went on to ask the Prime Minister to say what the attitude of the Government now was to that Declaration. His second point was that we were bound by the Charter of the United Nations to do everything we could to stop the conflict; he welcomed both Eden's statement that it was extremely important that hostilities should cease as soon as possible, and his announcement that the issue had been referred to the UN; indeed that the Security Council was at that moment discussing it. (In fact it was deferring consideration.) The third point related to Eden's announcement of the message to Egypt and Israel:

> We want to stop the hostilities; we want, I should have thought, both parties to withdraw themselves from the fighting area, but I must ask the Prime Minister under what authority, and with what right, he believes that British and French forces are justified in armed intervention in this matter before there has been any pronouncement by the United Nations upon it.[13]

Eden commented that Egypt's attitude to the Tripartite Declaration had been, to say the least, equivocal, and government-controlled newspapers in Egypt had made it clear on more than one occasion that she did not wish the

Declaration to be invoked on her behalf. As for the communication to the Security Council, it would have reached the Council by that time. On Gaitskell's third point,

> which I fully understand is the gravest, we do maintain, and I think I must fairly say, that there is nothing in the Tripartite Declaration or the Charter which abrogates the right of a Government to take such steps as are essential to protect the lives of their citizens and vital rights such as are here at stake. I ought to add [he said] vital international rights such as are here at stake.[14]

He undertook to report further to the House at 8 p.m. that evening, Gaitskell having already given notice that the Opposition intended to take the opportunity of the continuing debate on the Queen's Speech to hold a full day's debate the next day. In fact the exchange at 8 p.m. led to a debate. The Prime Minister began with a series of abstruse references to the Tripartite Declaration of 1950. Answering a point made by Hugh Gaitskell, he justified any apparent breach of the Declaration by 'the fact that Egypt has taken as her stand that she will not accept the implications of the Tripartite Declaration', and went on to refer the House to a White Paper issued in 1954. In any case Egypt was in breach of a Security Council resolution; also there were the continued threats against Israel. Referring specifically to questions from Labour backbenchers asking for an assurance that British and other troops would be withdrawn 'once the hostilities cease', Eden replied:

> Of course that will be so; certainly. It is our intention that they shall be withdrawn as soon as possible. The last thing that we want is an enduring commitment of that kind – the last thing.
>
> I have emphasized that we intend their presence at key points to be merely temporary. I have also explained that the purpose of that intervention is to seek to separate the combatants, to remove the risk to free passage through the Canal, and to reduce the risk, if we can, to those voyaging through the Canal.[15]

There was not a word about his overriding objective – to get rid of Nasser. Equally disingenuous was his last paragraph:

> I admit that the decision which Her Majesty's Government took, together with the French Government, was one which laid heavy responsibilities upon us. We thought that there was a fair and reasonable chance that these proposals might be accepted. With all respect to Hon. Gentlemen, I would ask them not to make up their minds. There is a fair and reasonable chance that they might be accepted. If they were, they offer by far the best opportunity of preventing this situation from growing into a far more dangerous one, affecting the whole of the Middle East. Hon. Gentlemen may, if they like, impugn our motives, because that was the decision we took and that was the spirit in which we took it.[16]

Hugh Gaitskell's speech on this debate and in successive interventions over the following weeks, for both his choice of phrase and the passion with which he spoke, were among the greatest of his career. Quoting the reasons Eden had given to explain the Government's motives for intervention, he said,[17]

Those are very grave words indeed. They amount, coupled with what the Prime Minister said in reply to a request from us, to an ultimatum to accept the proposals of the British and French Governments and, failing that, the British and French Governments will impose a solution by force. Therefore the possibility arises that before this House meets again British troops may be in action in Egypt. We did not feel that we could rise tonight, therefore, without a further discussion taking place . . .

I recognize, as I think we all do, that Israel has been subject to considerable provocation, that there have been many raids from Jordan and Egypt and lives have been lost, that threats have been made against her, that the latest action of combining the armed forces of Syria and Egypt and Jordan is a threat, that indeed, as we have said many times before, the purchase of arms from Czechoslovakia held out a very real possibility that within a fairly short time the balance would swing heavily on the side of Egypt and the Arab States . . .

I think the right place for judging the issue of whether or not there was aggression in terms of the United Nations Charter, and the exact degree of responsibility, is the Security Council of the United Nations.

I said this afternoon that we warmly welcomed the reference of this issue to the Security Council.

He did not, of course, know of the Government's determination to use the veto at that time. He then queried Israel's motives in advancing seventy to eighty or a hundred miles into Egypt and went on:

The difference between us – I am sorry to say this – lies in the action announced by the Prime Minister at the end of his statement which I read out at the beginning of my speech. Our first criticism of this is that it was taken independently by Britain and France at the very moment when this dispute was being referred to the Security Council. I cannot see any possible justification for that. Surely the right thing to have done would have been to have waited for the debate in the Security Council which was taking place this afternoon . . .

It is not our business to decide on our own that we should take independent action, even if it be, or appear to be, from our point of view police action. There is nothing in the United Nations Charter which justifies any nation appointing itself as world policeman. The great danger of the situation is that if we can do this so can anybody else. That is my first criticism and, I beg the Prime Minister to believe, a very grave anxiety of ours in this matter.

The second criticism is that I cannot see any legal justification for what it is proposed to do. The Prime Minister this evening gave a number of reasons why he felt that the Tripartite Declaration no longer applied. He said that

Egypt had denounced it. It is very odd that he should have left it until tonight to come forward with that argument. I should like the Foreign Secretary to tell us when it was that Egypt objected to the Tripartite Declaration. My recollection is that she objected from the very start to the Tripartite Declaration; and certainly in recent years, throughout the whole period since 1950, first of all our Government and then the present Government have repeatedly pledged themselves to abide by the Tripartite Declaration. It really is not good enough to come along at this last moment and say, 'Egypt is against it and therefore we no longer support it.'

The Prime Minister referred too to the Canal Zone evacuation Agreement, and he pointed out, which is perfectly correct, that there is an agreed minute which lays it down that an attack by Israel on one of the Arab States is not justification for the reoccupation of the Canal Zone by British forces . . .

The other arguments are no better. The fact that the Egyptians ignored and disregarded the 1951 Resolution of the United Nations is deplorable. We have repeatedly referred to it. But it has been known for the past five years. That is again no excuse, therefore, for suddenly coming along and saying we will not apply the Tripartite Declaration . . .

Finally, for the Prime Minister to come and tell us that, after all, the Egyptians have been getting a lot of arms from Czechoslovakia, strikes me as almost funny when I remember the debates earlier this year, in which we were protesting strongly because of the Government's refusal to allow Israel arms. For the Prime Minister now to come and defend this particular action on the ground that the Egyptians were allowed to have those arms and the Israelis were not, seems to me so feeble as an argument that I am surprised that he put it forward.

Our third criticism is that we are not satisfied with the degree of consultation which appears to have taken place either with other countries in the Commonwealth or with the United States of America . . .

I would therefore ask, what consultations took place with the Commonwealth, and what was the reaction of the other Commonwealth Governments? I would ask also whether the United States is in agreement with us on this. Is America supporting us? Is she giving us her full backing? If it comes to a vote in the Security Council on our action, if it is taken, can we be sure that the United States will vote with us, or are we doing this off our own bat without bothering whether the United States is going to support us or not? . . .

The first thing I would do – and this is what I am going to ask the Prime Minister to do – would be to refrain from using armed force until the Security Council has finished its deliberations.

The only other argument which the Prime Minister has put forward is that it is necessary to do this in order to protect British lives and ships in the Suez Canal. Very well. But suppose the news comes through that Israeli forces are being withdrawn towards the Israeli frontier, that they are far more than ten miles from the Suez Canal, is it still the intention of the Government, when there is really no danger whatever to British lives and shipping, to carry on with their ultimatum to Egypt and Israel and impose force if the ultimatum is refused?

. . . the Israelis have issued a statement saying that in fact this is not intended to be more than an attempt to wipe out the bases from which these raids are taking place and that they do intend to withdraw afterwards. If this is the case, how on earth can the Prime Minister possibly justify intervening when the Israelis are no longer near the Canal at all? He has also to show that there was no other way. In international law, I believe, there is provision, if the local authorities cannot maintain law and order, for a Government stepping in and rescuing their own nationals. But if that piece of international law is so interpreted as to justify armed intervention with an ultimatum of the kind that has been announced this afternoon – I suggest that it can be used in all sorts of circumstances and greatly to our detriment in all parts of the world.

I should have thought that if that was the case the Americans would also be concerned with the safety of their nationals and their shipping. Why have they not taken action of this kind? They have been content to tell their nationals to come home and to warn their shipping. In what has happened so far, I cannot see any possible justification for the use of force which we have heard about this afternoon.

The Prime Minister has not consulted the Opposition. I would like to place that on record . . .

We have had no discussions with the Prime Minister. I do not blame him for that – he has had very little time – but he made no attempt, if he wishes to have a united country on this issue, to find out whether it was possible . . .

Because we have very grave anxieties about the last part of the Prime Minister's statement, I am going to make an appeal to him. I ask him once again, as I asked him this afternoon, if he will defer any action by armed forces by Britain, and, if he can persuade the French, by the French as well, until after the Security Council has completed its deliberation and until we have had a further opportunity of discussing the matter in the House of Commons . . .

I must tell the Prime Minister that if he is unable to give that undertaking, which is a very reasonable one in view of what is happening in the Security Council today, and on the grounds that we do not think it right that this country should be put in grave danger of being involved in war in these conditions and in these circumstances, I regret to say that we shall have to divide the House.

Alfred Robens, winding up the debate, picked up a statement by Eden asserting that the Government had consulted the Commonwealth and he had gathered that the United States had been consulted. In that case why had the US State Department issued a statement that day saying that 'it had received no prior warning of the British and French intention to move troops into the Suez area if Egypt and Israel do not stop fighting'.[18] Denis Healey intervened to quote the Prime Minister's words, 'We have been in close communication with the United States Government', and Robens drew attention to the statement by Cabot Lodge, the US Ambassador to the United Nations, to the Security Council:

Failure by the Council to react at this time would be an avoidance of the responsibilities to maintain peace and security. The Government of the United States feels it imperative that the Council act in the promptest manner to determine whether a breach of the peace has occurred, to have a cease-fire ordered immediately and to obtain the withdrawal of Israeli Forces behind the frontier line. Nothing else will suffice.

If the Prime Minister would undertake not to take military action until the Security Council had discussed the matter, the Opposition would not press a Division at the end of the debate.

Selwyn Lloyd wound up. The strain was showing when he reacted against Opposition complaints that they had not been consulted before the Government lurched into war. 'Really, this idea that the Government of the day can take action only after prior agreement with the Opposition . . .' he began, when Hugh Gaitskell rose:

First, my Right Hon. Friend the Member for Llanelly [Mr J. Griffiths] and I saw the Prime Minister at 4.15, a quarter of an hour before the debate, and were given the statement. We appreciated seeing it at least 15 minutes before the debate, but that was not consultation. Secondly, I did not complain about failure on the part of the Government to consult us. I was making it plain that they did not do so, and that they could not expect, in the absence of that consultation and agreement with us, that they would automatically have unity.

Lloyd replied that the Government never suggested there should automatically be unity. They did not want a rubber stamp from the Opposition. They would do what they believed to be right in the interests of the country, and it was for the Opposition to do what they thought right. As for all the talk about 'dividing the House', if that occurred it would be the responsibility of the Opposition; in this serious situation that was something the country would not forgive.[19] Interrupted by the Liberal leader, Clement Davies, when he referred to the movements by the Israeli forces, he said,

Israeli forces are within a very few miles of Suez. They have been moving towards Suez, they are moving towards Suez and they are within very close distance of Suez. . . . There is also information of the increase of air activity, and I should have thought that it would be common sense to assess this as a threat to free passage through the Canal. And I believe that there is at the present time a threat of sufficient degree to require us to take straight away the action which we propose.

This statement was, of course, quite untrue; Israeli forces had not been near Suez, and were currently moving further away. Replying to the references which had been made to the United States, he ended his speech,

In a sense, the policeman has his hands tied behind his back. He has to wait a long time before he is allowed to play his part.

I myself believe that, if you have accepted that system, you are only safe if you also retain the rights of the individual countries to defend their own nationals and their own interests. [*Interruption.*] There are interruptions from the Opposition about Hungary. I really cannot understand their relevance . . .

In this matter we have never claimed that we have acted in agreement with the United States of America. (Hon. Members: 'Oh.') We have certainly been in close touch with the Government of the United States throughout this controversy, but we have never said that we have acted with their approval and authority. We believe that this is a decision which we and the French Government have had to take in our own right, and, really, it is a decision in the interests of the peace of that area.[20]

The House divided: Ayes (Labour) 218; Noes (Conservative) 270.

Suez dominated Parliamentary proceedings for each day of that week, including the Saturday. The proceedings for 31 October were in the control of the Opposition who earlier had given notice of debating the Armed Forces. In a statement on 'Business of the House' on that day, Rab Butler, Leader of the House, announced the change of business, at the same time saying that in view of the international situation the Prorogation of the House would not, as planned, take place on 1 November, but Parliament would continue to sit until the following Monday, the new session beginning the following day. Anthony Nutting resigned on 31 October.

Eden opened the debate, beginning with a reference to a meeting of the Security Council debate the previous day. He told the House that Israel had accepted the call to withdraw, and informed the House of the Israeli move on Sinai. Israeli troops were not advancing towards the Canal. To interruptions by Opposition members, he said:

We have no desire whatever, nor have the French Government, that the military action that we shall have to take should be more than temporary in its duration, but it is our intention that our action to protect the Canal and separate the combatants should result in a settlement which will prevent such a situation arising in the future. If we can do that we shall have performed a service not only to this country, but to the users of the Canal. . . . What would the future of the Middle East have been if, while denouncing Israel, we had done nothing to check these Egyptian actions . . .[21]

When Philip Noel-Baker interrupted to press him further about consultations with the Americans, Harold Davies, Labour MP for Leek, perceptively interrupted: 'No, the Right Hon. Gentleman has a card up his sleeve with Pineau.' The interesting thing was that Davies recognized Pineau far more than his Premier, Mollet, as the organizing genius of the operation.*

* In further debate the following day, Davies developed this reference, saying, 'The Jewish people are being dragged into this war. I am convinced that the speech of M. Pineau in France had something to do with the political manoeuvres that have been taking place since the beginning of the Suez crisis. M. Pineau said that he has other political cards up his sleeve' – *Hansard*, 1 November, col. 1653.

Eden took the opportunity of Gaitskell's question the previous day to go into a long disquisition on the Tripartite Declaration. Gaitskell, replying, pressed him to say whether, on the expiry of the ultimatum, instructions were given to British and French forces to occupy the Canal Zone. Eden, after much pressing, and for a time failing to find the relevant passage of his brief, replied that he had made it plain to the House that if no reply were received, 'we would take military action at the expiry of the period'. Gaitskell interpreted this as meaning that British and French troops were already on the move, and that this action involved

> not only the abandonment but a positive assault upon the three principles which have governed British foreign policy for, at any rate, the last ten years – solidarity with the Commonwealth, the Anglo-American Alliance and adherence to the Charter of the United Nations.[22]

On Commonwealth consultation, he asked what support the Government were getting – clearly not that of India, Pakistan and Ceylon. It was, he said, a remarkable and most distressing fact that Australia could not support us: on one UN resolution she abstained, on the other voted against us. Canada had expressed 'in the coldest possible language' their regret, and the New Zealand Prime Minister regretted the situation, the Foreign Minister proving unable to say whether he supported Britain or not.

On Anglo-US relations, we found ourselves actually vetoing a United States resolution in the Security Council. He quoted press reports that Dulles had described Franco-British action as 'a piece of trickery', and a Conservative newspaper comment that action was 'not only a reckless move which has brought the world to the edge of major war, but a calculated snub to President Eisenhower himself'. The Americans were further outraged by the fact that the air-drop came only hours after Britain's first veto had killed the American cease-fire proposal.

A strong point was that the action might create a precedent for Chinese intervention to protect their nationals in Hong Kong or Singapore. But he went on to challenge the Government about a Conservative newspaper report from Washington saying:

> There is no longer any doubt in the minds of American officials that Britain and France were in collusion with the Israelis from the beginning, and sanctioned the invasion of Egypt as an excuse to re-occupy the Canal Zone. Strenuous denials by British and French diplomats have failed to shake Washington's conviction that this was the case.

He also stressed the licence the Anglo-French action had given the Soviet Government to crush the freedom movement in Hungary, and ended by committing his party to oppose the Government's policy 'by every constitutional means at our disposal'.[23]

The following day, Thursday 1 November, after questions, the Defence Minister, Antony Head, made a statement, announcing bombing attacks on four Egyptian airfields: Almaza, Inchass, Abu Sueir and Kabrit. Ground-attack aircraft, shore and carrier-based, had carried out attacks on a total of nine Egyptian airfields that morning, and HMS *Newfoundland* had sunk the Egyptian frigate *Domiat* eighty miles south of Suez. They had no 'direct' information about Israeli movements, though reports indicated that paratroops were holding high ground twenty miles east of Suez, and in the north the Israelis claimed to have overrun the Egyptian position in Qasseina. Gaitskell's reaction was to condemn the bombing of Egypt, 'not in self-defence, not in collective defence, but in clear defiance of the United Nations Charter'.

At the end of supplementary questions, a Parliamentary situation occurred unprecedented in the memories of any of the members present. It arose from a point of order raised by Sydney Silverman, MP for Nelson and Colne.

> On a point of order, Mr Speaker, I would respectfully ask for your assistance and guidance to the House in what appears to be a completely unprecedented situation. The Minister of Defence has just made an announcement about the use of bombers and ships, the sinking of ships, the dropping of bombs, the destruction of property – (An Hon. Member: 'And life') – and the destruction of life in a country with whom apparently we are in friendly relations.
>
> There has been no declaration of war, there has been no breaking off of diplomatic relations. It looks as though the Minister has been telling the House of Commons that he has been using his authority to compel British subjects to commit illegal acts resulting in the loss of life. Is there anything that the House of Commons can do at this moment to make certain that those who have taken an oath of allegiance to Her Majesty are not required by that oath to commit murder all over the world?

As the questioning developed, Silverman, who was an experienced lawyer, rose again.

> Further to that point of order, Mr Speaker, may I draw your attention to the fact that there is one very important practical question involved in this? Some of our men may some day be taken prisoner by the Egyptians. What is their position? If they are carrying on activities of this kind on Egyptian territory in a state of war, that is one thing, and they have their rights, but if they are not, what is their position? Unless that question can be cleared up, there arises a most important constitutional difficulty . . .
>
> The issue raised is an extremely serious one, affecting the position of our Armed Forces. It really is essential that the Government should give us a reply on this vital issue of whether or not a declaration of war has been made, or is to be made in the very near future. I appeal to the Prime Minister, if he has any control over the situation left at all, to make a statement.[24]

When Mr Speaker refused to answer the question, Hugh Gaitskell rose:

> Further to that point of order, Mr Speaker – I understand you feel yourself
> unable to answer my Hon. Friend's question. Therefore, with your
> permission, I would like to ask the Government whether a declaration of war
> has been made?

One Labour MP after another rose when no answer was forthcoming.
Aneurin Bevan, saying that British soldiers, sailors and airmen had been
sent into action without the normal protection available to them, said:

> We want to know what protection they have should they fall into the hands of
> those against whom they are conducting operations. Can we have an answer
> to that question?[25]

The House was in a state of uproar, leading the Speaker to suspend the
sitting for half an hour, under Standing Order No. 24, namely 'Grave
Disorder having arisen in the house'.* When the House resumed, Gaitskell
challenged Eden, who said he would be able to give an answer which would
reassure the House, but on a considered statement rather than by question
and answer.

The debate was opened by James Griffiths, Labour's Deputy Leader. His
speech included the moving of a censure motion deploring the action of the
Government in resorting to armed force against Egypt in clear violation of
the United Nations Charter, thereby affronting the conviction of a large
section of the British people, dividing the Commonwealth, straining the
Atlantic Alliance, and generally damaging the foundations of international
order. Contrasting Churchill's phrase, 'Britain's finest hour', he referred to
his own humiliation at being present at Britain's worst hour. Pointing out
that over the years ministers had chided the Soviet Union for using the veto
in the UN, Britain, he said, had now used hers, outraging world opinion
thereby. He quoted the Foreign Secretary who, in excusing Britain's failure
to consult the UN before acting, had referred to the frustration of the
Security Council by the veto – 'it cannot act immediately . . . the
policeman'. Yet while he was making this speech, the UK delegate, on the
Foreign Secretary's instructions, was using the veto on Britain's behalf. He
challenged the Government to say whether they instructed their representative at the General Assembly, before whom the issue was being raised
that evening, to argue that Britain's action was in conformity with the UN
Charter.

Replying for the Government, the Prime Minister moved an amendment
to the Opposition Motion, asking the House to approve of

* The writer, after thirty-five years in the House, and having been present on a number of
occasions when Mr Speaker has suspended the sitting on grounds of 'disorder', cannot recall
anything to compare with the heat and passion of this occasion.

the prompt action taken by Her Majesty's Government designed to bring
hostilities between Israel and Egypt to an end and to safeguard vital
international and national interests, and pledges its full support for all steps
necessary to secure these ends.[26]

He did not, of course, mention the fact that the hostilities begun by Israel
were a put-up job on the part of Britain and France. He answered the
question pressed earlier, by saying that there had not been a declaration of
war by us:

The Geneva Convention applies to any state of armed conflict. Therefore, it
applies in the present conditions just as it applied in Korea. That is the
position of the International Red Cross in the matter.[27]

Hugh Gaitskell rose to pursue the matter.

The Prime Minister has made it perfectly plain that there has been no
declaration of war, but the question I put to him was whether we were in a
state of war. I am still not quite clear whether we are or not. He said that we
are in a state of armed conflict. Exactly what is the difference between war and
armed conflict?[28]

Eden replied:

We are in an armed conflict; that is the phrase I have used. There has been no
declaration of war. The Red Cross is in communication with them as with us.
We are all of us bound by the provisions of the Geneva Convention – Israel,
Egypt and ourselves.[29]

Eden stuck to his point that the Geneva Convention applied whether war
had been declared or not. 'We are in a state of armed conflict', as in the
fighting in Korea. On the general issue, Eden repeated his previous
arguments, and informed the House that Britain would put her case to the
General Assembly of the United Nations the following day.

Winding up the debate for the Opposition, Aneurin Bevan began by
saying that in more years than he cared to remember, even during the days
of the war, he could not recollect feeling running as high as it had done that
day, or such general uneasiness in the House as existed that day.

The fact of the matter is that mankind is faced with an entirely novel
situation. There has never been anything like it in the history of nations. Two
major events have completely cancelled ... all the finesse and the
sophistications of conventional diplomacy. There is nothing in the White
House, in London, in the Quai d'Orsay, or in the Kremlin that furnishes
statesmen with lessons in history to enable them to judge what to do in the
existing circumstances.[30]

All the arguments used by the Prime Minister to justify Britain's action were
standard: every country that attempts to justify itself uses language of this

sort. He went on to quote Hitler's ultimatum to Norway: 'we have only to substitute Egypt for Norway', he said, and quoted Eden's almost identical language. He did not, he said, blame the Government for not telling the US or the Commonwealth.

> their plans beforehand, because they were plans that could not be disclosed. What was wrong was not that the Government did not disclose the plans. What was wrong was the sort of plans that they had. Of course, it was not possible to tell Washington that we intended to invade Egypt within twelve hours – it might have leaked out. One cannot stab a man effectively if he is given too long notice beforehand. Therefore, the fault with the Government is that they have formed plans which in their nature were a violation of the confidence existing between ourselves and members of the Commonwealth.[31]

R. A. Butler, who, one imagines, did not relish the task, wound up for the Government. He spent some time dealing with Silverman's argument, summing up in this way:

> Her Majesty's Government do not regard their present action as constituting a war. (Hon. Members: 'Oh'.) It corresponds broadly to the situation in Korea. Nevertheless, they consider that we have complied fully with the spirit of Article 1 of the third Hague Convention . . . in warning Egypt by means of a statement of our requirements, accompanied by a conditional intimation that certain points in Egyptian territory would be occupied if that requirement was not complied with. That, therefore, is the legal position in regard to the background against which we have begun this action in the last few days.
> *Hon. Members:* Is there a war?
> *Mr Butler:* There is not a war, but there is a state of conflict.[32]

Continuing, he tried to explain the war. Because of the Egyptian arms deal and the military joint staff arrangements among Jordan, Syria and Egypt,

> There is no doubt that the Israeli nation felt itself ringed around and, while neither the House nor Her Majesty's Government should do anything to condone Israeli action, [sic] we have to treat the Israeli advance as a fact with which the Government had to deal . . .
> We had to deal with a position in which the Israeli attack upon Egypt could have been intended either to seize the east bank of the Suez Canal or to carry them across the Canal itself. Either of those circumstances could have prevented the free transit of goods and ships upon which this country depends.[33]

He then went on, perhaps unwisely, to deal with the deeper problem of Britain's motives. A Labour Member,* he said, had

> accused the Government of using the Israeli border incidents to provide a certain cloak of moral sanctity to enable them to follow up the plans which

* Wilfred Fienburgh, later killed in a car accident.

they have been cultivating and preparing for since the incident was first launched.

We do not accept that interpretation of our action.

He went on to list the components in the Government's peaceful search for a solution under the Charter – the eighteen-nation conference, the Canal Users' Association:

> We have had disappointments, but we had, up to this last incident, made some progress. Then came this emergency situation, and, as I have said, we hope still to pull a solution out of the nettle, disaster, which will be under the umbrella of the United Nations.
>
> I wish to reaffirm the statements made by the Prime Minister earlier this afternoon . . . that we do not seek to impose by force a solution of the Israeli-Egyptian dispute, or of the Suez Canal dispute or any other dispute in the area. We do not seek to negotiate by ourselves alone on any of those disputes. The sole object of the Anglo-French intervention is to stop the hostilities, to prevent a resumption of them, and to safeguard traffic through the Canal itself.[34]

Towards the end of his speech he produced a beautiful *double entendre*, of the kind known in those days, and indeed since, as a Butlerism:

> And the interpretation of British policy as I have given it, that we have been working up to this emergency (Hon. Members: 'Hear, hear') –
> *Mr Mikardo:* You gave the game away there, Rab.
> *Mr Butler:* I said that we have been working up to this emergency to obtain a peaceful settlement of the dispute; and now that we are faced with the fact of the emergency we have deliberately taken action which is controversial, yet highly courageous . . . in order to restore the respect for international law and order . . .[35]

There were three divisions at the end of the debate. On the first the voting was: Ayes (for Labour's motion) 255, Noes 324; on the second (the Government amendment): Ayes (for the amendment) 323, Noes 255; and on the third (the resolution as amended): Ayes 320, Noes 253. It was on that same evening that the UN General Assembly carried its resolution calling for a cease-fire. The vote was 64 for, and 5 against (Britain, France, Israel, Australia and New Zealand). There were six abstentions.

On Friday 2 November there was round-the-clock bombing of Egyptian military targets: warships and landing craft were slowly moving towards the coast of Egypt. The French were impatient, and Dayan, heavily committed in his own campaign in Sinai, worried. The French told him that they were frustrated by Britain's failure to move, whether through unwillingness or inability was not clear. They were pressing the British to advance their invasion date, at that time scheduled for 6 November: if Britain refused the French were ready to act on their own. Cooper records that he was called to the Embassy secret telephone, where Robert Amory, the deputy director of the CIA, was bawling at him,

> Tell your friends to comply with the cease-fire or go ahead with the goddam invasion. Either way we'll back 'em up if they do it fast. What we can't stand is their goddam hesitation waltz while Hungary is burning.

Amory was clearly not speaking for Eisenhower. America had her own command problems. Eisenhower was in the closing days of his campaign; Dulles was taken to hospital that night with terminal cancer. Cooper records that, making clear he was speaking on instructions, he told the Foreign Office Joint Intelligence Committee, 'Cease fire or get on with your landings. Present Washington with either an overnight stand-down or a fast *fait accompli*, and everything will be OK again.'[36]

The House met on the next day, 3 November – almost the only Saturday sitting in modern times. The Prime Minister opened with a statement:

The Prime Minister (Sir Anthony Eden):
    We move the Adjournment of the House in order that I may make the following statement in accordance with the undertaking that I gave yesterday to give the House as soon as I possibly could an indication of the reply we propose to send to the Resolution of the Assembly of the United Nations.
    I should first recall a statement which I made in the House in the course of my speech on 1 November, when I said this:

> The first and urgent task is to separate these combatants and to stabilize the position. That is our purpose. If the United Nations were then willing to take over the physical task of maintaining peace in that area, no one would be better pleased than we. But police action there must be to separate the belligerents and to prevent a resumption of hostilities.[37]

Since that statement was made, I have had consultations in London with the French Foreign Minister. As a result, Her Majesty's Government and the French Government are sending the following reply to the Resolution of the United Nations General Assembly:

> The British and French Governments have given careful consideration to the Resolution passed by the General Assembly on 2 November. They maintain their view that police action must be carried through urgently to stop the hostilities which are now threatening the Suez Canal, to prevent a resumption of these hostilities and to pave the way for a definitive settlement of the Arab–Israel war which threatens the legitimate interests of so many countries.
>   They would most willingly stop military action as soon as the following conditions could be satisfied:
>
> (i) Both the Egyptian and the Israeli Governments agree to accept a United Nations force to keep the peace;
> (ii) The United Nations decides to constitute and maintain such a force until an Arab–Israel peace settlement is reached and until satisfactory

arrangements have been agreed in regard to the Suez Canal, both agreements to be guaranteed by the United Nations;

(iii) In the meantime, until the United Nations force is constituted, both combatants agree to accept forthwith limited detachments of Anglo-French troops to be stationed between the combatants . . .

We have been in consultation with the Governments of Australia and New Zealand. (Hon. Members: 'And Canada?') I am coming to that. The House will understand the difficulties of timing in these consultations, but I have good reason to believe that those Governments will welcome my statement. We have also communicated the substance of the statement at once to the Governments of Canada and the United States, and to the Secretary-General of the United Nations.[38]

This was in fact the beginning of the climb-down. Britain and France had achieved none of their objectives. Nasser was still there. Britain was being forced to introduce oil rationing. Her relations with the United States, and indeed Canada, were at their lowest point for many years.

Hugh Gaitskell was clearly not disposed to exonerate Eden. He pointed out that the General Assembly's resolution, carried by 64 votes to 5, called on all parties to agree to an immediate cease-fire and halt the movement of military forces and arms into the area. Gaitskell said that reports of continuing, and indeed intensified, bombing by British aircraft, as well as the Prime Minister's attempt to haggle with the terms of the UN resolution, meant that Britain was not carrying out the call of the Assembly. The majority, he said, was larger than that on any previous resolution carried there. He went on to ask the Prime Minister, first, whether he was aware that the Egyptian Government had already announced their willingness to agree to an immediate cease-fire if all the other parties did so as well; second, whether Eden was aware that the Suez Canal was blocked 'and that the consequence of the intervention by Her Majesty's Government, far from facilitating the passage of ships through the Canal, has had precisely the opposite effect?' Thirdly, was the Prime Minister further aware that the Israeli Government had announced that the fighting in the Sinai Desert area was virtually at an end – therefore the original situation had substantially changed?

With Eden reeling against the ropes, Gaitskell stepped up the attack. Why was he insisting that the proposed United Nations Force should have to be maintained until both an Arab–Israel peace settlement had been reached, and until satisfactory arrangements had been agreed in regard to the Canal? While there was a strong case for a UN force to maintain such a presence until an Arab–Israel peace settlement was reached, what reason was there for such a police force to operate in the Canal Zone at all? (The true answer – which was not vouchsafed – was of course that control of the

Canal and the expulsion of Nasser were all that the operation and the collusion were about.) Finally, by what right was the Prime Minister insisting that until the UN Force was constituted, both combatants (Egypt and Israel) had still to accept the original ultimatum?[39]

On the last question Eden answered 'that it is in the Canal Zone that, "in our judgment" the danger had lain and still lies'. Gaitskell kept on pressing the point that the UN resolution demanded a cessation of all military operations: Eden was disobeying it. Although a debate was to follow, preceded by a statement on Hungary, questions continued on Eden's statement, and on a further one on the military position by the Defence Secretary, for nearly one and a half hours. After a statement on Hungary by the Foreign Secretary, the debate began. It was, as if by general agreement, confined to backbenchers until the two winding-up speeches from the Opposition and Government front benches.

James Griffiths was concerned to put three questions, one of which had been raised by Denis Healey. This related to Egyptian forces north of the Canal and the threat they posed to Israel, the greater in that Syrian and Lebanese forces had entered Jordan. The second and third were more direct. Would the Foreign Secretary give an undertaking that they would accept the United Nations solution for the future of the Suez Canal, and give that undertaking 'now, at this time'? The third related to the specific call by the General Assembly to 'all engaged in these hostilities – that includes Her Majesty's Government – to agree to an immediate cease-fire': he pointed out that the word 'immediate' had been used many hours before.

Selwyn Lloyd's reply[40] was pathetic. He was probably at the end of his tether, conscious too that, at least up to a point, he had been gravely misled. He refused to give the undertaking about withdrawal that Gaitskell and others had asked for on the ground, they had urged, that hostilities had terminated. This he denied. Israeli forces were now advancing on the Canal. 'That was continuing.' It was not true. Egyptian forces were also advancing on the Canal from the other direction:

> if someone does not intervene to separate the combatants, I am perfectly certain that there will be sustained hostilities, and the chance of their spreading will be very much greater. . . . We are certainly going to separate the combatants.

Gaitskell arose to correct Lloyd's statement that the Egyptians had not agreed, as the Israelis had, to withdraw ten miles from the Canal. He pointed out that the call to the Egyptians came from Britain, not the UN, and that the Egyptians had in fact accepted the UN Assembly resolution – they had agreed to the cease-fire providing that other parties to the dispute did so too.

On that same day, Saturday 3 November, Eden broadcast to the nation. Gaitskell demanded the right of reply, which was refused, a decision which today would appear incredible. I was with him at his home in Hampstead, drafting protests to the Director General and the Chairman of the Governors of the BBC. In the event he was allowed on the air on the Sunday. On 3 November, too, the French and British Governments rejected the United Nations call for a cease-fire, Israeli forces took Sharm-el-Sheikh: their military and political objective had been gained. Israel's ambassador to the UN was ordered to announce his country's willingness to accept a cease-fire forthwith, if Egypt would do the same. Their war was over. Meanwhile the French and British were still some distance from the starting-line.

On Monday 5 November, the Anglo-French invasion began with a paratroop drop on to a small airfield near Port Said. Confusion took over. The British and French commanders had their battle headquarters on different ships and it took hours to establish communication between them. Suddenly everything hit Eden. The Canadian Prime Minister sent Eden what was later described as 'the most blistering personal telegram ever to pass between two Commonwealth Prime Ministers'.[41] At the same time there was a flight from sterling. Before British troops had even landed, sterling reserves had fallen by $279 million (following the loss of $140 million in September and October), 15 per cent of Britain's gold and dollar reserves. Macmillan's memoirs show that he suspected the American Treasury of inspiring the run on the currency markets.[42] How far this was due to the results of speculation against sterling and heavy selling in New York, says Macmillan, 'is hard to know', though clearly he felt that selling by the Federal Reserve was far greater than what was needed to protect the value of the Americans' own reserves. In fact, the US was applying economic sanctions on a scale rarely seen before or since. With Eisenhower's full backing, the US Secretary to the Treasury, George Humphrey, was using financial pressure to the full, including master-minding the selling, holding up the scheme for emergency supplies of oil to Western Europe, and – when Britain went cap-in-hand to the US for a $1,000 million loan (plus a further loan of $500 million from the International Monetary Fund) – insisting that there would not be a cent unless Britain agreed to a cease-fire.[43]

Soon after these events I was given an interesting account by a prominent American lady living in London of a visit by one of the leading US journalists. As a matter of form, without any expectations, he had put in a request to both Eden and Macmillan, not expecting to be granted an interview by either. To his surprise each of them agreed to see him. Macmillan treated him like royalty, entreating him to use his influence to unlock the door of the US Treasury. Eden went further, and followed his entreaties by seeing the journalist (who has confirmed these facts to me) to and through the front door of No. 10, a courtesy which according to strict protocol applies only to heads of government and heads of state.

The Soviet Government, with Hungarian blood dripping from their fingers, not content with voting with the Americans in the US Suez debate, urged joint Russo-American military action to 'curb aggression' against Egypt. Less than ten years before, the Soviet Government had voted at the UN for Eretz Israel. Now Bulganin warned the Israeli Government that it was criminally playing with the destiny of its country and people – 'which raises the question of the whole existence of Israel as a state'.

What had in fact been going on in Washington and in the American Embassy in London is now available in a book published in the United States by Chester (Chet) Cooper in 1978, an account going far beyond the restrained memoirs of Eden and Lloyd.* In particular it describes the somewhat eerie relationship between the Embassy in Grosvenor Square and the Foreign Office in Whitehall. Chester Cooper, who had been appointed CIA contact with the FO Intelligence staff, records the story from his special vantage point. There were few secrets not known to the CIA, whether in London or Washington.

> Each day of that interminable week seemed to be more tense than its yesterday. I awoke every morning to a feeling that this would surely be the Moment of Truth: the British and French forces would land at Suez and the battle would be joined; and/or the Russians would either leave or subjugate Hungary. But the days passed and the tension mounted, and the relations between the United States and its old friends continued to deteriorate, and tempers continued to rise in Britain, and Eden hung on . . . it was hard to distinguish between the bad dreams of restless nights and the nightmares of frenetic days. . . . Anglo-American relations had sunk to a lower level than at any time since the Civil War.

It was in the early hours of 3 November that his telephone rang, and he was summoned to the Embassy to receive Robert Amory's message.

But that message is not the one Foster Dulles would have sent. In fact he sent no message: he was taken to hospital during the night, for an operation for abdominal cancer. The inexperienced – 'reportedly anti-British acting

---

* Chester Cooper is the author of *The Lion's Last Roar*, a detailed account of the Suez operation. I had come to know him in my first period as Prime Minister. President Lyndon Johnson had appointed him a member of a small team under Averell Harriman during the Vietnam War, to seek out any possibility of a negotiated agreement which would be defensible in Congress. It was when Kosygin visited Britain in 1967 that, at my request, the President authorized him to be in London during Soviet Premier Kosygin's visit to London. When Kosygin came to Chequers on the last day of his visit, Cooper was incarcerated in the historic Prison Room at Chequers, with a hot line to the White House. See *The Labour Government, 1964–70*, London, 1971, pp. 361–4.

secretary' – Herbert Hoover Jr was to be in charge for the next two months. Cooper passed on the message at that morning's meeting with the Intelligence Staff. Certainly, Cooper records, there had been a change of feeling in Washington, for a moment. But that was to reckon without Eisenhower, on the eve of his election.

One of Washington's retaliatory measures was to place an embargo on the supply of intelligence information to London. On the night of 5 November Cooper records that he telephoned his Washington chief, and told him that he would not be attending the Foreign Office Joint Intelligence Committee meeting unless Washington lifted its embargo on overseas intelligence. One subject they would be discussing was the warning Bulganin had issued to Britain and France. Washington, Cooper was told, took the Soviet threat 'very seriously', and there were 'reliable reports that the Air Defence Command in the Washington area had been put on an emergency basis'. He was, despite the decision to withhold intelligence material, instructed to attend the Foreign Office meetings each day in the week preceding the landings, unless the Foreign Office vetoed his attendance. When the Middle East situation came up, Patrick Dean, Deputy Under Secretary of State,* would ask hopefully, 'what do the Americans have on this?', to which Cooper had answered each time, 'nothing, I'm afraid'.

Just as he was leaving for the Foreign Office on the morning of the 6th, he was given the US assessment of the Bulganin threat to communicate to the Committee. However angry Washington was over the landings which they knew had taken place near Port Said, they were taking no chances with the Soviet *démarche*.

Cooper recalls the committee clerk answering the buzzer from the conference room:

> 'You may join them now, sir', she said coldly on her return. As I rose I reflected on *this* symptom of the new mood. In happier days, she had given me a wink and a smile and a 'Get-along-with-you-now'.[44]

(Cooper goes on to relate that, as he sat down, he heard a peal of church bells. Was it a warning of a Russian bomber force approaching? He learnt later that St Margaret's bells were 'striking joyous notes of marriage rather than ominous notes of war'). Asked if he had anything to report, he said,

> 'The United States Intelligence Board had an emergency meeting last night. They are convinced that the Russian nuclear rocket threat is a bluff. They seriously doubt that Moscow has either the long-range missile capability or the nuclear warheads to threaten Britain and France. They want you to know they do not believe there is any real danger.'
>
> 'Thank you,' Dean murmured, 'Tell Washington we are grateful for their views.'[45]

* Dean had attended the Sèvres meeting in Selwyn Lloyd's absence.

The United States was in the difficult position of not wanting to know, yet knowing all the time. Dulles had been preparing a speech for his only intervention in Eisenhower's election campaign, and the draft he had prepared made it only too clear that the State Department had prior knowledge of the Israeli attack which would signal the Anglo-French intervention. The CIA man, Robert Amory,* objected:

> Mr Secretary, if you say that and war breaks out 24 hours later, you will appear to all the world as *partie prise* to the Israeli aggression – and I'm positive the Israelis will attack the Sinai shortly after midnight tomorrow.**

The Americans in fact knew virtually everything about the invasion plans. Admiral Burke, chief of US Naval Operations, had actually talked to Lord Mountbatten who had told him that everything was 'in a hell of a mess' in Cyprus and Malta through Eden's repeated changes in the plans. Burke wanted to help the British with landing vessels, but Dulles vetoed the idea.[46]

In fact the British at high level had kept their American opposite numbers informed:

> practically every senior general, admiral and air marshal in the British armed forces was keeping the US Joint Chiefs informed of every move they were making.[47]

Dulles was anxious officially not to know, since, if this became known, Adlai Stevenson, Eisenhower's opponent in the Presidential election, could have exploited it. Where they appear to have been less than fully informed related to Israel: they were not clear whether the Israeli attack was an integrated part of the Anglo-French plan, or a smart move by the Israelis to take advantage of what they had heard of British and French intentions.

On that day, Monday 5 November, the House of Commons met for the Prorogation prior to the reopening of the new Parliamentary session on the Tuesday. The Foreign Secretary made a statement at the end of Questions.[48] Since the House had met on the previous Saturday, he said, the General Assembly of the UN, meeting in emergency Special Session, had passed three resolutions: the first, sponsored by African and Asian states, had called for a cease-fire, the halting of the movement of military forces and arms into the area, and the withdrawal of all forces in the area behind the armistice lines, the Secretary-General being charged with the task of obtaining compliance. The second, sponsored by Canada, requested the Secretary-General to submit within forty-eight hours a plan for setting up, with the consent of the nations concerned, an emergency international United Nations force to secure and supervise the cessation of hostilities, in

---

* A second cousin of Derick Heathcoat Amory, a member of Eden's Cabinet.
** As they did.

accordance with the terms of the cease-fire resolution of 2 November. The Secretary-General, the Foreign Secretary said, had sent a telegram drawing the attention of HMG to these resolutions, and requesting all parties to bring a halt to all hostile military actions in the area by 8 p.m. Greenwich Mean Time, the previous day. HMG, having invited French ministers to London for consultations, informed Mr Hammarsjköld that for this reason it was not possible to give him a definite answer within the time limit. Following the consultations with the French, they had sent a telegram to the Secretary-General early that morning, as follows:

The Governments of the United Kingdom and France have studied carefully the resolutions of the United Nations General Assembly passed on 3rd and 4th November.

They warmly welcome the idea which seems to underlie the request to the Secretary-General contained in the resolution sponsored by Canada, and adopted by the Assembly at its 563rd meeting, that an international force should be interpolated as a shield between Israel and Egypt pending a Palestine settlement and a settlement of the question of the Suez Canal. But according to their information neither the Israeli nor the Egyptian Government has accepted such a proposal. Nor has any plan for an international force been accepted by the General Assembly or endorsed by the Security Council.

The composition of the staff and contingents of the international force would be a matter for discussion.

The two Governments continue to believe that it is necessary to interpose an international force to prevent the continuance of hostilities between Egypt and Israel, to secure the speedy withdrawal of Israeli forces, to take the necessary measures to remove obstructions and restore traffic through the Suez Canal, and to promote a settlement of the problems of the area.

Certain Anglo-French operations, with strictly limited objectives, are continuing. But as soon as the Israeli and Egyptian Governments signify acceptance of, and the United Nations endorses a plan for an international force with the above functions the two Governments will cease all military action.

In thus stating their views, the United Kingdom and French Governments would like to express their firm conviction that their action is justified. To return deliberately to the system which has produced continuing deadlock and chaos in the Middle East is now not only undesirable, but impossible. A new constructive solution is required. To this end they suggest that an early Security Council meeting at the ministerial level should be called in order to work out an international settlement which would be likely to endure, together with the means to enforce it.

The third resolution, designed to implement the Canadian resolution, called for the establishment of a United Nations command to secure and supervise the cessation of hostilities in accordance with the terms of the earlier cease-fire resolution, and appointed General Burns, Chief of Staff of the United Nations Truce Supervision Organization, as Chief of Command on an emergency basis. 'Her Majesty's Government', said the Foreign Secretary, 'abstained from voting on this resolution.' (Hon. Members: 'Shame!')

> For although the steps called for in the third resolution might be considered to be a beginning, they are not in themselves likely to achieve the purposes set out in our message to the Secretary-General. We do not know that hostilities between Israel and Egypt have ceased or that they will not be resumed. The measures to be taken under the latest resolution would not be sufficient to ensure that.

Hugh Gaitskell, it was clear to those present, could hardly believe his ears:

> The House has heard with astonishment the statement of the Foreign Secretary on why Her Majesty's Government abstained from voting on the resolution of the United Nations General Assembly setting up an international force.[49]

Canada and New Zealand were prepared to contribute troops to this force. The UN, while supporting the proposition that countries providing troops should not be Security Council members, were willing to supply aircraft and supplies. Second, on the Canadian resolution to secure and supervise the cessation of hostilities – the cease-fire and withdrawal of combatants – why did the Government seek to insist that the international force was not merely to secure and supervise the end of hostilities, but also to secure a final settlement of the Suez Canal problem?

> Is the Foreign Secretary aware that by imposing that particular implication the effect is to confirm in the minds of the whole world that the real reason for British or French intervention here was not to separate the combatants but to seize control of the Canal?[50]

If they were to stick to that insistence they would effectively sabotage the whole idea of that force.

As questions were put from both sides of the House, the Opposition Leader continued to underline the importance of distinguishing between the setting up of an international force to deal with the Arab–Israeli question, and an international force to impose a solution of the Suez Canal problem. After further replies by the Foreign Secretary, Gaitskell asked,

> Is it still the case that as stated on Saturday, Her Majesty's Government's attitude to the proposal for an international force depends upon the acceptance by Israel and Egypt of this proposal?

Selwyn Lloyd's reply was, 'I think that for practical purposes that is bound to influence us.'

Tony Benn rose to quote the text of one of the Foreign Office's more fatuous broadcasts put out by the Supreme Command in Egypt, a copy of which he had obtained from the Foreign Office:

> It means that we are obliged to bomb you wherever you are. Imagine your villages being bombed. Imagine your wives, children, mothers, fathers and grandfathers escaping from their houses and leaving their property behind, This will happen to you if you hide behind your women in the villages. . . . If they do not evacuate, there is no doubt that your villages and homes will be destroyed. You have committed a sin – that is, you placed your confidence in Abdul Nasser.[51]

The Foreign Secretary said he was not aware of it. While these unrewarding exchanges were continuing, the Prime Minister intervened. Selwyn Lloyd gave way to him.

> I have had a flash signal from the Commander-in-Chief in the Eastern Mediterranean which affects even the discussion which is now taking place . . .
> This is the flash signal, which is, of course, subject to confirmation:
> Governor and Military Commander, Port Said now discussing surrender terms with Brigadier Butler. Cease-fire ordered.[52]

> (Hon. Members: 'Hear, hear.')

Later in the evening the House was summoned to the Bar of the House of Lords to hear the reading by the Lord Chancellor of the Queen's speech proroguing Parliament to the next session – the following day in fact. (The speech of course was as always drafted by the Government.) There was a single reference to Suez:

> My Government have been gravely concerned at the outbreak of hostilities between Israel and Egypt. They resolved, in conjunction with the French Government, to make a quick and decisive intervention to protect the lives of our nationals and to safeguard the Suez Canal by separating the combatants and restoring peace. My Government have proposed that the United Nations should take over responsibility for policing the area, as a prelude to a satisfactory settlement in the Middle East. They earnestly trust that this purpose will be achieved.[53]

On 6 November the Queen, with traditional ceremony, opened the new session of Parliament. Following ancient tradition the 'Address in Reply to the Gracious Speech' was moved and seconded by two Government backbenchers. It was then the Leader of the Opposition's turn, first to compliment them, then to make the definitive opening speech in a continuing debate due to go on until the following Monday.[54] Gaitskell made no excuse for leaving aside the usual comments on the legislative proposals contained in the Gracious Speech and proceeding straight to

Suez. Commenting on the Prime Minister's announcement of the cease-fire, he said,

> Unfortunately, this morning's news shows that there was certainly no general cease-fire and even that there is doubt about how far Port Said has surrendered.[55]

The previous day, he pointed out, Sir Pierson Dixon in New York, speaking on behalf of the Government, had announced that 'Great Britain would stop all bombing in Egypt'. Was that true? Reports were coming in from the Egyptians saying that bombing was continuing. He referred to the leaflet-dropping and supported a suggestion by Aneurin Bevan that the Government should produce a White Paper showing what the leaflets and broadcasts were saying.

Commenting on the unprovocative wording of the UN's cease-fire resolution, he asked why Britain could not have voted for it, and why, if the object of our continuing hostilities was to drive or force back the Israeli troops, were we attacking Egypt? Or was the Government's wish to continue hostilities directed to making way for the United Nations police force.

> Yesterday, for reasons which I completely fail to understand, the Foreign Secretary threw cold water on the whole idea so far as he could, and said that the force would not be adequate and would not do the job . . .[56]

Seven countries had offered to contribute to the international force, including three from the Commonwealth and three Scandinavian countries. He agreed with a Scottish backbencher who the previous day had said that the four great Powers should be ruled out – in any case three, Russia, Britain and France, 'have now been virtually condemned as aggressors by the Assembly of the United Nations'.

> That brings me to the next question I wish to ask about the object of continuing the fighting. We have heard from the Government from time to time that they believe that the fighting must be pushed ahead until either we or an international force gets into the Middle East, and that we must stay there until the problem of the Suez Canal has been solved. Yesterday, when I said that that seemed to be imposing a solution by force, the Foreign Secretary denied that that was so.
>
> I ask Hon. Members for a moment to reflect. What exactly is meant when one says that either we, the British and French, or an international force, must be in the Canal Zone and remain there until agreement has been reached? What is meant by 'agreement' here? Does it mean until a solution wholly satisfactory to Her Majesty's Government has been reached? Are we then to exercise, as it were, a right of veto? Suppose that negotiations took place and we said, 'No, we do not think that this is good enough. We are not going out until we get what we want'; if that is the case, how on earth can it be described as anything other than imposing a solution by force?

On the other hand, is it the view of the Government, when they talk in these terms, that some other body should settle the Suez Canal problem, that it should be for the Assembly, for instance, to decide what is a satisfactory solution, and that if the Assembly, on a majority vote thought that certain proposals were right and proper, Her Majesty's Government would accept them, and in that case would not only withdraw – our own forces might have been withdrawn already – but agree that the international force itself should be withdrawn? . . .[57]

Another object of continuing the fighting, he went on, was said to be to safeguard the Canal.

Let us consider where we are in respect of the Canal. I believe that it has now been blocked by eight ships, and with every hour that passes the prospect is that more ships and obstructions will be sunk in it.

Gaitskell was followed by R. A. Butler, who, as Leader of the House, was to make the traditional speech setting out the Government's legislative programme for the session and the Parliamentary arrangements he had in mind for getting it through. He took just thirteen minutes. Clearly regarding the whole Suez issue with elegant distaste, he was content to say that the Prime Minister intended to intervene at 6 p.m. When Eden came to reply[58] he said that during the night the UN Secretary-General had informed the Government that both Israel and Egypt had accepted an unconditional cease-fire, and asked Britain and France about their attitude. Accordingly HMG had telegraphed the Secretary-General:

Her Majesty's Government welcome the Secretary-General's communication, while agreeing that a further clarification of certain points is necessary. If the Secretary-General can confirm that the Egyptian and Israeli Governments have accepted an unconditional cease-fire and that the international force to be set up will be competent to secure and supervise the attainment of the objectives set out in the operative paragraphs of the Resolution passed by the General Assembly on 2nd November, Her Majesty's Government will agree to stop further military operations.

They wish to point out, however, that the clearing of the obstructions in the Suez Canal and its approaches, which is in no sense a military operation, is a matter of great urgency in the interests of world shipping and trade. The Franco-British force shall begin this work at once. Pending the confirmation of the above, Her Majesty's Government are ordering their forces to cease fire at midnight tonight unless they are attacked.[59]

He then referred to a message he had received from Washington, and recorded his reply.

I have received with deep regret your message of yesterday. The language which you used in it made me think at first that I could only instruct Her Majesty's Ambassador to return it as entirely unacceptable. But the moment is so grave that I feel I must try to answer you with those counsels of reason with which you and I have in the past been able to discuss issues vital for the whole world.

Her Majesty's Government have repeatedly said that the essential aim of the action taken by the British and French Governments was to stop the fighting between Israel and Egypt and to separate the combatants. This aim has now been virtually achieved.

As regards the future, you know that the Canadian Government have proposed the establishment of an emergency international United Nations force in the area. The General Assembly has taken the first steps to organize such a force. Her Majesty's Government fully approve the principle of an international United Nations force. Indeed, we suggested this ourselves.[60]

He had then, he said, included the text of the document to the Secretary-General which he had just read, and continued by reading his communication to Moscow:[61]

If your Government will support proposals for an international force whose functions will be to prevent the resumption of hostilities between Israel and Egypt, to secure the withdrawal of the Israeli forces, to take the necessary measures to remove obstructions and restore traffic through the Suez Canal, and to promote a settlement of the problems of the area, you will be making a contribution to peace which we would welcome.

Our aim is to find a peaceful solution, not to engage in argument with you. But I cannot leave unanswered the baseless accusations in your message. You accuse us of waging war against the national independence of the countries of the Near and Middle East. We have already proved the absurdity of this charge by declaring our willingness that the United Nations should take over the physical task of maintaining peace in the area.

You accuse us of barbaric bombardment of Egyptian towns and villages. Our attacks on airfields and other military targets have been conducted with the most scrupulous care in order to cause the least possible loss of life. Some casualties there must have been. We deeply regret them. When all fighting has ceased, it will be possible to establish the true figure. We believe that they will prove to be small. They will in any event in no way be comparable with the casualties which have been, and are still being, inflicted by the Soviet forces in Hungary.

The world knows that in the past three days Soviet forces in Hungary have been ruthlessly crushing the heroic resistance of a truly national movement for independence, a movement which, by declaring its neutrality, proved that it offered no threat to the security of the Soviet Union.

At such a time it ill becomes the Soviet Government to speak of the actions of Her Majesty's Government as 'barbaric'. The United Nations have called on your Government to desist from all armed attack on the people of Hungary, to withdraw its forces from Hungarian territory, and to accept United Nations in Hungary. The world will judge from your reply the sincerity of the words which you have thought fit to use about Her Majesty's Government.

Reverting to the Middle East, he went on:

> I must remind the House that the Israeli Government accepted our requirement and its forces remained about 10 miles from the Canal. I do not think that anybody who has followed the military story of recent days can have the least doubt that had the Israeli forces so wished they could have gone very much further forward than, in fact, they did. It is fair to say that their acceptance of this 10-mile limit has made its contribution to dividing the combatants.*

Certainly Dayan was never going to put himself in a position where he would be ordered to withdraw. His heavy fighting vehicles by this time were controlling Sinai, and his troops bathing in the warm waters of the Straits of Tiran.

Hugh Gaitskell rose to challenge Eden:

> My first question is this: as I understand, there is to be a cease-fire from midnight. I take it that we may presume that there will be no further movement of British and French troops into the Canal Zone. Would the Prime Minister confirm that that is the case?
>
> Will he also confirm that, in accepting the cease-fire, we are also accepting those other parts of the resolution which involve, in due course, as may be practicable, the withdrawal of our forces, as independent bodies, from Egypt?
>
> May I also ask him whether the statement that he made this evening supersedes completely the statement made by the Foreign Secretary yesterday as to this country's attitude to an international force; and the earlier statement in which we laid down a number of conditions? May I ask him to confirm – because this is important and he did refer to it later – that we now have dropped from our case, from any statement that is made, any condition about the settlement of the Suez Canal problem – so far, at least, as our forces are concerned, and so far as our consent and agreement to an international force is concerned?
>
> May I ask him, further, whether arrangements will be made as speedily as possible for discussions to take place with the Egyptian authorities regarding the withdrawal of our forces; and also on the matter to which he referred, namely, the speediest possible clearing of the Canal, because, clearly, that cannot be done without Egyptian co-operation? Finally, may we now take it that the objective set out in the leaflets dropped over Cairo, which was clearly to destroy – (Hon. Members: 'Oh') – the Egyptian Government, is now also abandoned by Her Majesty's Government?[62]

The Cabinet met at 10 a.m. on Tuesday 7 November and agreed to Eden's proposal for an immediate cease-fire. Mollet and Pineau desperately tried to persuade him to go on another two or three days, and he agreed to postpone the cease-fire for twelve hours – to 2 a.m., Cairo time, midnight GMT. The first intimation of the decision received by the British and

---

* This, as we have seen, was not the case.

French commanders, just after they had secured their beaches and were ready to fan out to their objectives, was when they heard of the decision on the BBC Overseas Service. Troops who had landed at Port Said made a determined last-minute attempt to break through to the Canal, but by the time the cease-fire came into effect they were just four miles short of their target, Qantara, the town on the Canal.*

On Thursday 8 November, after a brief report from the Defence Secretary on the military operations, the House debated the Opposition's vote of censure which for procedural reasons was tabled as an amendment to the Government Motion welcoming the Queen's Speech. Kenneth Younger moved,

> In view of the grave international situation and the division in the Commonwealth resulting from Your Majesty's Government's policy of armed intervention in Egypt, the Gracious Speech contains no reference to any proposal by Your Majesty's Government to convene forthwith a conference of Commonwealth Prime Ministers so as to bring to bear all the resources of the Commonwealth in support of the authority of the United Nations.

It is fair to say that by this time frontbench speakers were becoming a little repetitive, though Younger's remit was primarily to emphasize the effect of the Suez situation on Commonwealth solidarity, with particular reference to 'Hate Britain' riots in Pakistan, and to Lester Pearson's almost total detachment from Britain's policy. It was to remedy, or at least mitigate, the damage, that he specifically urged the Government to call a Commonwealth Conference.

Alan Lennox-Boyd, Secretary for the Colonies, had little to say except to repeat the by now familiar arguments about the separation of Israeli forces from Egypt, and the newer argument that the Government's foresight and vigour had created the prospect of the 'real creation of a United Nations Force'. Whether as a Cabinet Minister he was privy to all the facts which had created the Suez crisis is arguable, but if he was he must have almost choked when he proclaimed: 'The first news of the Israeli invasion of Egypt was received in London on the evening of Monday 29 October.'[63] George Wigg intervened to say, 'The Government knew of it long before', to which Lennox-Boyd made no reply.

Wigg's own speech was perhaps the most devastating backbench speech in the whole series of debates lasting a fortnight, even if one discounts his

---

* The military movements are fully described and analysed in Fullick and Powell, *Suez: The Double War*. They record that when the troops stopped in their tracks, a Swedish news reporter who had gone ahead of them, said, 'I cannot understand why you've stopped here, there isn't a single Egyptian soldier in Qantara, and the only one I saw in Ismailia was a fat officer getting into his car and driving frantically towards Cairo' (p. 167).

pro-Arab views of which he had never made any secret. On a Middle East visit he had already heard rumours of the Israelis mobilizing. Did not the 10th Hussars and the company of the Middlesex Regiment know what was going on? He recalled that there had been nine occasions in the last hundred years when operations had been the subject of a public inquiry: in the case of the Jameson Raid in South Africa, a Select Committee of the Commons had been set up. A better precedent, he felt, was the Royal Commission on the Dardanelles and Mesopotamia in the First World War. A great part of his speech was devoted, as a dedicated supporter of the Services, to condemn the lack of preparedness and the appalling shortage of relevant equipment, particularly tank-landing ships. He continued to press for a Royal Commission or Select Committee – the last thing the Government could have afforded to create.

The concluding speech for the Opposition was by Aneurin Bevan, scathing on Suez, but more directed to Commonwealth problems, especially the disillusionment of Commonwealth partners, and to the Soviet invasion of Hungary, while the backs of the Western nations were turned.[64] Peter Thorneycroft, President of the Board of Trade, wound up for the Government, again repeating the old 'separating the combatants' arguments.

> It is the simple truth that the battle was joined between the Israelis and Egypt. It is not unreasonable to suppose that Syria and Jordan would have joined in, or that the Egyptian Air Force would have inflicted massive retaliation. War would be raging today. Rightly or wrongly – and I concede the sincerity of those who hold a different view from us – we decided to intervene. I sincerely believe that if we had relied on resolutions rather than resolution, it would not simply be Budapest in flames tonight, but Tel Aviv, Cairo and the whole of the Middle East.[65]

These words strongly indicate that Thorneycroft was not in the secret about the collusion with France and Israel, but was speaking to a carefully sanitized brief supplied to him. There is, in fact, reason to think that this is so: indeed, as Board of Trade President, in close touch with the City, he had in his innocence put together a consortium to finance the building of a dam at Aswan. When he put the scheme to Eden he was quickly persuaded to forget it.

The House divided for the sixth time since 30 October: Ayes (Labour and Liberal) 262; Noes (Conservative) 320.

The following day, Friday 9 November, Eden began the proceedings with yet another statement. The UK representatives at the UN, he said, had voted on 7 November in favour of the resolution sponsored by Argentina and others. He could not forbear harking back and telling the House how on 1 November he had said that the first and urgent task was to separate these combatants and to stabilize the position. Then, he had said, if the UN were willing to take over the physical task of maintaining peace in that area, 'no one would be better pleased than we'. Her Majesty's Government, he said, welcomed the passing of the Argentine resolution, which approved the proposals of the Secretary-General for 'an emergency international United Nations Force'.

> Her Majesty's Government welcome the statement of the Prime Minister of Israel with regard to the withdrawal of Israeli forces and the intentions of the Israeli Government to co-operate with the projected United Nations Force. As soon as the force is in a position effectively to discharge its tasks, Her Majesty's Government, as has been repeatedly stated, are willing to hand over to it the responsibilities which they have assumed.[66]

He had been in contact with the French Government early that morning and confirmed that it was in agreement with what he had just told the House. On logistics, the Government would retain in being the ground organization of the RAF squadrons previously deployed in Cyprus and Malta, but it would now be possible for many of those squadrons to fly home. In an emergency, and with the ground organization retained, they could be redeployed in Cyprus and Malta within a matter of hours. As far as the Army was concerned, the Government would replace the assault units of paratroops and commandos with the equivalent in infantry battalions, and an additional infantry reserve would be held in Cyprus. Listening to him, one almost expected him to burst into the last verse of Rudyard Kipling's *Recessional*.

> Far-called our navies melt away.
> On dune and headland sinks the fire.
> Lo! all our pomp of yesterday
> Is one with Nineveh and Tyre . . .

Hugh Gaitskell began by welcoming Ben-Gurion's statement that Israeli forces were to be withdrawn from Egyptian territory. (Israel, in fact, held on to her gains in Sinai and the Sharm-el-Sheikh region.) He pressed Eden to make it clear that HMG was unconditionally agreeing to withdraw their troops from Egypt as soon as the international force arrived. He was clearly worried by Eden's insistence that 'the force must be able effectively to discharge its task'.

> Will he say that he will accept an assurance from the Secretary-General of the United Nations on this point, and not seek to decide that issue himself?

Eden continued to justify the original intervention, and the House passed on to the general debate on the Queen's Speech.

The usual arrangement for the five or six days of that debate is that after one or two days of general discussion, the House tries to deal with specific subjects. In Suez week, of course, each debate began with exchanges over Suez, and the early days were fully devoted to the fighting there. On the Friday, the Opposition had chosen home affairs, and a frontbench spokesman managed to sandwich in a speech on housing and other questions. Two members dealt exclusively with Suez, and the subject dominated the opening and closing speeches on both sides. In between, the debate was enlivened by speeches on prescription charges, shipowners' liability, films, oil, voluntary religious schools, subsidence, pensions, mental health, the cost of living, town and country planning, the National Coal Board, Africa, North Wales, wage demands, the safety and health of workers, and closing hours for shops. Some of those speaking on these subjects began with Suez, or interpolated Suez references into their speeches.

Even so, there was more to come. On Monday 12 November, the last day of the debate, it had been agreed that the House should hold one of its regular economic debates, and as Shadow Chancellor I had to move the Opposition amendment, 'at the end of the motion thanking Her Majesty for Her Gracious Speech', adding:

> but humbly regret, in view of the serious economic problems facing the country, which have been aggravated by the effects of the Government's policy in the Middle East, that your Majesty's Gracious Speech gives no indication that your Ministers intend to pursue policies adequate to deal with the situation.

In general, my remarks were on the already grim economic situation, to which Suez had now been added:

> For the past fortnight the House has debated the cost in political and moral terms of the Government's action in Suez. Today, we have to count the reckoning in economic terms as well. When I say 'economic terms' I do not mean merely the cost in terms of Government expenditure. We are no longer in the days of the nineteenth-century colonial wars, when the cost of these ventures could be reckoned in terms of another 2d on the Income Tax or another 1d on tea.[67]

The Chancellor, therefore, should not only tell the House what the events of the past two weeks meant on national expenditure, but he should also assess their wider economic effects on the balance of payments, on the gold reserves, on the strength and position of sterling, on exports, on production, on employment, and on our ability to aid Commonwealth development – 'if Hon. Members opposite could be persuaded any longer to take an interest in the Commonwealth'. The situation was already grave. Harold Macmillan, on taking over from Rab Butler as Chancellor, had engagingly set out the economic consequences of his predecessor as having held back exports, swollen our imports, forced us into balance of payment deficit, helped to reduce our reserves by a quarter, and driven up our domestic price level.

Even before Suez our gold and dollar reserves had risen only slightly, despite netting $177 million from the sale of the Trinidad oilfields. Our imports were rising sharply compared with our competitors, our exports losing ground. Overseas investment was falling off, and the previous rise in production giving way to stagnation. The cost of living index was getting out of control, and so forth.

> Now on top of this, piling Pelion upon Ossa, came the Government's ultimatum and all that followed it. I hope that the Chancellor or the Minister of Supply will tell the House frankly today what, in the view of their advisers, will be the economic consequences of this military action. After all, it was long prepared. What estimates did the Government make of its cost and its economic consequences? What estimate do they make now? In his Budget speech the Chancellor of the Exchequer referred to Mr Gladstone. I must remind him today of the words of Gladstone during the Crimean War. In his 1854 Budget speech, Mr Gladstone had this to say:
>
>> The expenses of a war are a moral check which it has pleased the Almighty to impose upon the ambition and lust of conquest that are inherent in so many nations. . . . The necessity of meeting from year to year the expenditure which it entails is a salutary and wholesome check, making them measure the cost of the benefit upon which they may calculate.[68]

The Opposition amendment to the Address was defeated by 321 votes to 259.

During this period of intense Parliamentary debate, the Labour Party had embarked on a nationwide anti-Suez campaign, under the slogan 'Law-not-War'. When the Shadow Cabinet had unitedly decided on fighting the Suez campaign, I pointed out that, while this decision was our clear duty, we must not assume that we should gain popularity in the country. Reminding them of the occasion during the Boer War (when the Liberal opposition was split) when Lloyd George was smuggled out of a Birmingham Town Hall disguised as a policeman to save his very life, I said that I hoped it would not be my lot to be sent to speak in Birmingham. I warned also that Labour would probably suffer in any by-elections. (So it proved: despite a marked swing to Labour in previous by-elections, the Chester by-election on 15 November showed only a marginal fall in the Conservative vote.)

I was, in fact, sent to Birmingham to speak on 4 November. The main hall was packed, as was a smaller hall linked by the public address system; vast crowds were assembled outside, also able to hear. Roy Jenkins, a Birmingham MP, accused Eden of causing 'enormous damage' to the chances of success of the Hungarian revolt against Russia 'for the sake of a squalid adventure in the Middle East'. The Prime Minister had driven himself, or allowed himself to be driven, into the position in which, to maintain his own prestige, he had set himself the objective of overthrowing the Egyptian Government. It was an object unworthy of a British Prime Minister, though he himself had no love for Nasser. The report of my own speech, of which a copy has been supplied by courtesy of the *Birmingham Post*, quoted me as saying that 'millions yet unborn may rue this week and curse the Government'. At one stroke Eden had endangered all three bases of British policy, relations with the Commonwealth, with the Atlantic community and support of the United Nations. To the people of Asia and the whole developing world Britain's aggression would mark her 'a bullying imperialist power imposing its will on a weaker, coloured nation'.

In my papers of that period I note a memo from the Israeli Embassy, enclosing an Egyptian 'Top Secret' Field Order dated 15 February 1956, to the Commander of the Egyptian Zone in Palestine and his officers in El Arish, Raffah, Khan Younis and Gaza:

> Para. 3. Every commander should be prepared and prepare his troops for the unavoidable war wth Israel, in order to achieve our supreme objective, namely annihilation of Israel and its complete destruction in as little time as possible and by fighting against her as brutally and cruelly as possible . . .
>
> Para. 4. . . . The National Guard – must complete training its volunteers for raiding operations, regardless of the training which they have had prior to their having taken part in battles. Training in every course must be finished within 7 weeks from their arrival at the battlefield.
>
> Para. 5. Our objective always is: annihilation of Israel. Remember that, and act for its fulfilment.

On 29 November, Suez again returned to the House of Commons agenda. The House was meeting without the Prime Minister. The strain of the crisis had hit him in his weakest point, his bile-duct. He was ordered by Lord Moran, his physician, to take a complete rest, and from 23 November to 14 December he was in Jamaica, staying at Golden Eye, the home of Mr Ian Fleming (author of the James Bond novels) and Mrs Anne Fleming.

Selwyn Lloyd made a statement on his return from New York, an interim statement, he said, as further discussions must take place with the French. Pineau was coming to London the following day. In New York, he said, he had made clear that HMG could not accept the Afro-Asian resolution, because it demanded an immediate withdrawal. A Belgian amendment, more acceptable to Britain, was tabled. The voting had been 23 in favour, 37 against, and 18 abstentions, including the USA. 'In other words, the majority of the Assembly either voted with us or abstained. That constituted a considerable shift of opinion.' The substantive vote, calling for immediate withdrawal was carried, he said, by a very large majority. But, he went on, clutching at every available straw, the vote was affected by the fact that the US delegate, Cabot Lodge, had said that he interpreted 'forthwith' to mean 'a phased operation'. The build-up of UN forces – by this time 1,400, and due to reach 2,700 by 1 December and 4,100 by the 15th – 'obviously . . . must have an important relationship to a phased withdrawal of our own and the French troops'. But he went on to say that there were other important matters to be considered, such as the speedy clearance of the Canal, and the negotiation of a final settlement with regard to the future of the Canal.[69]

This constant insistence on reopening the whole issue of the future of the Canal, which had dominated the affair now for nearly three months, was seized on by Aneurin Bevan:

> Is it not a fact that our insistence all the while upon having a clear declaration from Egypt about the future of the Canal is one of the chief causes of differences between ourselves and the United States?
>
> Is it not a fact that it is because it is assumed that we are trying to bring about a settlement of the question of the future of the Canal by force and not by negotiation that the difficulties have arisen? Is it not a fact that what the Government are doing all the while is attempting to associate the build-up of the United Nations Force in Egypt and the phased withdrawal of our own troops from Egypt with exacting from Egypt a declaration about the future of the Canal?
>
> Is not this the chief stumbling block between ourselves and the United Nations and the United States? Will the Right Hon. and learned Gentleman, when he makes his statement on Monday, bear in mind that the removal of that stumbling block is, in our opinion, the most important objective before the Government today?[70]

Lloyd stuck to his, by now, largely spiked guns. Clearing the Canal and the future of the Canal must be discussed with 'our French allies'. Jo Grimond then pressed him, asking if the House could take it

> that it is Her Majesty's Government's policy that we do not need to keep troops in Port Said until a final settlement is made about the future of the Canal?[71]

Lloyd replied:

> That is a question which I should like to consider. (Hon. Members: 'Oh.') If the Hon. Gentleman will refresh his memory as to the terms of the Belgian amendment, that referred to the application of the Resolutions
>
> > in the spirit in which they were adopted, particularly with regard to the functions vested in the United Nations forces.
>
> If he further refreshes his memory by looking at the Resolution of 2nd November, he will see that there is a very important point in that about the securing of free transit.[72]

The Foreign Secretary promised a further statement the following Monday. The Speaker refused to allow an immediate debate; these matters should be 'more happily gone into and more conveniently gone into' when the House had its promised two-day debate the following week.

The debate, which inevitably by this time involved a great deal of chewing of the old cud, was opened on 5 December by Selwyn Lloyd. His speech went over the whole history of the Suez affair, on lines by this time painfully familiar to the House. He was clearly nettled by the fact that his claim the previous week – that Her Majesty's Government's action had stopped the war from spreading – was greeted, he said, 'with a certain amount of hostility by most Hon. Members of the Opposition'. Denis Healey, a relatively new backbencher in those days, interrupted with a punishing question:

> The Right Hon. and learned Gentleman used a rather equivocal phrase when he said that we warned the Israelis on 29 October against action in other directions. Can he tell the House whether, at any time after 27 October, we warned the Israelis unequivocally against an attack on Egypt? If we did not, the whole case of the Government falls to the ground.[73]

The Foreign Secretary's confident answer was that HM Ambassador in Tel Aviv had warned the Israeli Government to use restraint and warned of the dangers if restraint were not used. Of course he had. He was not in the secret. But the Israelis knew exactly what Britain and France were doing, and would recognize – possibly they had been told – that the number of British ministers and officials who knew of the collusion was limited. Selwyn Lloyd, perhaps mesmerized by his own cover story, could by this time do no more than stick to that story. He even went so far as to quote at length a statement by Dulles which asserted: 'As the United Nations Force replaces those of the United Kingdom and France, the clearance of the Canal becomes imperative.'

The debate was noteworthy principally for the speech by Aneurin Bevan, who spoke immediately after the Foreign Secretary. He began by moving an amendment to Lloyd's motion, deleting every operative word and replacing it with the assertion –

> recognizing the disastrous consequence of Her Majesty's Government's policy in the Middle East, calls upon Her Majesty's Government to take all possible steps to restore Commonwealth unity, recreate confidence between our allies and ourselves and strengthen the authority of the United Nations as the only way to achieve a lasting settlement in the Middle East.[74]

Going right back to Eden's claim on 30 October that 'we seek to separate the combatants' and 'to remove the risk to free passage through the Canal', he commented:

In the history of nations, there is no example of such frivolity. When I have looked at this chronicle of events during the last few days, with every desire in the world to understand it, I just have not been able to understand, and do not yet understand, the mentality of the Government. If the Right Hon. and learned Gentleman wishes to deny what I have said, I will give him a chance of doing so. If his words remain as they are now, we are telling the nation and the world that, having decided upon the course, we went on with it despite the fact that the objective we had set ourselves had already been achieved, namely, the separation of the combatants.

As to the objective of removing the risk to free passage through the Canal, I must confess that I have been astonished at this also. We sent an ultimatum to Egypt by which we told her that unless she agreed to our landing in Ismailia, Suez and Port Said, we should make war upon her. We knew very well, did we not, that Nasser could not possibly comply? Did we really believe that Nasser was going to give in at once? Is our information from Egypt so bad that we did not know that an ultimatum of that sort was bound to consolidate his position in Egypt and in the whole Arab world? . . .[75]

Did we really believe that Nasser was going to wait for us to arrive? He did what anybody would have thought he would do, and if the Government did not think he would do it, on that account alone they ought to resign. He sank ships in the Canal, the wicked man. What did the Hon. Gentlemen opposite expect him to do? The result is that in fact, the first objective realized was the opposite of the one we set out to achieve . . .[76]

Why did we start this operation? We started this operation in order to give Nasser a black eye – if we could to overthrow him – but, in any case, to secure control of the Canal . . .

I put it again to the Right Hon. and learned Gentleman that if Hon. Members opposite had succeeded in what they wanted to do, they would have ruined the United Nations, because the very essence of the United Nations Force is that it is not attempting to impose upon Egypt any settlement of the Canal . . .[77]

We understand from the Hon. and learned Gentleman that at no time did the Government warn Israel against an attack on Egypt. . . . The fact is that all these long telephone conversations and conferences between M. Guy Mollet, M. Pineau and the Prime Minister are intelligible only on the assumption that something was being cooked up. . . . Did the French know? It is believed in France that the French knew about the Israeli intention. If the French knew did they tell the British Government? Did M. Guy Mollet, on 16 October, tell the British Prime Minister that there would be an attack on Egypt?[78]

He then led up to his most quoted passage:

What happened? Did Marianne take John Bull to an unknown rendezvous? Did Marianne say to John Bull that there was a forest fire going to start, and did John Bull then say, 'We ought to put it out', but Marianne said, 'No, let us warm our hands by it. It is a nice fire'? Did Marianne deceive John Bull or seduce him? . . .[79]

This passage has been reproduced in many of the books published at home and overseas, and has passed into the folklore of British Parliamentary debate. As he closed his speech, he drew a parallel between the Suez action and the Russian intervention in Hungary.

> The sound furniture of modern society is so complicated and fragile that it cannot support the jackboot. We cannot use the processes of modern society by attempting to impose our will upon nations by armed force.

On the second day of the debate, 6 December, the Chancellor of the Exchequer, who had played no mean part in setting up the Suez action, intervened. It was he whose panic at the run on sterling in New York had led him to change from the most hawkish of men on Suez to the most cooing of doves. While saying that he would not 'shirk the points of the past', which he proceeded consummately to do, Macmillan added that he felt he might be forgiven if he said something of the future, including some powerful passages condemning the Soviet Union – 'after the lancing of this wound and the draining of the poison the period of healing may well begin'.[80] The most interesting fact about Macmillan's speech was that, although one of the most eloquent speakers in the House, capable of holding its attention for half an hour, or indeed much longer, he spoke for only eighteen minutes, much of the time dealing with purely economic matters or attacks on the Soviet Government – not to mention giving way three times to Opposition interventions.

Hugh Gaitskell wound up for the Opposition, firm and clear, as he had been from his first Suez speech more than four months earlier, yet avoiding any tendency to gloat or use the shambles the Government found themselves in for factious opposition. He was content to sum up the position at the end of those four months and warn against any attempt to resist the decisions of the United Nations and the advice of the United States.

> The Suez Canal is blocked for many months, we are in great difficulties over oil supplies, we face financial and economic crises at home, we have lost any influence that we had in the Arab States, we have thrown the Arab States wide open to Russian influence, we have created very grave divisions in the Commonwealth, we have created a breach in the Anglo-American understanding which used to exist, and we have very seriously damaged our reputation for fair-mindedness, honesty and support for the United Nations.[81]

But he warned against those Conservative Members who, while not being entirely satisfied with what had happened, took the view that the real trouble was not so much that we began the operation, but that we failed to carry it through – 'They say that we should have gone on, that we should not have agreed to the cease-fire.'

Supposing we had pursued that line of action, what possible kind of solution could there have been? We should have found ourselves back again in the same position as we were in before we withdrew from Egypt with a very large army pinned down there and facing continual guerilla attacks. Would we, as a result of such action, have won any kind of friendship from the Arab States? Would we have secured that the oil flow continued? Of course not. In fact, had we done that, we should still have been up against the threat from Soviet Russia that was made the night before the cease-fire was agreed upon.

We should then have been obliged to ask the American Government whether they were prepared to give us their support in the event of Russian intervention, and I am afraid that there is no doubt that, so long as we found ourselves in that position, the American answer would have been 'No'. That is the simple straightforward answer to any Hon. Members who claim that really we should have faced the thing out, carried it through, ignored the cease-fire and dominated Egypt . . .

Rab Butler's reply to the debate was a classic, even by his standards. A few unwounding criticisms of Gaitskell, fewer arguments in support of the Government, that was all. Meandering between the United States, the Soviet Union and Hungary, and long-forgotten speeches of Nye Bevan, he succeeded in playing out time. He scarcely ventured into politics, but once when he claimed for the Government the support of the French Socialists, he went as far as saying that Marianne had jilted Gaitskell. An impenetrable reference to the ethical theories of Professor Gilbert Murray took him up to the time for the division, when there voted: Ayes (the Conservative lobby) 327: Noes 260.

The final debate of the year took place on the motion that the House 'do adjourn till Tuesday 22 January'. It was in one important sense different from its predecessors. In the press and elsewhere there had been growing disclosures of 'collusion' based on foreknowledge of the Israeli attack and prior agreement on the Franco-British response. Hugh Gaitskell opened the debate by reminding the House that the Government had given the impression that everything had to be done on 30 October in a tremendous hurry: we could not even wait for the Security Council to consider the matter, or hold any consultations with the United States because of the time factor.

The whole impression created, therefore, was that on 29 October, the night before, when the Israeli troops attacked Egypt, it came as a complete surprise to Her Majesty's Government.

The only other original comment made in this matter was the answer to a question which nobody had ever put, namely, did we, Great Britain, incite Israel to make this attack? The answer given was 'No'. What we asked, and what we continue to ask, was what prior discussions took place between the British and French Governments on the possibility of an Israeli attack on Egypt?

What plans were jointly made for Anglo-French action . . . ?[82]

Hugh Gaitskell was clearly not in full possession of all the facts about Sèvres and Paris, and the detailed military plans worked out with Israel. The reason for pressing this, he went on, was a statement made by Pineau:

> Yesterday the French Foreign Minister made the rather interesting and important statement . . . that France and Britain had for long realized Israel's predicament and had therefore decided together what action they would take if Israel began a preventive war.
>
> The first question which I put to the Prime Minister, therefore, is whether, in fact, such decisions were taken. Does the Prime Minister agree with M. Pineau and does he agree that decisions of this nature were taken? Were they taken on 16 October or 23 October at those secret meetings to which references have so frequently been made? . . .
>
> What we are asking is what discussions took place with the French against the possibility, to which M. Pineau's statement certainly may refer, and I believe does refer, that Israel would begin a preventive war against Egypt. What plans were made? Were these plans in fact the plans which were carried out in the ultimatum of 30 October and the succeeding day? Were they plans for the invasion of the Canal Zone of Egypt in the event of an Israeli attack upon Egypt? That is the question which I want to put to the Prime Minister.[83]

Gaitskell's final challenge was on the question of informing the United States, as a party to the Tripartite Declaration. The action

> apparently took place without the knowledge of the United States . . . what was there that we had in common with the French in this matter that we did not have in common with the United States? What was the reason for excluding the Americans, of keeping them in the dark, about what we were intending to do? . . .
>
> I come now to the last point I wish to put. I wish to ask the Prime Minister whether he accepts the statement of M. Mollet that the reason why the United States was kept out of these discussions, kept in the dark, and not made aware of any plans or intentions of the British and French Governments was that the British and French Governments felt convinced that the United States would disapprove of those plans and would do everything to prevent them from being carried out . . .[84]

The debate lasted one-and-a-half hours. Gaitskell's challenge was pressed by a number of Labour MPs, notably George Wigg, who had become an expert on the situation. On the Government side, the two most significant speeches were made by Eden himself, speaking immediately after Gaitskell and again at the close of the debate. (This was unusual: undoubtedly the normal course would have been to field another minister to reply.) Though Gaitskell had probed only about half-way into the collusion case, Eden rejected 'the charges', commenting somewhat strangely that there was not before him any 'charge of incitement. . . . Nor is there a charge of any prior agreement with Israel or foreknowledge.'[85]

I want to come to the last question: 'Did we have plans with the French, and discussions about plans with them?' Most certainly we had discussions about plans with the French. We have had them, roughly, from the beginning of August in one form or another – military discussions of some kind. They had been going on in various forms also in the tripartite discussions. What was different from the beginning of August and any earlier time was that we were moving out reinforcements to the Eastern Mediterranean, and so were the French. We both had forces there and, as a result, it was only proper – it would have been mad if we had not – to have some form of discussion with each other.

Eden then rode off on to questions Gaitskell had raised about Jordan. He rose again to wind up the debate, his speech lasting just six minutes:

On 26th October, we heard from our representative in Tel Aviv that Israel was mobilizing. It was not then known whether it was a partial or total mobilization. We sent instructions on the next day, 27th October, to our Ambassador at Tel Aviv, to make representations to Israel on the matter. It is quite true that he pointed out once again, not for the first time, that if there were an Israeli attack on Jordan, the United Kingdom would be bound to intervene in accordance with the Anglo-Jordan Treaty. That is quite true.

Our Ambassador also urged restraint on Israel in other directions, amongst other reasons because it was quite obvious that if Israel attacked any of the other Arab countries, whichever it might be, there was the possibility of Jordan becoming involved and a difficult situation being created for the United Kingdom . . .

I want to say this on the question of foreknowledge, and to say it quite bluntly to the House, that there was not foreknowledge that Israel would attack Egypt – there was not. But there was something else. There was – we knew it perfectly well – a risk of it, and in the event of the risk of it certain discussions and conversations took place, as, I think, was absolutely right, and as, I think, anybody would do. So far from this being an act of retribution, I would be compelled – and I think my colleagues would agree – if I had the same very disagreeable decisions to take again, to repeat them . . .

There was a relatively small attendance in the House, as is usual on Motions for the Adjournment. The Opposition called a division, the Government side prevailing by 165 to 85.

That was Eden's last speech in the House of Commons.

One issue arising in the Parliamentary debates was transferred to the correspondence columns of *The Times*. On 18 December there appeared under the heading in large capitals A CHARGE TO BE ANSWERED: ALLEGED COLLUSION WITH ISRAEL, a magisterial letter signed ATTLEE.

Sir – Everyone will be glad to know that the health of the Prime Minister has been restored and that he is back at work.

During his absence repeated requests have been made to his colleagues in both Houses of Parliament for a clear statement as to whether the British or French Governments knew in advance of the forthcoming Israeli attack on Egypt and whether the two Governments prior to October 29 discussed the proposal for military intervention in that event.

In particular Lord Jowitt, speaking with the authority of a former Lord Chancellor, in view of the circumstantial evidence asked for an enquiry.

No satisfactory answer has so far been given. Yet the worldwide rumours on this subject are so authoritative and persistent as to affect the reputation of Her Majesty's Government and so to prejudice the position of this country in future international negotiations.

Now that the Prime Minister is back, the country may reasonably ask that he should put an end without delay to an uncertainty which cannot fail to be damaging to the national interest.

Yours faithfully,
ATTLEE

House of Lords, Dec. 16.

Attlee's letter attracted no response from the Government. Dutiful letters duly appeared on successive days in Christmas week from Robert Boothby MP and Graham Page MP denying the charge on the basis of ministerial statements in the House.

Anthony Eden had not recovered as the result of his stay in the West Indies and resigned on medical advice on 9 January 1957. After a few days at Chequers he sailed from Tilbury to spend the rest of the English winter in New Zealand, on the invitation of Prime Minister Sidney Holland. Thanks to his retirement, the care of his devoted wife Clarissa, Winston Churchill's niece, and the skill of his doctors, he lived another twenty years.

I repeat from my *Prime Minister on Prime Ministers** an extract from Lord Blake's full-page tribute in the *Sunday Times*, when Eden died:

> If Aristotle was right in describing the tragic hero as the man who 'in enjoyment of great reputation and prosperity' brings disaster 'not by vice and depravity, but by some great error', then surely Eden was a hero in Greek tragedy if ever there was one in real life. Whatever his health, he could not long have politically survived this débâcle. It was left to Macmillan to achieve the silent transition from grandeur, masking, by a display of political legerdemain unequalled since Disraeli, a process which would have been insufferable if transacted in the naked light of day. When he quitted the scene six years later we had moved into a different world. Suez was almost as remote as Crimea.

* p. 303. I might add a personal note from the same page: 'In his retirement there were many of all parties who had reason to be grateful for his friendship and courtesy. I, for one, shall not forget that in 1976, though he was desperately ill and forbidden by his doctor to go to Windsor for the annual Garter ceremony, he wrote to me that though he could not be there all day and would have to miss my investiture ceremony, he would be there for lunch and for the installation in St George's Chapel.'

CHAPTER 11

The Six Day War

THE ORIGINS OF THE MIDDLE EAST WAR OF 5–11 June 1967 go back much earlier in the 1960s. Israel was restive about her enforced withdrawal from her gains in Sinai following the Suez campaign. It was a hard decision for her, only made possible by two guarantees. The first was the decision of the United Nations to create a peace-keeping force on the borders of Israel and Egypt. The second was President Eisenhower's pledge that the Gulf of Aqaba would remain open as an international waterway. The route from the southern port of Eilat, through the narrow Straits of Tiran into the Gulf of Aqaba was Israel's only route to the South, Southern Asia and the Far East, to Australasia and to continental Africa. Without that route her two-way trade with the world would depend on her Mediterranean ports, and a long passage through the Straits of Gibraltar and round the Cape. The shipping statistics for 1965 revealed that 15 per cent of her total imports, including about 90 per cent of her oil imports as well as 40 per cent of her exports of phosphates, were conveyed by the southern route.

In the middle 1960s an uneasy Middle Eastern truce gave way to a system of undeclared, clandestine war. A new and more militant government in Syria led to an escalation of the guerrilla raids into Northern Israel. The United Nations, whose record in the Middle East had been praiseworthy, found themselves unable to act. A series of terrorist raids for which Syria had claimed responsibility was the subject of a reference to the Security Council. The Soviet Union, who had moved from a policy of support for Israel to one of hostility, promptly vetoed what was at best a pussyfooting resolution. Israel took to retaliation and hit back at terrorist bases in Syria, who worked out a mutual defence aid agreement with Egypt. Raids and retaliation from both sides raised the danger threshold. On 12 May 1967 the Israeli Prime Minister, Levi Eshkol, warned that each act of terrorism would be answered by retaliation. The word spread round her Arab neighbours that Israel was mobilizing for a full-scale war. The US Government investigated and reported to the United Nations that the rumours were untrue. U Thant, the Secretary-General, made a similar declaration.

Moscow was stirring the cauldron, insisting that Israel was about to launch a war, hoping – so US intelligence reports warned – that President Nasser of Egypt would move into active military support for Syria. What the White House was hearing from the CIA was later confirmed by Nasser.

On 14 May, Nasser mobilized. Two days later he announced a state of emergency. In a broadcast that day he claimed that all Egyptian military forces were 'in a complete state of preparedness for war'. A similar announcement was made in Syria the following day. On 17 May the Egyptian Vice-President and Deputy Commander-in-Chief, Field Marshal Hakim Amer, 'requested' that the UN Emergency Force should be moved from their posts so that UNEF men would 'not be harmed if hostilities break out'. This was followed by an official demand to U Thant 'to terminate the presence of the United Nations Emergency Force in Egypt and the Gaza Strip'. U Thant, at fault in not referring the matter to the Security Council who had authorized their presence there, said that since UNEF had entered Egypt with the consent of the United Arab Republic's Government it could remain there only as long as that consent continued. He was immediately criticized in statements by George Brown in London and Lester Pearson in Ottawa. It was Pearson, who had proposed the stationing of UNEF, who said that such a decision was not in his view within the power of the Secretary-General. Nor had it been Hammarskjöld's view when UNEF was established. Paul Martin, Canada's Secretary for External Affairs, pressed the point that since the original decision had been taken by the UN, a move to reverse it would similarly require UN agreement. The Force had been engaged on patrolling the 117-mile-long Egyptian-Israeli frontier in Sinai and the Gaza Strip.

When U Thant withdrew the UN forces, he warned the Security Council that 'the position in the Middle East is more disquieting than at any time since the end of 1956'. He went on somewhat unconvincingly to condemn El Fatah activities, 'consisting of terrorism and sabotage', as a major factor in provoking strong reactions in Israel. From Israel, Prime Minister Eshkol that day cabled General de Gaulle, who did not reply until after Egypt's blockade of the Gulf had begun. Eban sent urgent notes to Couve de Murville, the French Foreign Minister, and to George Brown, warning that Israel's intention not to acquiesce in the blockade was 'solid and unreserved'. It was essential that President Nasser 'should not have any illusions'. The Israeli Ambassador in London was instructed to add:

> Our decision is that unless attacked we should not move against Egyptian forces unless or until they attempt to close the Straits to Israel-bound shipping. They have not yet done so.

In a letter I wrote to Eshkol I supported President Johnson, who had urged that any action by Israel should only be in response to a prior act by Egypt establishing the blockade, and went on:

> I am on public record as saying that the Straits of Tiran constitute an international waterway which should remain open to the ships of all nations. If it appeared that any attempt to interfere with the passage of ships through the waterway was likely to be made, we should promote and secure free passage. We stand by this statement. We think it important however that attention should be concentrated on free passage and not on the shore positions. If we are to give you the international support we wish, it must be based on your undoubted rights.[1]

Not only Israel's friends but Nasser must by that time have been fully aware that any attempts to close the Straits would be treated as an act of war.

On 23 May Nasser announced that the Straits of Tiran would be closed. His forces moved up the Straits and reoccupied the gun emplacements at Sharm el-Sheikh controlling the Straits of Tiran, the entrance to the Gulf of Aqaba. He said:

> We are in confrontation with Israel. In contrast to what happened in 1956 when France and Britain were at her side, Israel is not supported today by any European power. It is possible, however, that America may come to her aid.
>
> The United States supports Israel politically and provides her with arms and military material. But the world will not accept a repetition of 1956. We are face to face with Israel. Henceforward the situation is in your hands. Our armed forces have occupied Sharm el-Sheikh. . . . We shall on no account allow the Israeli flag to pass through the Gulf of Aqaba. The Jews threaten to make war. I reply 'Ahlan wa sahlan' – 'Welcome!' We are ready for war. . . . This water is ours.

President Johnson immediately issued a statement that Nasser's blockade was 'illegal' and 'potentially disastrous to the cause of peace', and publicly reaffirmed US support of the political independence and territorial integrity of all nations in the area.*[2] Dean Rusk, the Secretary of State, briefed the Senate Foreign Relations Committee and later reported to the President that there was general agreement there that the Arabs should not be allowed to drive the Israelis into the sea. But, they felt, the US should not go it alone: there should be a multilateral solution through the United Nations. The President agreed that this must be the first step. He told his advisers:

> I want to play every card in the UN, but I've never relied on it to save me when I'm going down for the third time. I want to see Wilson and de Gaulle out there with their ships all lined up too.[3]

His ambassadors in London and Paris were asked to check how far Britain and France were prepared to go along with a tough American line, in

* 'Although we cannot be sure, it seems likely that Nasser took this mortally dangerous action independently of the Soviet Union'.

particular how far each regarded the 1950 Tripartite Declaration as still effective. The reply from Paris was that the French believed it would be a mistake to invoke the Tripartite Declaration; that they were even wary, it was reported, of taking any moderating steps on their own. US Ambassador Bohlen concluded that they attached considerable importance to Soviet attitudes and were 'playing a careful game'. Johnson noted that, on the other hand, 'the British were actively seeking a way out of the crisis in full co-operation with us'.[4]

On the same day, the Cabinet was meeting in London. The subject was introduced by the Foreign Secretary, George Brown, at his superb best. George had never joined the majority in the Labour leadership which supported Israel, but in the Cabinet meetings during the crisis days of May and June 1967 he never wavered, and indeed journeyed to Moscow and Washington to make his weight felt against Arab aggression. Strangely it was to be Richard Crossman, the pro-Jewish convert of the 1946 Middle Eastern mission, who expressed all the doubts.

The critical situation in the Middle East which the Cabinet was facing can best be described in terms of retaliatory action undertaken by Israel in Jordan because of terrorist attacks from both Jordan and Syria. In consequence, Jordan, Syria, Israel and the United Arab Republic (UAR) had in turn felt obliged to adopt increasingly belligerent attitudes. The UAR had mobilized some 60,000 men, together with armoured force and air support along the Sinai frontier. The Palestinian Liberation Army had two divisions in the Gaza Strip. The massing of forces was greater than in the 1956 (Suez) crisis, when the Egyptian forces had been deprived of air support by Anglo-French bombing attacks on their landing strips and aircraft. The Israeli forces deployed were, for their part, much smaller, and there were indications that Israel had been caught unprepared.

Israel had repeatedly made it clear that she would regard the closing of the Gulf of Aqaba as a *casus belli*, since access to the port of Eilat was vital to her economy. Although her comparative position in relation to the UAR was considerably weaker than it had been in 1956, and great damage was likely to be done to her towns by air bombardment in the event of war, there was a grave risk that Israel would be tempted to launch a preventive war since her relative strength was likely to decline if she delayed, especially if access to the port of Eilat were cut off. The immediate problem, therefore, was to find means of dissuading Egypt from taking this step and thereafter of bringing the whole situation under control.

The United States were committed to intervene to prevent the destruction of Israel and wished to reactivate the Tripartite Declaration of 1950, which guaranteed existing frontiers in this part of the Middle East. This proposal could not, however, be acceptable to us, since it would involve a commitment to military action to maintain the frontiers, not only of Israel but also of the United Arab Republic; indeed reactivation would be harmful to our relations with the Arab states generally. The French Government, as the third party to the Declaration, took a similar view. The Soviet Foreign Minister, Mr Gromyko, had recently visited Cairo, and it was right to assume that the Soviet Government were concerned to support Syrian interests in order to reassert their position in the Middle East. In the circumstances George had proposed in the first place to call a meeting of the Security Council of the UN to consider the threat to peace in the Middle East and to pass a resolution calling for the Straits of Tiran to be kept open. It was now clear, however, that there was likely to be insufficient support to enable such a meeting to be called before the Secretary-General returned in two days' time from his visit to Cairo. Thereafter it was likely that the Soviet representative would prolong the discussions and eventually veto the resolution. It was unlikely that Israel would feel able to await the outcome of a meeting of the Security Council. We were joining with the United States Government, and such other maritime countries as could be enlisted in support, in announcing our intention to establish a naval force, whether under the auspices of the United Nations or not, to keep the Gulf of Aqaba open to the shipping of all nations, or to reopen it. It was in our view very desirable that such a declaration should be made at once, although no effective force could be assembled immediately. The United States had two ships which could be brought to the Gulf in a few days, but it would be necessary for ships of the US Sixth Fleet to pass through the Suez Canal, together with supporting British vessels from Malta. It would not therefore be possible to prevent the Gulf of Aqaba from being closed, but the assurances that it would be reopened offered the best chance of dissuading Israel from launching a preventive war. The declared purpose of the operation would be to assert maritime rights rather than specifically to assist Israel, and it would be unlikely to have any serious effect on our relations with the Arab states generally.

Not only Britain but the principal maritime powers acting together had declared in 1957 that they would support and assert the freedom of passage in the Straits of Tiran.* On that occasion we had said that we would assert this right on behalf of all British shipping and were prepared to join with

---

* The British delegate at the UN in 1957 had said: 'It is the view of Her Majesty's Government in the United Kingdom that the Straits of Tiran must be regarded as an international waterway through which the vessels of all nations have a right of passage. Her Majesty's Government will assert this right on behalf of all British shipping and is prepared to join with others to secure general recognition of this right.'

others to secure general recognition of these rights; and I was clear that it was in this spirit that we should act now. There was, further, a statement made in a foreign affairs debate during Harold Macmillan's last year as Prime Minister, in which he said, supporting President Kennedy's pledge on the Middle East:

> We regard the United Nations as being primarily responsible for the maintenance of peace in the area. If any threat to peace arises we will consult immediately with the United Nations and will take whatever action we feel may be required.[5]

This had been reiterated by me on 16 December 1964, again in a foreign affairs debate. Rab Butler, opening, had asked me to confirm what Harold Macmillan had said, and I replied,

> We certainly endorse what the Right Hon. Gentleman, the then Prime Minister, said some two or three years ago, in the quotation made by the Right Hon. Gentleman.[6]

Moreover, I had given an oral answer in the House on 13 April 1965 in reply to a question by Viscount Lambton, asking whether Her Majesty's Government were still committed to the tripartite agreement. The reply was:

> The Tripartite Declaration of 1950 was intended to express the policy of Britain, France and the United States at that time. It has not been retracted. I expressed the Government's deep concern for the peace and stability of the Middle East when, in the course of the Foreign Affairs debate on 16 December 1964, I endorsed Mr Macmillan's statement of 14 May 1963.[7]

Lord Lambton had put me in some difficulty when he had asked me whether my reply meant 'that England and France will stand by all the intentions of the tripartite agreement'. For President de Gaulle was anything but enthusiastic in these matters, as we were to learn in the course of the Six Day War. We were not surprised, still less was President Johnson, who records that on 24 May (the day after the Cabinet had given Thomson his instructions) Thomson, Rusk and State Department officials met to discuss the 1957 proposal based on the commitments made at the UN by 'the international community'.

On 30 May there was an exchange between Eshkol and Johnson.[8] Referring to Eban's meeting with the President on 26 May Eskhol said that the talks had had 'an important influence on our decision to await developments for a further limited period', adding, 'It is crucial that the international naval escort should move through the Strait within a week or two.' Johnson records that he and his advisers interpreted this as meaning that they had about two weeks 'to make diplomacy succeed before Israel took independent military action'. While intelligence reports early in June were to suggest that the Israelis would act earlier, they were still counting on the fortnight. On 2 June a senior Israeli diplomat spoke to Rostow, the President's close adviser, who reported that the two weeks would probably be measured from the previous Sunday and forecast that

> things . . . might happen in the week after next: that is, in the week beginning Sunday 11 June – although he indicated that there was nothing ironclad about the time period being exactly two weeks.[9]

Following the Cabinet line, 'The British', L.B.J. records, 'proposed two steps.'

> First, there would be a public declaration, signed by as many nations as possible, re-asserting the right of free passage through the Gulf of Aqaba. There was hope that the declaration might even be endorsed by the United Nations. Second, a naval task force would be set up, composed of as many nations as possible, to break Nasser's blockade and open the Straits of Tiran.[10]

L.B.J. then discussed 'the British proposal fully with key Congressmen and other interested Governments', beginning with Canada where he was due to go for EXPO '67, part of the celebrations of their centenary.

While George Thomson was meeting with the President I was off to Margate to address the annual conference of the Electrical Trades Union. Though the speech I had prepared dealt with productivity, prices and incomes, I began by reading a handout statement on the crisis, reaffirming the 1957 Declaration as set out above. It was on the same day that I sent a personal telegram to President de Gaulle warning him of the implication of the Egyptian threat to interfere with the free movement of shipping in the Gulf of Aqaba. We were, I told him, considering ways and means of concerting international activity to counter this threat. President de Gaulle's reply simply proposed consultation between the four powers: France, Britain, the United States and the Soviet Union.

Meanwhile Abba Eban had called in to Paris. He recorded that General de Gaulle received him 'with grave courtesy'. Even before he was seated the President said, loudly, 'Ne faites pas la guerre' – then added,

> at any rate don't shoot first. It would be catastrophic if Israel were to attack. The Four Powers must be left to resolve the dispute. France will influence the Soviet Union toward an attitude favourable to peace.[11]

Eban set out the Israeli position, ending by saying that Israel without Eilat would be stunted and humiliated. 'Israel without honour is not Israel. Our nation faces a stern choice.' When de Gaulle asked him what Israel would do, Eban answered:

Israel will resist. Our decision has been made. We shall not act today or
tomorrow, because we are still exploring the attitudes of those who have
assumed commitment. We want to know whether we are to be alone or
whether we shall act within an international framework.[12]

De Gaulle repeated that Israel should not make war: at any rate she should
not be the first to do so. Eban answered that Israel could not be the first to
'open hostilities' for that had already occurred. Nasser's blockade and
declaration were acts of war. De Gaulle kept on insisting that 'opening
hostilities' meant firing the first shot.

De Gaulle, I was to find, was obsessed with the question, 'who fired the
first shot?' On that he would decide which side to support. France's
declaration of 1957 on freedom of navigation was correct juridically, but
1967 was not 1957. Moreover, he went on, the Soviet Union must be
associated in a concerted effort by the Four. 'Il faut que les quatre se
concertent.' Eban complained that France's voice had not been heard
condemning Nasser's action of 22 May. De Gaulle defended the Soviet
Union and said that they were reconciled to Israel's freedom of passage in
the Gulf of Aqaba.

In the evening Edward Heath and Sir Alec Douglas-Home came to
No. 10 to express their concern and to be reassured that we were doing all in
our power not only to avert war, but also to stand firm on Britain's national
position on the maritime rights of all nations through international
waterways. From that moment the Government's policy was to have
bipartisan backing.

Abba Eban then arrived at No. 10 straight from Paris for an urgent
meeting to bring me up to date with the Israeli position. In harmony with
the Americans we were urging great caution. In his *Autobiography*[13] he
refers to his London visit in these terms:[13]

> My visit to London, although casually conceived and improvised, now took
> on more significance. The rhapsodic quality which had marked Israel's
> relations with France had never touched our dialogue with London – not even
> at the height of the Suez crisis, when we had a common foe. But British
> opinion was now in ferment. A weekly paper not usually friendly to our cause
> had even written of Israel's agony . . .
>
> In 1957 British support of Israel's right of navigation in the Straits of Tiran
> had been firm, although less vehement than that of France. My best hope in
> London seemed to lie in the heavy influence of public opinion on official
> policy, and on Harold Wilson's personal understanding of Israel's
> predicament . . .
>
> From the airport in London, I drove with Ambassador Remez to Downing
> Street. The London air was charged with familiar symptoms of crisis. The
> British public has a strange ritual at such times: it assembles in Downing
> Street and stares with silent gravity at those coming in and out of No. 10. As a

rule the crowds merely gaze contemplatively at the simple black door and at the policeman on guard, who returns the stare with defiant solemnity. As our car drew up, the Conservative leaders, Edward Heath and Sir Alec Douglas-Home, were walking away.

To Wilson I expounded my belief that Israel's three choices were: to surrender, to fight alone, or to join with others in an international effort to force Nasser's withdrawal from his present course. Israel would not live without access to Eilat or under the threat of Egyptian encirclement. Therefore the only choice was resistance, whether Israeli or international. My purpose was to examine, within a brief time, whether there was any serious intention of the maritime powers to act in accordance with their engagement.

Wilson's reply was forthright. The Cabinet had met that morning and had reached a consensus that the policy of blockade must not be allowed to triumph; Britain would join with others in an effort to open the Straits. Wilson said that I would be surprised if I knew who had supported firm British action in the Cabinet and who had opposed it. The implication was that the pro-Israelis such as Crossman had advocated a passive British stance. (This has since been confirmed in Richard Crossman's diaries.*)

During the next days we had something of a Foreign Office 'diaspora', with Thomson in Washington and Fred Mulley having a fruitless time in Paris. Meanwhile, George Brown was in Moscow, with the rare opportunity of a public lecture to the Soviet Foreign Affairs Institute, where he stated Britain's position with the utmost clarity and called on the Soviet Government to use their influence with the Arab countries to follow a policy of restraint. He received no encouragement, but we soon received evidence

---

* He was right about Crossman. Crossman was an educator, not a politician. In a BBC Radio 4 programme on the third volume of Crossman's Memoirs (reprinted in *The Listener*, 5 January 1979) I made this assessment:

Dick was above most things a scholar, even more perhaps a teacher. Cabinet, he felt, must reach its decision not in a fluffy way, not through vulgar departmental or even Parliamentary pressures, but in an academically defensible posture.

Dick was a great teacher, at Oxford, equally in the Workers' Educational Association. I followed him as a don at New College, Oxford, literally within days. I did not take his vacated post, for he was a classical philosopher, I an economist. But I taught many of his ex-students studying in the Final Honours School of Philosophy, Politics and Economics. From them I learnt a great deal. Dick was an unrepentant Platonist, driven into a still deeper concept of the ends justifying the means by his wartime work on black propaganda. But Platonist or not, he was a teacher. If a pupil, set to read him an essay on Plato, produced a simplistic Platonist essay drawn from the books, Dick annihilated him with devastating Aristotelian logic. So it was in Cabinet.

A Cabinet has to record the views of ministers on the issue before them, honestly, clearly, in many cases representing departmental views, it is true – to the point where Cabinet decides. But those views, honestly reached with or without departmental briefing, must be acknowledged as the views of the minister contributing to the decision. But not for Dick. He would seek, not as a Prime Minister must seek, to hear the voices, and on the basis of the views expressed, to summarize the Cabinet's decision; rather he would dissociate himself from a life-long personal belief, if he thought ministers were agreeing with him for the wrong reason.

that the Soviet Union was urging the utmost care on the part of its Arab friends.*

When the Cabinet met again on 25 May, we faced the new fact that the Straits of Tiran had been mined by the Egyptians. The Security Council had adjourned without a decision; U Thant had left New York for Cairo; President de Gaulle had put forward his four-power conference proposal with the idea of reducing tension.

Approaches by ourselves and the Americans to other maritime nations regarding a declaration on the freedom of navigation in the Gulf of Aqaba did not encourage the belief that there would be widespread support for robust action. The Foreign Secretary's discussions in Moscow suggested that the Soviet Union wished to avoid war in the Middle East, but was nevertheless giving strong support to the United Arab Republic. The immediate aim of the United States was to dissuade Israel from opening hostilities by providing her with an assurance that the right of innocent passage through the Gulf of Aqaba would be secured. It was intended to administer this to Israel when Eban arrived in Washington on 26 May after his Paris and London visits. Unless Israel could be brought to believe that the right of innocent passage would be assured by diplomatic action she was likely to take early military action to secure it, since if she had to fight in the end, delay would be to her military disadvantage. Very early assurances were therefore essential. The other Foreign Office Minister of State, George Thomson, was discussing in Washington a programme of diplomatic and possible military action with the United States Government designed to safeguard this right of innocent passage: any proposals that might emerge would be *ad referendum* to both Governments.

George Thomson in Washington was told to enter into no commitments with Washington at that stage about either military or naval action. The United Kingdom and the United States should press for effective action through the United Nations, in particular at the current meeting of the Security Council, to guarantee the freedom of passage through the Straits of Tiran and the Gulf of Aqaba. They would seek to ensure that any resolution included an endorsement of the principle of freedom of passage. Our view was that if the Soviet Union abstained, the principle would have received United Nations approval.** In the event of a Soviet veto, action by the maritime powers would nevertheless be seen to have received international support. Further to this, it should be known that we welcomed the initiative of the French Government and were seeking an urgent meeting in Paris to

* Kosygin told George Brown 'very earnestly' (Kosygin's phrase) at the end of the Moscow talks, 'Tell Mr Wilson that we have no interest in a flare-up and shall do all in our power to prevent conflict in the area.'
** This was when we were still assuming French concurrence.

pursue it with a view, if possible, to a quadripartite meeting in New York later that day of the Permanent Representatives to the United Nations of the four Powers. These moves should precede any further pressing of our proposal for the suggested international declaration by the leading maritime powers. Meanwhile we decided to try to associate the French Government as closely as possible with Britain and America in the proposal for such an international declaration when the time came to pursue it further. George was told that he should make clear in the discussions in Washington that the United Kingdom did not wish to seem to be taking the lead in a declaration on the freedom of navigation: any international force which might be established should not be solely Anglo-American. Any naval force, again, set up for minesweeping or escort duties in the Gulf of Aqaba, should include ships from other nations. It might take time before they could arrive on the scene, but this would be acceptable provided that the countries concerned associated themselves with the declaration and committed themselves to provide the ships.

We also took steps to ensure that the Prime Minister of Canada should be informed of the way we were seeking to go, so that he would be fully aware of our views before he himself met the President of the United States that day at the Canadian centenary celebrations.

Later that day I supplemented the Commonwealth Secretary's approach with a personal message to Pearson, seeking his support on the maritime declaration, and supporting the general line of President de Gaulle's four-power approach, while expressing doubts whether he would secure Soviet concurrence. (He did not.) At the same time I addressed a personal cable to President Johnson. This was the first I had sent during the crisis. We were in such close touch through our ambassadors that it had not been necessary: in any case George Thomson was already in the United States having detailed talks with Dean Rusk in Washington and Arthur Goldberg, US Ambassador to the UN, in New York. I was concerned that the President should realize that he would not be able to make any progress with de Gaulle and that we should not hold back with other contacts on his account. My message was mainly an analysis of de Gaulle's motives and a proposal that we should by-pass Paris in our planning. For his part the President sent me a lengthy message on the following day, assessing his talks in Ottawa. Pearson said that in his view we should all stay together to see if anything useful could be accomplished in the United Nations: failing that, he felt we should follow up 'the lines you have suggested', the maritime declaration.

On Saturday 27 May de Gaulle telephoned me, formally setting out his four-power proposals. On the same day I cabled Kosygin (the Chequers–Downing Street hot line was busy that day) formally commending de Gaulle's proposals. On the Sunday, I sent a lengthy assessment to Johnson.

I thanked him for his account of his talks with Abba Eban, but expressed the view that there was

> a serious likelihood that despite all your efforts and ours, when Israel's Cabinet meet tomorrow to consider Eban's report, you and we will find ourselves confronted with what could amount to an Israeli ultimatum – that if we do not give them even more categorical assurances than both of us have given so far about the right of passage through the Straits of Tiran, they will feel obliged to assert those rights by force in whatever manner and at whatever time seem most appropriate to them. This is the vital issue, closure of the Straits is what Nasser has gained. It concerns a vital Israeli interest.

I went on to stress the importance of what George Thomson was trying to achieve through the UN.

Meanwhile, in Moscow Kosygin was hotting up his own line to London, warning urgently of Israel's 'stepping up' of military preparations:

> Whether Israel commits this senseless act depends a great deal on the Government of Great Britain. There can be no two opinions on this. If Israel does not feel that she is getting encouragement she would not dare to go over the limit . . .
>
> The Soviet Union is in favour of a restraining influence but naturally not to the detriment of the legitimate interests of the Arab States. The measures that they are taking are of a defensive nature. Moreover, they are showing restraint and, as we know, they do not want a military conflict. Certainly if the guns start to fire it could be the beginning of serious events. *If Israel commits aggression and military action begins then we would render assistance to the countries which would be the victims of aggression* [author's italics].

On 26 May President Johnson received Abba Eban in Washington. Eban said that Israeli intelligence were reporting that Egypt was preparing an all-out attack. McNamara was doubtful: his intelligence groups had been into it thoroughly and advised that an Egyptian attack was not imminent. L.B.J. told him, 'All our intelligence people are unanimous that if the UAR attacks, you will whip hell out of them.' Eban, who was clearly willing to go to great lengths to avoid a pre-emptive attack, asked what the US would do to keep the Gulf open. The President referred him to his 23 May statement, and gave him a firm assurance, to be passed on to the Israeli Cabinet, that they would pursue vigorously any and all possible measures to keep the Straits open. But they had to work through the UN first: if that failed,

> then Israel and her friends, including the United States, who are willing to stand up and be counted, can give specific indications of what they can do.

He had to be sure of Congressional support before throwing his weight behind the proposed international naval force. The US, he said, was working hard to win support for the British plan from other governments:

Israel should concentrate their efforts on that. Then, with all L.B.J.'s Texan frankness, and use of surprise tactics, he warned:

> The central point, Mr Minister, is that your nation not be the one to bear the responsibility for any outbreak of war. . . . Israel will not be alone unless it decides to go alone.[14]

Eban was almost certainly one of those in Israel who wanted to see whether international action would be forthcoming before supporting immediate action to force the Straits. Just before the interview ended he asked,

> Again, Mr President, can I tell my Cabinet that you will use every measure in your power to ensure that the Gulf and Straits are open for Israeli shipping?

Eban records that the President said, 'Yes', and it appears that that was what Eshkol needed to persuade his Cabinet to wait. Johnson had telegraphed Eshkol while Eban was on his journey home. As Israel's friend, he must repeat more strongly what he had said to Eban. Israel just must not take pre-emptive military action. Rusk added a codicil to the President's message: the British and the United States were proceeding urgently to prepare the military aspects of the international naval escort plan, and other nations were responding vigorously to the idea. Eshkol was now ready to advise the Cabinet to wait for two weeks, and this they decided. 'It was not the Soviet warnings, but the American show of resolution which won the delay',[15] despite intelligence reports that the Egyptian forces in Sinai were in a state of chaos.

Britain and the US redoubled their efforts in the UN, but the potential maritime force did not rise above its membership of four: Britain, the US, the Netherlands and Canada. The Soviets were able to prevent the Security Council acting to secure the opening of the waterways. In the event Israel, however, was to move ahead of their pledge of two weeks. The final Washington message was on 28 May: hostilities began on 5 June.

When Cabinet met on Tuesday 30 May, the situation still remained grave, though Israel had up to that time been persuaded not to take military action. Eshkol in resisting pressure for a pre-emptive strike, was under attack at home. Our line continued to be that international action through the UN or by the assurance of the Great Powers should keep the situation under control. There was no immediate prospect of four-power talks as proposed by the French Government, because of the Soviet attitude.

Meanwhile it was already becoming known that the American President had given assurances to Eban on the latter's visit to Washington. Our aim in this very tense situation was to try to work for a holding resolution in the Security Council, at the same time working towards a negotiated solution. It was clear that we would not be able to revert to a situation in which the UAR would have no rights over shipping passing through the Straits, though, following the policies of successive Governments of both parties over recent years, we felt that Israel must be guaranteed the right of innocent passage through to Eilat. One idea was that the UAR might have a measure of control and inspection rights over the types of cargo allowed through, but with the types of cargo which were allowed to pass freely defined in such a way as to include oil in particular. To provide the background for such a settlement we were ready to canvass support for an international declaration in favour of the right of innocent passage through the Straits, meanwhile continuing with contingency plans to enforce this if all else failed. This was essential if action at the UN were to have any chance of success, and if Israel were to be deterred from a unilateral move. We could not at this stage assess which countries would support such a course of action, but in addition to the four countries who had offered their support, Sweden might also join the project. France seemed likely to support a 'holding' motion in the Security Council, asserting the right of innocent passage, but she would not take any part in canvassing support.

On 31 May there was an all-day debate in the Commons on the Middle Eastern solution. Opening the discussion with an appeal to the House to avoid raising the temperature of the dispute, George Brown surveyed the development of the problem over the previous twenty years. There had been no serious flare-up since 1957, and he referred to the importance of the UN Emergency Force acting as a buffer between the two sides in addition to maintaining a detachment at Sharm el-Sheikh. It was on this basis, and because of the firm declaration that there would be free passage for ships into the Gulf of Aqaba, that the Israelis had agreed to withdraw their forces from Sinai early in 1957. For nearly ten years the temperature had been kept down, but over the previous year a new and more dangerous pattern of incidents had emerged, in particular terrorist infiltration into Israel, with explosives directed at roads, bridges and railway lines. This had led to retaliatory action by Israel, which Britain had always made clear to Israel was not in Britain's view the right answer.

Unfortunately, he went on, in the Security Council, the highest organ of the UN charged with maintaining peace, there had been frustration. The Soviets, who twenty years ago had supported the General Assembly resolution which led to the creation of Israel, had switched their policy – 'one could hardly avoid saying cynically' – and become wholly one-sided in their action and behaviour.

> When the Israel Government are at fault, they are rightly criticized in the Security Council, and a resolution embodying that criticism can be passed.

When an Arab Government is at fault the Soviet veto is used against any resolution criticizing that Government.[16]

He referred to an incident the previous year when no action could be taken on a complaint to the Council by Israel about a terrorist raid, but yet soon afterwards an Israeli attack was made the subject of a condemnatory resolution, and he went on to give evidence of a stepping-up of violence which went unrebuked.

He then recounted the development of tension from the middle of May onwards, followed by Egypt's expulsion of UNEF, and by President Nasser's announcement of the closure of the Straits of Tiran to Israeli ships, and the carriage of strategic goods. He recounted the British delegate's 1957 statement that the Straits were an international waterway, through which the vessels of all nations have a right of passage, quoting Britain's commitment of that time. He cited, too, the Israeli Government's 1957 warning that they would regard any interference with their shipping as an act of aggression entitling them to take measures of self defence under Article 51 of the UN Charter, and the Conservative Government's statement to the UN that Her Majesty's Government would assert this right on behalf of all British shipping, and were prepared to join with others to secure general recognition of this right. He quoted his lecture in Moscow, and his appeal to the Soviet Union to work for peace. He went on:

> We are not setting out – to use the colloquialism – to 'topple' Nasser, as Hon. Members opposite once foolishly attempted to do.* But neither are we prepared to accept that he has the right to topple another Middle Eastern nation at the risk of plunging us all into war. . . . We would consider as acts of belligerence any unilateral act to close the Gulf of Aqaba or any acts of aggression committed by either side of the Israel–Arab border.[17]

He then urged the need for a restoration of the UN presence.

The leader of the Opposition, Edward Heath, began by saying that the situation was in some ways

> more dangerous even than the war in Vietnam. . . . There are dangers that raids and counter-raids – for example by the Palestine Liberation Army from the Gaza Strip – will, now that the United Nations Emergency Force has been withdrawn, escalate into war.[18]

He strongly supported George Brown in condemning the withdrawal of the UN Forces, saying that it was 'entirely incomprehensible' that this had been done without putting the matter to the Security Council or the Assembly. This decision he attacked on five grounds:

(i) it had exposed the Middle East to a much greater risk of conflict;

* A reference to Suez.

(ii) it had enabled the Gulf of Aqaba to be closed;

(iii) it had undermined the confidence of Israel which for ten years had been brought to believe that the United Nations was its main security – 'an invaluable asset to have gained after 1956 – and that asset has now been lost';

(iv) it had given President Nasser personally an immense increase of prestige because of the way in which the force was withdrawn;

(v) it had brought into question the position of United Nations forces elsewhere – and mentioned Cyprus as a specific case.[19]

He went on to underline the British interests involved, as described by the Foreign Secretary.

> But what happens if the United Nations fails to take action? The Secretary has clearly faced that question. He has said that he would attempt to get a clear declaration by the maritime powers of the position. This is to be welcomed. He is in consultation with other maritime powers now.

He would not, he said, press the Foreign Secretary on how the maritime nations should 'exert their rights', but 'the Foreign Secretary and the Prime Minister must realize that this is the key to the whole question'. There must be no delay, and he went on to say that 'the House looks to the Government to take the necessary action to ensure that this declaration is implemented if necessary'.[20] He welcomed the Government's acceptance of the proposal for a four-power conference, and regretted that the Soviet Union had rejected the idea. His speech ended by asking

> whether this will develop into an attempt to wipe out Israel once and for all. Surely the United Nations, which recognized Israel at once, and the Powers which helped to create Israel, cannot possibly allow a small independent country to be eliminated by those surrounding her.
>
> There is, secondly, the question whether this is an attempt to extend Soviet influence throughout the Middle East and down to the tip of Southern Arabia.[21]

It was a masterly statement and created an unequivocally bipartisan Parliamentary approach.

For the Liberal Party, Jeremy Thorpe gave the fullest possible party support to the Government and official Opposition line, and in the closing sections of his speech stressed that if we were not successful in preventing the blockade, 'that may well mean the despatch of British, American or other forces into the Gulf of Aqaba'.

Many backbench speeches supported the main frontbench speakers, though individually dedicated pro-Arab and pro-Israel MPs* took a simpler

---

* Notably Will Griffiths (Manchester Exchange) for the Arab side and Barnett Janner (Leicester North-West) advocating the Israeli cause.

line for one side or the other. Sir Alec Douglas-Home wound up for the Opposition, saying that George Brown's 'thoughtful review ... was generally accepted by the House as being a very constructive contribution with which to open the debate'. He made a new point that Egypt's expulsion of the UN Force had created a situation which, under Article 39 of the Charter, constituted 'a threat to peace'. He condemned Egypt's expulsion of the UNEF and the Secretary-General's acceptance of it. 'The plain fact of the matter is ... that Israel cannot stay passive while the life is slowly squeezed out of her.'[22] He was deeply concerned about the conduct of the Soviet Union, and hoped that Moscow would observe great caution, following the line she had taken:

> It is not the Soviet Communist method to go for direct confrontation, least of all with the United States. Their method is to cause the maximum amount of political confusion with the minimum deployment of power. Their actions in Cuba, Berlin and Vietnam confirm that diagnosis ...

He supported the Foreign Secretary on the assurance of free passage for international shipping in the Gulf of Aqaba, but said he would stress

> again and again the absolute importance of the time factor. Unless there is assurance of rapid action following a firm declaration, *then Israel must break out of the ring* [author's italics].[23]

With his experience of foreign affairs, and a deep sense of crisis, he was not, he said, going to press me on how the Gulf and the Straits should be kept open. I was, he said, going to see President Johnson and Mr Pearson,

> and I hope that, as a result of those visits, not only a firm declaration will be made, but that there will be a firm declaration that action will be taken. That, I believe, is the only way to save the peace.

Picking up references in the debate to Suez and Munich, he said:

> I myself have learnt the lesson at least from Munich that, if a dictator gets away with the loot the penalty we pay the second time is double or more.
>   The Prime Minister and Foreign Secretary can, therefore, rely on the full support of this side of the House in the course which the Foreign Secretary outlined. I believe that this is the right course lest our children pay the price of total war.[24]

The House was, give or take the odd maverick, completely at one, united, resolved, conscious of what so far unspecified action might have to be taken, and it was plainly giving this full backing, in the eyes of the country and of the world, to the Government whatever that action might be. My winding-up speech was inevitably restrained, thanking the House for the mandate we had been given. Whatever that mandate might mean in the ultimate no one could define. Few Prime Ministers have entered the last days of a world crisis so fortified by the House of Commons and – as I recited to the House – by our friends abroad, quoting in particular Australia, the Netherlands, New Zealand, Norway and Denmark, maritime countries all.

Cabinet met again the following day. Little had changed since our last meeting. A 'holding' resolution had been tabled in the Security Council. Contingency planning was continuing against the possibility that the use of force might have to be considered to secure the right of innocent passage through the Straits of Tiran and the Gulf. Three British ships had gone through the Straits and the Gulf unmolested, though no oil tanker had attempted the passage.

As soon as the Commons debate ended, I flew to North America. Before the crisis I had planned a week's tour across Canada, to take part in the celebrations of the centenary of the British North American Act. Unfortunately the trip across the Rockies to Vancouver had to be cancelled, as had a day to be spent at EXPO '67, Montreal, for the British day there. All I could do was to visit Ottawa for a long talk with Prime Minister Lester Pearson and some of his senior colleagues.

The Canadian Government fully supported our line, and indeed had proclaimed this in public and at the United Nations. Pearson's one doubt was whether we could get a sufficiently wide and representative group of maritime nations to impress the Egyptians. If we all asserted our position clearly enough it would be unlikely that there would be any interference with a British vessel passing through the Canal, or indeed with any ships from the maritime countries supporting the declaration. In any case we could provide naval protection. We might hope to persuade Nasser to remove the mines. But we would not be able to guarantee freedom of passage for an Israeli ship passing through the Canal, short of providing her with a naval escort: this was certainly not our intention. He made it clear that whatever demonstration was mounted, Canada would not play any direct part. He was, in any case, still sore at Nasser's action in demanding the removal of the UN Emergency Force, and critical of U Thant for tamely withdrawing the Force at Nasser's behest. The Canadians, he said, had felt that they had been bundled off home in the most inconsiderate and humiliating manner. I could not help feeling also that he was not going to play a leading role in any action taken, because he was still smarting at the treatment given to his Suez Canal Users' Association more than a decade earlier. Following an Ottawa press conference I was reported as describing Aqaba as the 'flashpoint', and saying that Lester Pearson and I were agreed that the solution must be sought through the UN. ' "Only if we fail", Mr Wilson added, "might other action have to be considered" in a statement on which he did not elaborate.'[25]

When I saw the President in the White House he told me that things were not going well in the Senate. Vice-President Humphrey and Dean Rusk had spent many hours there, and somewhat to their surprise, had run into considerable 'apathy and even resistance' to any positive action. I commented that while it was not fitting to express a view on another's political constituency, I felt that this would change when Senators and Congressmen received their weekend mail, especially from areas where the Jewish vote was strong. Hubert Humphrey, and Senator Ribicoff of New York, later told me that this was exactly how things turned out. The following day, after breakfasting with Hubert Humphrey, I flew to New York, where I lunched with U Thant – back from Cairo where he had made no progress.

As I left New York to fly home through the night, it was still possible that within forty-eight hours we should be giving the order for an international naval force, headed by the US and Britain, to sail through the Straits of Tiran. Had that order been given, L.B.J. would have very soon seen what he had visualized on 23 May: 'I want to see Wilson and de Gaulle there with their ships all lined up too' – though without de Gaulle.

Meanwhile in Paris a statement on the situation was issued on behalf of President de Gaulle, following a presentation on the Middle East by Couve de Murville to the Cabinet. The Ministry of Information quoted the General as having said:

1. that both Israel and the Arab states had 'the right to live';
2. that the worst thing that could happen would be the outbreak of hostilities;
3. that, if this happened, 'the country which is the first to use arms will have neither our support nor our aid';
4. that the problems of navigation in the Gulf of Aqaba, of the Palestinian refugees, and of the general relations between Israel and the Arab states should be 'settled by international decision'; and
5. that only the four great Powers which were members of the Security Council [i.e. the USA, the Soviet Union, Britain and France] should take part in such decisions.

On Monday morning, hardly more than twenty-four hours after I had left New York, I was awakened with the news that war had broken out in the Middle East.

From the moment the fighting began the international wires between presidents, prime ministers and foreign offices were alive. President Johnson records that he was wakened at 4.30 a.m. by a telephone call from Walt Rostow and spoke to Dean Rusk at 5.09, to agree the terms of a message for Rusk to send to Gromyko. At 7.57 the Defence Secretary came through to him, 'Mr President, the hot line is up' – the first time it had been used. Kosygin was waiting at the Kremlin end; both agreed, as we too were pressing, to go for a cease-fire through the United Nations.

By this time, because of the time difference between our countries, my own telegram was in Washington. Referring to my understanding with the President as we had parted on the previous Friday night, I recorded that

> you expressed some sombre belief that war between Israel and the Arabs could not be avoided, despite the efforts we had been making and discussing together earlier that day. This morning's news appears to confirm your estimate.

I went on to refer to the crisis contacts set up between our respective teams at all levels, in Washington, New York and London, and went on:

> the first thing we can try to do, I suggest, is to avoid the Security Council becoming hopelessly bogged down in sterile argument about which side is the aggressor. What we need is a clear demand from the Council for a cease-fire, after which a fresh attempt to thrash out a longer term settlement might be made.
>
> The French attitude is important to all this and we should do our best to make them face up to their responsibilities.

Before Cabinet met the following morning, Kosygin sent an urgent telegram:

> Military action in the Middle East continues. Moreover its scale is increasing.
>
> The Soviet Government is convinced that a resolute demand for an immediate cease-fire and the withdrawal of forces behind the truce line would correspond to the interests of restoring peace. We express the hope that this demand will be supported by the Government of Great Britain. We support it.
>
> Every possibility should be done [sic] to ensure the adoption by the Security Council today of a positive decision on this matter.

When Cabinet met that morning, I reported briefly on my talks with the President, now substantially outdated by events. Already it seemed clear that Israel had won a considerable initial victory against the air forces of the Arab countries. Numbers of Egyptian aircraft had been destroyed on the airfields and there had been no reports or claims of Egyptian air action. Although Syrian and Jordanian aircraft had been operating they had so far been largely ineffective. There was no truth in Egyptian reports that the oil refinery at Haifa had been bombed. Nor had there been any air raids on Tel Aviv, as claimed, and the shelling of the city from the sea had been ineffective.

It did not, however, seem at all clear that Israel was achieving a comparable success in the land battle in the South where a hard struggle was taking place: the Israelis were being reticent about its progress.[26] Heavy fighting was taking place in Jerusalem, where attempts to maintain a cease-fire had twice broken down after an initial acceptance by both sides. Israel had appeared that day to have taken the offensive against Jordan following shelling by Jordanian troops. We were taking administrative action to delay the shipment of arms to Middle Eastern countries while an assessment was being made of the attitudes and actions of other countries, including particularly those of France and the Soviet Union. The United States had stopped the supply of arms to both sides.

Our shipping had been warned to delay for twenty-four hours any approach to the Suez Canal, which was in any case reported to be closed. British dependents and other civilians were being evacuated from the most dangerous areas and preparations were being made for further evacuations if necessary. In the Security Council, a resolution confined to an appeal for a cease-fire had failed to gain the necessary support and we had to consider whether we might have to accept a resolution in less satisfactory terms, as the alternative to a most undesirable failure on the part of the Committee to agree on any resolution at all.

Reports reaching us suggested that Israel had succeeded in eliminating the Egyptian Air Force, a fact which would have a major effect on the land battle. There had been allegations by Egypt and Jordan that Israel had been given air cover by British and United States carrier-borne aircraft. This was completely untrue and, as far as we were concerned, physically impossible. There was no indication of any Soviet troop movements relevant to the Middle East situation.

Mr Kosygin had telegraphed me urging all possible efforts to put an end to the fighting. It contained none of the recriminations or allegations about the actions of British or other Western powers which were appearing in the Moscow press.

In the light of the Cabinet's discussion I replied to the Moscow telegram:

Many thanks for your message. I entirely agree that we should concentrate on obtaining a cease-fire. I think the best place to work for this at the moment is the Security Council. You can rely on our co-operation in achieving this as soon as possible, preferably today.

I learn that Lord Caradon is now trying to reach an agreement with Mr Fedorenko and their United States colleague, Mr Goldberg, on the basis of an expanded draft resolution which calls for a cease-fire, and in addition a withdrawal of forces, but *quote* without prejudice to the responsibilities, rights, claims or positions of others *unquote*. It also calls on both parties to work for the disengagement of their forces, and to reduce tension.

In our view, this expanded draft resolution would not be as good as a single cease-fire resolution, but we would certainly accept it. In any case we hope that present intensive negotiations now going on in New York will result in a unanimous resolution by the Security Council. . . . In the House of Commons today I said that we must get a solution which meets the honourable requirements of all concerned. This means we must work together to this end.

Please get in touch with me again if you have further thoughts on this dangerous problem. Warm regards.

By the time of the next Cabinet, two days later, the Israelis, having defeated the Egyptian forces in Sinai, had virtually ceased operations except against Jordan and Syria. Reinforcements for the UAR were, however, at that time reported to be on their way from Algeria, including fifty MiG aircraft, and if these were to reach Egypt the Israelis must be expected to act against them.

Israel had stated her willingness to accept a cease-fire provided that her Arab opponents were similarly agreeable, but so far only Jordan had shown herself willing. Reports were circulating that an Arab summit conference was to be convened, possibly by President Boumedienne of Algeria, to formulate a common policy on the cease-fire, on oil supplies, and on diplomatic relations with Britain and the United States.

Reports reaching the West about the Soviet Union suggested that they might table a resolution in the Security Council calling upon Israel to withdraw behind her original frontiers, but in view of the moderate attitude she had adopted diplomatically in circumstances of great difficulty, this now seemed unlikely to us. Their attitude in the UN and in relations with the West was in fact in sharp contrast to current Soviet propaganda, especially when compared with her broadcasts to the Middle East, which were now beginning to follow the UAR in propagating the lie that British and American aircraft had supported Israel in the Middle East fighting.

Two days after the fighting ended, on 9 June, when Cabinet met again, Nasser, following his defeat, had resigned and been promptly re-elected. Hostilities had broken out between Israel and Syria, otherwise the cease-fire had been generally respected. On Britain's behalf, Lord Caradon at the UN had recommended immediate action to relieve suffering in areas hit by the fighting. There was anxiety about oil supplies. It was not yet clear how far sanctions would be applied against Western nations. Apart from Iraq, the Governments concerned had done no more than place an embargo on tankers leaving for the United States or Britain, but production in Kuwait, Saudi Arabia and Libya had been stopped by action taken by the mobs. Contingency measures were being taken by the Government departments concerned to prepare for petrol rationing, should that become necessary.

That same day, Kosygin telegraphed me again:

Mr Prime Minister.

There is information that Israel is ignoring the Security Council Resolution which calls upon all the Governments concerned, as a first step to take forthwith all measures for an immediate cease-fire and for cessation of all military activities in the area.

This situation demands that the Security Council should use its powers to ensure the implementation of the decision which it itself has adopted.

In view of this we have submitted a proposal that the Security Council should meet at once to take effective measures for an immediate cessation of hostilities and the restoration of peace.

With respect

A. Kosygin
Chairman of the Council of Ministers
of the USSR

I replied:

Thank you for your further message of 7 June.

As I told you in my previous message, Her Majesty's Government are doing everything in their power to bring an end to the military conflict. To this end, as you know, we fully supported the resolution which your permanent representative to the United Nations put forward in the Security Council last night, calling for an immediate cessation of all military activities.

We welcome the fact that this was passed unanimously. I understand that the Jordan and Israeli Governments have already informed the United Nations of their acceptance of a cease-fire. There remains the problem of persuading the other combatants to do likewise. It is clearly essential that all efforts should be made to achieve this without further delay and to avoid further bloodshed. I know that you will do all in your power as we are doing to work to this end which is in our common interest.

On the same day I telegraphed Prime Minister Eshkol of Israel. I began by referring to the Security Council's call for a cease-fire and went on:

So far the dangers of outside intervention and escalation have been avoided, but any prolongation of the fighting will immeasurably increase these risks. I was glad therefore to note Mr Eban's welcome for the Security Council's cease-fire appeal in his speech at the Council.

The Security Council must clearly turn its attention to the further steps that are needed to secure a lasting peace. Without seeking at this stage to assess in any detail the form which this might take, I can assure you that Her Majesty's Government will work for a thorough examination of everything necessary for a constructive arrangement that will take account of the legitimate interests and aspirations of all the parties and will seek to eliminate the causes of past bitterness and conflict.

Indira Gandhi sent a telegram expressing her 'growing anxiety' and concern at the recent turn of events in 'West Asia'.* Indian Prime Ministers, irrespective of their own religious beliefs, never failed to tell their Western

* At a subsequent Commonwealth Conference, following a long debate on the 'Middle East', she accused us of being Euro-centric and said that they always called it 'West Asia'.

colleagues that there were ninety million Moslems in India. For the same reason Ayub Khan telegraphed me on the same day as Mrs Gandhi, urging us to use our influence 'in quest of the restoration of the Arab territories and the Holy Places in Jerusalem'.

Almost before some of our war correspondents could put pen to a telegram and get it encoded, the war, from the military point of view, was virtually over. To trace the main events, fighting had begun shortly before 8 a.m. (local time) on 5 June. The Israeli Air Force sent wave after wave of aircraft over Egyptian, Syrian and Jordanian airfields, and to the Iraqi base at Habbaniyah. Sixteen Egyptian airfields were put out of action in the first attack. Those in the north were destroyed by a daring stratagem. To by-pass the radar screen, which had been erected to deal with aircraft coming from the East or North, Israeli aircraft, keeping low, went well out to sea to the West and homed in on the air bases with little opposition.*

By the first night the Israelis had captured strategic bases in the Gaza Strip, location of the headquarters of the Palestine Liberation Organization (PLO). By the second day the Gaza Strip was occupied, as was the greater part of Jerusalem – opening up the 'Wailing Wall' and freeing the Hebrew University on occupied Mount Scopus. On the third day of the fighting, Israeli armour was driving on to the entrance to the Gulf of Aqaba, and Israeli paratroops, together with troops landed from patrol boats, captured the fortresses commanding Sharm el-Sheikh, and opened up the Straits of Tiran. That evening General Rabin, Commander-in-Chief, claimed total victory in the war against the UAR. On the fourth day, the Egyptian ambassador to the United Nations stated that his Government would accept a cease-fire if the Israelis would do so. Fighting continued on the Syrian front, especially with the shelling of Israel's border villages, kibbutzim and other settlements. By 9 June both sides, Syria and Israel, had agreed to the UN call for a cease-fire, but fighting continued. Israel's invasion of Syria via the Golan Heights, as far towards Damascus as Kuneitra, lent urgency to a cease-fire and the Syrians accepted the UN resolution.

The action was now transferred from the battlefronts to the peacemakers at the UN. But nothing was going to be the same again. President Johnson rode high. He had backed Israel and virtually without any direct help from him, Israel had won. But there was no longer a group of the 'Great Powers' who could be involved to veto a recourse to war. France had changed sides in

---

* In the subsequent inquest Britain and the United States were arraigned by Egypt for having played a leading part in the air bombardment which had virtually destroyed her air capacity. The reason for this charge was that the Egyptians thought, or affected to think, that the aircraft coming in from the West were from British or American aircraft-carriers. In fact, the US Sixth Fleet was nowhere near the area, and the two British aircraft carriers were hundreds of miles from the nearest point of hostilities, HMS *Hermes* at Aden and HMS *Victorious* at Malta.

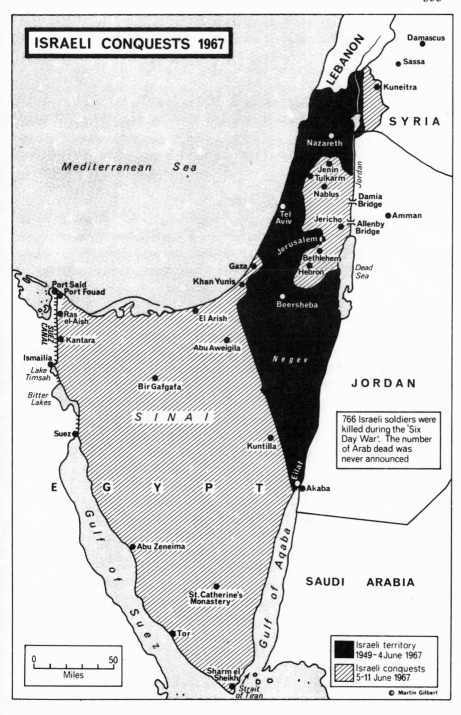

ISRAELI CONQUESTS 1967

Mediterranean Sea

LEBANON

Damascus

Sassa

Kuneitra

SYRIA

Nazareth

Jenin
Tulkarm

Nablus

Jordan

Damia
Bridge

Amman

Tel
Aviv

Jericho

Allenby
Bridge

Jerusalem

Bethlehem

Gaza

Hebron

Dead
Sea

Khan Yunis

Beersheba

Port Said
Port Fouad

Ras
el-Aish

El Arish

Kantara

Abu Aweigila

Negev

Ismailia

Lake
Timsah

Bir Gafgafa

JORDAN

Bitter
Lakes

S I N A I

766 Israeli soldiers were
killed during the 'Six
Day War'. The number
of Arab dead was
never announced

Suez

Kuntilla

E   G   Y   P   T

Eilat

Akaba

Abu Zeneima

SAUDI   ARABIA

St. Catherine's
Monastery

Tor

Israeli territory
1949-4 June 1967

Sharm el
Sheikh

Israeli conquests
5-11 June 1967

Strait
of Tiran

© Martin Gilbert

0   50
Miles

the midst of the confrontation, on the basis of the test her President had laid down – 'who would fire the first shot?' De Gaulle's branding-iron was set to brand Israel: he chose to disregard the fact, so clearly perceived by him three weeks before, that the closure by military means of the Straits was the first act of aggression. The Soviet Union had moved perceptibly, unhappily and clumsily into a pro-Arab posture. The Big Four were divided. France was looking beyond the Urals. No leader now voiced fears of Armageddon, in contrast, for example, with the anxious terms Premier Kosygin had addressed to Washington and London when he spoke as though the Third World War was at hand. None now warned that if Course A or Course B were rejected there would be war. There had been a war, and it had not escalated. It had destroyed no dynasty: all the dramatis personae at kingly or presidential level remained in power. Some had lost face, some had lost territory; Israel had survived, with more enemies than before, but with none capable of securing a victory should they seek a military replay. For six years she was to face hostility and bitterness, but not the threat of destruction.

In terms of prestige and influence, no country had suffered more than France, no statesman more than General de Gaulle. 'Paris est à vous', he had said only two months earlier before the Middle East crisis erupted, when, at Dr Adenauer's funeral, I had suggested that I should come over for a talk with him. My main purpose had then been to see whether there was any chance that he might think again about the veto he had applied when Harold Macmillan's Government had sought membership of the European Economic Community. In 1966 the Cabinet had discussed the matter from every angle, in long relaxed meetings at Chequers, and point by point round the Cabinet table in Downing Street. Before the Middle Eastern crisis, a date had been agreed, 19 June. British entry to the EEC, Vietnam, the strengthening of European political ties, Concorde, Anglo-French partnership in the design and production of a new generation of military aircraft – de Gaulle had without just notice cancelled the variable-geometry project: there was a great deal to discuss. But now it would be a President chastened by the events of six days at the other end of his Mediterranean, ignored by Moscow and with the hated Americans riding high. My own hopes were for progress on the EEC. Earlier in the year he had conceded that 'we had shown a willingness no longer to moor our British craft on the Eastern seaboard of America, or even to cruise around in mid-Atlantic, but in the Channel'. Not yet up the Seine. Looking back on those two sunlit days in Versailles, it is clear that our closeness to Washington over the Middle East crisis was fatal to any move on the EEC. What was still more striking was the effect of those recent days on an ageing and imperious statesman who felt not so much lonely – he had chosen his path of loneliness – as ignored, even impotent.

In preparation for our meeting I had sent him a long message setting out our hopes for the meeting and our general approach to some of the issues we should be discussing:

H.W. to President de Gaulle, 15 June 1967

M. de Courcel [French Ambassador to the Court of St James's] will have told you of the exchange of views I had with him last week about the possible topics that you and I might discuss when I have the pleasure of seeing you next Monday. While I believe you may share my view that we should not establish any formal agenda for what will, I hope, be essentially an informal and wide-ranging exchange of ideas about world problems generally, I expect we shall both agree on the need to take a hard look at the Middle Eastern situation and other possibilities that may now exist to bring about a definitive settlement there.

It is about that that I am now writing to you as a kind of prologue to our discussions.

You and I have both exchanged a number of messages in the past few days with Premier Kosygin: and our Governments have been in close touch with other friendly Governments. From the outset of this unhappy crisis we have, as you know, strongly supported your view that only if the four Great Powers were prepared to face up to their responsibilities could any hopeful issue result. This was the view that I urged on the Prime Minister of Canada when I saw him on 1 June, and I am glad to say that both then and in subsequent exchanges that I have had with him, Mr Pearson expressed his full support for it. Equally, I argued this with the President of the United States when we met on 2 June. Mr Johnson accepted the force of the case in so far as the UN Security Council was concerned but showed less enthusiasm for it as a general concept.

In my subsequent exchanges with Mr Kosygin I have equally urged the vital necessity for four-power co-operation and understanding if peace and stability are ever to be restored to that unhappy region.

Since then we have witnessed the series of events that resulted from the outbreak of fighting: the progressive weakening of the Soviet position resulting, as I believe, from their discovery of their inability to control a situation which they were at least partly responsible for creating: acquiescence in the unanimous cease-fire resolution in the Security Council and the latter's reluctant acceptance by the Arab powers.

But the cease-fire, as we both know, is only the first essential step in what is bound to be an excessively difficult and delicate advance towards a settlement of the Arab–Israel problem. I believe that all of us will now recognize that we are now confronted with a major choice in world affairs. Either we can seek to bring about an honourable settlement, in which the legitimate claims of all concerned, Israeli and Arab alike, will so far as possible be met: or we shall allow the rivalries between the local powers to be reflected and magnified by the rivalries between the Great Powers, leading either to a patched-up settlement which will satisfy no one or to no settlement at all – and in either case to an inevitable renewal of conflict: with the immeasurable dangers for world peace that this would entail.

In such a situation, the choice is clear. The problem is how to achieve this settlement while taking account not only of the interests of the Middle Eastern powers themselves, but also of those of the Great Powers which, as political realists, we must recognize react constantly on the area, on its resources and on its peoples. In the past, historically and again more recently, France and Britain have not always seen eye to eye about the Middle East. Indeed, in these latest weeks of crisis there have been substantial nuances of difference between us. But, as I say, the task now is to look to the future. And it seems to me that in fact our interests in the Middle East do now very much coincide. In my message to you of 28 May I hinted that, as the two European members of the Four Power Group, we might, by common action, achieve a common purpose. Developments in the past few days have strongly reinforced me in that view. This is not simply because we in Europe depend to an increasing degree on the oil supplies we derive from the Arab world, important as those are. It is also because we surely must ensure that decisions affecting the future of this key region must take due regard of the general politico-strategic world interests of the European powers, as well as of their obvious economic interests.

I am not of course suggesting a return to the kind of Anglo-French approach which characterized the disastrous 1956 excursion, nor am I suggesting that any joint public initiative by us both is necessarily required at present. Our position in the fighting, like yours, has been one of strict neutrality. Now we must surely work together to exert effective influence on the negotiation of a lasting and durable settlement. But I doubt whether Britain or France, acting individually, can expect to deploy such influence. If, however, we could establish a community of interest and of view about some of the problems that will face us in the coming weeks, then whether in a Four Power meeting at the United Nations, in some other forum, or more generally, we may perhaps ensure that the interests of Western Europe as a whole, as well as those of our two countries, are taken effectively into account.

This is the background against which I suggest we might discuss the Middle Eastern situation next Monday. I thought it might be helpful if I gave you this advance notice of my tentative thinking.

There were rumours that Kosygin and other leading Soviet ministers would attend the UN General Assembly, where the Russians were expected to call for a special debate on the Middle East. On 15 June I telegraphed L.B.J. about these rumours but advised that the two of us should not build up the occasion further by going ourselves, still less create an atmosphere of oratorical confrontation. He replied the following day:

Your messages of the last two days have been helpful as always. None of us can predict what situation may arise in the days ahead, but my present thinking is this. First, at the moment I doubt that anything useful can come from my personal participation in the General Assembly.

Second, from the beginning of this crisis I have not looked with favour on a Four-Power meeting outside the UN Security Council. It is something of an illusion that the Four Powers have the capacity to design and impose successfully a plan on the Near East. The States of the area have made it abundantly clear that they are not subject to effective control from outside. What the major powers can do is to try to create a climate in which the nations of the area themselves might gradually settle their affairs on a peaceful basis. But I am not confident that a Four-Power session is the best way to do this.

Moreover, I should think both of us would wish to avoid the possibility of having the four of us split or otherwise be strained in such a session.

I hope we can keep in close touch in the days ahead as the situation evolves, and we might wish to counsel together shortly after the smoke clears to assess the situation and see what is required to move things forward towards our common objective of stable peace in the area.

The next move was to be my visit to de Gaulle on 19 June. On the 17th he sent me a brief telegram in reply to my lengthy preparatory message, and in reply also to my inquiry about his talk with Kosygin:

> I had a talk here yesterday with Mr Kosygin. He struck me as disposed in the direction of a settlement which in the last analogy [*sic*] would be a peaceful one. But this will not be achieved without a great deal of toughness so far as he is concerned.
>
> We should have, on Monday and Tuesday, a full opportunity to discuss this problem as well as the other question of interest to our two Governments.
>
> My wife and I look forward to this opportunity of seeing you together with Mrs Wilson.

The President entertained us not in Paris but in the Trianon, Versailles. At mealtimes, or showing me over the Palace, or driving in his little car around the estate, he could not have been more affable and courteous. But in the work sessions it was clear that he was in a mood of total despair, almost resignation. A note I made at the time[27] describes the mood and his weary judgments.

We entered immediately into a discussion of the Middle East situation. The President was more depressed than I had ever seen him. This was partly, I think, because Mr Kosygin had virtually by-passed him; clearly the Soviet Premier's visit a few days before had not been a success. Not only had the USSR summarily rejected the President's proposal for Four-Power talks, but there was much discussion about a bilateral meeting between Mr Kosygin and President Johnson in the US. General de Gaulle felt he had been spurned and if this was so it was a sad ending to all his hopes about Franco-Soviet relations. But there was more than that. He believed that we were nearing a world crisis, that war, world war, could be very near and there was no one to listen to his warnings. He considered that Mr Kosygin, while taking a hard line about the need for Israel to retreat from the territory she had occupied and for the UN to condemn her 'aggression', had not formed any clear idea of what Soviet policy should be. For his part, he said, he had not given his guest any clear indication of French policy.

I explained our objectives and emphasized how we had supported the
French proposal for a Four-Power approach, which we still supported. We
had been very close in our basic approach, and we had both taken the same
line in cutting off arms; it was a disappointment that our lead had not been
followed. General de Gaulle then set out his apocalyptic attitude to the
world situation. The problem of Israel mattered less now than the grave
international context within which we had to consider the Middle East
position – a context which included such problems as the war in Vietnam,
the recent Chinese detonation of a thermonuclear weapon and many others.
We could not look at the Middle East alone, because these other factors
would encourage certain powers to stand out against any Middle East
settlement; he did not specify who these were. The world was now passing
through a very dangerous period. None of us – not Britain, not France, not
America, not Russia – was holding the reins any longer, nor likely to do so.
No one could say how long this would last, still less how it would end.
Nobody was in control of the situation. That was why he had proposed
Four-Power consideration. He would have insisted that the Four should
agree that whichever side struck first, Israelis or Arabs, should be
condemned as the aggressor. The US and Britain had supported the Four-
Power approach, but the Soviet Union had refused. Perhaps they were now
regretting this decision. But the war had broken out and now we were in a
different and totally incalculable period.

Let us look at the Middle East first, he said, and then at the wider
international scene. Public opinion in France – doubtless in Britain too –
was sympathetic to Israel: understandable after two thousand years of
history and the sufferings of the Jewish people, including the massacres of
the last war. In France, too, there was still a feeling of hostility towards the
Arabs, because of Algeria. But the Government must approach the problem
dispassionately. Britain, the US and the Soviet Union had created the State
of Israel. France had accepted this. Israel had taken root and flourished.

He offered no view on the Suez episode in 1956; he had not been in
charge at the time. But Britain and France had been forced to abandon the
Canal, while Israel, he said, had gained. The French Government of the day
had made a firm public declaration about free passage into the Gulf of
Aqaba, even when the Algerian war was producing bad relations with the
Arabs. But the situation had changed. The Algerian war was over. France's
relations with the Arab states had improved. She was on reasonably good
terms with many of them. Given this, there was no reason for France – 'or, I
would suggest, the United Kingdom' – to ruin its relations with the Arabs,
merely because public opinion felt some 'superficial sympathy' (his phrase)
for Israel because she was a small country with an unhappy history. France
had hoped that while supplying arms to Israel she could improve her

relations with the Arabs. I reflected silently that this was de Gaulle's genius, not only in the Middle East: he could supply arms to South Africa, yet seem to identify with emerging African countries. Trying to remain dispassionate, he had met the present crisis by saying that whoever attacked first was the guilty party. The guilty party proved to be Israel. She had been successful in the contest of arms, she had effected a drastic change in the balance of power in the Middle East, but she had created a situation which was more difficult than ever for the Arabs to accept. It might well be the case that no lasting agreement could be achieved for perhaps another quarter of a century. In effect, the two sides were still at war and they would stay at war.

Turning to the wider Middle East, he said his Government had noted our intention to withdraw from Aden. They welcomed this as friends of Britain. But we must recognize that the real reason why we were involved in the Middle East at all was because of our basic relationship with the United States. All our difficulties there, whether on oil or on the Suez Canal, would not be eased by withdrawal from Aden. It was for this reason: the Arab countries were hostile to the US because of American support for Israel, which 'rubbed off' on Britain because of our fundamental link with Washington. It was the same in the Far East. The French Government recognized our commitments in Hong Kong and Singapore. But here again, whenever international tension developed and we had to choose one side or the other, we always chose the same side. It was inexplicable to him, since it brought no benefit to us at all. The only realistic solution for Britain, as for France, was to have no external commitments. We, of course, might not agree: that would not affect France's friendship for us!

As I walked back on those slippery marble floors to my apartments, M. Burin de Roziers, the President's Chef de Cabinet, said he thought that the President was very depressed. Apocalyptic, I suggested. 'Ah,' he said, 'the General is seventy-six and has little to look forward to.' (I was sure he was referring to the General's disappointment following Mr Kosygin's visit.) I replied that I was fifty-one and, if I were to take so dejected a view, there would be no purpose in remaining in public affairs.

After lunch we became serious again. For about half an hour we discussed the Middle East situation and, in particular, the proposed Four-Power summit. I said that I was not disposed to go to New York unless he proposed to go. He said that he could see no point in going. It was impossible to predict how the situation would develop. Despite Mr Kosygin's inevitable need to strike attitudes in New York, he had received from him the impression of an almost physical attitude of uncertainty and indecision. He was quite sure that if he saw President Johnson he would receive exactly the same impression. No one was really in charge of the situation any longer;

nor would it be possible, until the lessons of the disastrous conflict between Israel and the Arabs had really sunk in – always assuming that general war had not broken out in the interval – to approach the question of a settlement in rational terms. And this would take a very long time. I suggested that this might be a negative view of the situation. A more positive view would be to work for a solution whereby all Arab states would recognize Israel's right to exist and her rights to enjoy freedom of navigation through the Straits of Tiran – and also through the Canal – while at the same time the Arabs would receive satisfaction of their claims as regards the settlement of the refugees. The President replied that this might be so; but any such settlement lay a long way ahead.

My assessment of de Gaulle's mood and his judgments was set out in a telegram to President Johnson on 23 June. It was mainly a recital of what the General had said, but on de Gaulle's general approach I included this judgment:

> I thought you might like to have a few highly personal impressions. I know you will treat them with particular care and for your personal eye only.
>
> The General was in a more gloomy and apocalyptic mood than I had ever seen him. I think he found his talk with Kosygin last Friday pretty shattering. I am not clear exactly what he hoped to get out of it – presumably an agreement to a four-power summit. In practice, Kosygin seems to have twisted his arm pretty hard to give straight support to the Soviet line and the General (who dislikes having his arm twisted) left him, as he told me in *quote* uncertainty *unquote* about France's attitude. But I think that the talk with Kosygin, and the Middle East situation as a whole, have forced him to face up to the realities of France's lack of effective influence in world affairs and to ask himself what his foreign policy has so far achieved. In his heart I believe he realizes that it has led him to something of a dead end. But he is too old, and I think physically too weary, to work out a new approach. In any event, this has never been something he does very readily. Given the reluctant recognition that France cannot fundamentally influence affairs, his response is a sad reflection of the old Maginot line approach – sitting behind his *quote* force de frappe *unquote*, watching the world move towards Armageddon. The general theme that ran through the whole discussion was that, as he put it at one point, the United States which was now the greatest power in the world behaved (as France and Britain had done in their hey-day) exclusively in her own interests. The only way for a medium-sized power like France (with, in his view, Britain) to conduct their affairs in such a situation was to disengage and *quote* to make it clear that America's quarrels are not our quarrels and their wars will not be our wars *unquote*. All this of course related primarily to Vietnam and the Middle East with [his references to] Vietnam in condemnation of yourself. This was his line with me: that there was no hope of a Middle Eastern settlement while the war in Vietnam continued to poison the world scene, and he gave as the main reason for France's withdrawal from NATO his determination to keep his hands free in this cataclysmic situation.

Britain's involvement with the United States made it inevitable that we should be dragged into your wars. It also affected us damagingly in such areas as the Middle East, where we were now suffering because we were regarded by the Arabs as indistinguishable from the pro-Jewish Americans.

The telegram then went on to summarize the opinions de Gaulle had expressed on nuclear questions and technological and industrial co-operation.

Here again his constant theme was our involvement with yourself and the danger that if we can [sic], all the weaker brethren in the Six, the *quote* poor Italians *unquote*, the Germans exposed to constant temptation, and the Dutch already on our side anyway would follow our lead and the whole thing would become an American-dominated Atlantic agreement. It was to prevent this that France was in the Community . . .

The outline of de Gaulle's gloomy philosophy and his acceptance of defeat was unutterably sad. It was the end of an era for France. He resigned in April 1969, after a national referendum had rejected his proposals for constitutional reform, and died in November 1970. From then on the influence of France in the United Nations and in world affairs declined until President Giscard d'Estaing began to seek a new role for her within the leadership of the EEC. She was no longer one of the 'Great Four' in the UN. Indeed there was now no inner cabinet of four. In world affairs the UN inevitably reflected the conflict of the United States and the Soviet Union, with Britain ranged on the American side and France seeking an intermediate but increasingly ineffective role. In de Gaulle's dying months no one sought her mediation. Splendid isolation remained a rousing theme for his increasingly confused perorations, but while achieving isolation, there was no splendour. Before long France's role seemed seldom to rise above midnight EEC arguments about the price of butter and subsidies from the bureaucrats administering the Common Agricultural Policy in Brussels. Her sole surviving grandeur came from issuing declamatory vetoes on British membership of the European Economic Community.

CHAPTER 12

Yom Kippur and After

THEY WERE AT PRAYER. The whole of Israel was at prayer. The most sacred day of the Jewish year, the Day of Atonement. The day was sanctified by Holy Writ. In the 23rd Chapter of the Book of Leviticus it is written:

> And the Lord spoke unto Moses saying:
>
> Also on the tenth day of this seventh month there shall be a day of atonement: it shall be a holy convocation unto you; and you shall afflict your souls and offer an offering made by fire unto the Lord.
>
> And you shall do no work on that same day: for it is a day of atonement for you before the Lord your God.
>
> For whatever soul shall not be afflicted in that same day, he shall be cut off among the people.

On 6 October 1973, at 2 p.m., the air raid sirens sounded. At 6 p.m., just as Yom Kippur ended, Prime Minister Golda Meir appeared on television: 'Because the news was so grave I was obliged to call a Cabinet meeting on Yom Kippur.' Already the army was being mobilized. In the Mea Shearim quarter of Jerusalem ultra-pious Hassidic Jews were loading army equipment into buses and cars.

This work relates to Britain's political reactions to Israel and her neighbours and initiatives concerning them. It does not purport to be a history of the Middle East, or an account of the wars between Israel and her Arab neighbours.[1] Nevertheless, in the case of the Yom Kippur War it is necessary to give a brief account of the fighting, the more so as the war had been in progress for ten days out of a total duration of eighteen before the serious issues it raised could be brought up in the British Parliament. The following pages therefore trace the main developments.[2]

The attack of 6 October was launched by Egypt across the Suez Canal, jointly with a powerful Syrian offensive on the Golan Heights. Jordan did not officially participate, but units of King Hussein's army were placed under Syrian military orders and joined in the Golan battles. Iraq, Morocco and Saudi Arabia were subsequently reported to have contributed units. Despite Egyptian and Syrian allegations that Israel was the aggressor, UN truce observers in the war areas placed the onus plainly on Egypt and Syria, and so reported to New York.

On that morning Egyptian forces, supported by an intensive deployment of Russian-supplied SAM-2 and SAM-3 missiles, crossed the Canal at five points, carrying 400 tanks across on pontoons. They breached the Bar-Lev line, the string of outposts on the East Bank, and fanned out into a 100-mile front. This enabled them by Sunday 7 October to drive eastward into Sinai. Israeli Phantoms went into the attack, but withheld details of the numbers shot down. On 8 October Cairo claimed that the whole East Bank had been occupied, as well as Qantara – the key in earlier operations. Egypt continued to claim massive destruction of Israeli tanks and aircraft – forty-three in the early strike – Israel remaining silent, but an authoritative journalist on the Israeli side conceded that Israel was engaged in 'one of the most bitter battles in her history'. Major-General Aharon Yariv, assistant to the Chief of Staff, stated that Israeli forces had evacuated most of the Bar-Lev line, but had established a 'firm base for operations' two to three miles, and in some areas four miles, east of the Canal. He went on to say that the situation would not be easily redressed. There was 'still a lot of fighting' ahead, and 'it is not going to be a short war'.

For the next three days the situation on the western front was fairly stable, the Syrian front taking most of the hard blows, but on 13 October the last Israeli fortified position on the East Bank was cut off and captured. The following day Tel Aviv announced that Major General Avraham Mendler, commander of the Israeli armoured forces in Sinai, had been killed in action. Egypt's Mirage forces attempted to bomb Tel Aviv, two being claimed as shot down by the Israelis. These had been supplied by France who, at the time of the agreement with Egypt, had given a categorical assurance that they would not be sent to 'battlefield countries', but used solely in the defence of Libya. Egypt and Libya denied that any Mirages had been in action, and France accepted this assurance.

On Sunday 14 October the Egyptians on the East Bank launched a great offensive with 100,000 troops along the entire 100-mile front, directed mainly against the Mitla Pass, one of the three gateways into Israel. For five days a great tank battle continued: a senior Israeli spokesman said that more tanks were involved than in Montgomery's attack at Alamein or the Nazi invasion of the Soviet Union in 1941. While the tank battle continued to rage, the Israelis, on 16 October, counter-attacked with a successful invasion of the Canal's West Bank. A security blackout on the invaders' whereabouts was enforced, Mrs Meir simply informing the Knesset on the day the operation took place.

From 17 October the Sinai battle began to go Israel's way. At the same time Israel's bridgehead on the West Bank was being widened and reinforced. General Dayan claimed that Israel had secured the initiative on both the Sinai and Syrian fronts, this time warning that 'there is no shutting our eyes to the heavy price we are paying'.

By the 20th Tel Aviv was able to announce that Israeli forces west of the Canal – originally described as a limited commando operation – held a bridgehead twenty-five miles long and nearly twenty miles deep, and that they had overrun, destroyed or captured many of the SAM missile sites, and had fought their way to within seventy miles of Cairo. Simultaneously it was claimed that Israel had achieved total air superiority on the Sinai front.

Meanwhile the UN had been active, and by 22 October Egypt and Israel had agreed to a cease-fire. By this time 12,000 Israelis, deploying 200 tanks, were holding a menacing bridgehead of 500 square miles around the Great Bitter Lake and had cut the Cairo–Ismailia road.

Heavy fighting went on despite the two sides' agreement to the cease-fire, which finally became effective on the 24th. (On 26 October it was reported that, with the co-operation of the International Red Cross, the delivery of 200 units of plasma with 200 units of blood to the Egyptian Third Army, was completed by the Israelis.) All this time the United States Government was active in monitoring Soviet involvement and naval movements. On 10 October the US State Department official spokesman had announced that the Soviet Union had carried out a large airlift of 'very big tonnages' of military equipment to Egypt and Syria, warning that if the Soviet airlift became 'massive' it would 'tend to put a new face on the situation'. The United States, he explained, was 'exercising restraint' in the Middle East fighting and 'expected all concerned' to do the same. The spokesman called attention to a statement which the Secretary of State, Henry Kissinger, had made earlier in the week that détente 'cannot survive irresponsibility in any area, including the Middle East'. Five days later the State Department announced that the United States had now begun an 'appreciable' airlift of military supplies to Israel to offset what had become a large Soviet airlift of military supplies to Syria and Egypt. Washington said that 4,000 tons in all of military equipment in 280 flights had been supplied by the Soviet Union via Hungary and Yugoslavia, then down the Adriatic and across the Eastern Mediterranean. Washington also let it be known that the Soviet Fleet in the Eastern Mediterranean had been reinforced to over eighty warships – its highest ever deployed in this area – including missile cruisers, destroyers, a helicopter carrier, submarines, amphibious vessels and landing craft. Press reports added that the Soviet missile cruiser *Sverdlov* and two missile destroyers had passed through the Dardanelles to join the fleet already deployed by the Russians. The US Sixth Fleet was therefore further reinforced – including the carriers *Independence*, *Franklin D. Roosevelt* and *John F. Kennedy*.

While Alexei Kosygin was visiting Cairo, President Nixon formally asked

Congress on 16 October for $2,200 million (£900 million) in immediate military aid to Israel: this was needed to prevent a 'substantial imbalance' of military power in the Middle East. He did not have to press: sixty-seven Senators had introduced a resolution asking for *unlimited* aid for Israel to offset Soviet help for the Arab states. At the same time a resolution by 220 Congressmen had been presented to the House of Representatives.

> The US deliveries had begun on 13 October, when at 3.30 p.m. thirty C130 transports were on their way to Israel. By Tuesday we were sending in a thousand tons a day. Over the next few weeks there would be more than 550 American missions, an operation bigger than the Berlin airlift of 1948–49. I also ordered that an additional ten Phantom jets be delivered to Israel.[3]*

Meanwhile Britain's Foreign Secretary, Sir Alec Douglas-Home, was addressing the Blackpool Conference of the Conservative Party. In a somewhat stuffy speech, very much head down, on 12 October he said he was doubtful whether a settlement could now be reached between the combatants without the help of others, the Secretary-General of the United Nations, or perhaps a wider international conference in which the combatants would take part. But he went on to say that he had 'been certain that it would not be psychologically possible for the Arabs to go on gazing indefinitely at their own lands without the eruption of war'.

The Conservative Conference precluded a recall of Parliament.

It was Labour who provided all the activity. As soon as the news of the invasion became known I telephoned the Israeli Ambassador to the Court of St James's, Michael Comay, and made an immediate appointment to see him and be briefed. Thereafter I was in contact with him each day to hear of developments. The first thing he told me was that Mr Heath's Government had placed an embargo on the shipment of spares and ammunition to Israel needed for the Centurion tanks Britain had supplied when Labour had been in power. As soon as the Prime Minister, Edward Heath, returned to London, I went to No. 10 to press him to change Government policy on spares and ammunition. When he refused, James Callaghan and I took up the issue publicly.

At a Cabinet meeting the next day concern must have been expressed about our demand that spares and ammunition be exempted from the ban on arms shipments, for James Callaghan and I received a telephone message from No. 10 asking if we would see Sir Alec in the Foreign Secretary's room at the House.** Sir Alec appealed to us to support the Government's

---

* Nixon was involved in these decisions just as the Watergate crisis reached its climax. (On Friday 12 October the US Court of Appeals ruled against Nixon on the question of surrendering the Watergate tapes.)

** Opposition leaders (of both parties) have a strong predilection for going to No. 10 to make representations. Equally, Prime Ministers (of both parties) like to see the meetings take place in the Palace of Westminster unfrequented by TV and press cameramen.

position. James Callaghan loyally said that I was the Leader of the Party and that, while he did not feel as strongly as I did, I was the boss and he supported my line. I declined to cease pressing our demand. Parliament met on 16 October. The Foreign Secretary made a statement:

> When the hostilities broke out, Her Majesty's Government called for an immediate cease-fire, and suspended all shipments of arms to the battlefield. We did this because we considered it inconsistent to call for an immediate end to the fighting and yet to continue to send arms to the conflict. This seems to me to be the best posture from which to make an effective contribution to a constructive settlement. As regards the effect of the embargo we have supplied a limited number of arms to both sides in recent years. Whereas in 1967 an embargo would have discriminated against Israel, it is now even-handed. I would like to add here that British military facilities overseas have not been and are not being used for the transit of military supplies to the battlefield.
>
> We have also sought to bring the Security Council into action at once, but neither side was willing to contemplate a cease-fire, except on terms totally unacceptable to the other. The Security Council has met several times but has been unable to find a consensus on any action . . .[4]

James Callaghan, Opposition spokesman on foreign affairs – 'shadow Foreign Secretary' – responded:

> I think that the major criticism being made of Her Majesty's Government at the moment concerns this question of the arms embargo and whether it is even-handed. The Government say that their intention is that it should be. But will the Right Hon. Gentleman reconsider this question of the supply of arms? I think that it is basically a matter of ammunition for the Centurion tanks, and it may be spare parts as well, although my information is that basically it is ammunition. Is it the case that the Israelis had a shipment ready to go before the battle broke out, that it was delayed purely on the technical ground that another consignment would be ready within a few days and that the battle started between those two dates? If that is so and if the Government wish to be even-handed, ought not they to allow this consignment of ammunition, and possibly the spare parts as well, to go to Israel in order to preserve the neutral position which they say they intend to adopt?

Jim supported Sir Alec's Security Council approach, and went on:

> The Right Hon. Gentleman did not refer to the problem of oil supplies. I hope that he will make it clear to anyone who is using such threats that we are not likely to be intimidated by threats of dislocation to our oil supplies and that such threats will not cause us to change a policy which we believe to be right. That would be monstrous. If we were to pay such a price now we would merely find that the price escalated on a second occasion. If that suggestion is ever put forward, I hope that the Foreign Secretary will deal with it summarily despite the dislocation that it might cause . . .[5]

Sir Alec again expressed his view that he did not think one side would come off better than the other. The Leader of the House then rose to announce the week's business which provided that on the Thursday, two days later, there would be a debate on the Middle East. Sir Alec stuck to his guns; there were to be no spares and ammunition for either side.

Commenting on HM Government's decision, Abba Eban said,

> The relief of the Cabinet and the General Staff [at the American supplies] was deepened by our parallel knowledge that European countries, including Great Britain, were pulling back in panic before the Arab threat to withhold oil supplies. European Governments were not only denying Israel new armaments; they were even forbidding the export of ammunition and spare parts necessary to put existing equipment to work. The decision of Edward Heath and his government in London came as a specially harsh blow at its lowest point in her ordeal. The quantities at stake were not vast, and the material effect to us perhaps not decisive, but the British example affected other European countries. Moreover, British leaders should have been the first to recall the crucial influence of morale and solidarity in lonely hours. Some months later when a British Minister, Sir Keith Joseph, came officially to Israel for Ben-Gurion's funeral, he admitted to me that the Conservative Cabinet never understood how deep a wound its embargo would leave in Israeli opinion. It was only when Harold Wilson's Labour Government came to power that the scar in our relations began to heal.[6]

The Parliamentary Committee ('Shadow Cabinet') of the party had met two evenings earlier to discuss the line. In view of the clamp-down on the supply of spares and ammunition I demanded a three-line whip and met fierce resistance, particularly from Roy Jenkins who, after his resignation from the Shadow Cabinet over the EEC issue[7] in 1973, had finally decided to return to us, and had been elected in the month of Yom Kippur. In the event, I was moved to say,

> Look, Roy, I've accommodated your [expletive deleted] conscience for years. Now you're going to have to take account of mine: I feel as strongly about the Middle East as you do about the Common Market.

I knew there would be heavy abstentions, even cross-voting – and indeed there were meetings to plan them – and the Chief Whip, with my agreement, greeted all approaches on this question with great tolerance. In the event there were not only many abstentions but considerable cross-voting, some Conservatives going into our lobby.*

* Many observers of British politics have been surprised by the fact that Labour left-wingers, who in earlier years were mainly strong supporters of Zionism and Israel, should have developed a marked adherence to the Palestinian cause. Michael Foot, who as a close associate of Aneurin Bevan had shared his views on Israel, explained the change of attitude. He was speaking at a memorial meeting for Will Griffiths, MP for the Exchange Division of Manchester and, in the 1940s, Parliamentary Private Secretary to Aneurin Bevan. Many

Opening the debate, I referred to the death on the Golan Heights of a distinguished British journalist, Nicolas Tomalin:

The House today is debating a tragedy. It is a tragedy first in terms of the heavy casualties on both sides and, unless peace comes quickly, of the inevitability of many, many more casualties. Many of us throughout the House have friends, both Jew and Arab, suddenly torn from their families by the outbreak of fighting, many will not return, and daily each of us waits anxiously for bad news.[8]

When, from our different approaches, we analyse the events which have led to this fresh outbreak of fighting, we are faced with a further tragedy – the tragedy of missed opportunities, of six years of attempts to bring the parties together, to reconcile under the wide sweep – and it is a wide sweep – of Resolution 242 what proved for so long to be irreconcilable claims and demands – on Israel's side the acknowledgment of her right to exist as a nation, her right to secure defensive frontiers, as Resolution 242 sets out; on the Egyptian and Syrian side, their claim based on the resolution's denial of the right of any nation to acquire territories by force; and the problem, far older than those created by the Six Day War, of the Palestinians who lost their homes, in what they too regard as the land of their fathers, in 1948.

This is a problem that I have constantly raised. I have raised it in Israel, in private and in public, and as many of my Hon. Friends know, I have spelled it out on the record at Jewish gatherings in this country. Let there be no argument about this. The Palestinian problem must be dealt with not only in any ultimate permanent solution but even in a temporary and limited solution.[9]

For many years peace was kept by the Tripartite Declaration, which perished with Suez. It was, I think, the then Conservative Government in this country who said that the Tripartite Declaration and guarantees were dead. For 10 years longer the United Nations carried out its peace-keeping role, but that was rudely shattered by U Thant's regrettable decision to recall the United Nations troops when asked to do so by President Nasser. I am not simply saying that now. I said it to U Thant at the time and, indeed, publicly.

From then on, Israel decided that her security could be entrusted to none but her own fighting men. Her neighbours have shown this month that they take the same view about their security. But the Right Hon. Gentleman is right to canvass the idea again. We may have to return to it.

Apart from the question of the arms embargo, I do not want to press too many points of basic disagreement. There are disagreements, and it is

---

people, he said, were surprised at this great change in support: Will Griffiths was entitled to the credit. During the war he had been an ophthalmic optician in Montgomery's Army. When the British moved into Cairo, Griffiths remained there for several months, treating those with eye injuries, the effects of sand and so forth. During this period he made contact with a great many Egyptians, not the richer sort, but the fellahin, and it was they who converted him to the pro-Arab cause. Today, there are one hundred and twenty Labour MPs and twenty members of the House of Lords who are members of the Parliamentary Group of Labour Friends of Israel, but also certainly a quite considerable number who support the Palestine cause. The Conservative Friends of Israel are even more numerous.

absolutely fair to say that, where they occur, they occur on each side of the House. No Party can claim today to put forward homogeneous views, either supporting the Foreign Secretary's policy and basic attitude or opposing them. The only disagreement I would refer to at this point is this: there will be many of us who regret that the Right Hon. Gentleman, having over the past year on a number of occasions voted for and, indeed, on three occasions having sponsored, separately or with the French Government, resolutions condemning Israel for alleged military raids, should have remained silent in condemning the vastly greater act of aggression on the Day of Atonement. Whether or not Right Hon. and Hon. Members on either side of the House like it, I did condemn that aggression and I re-emphasized it early on the following Sunday morning. I stand by what I said.[10]

Britain has been a principal supplier for the Israeli army and navy, most of all for tanks, guns mounted on tanks, ammunition for those guns, and spares. This war, like that of six years ago, is a war predominantly of tanks, anti-tank weapons and aircraft, but now with the new dimension of lethal missiles.

Successive British Governments have supplied Israel, as we have supplied Jordan, in good faith. On Tuesday, some Hon. Members on both sides of the House challenged the good faith of the present Government for their action in dishonouring contractual obligations at the very moment of Israel's greatest need. One Right Hon. Gentleman was reported as having gone so far, outside the House, as to compare them with a dud insurance company which continued to collect premiums but failed to honour the contract when a claim had to be met. I hope that the Government would agree that where arms have been supplied on a continuing basis, only absolutely overriding considerations could justify failure to honour the letter and the spirit of the contract.

I referred to a statement made on 8 June 1967 by the then Foreign Secretary, Michael Stewart, three days after the Six Day War began:

We have no positive response from the Soviet Government about arms supplies and it is clear that for the time being there is no immediate prospect of a general embargo. We are, therefore, reverting to our normal practice of scrutinizing applications for arms in each particular case, and we are, naturally, doing so particularly carefully in the present situation.

I should like, however, to remind the House of the reaction of the Right Hon. Gentleman, the present Foreign Secretary to a statement by the then Foreign Secretary. Having referred to something else which the then Foreign Secretary said about the Arabs' oil embargo, the present Foreign Secretary said:

'We would support, too, the Right Hon. Gentleman's decision on arms as long as the Russians do not co-operate. There are rumours that arms are going into Alexandria' – obviously Russian arms – 'The Government's decision is right.'

The Right Hon. Gentleman said in 1967 that the Government's decision was right. But if it were right then, why is it wrong today?[11]

I say this to the Right Hon. Gentleman, and I say it in all seriousness and not in a contumacious manner. He will, I think, have cause to remember the international problems of the 1930s, in part dominated by the Spanish Civil War. There is almost a ghoulish similarity – (*Laughter*). This is not a laughing matter. The Hon Gentleman could laugh as much as he liked yesterday, but I ask him not to do so today. There is almost a ghoulish similarity in what is happening now and what happened during the Spanish Civil War, including the use of a localized war to test the products of super-Power military technology, hitherto untested, and with no loss of blood on the part of those supplying the technological weapons. (*Laughter.*) I wish that Hon. Members would be serious. This is too important a debate for an attitude like that.

The other parallel with the Spanish Civil War is this: Britain's role in the Spanish Civil War was a policy of what was called – in capital letters – Non-Intervention. That was the posture of the Conservative Government towards the Spanish Civil War and I must remind the Right Hon. Gentleman that statesmen who elevate a posture of non-intervention into an act of State must sometimes expect to be asked, 'Who are you non-intervening against?' That was the position in the Spanish Civil War. I believe that it is the position today.

Between 1968 and 1970 the Israeli Government repeatedly pressed the Labour Government to supply Chieftain tanks in place of Centurions. We had similar requests from Libya. One of the arguments used by the Israelis was the likelihood – indeed, the certainty in their minds – that in time the Arab forces would be supplied with Soviet T62s. It was a difficult decision for us to make.

We informed the Israeli Government that we could not at that time accede to the request for Chieftains. But there was an understanding between the Labour Government and Israel that if at any time the Soviet Government started to supply T62s to Israel's neighbours we would make Chieftains available in strength.

In this fight, many hundreds – the Government know the figure, and I know it – of T62s have been deployed against Israel, on both the Sinai and Syrian fronts. The intelligence facilities available to Her Majesty's Government are such that Ministers must have known of the supply of T62 tanks. They cannot deny it. Both of us know. The Right Hon. Gentleman, the Prime Minister and I know the quality of the intelligence sources. Therefore, they must have known not only of the understanding which we had with the Israelis, but also of the supply of T62s to Israel's neighbours.

But the understanding which my Right Hon. Friend the Member for Fulham [Mr Michael Stewart], then Foreign Secretary, can confirm, has clearly not been accepted by the present Government.[12]

The Foreign Secretary replied to the questions on arms supply:

I am not giving away any secrets when I say that we supply Centurion tanks and ammunition to Jordan as well as to Israel. Does it make sense, when a war has broken out, to go on supplying both countries so that the war will escalate? I will of course keep this whole matter under review as the war proceeds. However, I am sure that the embargo provides us with the best posture for a peace-making effort. That is what matters. The war should be stopped. There should be a cease-fire and we should get down to negotiations about a settlement.[13]

Sir Alec was under strong pressure from the Liberals and from pro-Israeli Conservatives, notably Hugh Fraser. He conceded that the Government had been training Egyptian helicopter pilots, and supplying arms to Jordan, and said,

I have made no secret of the fact that there were contracts. We have not broken the contracts. We have suspended them. (*Interruption.*) I think the laughter is a bit too soon. . . . I will certainly make a full statement in the debate on what my Right Hon. Friend said is a fair balance . . .[14]

At the end I intervened to press Sir Alec further:

The Right Hon. Gentleman has just said that in this situation – and we all accept this – it is difficult to know whether any course is right or wrong. In that spirit, may I ask the Right Hon. Gentleman to look again at the arms embargo? Is he not aware that this must mean that one side has its hands tied by the immobilization of tanks, which it bought for its own defence, by the failure to send ammunition for guns supplied by this country, attached to tanks supplied by this country?

Secondly, when the Right Hon. Gentleman refers to the 1967 embargo – and I should not want to contradict anything that he said – may I ask whether he is not aware that that was announced by the then Government on the basis that we were trying to give a lead and we would have to end the embargo if the lead were not followed? That lead was not followed, and we ended the embargo.

Does not the Right Hon. Gentleman recognize that there is a difference on this occasion – namely, that even before Her Majesty's Government applied the embargo, and before Russia came into the picture, certain countries in North Africa – Libya, Algeria and others – made clear that they would supply arms and would not honour any embargo, and have now started supplying them? Will the Right Hon. Gentleman recognize that the present basis is different from that on which we announced an embargo?[15]

But there is another argument in my mind and that of many of my Hon. Friends. I recognize that this will have no appeal to Hon. Members opposite. Perhaps they will switch off listening for the moment. It is something which concerns us more than them, and I do not apologize.

Israel is a democratic socialist country. More than that, it is a community with a national wealth as well as national burdens shared in common. It is a country which, despite her prodigious arms burden, has established a remarkable record in the social services and care for people, especially for her children. (An Hon. Member: 'Palestinians?') It is now producing better facilities for educating Arabs than they ever had before 1967. I have seen them, as other Hon. Gentlemen have. By certain very difficult tests Israel's record in education, one of the social services, is the finest in the world with the exception of Canada, and I should be prepared to give my evidence for that.

Therefore I believe that something is owed by some of us to the only democratic social State in that vast region. Indeed, by any test that would apply it is the only democracy in that region, and I bitterly regret that at this time more of my fellow democratic Socialist leaders in the Socialist International have not declared where their loyalties lie. Some are corralled in the Foreign Secretary's EEC – the see-no-evil, hear-no-evil, speak-no-evil camp. But the silence has not been confined to them.

I must before I close refer to oil, as the Right Hon. Gentleman did. I agree with the Right Hon. Gentleman. We must not be blackmailed by oil sanctions. No one underestimates the gravity of what is happening on this front – the cost, simply, of the increase in prices and its effect on inflation in this country. We had to face the same situation in 1967. I hope that I may show a little more understanding to the problems of the present Prime Minister than he did then, because that was a most important factor leading to the devaluation in 1967. I understand the position, but we must not be blackmailed. We must decide what is right as a nation, as a Government, as a Parliament, and abide by it. Danegeld is Danegeld, whether exacted by pillagers from the Kattegat or by oil-rich monarchs and presidents.

But the characteristic of Danegeld through the ages is insatiability. They come again. Their appetite feeds on appeasement . . .[16]

I went on to welcome Sir Alec's statement that questions of oil supply did not enter into the reasons underlying the Government's policy.

In the debate which followed, and more particularly in the vote, some committed Labour friends of the Arab standpoint supported the Government; equally, Conservative friends of Israel spoke and voted with the Opposition. There voted, For, 251; Against, 175, a Government majority of 76. The tally as recorded in the issue of *Hansard* published next morning showed that 17 Conservative Members voted with the Opposition and 15 Labour Members voted with the Government. The Liberal Party voted against the Government.

On 22 October the Security Council issued its call to the combatants in Resolution 338.

The Security Council

Calls upon all parties to the present fighting to cease all firing and terminate all military activity immediately, no later than 12 hours after the moment of adoption of this decision, in the positions they now occupy;

Calls upon the parties concerned to start immediately after the cease-fire the implementation of Security Council resolution 242 (1967) in all of its parts;

Decides that, immediately and concurrently with the cease-fire, negotiations start between the parties concerned under appropriate auspices, aimed at establishing a just and durable peace in the Middle East.

Four days later the cease-fire was agreed at the UN. Another two days, and the fighting ceased.

The inquest did not. Labour MPs continued to harry the Government Front Bench, who took refuge in the fact that the warring parties were sending representatives to Geneva to negotiate a final settlement.

Golda Meir, the Israeli Prime Minister, was anxious to state Israel's case to the European Socialist leaders, a number of whom she felt had betrayed her in her country's most dangerous hour and had given comfort to her country's enemies. She telephoned me to propose a conference of the Socialist International (the confederate body of the world's Labour and Democratic Socialist Parties). She asked me to approach Anker Jørgensen, the Danish Socialist premier, to inquire whether his party would host such a gathering. He demurred, so I offered London. The conference met on Monday 12 November. Among those attending were Bruno Kreisky, the Austrian Chancellor; Edmond Leburton, the Belgian Prime Minister; James Callaghan, Shadow Foreign Secretary and then chairman of the British Labour Party; François Mitterrand, the first secretary of the French Socialist Party; Willy Brandt, Leader of the German Social Democratic Party; Justin Keating, the Minister of Trade and Industry in the Irish Republic; Brendan Halligan, the secretary of the Irish Labour Party; Dom Mintoff, the Maltese Prime Minister; Sir Seewoosagur Ramgoolam, the Prime Minister of Mauritius; Joop den Uyl, the Dutch Prime Minister; Trygve Bratteli, the Norwegian Prime Minister; Olof Palme, the Prime Minister of Sweden, and Pietro Nenni, President of the Italian Socialist Party.

The Times report on 12 November was an accurate account of my press briefing at the end of the conference, where the discussion had been so disjointed and diffuse that I had, half an hour before press and TV (thirty-five cameras), to ask what I could fairly report as nothing had been agreed. In the end it was suggested that we were agreed that any resolution should be within the terms of (Britain's) UN Resolution 242, Golda Meir insisting that we should now bracket with it the new text, 338, which she regarded as being helpful to Israel. This was agreed.

The Times summed up in these words:

Mrs Golda Meir, the Israel Prime Minister, yesterday spoke to socialist leaders in London for nearly an hour, but probably failed in what she hoped to achieve.

Although she received individual support for Israel's case at a meeting under the aegis of the Socialist International, the socialist leaders also decided to consider setting up a study group to establish relations with the Arab countries.

No communiqué was issued after the conference, and it seemed clear that Mrs Meir had failed to get a pledge of support from the Socialist International for the Israel cause. She is to hold her own press conference in London today.

The conference had been called at the instigation of Mrs Meir, with the backing of Herr Willy Brandt, the West German Chancellor.

Mr Harold Wilson, leader of the British Labour Party, told a press conference afterwards that although he had been deeply afraid that there might have been a confrontation, the conference had been more comradely than one might have expected.

Mrs Meir had spelt out the Israel case. She had told the 21 socialist leaders – nine of whom were Prime Ministers – of the tragedy of the Middle East conflict, not only for the mothers of Israeli sons who had been killed, but also for the Arab mothers.

Mrs Meir said that in terms of population, Israel had lost two and a half times as many soldiers killed as the United States had in ten years in Indo-China. Israel was a small country and during the conflict had felt at times very alone.

Mr Heath received Mrs Meir on the day after the conference. She had told me she was not anxious to see him, having regard to the Government's refusal of spare parts and ammunition. I insisted that she should do so, and later received the impression that she expressed herself with, if anything, even more than her customary vigour.

It was interesting that a London Conservative evening paper made the story of her brief visit to Downing Street their main front-page headline. For why? There was a by-election in Hove three days later. The Conservatives were in trouble, and very many British Jews live in the Brighton area. Golda's call on Ted proved a great help to him: there was no suggestion that she was in London on Labour's invitation. (Hove was held by the Conservatives on a minority vote, the general election majority of 18,648 falling to 4,846.)

The terms of settlement were soon agreed, Egypt continuing to accept *force majeure* Israel's 'illegal' hold over Sinai, the Negev and the Eilat approaches. But mutual aggro continued over the Gaza Strip and Israel's occupation of settlements in the desert, and their plans to build new settlements. One of these, near the mini-oilfield of Abu Rodeis, was particularly sensitive, and the US quickly perceived that there must be a settlement if the danger of a new war, or at least continuing local hostilities, was to be averted. Through Dr Kissinger, pressures began for a negotiated local rearrangement of boundaries to reassert unequivocally Egypt's right to the oil sites.

Richard Nixon left the White House in 1974 and was replaced as President by Gerald Ford, who, on Vice-President Agnew's disgrace, had been selected as Vice-President. Earlier in the year the Labour Party had won the General Election in Great Britain and I was back at No. 10 Downing Street. Ford was new to foreign affairs, but as I noticed in subsequent meetings with him in 1974 and afterwards, he had fully mastered the tutorial briefings of Henry Kissinger, shortly to be moved up to Secretary of State.

In the spring of 1975 the President was becoming increasingly restive at Israeli tactics, including their border raids, east and west, but mainly on the Lebanon border. When I met him on a set-piece Prime Ministerial visit in February, still more when I called on him on my way home from the Commonwealth Prime Ministers' Conference, held in Jamaica in May 1975, he outlined with increasing emphasis his strictures on Israeli policy. What he wanted me to do was to communicate his views, amounting almost to threats of a fundamental reappraisal of US–Israeli relations, to Jerusalem in the hope that Israel would be more restrained in her threats against Egypt.

We met in the Oval Room in the White House, James Callaghan and myself, the President and Henry Kissinger, together with two officials – General Scowcroft for the President, and Sir John Hunt, Cabinet Secretary, on our side. Ford was very direct, no doubt intending that my close relationship with Israel would lead me to pass on the warning he was anxious to register. As we left the Oval Room, Henry Kissinger underlined what the President had said. In the next few weeks, certainly by June, the President would have carried out a fundamental reappraisal, and whatever decision he might reach, the Israelis should not take him for granted. Kissinger called on me in London the following month and reiterated the warning. The reappraisal might be announced in June, or be deferred until July – not later. Nothing was heard of it in June, but I was told that we should be discussing it 'in the margins' of the all-Europe Conference at Helsinki at the end of July.*

Delegates assembled in Helsinki on Tuesday 29 July. On the Wednesday morning James Callaghan and I had breakfast with the President and Henry Kissinger. The main subject we discussed was the increasingly serious situation, as they now regarded it, in the Middle East. Gerald Ford's 'agonizing reappraisal' was about to be made public. Unless there were real moves to a peace settlement amounting to a palpable change in Israel's attitude to her Arab neighbours, particularly in Sinai, Washington's traditional support of Israel would give way to a much more pragmatic and tough approach. The Americans again wanted to use my close relations with Israel to get the message across. Late the previous night I had had a visit from Eppi Evron, a former minister at Israel's London Embassy, and at the time of writing Ambassador to the United States. He explained that, having been working very hard, he had decided to take a holiday and had borrowed

---

* The Governments invited were from all the countries of Europe, plus the United States and Canada in view of their close ties with and commitments to Europe.

the Helsinki apartment of the Israeli Ambassador to Sweden, who was also accredited to Finland.

I received a series of telephone calls from Gideon Rafael, the Israeli Ambassador in London. To both I administered the American message. Kissinger was going to put a stop to his shuttle service between Israel and Egypt, in which he found himself carrying negotiating points from one to the other, and from now on he was available only when the two sides could find a policy on which they could agree. He would be prepared to make one more visit only, and that would be to 'tie up the terms of an agreement between the two parties'. Not only did the Israelis want a more advantageous territorial settlement than the US thought possible or reasonable. Kissinger was trying to negotiate an agreement between two parties which was difficult enough: the Israelis were making it still more difficult by continually shouting the odds in public as to what they could and could not accept. In passing this on to Jerusalem via Ambassador Evron, I used Attlee's famous phrase about Churchill, who had got into Parliamentary difficulties by an ill-judged intervention: 'Trouble with Winston: nailed his trousers to the mast, can't climb down.'

There was another message I wanted to get through to Israel. Plans were advanced in the United Nations to expel Israel from the Organization. It had been actively canvassed with delegates from the developing countries. who were ready to vote for it, thus ensuring that it would be carried. Britain, the US and most West European countries would vote against it. I told Eppi Evron that on the way home from Helsinki, European socialist leaders were stopping off in Stockholm for a meeting of European members of the Socialist International. My strong message to Prime Minister Rabin was that he should be present at Stockholm so that we could concert our policies on the Afro-Asian threat at the UN. Rabin in fact was there, and useful publicity was given to our unanimous decision to oppose the expulsion of Israel, or indeed any other state. In the event no such motion came up before the UN.

On 31 July President Ford, Giscard d'Estaing and Helmut Schmidt joined us for lunch at the British Embassy. Once again Gerald Ford issued his warning to Israel, perhaps in the belief that the others, as well as Britain, would pass the message through to Jerusalem. He began by condemning Israel for going public during delicate negotiations. He was not going to put American troops into any peace-making role, for example in the Sinai passes between Israel and Egypt. The Israelis should be made to understand that if the agreement they were working for did not materialize by the end of August, he would make his long-threatened statement of reappraisal early in September. Ford's hope that Giscard d'Estaing would make common cause with the US and Britain in seeking an agreement in Israel was disappointed.

Giscard flatly refused to be associated. It was, in fact, due to Giscard that the Middle Eastern question had become an issue between members of the European Economic Community. As a preliminary to the Labour Government's insistence on 'renegotiating' the terms of Britain's entry to the EEC, as negotiated by Mr Heath in 1973, President Giscard d'Estaing of France, which then held the EEC chair, organized a meeting of Heads of Government in Paris in December 1974. We lunched at the Elysée and then adjourned to a drawing-room, where he launched a discussion on Israel and her neighbours, clearly having prepared the ground with Chancellor Helmut Schmidt of Germany. Both of them took a strong anti-Israeli line, which provoked me to argue the contrary case. All our colleagues then joined in and, as we left for the afternoon formal session, I checked with the Prime Ministers of Belgium and Luxembourg. My calculation was that the Giscard–Schmidt thesis had been opposed by 5 to 4, but my colleagues reckoned it was 6 to 3.

Up to the time of writing, in 1980, there have been no developments in Israel, or in her relations with her neighbours which have involved Britain. A study of *Hansard* reveals some forty Parliamentary questions, nearly all written, with written answers, and with the barest mention in debates. Some of the later questions, again mostly written, show some evidence of left-wing inspiration, mostly designed to secure an answer critical of Israel.

In the spring and summer of 1978 – I had resigned the Premiership two years earlier – the press headlined cases of murder and attempted murder, two bomb explosions in Jerusalem, Israeli bombing and armed forays directed against Lebanon and Syria, the shooting in London of members of the crew of an El Al airliner, and the murder of Said Hammami, a friend of mine, the European representative of the Palestine Liberation Organization, by a Palestinian extremist who broke into his London office and shot him dead. On the other side, Israel was accused by the Syrian Government on 12 April 1978 of 'seriously escalating' the Middle Eastern conflict by fitting a booby-trapped listening device to the main Damascus–Amman telephone cable to monitor communications between Syria and Jordan. Syrian experts examining the monitoring system exploded the device, killing eight Syrian soldiers and four civilians and, the Syrian statement complained, releasing radioactive particles.

It was an American initiative, however, which brought greatest prominence during this period to Arab–Israeli relations: the tripartite talks between President Carter, President Sadat and Prime Minister Begin in September 1978.

On 8 August Washington announced that President Sadat and Mr Begin had accepted President Carter's invitation to join him at Camp David, the

President's country residence, named by President Eisenhower after his son. On 17 September the two leaders signed in Jimmy Carter's presence two preliminary agreements intended to lead to the negotiation of a treaty of peace within three months. Unfortunately a dispute broke out between Israel and Egypt about the duration of the agreed ban on new Israeli settlements on the West Bank, Menachem Begin arguing that the provision lasted only three months, on his assumption that the negotiations to set up a self-governing authority in the West Bank and Gaza areas would be concluded in the three months' limit set for bilateral agreement on a peace treaty.

Certainly nothing achieved in Camp David has led to any improvement in the relations between Israel and her other neighbours, Syria, Lebanon and Jordan. Indeed, they have worsened, especially since President Sadat's visit to Israel, Menachem Begin's return visit and Sadat's second visit. Arab – and particularly Palestinian – hostility to Sadat has grown. He has virtually become *persona non grata* with the rest of the Arab world.[17]

This study of the impact of Zionism – Balfour, Churchill, the Mandate and the surrender of the Mandate, wars, rumours of war, dictated settlements and the rare voluntary agreement – right up to the present time, has recorded the slow fulfilment of Weizmann's dream.

So at the time of writing, the historic Camp David agreements seem for the foreseeable future to have measurably improved relations between Israel and Egypt, while sharpening the hostility of the rest of the Arab world against Israel, and indeed against Egypt. But partly – and by no means exclusively – because of the cost of maintaining Israel on an almost permanent quasi-military régime, Israel's economy faces great strains. Her overseas payments deficit has reached £1½ billion a year, over £370 per head of the population, man, woman and child. In his book, *Story of My Life*, Moshe Dayan highlights the burden of military preparedness:

> According to the figures published by the Institute of Strategic Studies in London, Israel maintains in *peacetime* an army whose size and cost, in proportion to her population and economy, greatly exceeds those in other countries. The Air Force and armor represent 80 per cent of Israel's military strength – and if this figure is compared with the situation in other countries, it offers a true reflection of her burden. According to the Institute's figures for 1974–75, Britain, with a population of 56.4 million, maintained 900 tanks and 500 combat aircraft, and France, with a population of 52.4 million, had 950 tanks and 461 planes. In the same comparative table, Israel, with a population of only 3.3 million, had 2,700 tanks and 461 warplanes. In further contrast, Egypt, Syria, Jordan and Iraq, with a total population of 58.6 million, maintained 6,600 tanks and 1,189 combat aircraft.[18]

That is part of the problem. But no less significant and worrying has been the impact of inflation and the nationwide reaction to it which has simply aggravated and intensified it.

There is hardly a man of military age who, if a further war came, would not lay down his peacetime pursuits, lay down his life too. But those same men are responsible for the debauching of Israel's economic life. At the time of writing, inflation has reached a year-on-year rate of about 160 per cent, and many serious observers inside and outside Israel believe that it has now become endemic and self-generating. The system of Government – factions rather than parties, cobbled coalitions – has created a political and administrative system dedicated to drift.

Israel, in such years of peace as she has been vouchsafed, has achieved miracle after miracle in creating new industries, new technologies, great advances in science, driven back the desert and created vast areas of high agricultural fertility, producing fruit, flowers and vital raw materials for her own use and for export. Few, if any, of those who eighty years ago and more preached the new Zionist dream could have foreseen these achievements, even with the full flow of billions in dollars and sterling from the diaspora. But none at all could have foreseen the deterioration in economic morale and this present destructive refusal to sacrifice their demands for higher living standards in order to make their country viable.

It would be a terrible epitaph if some dedicated Zionist or friendly Gentile were forced to sit down and write the story of a people who created a nation, who fought war after war to assert their freedom, who conquered desert and mountain range, overcame starvation and primeval drought, but who perished on the altar of short-term, self-delusive personal advantage.

Postscript
June 1980

IN MID-APRIL THIS YEAR I visited Israel to make the principal speech in the commemoration of the life and achievements of Yigal Allon, my closest friend among all the Israelis. The impression I formed of Israel, under Menachem Begin's Government, was the unhappiest I have known. In addition to the inflation rate, Israel at this time suffers from a theocratic and bitterly divided Government. Begin is obsessed with the divisive question of Jewish control over the disputed West Bank. Following Dayan's resignation from his Government in October 1979, General Weizman, nephew of Israel's first President and a member of Likud, has resigned from the Government and is now publicly – lethally perhaps – attacking Begin. The Prime Minister, for his part, brought Shamir into his Government, leader of the Stern faction which murdered Churchill's close friend, the Middle East High Commissioner Lord Moyne. Shamir was appointed Foreign Secretary and, following Weizman's resignation, Begin sought to move him to the vacant Defence post, which immediately led to resignation threats: Begin himself then took over Defence.

At the time of going to press, there is also great confusion and provocation about the Begin Government's activities on the West Bank and in the Gaza Strip, as well as in his decision to move his office to one of the most hotly contested areas of Jerusalem.

The international guild of retired Prime Ministers has an unwritten rule of not interfering in the internal affairs of friendly countries. At the risk of breaching that doctrine, I have at least felt it necessary to express my anxieties about the present state of affairs in Israel. By the time this book is printed, maybe a great deal will have happened: public opinion polls show a great rallying to the opposition Labour Party led by Shimon Peres, currently calling for an early general election. Many of Israel's overseas friends would welcome a Government of National Unity led by the leader of the party gaining the most seats. That must be for Israel's politicians to decide. For my part, I should commend a different system of elections.

Political philosophers for centuries have drawn the distinction between legislatures elected by *scrutin de liste* and those where *scrutin d'arrondissement* applies. Israel has the former system. In that small country each major party submits a list of candidates usually equal to the number of Knesset seats, placing them in order of precedence. Thus if the party secures, say, thirty-five seats, the top thirty-five become members, number thirty-six and the others being left out in the cold. It is difficult to imagine a more invidious task for any democratic leader. I cannot imagine any party leader wishing to be faced with the task of deciding whether to put a left-wing Scot ahead of a right-wing Englishman, and even the National Executive Committee of the Labour Party might find it a difficult task.

I have in fact found considerable, indeed surprising, support in Israel for a system based on individual constituencies, despite the prior requisite that Israel must decide first exactly where its national boundaries lie. Even in so small a country there would be a great advantage in a member of Parliament being able to commune with a body of local constituents. The British House of Commons derives its name from House of Communes or Communities, and, whatever our faults, we have been able to claim that our Lower House represents, and draws ideas and inspiration from, radically different local communities. Israel is perhaps not too confined or beleaguered a state to learn from our experience.

Appendices

I

Extract from the Peel Report: immigration figures

2. The following statistics show the authorized immigration from September, 1920, to the end of 1936:—

Year	Recorded Immigration	
	Jews	Non-Jews
1920 (September–October)	5,514	202
1921	9,149	190
1922	7,844	284
1923	7,421	570
1924	12,856	697
1925	33,801	840
1926	13,081	829
1927	2,713	882
1928	2,178	908
1929	5,249	1,317
1930	4,944	1,489
1931	4,075	1,458
1932	9,553	1,736
1933	30,327	1,650
1934	42,359	1,784
1935	61,854	2,293[*]
1936	29,727	1,944[†]

[*] Of these 903 were Arabs.   [†] Of these 675 were Arabs.

Poland supplied the largest proportion of these immigrants, the countries next in order as sources of supply being Russia, Germany, and Roumania. In recent years immigration from Russia has almost entirely ceased, and her place has been taken by Germany, which comes second in the list of countries from which immigrants arrive. The Department of Migration estimates the numbers of the Jewish community in Palestine in 1936 at 370,483 out of a total population in that year of 1,336,518, or just on 30 per cent. of the population. To the above-mentioned figure of 370,483 must be added a considerable figure for the numbers of illegal Jewish immigrants in Palestine.

II

*Memorandum by Sir Bernard Braine D.L., MP**

In 1947 I was invited by the War Office to give a series of lectures to British troops in North Western Germany.

On the morning of 6 September, following a lecture to the 1st Battalion Sherwood Foresters in Hamburg, a Sergeant, whose name I cannot recall, asked me if I would have supper with him that evening. He told me that he was troubled about certain matters and wanted my advice. He was a pleasant and well-educated man and I readily agreed.

For weeks previously the newspapers at home had been full of disturbing stories from Palestine where the army had been trying to cope with an increasingly violent and emotive situation.

In July the cargo ship *President Warfield* (*Exodus*) carrying 4,554 illegal Jewish survivors of the holocaust had been intercepted off the coast of Palestine. They were now being forcibly shipped back to Europe in three British ships and after attempts had been made to land them in France, their destination was rumoured to be Germany.

On 31 July, before I left home, two British Sergeants, kidnapped in Palestine by Jewish extremists, had been found hanged, their bodies booby-trapped, in an orange grove at Nathanya, and some newspapers were beginning to say that the situation was too hot to handle and it was time for us to leave Palestine.

Not unnaturally I was questioned about all this at the end of my lectures and I sensed that some officers and men were uneasy about the situation.

On the afternoon following my lecture to the Sherwood Foresters I was driven, at my request, to the site of the infamous Belsen concentration camp. All that remained were the huge mass graves of the tens of thousands who had perished there before and after the liberation. It was a shattering experience.

It was then that I learnt, to my horror, that nearby was the main collecting point for all remaining Jews in the British zone, including survivors of the Belsen Camp. That this could be sited so close to where vast numbers of people had died in such cruel circumstances seemed beyond belief.

Clearly this provided an opportunity to find out what survivors of the holocaust felt about British policy in Palestine. I entered the camp and asked the watchman at the gate, a small quiet man who spoke a little English, if I could see whoever was in charge. He took me to the Camp Office and while we walked I asked him what he himself hoped to do. He replied that he was going to Palestine by one means or another. Where else could he go? He had lost his wife, children and parents in one of the death camps; he had nothing left save hope of Zion.

The Camp Commandant was a burly cockney who had served in the Royal Artillery and who I imagine had been appointed to take charge by the Jewish Agency. I asked him the same question. He did not answer, but called together about a dozen camp leaders and told me to put the question to them. They came

---

* Hearing that I was writing a book on *The State of Israel in British Politics*, Sir Bernard Braine, MP for the Thanet constituency, prepared this memorandum arising out of his own experiences in relation to the Belsen concentration camp.

from all over Europe, some had been partisans, some had been freed from Belsen, but all had lost close relatives and friends in the death camps. In their view Europe had rejected the Jews. There was no future for them there, nor were they interested in starting new lives in Britain or America. They were determined to go to Palestine and shape a new destiny for themselves.

They made a special point of saying that they did not approve of violence. They had seen enough of it, but were prepared to fight for a Jewish homeland, if necessary. They left me in no doubt whatsoever as to their determination to go to Palestine by hook or by crook.

I returned to Hamburg and that evening had supper with the Sherwood Forester Sergeant. He told me that although he bore a British name, he was of German-Jewish origin, having been sent to Britain as a child in the early 1930s. He had been given a British identity and as soon as he was old enough had joined the British Army and had been trained as a paratrooper. He told me that he had been detailed to take part in an operation the following day (7 September) to remove illegal Jewish immigrants from one of the ships bringing them back from Palestine and, if necessary, force would have to be used. He was deeply distressed about this and had made up his mind to disobey orders.

Although I learnt later that these hapless refugees were not to be taken to the Belsen Camp, but to two other former concentration camps near Lubeck, I do not think that either of us knew this at the time and I could fully understand the Sergeant's terrible dilemma. I told him that he had the right to appeal to his Commanding Officer, should exercise this without delay, and somehow get a message to me if he ran into any difficulty. As it happened the disembarkation was delayed by fog and did not begin until 8 September. I did not hear from him again and have always presumed that he was relieved of a duty which he should not have been ordered to undertake in the first place. When I returned home I reported all this to a Jewish Agency representative in London.

Ironically, while I was in Hamburg I had the distinct impression that even the German civilian population was horrified that we were bringing these refugees back to the country where they had suffered so much, and I think this itself was upsetting to the troops. What struck me at the time was not merely the inhumanity of what was being done and the psychological blunder of bringing these people back to the hated soil of Germany, but the sheer futility of it all at a time when we had lost control in Palestine itself.

20 November 1979   Bernard Braine

III

An Exchange of Letters Between Attlee and Truman, 1945

When Attlee, apparently to his great surprise, found himself Prime Minister at the head of an unchallengeable majority, there awaited him at No. 10 Downing Street a letter from President Truman, addressed to Churchill on 24 July 1945:[1]

To: The Prime Minister.   The White House,
From: The President.   Washington.
                                                          July 24, 1945.

There is great interest in America in the Palestine problem. The drastic restrictions imposed on Jewish immigration by the British White Paper of May, 1939, continue to provoke passionate protest from Americans most interested in Palestine and in the Jewish problem. They fervently urge the lifting of these restrictions which deny to Jews, who have been so cruelly uprooted by ruthless Nazi persecutions, entrance into the land which represents for so many of them their only hope of survival.

Knowing your deep and sympathetic interest in Jewish settlement in Palestine I venture to express to you the hope that the British Government may find it possible without delay to take steps to lift the restrictions of the White Paper on Jewish immigration into Palestine.

While I realize the difficulties of reaching a definite and satisfactory settlement of the Palestine problem, and that we cannot expect to discuss these difficulties at any length at our present meeting, I have some doubt whether these difficulties will be lessened by prolonged delay. I hope, therefore, that you can arrange at your early convenience to let me have your ideas.

Attlee sent a brief acknowledgment:

                                                                 Berlin
                                                           31st July 1945

Memorandum to the President from the Prime Minister.

'I have read your memorandum of July 24 about Palestine. You will, I am sure, understand that I cannot give you any statement on policy until we have had time to consider the matter, and this is simply to inform you that we will give early and careful consideration to your memorandum.'

Truman had sent the Dean of the University of Pennsylvania Law School, and US representative on the Intergovernmental Committee on Refugees, Earl G. Harrison, on a European mission to report on the refugee problem. In the light of this, Truman wrote to Attlee on 31 August enclosing a copy of the Harrison report:

In view of our conversations at Potsdam I am sure that you will find certain portions of the report interesting. I am, therefore, sending you a copy.

I should like to call your attention to the conclusions and recommendations – especially the references to Palestine. It appears that the available certificates for immigration to Palestine will be exhausted in the near future. It is suggested that the granting of an additional one hundred thousand of such certificates would contribute greatly to a sound solution for the future of Jews still in Germany and Austria, and for other Jewish refugees who do not wish to remain where they are or who for understandable reasons do not desire to return to their countries of origin.

On the basis of this and other information which has come to me, I concur in the belief that no other single matter is so important for those who have known the horrors of concentration camps for over a decade as is the future of immigration possibilities into Palestine. The number of such persons who wish immigration to Palestine or who would qualify for admission there is, unfortunately, no longer as large as it was before the Nazis began their extermination programme. As I said to you in Potsdam, the American people, as a whole, firmly believe that immigration into Palestine should not be closed, and that a reasonable number of Europe's persecuted Jews should, in accordance with their wishes, be permitted to resettle there.

I know you are in agreement on the proposition that future peace in Europe depends in large measure upon our finding sound solutions of problems confronting the displaced and formerly persecuted groups of people. No claim is more meritorious than that of the groups who for so many years have known persecution and enslavement.

The main solution appears to lie in the quick evacuation of as many as possible of the non-repatriable Jews, who wish it, to Palestine. If it is to be effective, such action should not be long delayed.

Very sincerely yours,   HARRY TRUMAN

Attlee began firmly to resist the President's pressure and pointed out that not all the immigration certificates available to the refugee organizations had been taken up. On 16 September he sent the fuller reply he had promised:

Prime Minister to President Truman.   16.9.45
I am now in a position to give you a considered reply, which I am telegraphing in order to save time, to your letter of August 31 enclosing a copy of Mr Harrison's report.

I am sure you will appreciate the very grave difficulties that have confronted our representatives on the Control Commission, and from my own investigation of the matter it is quite clear that they have endeavoured to avoid treating people on a racial basis. Had they done this, then there would have been violent reactions on the part of other people who had been confined to these concentration camps. One must remember that within these camps were people from almost every race in Europe and there appears to have been very little difference in the amount of torture and treatment they had to undergo. Now, if our officers had placed the Jews in a special racial category at the head of the queue, my strong view is that the effect of this would have been disastrous for the Jews and therefore their attempt to treat them alike was a right one. After all, the situation in Central Europe is appalling. The number of displaced persons, refugees from concentration camps, the violent driving of people from one territory to another, is one of the most horrible events in human history. So concerned are we about the starvation generally in that area that we have been taking steps to try and prevent epidemics arising and spreading to other countries. On this matter we shall be communicating with the State Department as soon as possible.

With reference to immediate relief there is a camp at Philippeville, North Africa, capable of taking 30,000 and another one at Felada with a capacity of 5,000. I suggest that, in order to relieve immediate suffering, these two places be used. I understand that UNRRA have it under their control. It would of course involve our Commanders in the task of sorting them out. This, however, should relieve the situation.

In the case of Palestine we have the Arabs to consider as well as the Jews, and there have been solemn undertakings, I understand, given by your predecessor, yourself and by Mr Churchill, that before we come to a final decision and operate it, there would be consultation with the Arabs. It would be very unwise to break these solemn pledges and so set aflame the whole Middle East. I know you realize that, as things are, the responsibility of preserving order with all the consequences involved rests entirely on this country.

As I mentioned in my earlier telegram, the Jews are not now using the numbers of certificates available and up to the present have not taken up the 1,500 available for this month which were offered them. Apparently they are insisting upon the complete repudiation of the White Paper and the immediate granting of 100,000 certificates quite regardless of the effect on the situation in the Middle East which this would have.

In addition to this problem we are engaged upon another related one and that is India. The fact that there are ninety million Moslems, who are easily inflamed, in that country compels us to consider the problem from this aspect also. Therefore, while sympathizing with the views of Mr Harrison and weighing them very carefully, we believe that the suggestion which he has made raises very far-reaching implications, which would have to be most carefully balanced against the considerations which I have set out above.

He then set out the problem the Government was facing as a result of the conflicting and incompatible claims of Arabs and Jews:

Both communities lay claim to Palestine; the one on the ground of a millennium of occupation, the other on the ground of historic association and of an undertaking given it to during the First World War. The antithesis is thus complete.

The repercussions of the conflict have spread far beyond the small land in which it has arisen. The Zionist cause has strong supporters in the United States, in Great Britain, in the Dominions and elsewhere; civilization has been appalled by the sufferings which have been inflicted in recent years on the persecuted Jews of Europe. On the other side of the picture, the cause of the Palestinian Arabs has been espoused by the whole Arab world and more lately has become a matter of keen interest to their ninety million co-religionists in India. In Palestine itself, there is always serious risk of disturbances on the part of one community or the other, and such disturbances are bound to find their reflection in a much wider field. Considerations not only of equity and of humanity but also of international amity and world peace are thus involved in any search for a solution . . .

In regard to the immediate future, His Majesty's Government have decided that the only practicable course is to maintain the present arrangement for immigration. The Government of the United States will realize that His Majesty's Government have inherited, in Palestine, a most difficult legacy and their task is greatly complicated by undertakings, given at various times to various parties, which they feel themselves bound to honour. Any violent departure decided upon in the face of Arab opposition, would not only afford ground for a charge of breach of faith against His Majesty's Government but would probably cause serious disturbances throughout the Middle East, involving a large military commitment, and would arouse widespread anxiety in India. Further, the Arabs have not forgotten the assurances given by the late President Roosevelt and by President Truman, to the heads of Arab States, of their desire that no decision should be taken in respect to the basic situation in Palestine without full consultation with both Arabs and Jews. It can hardly be contended that a decision to depart from the present policy in respect of immigration would not constitute a decision in respect to the basic situation in that country.

Truman was under increasing pressure from American Zionist leaders to reject any British proposals which excluded the proposal that 100,000 refugees should be admitted at once to Palestine. Attlee finally agreed at a meeting in Washington with the President (on atomic energy) to setting up the joint Commission of Members of Parliament and of Congress.

On 31 July, as recorded on page 174 above, Truman pulled the rug from under the feet of Attlee and Bevin by his statement rejecting the entire line of the British proposals.

Source Notes

INTRODUCTION: *The Diaspora*

1. Abba Eban, *My People*, London, 1968, p. 104.
2. Psalm cxxxvii, I.
3. Eban, *My People*, pp. 104–6.
4. Royal Commission on Palestine (Peel Commission), 1937, Cmd 5479, p. 8.
5. Amos Elon, *The Israelis, Founders and Sons*, London, 1971.
6. Peel, Cmd 5479, p. 11.

CHAPTER 1: *The Zionists*

1. Leon Pinsker, *Auto-Emancipation*, published anonymously in Berlin in 1882.
2. In addition to general histories of the period and the biographies of his contemporaries, see in particular Amos Elon, *Herzl*, London, 1975.
3. Elon, *Herzl*, p. 112.
4. Elon, *Herzl*, p. 115.
5. Elon, *Herzl*, p. 127.
6. Edward Crankshaw, *The Shadow of the Winter Palace: The Drift to Revolution, 1825–1917*, London, 1976, pp. 282–3. See also pp. 371–3 for the growth in 1908–9 of the 'Union of the Russian People' and the 'Society of Michael the Archangel', with their Black Hundred Gangsters and their vicious anti-semitism; and in 1911 the murder by a Jew, D. G. Bogrov (also a Social Revolutionary and police agent), of Stolypin, the Czar's first minister.
7. Elon, *Herzl*, p. 179.
8. Chaim Weizmann, *Trial and Error*, London, 1949, p. 115.
9. Simon Schama, *Two Rothschilds and the Land of Israel*, London, 1978, p. 17. The two Rothschilds were Baron Edmond de Rothschild (1845–1934) and his son, Baron James de Rothschild (1878–1957).
10. Schama, *Two Rothschilds . . .*, pp. 66–7.
11. Chaim Weizmann, 'Letters and Papers', vol. 6, p. 117; the quotation reported is in

Schama, *Two Rothschilds . . .*, p. 193.
12. Weizmann, *Trial and Error*, p. 12.
13. Weizmann, *Trial and Error*, p. 29.
14. In 'The Biographical Facts' in *Chaim Weizmann, Statesman of the Jewish Renaissance*, ed. Dan Leon and Yehuda Adin, Jerusalem, 1974 (for the centenary of Weizmann's birth).
15. Weizmann, *Trial and Error*, p. 15.
16. Weizmann, *Trial and Error*, p. 15.
17. Weizmann, *Trial and Error*, p. 118.

CHAPTER 2: *Balfour, Churchill and the Mandate: 1905–22*

1. Blanche E. C. Dugdale, *Arthur James Balfour*, vol. 1, London, 1939, p. 433.
2. Dugdale, *Arthur James Balfour*, vol. 1, p. 435; Weizmann, *Trial and Error*, pp. 143–4.
3. Dugdale, *Arthur James Balfour*, vol. 1, p. 435.
4. Dugdale, *Arthur James Balfour*, vol. 2, p. 217.
5. Weizmann, *Trial and Error*, pp. 161 and 164.
6. H. M. Blumberg, *Weizmann: His Life and Times*, Israel, 1975, p. 42.
7. Weizmann, *Trial and Error*, pp. 191–2.
8. Earl of Oxford and Asquith, *Memories and Reflections, 1852–1927*, vol. 2, London, 1928, pp. 59–60.
9. Asquith, *Memories and Reflections*, pp. 66–7.
10. Asquith, *Memories and Reflections*, pp. 219–20.
11. Lloyd George, *War Memoirs*, London, 1933, vol. 2, p. 586.
12. The map as it finally emerged is reproduced in the end-papers of Roger Adelson's *Mark Sykes, Portrait of an Amateur*, London, 1975, by far the best account of the historic Sykes-Picot transactions.
13. Weizmann, *Trial and Error*, p. 85.

14. A letter from Weizmann to Sir Ronald Graham, Assistant to the British Foreign Secretary, 13 June 1917, as part of his campaign to hasten the Balfour Declaration. Blumberg, *Weizmann . . .*, pp. 54–5.
15. Weizmann, *Trial and Error*, p. 235.
16. Weizmann, *Trial and Error*, p. 220.
17. For the authoritative account of Allenby's Jerusalem campaign, see Brian Gardner, *Allenby*, London, 1975, pp. 115–64. Lawrence's capture of Aqaba is described on pp. 135–8. For his destruction of a Turkish supply train by hidden explosive, see pp. 141–2.
18. Gardner, *Allenby*, p. 160.
19. Weizmann, *Trial and Error*, p. 200.
20. Christopher Sykes, *Cross Roads to Israel*, London, 1965.
21. Sykes, *Cross Roads to Israel*, p. 24.
22. Weizmann, *Trial and Error*, pp. 280–81.
23. Weizmann, *Trial and Error*, p. 308.
24. Kenneth Rose, *Superior Person*, London, 1969, pp. 89–90.
25. *Hansard*, vol. 128, cols 1398–1401.
26. Martin Gilbert, *Winston Churchill*, London, 1975, vol. 4, p. 527.
27. Gilbert, *Winston Churchill*, vol. 4, p. 484.
28. Sykes, *Cross Roads to Israel*, p. 64.
29. For the full text of Churchill's statement, and of his reply to the Jewish deputation which followed the Arabs, see Gilbert, *Winston Churchill*, vol. 4, pp. 564–9.
30. Gilbert, *Winston Churchill*, vol. 4, pp. 570–71, 574, 597.
31. Gilbert, *Winston Churchill*, vol. 4, p. 589.
32. *Lords' Hansard*, vol. 820, col. 994.
33. *Lords' Hansard*, vol. 820, cols 1008–19.
34. *Hansard*, vol. 150, col. 1055.
35. *Hansard*, vol. 150, col. 1939.
36. *Hansard*, vol. 151, cols 1548–9.
37. *Hansard*, vol. 151, col. 1947.
38. *Hansard*, vol. 152, cols 215–16.
39. *Hansard*, vol. 154, col. 209.
40. *Hansard*, vol. 155, col. 531.
41. *Hansard*, vol. 155, col. 831.
42. *Hansard*, vol. 156, col. 297.
43. Ibid.
44. *Hansard*, vol. 156, cols. 297–8.
45. *Hansard*, vol. 156, col. 298.
46. *Hansard*, vol. 156, cols 332–5.
47. See Harold Wilson's *A Prime Minister on Prime Ministers*, London, 1977, pp. 155–7.
48. Weizmann, *Trial and Error*, p. 239.
49. Weizmann, *Trial and Error*, p. 241.
50. Weizmann, *Trial and Error*, p. 333.
51. In this account, I am indebted to Joseph Fraenkel's *Louis D. Brandeis, Patriot, Judge and Zionist*, published by the Hillel Foundation, 1959.

CHAPTER 3: *The Partition Question*

1. *Lords' Hansard*, vol. 54, col. 669.
2. Royal Commission on Palestine (Peel Commission), 1937, Cmd 5479, p. 41.
3. Peel, pp. 43–5.
4. Peel, p. 46.
5. Peel, p. 48.
6. Peel, p. 54.
7. Peel, p. 57.
8. Ibid.
9. Peel, p. 66.
10. Shaw Report, Cmd 3530, p. 64.
11. Peel, p. 71.
12. Peel, p. 74.
13. Peel, p. 75.
14. Peel, p. 78.
15. Peel, pp. 107–10.
16. Peel, pp. 110–12.
17. Peel, pp. 380–93.
18. Peel, pp. 382–6.
19. *Hansard*, vol. 326, col. 2236.
20. *Hansard*, vol. 326, col. 2247.
21. *Hansard*, vol. 326, col. 2259.
22. *Hansard*, vol. 326, col. 2330.
23. *Hansard*, vol. 326, cols 231–2.
24. *Hansard*, vol. 326, col. 233.
25. *Hansard*, vol. 326, cols 2365–6.
26. Cmd 5854.
27. Ibid, p. 235.
28. Cmd 242.
29. Cmd 5854.

CHAPTER 4: *Holocaust and War*

1. Martin Gilbert, *Exile and Return*, London, 1978, p. 220.
2. Gilbert, *Exile and Return*, p. 221.
3. Gilbert, *Exile and Return*, pp. 220–21, where seven of the 133 cases are set out in detail. The account of this and the other atrocities set out on pp. 91–104 are mainly taken from Gilbert. For the wartime holocaust, see Gilbert, op. cit., pp. 252–67; also his books *The Holocaust*, London, 1978, containing twenty-three maps plus other illustrations; and *The Jews of Russia*, London, 1976, with twenty-six maps, plus illustrations showing the sites in Germany and in occupied countries where mass murders took place. Also Lucy S. Dawidowicz, *The War against the Jews, 1933–1945*, London, 1975.

4. See Frederic Morton, *A Nervous Splendor: Vienna 1888-1889*, London, 1980, pp. 292, 301, 305-7.

5. Gilbert, *Exile and Return*, p. 132.

6. Gilbert, *Exile and Return*, pp. 158-9.

7. Gilbert, *Exile and Return*, p. 162.

8. Ehud Avriel, *Open the Gates*, London, 1975, p. 16.

9. Martin Gilbert, *Final Journey*, London, 1979.

10. For a detailed account of his capture, see Dennis Eisenberg, Uri Dan and Eli Landau, *Mossad, Israel's Secret Intelligence Service*, London, 1978, pp. 25-40; the names of some of the captors may have been changed in this book to avoid blowing their cover in respect of other operations.

11. See Harold Wilson, *A Prime Minister on Prime Ministers*, pp. 180, 253.

12. Compare chapters on Baldwin (pp. 166-88) and Chamberlain (pp. 213-38) in Wilson, *A Prime Minister on Prime Ministers*.

13. Wilson, *A Prime Minister*..., pp. 226-8.

14. Weizmann, *Trial and Error*, pp. 494-5.

15. Weizmann, *Trial and Error*, p. 496.

16. Lord Bethell, *The Palestine Triangle*, London, 1979, p. 64.

17. I am indebted to Kenneth Rose for the information that Elliot and Baffy Dugdale were very close friends indeed.

18. See Bethell, *The Palestine Triangle*, for Baffy Dugdale's account of her call on him in the Colonial Office to tell him 'that he had broken the love and loyalty of the Jews which she had thought unbreakable, and ruined the fair name of Britain'.

19. *Palestine, Statement of Policy*, Cmd 6019.

20. Ibid, p. 2.

21. Cmd 1700.

22. Cmd 6019.

23. Cmd 6019, p. 6.

24. Cmd 6019, p. 8.

25. *Hansard*, vol. 248, cols 751-7.

26. Cmd 6019, p. 9.

27. Cmd 6019, pp. 10-11.

28. Cmd 6019, p. 12.

29. *Hansard*, vol. 347, cols 1937-54.

30. *Hansard*, vol. 347, col. 1941.

31. *Hansard*, vol. 347, cols 1944-5.

32. *Hansard*, vol. 347, col. 1955.

33. *Hansard*, vol. 347, col. 1994, 22 May 1939.

34. *Hansard*, vol. 347, col. 2002.

35. *Hansard*, vol. 347, col. 2039.

36. *Hansard*, vol. 347, cols 2167-79. This is quoted at length as being one of Churchill's greatest speeches, the 1939-45 speeches apart.

37. *Hansard*, vol. 347, cols 2168-9.

38. *Hansard*, vol. 347, col. 2169.

39. *Hansard*, vol. 347, cols 2169-70.

40. Sykes, *Cross Roads to Israel*, p. 249.

41. Sykes, *Cross Roads to Israel*, p. 246.

42. Sykes, *Cross Roads to Israel*, p. 249.

43. Bethell, *The Palestine Triangle*, pp. 94-5.

44. See Abba Eban, *My People: The Story of the Jews*, New York, 1968.

45. Sykes, *Cross Roads to Israel*, p. 293.

46. House of Commons, 17 November 1944, *Hansard*, vol. 404, col. 2242.

CHAPTER 5: *Britain Puts Back the Clock*

1. R. H. S. Crossman, *Palestine Mission*, London, 1947.

2. Labour Party Conference Report, 1943, pp. 188-9.

3. Report of the National Executive Committee for 1943-4, p. 9. See also Hugh Dalton's *Memoirs: The Fateful Years 1931-45*, vol. 1, 1953, vol. 2, 1957, London, pp. 425-6.

4. 1944 Labour Party Conference Report, p. 9.

5. 1945 Labour Party Conference Report, p. 103, 'Let Us Face the Future'.

6. 1944 Labour Conference Report, p. 9.

7. Attlee's speech moving the 'International Post-War Settlement' section of the report, 12 December 1944, cols 130-33; the statement at the end of the general debate, col. 141.

8. See Wilson, *A Prime Minister on Prime Ministers*, p. 291.

9. Clement Attlee, *Autobiography: As it Happened*, London, 1954, p. 153.

10. 1946 Labour Party Conference Report, 12 June, p. 165.

11. See Wilson, *A Prime Minister on Prime Ministers*, pp. 293-4.

12. Circulated as CP (45) 156, 8 September 1945.

13. Cmd 6019.

14. See Harold Wilson, *The Governance of Britain*, London, 1976, pp. 169-73.

15. Harry S. Truman, *Memoirs, Volume II: Years of Trial and Hope 1946-53*, New York and London, 1956, p. 140.

16. Truman, *Memoirs*..., p. 144.

17. Truman, *Memoirs*..., p. 145.

18. Truman, *Memoirs*..., pp. 145-66.

19. Truman, *Memoirs*..., pp. 149-51.

20. Forty-five points according to Attlee, *A*

Prime Minister Remembers, p. 196.
21. *Hansard*, vol. 416, col. 1926.
22. *Hansard*, vol. 416, cols 1926 *et seq*.
23. *Hansard*, 21 February 1946, vol. 419, col. 1367.
24. Abba Eban, *An Autobiography*, London, 1978, p. 59.
25. Crossman, *Palestine Mission*, pp. 26–7.
26. See Wilson, *A Prime Minister on Prime Ministers*, pp. 278–9, 294.
27. Truman, *Memoirs . . .*, p. 156.
28. Truman, *Memoirs . . .*, p. 157.
29. Truman, *Memoirs . . .*, pp. 158–9.
30. Truman, *Memoirs . . .*, p. 160.
31. For the origin of this phrase, see the chapter on Churchill in Wilson, *A Prime Minister on Prime Ministers*, p. 256.
32. See Menachem Begin's *The Revolt, Story of the Irgun*, New York, 1951, and Harry Sacher's *Israel, The Establishment of a State*, London, 1952, particularly chapter IX, 'Agency and Irgun'.
33. For an authoritative and detailed account, see Bethell, *The Palestine Triangle*, pp. 248–52. Bethell reports that the volume of Hebrew documents removed would have taken the 'qualified British policeman'several years to go through, adding that there were, it was said, only five men in the British police force qualified to produce a British translation.
34. *Hansard*, vol. 424, cols 1795–8.
35. *Hansard*, vol. 424, cols 1859–67.
36. *Hansard*, vol. 424, cols 1867–78.
37. *Hansard*, vol. 424, cols 1904–12.
38. Truman, *Memoirs . . .*, p. 160.
39. Truman, *Memoirs . . .*, p. 161.

CHAPTER 6: *Bevin Moves the Reference Back*

1. *Hansard*, vol. 426, cols 959 *et seq*.
2. *Hansard*, vol. 426, cols 964–9.
3. *Hansard*, vol. 426, cols 970–7.
4. *Hansard*, vol. 426, col. 979.
5. *Hansard*, vol. 426, cols 1246–58.
6. *Hansard*, vol. 426, cols 1246–52.
7. *Hansard*, vol. 426, cols 1251–3.
8. *Hansard*, vol. 426, col. 1255.
9. *Hansard*, vol. 426, cols 1257–8.
10. Truman, *Memoirs . . .*, p. 162. This contrasts sharply with Attlee's judgment: 'a good many of them ran away from the real problem. They had a sort of conception that you could get both sides to live in peace with the other. You couldn't.' *Autobiography*, pp. 181–2.
11. *Hansard*, vol. 427, cols 1681–2.

12. *Hansard*, vol. 427, col. 177.
13. Hugh Dalton, *High Tide and After*, vol. 2, London, 1962, pp. 425–7.
14. Dalton, *High Tide and After*, p. 147.
15. Dalton, *High Tide and After*, p. 149.
16. Dalton, *High Tide and After*, p. 151.
17. Dalton, *High Tide and After*, p. 189.
18. Dalton, *High Tide and After*, p. 190.
19. *Hansard*, vol. 433, col. 989.
20. *Hansard*, vol. 433, col. 1907.
21. *Hansard*, vol. 433, col. 1914.
22. *Hansard*, vol. 433, col. 1915.
23. *Hansard*, vol. 433, cols 1917–18.
24. *Hansard*, vol. 433, col. 1930.

CHAPTER 7: *Eretz Israel*

1. Isaiah xi, 11–12.
2. Eban, *An Autobiography*, p. 72.
3. Gilbert, *Exile and Return*, p. 295.
4. See Eban, *An Autobiography*, pp. 73–4, for an account of his lobbying.
5. Quoted in Gilbert, *Exile and Return*, pp. 302–3.
6. UNSCOP Report to the General Assembly, vol. 1, chapter VI.
7. Eban, *An Autobiography*, p. 96.
8. Moshe Dayan, *Story of My Life*, London, 1976, p. 59.
9. *Hansard*, vol. 445, cols 1208–9.
10. *Hansard*, vol. 445, col. 1212.
11. *Hansard*, vol. 445, col. 1221.
12. *Hansard*, vol. 445, cols 1381–8.
13. Truman, *Memoirs . . .*, pp. 158, 160.
14. Eban, *An Autobiography*, p. 102.
15. Truman, *Memoirs . . .*, p. 161.
16. Jonathan Daniels, *Man of Independence*, cited in Eban, *An Autobiography*, p. 104.
17. Eban, *An Autobiography*, pp. 110–11.

CHAPTER 8: *Why Do the Nations . . .?*

1. Gunther Rothenburg, *The Anatomy of the Israeli Army*, London, 1979, p. 47, to which book I am indebted for this brief account of the post-independence fighting.
2. Harry Sacher, one of the three Manchester Zionist leaders before and during the First World War, has written a much more detailed account of the fighting in 1947–9, in which he himself took part: *Israel, The Establishment of a State*, pp. 219–309. See also Bethell, *The Palestine Triangle*.
3. Sacher, *Israel, The Establishment of a State*, p. 127.
4. Rothenburg, *The Anatomy of the Israeli Army*, p. 56.
5. *Hansard*, vol. 460, cols 925–6.
6. *Hansard*, vol. 460, cols 929–30.

7. *Hansard*, vol. 460, cols 933–5.
8. *Hansard*, vol. 460, col. 937.
9. *Hansard*, vol. 460, cols 943–5.
10. *Hansard*, vol. 460, cols 944–5.
11. *Hansard*, vol. 460, cols 947–8.
12. *Hansard*, vol. 460, col. 950.
13. *Hansard*, vol. 460, col. 951.
14. *Hansard*, vol. 460, col. 952.
15. *Hansard*, vol. 460, col. 956.
16. *Hansard*, vol. 460, col. 961.
17. *Hansard*, vol. 460, col. 1042.
18. *Hansard*, vol. 460, col. 1049.
19. *Statistical Abstract of Israel*, Central Bureau of Statistics, Jerusalem, 1975, p. 394.

CHAPTER 9: *Tangled Web*

1. Harold Macmillan's *Memoirs*, vol. 4, *Riding The Storm*, London, 1971, pp. 198, 200. His successful tour of the Commonwealth after he became Prime Minister after the Suez disaster provided the answer when he used the phrase, 'wind of change'.
2. *Hansard*, vol. 557, cols 918–19.
3. Selwyn Lloyd, *Suez 1956: A Personal Account*, London, 1978. This book was completed just before his death in May 1978 and published posthumously.
4. *Hansard*, vol. 557, cols 1603–4.
5. *Hansard*, vol. 557, cols 1605–6.
6. *Hansard*, vol. 557, cols 1610–12.
7. *Hansard*, vol. 557, col. 1638.
8. *Hansard*, vol. 557, col. 1638.
9. Ibid.
10. Anthony Eden, *Full Circle: The Memoirs of Sir Anthony Eden*, London 1960, p. 431.
11. Quoted in Chester Cooper, *The Lion's Last Roar*, New York, 1978, pp. 111–12.
12. Eden, *Full Circle . . .*, p. 437.
13. Eden, *Full Circle . . .*, p. 439.
14. Cooper, *The Lion's Last Roar*, pp. 118–19.
15. Cooper, *The Lion's Last Roar*, p. 120.
16. Cooper, *The Lion's Last Roar*, pp. 127–8.
17. Cooper, *The Lion's Last Roar*, p. 129.
18. Cooper, *The Lion's Last Roar*, p. 126.
19. Robert Murphy, *Diplomat Among Warriors*, London, 1974, p. 470.
20. Dwight D. Eisenhower, *Waging Peace: The White House Years 1956–61*, vol. 2, London, 1966, pp. 666–8.
21. Lloyd, *Suez 1956*, p. 132.
22. *Hansard*, vol. 558, col. 3.
23. Lloyd, *Suez 1956*, p. 135.
24. Cooper, *The Lion's Last Roar*, p. 133.
25. Macmillan, *Memoirs . . .*, p. 127.
26. Lloyd, *Suez 1956*, p. 152.
27. Lloyd, *Suez 1956*, pp. 158–9.
28. Anthony Nutting, *No End of a Lesson*, London, 1967 (the title is based on Rudyard Kipling's poetic commentary on the Boer War), p. 70. Nutting's informative book fills in many of the inconvenient details which Suez ministers would have preferred should go unrecorded.
29. Lloyd, *Suez 1956*, p. 160.
30. Lloyd, *Suez 1956*, p. 161.
31. Lloyd, *Suez 1956*, p. 163.
32. Lloyd, *Suez 1956*, p. 170.
33. Lloyd, *Suez 1956*, p. 172.
34. Nutting, *No End of a Lesson*, p. 89.
35. Lloyd, *Suez 1956*, p. 173.
36. Lloyd, *Suez 1956*, pp. 173–4.
37. Lloyd, *Suez 1956*, p. 182.
38. Lloyd, *Suez 1956*, pp. 192–3, and Christian Pineau, *1956, Suez*, Paris, 1976, pp. 149 *et seq.*
39. Lloyd, *Suez 1956*, p. 188.
40. Roy Fullick and Geoffrey Powell, *Suez: The Double War*, London, 1979, p. 85, a summary of the protocol based on harmonizing the Dayan and the Pineau versions.
41. Dayan, *Story of My Life*, p. 193.
42. Lloyd, *Suez 1956*, p. 173.
43. Dayan, *Story of My Life*, p. 150.
44. Dayan, *Story of My Life*, p. 151.
45. Dayan, *Story of My Life*, p. 157.
46. Dayan, *Story of My Life*, p. 160.
47. Dayan, *Story of My Life*, p. 161.
48. Dayan, *Story of My Life*, p. 176.
49. Dayan, *Story of My Life*, p. 181.
50. Dayan, *Story of My Life*, pp. 181–2.
51. Ibid.
52. Dayan, *Story of My Life*, p. 190.
53. Dayan, *Story of My Life*, p. 192.
54. Dayan, *Story of My Life*, pp. 192–3. Roy Fullick and Geoffrey Powell (*Suez: The Double War*) point out that Pineau's account was slightly different from that published by Dayan: their own summary is briefer than either.

CHAPTER 10: *A Canal Too Far*

1. Fullick and Powell, *Suez: The Double War*, pp. 192–3. They point out that General Jacques Massu was irritated at the constant British references to Arnhem.
2. Eisenhower, *Waging Peace . . .*, p. 75.
3. Cooper, *The Lion's Last Roar*, p. 165.
4. Eden, *Full Circle*, pp. 525–6.
5. Assemblée Nationale, *Débats, Journal*

Officiel, 20 December 1956.
6. Eisenhower, *Waging Peace...*, pp. 678–9.
7. Cooper, *The Lion's Last Roar*, p. 167.
8. Eban, *An Autobiography*, p. 214.
9. Cooper, *The Lion's Last Roar*, p. 166.
10. Cooper, *The Lion's Last Roar*, p. 173.
11. *Hansard*, vol. 558, cols 1274 *et seq.*
12. *Hansard*, vol. 558, col. 1275.
13. *Hansard*, vol. 558, cols 1275–6.
14. *Hansard*, vol. 558, col. 1277.
15. *Hansard*, vol. 558, col. 1343.
16. *Hansard*, vol. 558, col. 1344.
17. *Hansard*, vol. 558, cols 1345–51.
18. *Hansard*, vol. 558, cols 1371–2.
19. *Hansard*, vol. 558, cols 1373–4.
20. *Hansard*, vol. 558, col. 1378.
21. *Hansard*, vol. 558, col. 1448.
22. *Hansard*, vol. 558, col. 1454.
23. *Hansard*, vol. 558, cols 1455–6.
24. *Hansard*, vol. 558, cols 1622–3.
25. *Hansard*, vol. 558, cols 1624–5.
26. *Hansard*, vol. 558, col. 1639.
27. *Hansard*, vol. 558, col. 1641.
28. Ibid.
29. Ibid.
30. *Hansard*, vol. 558, col. 1708.
31. *Hansard*, vol. 558, cols 1713–14.
32. *Hansard*, vol. 558, col. 1719.
33. *Hansard*, vol. 558, col. 1723.
34. *Hansard*, vol. 558, col. 1726.
35. *Hansard*, vol. 558, col. 1727.
36. Cooper, *The Lion's Last Roar*, pp. 181–2.
37. A reference to *Hansard*, vol. 558, col. 1653, 1 November 1956.
38. *Hansard*, vol. 558, cols 1857–8.
39. *Hansard*, vol. 558, cols 1858–63.
40. *Hansard*, vol. 558, cols 1911–15.
41. James Eayrs, 'Canadian Policy and Opinion During the Suez Crisis', International Journal, Canadian Institute of International Affairs, Toronto, vol. 12, no. 2, 1957, p. 101.
42. Macmillan, *Memoirs...*, p. 164.
43. Cooper, *The Lion's Last Roar*, p. 192.
44. Cooper, *The Lion's Last Roar*, p. 200.
45. Cooper, *The Lion's Last Roar*, p. 200.
46. Leonard Mosley, *Dulles*, New York, 1978, pp. 416, 417.
47. Ibid.
48. *Hansard*, vol. 558, cols 1956–7.
49. *Hansard*, vol. 558, cols 1955–8.
50. *Hansard*, vol. 558, cols 1958.
51. *Hansard*, vol. 558, col. 1963.
52. *Hansard*, vol. 558, col. 1966.
53. *Hansard*, vol. 558, col. 1980.
54. *Hansard*, vol. 560, col. 16.
55. *Hansard*, vol. 560, col. 27.
56. *Hansard*, vol. 560, cols 29–30.
57. *Hansard*, vol. 560, cols 31–2.
58. *Hansard*, vol. 560, cols 75–81.
59. *Hansard*, vol. 560, col. 76.
60. *Hansard*, vol. 560, cols 77–8.
61. *Hansard*, vol. 560, cols 75–8.
62. *Hansard*, vol. 560, col. 82.
63. *Hansard*, vol. 560, col. 291.
64. *Hansard*, vol. 560, cols 384–93.
65. *Hansard*, vol. 560, col. 399.
66. *Hansard*, vol. 560, cols 421–4.
67. *Hansard*, vol. 560, cols 571–2.
68. *Hansard*, vol. 560, col. 580.
69. *Hansard*, vol. 561, cols 579–80.
70. *Hansard*, vol. 561, col. 582.
71. *Hansard*, vol. 561, col. 583.
72. *Hansard*, vol. 561, col. 584.
73. *Hansard*, vol. 561, col. 1259.
74. *Hansard*, vol. 561, col. 1268.
75. *Hansard*, vol. 561, col. 1270.
76. *Hansard*, vol. 561, col. 1271.
77. *Hansard*, vol. 561, col. 1274.
78. *Hansard*, vol. 561, cols 1276–7.
79. *Hansard*, vol. 561, col. 1277.
80. *Hansard*, vol. 561, cols 1470–71.
81. *Hansard*, vol. 561, cols 1557–8.
82. *Hansard*, vol. 562, col. 1486.
83. *Hansard*, vol. 562, cols 1487–8.
84. *Hansard*, vol. 562, cols 1489–90.
85. *Hansard*, vol. 562, col. 1491.

CHAPTER 11: *The Six Day War*

1. Eban, *An Autobiography*, pp. 327–8.
2. L. B. Johnson, *The Vantage Point: Perspectives of the Presidency*, New York, 1972, p. 291.
3. Johnson, *The Vantage Point*, p. 292.
4. Johnson, *The Vantage Point*, p. 293.
5. *Hansard*, vol. 677, col. 142.
6. *Hansard*, vol. 704, col. 416.
7. *Hansard*, vol. 710, col. 1152.
8. Johnson, *The Vantage Point*, p. 294.
9. Ibid.
10. Johnson, *The Vantage Point*, p. 293.
11. Eban, *An Autobiography*, p. 341.
12. Eban, *An Autobiography*, p. 342.
13. Eban, *An Autobiography*, pp. 345–6.
14. Eban, *An Autobiography*, p. 359.
15. Eban, *An Autobiography*, p. 370.
16. *Hansard*, vol. 747, col. 104.
17. *Hansard*, vol. 747, cols 110, 112.
18. *Hansard*, vol. 747, col. 115.
19. *Hansard*, vol. 747, cols 119–20.
20. *Hansard*, vol. 747, cols 122–3.
21. *Hansard*, vol. 747. col. 125.

22. *Hansard*, vol. 747, col. 194.
23. *Hansard*, vol. 747, cols 197–8.
24. *Hansard*, vol. 747, cols 198–9.
25. *Keesing's Contemporary Archives*, 10–17 June 1967, p. 22077.
26. For an account of the fighting, including the Jordanian and Syrian conflict and the war at sea and in the air, see Rothenberg, *The Anatomy of the Israeli Army*, pp. 135–52.
27. See Wilson, *The Labour Government, 1964–70*, pp. 402–13.

CHAPTER 12 : *Yom Kippur and After*

1. For a detailed and authoritative account from the Israeli point of view, see Eban's *An Autobiography*, pp. 500–536.
2. For the most authoritative, military account of the war, see Dayan's *Story of My Life*, pp. 375–451.
3. *The Memoirs of Richard Nixon*, New York, 1978, pp. 927–8.
4. *Hansard*, vol. 861, cols 30–31.
5. *Hansard*, vol. 861, cols 32–3.
6. Eban, *An Autobiography*, pp. 513–14.
7. See Harold Wilson, *Final Term: The Labour Government 1974–76*, London, 1979, p. 51.
8. *Hansard*, 18 October 1973, vol. 861, col. 427.
9. *Hansard*, vol. 861, col. 428.
10. *Hansard*, vol. 861, col. 430.
11. *Hansard*, vol. 861, cols 431–2.
12. *Hansard*, vol. 861, col. 437.
13. *Hansard*, vol. 861, cols 33–4.
14. *Hansard*, vol. 861, cols 37–8.
15. *Hansard*, vol. 861, col. 40.
16. *Hansard*, vol. 861, cols 440–41.
17. The implications of the Camp David meetings form the theme of an analytical article in *Foreign Affairs*, New York, vol. 57, no. 3, 1979, pp. 613–32, which not only sets out their positive and negative consequences, but also shows an uncanny degree of prediction about their implications for 1979 and 1980.
18. Dayan, *Story of My Life*, p. 512.

APPENDIX III

1. The letters on pp. 384–7 are set out in full in Francis Williams, *A Prime Minister Remembers*, London, 1961.

Index

395

990.17

HAROLD WILSON

CHARIOT OF ISRAEL

DEMCO